AF352756

JOHN YOUNG: THE HISTORY PROJECTS

EDITED BY
OLIVIER KRISCHER

CONTENTS

INTRODUCTIONS

PART ONE

PART TWO

THE MEDIUM OF HISTORY:
AN INTRODUCTION TO
JOHN YOUNG: THE HISTORY PROJECTS

Olivier Krischer

This book begins with one artwork (pictured opposite) from a large installation within a body of artworks known as the History Projects, by Hong Kong-born Australian artist John Young Zerunge (楊子榮). Titled *Void* (2017), the work was made with chalk on paper prepared with blackboard paint, so that it forms a small chalkboard—a medium and process that is a key feature of the mature History Projects. This particular 'drawing' looks empty, but the feint cloud of effaced chalk leaves a trace of something that was once here. This cloud might be seen as an absence, a loss even, yet it speaks to the way a chalkboard accommodates erasure, facilitating a complex yet familiar process of drafting, erasing and re-drafting. We may recall this tactile process from childhood experience (remember your dry and dusty fingers?); and this too—this feeling-knowing—is a key part of the History Projects. The chalkboard is a space of play, of learning, of possibility; it is not a monument, it is a palimpsest. This simple work, more a stage in a process than an 'image', is a fitting place to start the conversation that unfolds in the pages that follow.

Originally a student of philosophy and painting, John Young has long seen art practice as a form of knowledge production, an aesthetically grounded intellectual endeavour of thinking through making, and this book is edited and designed to highlight both dimensions of the History Projects. In the 1980s and 1990s, Young was at the forefront of explorations of authenticity and cross-cultural identity in appropriation art, and the critical juxtaposition of visual traditions in paintings and mixed-media works. The History Projects, however, marked a major shift in Young's practice towards an aesthetic engagement with both diasporic memory and public history, embracing archival research alongside the development of an aesthetic form that sought to articulate, indeed embody, an ethical responsibility to the past.

The problem of dealing with history in an art of the present has been a concern for the theorisation of an ostensibly global contemporary art for many years. In his most recent formulation of an 'art to come', Terry Smith, for example, states the basic dilemma by asking: 'What does it mean to say, in the same breath, that contemporary art is an art to come and is also subject to—indeed, calls out for—historical interrogation?'[1] A decade ago, Peter Osborne pointed out that the very category of the contemporary is 'empirically problematic', a kind of idealistic fiction, since there is no subject position that can really occupy it, yet it continues to function as if there were—'as if the speculative horizon of the unity of human history had been reached'.[2] Here the contemporary, an 'as if' that reaches temporally in all and no directions, is patently utopian and (for Osborne) negative in its typically apolitical nature. Yet this as-if can also be seen as a positive space of 'productive imagination', in that it is able to project a unity on different places and times. But for art to articulate such a global, translational space, the subject-position of its production must be able to in some way reflect 'something of the structure of "the contemporary" itself'.[3] Young's History Projects emerged from recognising and facing such an impasse.

Void 2017
Chalk on blackboard-painted
archival cotton paper, 100 × 70 cm

Between 2005 and 2019, Young completed eleven cycles of artwork that he came to label collectively as 'The History Projects' from around 2010. In their mature form, each is a series or group of artworks that typically comprise digital prints, oil paintings and chalk drawings, but have also included textiles. These have predominantly been exhibited as installations, a mode of display that eventually developed a characteristic grid formation, presenting works of image and text in complex juxtapositions. Across this book, each project is addressed through a variety of texts, including academic essays as well as email correspondence, interviews, poems, republished essays, archival letters and even sermons. This range of textual reflections registers the inherent diversity in the source materials of these works, as well as the collaborative relationships Young forged through their production, reception and critique. This book is therefore structured as a critical reference and guide to the aesthetic and conceptual development of the History Projects, which necessarily features many voices.

Presented in two parts, the book assumes a chronological path, charting the trajectory of each project's development, with a basic outline of the work's underlying narrative or context. These brief introductions include Young's voice in the form of original artist statements as well as recent reflections on the works, recognising shifts in Young's approach or thinking about the Projects. Young's work has interrogated historical and art historical structures, and the book actively embraces such conceptual concerns. The individual essays and conversations frequently reach between and beyond the History Projects. The details of Young's biography—often cited to situate his work, and particularly the diasporic perspective of the History Projects—reappear in different ways throughout the book, to accumulate between authors, rather than be presented as a fixed, linear narrative. It is in such a space, with its echoes and silences, that resonances form. In this sense, this has been conceived as a workbook, which could be read cover to cover, or used as a resource to which one returns intermittently.

One might expect the chronological presentation of the projects to emphasise the way in which Young develops and refines the mature grid-based form of the later History Project installations, combining chalk drawings and digital prints. However, here the teleological implications of chronology are subtly challenged from within by the unruly nature of the works and the creative process, as well as the lateral connections made by writers. A nuanced reading of the projects reveals the elliptical nature of their material and conceptual development: we notice parts of earlier research and aesthetic strategies that re-emerge and transform at later stages, sometimes consciously and at other times in more intuitive or organic ways. One constant, however, is a productive tension between ostensibly empirical history represented from the archive, and more mythical or lyrical renditions of the past, of collective and individual memory and imagination, referenced in the uncanny legacies of visual symbols and motifs, in poetry and, of course, art's own histories.

For instance, it may seem unlikely to begin a discussion of the History Projects with the collaboratively produced and officially commissioned textile piece *Open World* (2008), yet the discussion of this elaborate work's production, between Young and the team of expert weavers at the Australian Tapestry Workshop, also reveals Young's attempts to share and even relinquish artistic control in the pursuit of an ethically grounded art practice. Such byways form, then, a refrain or chorus which reminds us of the importance of creative process—of tactile making—even in the face of monumental 'History'.

This chronological framework also shows that the major early works in the History Projects, such as *Bonhoeffer in Harlem* (2009), were developed for contexts outside of Australia, dealing with moments of global history. This is significant, given the way in which the presentation of the History Projects has been framed since their wider exhibition in Australia: namely, while the later projects indeed focus on the often unrecognised and seldom visualised Chinese Australian histories of nineteenth and early-twentieth-century Australia, the History Projects overall are forged from and continue to confront more inclusive and abstract concerns. A number of authors in this volume suggest that Young's later History Projects constitute some of the most significant 'history paintings' in recent Australian art. Yet, far from denying the significance of 'local' histories, to understand this broader implication of the work is to recognise the ways in which the critical concerns of the History Projects complicate and transcend localised identity politics, and its stubborn limitations in Australian cultural discourse. Even as they are rooted in specific (hi)stories, Young's projects work to expand the spaces in which 'other' voices, particularly diasporic voices, can speak, beyond autobiographical and identitarian narratives.

BARNES, CLARK AND THE HISTORY PROJECTS

As a volume that emphasises a range of perspectives, reflecting the projects themselves, this book begins with two distinct overview essays by **Carolyn Barnes** and **John Clark**, which frame the History Projects in the context of Young's broader practice. Barnes, who has written extensively on the development of Young's work, highlights the ways in which these projects build on and diverge from his earlier aesthetic strategies.[4] In the context of Australian art history and drawing on continental philosophy (which was part of Young's university education too), Barnes proposes the History Projects as a critical reworking of the concerns of history painting from a more complex, diasporic subject position. This signals the diasporic and specifically Asian Australian histories that remain largely unseen or denied in frameworks of Australian art, history and identity, compared to, for example, the complexity of the discourse that has developed on indigeneity and contemporary art.[5] Barnes calls the projects a 'counter-pedagogy', operating not only at the level of their underlying archival materials but, importantly, animated by the affective labour Young takes on by sharing the act of learning and sense-making as an open process, especially in his use of installation, as a medium that 'invites the subject inside'.[6]

Young's work has been deeply engaged with art's history, and the 1991 conference 'Modernity and Post-modernity in Asian Art', organised by John Clark in Canberra, has been cited by Young as inspirational in its recognition of non-Euramerican modern subjectivities at an early turning point in his career. Here, Clark expands on his detailed discussion of Young's work in the theorisation of 'the Asian modern', in which Young is not the only Australian artist to be included.[7] Tracing five stages to Young's work and life, Clark focuses on how art can be a means to 're-awaken the past in the present', in ways that also trouble postmodern or postcolonial claims on the contemporary—a dilemma Young has sought to confront, and to which Clark draws suggestive parallels to Chinese Indonesian artists who have addressed anti-Chinese violence of the 1960s in Indonesia. Clark's reading of the History Projects from the perspective of an Asian modernity, in which Australia is unapologetically implicated, forms a complex foundation on which the transnational subject of Young's oeuvre is cast as radically 'historical'—refusing narratives of (re)discovery or futurity that preface discussions of Asia and diaspora generally in Australia.

BONHOEFFER, SAFETY ZONE AND POEISIS

The History Projects are marked, in part, by their commitment to a process that is lived, embodied and collaborative. Part One begins with an interview by **Venita Poblocki** with Young and weavers from the Australian Tapestry Workshop, who worked on *Open World* (2005), a large tapestry that was gifted to China's Jiangsu Province, which has been a sister state of Victoria since 1979. This work, and the conversation, underline important facets of the later History Projects, including cross-media experimentation and collaborative production in which artistic, authorial agency is consciously shared or relinquished. *Open World* saw Young conducting research in Nanjing—Jiangsu's provincial capital, and once the capital of China—which built on the cross-cultural interests of his earlier *Double Ground Paintings* (1993–2005). By contrast, I (**Olivier Krischer**) discuss in my essay, how it is really Young's 2008 work *1967Dispersion* that connects the artist's diasporic experience—being sent to Australia following the 1967 riots in Hong Kong—to global contemporary processes of conflict, capitalism and displacement. It is in this series that Young first started to develop a particular aesthetic language for critically engaging history visually, in the juxtaposition of digital prints from archival photographs with abstracted oil paintings.

Young's aesthetic methodology and focus on transcultural humanitarianism are then unpacked in a series of texts on his two pivotal projects *Bonhoeffer in Harlem* (2009) and *Safety Zone* (2010). Introducing these projects in the context of their work on art and human rights, **Caroline Turner** and **Jen Webb** draw attention to the role of contemporary artists such as Young in 'witnessing, interpreting and communicating' amid the increasingly complex context of postcolonial globalisation. Their reflection brings the reader from the broader perspective of the introductory essays into the detailed essays on specific projects, through the lens of ethical practice in art.

In her essay on the project *Bonhoeffer in Harlem*, **Sylvia D. Volz** details the historical narrative of Dietrich Bonhoeffer (1906–1945)—the Lutheran pastor and theologian known for his resistance to German National Socialism—and highlights the way Young chose to focus on the transcultural dimension of Bonhoeffer's experience of community in the face of discrimination against the Black community in late 1920s Harlem, New York. Complimenting this critical reflection on Young's project in Berlin are a range of texts that reveal the complex research and collaborations underpinning this formative work, including a 1931 letter sent by Bonhoeffer to his grandmother, which shares his Harlem experience and political awakening, as well as a speech and a sermon from the exhibition opening, which reveal the significance of the project for the contemporary Berlin community where it was staged, in St Matthäus Church, where Bonhoeffer was originally ordained.

Safety Zone deals with the Nanjing Massacre of 1937, in which Young focuses on the committee of foreigners who remained in the city to try to protect Chinese civilians from the ravages of the invading Imperial Japanese Army. Two historical essays by **Thomas Berghuis** and **Jacqueline Lo**, published in response to this project, form an important insight into not only the discursive development around the History Projects but also how Young has engaged with critical writing about these works as part of his artistic process. Prefacing Berghuis' 2011 essay 'Situational Ethics' is part of the e-mail correspondence between Berghuis and Young that shaped the development of Berghuis' concept of 'situational ethics'. Similarly, in an introductory note to the republication of her important essay, Lo prefaces the role of empathy in *Bonhoeffer in Harlem* and *Safety Zone*, referring to these works as part of a search for a 'cosmopolitan ethics' that appears even more timely today.

In a major new essay for this volume, **Marc Glöde** takes this discourse a step further by providing a detailed critical reflection on the discursive development that appears between *Bonhoeffer* and *Safety Zone*. Glöde argues that in *Safety Zone* Young invites— or even compels—the viewer to identify with different sides of historical trauma, including through its spatial installation in symbolic, sacred spaces such as churches in Berlin and Bamberg. This expands the critical discourse around the History Projects by registering the important movement between projects from a search for ethical role models to a more self-reflexive sense of personal implication and ethical responsibility. Dealing with the complexity of these multi-media, multi-panel works, Glöde's reading advocates a slower mode of looking which builds on issues of ethics and diasporic memory raised by Berghuis and Lo.

Presenting Young's projects chronologically reveals potential segues and connections between the History Projects and other series that would otherwise be presented separately, but are drawn together here to encourage cross readings. Two examples of this are the series *The Macau Days* and *New Wolf of Rome*, both dating from 2012. These form part of a significant transition, after which Young began developing History Projects that were focused on narratives of Chinese Australian history. They highlight the importance of symbolism, poetry and allegory, and their enduring affective power, which is often simmering below the surface of works in the History Projects but becomes more legible through these two series. In this sense, they might signal a movement from the global concerns of the earlier projects.

The Macau Days was developed from a melancholic sense of loss. This loss was not only for a Macau that Young knew from visits as a child, but also for what this tiny point on the world map represented as a node of transcultural, Eurasian history. The project was exhibited in a few iterations over subsequent years, in both Hong Kong and Australia, and in 2017 Young also collaborated on a related publication with writer **Brian Castro**, whom he joins here in a conversation moderated by **Jennifer Mackenzie**, to discuss ways of processing historical imagination from a diasporic perspective. Castro's voice is also present in a selection of poems from that publication. In her related essay, **Claire Hielscher** extends her critical reflection on *The Macau Days* exhibition project through a parallel discussion of another series, *The New Wolf of Rome*, which applies visual strategies developed in the History Projects—digital prints from archival photographs paired with chalkboard drawings. With its references to the Roman founding myth of the 'she-wolf', ancient Chinese nature poems, and Jungian symbols, Heilscher discusses how the work forms a haunting meditation on a past that is deeper than history or memory, and seems to endure in such aesthetic echoes.

DIASPORIC HISTORIES AND THE POLITICS OF DISPLAY

The essays in the second half of the book address the History Projects focused on diasporic—particularly Chinese Australian—histories, which are based on research facilitated by an Australia Council grant Young received in 2013. It is important to recognise that while these later projects are concerned with Chinese Australian identities and acts of benevolence in the face of historical discrimination and violence, Young's aesthetic methodology was developed earlier in his practice. In so doing, we are compelled to draw these local histories—that are often vitally important for families or communities with whom Young has worked closely—into broader critical concerns. These projects illustrate the impact of diasporic historical imagination in contemporary artistic practice, even as they join other voices in emerging historical work that seeks to address the denial and repression of Chinese and Asian Australian histories. This also underlines the significant processes of learning Young undertook to treat this subject. Young is a Hong Kong-born Australian artist of complex, affluent heritage, with only tangential connections to the colonial Australian context of these works. To simply frame them—the artist, and the subjects of these works—in the same space serves, it seems, to again limit the potential for such work to implicate a wider community of concern. The texts in this section resist seeing these projects as 'natural' ground for Young, and so better appreciate the way his treatment of such history actively complicates the more familiar frames through which diasporas are represented, such as through personal stories of migration and cultural communities, rather than political or transcultural individuals. In this respect, the works intervene more contentiously, more radically, in the politics of who has the right to speak and be heard, to write and be read, to remember and be remembered in 'Australia', even now.

Such political significance simmers through essays by **Nadia Rhook, Sophie Loy-Wilson** and **Mikala Tai**. Echoing the exploration of poeisis suggested above, Rhook, who works between the disciplinary territories of history and poetry, prefaces her detailed exploration of Young's project *1866: The Worlds of Lowe Kong Meng and Jong Ah Siug* (2015) with her poem *The Greeting*. This poem, like her essay, explores the premise of Young's exhibition, and particularly his embroidery *The Meeting* (2015), which imagines that the wealthy Lowe and the abject, institutionalised Jong, may have crossed paths in 1866 in Victoria, despite their radically different migrant experiences. As Rhook's poem suggests: 'even after all tongues are untied / some walls remain more soundproof than others'. In her essay, Rhook points to the potential of imagination in historical work that seeks to address pasts that have been denied or forgotten, and often literally buried.

This process of burying and unearthing is explored by Loy-Wilson too, who reflects on Young's work as a form of 'truth telling' from her perspective as an historian. Combining this with a frank and confronting account of recent field trips researching Chinese gold-rush era presence in a number of country towns in New South Wales, Loy-Wilson details the sites of historical violence she is compelled to confront. The way in which such histories lie unseen yet just beneath the surface of the landscape— 'lying in the mud', as Loy-Wilson provocatively suggests—inevitably ties episodes of anti-Asian violence in Australia to other repressed histories that are only now emerging from the land, like the Frontier Wars.[8] In this respect, it is significant that the essay includes Young's project *None Living Knows* (2017), a series of sublime abstract paintings that seeks to visualise events that were never documented—namely the overland trek, across thousands of kilometres, from the northern port of Darwin to distant north-eastern goldfields like Palmer River, by Chinese miners avoiding a prohibitive poll tax that was imposed in Queensland between the late 1890s and early 1900s. These treks, which led to deaths en route, remain largely unknown in Australian history.

Young's project *The Burrangong Affray* (2018) directly addresses the potential intersections between Chinese gold rush migration and colonial violence through the Lambing Flat riots of 1861, the largest racially motivated attack in Australia's history. Then director of 4A Centre for Contemporary Art, Mikala Tai writes about this project from the perspective of a participant observer, discussing not only the final exhibition but also the significant research and field trips they undertook, and the collaboration Young formed with the other participating artist, Jason Phu.

As Tai notes, the racist reaction to the exhibition online—as well as the failure of this and other projects on Chinese Australian history to find their way into a public collection—speaks to the ways 'safe white spaces' can still characterise Australian society, and its art world. Recalling the 'counter pedagogies' framed by Barnes in her introductory essay, Tai instead critically positions the works in *The Burrangong Affray* as some of the most significant Australian 'history paintings' to have been produced in recent memory.

At least one of Young's projects on Chinese Australian histories has had a more direct public impact. In 2015 he completed *Open Monument* (2015) in the historically significant gold rush town of Ballarat. In his interview with **Venita Poblocki** regarding this work, Young highlights the sense of responsibility to community and the different forms of collaboration that accompanied this permanent installation, one that was designed to change along with the local community, over time.

In *Modernity's End: Half the Sky* (2016), curated by Poblocki, we find something of a companion piece to *1866*, this time exploring the lives of two Chinese Australian women—Daisy Kwok and Alice Lim Kee—who further complicate diasporic narratives through their positions as women moving not *to* but *from* Australia: both travelled with family to the cosmopolitan Shanghai of the 1930s, where they formed part of the city's cultural elite, in stark contrast to their positions in White Australia. For this project, Young invited two Chinese Australian woman artists, **Cyrus Tang** and **Pei Pei He**, to produce works responding to these women's lives, and whose artist statements are included here too.

The final essay, by **Claire Roberts**, concerns the ongoing series *Fairweather Transformations*, which echoes aspects of *1967 Dispersion* in its deployment of abstract oil painting, as well as the commitment to alternative frameworks of history seen in works such as *The Macau Days*. Here, however, Young connects through art history and practice to an artist who fascinates him personally and aesthetically, for his crossing of cultures and visual canons. Young 'processes' Fairweather's work through his own digital mediation, creating a computer-generated abstract image, which is in turn hand-painted onto a canvas in oil. Young's *The Chinese Room (Mangrove)* (2022), for example, is a transformation, through this process, of Fairweather's original *Mangrove* (1961–2) from the Art Gallery of South Australia. Just as *The Macau Days* points to the poetic and mythical as ways of making sense of the past, Roberts' essay recognises the deep engagement Young has had with Australian art history, and the ways in which this visual, procedural dialogue with the work of Fairweather makes transformation into an act that creates—or reveals—another form of live connection with other pasts.

Indeed, the lyrical or poetic has a crucial, transformative power in our approach to history, as we see in Young's series *The New Wolf of Rome*. In its original Greek form poeisis meant 'to make' or create. It was this implication that Heidegger took up in his reflections on technology, pointing to the philosophical use of 'poeisis' in Plato's Symposium, where it suggests a 'bringing forth', from nonexistence to existence— not only in terms of an artisan fashioning materials, but also like a blossom coming into bloom: a bringing forth from within the form itself. For Heidegger, this sense of revelation was part of his understanding of 'truth'.[9]

Finally, two conversations punctuate Part Two. First, Young's conversation with curator **Matt Cox** builds on the experience of *Open Monument* and the institutional politics of display, while also drawing on connections to Cox's capacious curatorial practice, in which collaborations and histories of Asian art inform a research-led creative methodology that similarly strives to embody an ethical position. Rounding out the volume is a conversation with **Aaron Seeto**, who has engaged with Young as an artist, curator and former director at 4A Centre for Contemporary Asian Art —an important exhibition platform that Young helped to establish in the mid-1990s. Conceived as a coda, in this wide-ranging conversation Seeto draws on different periods of Young's practice, before and beyond the History Projects, from some of Young's earliest minimal, conceptual works through to the present. While the conversation looks 'back', it brings us full circle, transforming in subtle ways our perspective not only on the History Projects but also on Young's practice as a whole.

In 2005, when we might imagine Young was starting on a path that would lead, in a few years, to the first History Projects, the British-born Australian historian of Japan, Tessa Morris-Suzuki published a small but incisive volume titled *The Past Within Us: Media, Memory, History* (2005). Writing for an audience of history colleagues and students, she argues that East Asia's history textbook controversies, and indeed 'history wars' generally, are played out across a range of media:

> Our visions of history are drawn from diverse sources: not just from the narratives of history books but also from photographs and historical novels, from newsreel footage, comic books and, increasingly, from electronic media like the internet. Out of this kaleidoscopic mass of fragments we make and remake patterns of understanding which explain the origins and nature of the world in which we live. And doing this, we define and redefine the place that we occupy in that world. Often, in fact, it is the snippets of vision and sound—seconds of newsreel, stark caricatured faces—that continue to frame our picture of the past even when the details of the accompanying narratives have been forgotten.[10]

It is telling how this account of the need to address the *medium* of history resonates with the kaleidoscopic, fragmentary, remediated nature of the past explored in the texts of this volume. Morris-Suzuki goes on to call for the need to recognise:

> [O]ur understanding of history is never just an intellectual matter; any encounter with the past involves feeling and imagination as well as pure knowledge … [A]cademic history has tended to be too wary of emotions, too prone to treat historical knowledge as though it were a form of pure reason existing beyond the sullying realms of passion, fear, hope or sheer pleasure.[11]

As Loy-Wilson suggests, the History Projects acknowledge and embrace these 'sullying realms' and invite us to get our hands 'dirty', dealing with the grit of history. As the diversity of voices here demonstrates, these projects acknowledge and present themselves in all their limitations, as ongoing conversations. 'The past is never dead,' wrote William Faulkner, 'it's not even past'. History here is unfinished business—and hence an invitation to action.

1. Terry Smith, *Art to Come: Histories of Contemporary Art*, Duke
    University Press, Durham, NC, 2019, p. 1.

2. Peter Osborne, *Anywhere or not at all: Philosophy of Contemporary Art*,
    Verso, New York and London, 2013, p. 23.

3. Ibid., p. 28.

4. Such as the monograph Carolyn Barnes, *John Young*, Craftsman
    House, Fishermans Bend, Victoria, 2005.

5. Consider, for example, Ian McLean (ed.), *How Aborigines Invented
    Contemporary Art*, Power Publications, Sydney, 2011.

6. See Carolyn Barnes, 'The History Projects: Aesthetics and
    unorthodox pedagogies', in this volume, pp. 16–23.

7. John Clark, *The Asian Modern*, National Gallery Singapore,
    Singapore, 2021.

8. Since Henry Reynolds' pioneering book *The Other Side of the Frontier:
    Aboriginal Resistance to the European Invasion of Australia* (1982),
    Australia's frontier wars have become a firmer part of a mainstream
    national historical identity, in works such as *The Australian Frontier
    Wars 1788–1838* (2002), by John Connor, an academic at the
    Australian Defence Force Academy at the time. While there remains
    a small but significant debate about the particulars of such history,
    even at relatively conservative public institutions such as the
    Australian War Memorial, there is recognition of a need to present
    this history more substantially. It has also been the subject of a
    recent documentary television series titled *The Australian Wars*
    (2022), directed by Indigenous (Arrernte/Kalkadoon) filmmaker
    Rachel Perkins.

9. Martin Heidegger, 'The Question Concerning Technology', in *The
    Question Concerning Technology and Other Essays*, William Lovitt
    (transl.), Garland Publishing Inc., New York and London [1954] 1977,
    pp. 11–12.

10. Tessa Morris-Suzuki, *The Past Within Us: Media, Memory, History*, Verso,
    New York and London, 2005, pp. 2–3.

11. Ibid., p. 27.

THE HISTORY PROJECTS: AESTHETICS AND UNORTHODOX PEDAGOGIES

Carolyn Barnes

John Young's History Projects encompass eleven series of works investigating different episodes in modern history, many with a connection to the Chinese diaspora or cases where individuals risked their lives to come to the aid of others. Woven into the visual fabric of the works is a wealth of historical detail. The titles of the different series—*1967Dispersion* (2008), *Bonhoeffer in Harlem* (2008), *1866: The Worlds of Lowe Kong Meng and Jong Ah Siug* (2015), *The Burrangong Affray* (2018)—often identify the people, places or events that inhabit the works. Many works incorporate contemporaneous photographs or extracts from historical documents, but the History Projects don't deliver a history lesson in the standard sense. What you learn is grounded in aesthetic experience and dialogical conceptual relations, informed by artistic critique and Young's personal experience of displacement. Past and present, critical insight and lived history thus collide in these works, which see Young stepping away from the globalised condition of contemporary art, from the noise of social media and the historical amnesia it creates, challenging us to commit to considering not only how we got here, but what the past was for those who lived it.

The History Projects strike a note of caution here. They resist the temptation to look back at history and think that we can readily understand it, or that our experiences, issues and outlooks equate with those of previous people and times. To surrender to this tendency is to limit what the past is. Instead, Young's History Projects offer an elusive version of 'history painting', being steeped in aesthetic experience that is coeval with discursive thought. Crossing boundaries of time, place or culture attains a crucial felt dimension, providing a demanding form of access, as Young explains it, 'to particular ethical values that have been denied us in this wicked era'.[1] As with all of Young's work, the History Projects incorporate a self-reflexive interrogation of chiefly European pictorial traditions, a version of history painting grounded in various conceptual and post-conceptual practices of the 1960s and 1970s, and postmodern appropriation strategies from the 1980s. In refusing to reduce painting and photography to mere depiction, Young's treatment of images plays an important conceptual role in the works' reception. The complex sequence of inversions and iterations to which he submits the pictorial content of the History Projects mirrors complications in framing the object and subjects of history at this time, in which pasts and facts are under sustained attack. The History Projects exemplify an ethics of receptivity to history for an era in great need of alternative pedagogies where history is concerned.

NEW HISTORY PAINTINGS

From the seventeenth century to the 1850s, history painting—the painting of subjects from classical history and mythology and the Bible, and later from historical events— was the most highly valued of the genres of painting for the instruction it afforded. History painting was a foundational genre in Australian colonial art, being used to represent the appropriation and settlement of Indigenous land as somehow heroic. The rise of modernism in the second half of the nineteenth century, with its embrace of more quotidian subject matter, sidelined the elitist didacticism at the heart of history painting. Charles Reep argues that within modernism 'overt instruction' in a work of art made it 'less valuable as a source of instruction'.[2] In working through non-cognitive dimensions—perception, imagination and intuition—Young's History Projects explore how historical forces inform the subject of the viewer, aesthetic experience having an important mediating role in this process. They are educative, but never dictate a lesson.

This can be deduced from the nature of the works but understanding the processes of artistic enactment that bring them into being is also important. Paradoxically perhaps, for Young, a strong measure of auto-didacticism is involved in the works' production. Each series in the History Projects is forged from the interaction of critical reflection in the research phase and the development of a feeling for the subjects of history during the making phase. Sifting through and selecting images, experimenting with image combinations, digitally manipulating images to negate their recognisable content, then painting the results, writing out sections of historical text—these are all ways for Young to vicariously experience history, its erasure and reclamation in the present. If each series starts with facts and ideas, the development and interplay of the works' aesthetic, conceptual and material elements—the essence of their 'artfulness'— is pivotal for Young. In the process of making, critical consciousness and elements of the pre-modernist and modernist pictorial traditions merge, pointing to Young's interest in philosophical speculation on the embodiment of reflective judgement in art, as first proposed by philosopher Immanuel Kant, who subsequently perceived an alliance between aesthetics and ethics through their shared basis in value judgements.

Through the act of making, Young expends actual and affective labour on our behalf, retrieving particular events from the flux of history, identifying meaningful correspondences between instances—such as the perilous intercession on behalf of others of Dietrich Bonhoeffer in Nazi Germany, John Rabe in Japanese-occupied Nanjing and James Roberts amid the anti-Chinese riots in 1860s Australia—adding aesthetic experience to historical fact through the performative process of production. For Young, the latter is especially exemplified in the many chalk drawings on black

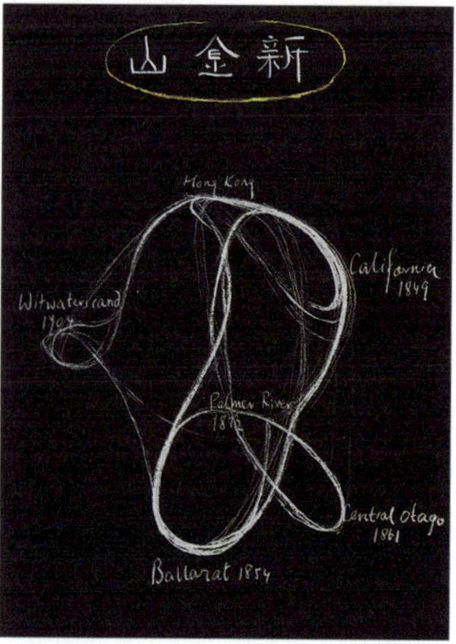

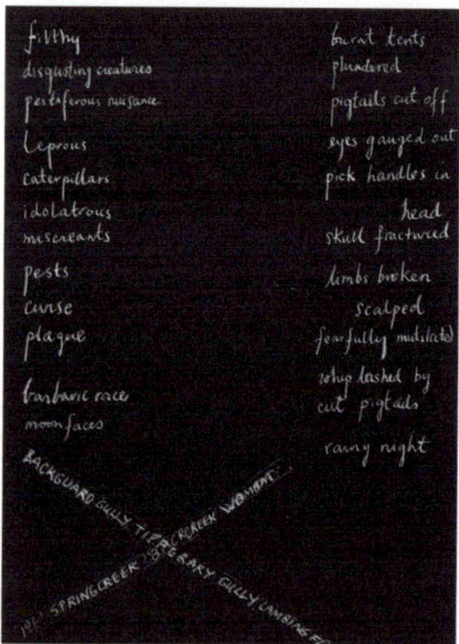

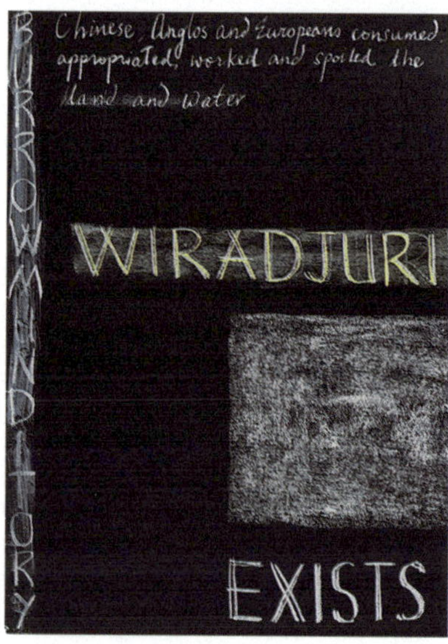

New Gold Mountain 2018
Burnt Tents 2018
Wiradjuri Exists 2018
Chalk on blackboard-painted archival
cotton paper, 100 × 70 cm each

ground that appear across The History Projects, such as those from the series *The Burrangong Affray* (2018). In the drawing *New Gold Mountain* (2018), for example, Young replicates a process of rote learning from a bygone era by writing out the names of the various goldfields to which people from China, especially southern China, journeyed in the nineteenth and twentieth centuries, dating the start of each gold rush: California 1849, Ballarat 1854, Central Otago 1861, Palmer River 1872, Witwatersrand, 1904. Connecting the place names is a sequence of looping lines drawn over many times in the way a child learns to form letters in their early school years.

The series *The Burrangong Affray* explores the Lambing Flat riots of 1861, a sequence of violent anti-Chinese demonstrations that happened in the Burrangong region of northwest New South Wales. In *Burnt Tents* (2018), Young writes out a list of racial slurs down the left-hand side of the black, monochrome sheet, highlighting the attitudes that motivated the demonstrations. Down the right-hand side of the sheet, he writes out a list of violent acts inflicted on the Chinese miners by other colonists. At the bottom of the sheet, in two crossing lines, Young writes out the names of the long-forgotten goldfields around Burrangong where the riots took place: Back Creek, Blackguard Gully, Lambing Flat, Spring Creek, Stoney Creek, Tipperary Gully and Wombat. A third drawing, *Wiradjuri Exists* (2018), highlights how the miners— both Anglo-European and Chinese—ruined the land and water through their mining practices. This is Indigenous land and water, no permission was sought, or compensation paid for its exploitation. The History Projects broach the devastating world-historical effects of colonisation and diaspora, as Young explains, 'the works are not intended to be didactic to a public'.[3] Rather, through the process of drawing, painting, performance or writing, Young works with the residue of historical phenomena to learn for himself something of their historical meaning and ethical significance.

TOWARDS A DIASPORIC AESTHETICS

Young began making art at the end of the 1970s, a period of uncertainty for contemporary art. The main clarity in art practice came from what was being negated, the radical conceptual critique of art and its institutions rejecting visual art's traditional focus on aesthetic experience, manual mastery and self-expression. Conceptual art contested artworks' social and economic purpose within the gallery/museum system via the rise of a range of anti-art strategies. As the role of aesthetic experience and the formalistic properties of a work of art were delegitimised, an art of ideas and tactical thinking came to the fore. Young, for example, privileged chance and mathematical progressions over aesthetic decision-making in his work of the late 1970s and early 1980s.[4] The critique of art world frameworks and structures sustained contemporary art practice for only so long. Lacking the collective purpose that formal investigation had afforded modernism, discourses of inauthenticity and denaturalisation in a postmodern age came to occupy many artists. For a long time, Young's work reflected a new negative position founded on a sense of the artifice of a wholly constructed world, with his painting practice revolving around a range of hybrid conceptual-visual mechanisms to accommodate the assortment of pictorial genres and sources he used to explore problems of art and culture in postmodernism in three major painting cycles: the *Silhouette Paintings* (1987–89), the *Polychrome Paintings* (1989–92) and the *Double Ground Paintings* (1993–2005).

The *Silhouette Paintings* referenced reactionary *rappel à l'ordre* painting of the 1920s and 1930s and modernist values of truth-to-materials, suggesting all art was open to cooption and decadence. The *Polychrome Paintings* explored modernism's closure to further development, many works broaching the ideological struggle between high art and mass culture in modern aesthetic theory. The *Double Ground Paintings* addressed cultural flattening and rupture, temporal and spatial compression, shifting centres and peripheries, and questions of origin and identity amid globalisation. In each cycle, Young took the role of the 'cultural intermediary', appropriating, combining and recontextualising heterogeneous visual content.[5] The high proportion of borrowed content contrasted to the emphasis on originality and formal progress in modernism, alerting us to the fact that the preservation of cultural forms was more the norm in art history. The appropriated images in all three cycles echoed the conventional genres of Western painting—still life, figure painting, nature views, scenes of everyday life—but in a debased form, filtered through popular photography of the 1930s and 1940s. Young, however, had little interest in celebrating popular taste or exploring the differential basis of aesthetic judgment and values in different cultural contexts. Ambiguous, inauthentic and sentimental, the character of the material and its juxtaposition addressed Young's sense of the displacement of meaning and identity in the present, that contemporary subjectivity was increasingly alienated and fractured. This was not just a disinterested, intellectual critique of the failure of grand modern attempts to offer meaning, transcendence and truth. It was linked to Young's deep sense of having a diasporic, nomadic relationship to the world and his existence.

In 1967, as an eleven-year-old, Young's parents had sent him to school in Sydney as insurance against the potential spread of the violence from China's Great Proletarian Cultural Revolution to his native Hong Kong. Young has visited Hong Kong many times since coming to Australia but has never returned to live there. Benzi Zhang argues that complexity and ambivalence are integral to the expression and definition of identity in diaspora. Diaspora, he comments, is 'not only a movement across the borders of a country but also the experience of traversing boundaries and barriers of space, time, race, culture, language and history'.[6] In search of cultural foundation, the backgrounds of Young's *Double Ground Paintings* mostly reference Asian culture and history, beginning with reproductions of works by Giuseppe Castiglione, a Jesuit missionary and artist who lived in China between 1715 and 1766. The scholarly Castiglione's time in China represents a significant early encounter between European and Chinese culture. Mostly, however, the *Double Ground Paintings* expose the clichéd and intransigent imaginaries bound up in transversal cultural relations, with other pictorial elements reflecting stereotyped projections of Asianness—romantic, banal or disparaging—that relate to prosaic Western cultural tropes, such as the representation of the sublime through mannered landscape imagery or the use of portraiture and figure painting to capture intangible states of mind and being.

The *Double Ground Paintings*, informed by Young's situation as insider and outsider to more than one culture, use the diasporic experience to model broader issues of identity formation, cultural meaning and their splintering in globalisation. To address the multi-stranded complexities of identification and meaning, Young developed a system of internal relations within his paintings based on the juxtaposition, layering and stacking of appropriated images. In certain subsets of the *Double Ground Paintings*, Young also manipulated the background images digitally to disguise their original representational content. The resulting distorted forms and patterned fields identified a new visual sublime and agent of estrangement within digitisation, pre-empting more recent concerns about the ontology of images in an age of artificial intelligence, digital technology and the phenomena of 'deepfake' audio and video recordings. The *Double Ground Paintings* recognise the role of reproductive technologies in the dissemination and recontextualisation of images and contrast historical and contemporary techniques of representation. Images copied from photographs are hand-painted onto digitally printed grounds. The residue of the human in the act of copying resists the complete subordination of culture and experience to the technological, but no image is produced directly from life. What is painted derives from book and magazine plates or staged studio photographs, the cycling of pictorial content through several mediums identifying representational practices as a source of meaning in themselves.

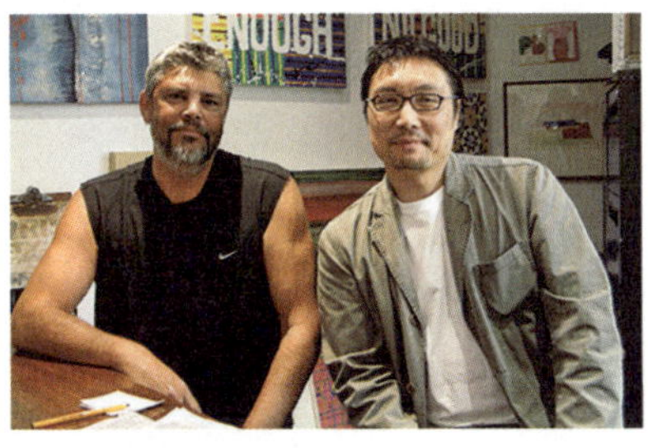

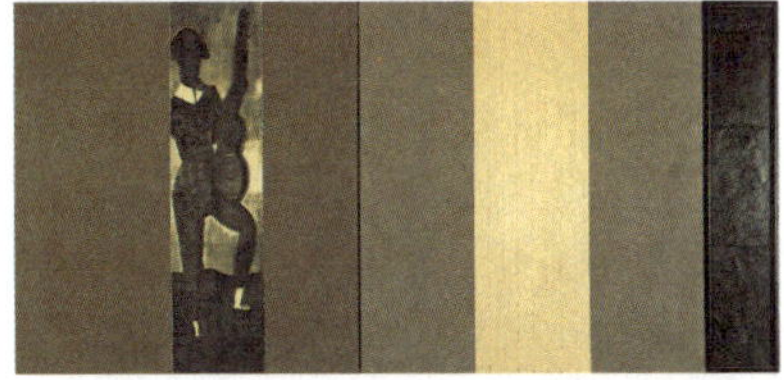

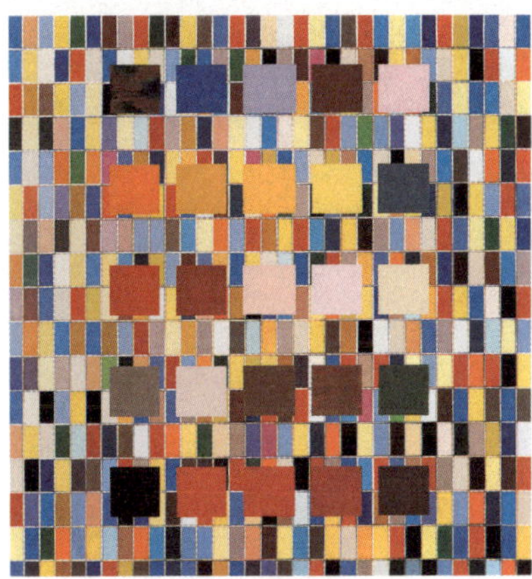

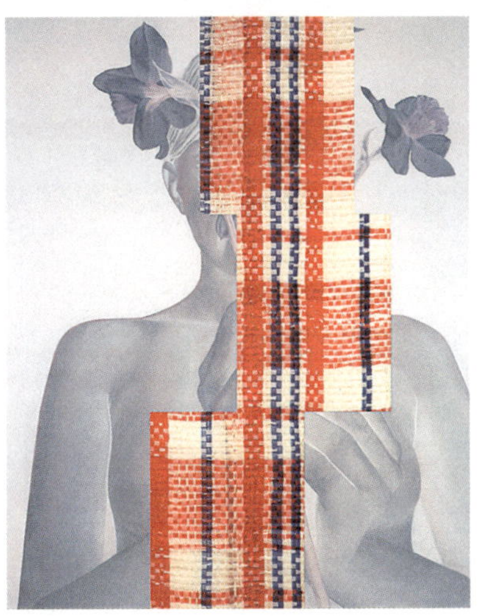

Left to right: Gordon Bennett and the artist, Bellas Milani Gallery, Brisbane, 2005
Photograph by Josh Milani

Charred Head Silhouette Painting 1988
Oil on linen, etched slate, wooden frame, 183 × 372 cm
Private collection, Perth

A Sudden Rush of Devotion 1989
Oil on linen, 183 × 168 cm
Private collection, Melbourne

Sanctuary 2003
Digital print and oil on linen, 195.5 × 151 cm
Collection of Salim Trust, Melbourne

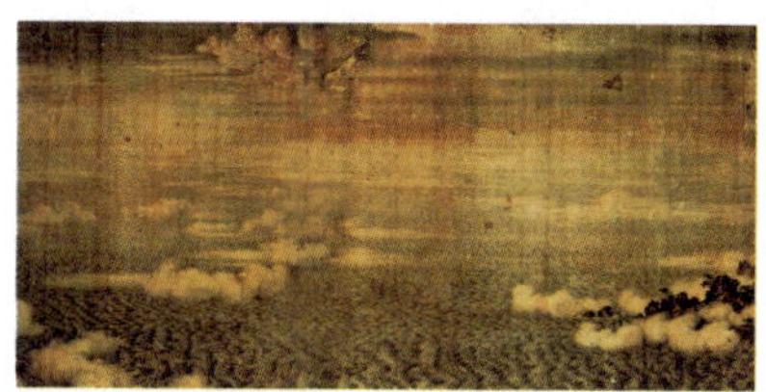

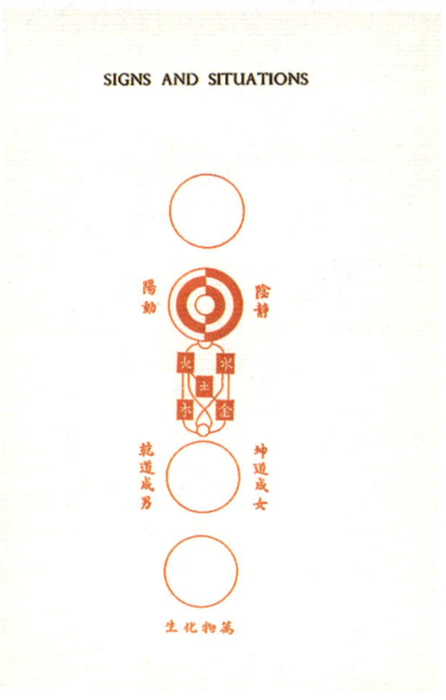

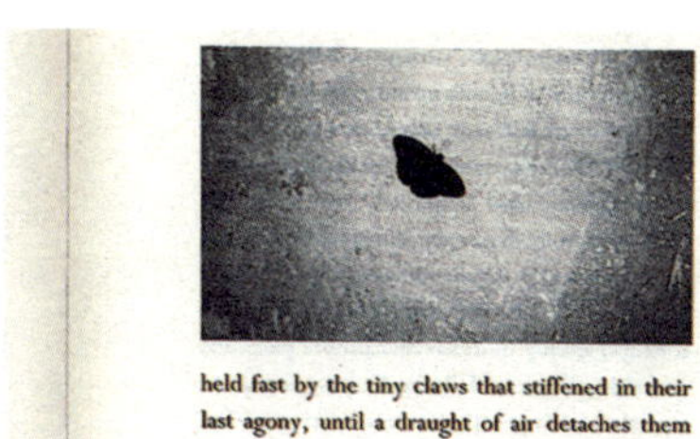

Giuseppe Castiglione (Lang Shining
郎世寧, 1688–1766)
Rising Sun Against Oceanic Sky
海天旭日圖 c. 1765
Ink and colour on silk, 93.7 × 182.2 cm
Collection of The Palace Museum, Beijing
Artist's note: Believed to be the last painting
completed by Castiglione.

Chinese mystical diagrams in Kenneth White,
The Most Difficult Area, Cape Goliard Press,
London, 1968

Detail of page 33 from W. G. Sebald,
Austerlitz, Penguin, London, 2001

NEW MODELS AND VALUES

Since around 2006, however, Young has worked to transcend the institutionalised situation of contemporary art and the way this limits meaningful exchange with the wider culture to explore the nature of memory and the shaping of history. Young considers the years he spent exploring problems of meaning and representation through the play of diverse semiotic resources as an artistic apprenticeship during which he was only developing the formal vocabulary and syntax to say something through art.[7] The present is informed by very different ideas about the nature and purpose of contemporary art. Nicolas Bourriaud, for example, has notably argued that criteria of social interaction have supplanted aesthetic values in contemporary art, with collaboration, participation, and intervention in contexts beyond the art world, and approaches grounded in research, defining contemporary practice.[8] By contrast, Boris Groys sees contemporary art practice as wholly circumscribed by the art system. No longer is art the object of aesthetic contemplation as it was in the modernist period, rather the artist's role is the production of their public self while a new 'democratic' art public expects art to examine 'the issues, topics, political controversies, and social aspirations that move … its everyday life'.[9]

Exploring a self-referential semiosis has been an undercurrent in Young's work, providing a fulcrum for investigating the forces at work on the individual and the collective in and between cultures. Since 2006, he has increasingly come to question whether contemporary art's dissection of signifying practices has been complicit in the denial of cultural and social agency. For Marc James Léger, 'Among the keystones of the postmodern notion of the multitude of decentred struggles we find the repudiation of universality … and the kind of ultrapolitics that depoliticises the culture wars and identity conflicts that are generated by the capitalist system'.[10] Young's current interest is to engage the whole of culture and society, not just the art world, using painting to address the lack of knowledge around historical events. Previously, aesthetic effects in his work acknowledged capitalism's success in aestheticising the whole of social experience to the detriment of the relevance of art. In the History Projects, aesthetic and material form are mediums of commentary, although Young does not assume his works' reception to be uniform given the differently constituted and positioned subjects who make up a broad viewing audience.

Young's models of practice in these projects come primarily from literature and film rather than visual art, notably the works of the Scottish poet Kenneth White, the German academic and writer W. G. Sebald, and the German filmmaker Hans-Jürgen Syberberg. Each addresses decay and destruction—of nature, historical epochs or memory—merging creative practice with critical historiography, controversially so in the case of Syberberg.[11] White and Sebald share a concern for the artist's responsibility to society and history. White's idea of geopoetics—where the subject of writing is the pure poetry of the natural world—seeks to realign human relations with nature by restoring poetics to the core of culture.[12] Sebald adopted the Frankfurt School philosophy that artworks should reflect a dialectical response to their historical circumstances, although, as Ben Hutchinson argues, Sebald launches each act of resistance from an aesthetic standpoint.[13] In the case of the work of Syberberg, Young's interest is more in the way form influences reception, the evident artifice of the *mise-en-scène* in Syberberg's films prompting the viewer to question their own signifying structures. The Taiwanese filmmaker Ang Lee is also an inspiration to Young, for his ability to work with subject matter from a diversity of cultural and social contexts, developing new representational languages through which to do this.

Where Young's previous interest was in capitalist globalisation and the rationalities and technologies of its culture and creative industries, the work of Lee, Sebald, Syberberg and White has inspired him to reorient his practice to advance a double-layered view of history via the stories of lesser-known historical figures and events in which barbarism did not wholly suppress the good. Within the History Projects, series such as *1967Dispersion* (2008), *Bonhoeffer in Harlem* (2009), *Safety Zone* (2010), *The New Wolf of Rome* (2012) and *The Macau Days* (2012) examine specific episodes of history within larger catastrophic events such as revolution and world war. *1967Dispersion* deals with political turbulence in Hong Kong in the summer of 1967, the exhibition title referencing both the breaking up of Maoist protests by the colonial government and the flight of many Hong Kong citizens, including Young, to other countries in the wake of the violence. *Bonhoeffer in Harlem* examines how the experience of racial oppression in New York in 1930 influenced active resistance to Nazism on the part of the German Lutheran pastor and theologian Dietrich Bonhoeffer. *Safety Zone* concerns the efforts of fifteen American and European missionaries and businesspeople in Nanjing in 1937 to save at least 200,000 Chinese citizens from death at the hands of the advancing Japanese army. *The Macau Days* focuses on the merchant port of Macau as a key staging post for Anglo-European encounters with China and Japan, contrasting this rich period of cross-cultural exchange with Macau's current incarnation as a phantasmagorical international gambling centre.[14]

COUNTER-PEDAGOGIES

In developing new counter-pedagogies in the History Projects, Young gives affective form to informational exchange. Although each exhibition seeks to preserve or reclaim the memory of a historical figure or situation, the use of sensory encounter for this purpose signals Young's contingent interest in the nature and process of memory production. The past is an infinite source of subject matter for remembering, collective memory being selectively shaped by its socio-historical context. In his work on time, the French philosopher Gilles Deleuze depicts memory formation as a fluid, two-way process, rather than a linear and cumulative one, a movement in time in which a vestigial past continues to act on the present.[15] Here Deleuze draws on Henri Bergson's earlier representation of the present as the condensation of the whole of the past in a moment, depicting the present as an emergent state in which the immediate experience of the world is continuously falling away.[16] James Williams argues that a primary concern in Deleuze's metaphysics of time is 'questions of genesis as they impinge on action'.[17] In his major work on time, *Difference and Repetition* (1968), Deleuze discusses the problems of retrieving and protecting the past through representation, not for the past's own sake, but in terms of how to exist with and act on the past in the present.[18] Deleuze cites Proust's approach to reminiscence as establishing a pure past that transcends what the past was in its own present without veering into idealisation.[19]

The return of the past as difference is pivotal to Deleuze's account of time, seeing him characterise the recovery of lost pasts as an endeavour suspended between actualisation and virtualisation.[20] Young's acquaintance with Deleuze comes through his reading of Deleuze's writing on cinema, which in exploring temporality in cinema offers a slightly less complex model for the representation of time that admits analogy, metaphor and direct representation.[21] Young's approach to history painting uses such means to reflect Deleuze's idea of a pure past that encompasses the quality of the infinitive with simultaneous 'surface intensities' in its representation to return perpetually as difference.[22] In certain painting cycles in the History Projects, Young works with a historian's attention to detail and interest in interpretation, while using the aesthetic treatment

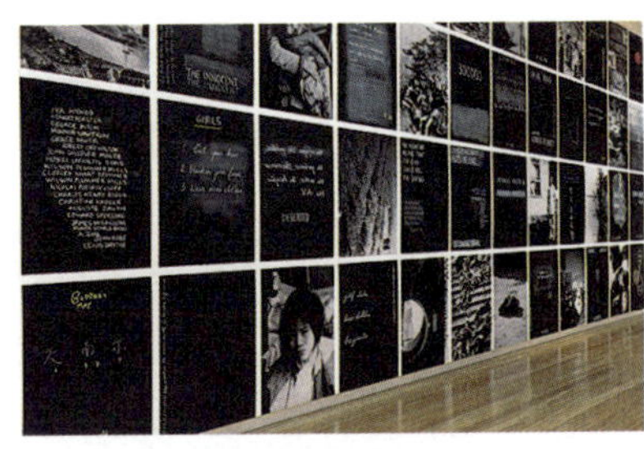

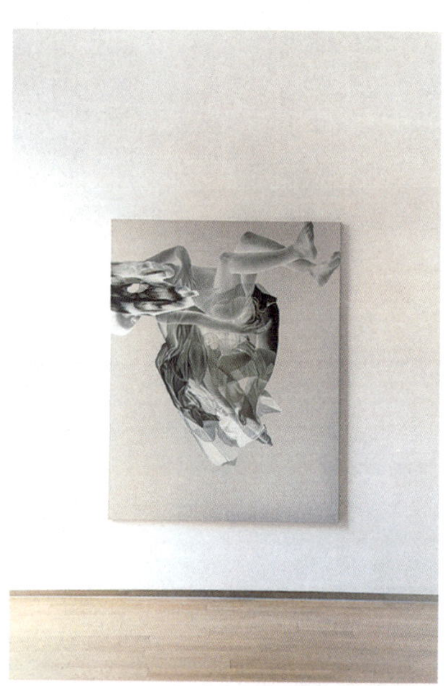

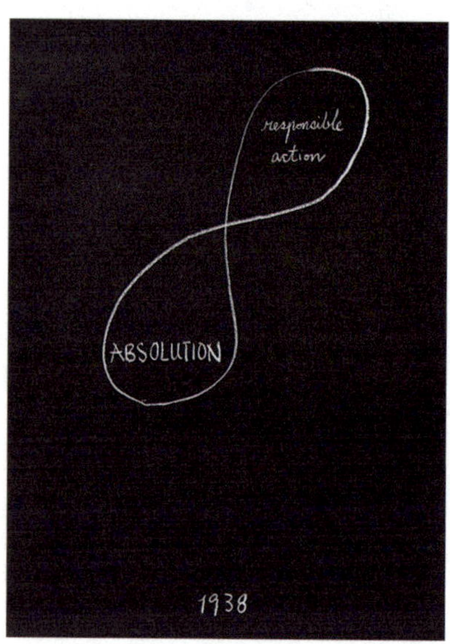

*Mazu, Goddess of the Sea II
(The Drowning of Mazu)* 2012
Installation view, 10 Chancery Lane Gallery,
Hong Kong, 2012

Responsible Action/Absolution 2008
Chalk on blackboard-painted archival
cotton paper, 100 x 70 cm

of pictorial materials to suggest the multiplicity of relations bound up in time, highlighting their asymmetrical nature and hence the past's resistance to fixity, resolution and completeness in evoking the processes involved in its forgetting and recovery. Certain paintings in *The Macau Days*, for example, exemplify this in their tangle of pictorial content—some elements presented as filmy traces, others as more solid forms—suggesting the elusive, synthetic processes bound up in memory, resulting in the uneven convergence of past and present according to which things from the past exist in the present in different intensities.

Within the corpus of the History Projects, different visual metaphors reveal something of the emotional and epistemological distance to be covered to engage the past. Monochrome images, negative images, images that expose the processes of reproduction, figures that defy gravity, otherworldly forms, visual manipulation that stretches the limits of representation, realism, abstraction, indeterminate spatial planes, alone and in combination—such distancing effects are the substance of Young's historiography. Mostly, his 'history paintings' have the quality of apparitions, echoing Deleuze's idea that the past, in contrast to the sense of the immediate present, encompasses nothing specific, but at the same time cannot be dismissed as fictional or intangible.

BRINGING THE SUBJECT INSIDE

Importantly, as a set of inherently synthetic projects, the individual works in each series gain their full impact and meaning when brought together in the form of an exhibition through installation strategies, such as the use of banks of works on paper that occupy whole walls of a gallery. The use of installation to unite the archaic and fragmentary is common among artists who work conceptually with the material of history. In 2004, Hal Foster drew attention to this distinct tendency in contemporary art through which artists used invented archives comprised of remediated images, texts and objects to foster historical mindfulness, using installation to bring coherence to these collections of materials. For Foster, this 'archival impulse', exemplified for him in the work of artists including Gerard Byrne, Tacita Dean, Douglas Gordon, Thomas Hirschhorn and Pierre Huyghe, was a way 'to make historical information, often lost or displaced, physically present'.[23] The unorthodox pedagogies Young employs in the History Projects retrieve and juxtapose remnants of the past, with the titles of the different works and series, when combined with written content within the select works, providing a textual index that is augmented by the aesthetic, conceptual and material characteristics of the works.

Jungmin Lee argues that 'the terminology of "Installation" reveals an inward movement and thus an effort to bring the subject inside'.[24] In the exhibitions of *Safety Zone* (2010), *1866: The Worlds of Lowe Kong Meng and Jong Ah Siug* (2015) and *The Burrangong Affray* (2018), for example, banks of images cover entire walls of the gallery, towering over the viewer to form a plane of vision, the *in situ* corporeal experience intensifying the encounter with the work's subject matter so as to afford the past a living presence. Young's approach to installation takes much from the model of cinema, which uses duration, the editing and sequencing of images, and sensory immersion to show the relationship between things. In each group of works, reproductions of historical photographs in combination with chalk drawings harness cinema's language of reference and representation, its modes of experience and sensibility, but in contracted form. Familiarity with the role of characters in embodying positive and negative attributes and delivering narrative content amplifies the sense of density in the actual representational content.

From the sixteenth to the mid-nineteenth century, academic
history painting was central to Western art, being grounded in
the effort to transmit moral understanding from past to present.
Under the conditions of modernism, the locus of art shifted to
firstly capturing the essence of modern life, then articulating the
aesthetic basis of painting as forms of communicable knowledge.
Postmodernism reflected a complete scepticism towards the
principles of verifiable knowledge. Recently, knowledge exchange
has been restored to the core of art practice, albeit while
embracing the idea of its multi-sided perspectivism, with current
participatory and community-based forms of art engagement
seeking to confront fixed categories, discourses, meanings and
representations that entrench hierarchical values, power or
inequity.[25] As a substantial body of work, John Young's History
Projects are dedicated to knowledge production, challenging
collective forgetting on the basis that the present remains in
the hold of the past.

The traditional nature of painting has to an extent invalidated
painting as a medium of communication for many artists, the
state of contemporary visual art reflecting a 'post-medium'
situation. Against the flood of competing stimuli in the present,
Young approaches painting as a space for focused subjective
connection with history. Both imagistic and poetic approaches
to representation from film and literature and modern art's
far-reaching experimentation with forms and materials are a
presence in the History Projects. The works simultaneously play
off relations between image and text and the medium-specific
capacities of painting and photography to present a revitalised
post-conceptual version of history painting, the reanimation
of archival content re-infusing the genre with new critical force
and productivity. The History Projects awaken us to categories
of historical and human experience to enrich our sense of
history. Works of art, at their best, stand as prototypical
opportunities for experience. In a world in which everything
has become a commodity and everyday life a projection of
consumption, the History Projects seek to add duration and
empathy to the process of reflecting on history, via the aesthetic
and the sensory, not to instruct us in what to think about
history, but rather to actualise our powers of ethical judgement.

1. Email correspondence with the artist, 22 September 2020.

2. Charles Reep, 'What's Wrong with Didacticism?', *British Journal of Aesthetics*, Vol. 52, No. 3, 2012, p. 271.

3. Email correspondence with the artist, 22 September 2020.

4. For a discussion with John Young on some of these earlier works, see the conversation with Aaron Seeto in this volume, pp. 394–414.

5. The term 'cultural intermediary' is proposed by Pierre Bourdieu in *Distinction: A Social Critique of the Judgement of Taste*, Harvard University Press, Cambridge, UK, 1984.

6. Benzi Zhang, 'Identity in Diaspora and Diaspora in Writing: the poetics of cultural transrelation', *Journal of Intercultural Studies*, vol. 21, no. 2, 2000, p. 125.

7. See the discussion on early projects, from the late 1970s for example, with Aaron Seeto in the Coda to this volume, pp. 394–414.

8. Nicolas Bourriaud, *Relational Aesthetics*, Simon Pleasance and Fronza Woods (transl.), Les Presses du Réel, Dijon, [1998] 2002, p. 11. Young's development of a methodology that embraces ethics as art practice, dubbed 'situational ethics' by Thomas Berghuis, included a critical response to Bourriaud's then popular theorisation of 'relational' artworks. See the correspondence between Young and Berghuis in this volume, p. 122.

9. Boris Groys, *Going Public*, Sternberg Press, Berlin, 2010, p. 12.

10. Marc James Léger, 'Avant-Garde and Creative Industry', *Creative Industries Journal*, vol. 3, no. 2, 2010, p. 152.

11. On Syberberg, see the essay in this volume by Marc Glöde, p. 148.

12. Pierre Jamet, 'The Poetry and Ideas of Kenneth White: A Perspective from France', *Scottish Literary Review*, vol. 1, no. 1, 2009, p. 103.

13. Ben Hutchinson, 'The Shadow of Resistance: W. G. Sebald and the Frankfurt School', *Journal of European Studies*, vol. 41, no. 3–4, 2011, p. 276.

14. For fuller accounts of these projects, see for example the essays in this volume by Krischer on *1967 Dispersion*, p. 60; Volz on *Bonhoeffer in Harlem*, p. 92; Glöde on *Safety Zone*, p. 154; and Hielscher on *The Macau Days*, p. 209.

15. Gilles Deleuze, *Bergsonism*, Zone Books, New York, 1988.

16. Gilles Deleuze, *Difference and Repetition*, Paul Patton (transl.), Continuum, London, 2004, p. 103.

17. James Williams, *Gilles Deleuze's Philosophy of Time: A Critical Introduction and Guide*, Edinburgh University Press, Edinburgh, 2001, p. 1.

18. Ibid., p. 77.

19. Deleuze, *Difference and Repetition*, pp. 121–24.

20. Williams, *Gilles Deleuze's Philosophy of Time*, p. 74.

21. Ibid., p. 162.

22. Ibid., p. 163.

23. Hal Foster, 'An Archival Impulse', *October* 110 (2004): 4. http://www.jstor.org/stable/3397555.

24. Jungmin Lee, 'Modes of Exhibition as Mediated Space: Projection Installation as Spectatorial Frame', *Art & Education*, http://www.artandeducation.net/paper/modes-of-exhibition-as-mediated-space-projection-installation-as-spectatorial-frame/, accessed September 2012.

25. Katarzyna Kosmala, 'Temporality and alteration of social boundaries in the making of an art installation', *Creative Industries Journal*, vol. 4, no. 1, 2011, p. 65.

JOHN YOUNG: PAINTING SIMULACRA AND A RE-ENVISAGED HISTORY

John Clark

The work of John Young intends to re-envisage history, including, eventually, the history of the Chinese in Australia.[1] The intention is such in terms of the two meanings postulated by art historian Michael Baxandall: that the notion of intention is 'descriptive of a relationship between a picture and its circumstances' and that as a 'pattern posited in behaviour, it is used to give circumstantial facts and descriptive concepts a basic structure'.[2] Baxandall explains the causations that led to particular pictures in terms of those induced from the structure of the work's relation to the situation in which it was made, and as an inferable pattern of behaviour in the maker or the overall procedures of making. It is in the latter that the artist's own notion of making and why a particular work was made—that is, their artistic will or intention—can be assessed.

Baxandall pursued his analysis with solid, reproducible works of art that might be deemed permanent for the purposes of appreciation and understanding. However, works of art can also be impermanent and indeed, we can suppose it is because the aesthetic situation of their appreciation is so historically subject to the values of the audience and the artist that they may be contested. They can also be imbricated within other sets of values and the notion of who and whose values are to rule, to serve as a hegemon. This will be so in any particular situation of historical interpretation of an artwork with a set of values that are not those of its maker or first audience, or with values that are used to re-historicise a work with a new set of values hidden in the original. These are sometimes not apparent to the original maker.

In this light, the work itself is impermanent—whatever the physical durability of its materials or visual technology—and what constitutes any regular recurrence of aesthetic appreciation, must be due in part to the ability of those who set the aesthetic values for a culture to impose or continue to impose them. The ability to re-awaken the past in the present is one of the features of historical memory most relevant to art, into which any set of aesthetic values now dominant for a culture or a set of interpreters, such as postmodern art critics or curators, interpose.[3]

One might propose that the very impermanence of art historical reality allows it to be recuperated, even under contestation by those dominant aesthetic values in a different time, or when those values are held by a different hegemon.[4] The very attractiveness of looking at art from other cultures, which themselves incorporate values of more than one culture, is that the values the works carry become part of a liminal space for their re-construction, or rather that those makers who cross cultural boundaries are equipped to live in a liminal state where their own hybridity permits a re-valuation.

The linkage of artist, artwork, and audience is unstable across time. A clear Chinese example is the pair of paintings by Hou Yimin: *Liu Shaoqi and the Miners of Anyuan* (1964) and *Chairman Mao with the workers of Anyuan* (1977). These were originally intended as a pair but the first one was destroyed during the Cultural Revolution because its subject was Liu Shaoqi, a Chinese revolutionary, politician and theorist and the then Chairman of the People's Republic of China, who was persecuted to death in the Cultural Revolution. The surviving painting, in the National Art Museum of China in Beijing, is a later re-painting by Hou. Likewise, its intended pair was supposedly begun at the same time but could not be completed in the political atmosphere of the early 1960s and was worked up by the artist from his surviving sketches from 1976 to 1977. Under certain conditions the permanence of the artwork is stable only in the artist's intention and almost impossibly impermanent in the actual world.

Furthermore, the events depicted can be so unstable—that is, historically contested—or have been overlaid with such later meanings, that the work itself cannot come into the world until much later when the hegemon has changed. This is very clear in Indonesia with FX Harsono's artwork, *Darkroom* (2009), which depicts the massacres of ethnic Chinese during the War of Independence (1947–1948), when some were suspected of spying for or collaborating with the Dutch. Given the social position of Chinese in the Dutch colonial Indies, this would have been hardly surprising. But the making of an artwork to commemorate them only became possible in the post-Suharto era, when Harsono discovered a number of images of bodies being disinterred among his late father's photographs. His father was the town photographer and when the bodies of the Chinese victims were given proper burial between 1949 and 1951, after Independence, his father was employed to take photographs of the bones as they were disinterred before re-burial. Harsono made a very large installation work of this material that was shown in 2010 in Yogyakarta.[5]

But this interpretation of the issue of restitution of a historical event is not quite so clear-cut. As a teenager in 1965, Harsono had witnessed the massacre of Chinese accused of being communists, but he could not make a work about this until much later, after the hegemon had passed on. In other words, one permissible reconstitution of history via re-visualisation was overlying a much more recent and more atrocious event that was nearer in time but could not yet be properly worked out.[6]

History is embodied in particular lives, in the creative life of artists among others. These lives often tell us, through the artist's works, which events or subjects have been allowed into history and what is controlled or deflected from it by a mainstream agenda. This is clear in Australia, where since the 1970s, an Anglo-Celtic mainstream has more widely accepted immigrants, often from China. But China has a much older and deeper relationship with Australia and much of this history is only now emerging. Bearing these two different histories of China overseas in mind, let us now consider the life and work of one artist, John Young, as their focus.

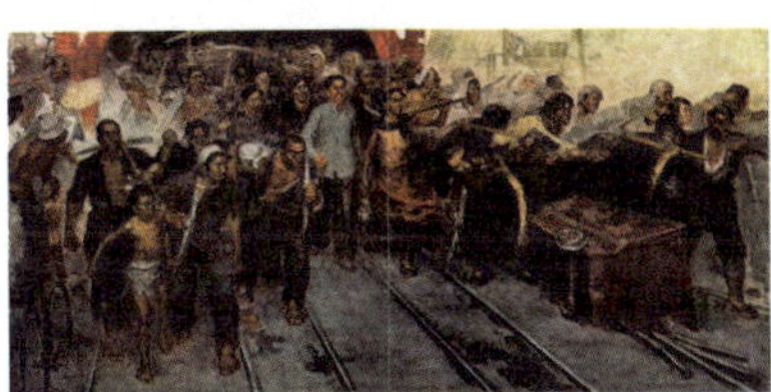

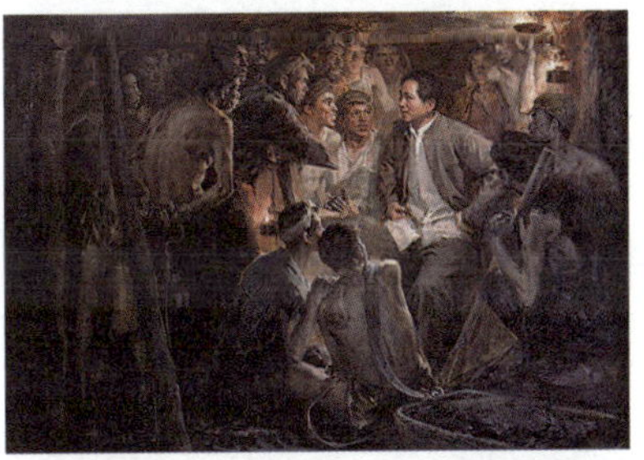

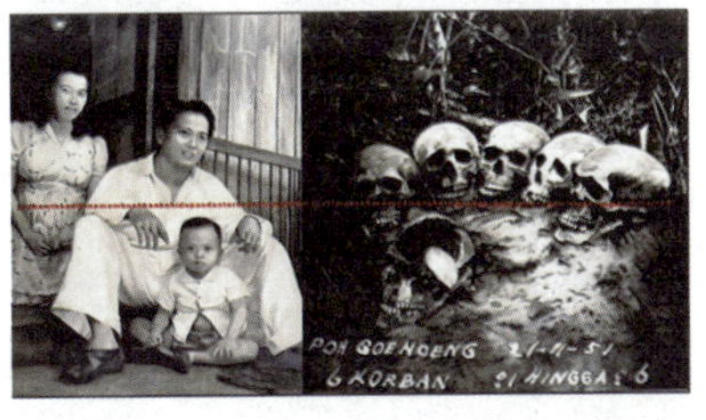

Hou Yimin (候一民, 1930–2023)
Liu Shaoqi and the Miners of Anyuan 1961/1977
Oil on canvas, 160 × 330 cm
Collection of National Museum of China, Beijing
Artist's note: The original 1961 painting was apparently destroyed in the Cultural Revolution and repainted by Hou in 1977.

Hou Yimin (候一民, 1930–2023)
Chaiman Mao with the Workers of Anyuan 1977
Oil on canvas, 182 × 254 cm
Collection of National Museum of China, Beijing
Artist's note: This painting was completed from the pre-Cultural Revolution sketches that survived.

FX Harsono (1949–)
Preserving Life, Terminating Life #2 2009
Oil, acrylic and thread on canvas, diptych, 200 × 350 cm
Collection of Singapore Art Museum; image courtesy of the artist

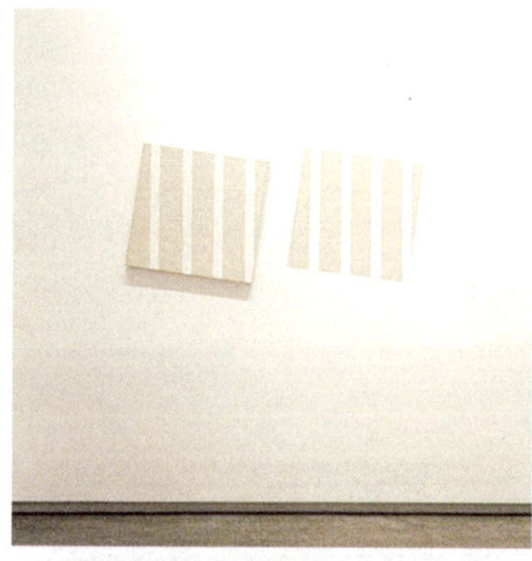

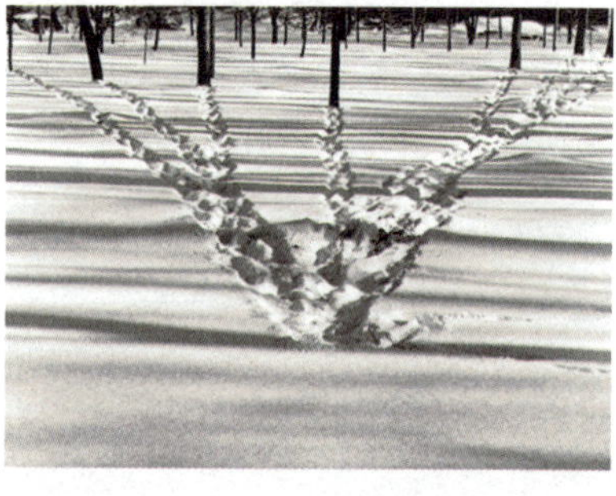

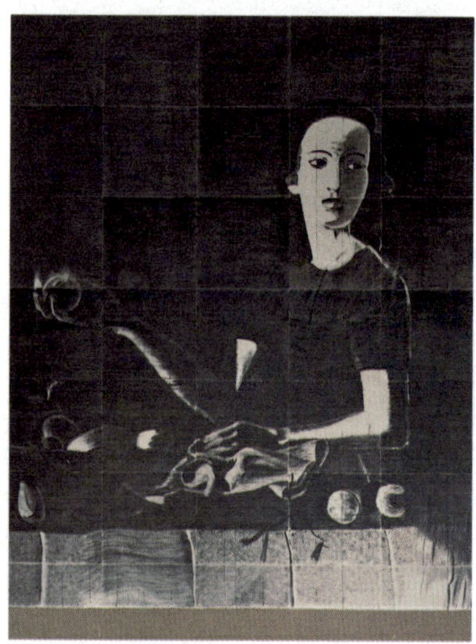

Propositional Limits - Visual Paradox 3 and 4 1978
Canvas with industrial gloss paint and canvas
on wall, two units, 55 × 55 cm each

Manchurian Snow Walk (completed) 1979
Silver gelatin print, 60.5 × 80 cm

The Pink Fruit 1987
Oil on linen, 167.5 × 122 cm
Private collection, Melbourne

Young's personal life, artistic development and cultural location in many ways form a paradigm case for the placement of art both internationally and in Australia in the late twentieth and early twenty-first centuries. Because he moved from Hong Kong to Australia in 1967, and later made international travels to Europe, his biography is also a marker for interaction between the local and the transnational, both of which bracket the national. The diasporic exerts pressures in both inward and outward directions. Young situates for us the issues of a re-constituted Australianness with its many obscured, even occluded, narratives of what it is to be both Asian and Australian. China is both a culturally specific and primal identifier for those of Chinese heritage, but it is now also far more generally a marker for what is the Asianness of Australia itself, in geographical location, political and familial history, and in cultural identification. These are issues linked to the colonial and its heritages in a postcolonial situation where they are more visible due to the very length of postcoloniality in Australia. Some would see such visibility as due to the reluctance of Australia to relinquish its own (British) coloniality in a state that, at least in name, became independent in 1901. This was a refusal that extended up to the failed referendum on the Republic in 1999, when Australia declined to determine that its head of state should be autochthonous. This long, and some would say still unrealised, withdrawal from the colonial allows us to see the temporal longevity and historical complexity of these residues of a once colonial history and their problematic expression in art forms more clearly than if there had been an abrupt rupture with the hegemony of the once-colonising power.

Indeed, the Australian postcolonial situation, overlapping here as it does with questions of a hybrid cultural and personal identity with Asia, including China, can make us think there are extremes and variabilities in the rupture with the past and the projection of a future. Historical permanence and impermanence of the national entity and its cultural representation in Australia overlap with the issue of cultural affiliation, and the formation of different types of identity within Australia and its region. In other words, a *temporal* or historical variation is over-mapped with the consequences of a *spatial* or geographical placement. These variations may be as well known to individual artists and expressed in their work as they are so little understood, and may be passed over or even rejected by a mainstream art culture.

Yet quite distinct from his situation as an artist within Australian culture, the development of Young's art itself is every bit as complicated. One would expect this of an artist who came of age at a time in the late 1970s to early 1980s, when critical art theory and the formal discourses of conceptualism struck the art world of Australia, as elsewhere in Japan, Korea, and Southeast Asia for example. Whether or not art theory and conceptualism were ideal frames for understanding identity issues, they were nevertheless the ones Young dealt with in forming his own art.

Some of Young's important statements regarding the formation of his art will emerge in what follows. It would be superfluous to repeat them all here, but I will examine features of Young's personal and artistic development, before tracking some of his theoretical writings and other explicatory descriptions.

FIVE PHASES

Young's development is marked by the turns of five major phases. The first, in the late 1960s to late 1970s, was his arrival in an Australian Jesuit high school. Later in the 1980s, Young's texts were to be secular and unconcerned with theology, but one cannot help feeling that the legacy of his verbal and visual expression must owe something

to this early Jesuit education. This was followed by his training first as a philosopher
and then as an artist in Sydney. One could say that, for an artist, he is unusually well
trained to think, but his interest in art is parallel to this intellectual formation and not
separate nor indeed successive.[7]

The second phase through to the mid-1980s is one of stylistic positioning within the
domain of postmodern conceptualism—expressed in a philosophy-derived trajectory
which questions the ontological status of visual propositions—seen in his 1978
Propositional Limits–Visual Paradox series. This phase included journeys that separately
marked his affiliations with both China and Europe, including a conceptual walk in
Harbin, in northeast China, in 1979, and a one-minute one-person show in Rosroe,
Ireland, in 1982, in the house where Ludwig Wittgenstein (a particularly influential
figure from Young's philosophy studies) completed his *Philosophical Investigations*.

Young's third phase includes extensive work with the iteration of figurative images
across a number of culturally associative layers in the same work. These began with
debts to European late modernism, such as the late André Derain (*The Bacchantes*,
c. 1945) in the 1986 *Silhouette Series*, but soon moved to the elaborate series of large
coloured tesselations, some with what might appear to be a narrative element in the
top of the frame. They were followed by the narrative over-layering of the *Polychrome
Paintings* of 1991 to 1992 and the masterly formalesque ground and surface image
switching of the *Double Ground Paintings* from 1995. These paintings displayed
bravura formal innovation through their use of multiple digitised images which
were then painted in oils, often by studio assistants. Young had been increasingly
concerned with, on the one hand, the lack of patronage for contemporary art by Asian
Australians and, on the other, by the resistance of mainstream art culture to heritage
references by Asian artists. To address these issues, in 1995 he was involved in setting
up the Asian Australian Artists' Association (Gallery 4A), now the 4A Centre for
Contemporary Asian Art, Sydney, but soon became disillusioned by the excessive
Asianisation of Asian Australian artists—what we may call reverse exoticisation, due
to the mood in cultural politics of the time. By 1997 he had left Gallery 4A, married
and moved to Melbourne. He was later involved again in 4A as a Board Member
for many years.

The fourth phase was one of a concern with ethical and transnational historicism
and, separately but in parallel, with a re-mediated decorative abstraction. Young had
been careful to connect with the political class who dispense art commissions and
was asked by the State Premier of Victoria, Steve Bracks (himself of Lebanese family
background), to design a work to commemorate links between Victoria and Jiangsu
Province. For this, Young produced a design which was woven into the tapestry
Open World (2005) which now hangs in Nanjing Library.

Almost in parallel, Young began a series of abstract paintings from 2007 based
on a computer transformation of an image selected from several thousand images
randomly downloaded from the internet overnight. This image was transformed, then
blown up and copied into an oil painting field. It was also this technique that Young
deployed in the design for a tapestry made to hang in the St Matthäus Church, Berlin,
where there is a commemorative memorial to the heroic Pastor Dietrich Bonhoeffer
(1906–1945), who was martyred by the Nazis for his resistance. Young also used
writings in German, Chinese and English on paper prepared with blackboard paint,
in the manner of lecture notes by the anthroposophist Rudolf Steiner, which were later
referenced by Joseph Beuys.[8] In 2009, the *Bonhoeffer in Harlem* series was exhibited
in Berlin and ultimately became a permanent exhibit at a church in Bamberg.

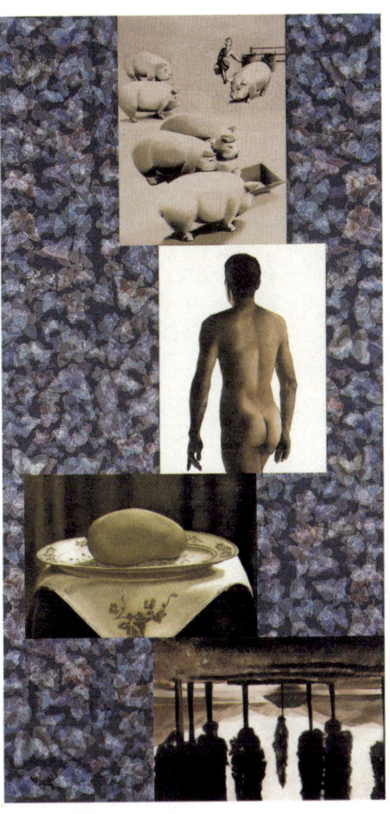

That bright red star 2000
Digital print and oil on canvas, 288 × 138 cm

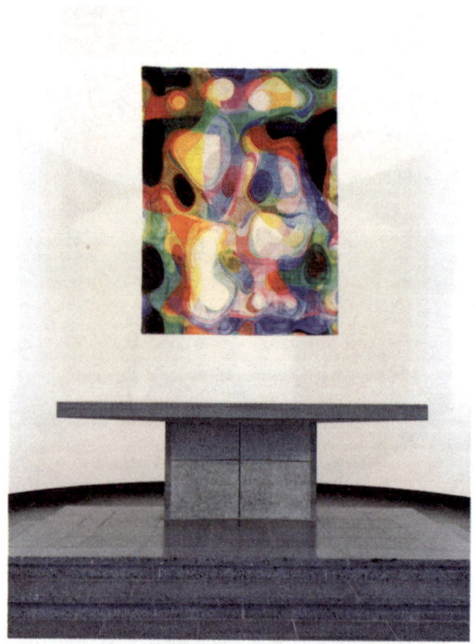

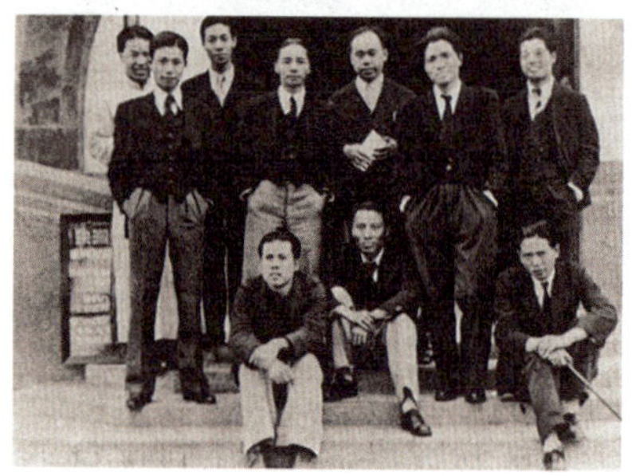

This work does not exist as a singularity, nor does its installation allow for a single, permanent set of iterable aesthetic experiences. Indeed, there are many layers of temporality at play in the Australian discourse of Young's works: the thoughts of Young on the ethicality of *Bonhoeffer in Harlem*; the affect on national perception as a result of the musealisation of the Nanjing Massacre; the location of three physical sites in Berlin, New York, and Nanjing; the viewing of all these works from a culturally hybrid Australian viewpoint, one which is not causally linked to the referenced events.

Young returned to research he had already done on Nanjing for the 2011 work *Safety Zone*. He met the grandson of John Rabe (1882–1950), the Siemens' manager in China and Nazi Party member who was one of the international committee members responsible for saving 300,000 Chinese people during the Japanese Rape of Nanjing. Rabe thought 250,000 of the Chinese population were saved so the figure of dead may have been about 50,000, but other estimates are much higher.[9] Young went on to think beyond the narrow preoccupation with the reception of Asian Australians and their art in Australian culture to broader questions of how someone who had not experienced these horrendous events of twentieth-century history could legitimately reconstitute them as the subject of an ethically concerned artwork from a transnational position.

In the fifth phase of Young's development, he has continued the abstract painting transformations of downloaded images, as a sort of pure painting of our age. *Storm Resurrection* was shown in 2016 in Shanghai, based on photographs of the Storm Society (Juelanshe), a Chinese avant-garde art group which Young learnt about from a paper presented at an academic conference in Canberra, in 1991.[10] But in the 2010s, he continued the transnational ethical exploration developed for his *Bonhoeffer in Harlem* and *Safety Zone* projects, to re-envisage historical Chinese Australian interactions, in particular the historical placement of Chinese in Ballarat and their subsequent effacement from Australian history. Young has reconstituted this history via primary research on documents, the assembling of photographs from family records, and by a type of visual memorialisation.

This would take the form of a public monument with photographs laser-cut into granite, in Ballarat in 2015, and in the revisualisation of Chinese lives in Australia from family and other records, as well as texts shown as large photographs or written in white chalk on paper painted with blackboard paint in *Modernity's End: Half the Sky* (2016). This series shows images of two Australian-born Chinese women, the journalist, Alice Lim Kee, and the mother and later translator, Daisy Kwok from the family who managed the Wing On department stores in Shanghai in the 1920s and 1930s. Young again displays the device of chalk writing in English in alternation with the images, a faux-naïf but particularly effective way of introducing comments on the images or half-citations from other documents and letters.

Here, history is presented to the viewer as not-fixed and subject to new construction in the hands of its successors—its familial or community inheritors. History is no longer due to the habitual or permanent deflection or occlusion of the dominant trajectory of the cultural mainstream. By such images, one group of inheritors claims the right to construct its own sometimes transitory or 'impermanent' relation to the mainstream. But that construction can be seen the other way around, as permanent from a position of mainstream hegemony. This claims 'permanence' for its historical views, even if these can and do change.

Some of these issues become particularly clear when we look at Young's own art theoretical and critical writings, because they have in various guises preoccupied him throughout his career. I cannot claim to deal with the full complexity of his thought here, but I think it is productive to take up a few of these ideas.

YOUNG'S ART THEORIES AND THEIR SOURCES

Early on, Young was attracted to chance photographs, made without use of the viewfinder. His first exhibition in 1981 was of a single, random, reflected image taken in Amsterdam, which he showed for one minute in the cottage in Ireland where Wittgenstein had finished his *Philosophical Investigations*. Here Young was bringing together his continual preoccupations with the conceptual status of an image and the paradox in scientific writing: 'namely the coexistence of apparently rigorous rationalism with a more imaginative, metaphorical aesthetic dimension'.[11]

Young, who studied mathematics, history of science and art history (then called Fine Arts) at the University of Sydney, marked off the following section in the book *Against Method* by the theorist of epistemological anarchism, Paul Feyerabend:

> The epistemological anarchist has no compunction to defend the most
> trite, or the most outrageous statement. While the political or religious
> anarchist wants to remove a certain form of life, the epistemological
> anarchist may want to defend it, for he has no everlasting loyalty to, and
> no everlasting aversion against, any institution or ideology.[12]

In this free epistemological space, it is unsurprising that Young was also among the first Australian artists to pay due attention to Baudrillard's theories of the simulacrum. Due to this, in 1981 Young jointly authored, with Terry Blake, an essay in the then leading Australian art theoretical journal, *Art & Text*, in which he moves from the evacuation of the sign to its counterweight, the death of the author/artist:[13]

> The hermit responds to the death of the code with a gesture of mourning
> and isolation. Carefully he goes over images of death and decay rendering
> them with a perfectionist delight in craftsmanship. But the work of
> cultural mourning, this progressive detachment of the hermit from all
> the cultural contents is accompanied by the discovery of the craft itself as
> value. By an impersonal immersion in the craft, the hermit comes to *mourn
> the myth of his own subjectivity*, the death of the artist.[14]

Thus, what is evanescent or transient for Young will be the intellectual frame for the next thirty-five years of his work, firmly based on a critical break between a supposed univalent relation of the artist and the work itself. This cut is also the logical support that overturns a singular reading by the audience or denies a hegemonic interpretation like that of the state or other nation-proclaiming avatars. The artist's relation with his work is so de-constructed or bracketed that the notion of a permanence in the artwork itself is called into question. Perhaps, too, this may be why the position of avant-gardists, or of the avant-garde hermeneutic, is so similar between artists who may have quite different stylistics, material practices or cultural and historical contexts.

In an interview with an art critic in 2002, Young noted how he had been given a sudden release into what was, if not a permanent discourse, then certainly a position

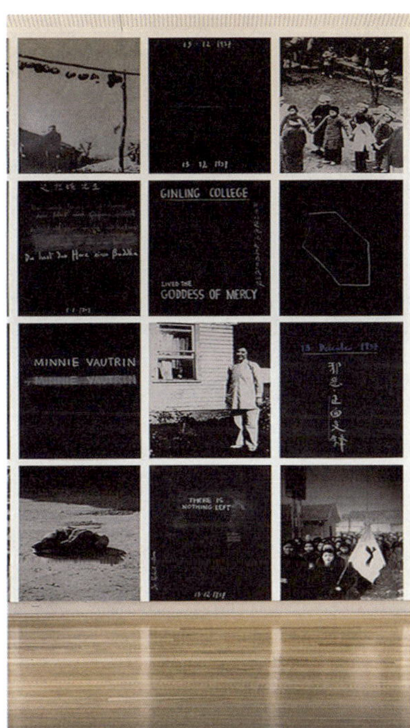

Detail of *Safety Zone* 2010
Installation view, *John Young: Diaspora Psyche*,
Bunjil Place, Narre Warren, 2021

29

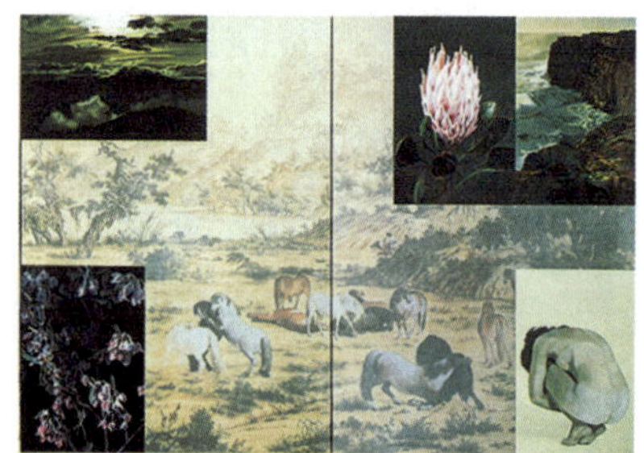

that had escaped the hegemony, which by the early 1990s was promoted by critics, theoreticians, and, slightly later, curators.

> Sean Lowry: Nonetheless, you must have found that a distance exists between your own artistic process and the critical rhetoric that can often surround your work.
>
> John Young: In the 1980s it was postmodernism, and in the early 1990s a lot of my 'postmodern' friends just slipped away to other disciplines, but I got a sudden rebirth through this curious thing called 'Regionalism'. It is a very obvious Asianisation, bringing Asia into the discourse of Western art or confronting it directly or on the side.
>
> SL: I guess to be part of that whole postcolonial multiculturalism in the early 1990s you needed an identifiable platform.
>
> JY: But I was fairly unpopular in that situation too because a lot of Chinese artists were exoticising themselves in the way in which, in advertising, people consciously exoticise themselves. I see that happening in the art world still. I learnt […] that cultures are more translatable than incommensurate. Artists who claim untranslatability are at times claiming a power to say anything without any accountability.[15]

Even by 1983 Young was beginning to think of images not as single concatenations but as discretely layered in two planes on top of and visible through each other, and it is a third 'figure' or a consciousness at their intersections which governs how they are entangled. This 'witness' or 'protector' was called a Third Man by critics deploying the theories of Michael Serres:

> [the Third Man] untangles, interlaces, twists, assembles, passes above and below, rejoins the rational, the irrational, namely, the speakable and the unspeakable, communication and the incommunicable.[16]

These intersections were clear or obscured and could be used for references to previous artworks, or as Young was soon to develop them in 1993, as actual reproductions from culturally specific and presumed culturally distinct art worlds. Young wanted to paint later images without them being framed by a ground. In fact, he specifically wanted to envisage multiple narratives which were obvious by the cultural source of the images, whether they be 'academy nudes' or 'Chinese landscapes'. He was concerned with the mundane or kitsch qualities of images in everyday discourse but also to show how there was a relationship of dependence between both aspects:

> Narratives, patterns, marks digitally printed on the background: areas of painted generic photographic images in the foreground. The paintings are worked from all four sides. The structure aims to make you feel as if the images in the foreground and the background have belonged together all the while—a sort of necessary dependency. This diabolical structure may naturalise the foreground into the background, or mimic the way that resonance can determine our everyday attitudes towards images.[17]

Detail of *Castiglione's Dream* 1996
Digital print, synthetic polymer paint and oil
on canvas, four panels, 219.5 × 613.6 cm
Collection of National Gallery of Australia,
Canberra

DIASPORIC IDENTITY AND HISTORY

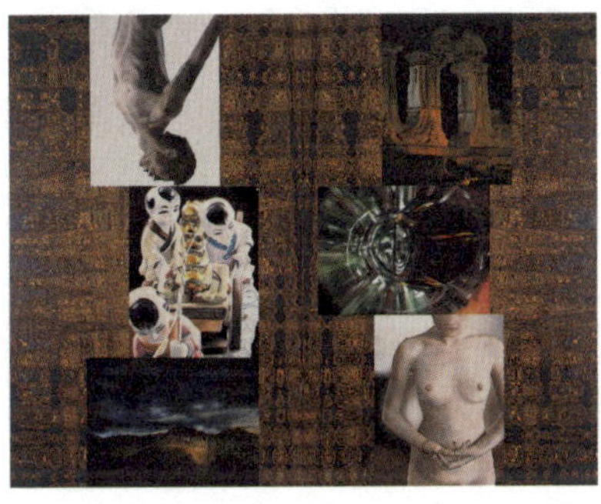

The caesura in Young's work that took him away from postmodernist and conceptual mirror effects of discourse—or the breaking of historical continuities through the abandonment of hierarchy as a device for linking references—was the conference 'Modernism and Postmodernism in Asian Art' which he attended in 1991.[18] This conference showed him the historical differences and cross-national contiguities between different kinds of modernity in Asian cultures. He subsequently felt more empowered to pursue a set of Chinese references alongside Western ones; something his previous philosphical training and art world placement had not allowed him to do.[19] Indeed, that an intellectual position advanced for 'Asia' as a construct could be valid in Australia for a person of both Chinese and Western heritages without any superficial hybridisation, which allowed for the interweaving but also identitification of discrete cultural strands, was experienced by him as a liberation.

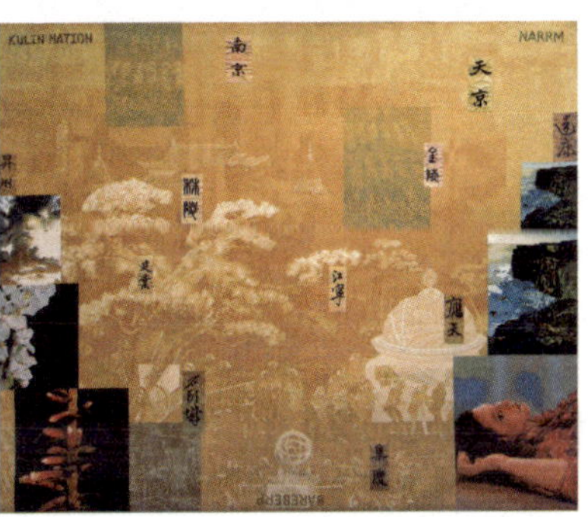

It may be that by the 1990s the high theorisation of the 1980s had passed its relevance, or was simply exhausted. Perhaps all intellectual and visual references made available by international travel were, by this period of early globalisation, sufficiently broad to allow heterogenous juxtaposition of text, figurative images and abstractions as a visual technique. These were shortly to be greatly expanded by the virtual travel of the World Wide Web from around 1993. However, individuals, like cultures, have a history, and Young felt that the Australian culture he was in did not significantly permit him to articulate the other culture which he had carried from childhood, that of a Hong Kong Chinese. This was not what he had encountered equally deeply as Australian, but the construction of art discourses in Australia as 'national' shut off this heritage. Indeed to connect too much with it in an Australian space might be regarded as subversive or even treasonous.[20] Around 1994 Young began to be more aware that he had a set of values which he wanted to describe and to do so through figurative painting, a language whose limitations he was keen to test:

> [M]y interest is in attempting to describe a lot of different values which are inherent in Chinese culture, for example, but using one language which is figurative painting. You tend to run against the walls of language. Sometimes if a person from the West sees these paintings they would tend to think it is a bit kitsch or nonsensical, but what interests me is this idea of attempting to describe values in a pictorial language where you continually run against the walls of that language.[21]

It was Young's commission to design a tapestry presented by the State of Victoria to the Province of Jiangsu, China in 2005 that was to prove a major re-articulation of his diasporic situation towards a transnational cosmopolitanism. The visual theme of a Chinese silk tapestry was taken from a Chinatrade painting from about 1793 that is now at the National Maritime Museum, Greenwich, in the UK. This painting depicts foreigners bearing gifts to a Chinese monarch, but they are viewed in the tapestry from the back in a 'negative' weave. An external viewer is thus 'woven' into an eighteenth-century view. Whilst Young was not to address the Nanjing Massacre at this stage, he did find out more about it during a visit to Nanjing.

An intervening visit to Berlin took Young to the locus of his next major work and installation at the St Matthäus Church in Berlin, where he was brought by the

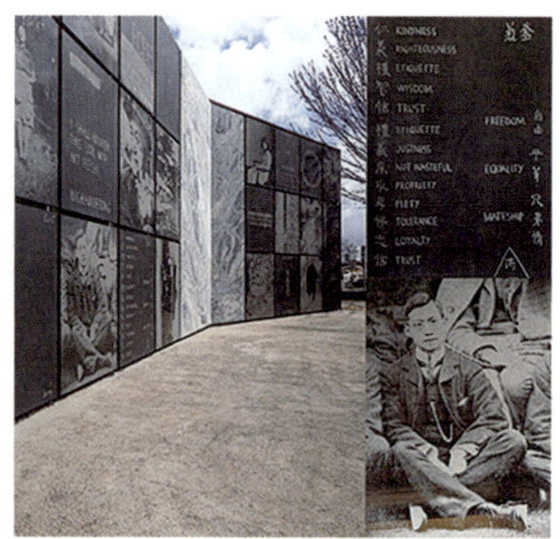

important German gallerist Alexander Ochs. He began to conceive of a very large multi-work installation on themes drawn from the life of Pastor Dietrich Bonhoeffer, who is remembered in that church.[22]

Young began to work with the notion that diaspora permitted, even enabled, an ethical position about ideas and historical realities with which the artist was not directly connected, either in his own life or in the associations of the histories of the cultures he inhabits. Impermanence of historical connection directly facilitated the realisation of a kind of permanent historical truth that allowed his work an ethical expressive power. In a sense, the formal issues due to the impermanence of the aesthetic event for the artist and the audience in constructing a multi-layered work with historical references, became identified with a more permanent potential given by his diasporic mobility.[23] Indeed Young's ethical position so complexly overlaps the positions derived from his understanding of Bonhoeffer's life and sacrifice that, because of Young's earlier conceptualism which masked intentions within formal procedures, in *Bonhoeffer in Harlem* artistic choice of formal means became indistinguishable from an ethical, and hence intentional choice of values.

One could say that in *Safety Zone* (2010), Young handles Chinese historical material as a precursor of his return to Australian subjects and his work on Chinese Australian historical images. As noted above, Young had visited Heidelberg to meet the grandson of one of the foreign heroes of the Nanjing Massacre, John Rabe, but this was a few years before he had conceptualised the work. Young follows a kind of spiral and non-linear procedure of aesthetic and historical awareness accompanied by research, which is actually a permanently recurring method reinforced by the practice of exposure to visual realia and texts. These may be found in the diary of John Rabe shown to Young by Rabe's grandson, where all references that the artist acquires and knows at some point will be transformed. He is allowing a diasporic imagination to find space for inspiration rather than to simply pursue the factual iteration of history. But this is partly due to Young's resistance to the current exigencies of the globalised art world, which he thinks exacerbate ethical indifference:

> Young sees a role for art in linking the present to 'a world of forgotten stories, discarded objects, and memories … Making art not only means to recollect stories, but to reawaken an intrinsic ethical impulse in the present.'[24]

Certainly in these historical works, Young is trying to find a reciprocality with the historical or cultural 'Other'.[25] His sense of history is to re-awaken its effect in the Other-directed present, rather than indulge in a passive, self-directed melancholy associated with cross-cultural existence. While poignant, as Berghuis explains: 'Young is also conscious of the need to move beyond such a state of loss and "search for an active principle" in engaging the ethical dimension of cross-cultural exchange for individuals, groups and societies'.[26]

In several large later installations and exhibitions, such as *1866: The Worlds of Lowe Kong Meng And Jong Ah Siug* at Melbourne's ARC ONE Gallery in 2015, and *Open Monument*, a three-year public art project commissioned for Frazer Reserve, Ballarat, Young has juxtaposed images and texts from different kinds of Chinese lives on and off the Gold Fields, as well as the different and impermanent meaning of the ways historic Chinese in Australia interacted with Anglo-Celtic society. Lowe Kong Meng ended up as a distinguished merchant able in 1878 to co-author polemics in English on behalf of Chinese in Australia.[27] But Jong Ah Siug:

Transculture, part of *Open Monument* 2015
Architectural monument, 430 sq m
Len T. Fraser Reserve, Ballarat

after recovering from an altercation was condemned to 33 years of
incarceration in lunatic asylums until his death in 1900. The only thing
left today of his life is a small hand-written diary, no bigger than one's
palm, that tried to prove his sanity and innocence.[28]

Young has sought in these works to re-visualise Chinese Australian history that is
full of situations discarded by the Anglo-Celtic mainstream and of occluded personal
experiences only recently allowed into the space of multicultural expression of
'Australianness'. With about 12% of the total population speaking an Asian language[29]
and another 20% or so having some kind of Asian family heritage or link, it is indeed
surprising how little Asian cultural material has been accepted into the Australian
mainstream, with the exception of cuisine.[30] To some extent this exclusion is part, now,
of the unresolved issues of multiculturalism where cultural affiliations or heritage are
accepted as decorations and not part of core values.[31] Such exclusion is also due to the
inherently unstable or insecure nature of Australian nationalism, founded as it is on
rejection of the former colonial hegemon, but dependent as it still is on the former
colonial centre in the United Kingdom, even with the addition of a new centre in
the United States of America since 1945. Clearly since Australian identity has been
so impermanent but contested by the Anglo-Celtic hegemony, and the nature of its
relations with Indigenous forebears and Asian neighbours has been so suppressed
until at least the 1970s (including formal exclusion by the White Australia Policy),
an Asian Australian artist of whatever socially recognised distinction is always going
to have to encounter the suppressions of the past. They might even resist the role of
exotic decoration that they may be forced or expected to provide in the present.

Young has brought this conundrum to a peak of visual representation by firstly doing
work that neither hides nor exoticises the Chinese side of his multiple heritages, and
secondly, that formally displays the overlay of images that the two cultures seem to
be visually inclined to refuse, except as discrete genealogies of images. Furthermore,
partly through his Nanjing work, and partly through his understanding of figures such
as Bonhoeffer, Young has stood well outside Australian history to treat ethically issues
that have no direct concern for Australian nationalism. In a sense, he has adopted
a position that is above or beyond Australian connotations by his denotative grasp
(or careful formalist treatment) of two among many great historical horrors of the
twentieth century.

At the same time, Young has continued his work in abstract painting discourses while
also turning to look at visual representations of Chinese history in Australia. There
is no sign yet of a synthesis between this work and mainstream Anglo-Celtic art
culture, nor indeed a recognition of either Young's historical scale or his art's historical
importance as a presenter of an alternative visual history. This provides for a powerful
and ethical critique of Australian mainstream historical constructions of Chinese,
amongst other Asians.

It could be, pessimistically considered, that over time these exclusions will get more
rigid and shutout more of the non-Anglo-Celtic pasts, however much they constitute
part of Australian history. But I prefer to remain optimistic and think that the
pressures of globalisation and the changes in Australian population dynamics, as well
as a greater recognition of the Indigenous peoples of Australia, will at some point lead
to fuller understanding of the significance of Young's achievements in the art world.
These have provided creative possibilities for the generation of new Australian art
discourses to deal with Australian histories, so long as mainstream culture accepts
and works with them.[32]

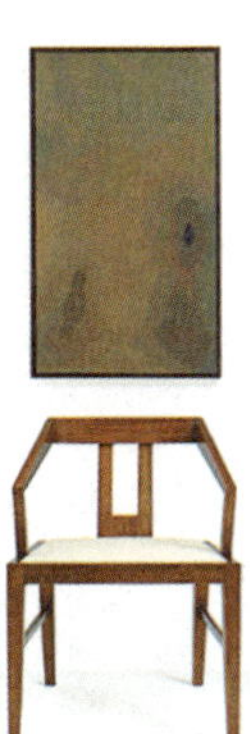

1. The last two thirds of this essay form part of a chapter-length case study in my book *The Asian Modern*, National Gallery of Singapore, Singapore, 2021.

2. Michael Baxandall, *Patterns of Intention: On the Historical Explanation of Pictures*, Yale University Press, New Haven, 1985, p. 42.

3. Collingwood writes: 'Historical knowledge is that special case of memory where the object of present thought is past thought, the gap between present and past being bridged not only by the power of present thought to think of the past, but also by the power of past thought to reawaken itself in the present'. See R. G. Collingwood, *The Idea of History*, Oxford University Press, Oxford, [1946] 1961, p. 294.

4. Keith Moxey writes: 'If contemporaneity is conceived as a temporal framework in which many nonsynchronous forms of time jostle against one another, only the art of those times and places that corresponds with dominant ideological paradigms will be privileged'. K. Moxey, *Visual Time: The Image in History*, Duke University Press, Durham, 2013, p. 18.

5. FX Harsono, *Memory of a Name, Re-writing the Erased* (2009), exhibited at Langeng Foundation, Yogyakarta, 2010.

6. Indeed, it is only recently that another Chinese Indonesian artist, Dadang Christanto has been able to do work which directly and explicitly refers to the 1965 massacre, and perhaps only then because he has lived abroad, in Australia, since 1999.

7. The phases of Young's development may also be associated with his gallery connections as shown below:
    Phase II   1982, joins Yuill/Crowley Gallery, Sydney
    Phase III 1987, joins United Artists Gallery, which became Anna Schwartz Gallery, Melbourne
               1993, joins Sherman Galleries, Sydney
    Phase IV   2006, joins Alexander Ochs Galleries, Berlin & Beijing
               2007, joins 10 Chancery Lane Gallery, Hong Kong.
    Phase V   2014, joins Pearl Lam Gallery, Singapore & Shanghai
               2015, joins ARC ONE Gallery, Melbourne

8. See the essay by Sylvia D. Volz in this volume, pp. 92–99.

9. The then US ambassador to Berlin noted on 14 December 1937 that the Japanese boasted of killing 500,000. For a detailed and nuanced historical survey see 'Massacre at Nanjing' in Rana Mitter, *China's War with Japan, 1937-1945: The Struggle for Survival*, Penguin Books, London, 2013, pp. 137, 119–40.

10. The paper was Ralph Croizier, 'Post-Impressionist in Pre-War Shanghai: The Juelanshe (Storm Society) and the Fate of Modernism in Republican China', in John Clark (ed.), *Modernity in Asian Art*, Wild Peony, Sydney, 1993, pp. 135–54.

11. Graham Coulter-Smith et al., *John Young: Silhouettes and Polychromes 1979–1992*, Schwartz City Publications, Melbourne, 1993, p. 20.

12. Paul Feyerabend, *Against Method: outline of an anarchistic theory of knowledge*, New Left Books; Humanities Press; London; Atlantic Highlands, 1975, p. 189, as cited in Coulter-Smith et al., *John Young*, p. 20.

13. Terry Blake was a guitarist for the post-punk band The Slugfuckers, with which John Young was involved, and later became an academic philosopher based in France.

14. John Young and Terry Blake, 'On Some Alternatives to the Code in the Age of Hyperreality; the Hermit and the City-Dweller', *Art & Text*, issue 2, Winter 1981, p. 17.

15. Unpublished conversation between Sean Lowry and John Young on 24 October 2002, at Sherman Galleries, Sydney. Transcript supplied by the artist. Young is referring to the 1991 conference 'Modernism and Postmodernism in Asian Art', discussed below, n. 18.

16. Michel Serres, *Hermes: Language, Science, Philosophy*, John Hopkins University Press, Baltimore, 1981, pp. 131, 52, cited in Rex Butler and Keith Broadfoot, 'The Art of the Third Man', in *Objective Gesture, John Young, Selected Works 1986-1987*, Sydney, 1987.

17. A statement by John Young on the *Double Ground Paintings* in 1997, cited in Carolyn Barnes, *John Young*, Craftsman House, Fishermans Bend, Victoria, 2005, p. 121.

18. Convened by the author, the conference 'Modernism and Postmodernism in Asian Art' was held at the Humanities Research Centre, Australian National University, Canberra, in 1991. Most of the conference papers were published in John Clark, *Modernity in Asian Art*, 1993.

19. Young also expressed this to me in several private conversations at Ballarat in May 2016.

20. As Barnes, in *John Young*, p. 60, notes: 'When Australian-Asian artists advocated their 'Asianness'—outside their use of the representational languages and symbols of Asian culture in their work—they positioned themselves outside all discourses of Australian identity except multiculturalism which had lost most of its authority by the late 1990s. The idea of the Australian-Asian artist, although a factual reality, was inherently paradoxical: the decision to express cultural allegiances outside a performative Australianness suggesting not only a lack of identification with Australia but a capacity to subvert the idea of Australian culture'.

21. Interview with John Clark, Sydney, 13 March 1994. Parts of this interview appear in *Asian Art News*, vol. 4, no. 3, May/June 1995, and in John Young, *The Double Ground Paintings*, Australian Art Promotions, Sydney, 1995.

22. *Bonhoeffer in Harlem*, 2009, comprises three work complexes: 1. portfolio of eleven conceptual works, eight chalk drawings on black board paint on paper, three digital inkjet prints; 2. one large format abstract silk tapestry; 3. two abstract paintings taking up the motif of the tapestry. Both 2 and 3 are elaborate computer-generated abstract transforms of the images of stained-glass windows found at the Abyssinian Baptist Church in Harlem, New York, where Bonhoeffer preached and where he had learnt he must oppose racism in any form. This resulted, after his 1931 return to Germany, in his own public opposition to the persecution of the Jews, his association with the anti-Nazi resistance from 1938, his arrest in 1943, and his eventual execution at Flossenbürg in 1945. For details of Bonhoeffer and this project, see the essays by Lo, Volz and Glöde in this volume, as well as Alexander Ochs et al., *John Young: Bonhoeffer in Harlem*, St Matthäus Church, Berlin, 2009).

23. The works are full of art historical references too, especially to Steiner and Beuys as noted above.

24. Young quoted in Berghuis, 'John Young: Situational Ethics', in *Art & Australia*, vol. 48, no. 3, 2011, pp. 440–43, republished in this volume, p. 134.

25. As Lo indicates: 'As a creative act, the artworks bridge personal and collective memories, producing new narratives of social belonging, new affective capacities across diasporas and challenge us to rethink collective responsibility'. See Lo, 'Diaspora, Art and Empathy', in *John Young: The Bridge and the Fruit Tree*, Drill Hall Gallery, Australian National University, Canberra, 2013, p. 41, republished in this volume, p. 137.

26. Berghuis, 'The Situational Ethics of John Young', republished in this volume, p. 134.

27. See the pamphlet, L. Kong Meng, Cheok Hong Cheong, and Louis Ah Mouy (eds), *The Chinese Question in Australia, 1878–79*, F. F. Bailliere, Melbourne, 1879, inter alia at Rare Books, Fisher Research Library, University of Sydney, a scan of which was kindly provided by John Young.

28. From the catalogue *1866: The Worlds of Lowe Kong Meng And Jong Ah Siug*, ARC ONE Gallery, Melbourne, 2015.

29. For a recent discussion see 'Are we Asian yet? It's complicated', p. 73, in George Megalogenis, 'The Rookie PMs', *Australian Foreign Affairs*, no. 5, February 2019, pp. 55–75.

30. Tim Soutphommasane, 'Australia's Asian-Ness Is Barely Visible', *The Sydney Morning Herald*, 5 November 2012, https://www.smh.com.au/politics/federal/australias-asian-ness-is-barely-visible-20121104-28ryq.html: 'Some of us seem to believe that Asia is something out there, wholly apart from us. In fact, there is already a lot of Asia within Australia. Thus, many of us

overlook our existing Asia literacy. This is one of the inbuilt
benefits of a multicultural Australia: we have a strong platform
for extending our relations with the region. Benjamin
Herscovitch of the Centre for Independent Studies argued in
a recent paper that our cultural diversity means there are more
than 2 million speakers of Asian languages in Australia, including
some 650,000 speakers of Chinese.'

31. Benzi Zhang argues [about Canada] via Barnes, 2005, p. 47,
citing Benzi Zhang, 'Identity in Diaspora and Diaspora in Writing:
The Poetics of Cultural Transrelation', *Journal of Intercultural
Studies*, no. 2, August 2000, p. 126: 'mosaic multiculturalism
means a centre-periphery structure in which Asian cultural
inheritances are treated as "foreign" festoons that would
bedeck but never become a central part of national identity'.

32. One should remember there is a line between the small and
fractious art world and the wider one of political forces
favouring closer Australian mainstream recognition of its
links with Asia, problematic as these still remain. Rather
than the inclusion and re-formation of Asian visualisation in
the wider Australian discourses being the issue, one may
consider pessimistically that these may have lost the ability to
see freshly at all. Young has not lacked powerful connections
to corporate and political patrons, such as the then Victorian
State Premier Steve Bracks who supported his Nanjing Tapestry
project in 2007, and the then Prime Minister Kevin Rudd who
wrote a message for his 2009 Berlin exhibition catalogue.
Young is broadly collected by state galleries and the National
Gallery of Australia in Canberra. But this does not indicate that
the significance of his work is immediately recognised by art-
world peers of the same generation. His lack of inclusion in
the 2016 survey of contemporary Australian painting at the
Australian Centre for Contemporary Art in Melbourne testifies
to a narrow localism, which extends to many other artists too.

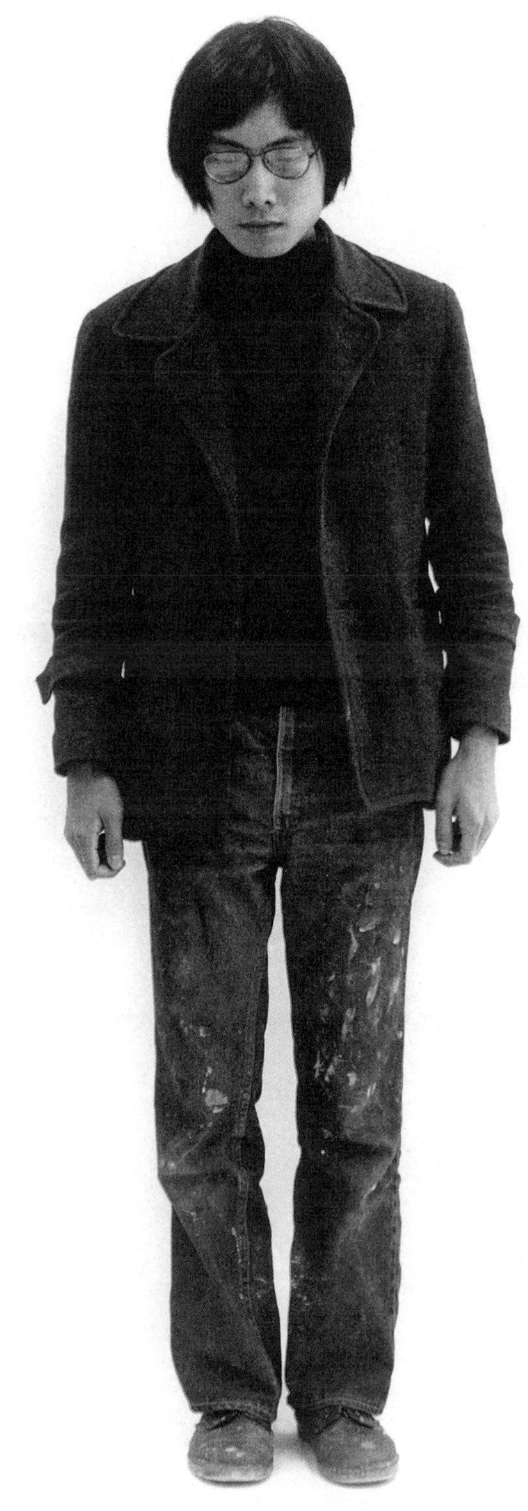

John Young in his studio
Glebe, Sydney, 1981

PART ONE

OPEN WORLD

2005

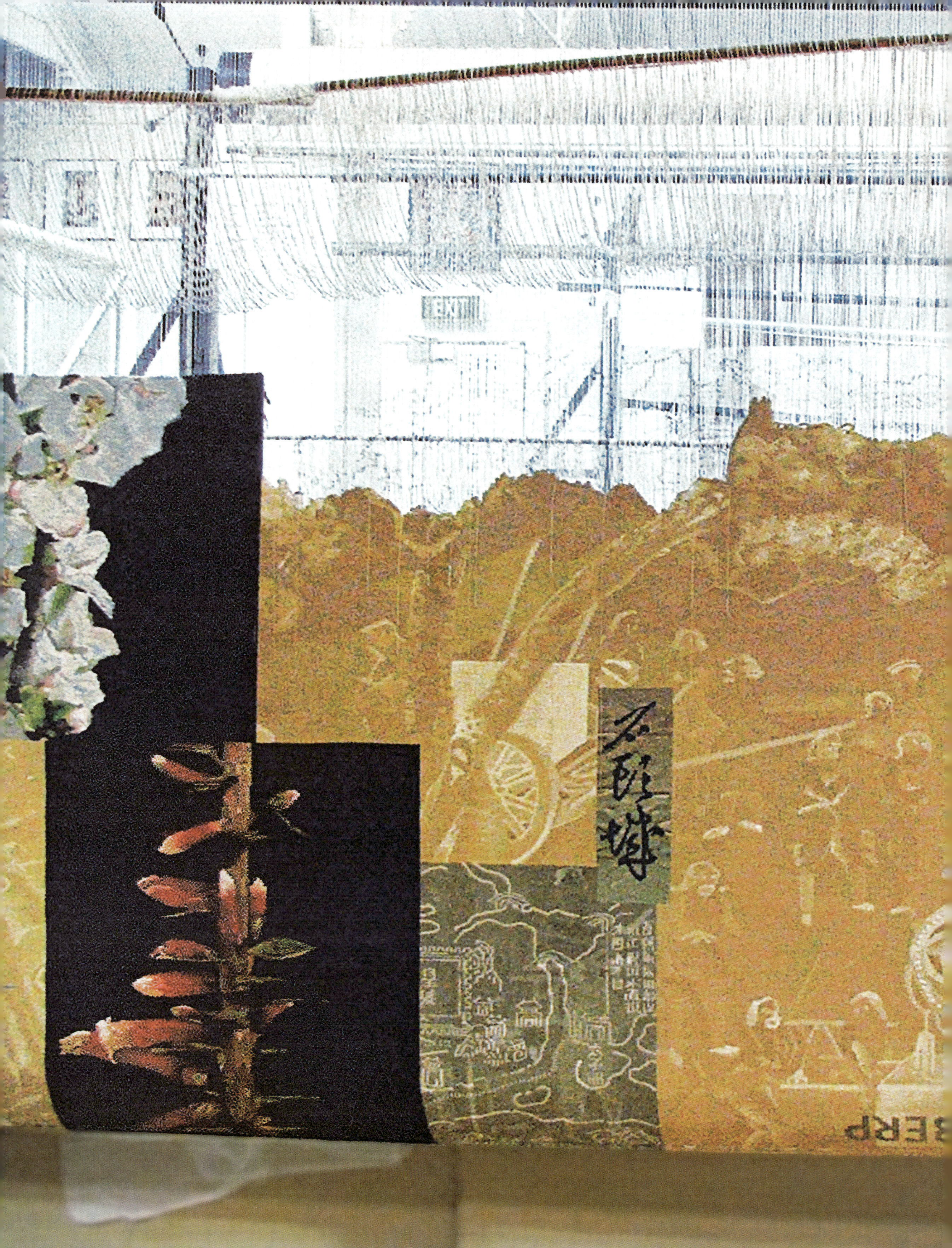

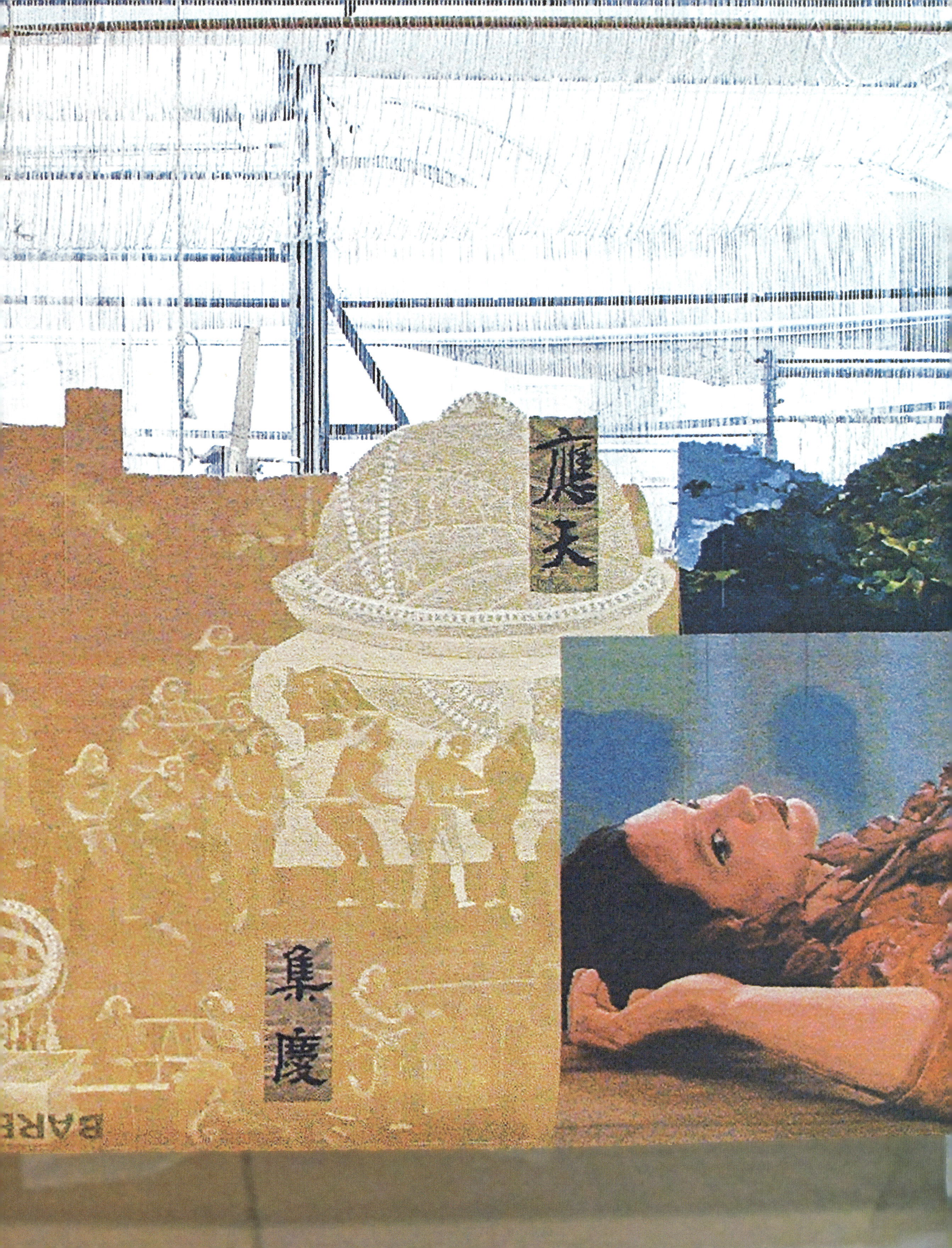

應天
集慶
BARE

OPEN WORLD

Open World (2005) is a tapestry commissioned by the State Government of Victoria as a gift to mark the twenty-fifth anniversary of sister state ties with Jiangsu Province, China. Digitally composed by Young, it was produced by the Australian Tapestry Workshop, taking over nine months to complete. Working on *Open World* was the first time the Workshop used digital composition, and, in consultation with Young, they developed new techniques to weave layered, translucent images prompted by his designs. The work is now permanently exhibited at Nanjing Library.

The tapestry's background is a negative image of a *kesi* 緙絲 ('cut silk') tapestry depicting the arrival of a European planetarium and celestial globe at the Summer Palace of the Qing dynasty emperor Qianlong, in September 1793, in Beijing. Interwoven into this depiction of the introduction of Western knowledge and cartographic systems being introduced to China are translucent images of historic texts and diagrams of the voyages of the intrepid Ming dynasty mariner and Chinese Muslim admiral Zheng He (c. 1371–1433), sourced from the Nanjing library archive. Layered onto this ground are photorealistic images of Victoria's scenic Great Ocean Road, the common heath and cherry blossom (floral emblems of Victoria and Jiangsu), and a supine Eurasian woman dressed in red. Finally, silk badges inscribed with various historical Chinese names for the city of Nanjing, written in the calligraphic style of the corresponding era, are inlaid over the foreground. These form a dialogue with the Indigenous place names for the area of Melbourne, which are arranged around the tapestry's boundaries: *Kulin Nation, Naarm* and *Bareberp*.

Given total freedom to compose the work, Young made an initial research trip to Nanjing in 2004, where he viewed precious Buddhist texts and Zheng He's notes at the Nanjing Library. Young also consulted with local historians and calligraphers to develop his composition, the mode of which—combining historical background images with generic images layered onto the foreground—is an elaboration of strategies developed in Young's *Double Ground Paintings*.

Reflections (2022)

I was asked to make this work with the Australian Tapestry Workshop at a turning point. I had just completed a twelve-year cycle of works, *The Double Ground Paintings* (1993–2005), which, among other things, hoped to develop a process, structure and form to lay out clearly transcultural, transhistorical and kitsch everyday imagery. In essence, it was a hope towards poetic description, and a relation of imagery in the work that evaded literalism or direct representation.

For the composition of *Open World*, the subject matter was gifting and reciprocity, so I felt every aspect of the work's process and content needed to demonstrate this: from the use of historical imagery that demonstrated gifting to the 'gifting' of new creative processes to the Workshop, such as the use of digital composition and the weaving of transparent imagery. Self-referential as it may be, the tapestry was a gift from Victoria to Jiangsu, about gifting. My work *Give and Take* (2001), now in the collection of the National Gallery of Australia, was something of a precursor to this work. Yet, it was this attitude about the autonomy of the work that perhaps prompted me to look outwards, from myself and in the art making, towards history, events, proximity and atonement. Thus, this moment was a sort of turning point, from the processes of the *Double Ground Paintings* (1993–2005) to the History Projects, which subsequently occupied another fifteen years.

pages 38–39
Open World on the loom
Australian Tapestry Workshop, Melbourne, 2005

MAKING *OPEN WORLD*: A CONVERSATION WITH THE AUSTRALIAN TAPESTRY WORKSHOP

An interview with John Young, Australian Tapestry Workshop director Antonia Syme and weaver Amy Cornall, moderated by Venita Poblocki, 12 October 2020.

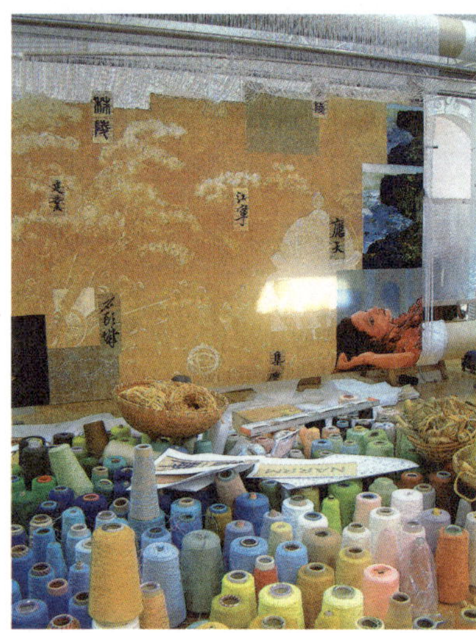

Open World on the loom with spools of dyed thread, Australian Tapestry Workshop, Melbourne, 2005

Venita Poblocki: The Open World tapestry was commissioned in 2004 by the State Government of Victoria as a cultural gift for Victoria's sister state, Jiangsu Province. John, do you know why the Victorian Government asked you to produce an artwork that would be translated into another medium by the Australian Tapestry Workshop, as you hadn't done that prior to this project?

John Young: This was the first time I was asked, and I was very grateful that they asked me for a start. I think it was Michael Nation and Penny Hutchinson [from Arts Victoria] who actually invited me to do this work, and I hope it was because they thought that I had some sort of bicultural understanding as to how different people comprehend visual imagery. So, I thought a way to go about this was perhaps to acknowledge the liminal space between different cultural comprehensions. And this acknowledgement is precisely the message, or the gift of the work. I was also well aware of the questionable intentions of soft power and diplomacy in this. That is to say, to make the artwork work, so to speak, to weaponise it, in other words. But for me, good art has always been really first and foremost the form and the craft of the work, and its lack of functionality. Good work doesn't need to work for anything else. It's an end in itself. To me, the aim was to make a work that allows us to enter into a space of awe, into a space which is a reciprocality of differences. And also, a space where you can experience the virtuosity of the craftsmanship in the work. This is why I feel the tapestry is not just a diplomatic gift. It was really necessary to make a true artwork that addresses gifting—since gifting was part of its facture. That was the goal of it, I think.

VP: Speaking of true craftsmanship, Antonia, I'll bring you into the conversation. The Australian Tapestry Workshop obviously has an outstanding reputation for innovation in contemporary handwoven tapestries. As I understand, it's one of a small handful in the world who are dedicated to the production of handwoven tapestries. It is a central aspect of the workshop's vision to collaborate creatively to produce tapestries of artistic merit. The Workshop has worked with numerous Australian and international artists, architects, designers such as Emily Kngwarreye, Jørn Utzon, and so on. How do you first approach such collaborations? And, from a technical point of view, are there parameters that must first be set? How do you consider the weaving technology in the creative process? How does that synergy work?

Antonia Syme: We start with the artist or designer or architect, whoever we're working with, and we really try and encourage them to understand as much as they possibly can about the process of tapestry weaving, and the extraordinary skills that the weavers can bring to their work. We encourage them to visit the tapestry workshop, if possible, but otherwise, we give them insight into the structure of tapestry, the form, the ability of the weavers to interpret their design in tapestry form and answer any questions about the process that they have. We don't try to replicate traditional tapestry masterpieces such as *The Lady and the Unicorn* or other medieval or Renaissance tapestries. We set our practice in the twentieth and now twenty-first centuries, where our weavers and artists work together in this extraordinary contemporary art form. Increasingly, artists want to explore different media. We encourage artists to work with tapestry as an extension of their art practice. Indeed, that's one of the reasons we were founded, because many artists were wanting to work with tapestry, but were having to go overseas to be able to fulfill that desire.

The weavers have an extraordinary colour sense. We have 370 wool colours and 200 cotton colours, and we can have up to thirteen different colours on any one bobbin. We can create extraordinary subtlety, complex layering of images and effects, and John is very aware of this versatility. That's why working with him on a second tapestry was challenging, because he wanted to push our boundaries. He had a really clear understanding of how we worked after his first tapestry, and he pushed the weavers further with the second tapestry.

Every project is different, every artist is different, but essentially we help artists understand the medium and its capabilities and we explore the artist's design concepts and intent, so we can come to a common point. The weavers produce a series of experimental samples where they explore the possible interpretations. They'll make a collective decision with the artist about the most successful approach to realise the artist's vision in tapestry. It's a very collaborative and exciting process.

VP: John, in this collaborative process of working with such skilled weavers, there must have been a period of knowledge exchange and insight that took place between you and the weavers prior to commencing the design. How did this inform your final artwork design? Did it play into what you produced in the end? And can you elaborate on the process of transferring your design to a tapestry?

JY: It was quite a long time ago. Amy, correct me if I'm wrong, I think we just had some short meetings. I don't think we had a really big meeting.

Amy Cornall: I think you would have given a presentation, an artist's talk, which would have given us an insight into your work. Then we would have had a discussion, first looking at your imagery, and then woven some samples and gotten some feedback from you on what works for you. The back and forth, really.

JY: That's right. It was back and forth, because it was a continual process of learning and connection. For me, being my first tapestry, it was really a discovery of the differences in capabilities of the mediums of weaving and painting. That was a very interesting revelation. I knew that the workshop was one of the best in the world in translating contemporary art into tapestry form. What was actually most interesting was, once again, what could come out of this. Not a painting, and not a traditional tapestry, but a sort of hybrid object: one that has taken the technical challenges from both sides from painting and from tapestry and created a new sense of viscerality, of physicality, of skill, which is not in painting. What I really admire is that the tapestries tend to create a sort of texture, which accompanies any image. It's a physicality in feel and in sight that is not as primary in painting.

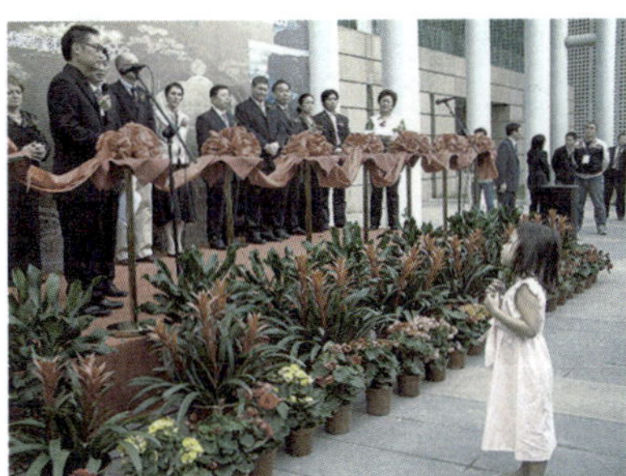

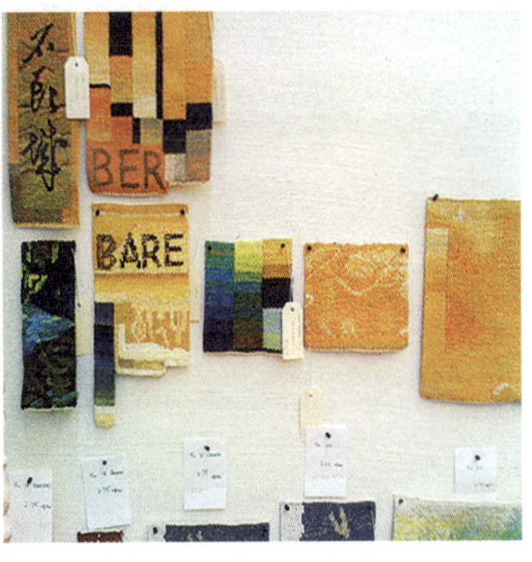

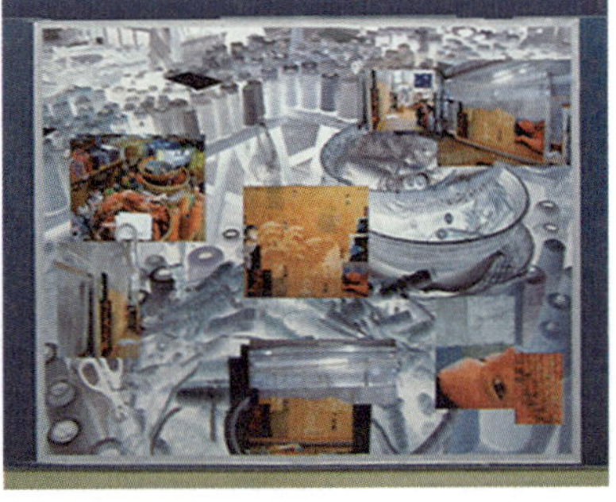

Charlotte-Persia Young in front of the inauguration ceremony for *Open World*, Nanjing Library, Nanjing, 2007

Preparatory studies for *Open World*, Australian Tapestry Workshop, Melbourne, 2005

Tapestry Notes 2 2007
Digital print on canvas
Installation view, *Open World*, Nanjing Library, Nanjing, 2007

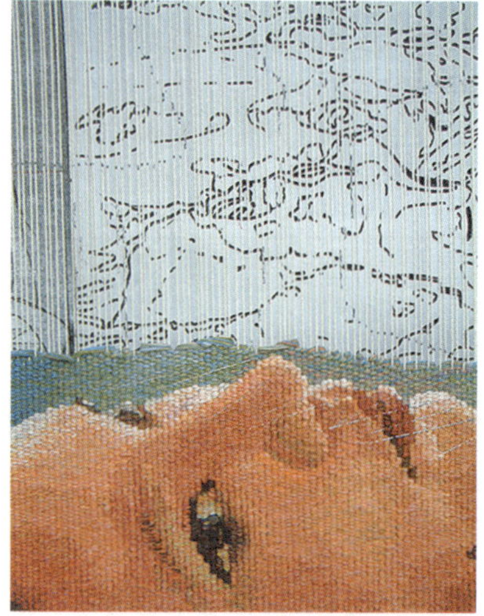

Details from *Open World* 2005
Woven at the Australian Tapestry Workshop
by Amy Cornall, Rachel Hine, Milena Paplinska
and Caroline Tully
Cotton and wool tapestry, 330 × 365 cm
Collection of Nanjing Library, Nanjing

VP: Did that physicality play into your final design as well?

JY: Yes, I think that regardless of what happens in a tapestry form, that physicality is always there, you know, unless the image tends to overtake it, or something like that, which I doubt. Most of the time, it's there. The other issue is that it was the first work that the Workshop had done from an electronic composition. So, with my own work, with the *Double Ground Paintings*, I had explored the relationship between electronic composition and painting. And as you know, electronic composition has a sort of poverty in its flatness, and its disembodied-ness. It's a very flat and disembodied screen-based sort of thing. Whereas painting is very rich and visceral, which speaks to our body, and so does tapestry. So, in that sense, there was a very interesting exploration, between this idea of the original composition, all the way to the making of it. From something which is fairly conceptual to something corporeal, both are equally as important. I don't work with the idea that the concept is most important, and then everything else is relegated to that, you know. That's a very chauvinistic way of looking at things. That was why I really thought there was a hybrid object that came out of all this, and that it was actually something that tested the boundaries of both media, of painting and tapestry.

VP: Do you feel there are aspects from this process that have informed your work going forward, even when you're not working with tapestry? Or was it specific to this medium?

JY: More so much later on. I did a tapestry, a rug actually, for *Bonhoeffer in Harlem* (2009), which was woven by Tibetan refugees living in Nepal, guided by a wonderful weaver called Dolma Lob Sang. They only had very poor colours, because their workshop didn't have much choice of materials and things like that. Initially I found the result disappointing and felt that it went against my will. In the end, I felt I actually had to accept that, and give up my own intentionality, because I really felt it is what it is. The tapestry was woven in an extremely poor place, between Tibet and Nepal. That experience really changed my own sense of the artist as having or insisting on their own intention. My will got in the way of the awe we can feel for reciprocality, and so once the will was abandoned, the object that emerged became an expression of that reciprocality. On the other hand, with the Australian Tapestry Workshop it was very different. This workshop is extremely apt and very skilled in working with contemporary art, and we had a huge choice. The virtuosity is completely different. In that sense, while there was still a lot of acceptance and exchange required from both sides, I think that it was a different process, you know, to work with a context of poverty. In both experiences the capacity for the weavers to work with the design was entirely dependent upon their respective realities, their cultural expectations, and the resources at hand. These sorts of material realities have to be accepted as a part of the process of the work, otherwise it's exploitation.

VP: John, I wanted to focus on *Open World* itself. It's quite a structured composition, which is very much in line with your *Double Ground Paintings*. It contains a layered dialogue of historical contemporary images, both Western and Chinese, portraiture and landscape, photographic and painted images, English and Chinese texts. It presents multiple ways of being read. Can you take us through the significance of these image choices and the assemblage and layering of the images?

JY: The structure of the *Double Ground Paintings* is usually that the background is a historic image, and the images in the front are usually generic images, from travelogue magazines or flower books. But when you put very generic images in front of the background, which is usually historic, the meaning of it changes, and this somehow tends to relate to this background context. However, in this particular tapestry, it is a little bit more complex, which I won't really talk about now. But, basically, it forms a sort of scaffold, to primarily show up a lot of the virtuosity of the weaving. I think that was very important, and what it's capable of, you know. One can achieve an almost trompe-l'oeil effect or astounding hazes of colour fusion, or a molecular sense of constancy and focus in tapestry, in weaving.

VP: Can you speak specifically to the background image of the original Chinese silk embroidery—the negative weave of the original?

JY: Whether you're looking from a Chinese or European point of view, this image rendered in negative more often than not signifies a remoteness, or an otherness, or unfamiliarity. What interested me with this silk embroidery … I can't remember what year it was made. Oh, it was around 1793. What interested me about this embroidery was that it was a depiction of Westerners, more likely Jesuits, actually, bearing gifts representing a Western cosmology—celestial spheres or orbs, to the Emperor of China. And so, we're looking at a sort of very interesting incommensurability of worldviews and knowledge systems here. You've got these Jesuits, bringing the Western worldview into China, which is not understood, but it's still a gift. The dynamism in almost saying, 'Look how different these differences are', I'm bringing these different things to you.' These celestial spheres are gifts, from a different knowledge system to the Chinese. So, in this, there's this sort of gifting of something of great value from one worldview, and then for the other worldview. They didn't actually understand it, but they accepted it as something of great value. This reciprocality is not unlike the gifting of a contemporary artwork based on Euro-American modernist visual conventions to a different cultural context like Nanjing. *Open World* was like a weird sort of analogy of this reciprocality that can happen with different worldviews and the acceptance of a gift. The other thing is that the negative image, due to one's unfamiliarity with it, slows down your reading of it literally. It gives you a space to slow down and not feel you have to wrap up the meaning behind something straight away. What it does then, is to amplify a space or a world that is open enough, I guess, for differences. The incomprehensible wants to coexist, and that's why I tried to create a lot of space in this work; a scaffold to hold all these rich differences.

VP: Amy, were there particular challenges in achieving a negative weave from this image?

AC: In a negative image, all of the colours are inverted, warm and cool are flipped, and also the highlights and shadows are reversed. So, where shapes would normally recede, they advance and vice versa. Everything, as John said, becomes a little bit removed, a bit abstracted and obscured. It's like a separation between what we are creating and the reference image, the Chinese silk embroidery. That separation, as interpreters, as weavers, gives us the freedom to create something new, to create something that's really beautiful and luminous, and to take that composition that John has given us and to give it a new form. The background area, based on the Chinese silk tapestry, makes up a large proportion of *Open World*, it's probably about eighty to ninety percent. There's a strong mood that's created by that whole area. It's really dominant, despite being quite a subtle, soft, and faded image; it sets the mood for the whole piece. While we're weaving, we are considering multiple

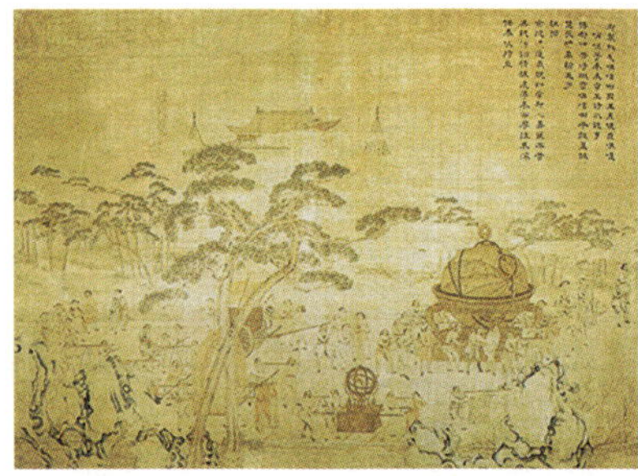

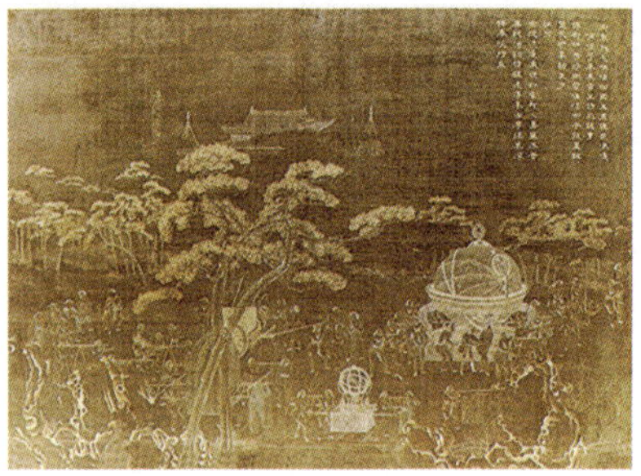

Anonymous
*Arrival of a planetarium and celestial globe at
the Summer Palace of the Emperor of China* 1793
kesi 緙絲 silk tapestry, 121.5 × 160 cm
Collection of National Maritime Museum,
Greenwich, London

The artist's digital negative of the *kesi* tapestry,
used as the background for *Open World*

things simultaneously: we're thinking about the small sections that we're working on; how they fit into that overall context of the whole image; and how they appear close up as we're weaving them; and also how it will appear from a distance, because it's generally a monumental scale, and it may not be viewed close up, it may be viewed from maybe ten or more meters back. So, we have to think about everything simultaneously, as well as retaining the artist's intention, their meaning, the feeling of the work, as well as considering the very basic things of tone and form and line and contrast. So, everything at the same time.

VP: This feeling you mentioned can become particularly apparent in John's use of image transparency. I don't know if you had dealt with that before or if this was unusual. Is that technically difficult to achieve? How did you manage the layering and subsequent transparency of the design?

AC: It's something that we're doing more and more I feel, because we're finding that it's really effective. It's a surprising thing to us as well, because you think of both painting and tapestry as being opaque or heavy, but what you're actually playing with is light and colour. You're creating an illusion by manipulating the light and the colour in the wool and the cotton, and how they play off each other. Basically, you're creating a sense of transparency by blending different tones, different colours together, all together on the one bobbin. And we're mixing every colour combination by hand, and we're making that decision in the moment, quite immediately. As we progress from the bottom of the tapestry right up to the top, we're making thousands of little tiny decisions about colour and tone. This gives us the ability to make those really subtle shifts that Antonia mentioned earlier. You can do things like merging two images together quite seamlessly and see them both at the same time. I think John played with this a little bit more in his next tapestry, where he had multiple portraits of Kenneth Myer overlaid on top of each other, which I suspect would have been a significant challenge for whoever was weaving that area. I wasn't involved with that particular project. But we've incorporated transparency in many projects. We wove a fantastic tapestry with David Noonan, where basically the whole tapestry was two images overlaid and you could almost look into it. There was a genuine feeling of space, and you could almost fall into it. One of my favourite things to attempt and to weave, is to get that light and that transparency, and that fabulous illusion that you're looking at something more than what's in front of you.

JY: Can I just say a little bit about that, too? I first noticed the workshop could do this transparent effect from their tapestry of a Patrick Heron watercolour, from many years back. But I want to say something about the transparent images in *Open World* and the significance of ambiguity. Before I started this particular composition, I was invited to Nanjing to learn about the city. In Nanjing, there was a whole series of different libraries that held a lot of precious books and Buddhist scriptures that they showed me. One of them was actually an ancient book that had a lot of place names in it. These place names were documented by the explorer Zheng He in 1421, the great Chinese- Hui Muslim admiral explorer, who also, by the way, had his shipyards in Nanjing. He definitely explored the Indian Ocean, all the way to the edge of Africa. Gavin Menzies' book called *1421: The Year China Discovered America*, speculated that Zheng actually sailed all the way down to Warrnambool. If you go to Warrnambool Museum, you can still see some Chinese model boats that they surmise were similar to wrecks off the shore, you know, part of Zheng He's armada—but we don't really know. He certainly got down to maybe Java, though the place names in the ancient books were obscure, it's modal. In *Open World* these records exist in the veiled world of possible truths. There are three rectangles in there that Amy actually did with such accomplishment with her colleagues to actually get that transparency working.

AC: That was great fun, by the way. I was looking through my photos before and have an image of myself weaving one of those exact panels that you're talking about. There was a great deal of levity on that project and I look back to that time with great fondness.

VP: John, in the final tapestry you also incorporate a lot of text, including Indigenous place names and references to Zheng He's apparent travels. Was that the first time you engaged text so prominently in your artworks?

JY: Yes. Ironically, after saying a work needs no functional use, there was a practical reason behind starting to use text as well. Well maybe not ironic, more like a ruse. You see the nature of this particular tapestry is that it's a contemporary artwork based on a Western modernist vocabulary, and it was going to be hung permanently in the Nanjing Library, where the public is not necessarily familiar with contemporary Western art whatsoever. So how are they going to get something out of it? I mean, other than just producing a literal iconic populist image tapestry that is artistically pointless, how do you give a viewer genuine time to have a meaningful connection with it and move into the tapestry and experience its qualities? So, I came up with this scenario which guided my design. I imagined a grandfather holding his granddaughter's hand in China standing in front of the tapestry, and thought, how would they look at this tapestry? Then I thought, maybe I should put all the historic names of Nanjing into the tapestry. So, these Chinese words on the tapestry are historic names of Nanjing from different dynasties—like '南京' (*nanjing*), which means Southern Capital, or '天京' (*tianjing*), which means City of Heaven or Heavenly Capital, or another name, '江寧' (*jiangning*), which means Tranquil River. There are a few different names from different periods. In fact, for the tapestry, the Chinese names were scripted by a learned calligrapher in the calligraphic styles consistent with their time. For me, I hoped that was a key for this grandfather and his granddaughter to unlock this tapestry. Standing in front of the tapestry becomes a sort of fascination, a lesson for the granddaughter about where she comes from.

It was a way for them to go into the constellation of reading of the tapestry, and then maybe they would realise that there are these Indigenous names like 'Naarm', and they would say, 'Oh, maybe that name has significance to Australia'. The weaving was so great you can even experience the weight, the tempo, the viscosity of the ink of these scripts—in a tapestry! It could have been clumsily woven and the reading would have been ignored, since Chinese people attribute calligraphy as the highest art form, and so much meaning dwells in the calligraphic scripting. This is sort of a way of bringing people in through the text and their recognition of difference, of quality. That was how I tried, with the help of the weavers to use text for the first time.

VP: A key aspect of *Open World* is the overwhelming sense of history, time and place. There are representations of multiple human and natural worlds—from the real to the surreal, and imaginary spaces to historical places. Can you speak to this reimagining of place in history? Do you consider *Open World* to be your first work within the historical projects, by drawing on these real and reimagined elements?

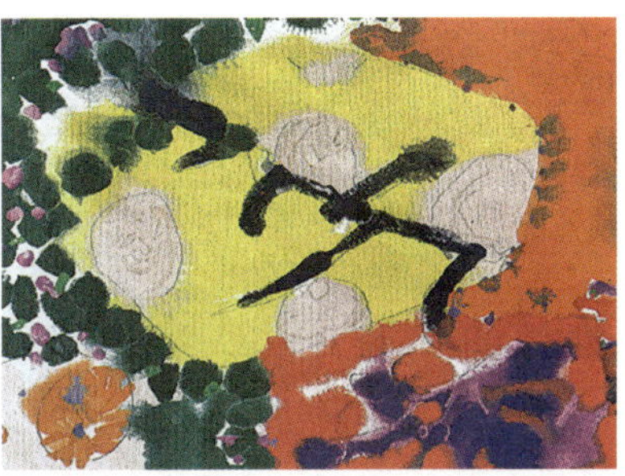

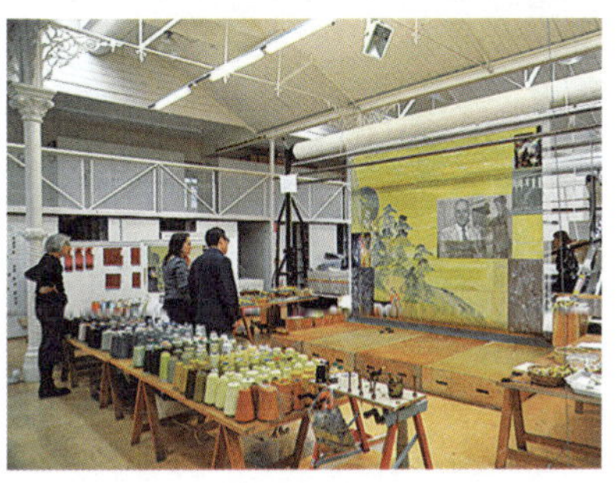

Detail from
Patrick Heron (1920–1999)
22 July 1989 1999
Woven at the Australian Tapestry Workshop
by Cheryl Thornton and Caroline Tully
Cotton and wool tapestry, 145 × 198 cm
Private collection

Left to right: Sue Batten, Melina Paplinska,
and John Young
Production view of *Finding Kenneth Myer*,
Australian Tapestry Workshop, Melbourne, 2011

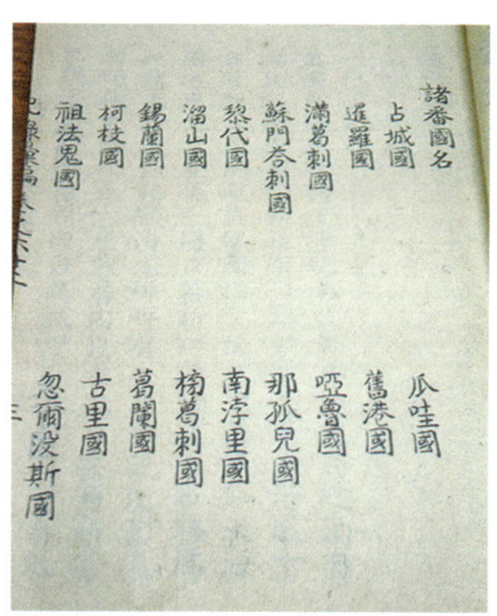

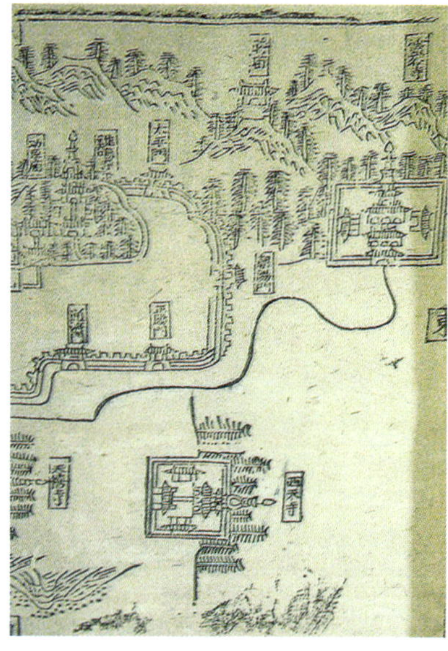

Internal page views of a list of exotic place names from Australasia and a map of Zheng He's 郑和 shipyard in Nanjing, sourced from books that recorded Zheng's 1421 Indian Ocean voyage
Collection of Nanjing Library, Nanjing

JY: Well, precisely that actually. For me history and memory is always a reimagining. To me, it's not so much an unearthing or a verification of facts. It's always a reimagining, it's modal. Particularly memory. It's sort of an empathy in reimagining something which is very remote, to celebrate becoming the unfamiliar. That's one thing I've learned subsequently from doing the History Projects. So yes, I think that this tapestry kickstarted me in looking at reimagining memory, and history, and trying to have a sense of empathy towards difference. That's why I really attribute this as one of the earlier History Projects, perhaps. Maybe my early cycles of work say 'There is difference', and this latest cycle probably tries to resonate the proposition, 'We can become different'.

VP: Antonia, just finishing with a question for you. We have so much admiration for what you and your team achieve. I just wanted to know—how do you see the workshop fitting within the context of Australian art history? What do you feel are the future directions for the Workshop?

AS: We've only been going for forty-six years, but I think in that time we have made a significant contribution to the visual arts and to the cultural life of Australia and I'm really hoping that we can continue to expand that. We've been working with the Sydney Opera House, and I'm excited to see that the current CEO Louise Herron is absolutely embracing tapestry. There's a lovely program that they're doing online about the various tapestries in the Opera House. One of course is our Jørn Utzon tapestry that was designed to hang in the Utzon Room and celebrates the reengagement of Utzon with the Sydney Opera House. There are the beautiful John Coburn tapestries, which were the stage curtains, and the recently acquired Le Corbusier. So, places like the Opera House are now expanding their engagement with tapestry in a really meaningful, public way. Also, we're really excited about our relationship with architects through our international Tapestry Design Prize for Architects. We're about to have our fourth iteration of the prize, which was designed very specifically to reengage architects with tapestry. There was a very strong engagement with the early modernists and tapestry, but tastes changed. It is stimulating to connect architects with our work, and to reach an international audience of architects around the world.

VP: Absolutely. We have incredible respect for what you and your whole team accomplish. It's outstanding on a world scale.

AC: Can I just mention all of the other weavers who were on that project? It was led by Milena Paplinska. The other two weavers on the project were Caroline Tully and Rachel Hine. I was the most junior weaver on that project. I think it was only my second major tapestry after completing art school, so it was a little bit daunting. And a long time ago.

JY: As a matter of interest, did you have a division of strengths? I remember Milena was very good in rendering portraits.

AC: Absolutely. Milena wove the figure that's in the bottom right-hand corner. I think everybody has their own strengths. You do get a little bit shunted towards the things that you are particularly good at, but occasionally they like to throw you a curveball and give you something that's really, really hard and that you've not done before. But you're sitting with two or three other people who are incredibly experienced, and you can pick their brains while you work. It's kind of like an in-house mentoring program while you work. As a learning environment, it's fantastic, really.

AS: I remember speaking to one of the weavers at Dovecot Studios in Edinburgh—which is the model on which we were founded, and he was retiring, I think at seventy [years of age], and he said he still loved it, because he was learning every day. There was always something new to learn. I've been working at the Workshop for eleven years now and the weavers' abilities to seemingly nonchalantly mix these incredibly complex bobbins and weave these beautiful tapestries is extraordinary.

VP: Are you a weaver Antonia?

AS: I have tried weaving many years ago, but the weavers are professional, and it is a job for experts.

Just to make a brief point about what John was talking about with the colours—we have a rich palette. With paint, you mix paint and you get a new colour, but with tapestry, you have all these colours mixed together on the bobbin and your eye will do the mixing. So, you have this incredible vivacity of colour and texture that you just don't have by using flat colour and single colours. It just gives it a lusciousness, a tactility and presence that's quite extraordinary. I don't know how else to explain it, you'd probably do better than me, John, on that one.

JY: Not really, as you were saying that a picture came to memory from the first time that I walked into the National Gallery in London. The first painting that you see is [Georges] Seurat's *Bathers at Asnières* [1884], and pointillism, you know the way that the colours actually fuse from a distance is the sort of thing that reminds me of tapestries. It's quite amazing.

I just want to say I've got nothing but the greatest respect for the weavers—Amy, Milena, Rachel and Caroline—there is a truth they have woven into the tapestry which is so instructive and timeless. This object is not my object. This object is something that came out of the Workshop, and it's gone into a different context now. I hope some people will get something out of it, someday. I learnt a lot about how historic images resonate in doing this tapestry. I hope that it continues to open up a lot of technical challenges as well, in the future.

AS: I look forward to our next tapestry with you, John.

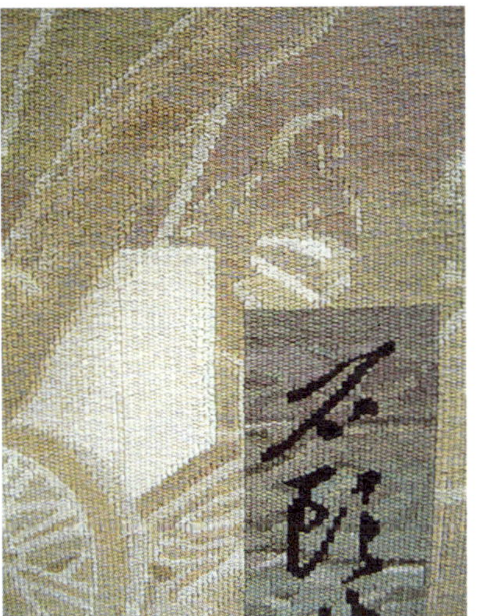

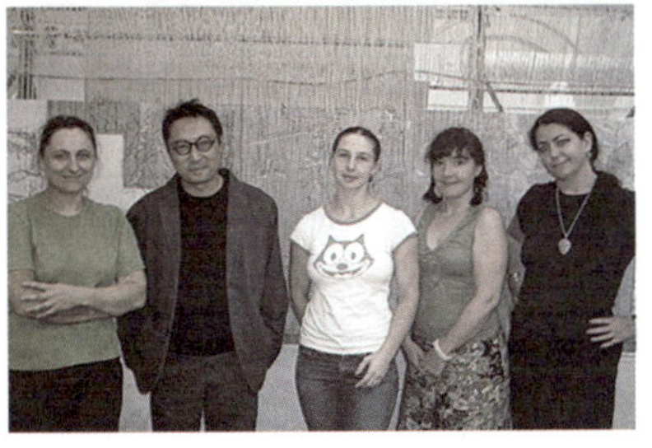

Details featuring calligraphic historical names of Nanjing from *Open World* 2005

Left to right: Melina Paplinska, John Young, Amy Cornall, Rachel Hine and Caroline Tully Australian Tapestry Workshop, Melbourne, 2005

Rachel Hine

What I remember about weaving *Open World* was the overwhelming size and importance of this piece—it being a gift to a sister city, to be hung in one of the biggest libraries in the world.

Aside from the 'photographic' elements that needed to be woven, the challenge of the golden colour of the silken-like drapery of the body of the tapestry was something I had to put my mind to. After many different samples were woven by the team, I remember coming across what would turn out to be the colour DNA of the project. Combining a selection of colours wherein the hues could be shifted towards warmer and cooler tones by adding or taking away certain colours, I remember feeling like we were going to be able to do it justice.

The historical references were fascinating and very pleasing to weave. I also remember taking great care in weaving the Chinese characters, so as not to represent the wrong word or meaning. *Open World* was truly my favourite tapestry of those I had the pleasure to be a part of.

Milena Paplinska

The John Young tapestry started in early 2005. I believe this was also the first year of Kate Derum's leadership as Artistic Director of the then Victorian Tapestry Workshop. I remember that she was quite easy-going and relaxed about the whole process and open to any suggestions, except for one thing: I was told I must weave the panel with the female model's face.

We had numerous meetings with John and spent a lot of time learning about what the different elements of his artwork were and about their meaning. We made sure that we understood his ideas and creative thinking process. I felt that John was open to collaboration with the Workshop and trusted us with his design, without hesitation.

My idea, as a general approach, was to let all the weavers choose what they wanted to do. That was quite a different approach to our usual process at the workshop. Many team leaders allocated areas that they wanted each weaver to work on. In the case of the John Young tapestry, I really wanted all weavers to connect emotionally to the parts of the design they worked on and to feel passionate about them. I always believed that such a mindset was a great start to any creative process.

My approach to the composition of the artwork was that all side panels were treated as separate images. Each one of them had their own colour palette set up on the tables. However, we made sure that all of them had the same intensity of colour and contrast. So, they were balancing each other within the entire design.

The background of the tapestry evolved from a tonally close, almost solid quality at the bottom, to something very airy, transparent, almost translucent at the top, with an addition of subtle blue cotton in the mixes that visually connected it to the side panels and the beautiful, crisp Chinese calligraphy.

We had one issue with the gold colour of the background. Our range simply did not include this colour at the time. So many different samples in wool and cotton were dyed in collaboration with the dye shop for this project. In an elimination process we came up with a colour that was so desirable that it later became a permanent in the workshop's range. I hope it is still there!

We used many cotton threads within our mixes against flat wool to achieve beautiful, sharp edges and contrasts. As for the transparency, our mixes included dark and light threads with some in-between to get the illusion of layers within the top part of the middle image and background.

Also, as we approached a more open area, I made the decision to unify the pallet of the background and to use the same mixes across the top part of the design to close up the composition. To produce such a strong, beautiful tapestry with such a strong meaning is a credit to the incredible collaboration between John and us weavers, and a fantastic team effort.

I think Caroline did an exceptionally good job. She has always been a very reliable weaver and at that time both of us had comparable weaving experience. It was a pleasure and great support and so much fun to have her there, just weaving away! Amy, you were also great with getting these contrasts and transparencies so beautifully and almost effortlessly. As the youngest weaver on our team, you were trouble free and an absolute pro with Chinese calligraphy and also a really good hard worker! Rachel, as an artist in her own right, achieved the most growth as an interpretative weaver and in all technical aspects of weaving during this time. In my eyes, she had the most challenging task and she came out of this as a winner. In 2011, I worked with John Young again on a tapestry *Finding Kenneth Myer*,[1] which was commissioned by the Myer family for the National Library of Australia.

1. John Young collaborated with the Australia Tapestry Workshop for a second time in 2010 and 2011 to produce the tapestry *Finding Kenneth Myer*, commissioned by Lady Southey and the Myer Family for the National Library of Australia, Canberra

AUSTRALIAN TAPESTRY WORKSHOP: WEAVERS' PROFILES

AMY CORNALL studied Fine Art at Monash University, completing an Honours Degree majoring in Tapestry. She began working as a professional weaver at the Australian Tapestry Workshop (ATW) in South Melbourne in 2004, collaborating with other artists and weavers to create contemporary tapestries on a large scale. These include the last in a suite of six Roger Kemp tapestries that hang in the Great Hall of the National Gallery of Victoria (NGV) International in Melbourne, and Alice Bayke, designed by Yvonne Todd, commissioned for the Gallery of Modern Art in Brisbane. She is currently a Senior Weaver at the ATW.

ANTONIA SYME was the Director of the Australian Tapestry Workshop between 2009 and 2023. Her 40-year career reflects her enduring commitment to cultural heritage and community service. Syme is a specialist in contemporary art, craft and design, developed through exhibition curation, collections management and conservation, and gallery management. In 2020, Syme was made a member of the Order of Australia AM for her significant service to visual arts administration, and to maritime archaeology. She was the recipient of the William J. Mitchell Prize by the International Chapter of the Australian Institute of Architects in 2020, and was awarded a place in the Royal Collection Studies course, Windsor, in 2019, supported by a Nina Stanton Scholarship.

CAROLINE TULLY holds a Bachelor of Arts (Fine Art) from Monash University, Graduate and Postgraduate Diplomas in Classics and Archaeology as well as a PhD in Aegean Archaeology from the University of Melbourne. She is an author, scholar and Honorary Research Fellow at the University of Melbourne. Tully was a professional tapestry weaver with the Australian Tapestry Workshop from 1996 to 2010.

MILENA PAPLINSKA took part in a Weaver Exchange Program in 2015 and travelled to Scotland, Dovecote Studios as well as London. The same year she visited China and has since travelled to Italy, France, Poland and India. After 20 years of working in tapestry weaving, she made the decision to use her creativity in a different way, utilising her people skills and knowledge of languages and digital technology to work with the older generation in a disability field. She also works in the community and supports her family business.

RACHEL HINE holds a BA Masters Degree in Fine Art (Tapestry) from Monash University. She lives and works in Geelong, and has a prolific and highly successful studio practice. Her focus is on presenting contemporary tapestry weaving and creating a context that makes sense in this modern world. Most recently she has been included in a publication called *The Weaving Explorer*, by Gwen Steege and Deborah Jarchow. Hine exhibits her tapestries and paintings regularly and has had a large-scale tapestry acquired by Geelong Gallery.

Open World 2005
Woven at the Australian Tapestry
Workshop by Amy Cornall, Rachel Hine,
Milena Paplinska and Caroline Tully
Cotton and wool tapestry, 330 x 365 cm
Collection of Nanjing Library, Nanjing

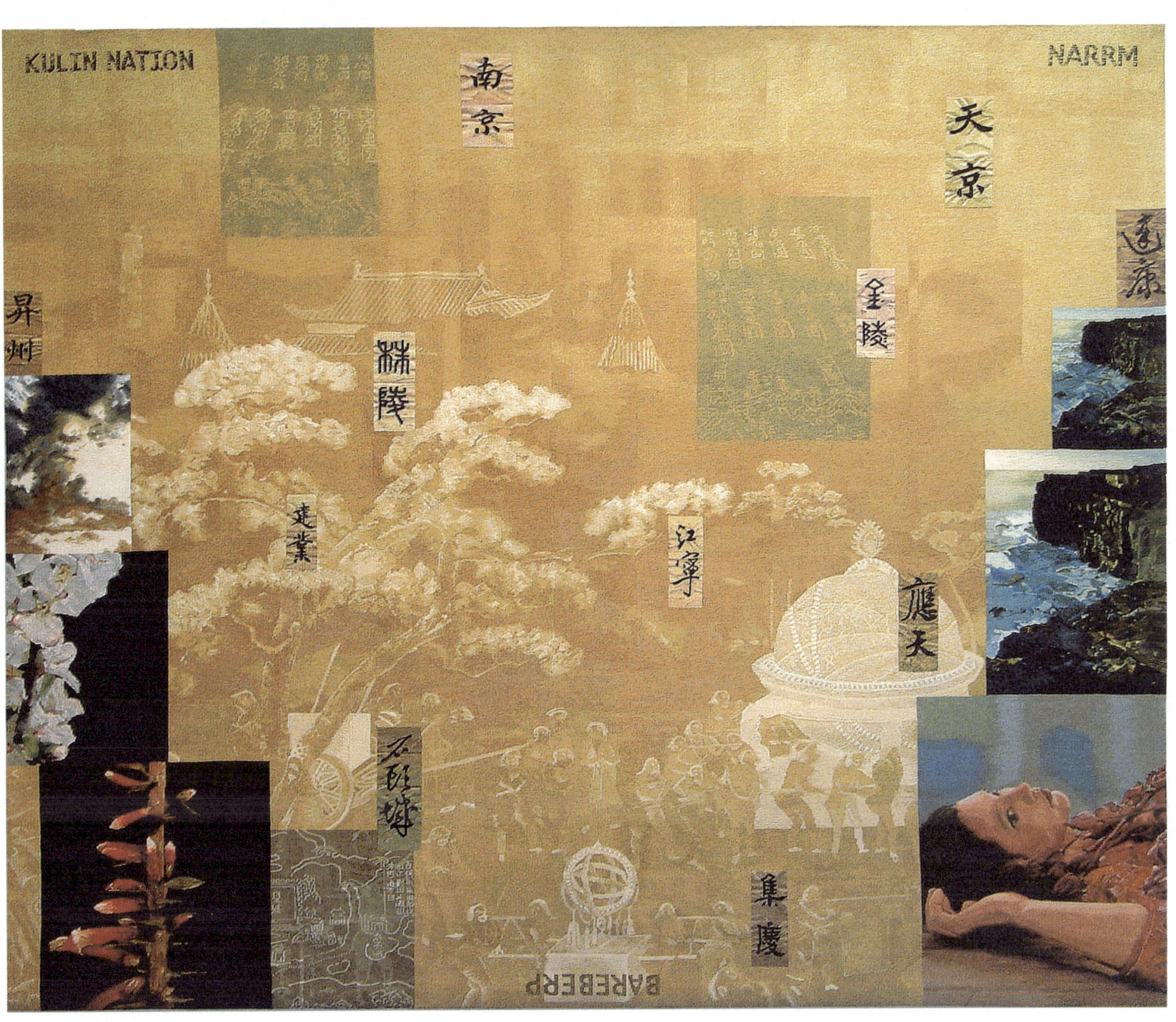

KULIN NATION
NARRM
南京
天京
昇州
金陵
遠康
秣陵
建業
江寧
應天
石珵城
集慶

1967DISPERSION

2008

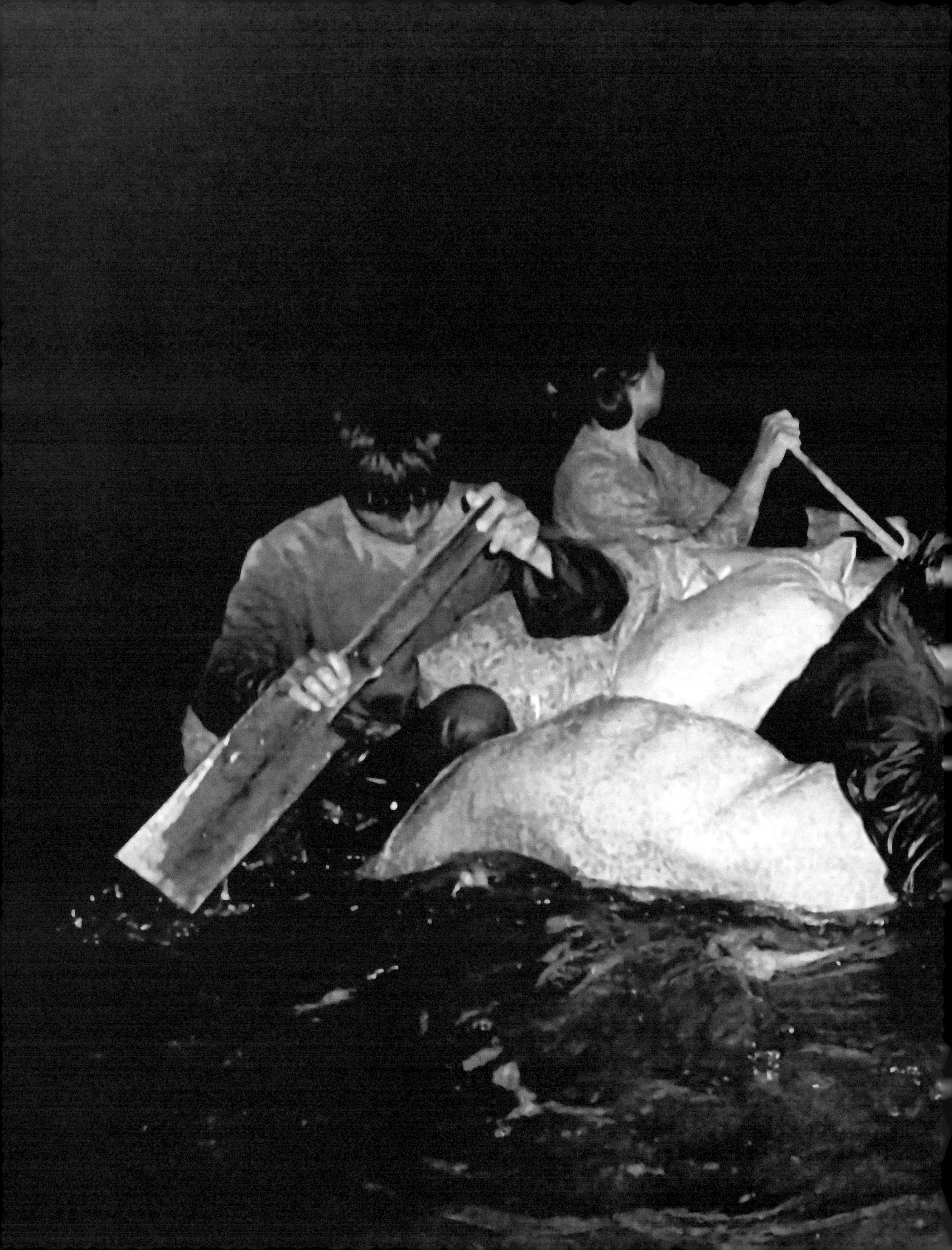

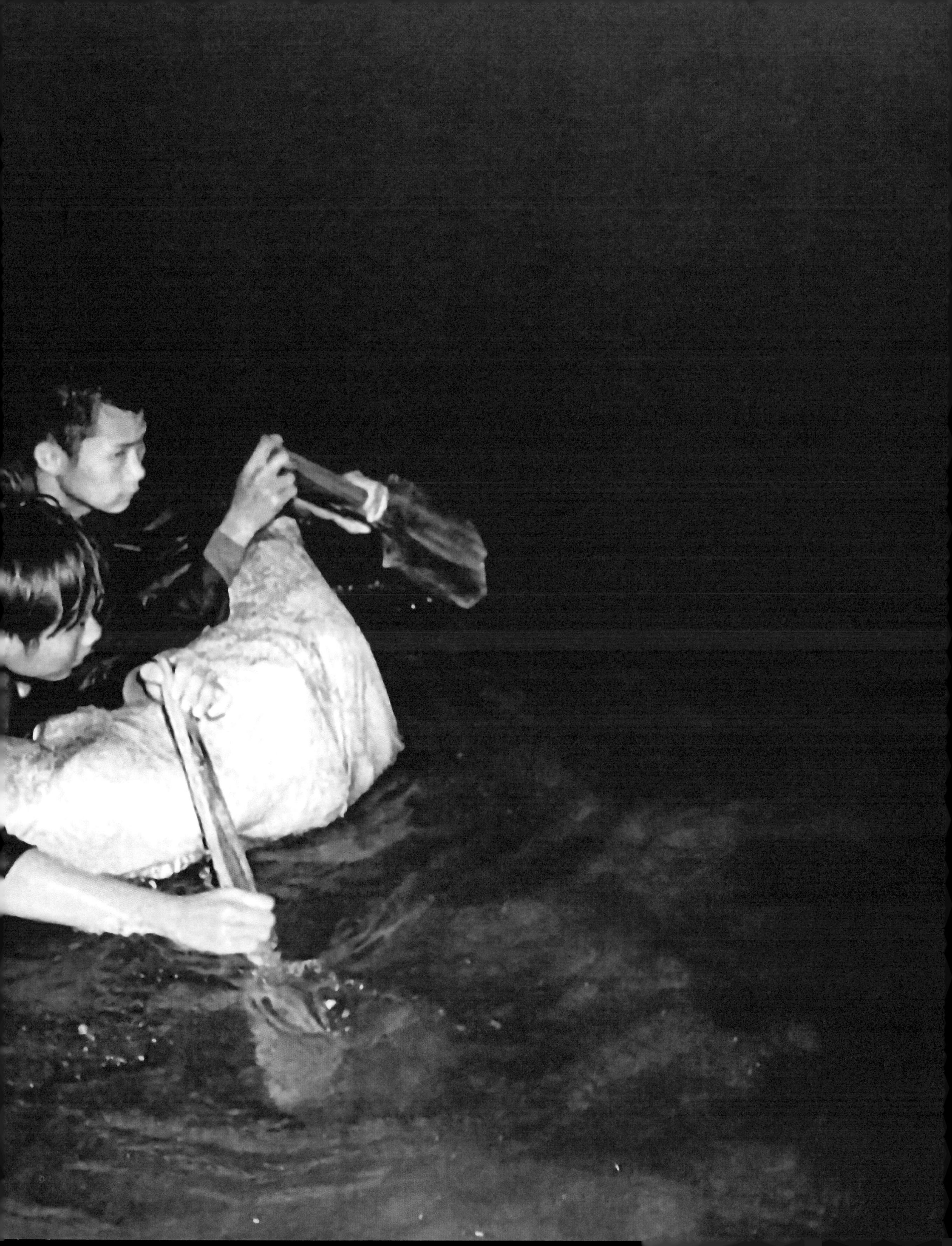

1967DISPERSION

In April 1967 the Hong Kong Artificial Flower Works, in Kowloon's San Po Kong, fired some 650 workers for refusing to accept new work regulations. The resulting strikes and demonstrations by leftist unions—fomented by the editorialising of the local branch of the mainland Chinese Xinhua ('New China') News Agency and the political ripples of the Cultural Revolution (1966–77) on the mainland—escalated into a prolonged and violent anti-colonial campaign. Within the year, 51 people had died, 1936 were convicted and the territory was effectively brought to a standstill by a spate of public bombings. Seen by the British colonial government as an insurrection, the riots expedited the introduction of a wide range of social reforms and policies fostering local identity. That year the term *heung gung yan* 香港人 ('Hong Kong People' or Hongkonger) appeared in the local press for the first time. However, the instability that the riots brought also triggered an exodus of people and capital from the territory.

1967Dispersion consists of seven multi-panelled paintings, each combining digital printing and oil on linen. The project marks Young's first use of archival photographs in the creation of his work. Here, the photographs are drawn from news coverage by the *South China Morning Post*, the local English-language newspaper. An inflection point in the artist's practice, the work does not yet incorporate historical photographs in the kind of grid installation that forms the template for later History Projects. Instead, they are digitally printed at scale onto linen and juxtaposed with abstract colour fields or photorealistic oil paintings of plastic flowers in *Riot – Flowers*, or a red plastic bucket in *Wishforce*. *1967Dispersion* also marked the first time Young paired archival photographs with digitally composed abstract paintings, which began as individual works from his *Naïve and Sentimental* series (2006–).

Studio notes (October 2008)

While working in my Melbourne studio in the winter of 2007, it suddenly occurred to me that it was the fortieth anniversary of my initial departure from Hong Kong. In that winter, I read Walter Benjamin's recollections of his childhood years in Berlin. He was at once fascinated, melancholic and plagued by the phantoms of that time. Those from a diaspora—the Jews, the Irish, the Polish, the Chinese—can tell you precisely, and in meticulous detail, why and how they left the land that bore them. More often than not, the reasons for leaving were abject. The year of 1967 in Hong Kong was no exception.

1967 was a year of drought, floods and riots. The droughts and floods were God's will. The riots were men's. Hong Kong became the fault line of ideologies—between the 'Great Proletarian Cultural Revolution' and the safeguarding of one of the last promising capitalist experiments of the British Colonial Empire. I left Hong Kong, as a child, with a C-class British passport. Then I began to see the documentary photos from newsprints—the horror on the faces of the poor British bomb disposal experts, immediately after their limbs were blown off by 'pineapples', those makeshift bombs in shopping bags that you stay well clear of at tram stops.

It's well known, how the riots started at a plastics flower factory. Plastics was the roaring industry at the time—the dolls, the flowers, the Red-A buckets I bathed with—signs of modernity, signs of capitalist oppression, signs of modular utility, signs of fat cats to come.

The abstracts that accompany the images are meticulously painted in oils, but originally generated out of thousands of images, technologically. These 1960s high-modernist-looking abstracts make you feel that, just perhaps, the riot scenes had been related to them all along.

Reflection (January 2022)

The realm of the present always includes the interpenetration of the past and the present. Our society's comprehension of time went horribly wrong in the progressive late twentieth century when it came to dealing with the present. Its conception of the present never had any sense of extension and contraction. The future is now exploited for its primacy. The diasporan's time enlightens us. The temporal co-existence of the past and the present, which is the fundamental psychic condition for those in a diaspora, displaces the compulsion to understand one's existence in spatial terms. Diaspora or dispersion—the movement of people—is never only from A to B, from one location to another; that is, a quantitative spatial thinking. Nor is the nature of diasporas only predicated on the numerical, on peoples' transit. It is an escape, a duration, a flux, an endless creative combination.

pages 56–57
Central panel of *Dispersion* 2008
Digital print and oil on linen, three panels, 85 × 375 cm
Collection of M+, Hong Kong

LETTING THE PAST IN:
RECONCILING HISTORY IN
JOHN YOUNG'S *1967 DISPERSION*

Olivier Krischer

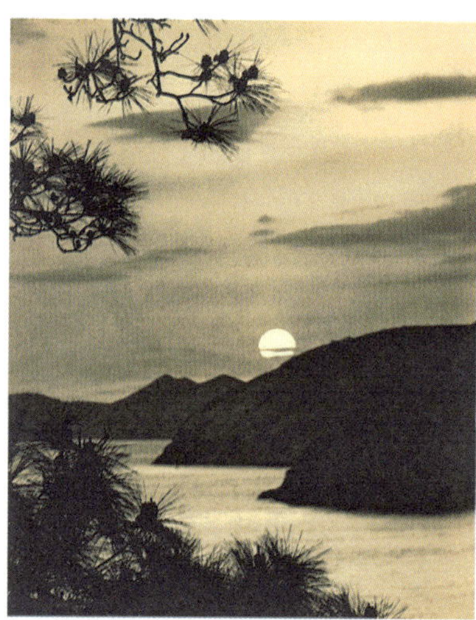

Repulse Bay, Hong Kong, c. 1960s
Photograph by the artist's father,
Norman Sze Kuen Young

History begins in the present. It seems to anchor the past even as we, and it, drift our separate ways. But there are pasts that do not wish to be anchored at all; pasts that prefer to slip away in the current, to recede into memory, under the veil of night. How to reconcile with the past, when it is precisely that from which we flee, or which has cast us away? How can we find a way back, if only to move on?

STILL WATERS

And so we begin on a threshold: we are looking at a setting sun across the calm waters of Repulse Bay, on the affluent southern shores of Hong Kong Island. It is some time in 1956. At another time this year, perhaps before, perhaps after, John Young is born into this view. In October, in faraway Kowloon, simmering tensions between the communist and nationalist groups in Hong Kong will finally erupt into the Double Ten riots, leaving over fifty dead and hundreds injured. The ripples of decolonisation and Maoist politics will soon wash over Hong Kong, but this year the colonial authorities conclude that the conflict stems from just another exile, another migrant, posing little challenge to the status quo.

But we see none of this history here. This carefully composed image, photographed by Young's father from the family's home, keeps tension at bay; like the setting sun, it hovers outside time, seemingly beyond the reach of a historical gaze.[1] Such pictorialism—rendered clichéd by preceding decades of modernist and leftist visual culture—was popular in the circles of salon photography, enjoying, like certain modes of ink painting, a kind of dual identity. It speaks of tradition, of culture, yet it is transnational; it is local, yet cosmopolitan. It is hardly a coincidence that such visions circulated across the Sinophone diaspora of Cold War Asia, including in Hong Kong.

Are we looking into the past? While the camera lends our view a kind of veracity, it is quickly tempered by a culturally conditioned aesthetics which takes the viewer (who knows how to see it) beyond the now, to meander into other times and places: the hills recede into a distance they define; the diagonal stretch of water charts a journey for the embodied eye; clouds are layered across an ever-setting sun, inviting self-reflection and suggesting cyclical time. Tree branches—perhaps pine, one of the 'four gentleman' (四君子) of the Chinese literati canon—open a bridge to the *au-delà*, beyond the frame, an expanded world in which the viewer is subtly immersed, in which they actively see rather than distantly observe.

This self-consciously privileged view, outside time yet of its moment, is a complex point of departure to discuss the relationship of Hong Kong to the historical turn in Young's work.

The 2008 series *1967Dispersion* marked a significant conceptual and formal transition in John Young's oeuvre, from the rhetorical deconstruction and transcultural exploration of his earlier series into a new critical engagement with history and memory. Considered by Young to be the first of his History Projects, *1967Dispersion* is anchored by Hong Kong's 1967 riots, a period that would usher in far reaching social and policy changes in colonial Hong Kong. It was also the catalyst for one of the 'flights' (to use Young's term) or displacements of the Hong Kong population, including his own. Significantly, the individual mediation of history meant forming a new relationship to the documentary photographic image, an ethical relationship that animates the subsequent History Projects. It is this relationship to the image and its mode of production that embodies what Young calls 'an ethical responsibility'.

When this series was first exhibited in 2008, Young associated the historical turn in his work with the realisation, in the winter of 2007, that it had been forty years since his arrival in Australia.[2] While reading German philosopher and critic Walter Benjamin's memoirs of childhood in Berlin, Young recognised the potential to forge 'a new praxis' through a critical engagement with (personal) history and memory. Benjamin was no stranger to displacement, having moved around Germany with his family and for studies, later going to Paris in exile from the Nazi regime, from 1932. His 'memoir' was an attempt to construct a philosophy woven from a critical reflection on his formative years, but Benjamin considered it a failure and it was not published until after his death.

Benjamin's sensitivity to the relationship between displacement and historical consciousness continues to trouble the contemporary. Art historian T. J. Demos begins his book *The Migrant Image* (2012) by recalling Benjamin's poetic reading of Swiss artist Paul Klee's 1920 monoprint *Angelus Novus*. Made using an oil transfer method Klee developed, which produced a distinctly fragile line over which he added watercolours, this was a work Benjamin had acquired in 1921 and carried with him among his papers. Demos draws on Benjamin's reference to this from his 'Theses on the Philosophy of History', written in 1940 but published posthumously, in which Klee's image is that of the angel of history. Writes Benjamin:

> His face is turned toward the past. Where we perceive a chain of events, he sees one single catastrophe which keeps piling wreckage upon wreckage and hurls it in front of his feet. The angel would like to stay, awaken the dead, and make whole what has been smashed. But a storm is blowing from Paradise; it has got caught in his wings with such violence that the angel can no longer close them. The storm irresistibly propels him into the future to which his back is turned, while the pile of debris before him grows skyward. This storm is what we call progress.[3]

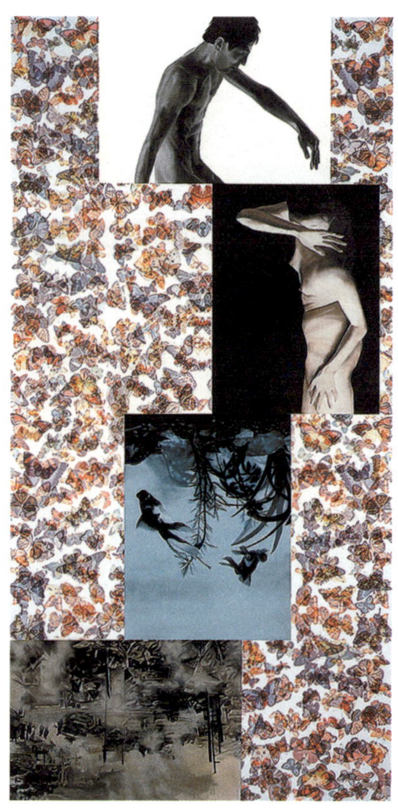

Demos suggests Benjamin's melancholic account of historical time represents 'a philosophy of complex temporality that in effect renders us all perpetual refugees in the fleeting present.'[4] Writing in the shadow of fascism, Benjamin recognised how ideological conflict extends over the past, threatening to disrupt or even vanquish not only what could be, but also what had been. In this sense, he argued that 'hope' comes not from the future but rather from a vanquished past that resists domination. For Benjamin, it was the historian—the historical materialist more specifically, in his conception—whose duty it was to continue 'fanning the spark of hope in the past' (Thesis VI).[5]

RESPONSIVE IMAGES

Looking at the arc of Young's work from the 1990s and 2000s, however, we can trace concerns regarding history, memory, power relations and displacement developing in the broader philosophical and formal shifts in his practice throughout this period. Young's awareness of his social and cultural context made him feel that postmodernism was largely 'a crisis of Western mastery', which amounted to a 'notional critique of culture that was largely silent on underlying social forces'.[6] Moving on from the procedural and strategic void of the *Polychrome Paintings* series, in the *Double Ground Paintings* series Young explored 'cultural identity, hybridity and difference in a postmodern, postcolonial age'.[7] This series developed his interest in the technology of copying, evident in his earlier use of photocopies in the *Silhouette Paintings* (1985–1988). Young used scanned and digitally printed images from the classical canons of Europe and China, onto which were layered hand-painted images of generic landscapes, flowers, *objets d'arts* or nudes. While he retained the practice of painting, Young enlisted it into a different economy by collaborating with peers and employing assistants. The combined intention was to naturalise distinct scopic regimes while retaining a 'volatility' that refuted a singular historical vision, and instead 'embrac[ed] relativism over singularity and truth'.[8]

By the late 1990s, however, Young's experience at the forefront of multicultural Australia's cultural industry made clear the political dilemma of transcultural positioning. On the one hand, Young had represented Australia on the world stage, including the 1995 exhibition *Antipodean Currents* at the Guggenheim Museum in New York. Yet, in Australia and its art world, Young and other Asian Australian colleagues recognised the persistent lack of a critical space for complex cultural identities.[9] In Australia, as elsewhere, a multicultural rhetoric existed alongside sometimes brazen xenophobia, exemplified by the emergence of the openly anti-immigration politician Pauline Hanson as a Liberal candidate in the 1996 federal elections, and her subsequent establishment of the right-wing One Nation party the following year.[10] Importantly, Young was also concerned with urgent political realities, including the fate of Hong Kong, where members of his family remained, following the 1997 transition to Mainland Chinese rule. As he recently reflected:

> The changing political and cultural nature of Hong Kong after the Handover really, in retrospect, galvanised something in my overall intentions in making art … there was an urgency and a certain responsibility of engagement beyond the syntactic or cultural-civilisational responsibilities in a work. Bringing memories, especially personal memories, into a work gave me an acute responsibility [towards] my reflections of my own past—and later, in the other History Projects, other people's pasts as well.[11]

Hong Kong Burns 2000
Digital print and oil on canvas, 288 × 138 cm

Historically a port city, Hong Kong has been a place of arrival and departure, only partially 'present' perhaps, in its relentless projection towards a possible future. The announcement of the handover of sovereignty to Mainland China in the early 1980s changed the nature of time for the British colony. In either apprehension or anticipation, all at once, one knew when the present ended. A countdown had begun in which the present slowly but surely drip, dripped into the past. For some, time seemed no longer to be moving forward; instead, it was hurtling into the past—but what and where was this unknown and uncharted past? For many in Hong Kong at the time, in the arts and media, this slippage fostered an anxious search to recognise, in the fragments of time revisited, some common ground on which to rally in the face of uncertainty.

Perhaps Young's first direct reference to Hong Kong emerged in the provocatively titled *Hong Kong Burns* (2000), part of the *Patterned Grounds* series of oil paintings on digitally printed canvases. In this work, Young adapts the *Double Ground Paintings* schema to compose an allegory of Hong Kong's uncertain fate at the intersection of colonialism, global capital and the precarious assurances of the 'One Country, Two Systems' principle.[12] The butterfly-patterned textile of the background is said to suggest the transient nature of national and cultural boundaries in an age of global trade and rapid technological change. On this ground, Young positions hand-painted monochrome images: a male and female nude, each in an awkward pose, who look clumsily 'human' rather than allegorically strong or youthful; an inverted image of goldfish—usually an auspicious Chinese symbol—that renders them inert or lifeless; and an upturned grey image in the lower left, which turns a documentary image of a fire in one of Hong Kong's old squatter villages—the kind that were home to nearly a quarter of Hong Kong's population in the 1960s, and survive in pockets to this day—into an abstract graphic element.[13]

In the *Refugee Patterns* series, however, the layered composition of hand-painted images on digitally printed ground moves from a symbolic to a more narrative relationship, from which one might even suggest a resonance with the issue of refugees and concerns for post-handover Hong Kong. In 2001, in what became known as the Tampa Affair, the Liberal Howard government in Australia had denied entry to a Norwegian ship carrying hundreds of refugees rescued at sea, successfully turning a humanitarian crisis into a national security issue. Despite international condemnation, the September 11 attacks in New York and Washington gave credence to the Australian government's portrayal of asylum seekers as potential criminals.[14] In these years, Young also remained highly engaged in Hong Kong: he completed a public art commission for the expansion of North Point MTR subway interchange in 2001, and was even shortlisted to represent Hong Kong at the Venice Biennale in 2003—the same year that Hong Kong's annual 1 July protests attracted half a million people opposing proposed anti-sedition laws, just as the SARS epidemic subsided.[15]

In *Red, Blue* (2003), from the *Refugee Patterns* series, images of a makeshift raft suspended on open ocean are layered onto a digital print of a woven red, white and blue plastic fabric. This *hung baak laam* (紅白藍 'red-white-blue') fabric has commonly been used in Hong Kong as a form of urban shelter on construction sites and hawker stalls, and was first transformed there into the familiar carry bags used by the city's migrants, cross-border traders and domestic helpers—highly mobile, visible, yet precarious communities. As a symbol of grassroots cultural identity, it has been employed by a number of Hong Kong artists to make sculptures and installations.[16]

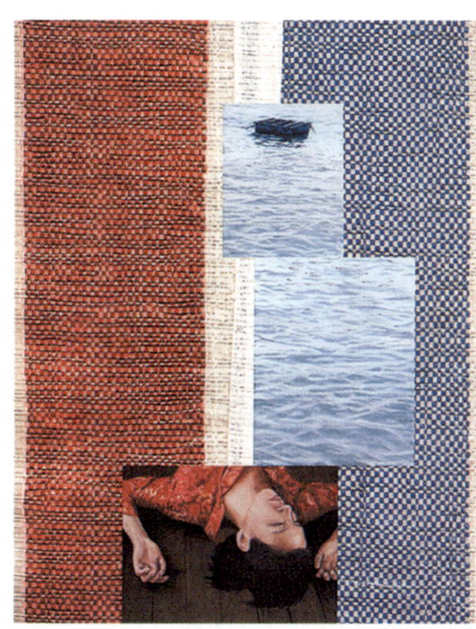

Red, Blue 2003
Digital print and oil on linen, 200 × 150 cm
Private collection, Berlin

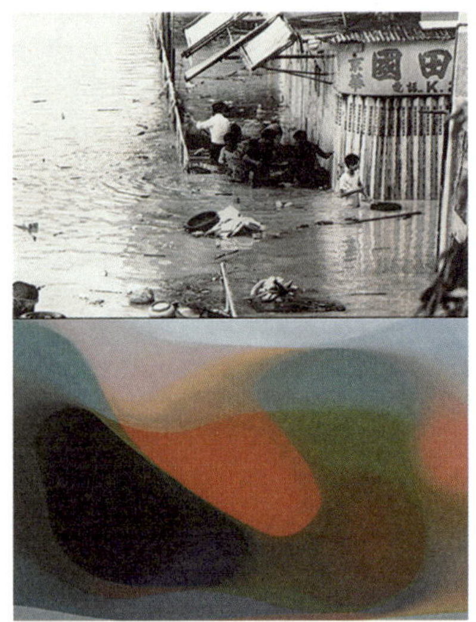

In Young's work, it has a more global currency, yet the lateral resonance with the cultural politics and historical dimensions of Hong Kong points to developments that come to fruition in *1967 Dispersion*. Rather than the kind of 'rhizomatic' effect of the layered images in the *Patterned Ground* series, here the composition fosters a narrative resonance: the expanse of open ocean deepened through its repetition, while its oppressive calm seems to be echoed in the model's gaze.

RECUPERATING ETHICS

In *1967 Dispersion* Young sets an agenda that has characterised the History Projects, both in the relationship between art making and historical research, and in a new relationship to the photographic image. The series forms a cycle of seven works that resist a linear, chronological retelling of history. Instead, they 'stage a process of remembering'[17] —as Jacqueline Lo has written of Young's *Bonhoeffer in Harlem* (2010)—which Carolyn Barnes has associated with Deleuze's idea of memory formation in *Difference and Repetition*.[18] Importantly, in *1967 Dispersion*, Young formed a new approach to images, not as truths or cyphers but as artefacts eliciting a kind of custodianship.

As he explains:

> Formally, I had to gain an understanding of … the documentary press photograph—how its apparent factuality is such a powerful rhetoric; [how] its literalness and didacticism demands a sort of ethical responsibility for any artist who wish[es] to employ them. As these images of the time wedge themselves into our memory, like it or not, they almost become the yardstick in our re-imagining of that trauma.[19]

In *1967 Dispersion*, rather than reconstructing a historical event, Young explores what he refers to as 'pressure points', including not only the environmental and political events but also their underlying conditions and impacts.[20] This leads away from a linear reading of the history and instead to a cyclical sense of narrative. For example, the central image of an overloaded dinghy recalls the arrival of desperate migrants, as much as it refers to their 'flight' from or to Hong Kong. The repeated abstract paintings that flank this documentary image add depth to the night that envelops this desperation.

We might glean, from the documentary images, elements of the historical 'record' that form the contextual backdrop to the dispersion signalled in the series' title. In *Flood*, a diptych image is comprised of a digitally printed news photo above and a hand-painted abstract canvas below. The photographic image is cropped, focusing on the struggle of people navigating the waist-high waters around a shopfront, on what would have been a commercial thoroughfare. As with other images in this series, the contrast has been intentionally manipulated. The dynamic effect of water is echoed in the digital printed image in *Folks*, yet, with its closely cropped and slightly out-of-focus image, it is rendered almost abstract—its surface effect of mottled abstraction seemingly mirrored in the painted canvas below.

Hong Kong suffered drought and water shortages into the 1960s, but in 1966 torrential rains flooded the city, wrecking infrastructure and leaving thousands homeless. In its wake, a significant fare increase for the Star Ferry (the main public transport across Hong Kong harbour) sparked a public petition. The situation escalated when a local man launched a hunger strike at the terminal, which drew a group of sympathetic protestors, who were then met with a harsh police response. Riots broke out, leaving dozens injured and over a thousand arrested.

In May 1967, disputes over wages and working conditions at a plastic flower factory again led to clashes with police. This time, perhaps buoyed by the success of communist agitation in Macau five months earlier, the Chinese Government officially protested to the British Embassy in Beijing and organised anti-British demonstrations and media campaigns in Beijing and Guangzhou.[21] Hong Kong leftists and communists launched protests, strikes and propaganda campaigns, but when the administration shut down leftwing media and carried out raids and arrests, some radicals started a violent bombing campaign that continued well into 1968. This eventually included around 253 explosions, 1500 'true bombs' and thousands of hoaxes.[22] In an attempt to curb the campaign and restore order, a curfew was declared, limiting movement after 8pm.

Riot appears to present a news image from the heart of the violence: flames and smoke are bellowing high in the air beside a block of dense apartments. Residents line the balconies, shoulder to shoulder, as they look down at the crowd running from multiple blazes. Some are trying to scale the railings to safety; debris is strewn across the emptying streets. A car, its bonnet cocked, looks hastily abandoned; a dented oil barrel lies on the road nearby. *Riot–Fire*, serves to isolate the elemental force of the fire, its abstraction heightened by the canvas below, which (as in *Folks*) appears to mimic the atmospheric dynamic of the accompanying cropped image.

In the broader context of the ensuing Cold War and a process of decolonisation that had seen dozens of anti-colonial agitations waged across the waning British Empire, the colonial administration had initially described the violence of 1967 as the 'Hong Kong emergency'.[23] Yet, a decisive local factor was the very structure of Hong Kong's boom-era economy, which had relied on an abundant supply of cheap refugee labour to pivot from regional exports to manufacturing. By the 1960s, despite labour reforms proposed in London, local industry was resisting reform to maintain the lucrative status quo. Underlying leftist politics was therefore a genuine grievance with the colonial government's failure to address labour conditions and the complicity of industrialist elites.

As global capital seeped into the colony, the 1960s was also a time in which the concept of 'Hong Kong people' began to emerge from both a top-down policy and more grassroots cultural trends. Government programs in public housing, originally for public health reasons, began to shape ideas of daily life and improve social welfare. As society became more prosperous, popular culture in Cantonese films, music and publishing informed and reflected local identity in turn, as did the general acceptance of a kind of cosmopolitan 'East meets West' identity in the increasingly middle-class society, however limited this reality was for the territory broadly. These factors contributed to a sense in which Hong Kong felt increasingly distinct from mainland China as well as Taiwan, a trend encouraged by the colonial administrators.[24] A particular manifestation of this was the emerging consumer culture for export goods, including textiles and plastics, promoted through manufacturing 'exhibitions' and festivals that made shopping into a social event. Such goods were promoted as the fruits of local industry and symbols of a modern, international city.[25]

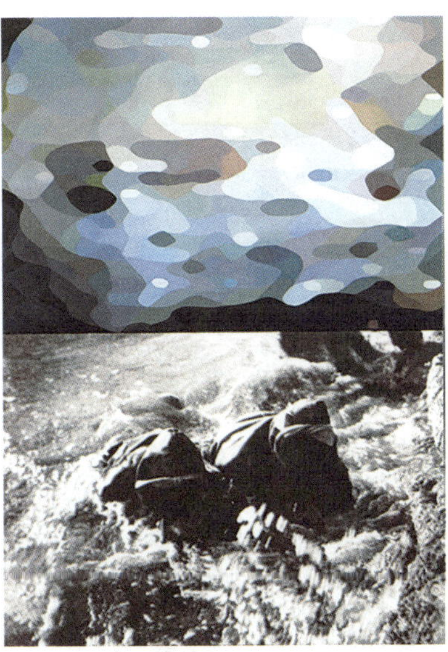

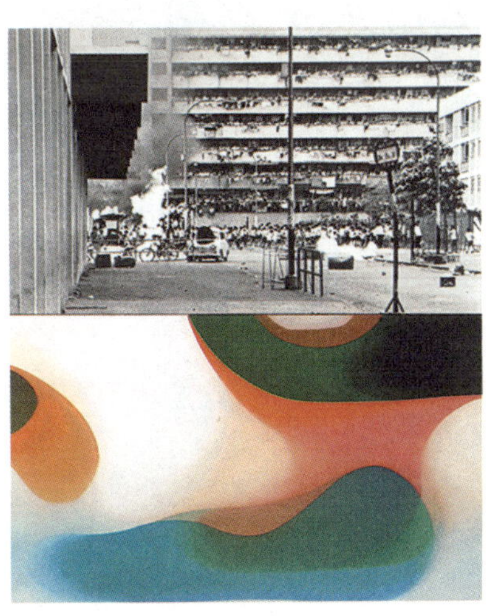

Folks 2008
Digital print and oil on linen, two panels,
169 × 118 cm

Riot 2008
Digital print and oil on linen, two panels,
170 × 125 cm
Collection of M+, Hong Kong

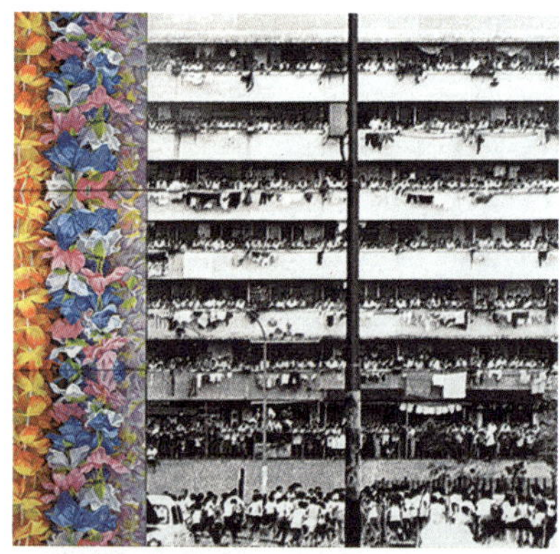

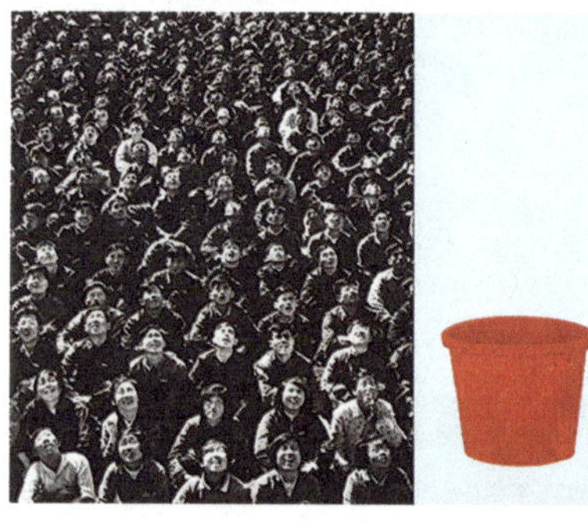

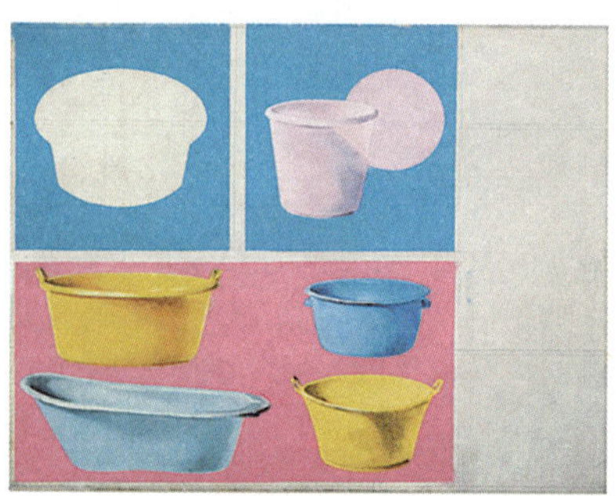

Riot – Flowers 2008
Digital print and oil on linen, four panels,
147 × 146 cm
Collection of M+, Hong Kong

Wishforce 2008
Digital print and oil on linen, two panels,
151 × 180 cm
Collection of M+, Hong Kong

Sigmar Polke (1941–2010)
Plastik–Wannen (Plastic Tubs) 1964
Oil and graphite on canvas, 94.6 × 120 cm
Private collection; image courtesy of Sotheby's

In *Riot – Flowers*, Young directly references this context by juxtaposing a cropped image of the riot alongside images of plastic flowers. These are in fact three identically painted panels, replicating the industrial mode of production at the heart of not only their manufacture, but also the labour conditions that sparked the riots.

This relationship helps to unpack *Wishforce*, in which an anonymous mass of seated Mainland Chinese, with uniform clothes and hair, gazes skywards, alluding to the cult status of Mao, who was exalted in song and dance as the 'red sun' of the Cultural Revolution, his people turning to him like sunflowers.[26] According to Young, the image was likely sourced from an edition of *China Pictorial*, one of the few magazines officially allowed during the Cultural Revolution, which was instrumental in promoting the Maoist revolutionary line. Alongside this, Young places a seemingly nondescript red plastic bucket, in fact an iconic everyday consumer item in 1960s Hong Kong, which many (including Young) remember using to bathe as children. Such references signal Young's acute awareness of the historical privilege of his family's pioneering success in the early plastics industry, which secured his passage to Australia, even as it imbricates with the conditions that underlie the political violence causing his departure.[27]

However, *Wishforce* is also significant for the way it simultaneously references another distinct historiographical framework: that of art history. In addition to the local and political references of the bucket and the Maoist propaganda image, this painting references the work of German artist Sigmar Polke, who grew up in the early years of the German Democratic Republic (East Germany) before fleeing with his family, via West Berlin, to settle in Düsseldorf in 1953. In 1964, when he painted *Plastik–Wannen* (Plastic Tubs) (1964)—which Young acknowledges as an important reference[28]—Polke had just founded 'Capitalist Realism', along with Gerhard Richter and Konrad Fischer-Lueg. Polke's paintings in this short-lived style depicted everyday consumer items like men's socks, plastic goods and chocolate bars (tariffs on which had just been lifted).[29] Importantly, this Pop sensibility emerged in a radically different cultural context to its postwar American counterpart, as West Germany grappled 'to come to terms with the past' (*Vergangenheitsbewältigung*)—a key cultural concept at the time.[30] Polke's work therefore marks a locally situated response to modern industrialisation and capitalist consumption that resonates with Young's *Wishforce* in subtle, insightful ways. More broadly, such an oscillating set of references—to personal, political, cultural and artistic pasts—crucially expands the terrain of 'history' in this series beyond the factual and autobiographical, in ways that Young would develop later in series such as *The New Wolf of Rome* and Young's dialogue with the art of Ian Fairweather, the *Fairweather Transformations*.

Understanding the ways that Capitalist Realism simultaneously invested in and questioned painting amid industrial and technological change, Young's complex relationship to capital and the legacies of a late modernist avant-garde are embedded in the mode of abstraction he developed, which was paired with photographic images for the first time in *1967Dispersion*. At this earlier stage in his process, Young's abstracts were produced by feeding random internet images through automated Photoshop filters, then subjectively selecting from the hundreds of results, with the final choices being hand-painted in oil on canvas. While Young had long been interested in the element of chance or random processes of creation as 'distancing strategies'[31], here such elements move beyond the conceptual frisson of modernism: they are suspended between chance and intention (in their manner of selection), automation and artisanship (in their mode of production), with an added layer of (art) historical criticality. Young has explained this in terms of a complex intertextuality:

Transformed from thousands of images overnight, these abstracts evoke,
but do not lay claim to 'truths' like the documentation photo. At times,
they remind us of 60s Greenbergian modernism, the time of high
capitalism and its 'progressive' global colonial abstraction. Like Hegel's
spirit, Marx had to turn him on his head. In *Riot* we see the underbelly
of this sort of sweet capitalistic abstraction—exploitation, leading to riots
by the factory workers. This was precisely the darkness that I left Hong
Kong with in 1967, as an eleven-year-old—not the trauma of violence
on the streets, but the trauma of capital, and its ultimate exploitation.
The movement of people, the origins of diasporans are often not just
away from the violent events, but an escape from exploitation.[32]

RECONCILING HISTORY

Young's 'ethical impulse' to identify with this exploitation, with marginalised
histories through the intermediary position of the diaspora—the migrant, the
émigré, the exile—resonates with Demos' reading of modernity's 'darkness'
(after Benjamin), which casts us all as 'perpetual refugees'. This remains a position
of fertile, yet only vague, potential. As Demos suggests, '[A] politics of migration
beckons, a politics that leads to an openness to the unfamiliar and the untimely,
to a sensitivity regarding how one's own form of life connects inevitably to others
far away and in the past, and does so in both positive and negative ways, with
accompanying debts, responsibilities, and solidarities'.[33] For Young, however, there
is perhaps less of a sense in which all such resonance is 'inevitable'. Rather, his
ethical impulse refers to a more specific relationship, and his projects have identified
particular instances of 'transcultural humanitarianism'.[34] In the later development
of the History Projects, Young has courted heroism, even aspects of nostalgia.
'What the ghostly remains of other pasts recall', writes Peter Fritzsche, 'is the
fact of other presents and other possibilities'.[35] This speaks to Benjamin's
insistence that our task was to 'brush history against the grain'.[36]

Given the strong relationship between art making and research, or knowledge
production, at the heart of this historical turn in Young's work, it is productive to
consider these projects as a form of 'historical subjectivity'. This is not the inverse
of a scholarly objectivity but rather, in the context of academic history writing
for example, a practice that 'begins with the individual scholar's perception of her
connection to, and distance from, the past, and … is sustained through the historian's
decision to make that perception integral to her scholarship'.[37] Such a position
expresses a consciousness that Susan Crane describes as 'connected separation'.[38]
Perhaps this is the most straightforward image of the structure Young developed
to let the past in, as a form of reconciliation.

1. This image was published in Carolyn Barnes, 'Towards a Layered Imaginary', in Carolyn Barnes, ed., *John Young,* Craftsman House, Fishermans Bend, 2005, p. 27.

2. John Young, 'Studio Notes' to the 2008 exhibition of *1967 Dispersion* at 10 Chancery Lane Gallery, Hong Kong.

3. Walter Benjamin, 'Theses on the Philosophy of History' (Thesis IX), in Hannah Arendt (ed.), *Illuminations*, Harry Zohn (transl.), Schocken Books, New York, 1969, pp. 257–58.

4. T. J. Demos, *The Migrant Image: the art and politics of documentary during global crisis*, Duke University Press, Durham, NC, 2012, pp. 1–2.

5. On this reading of Benjamin's Theses, see Ronald Beiner, 'Walter Benjamin's Philosophy of History', *Political Theory*, vol. 12, no. 3, August 1984, p. 426.

6. Barnes, 'Towards a Layered Imaginary', p. 41.

7. Ibid., p. 49.

8. Ibid.

9. The 1990s witnessed, however, numerous counter-narratives regarding Australian engagements with Asia. Australian academic of Chinese, Indonesian and Dutch background Ien Ang critically explores the dilemma of 'Chineseness', and the paradox of Australia's self-image as a 'Western' nation, in *On Not Speaking Chinese: Living Between Asia and the West*, Routledge, Oxfordshire, 2001.

10. One response was the establishment of the Asian Australian Artists' Association and Gallery 4A, in 1995, by Young and a number of peers from theatre, visual arts and criticism. See Barnes, 'Towards a Layered Imaginary', especially the section 'The question of the art system' (pp. 53–64); and more recently Tian Zhang, 'Talking and not talking about race: curating Asian-Australian identities in the early years of 4A', *4A Papers*, Issue 6, May 2019, https://4a.com.au/articles/race-curating-asian-australian-identities-tian-zhang.

11. John Young, email communication with the author, 11 October 2020.

12. 'One Country, Two Systems' (*yiguo liangzhi* 一国两制) is a constitutional framework developed by China in the early 1980s, attributed to then Chinese leader Deng Xiaoping, which is intended to assert the 'One China' principle while allowing for distinct systems of local government, law and trade in post-handover Hong Kong until 2047. The same framework has guided the governance of Macau following its handover from Portuguese rule in 1999, and has been touted as a principle for Taiwan's 'reunification' with the Mainland. Following the 2019 protests in Hong Kong and subsequent introduction of the National Security Law in June 2020, official interpretation seems to have shifted to openly prioritise national unity, seen in the prominent public display of the slogan *yiguo shi gen, yiguo shi ben* 一国是跟，一国是本—meaning 'One Country is the Root, One Country is the Foundation'.

13. Barnes, 'Towards a Layered Imaginary', p. 48.

14. The ship was forced to Nauru, leading to the establishment of the so-called Pacific Solution of offshore detention for asylum seekers arriving by boat to Australia. See Judy Johnston, Guy Callender, 'One Impact of 9/11 in the Australian Context: Government's Public Management Response to Asylum Seekers', *Administrative Theory & Praxis*, vol. 24, no.3, September 2002, pp. 603–6.

15. Young's candidacy was withdrawn by Hong Kong officials due to his residency status. See Barnes, p. 64.

16. Early examples include Doris Wong Wai Yin's *Home Moving Furniture* (2002). In November 2004, artist-designer Stanley Wong (known as Anothermountainman) curated the exhibition *Building Hong Kong: Redwhiteblue* at the Hong Kong Heritage Museum, and his own works in this material were part of the Hong Kong Pavilion at the 2005 Venice Biennale.

17. Jacqueline Lo, 'Diaspora, Art and Empathy', originally published in *John Young: The Bridge and the Fruit Tree*, Drill Hall Gallery, Australian National University, Canberra, 2013, pp. 19–43, republished in this volume with a new introduction, see pp. 137–47.

18. Carolyn Barnes, 'Aesthetics and memory work in the recent painting of John Young', *John Young: The Bridge and the Fruit Tree*, Drill Hall Gallery, Canberra, 2013, p. 61.

19. John Young, email correspondence with the author, 8 October 2020.

20. This also relates to the intentionally jarring juxtaposition of '1967' and 'Dispersion', which Young attributes to his interest in a dialectical process: forcing two elements together to suggest and potentially produce a third.

21. Left-wing protests in Macau on 2–3 December 1966 (the '12.3 incident') eventually led to the capitulation of the Portuguese colonial authorities and the reinstatement of de facto Chinese rule (for example, control over policing and many other government functions) under a Portuguese governor. See Robert Bickers, 'On not being Macao(ed) in Hong Kong: British official minds and actions in 1967', in Robert Bickers and Ray Yep (eds), *May Days in Hong Kong*, HKU Press, Hong Kong, 2009, pp. 56–57.

22. According to records from the Foreign & Commonwealth Office, in the United Kingdom National Archives, summarised in Bickers and Yep (eds), *May Days in Hong Kong*, p. 7.

23. Ray Yep and Robert Bickers, 'Studying the 1967 riots: An overdue project', in Bickers and Yep (eds), *May Days in Hong Kong – Riot and Emergency in 1967*, pp. 1–18.

24. See Matthew Turner, '60s/90s: Dissolving the People', in Pun Ngai and Yee Lai-man (eds), *Narrating Hong Kong Culture and Identity*, HKU Press, Hong Kong, 2003, pp. 26–29.

25. Ibid., p. 28.

26. During the Maoist era, numerous propaganda posters picture Mao surrounded by actual or stylised sunflowers, denoting the adoring

masses. See, for example: 'Sunflower', *chineseposters.net*, Chinese Poster Foundation, https://chineseposters.net/tags/sunflower. This was poignantly referenced in Ai Weiwei's *Sunflower Seeds* (2010).

27. Young's father, a successful agent for a British firm in the 1930s, established the Yuen Hing Hong Co. Ltd. with Young's mother in the 1940s. This became, by some accounts, the leading distributor of raw plastic during the consolidation of the local industry in the late 1950s, with Young senior also serving as chairman of the Hong Kong Plastic Manufacturers Association. See notes on the Industrial History of Hong Kong Group, 23 February 2017, https://industrialhistoryhk.org/yuen-hing-hong-company-ltd-initial-notes.

28. John Young in conversatin with the author at his studio, Melbourne, 1 April 2022. John Young also refers to Sigmar Polke's work in his conversation with Matt Cox in this volume, see p. 361. From the mid-1960s Polke also made paintings that reproduced the dot matrix cheap newsprint images, often painting directly on found fabrics rather than canvas.

29. Kathrin Rottman, 'Polke in Context: a chronology', in Kathy Halbreich et al (eds.), *Alibis: Sigmar Polke, 1963–2010*, The Museum of Modern Art, New York, 2014, p. 25; also Sean Rainbird, 'Seams and Appearances: learning to paint with Sigmar Polke', in Judith Nesbitt (ed.), *Sigmar Polke: Join the Dots*, Tate Gallery Publications, London, 1995, pp. 10–12.

30. Rottman, 'Polke in Context: a chronology', p. 25. Originally referring to feelings of anger, remorse and responsibility in German postwar society towards the rise of Nazism and the Holocaust, this compound noun—combining *bewältigung* ('coping or coming to terms with') and *Vergangenheit* ('the past') came to describe a broader cultural process of soul searching regarding German identity.

31. Wendy Walker, 'Making a case for the interrupted dance', *Passages—Brian Castro, Khai Liew, John Young*, TarraWarra Museum of Art, Healesville, Victoria, 2012, p. 20.

32. John Young, email correspondence with the author, 8 October 2020.

33. Demos, p. 249.

34. Genevieve Trail, 'Plurality of Memory: History Projects, Diaspora and Nationalism', *Divan: A Journal of Accounts. Art, Culture, Theory*, vol. 8, September 2020, p. 100.

35. Peter Fritzsche, 'Specters of History: On Nostalgia, Exile, and Modernity', *The American Historical Review*, vol. 106, no. 5, Dec 2001, p. 1592.

36. Walter Benjamin, 'Theses on the Philosophy of History', pp. 257–8.

37. Susan A. Crane, 'Historical Subjectivity. A Review Essay', *The Journal of Modern History*, vol. 78, no. 2, June 2006, p. 434.

38. Crane, p. 435.

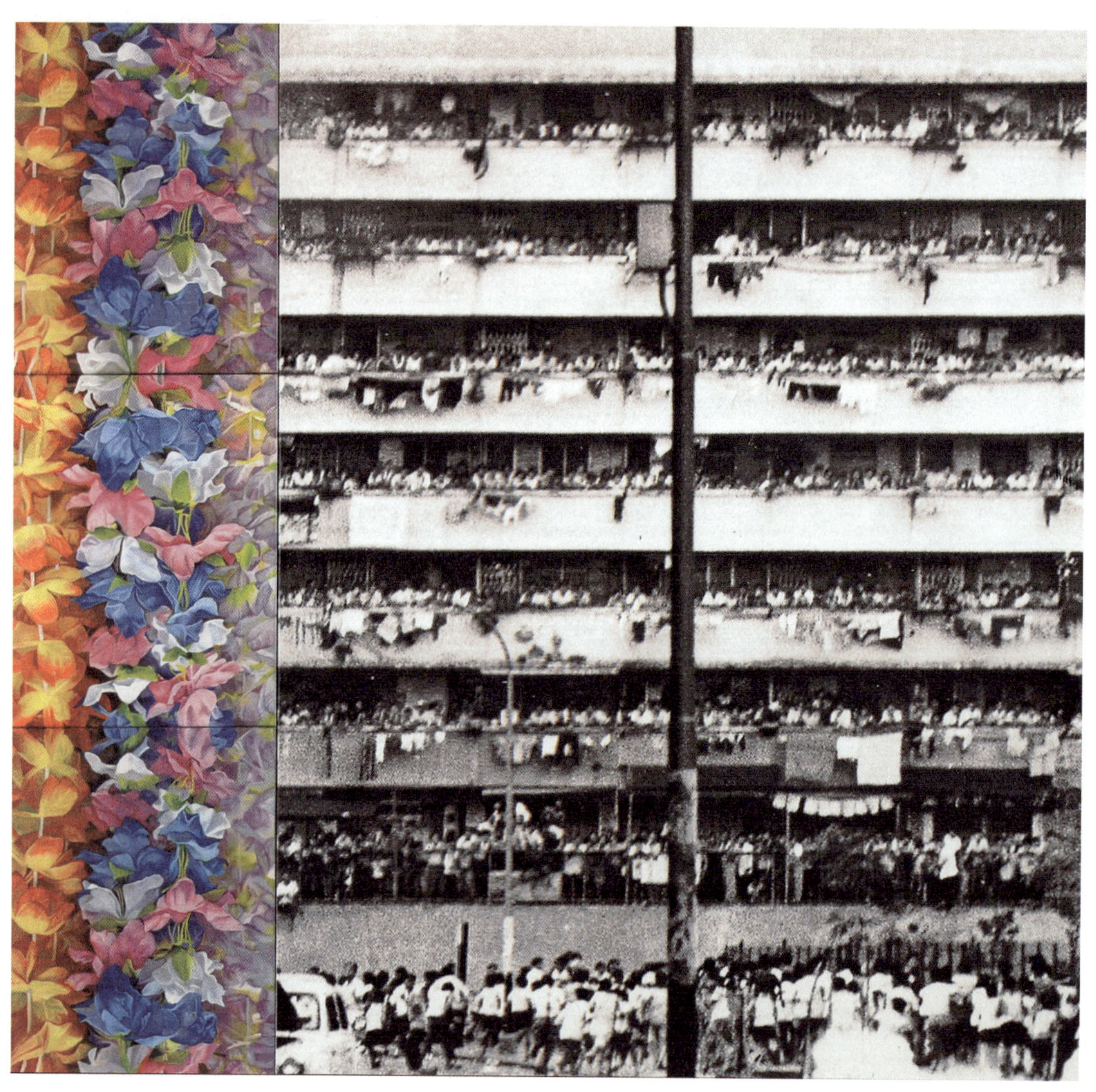

Riot — Flowers 2008
Digital print and oil on linen, four panels,
147 x 146 cm
Collection of M+, Hong Kong

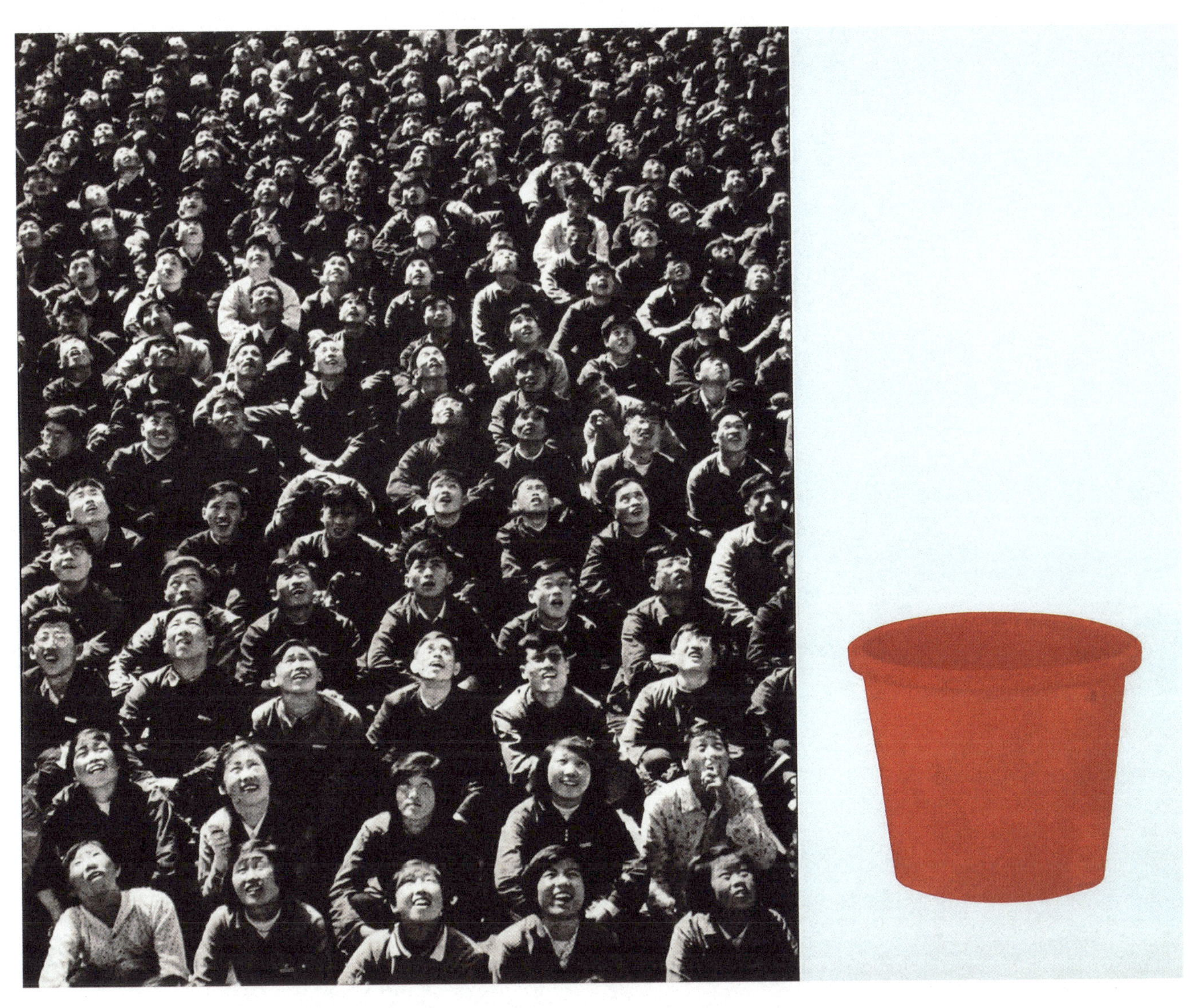

Wishforce 2008
Digital print and oil on linen, two panels,
151 x 180 cm
Collection of M+, Hong Kong

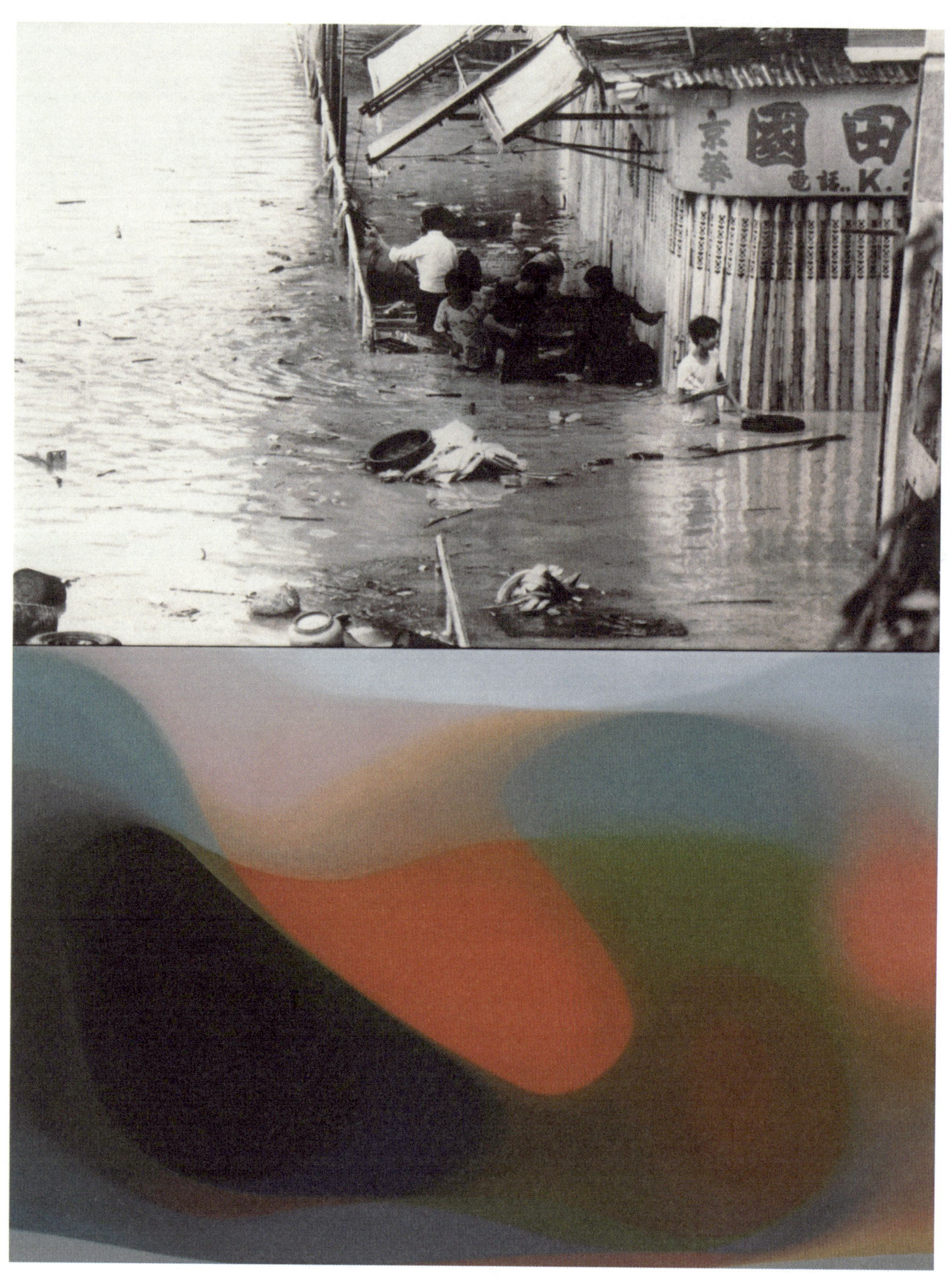

Flood 2008
Digital print and oil on linen, two panels,
170 × 125 cm
Collection of M+, Hong Kong

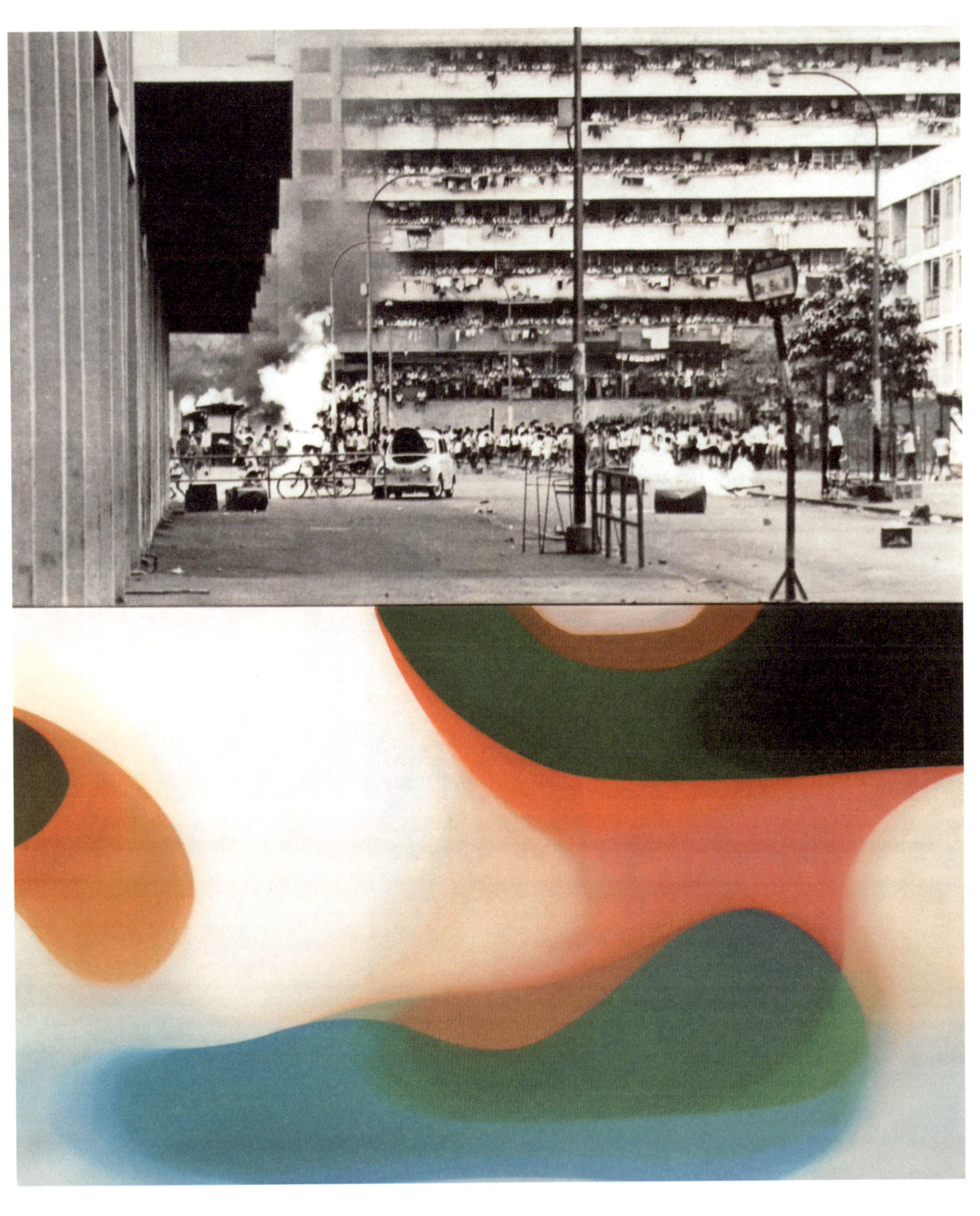

Riot 2008
Digital print and oil on linen, two panels,
170 × 125 cm
Collection of M+, Hong Kong

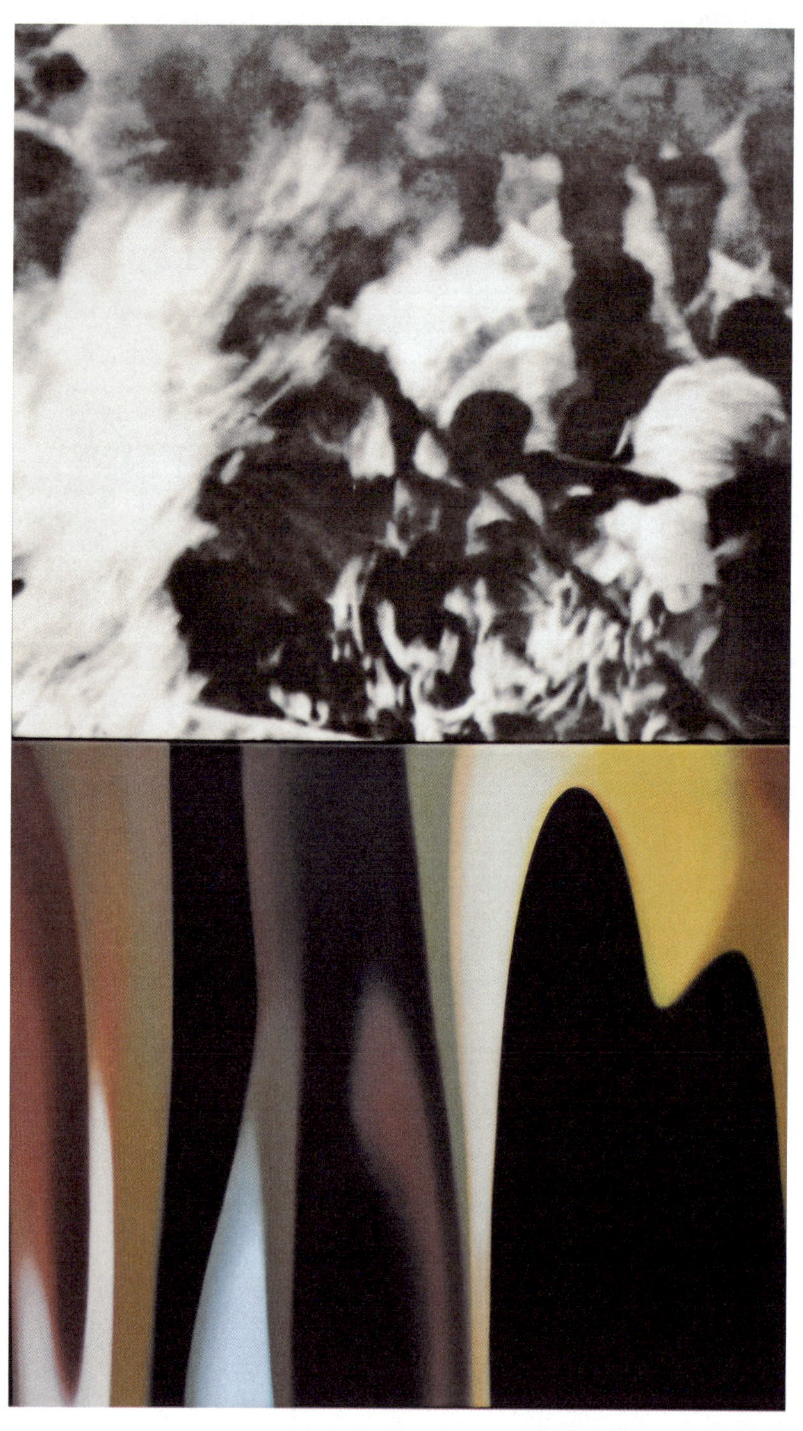

Riot – Fire 2008
Digital print and oil on linen, two panels,
170 × 98 cm

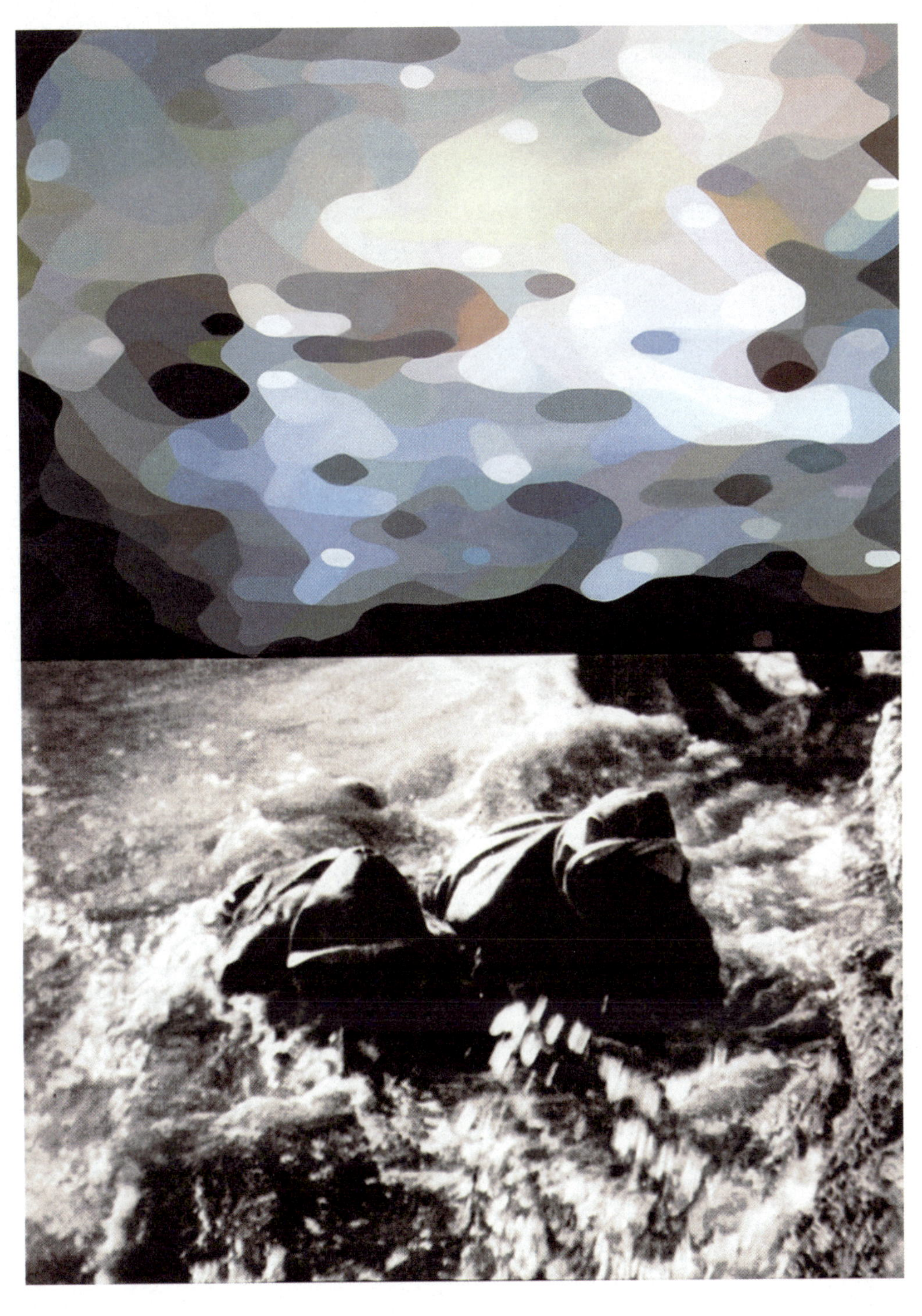

Folks 2008
Digital print and oil on linen, two panels,
169 x 118 cm

☷☱ ☷☱
19   19.

Approach

'becoming great'
What becomes great are the two
strong lines growing into the hexagram
from below, the light-giving power
expands with them.

The approach of what is strong and highly placed
in relation to what is lower.

Approach has supreme success } work with determination
Perseverance furthers.   and perseverance to
When the eight month comes   make full use of the
There will be misfortune   propitiousness of the time.
                                 Spring does not last for ever

                                 If we meet evil before it becomes reality — before it has
                                 even begun to stir, we can master it

The earth above the lake
The image of approach
Thus the superior man is inexhaustible
In his will to teach,
And without limits
In his tolerance and protection of the people

Just as the lake is inexhaustible in depth.
So the sage is inexhaustible in his readiness to teach mankind.
The sage sustains and cares for all people and excludes no part
of humanity.

GLOBALISATION, IDENTITY, AND TRANSCULTURAL ETHICS IN THE ART OF JOHN YOUNG ZERUNGE

Caroline Turner and Jen Webb

The role artists can play in cultural and social transformation has been shown to be a critical one: they witness, interpret and communicate through visual languages in a way that increases our cultural understanding of complex issues; reviving memory, confronting trauma, and potentially contributing to defining a shared sense of humanity. John Young has created art over many years that offers responses to dilemmas that are of critical concern to all humanity, including the ethics of human relations, especially in transcultural settings.[1]

The latter part of the twentieth century and the early twenty-first century introduced greater complexities across the world, marked by a rapid increase in globalisation and increasing connections between people, to the point where new and extended global interactions now have enormous impact on individual lives. As historian Wang Gungwu wrote in 1993, 'the modern world … has made people aware of similarities and differences among themselves to an extent never dreamed of in the past. Being thus aware, people can never be the same again.'[2] These changes have generated new debates about identity, differences and transcultural relations, and are a key element in the experience of many artists, including Young.

Born in Hong Kong, Young has conducted his vocation mainly in Australia. Often framed as an Australian or Asian Australian artist, he has exhibited in Australia, Europe, North America and Asia. His art exemplifies the complexities and challenges of identity in global contexts: a reminder of the plurality of identity and its variability that, to use Stuart Hall's term, is never complete— it is always in a process of becoming, and so is something that 'belongs to the future as much as to the past'.[3]

The late Chinese French artist Chen Zhen characterised his own transcultural journey from Shanghai to Paris—from China to the West—in the late 1980s, in terms of what he called 'transexperiences'. He described 'transexperience' as 'a kind of fusion-transcendence of experiences … which summarizes vividly and profoundly the complex life experiences of leaving one's native place and going from one place to another in one's life'.[4] This complex form of belonging and detachment can, Chen suggests, result in a type of 'cultural homelessness, namely, you do not belong to anybody, yet you are in possession of everything'.[5] Though there may be loss, the result may be an enriching change, with transexperiences providing a creative catalyst for art, including an art that bridges cultures.

John Young's art, we suggest, needs to be seen also in the context of the emergence of a new global art that has developed in the last thirty years, one that also marked the beginnings of a troubling of the binary of East/West

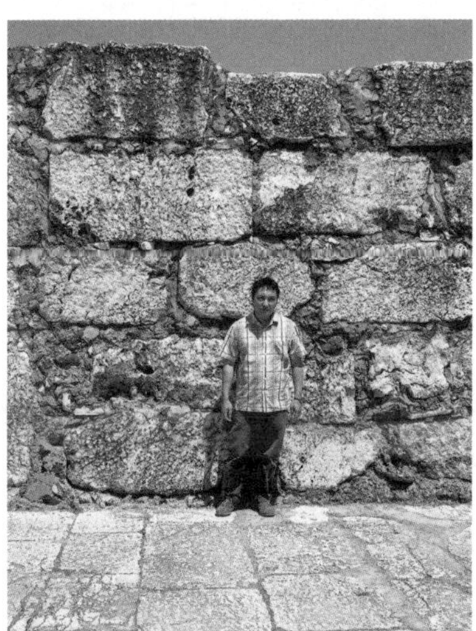

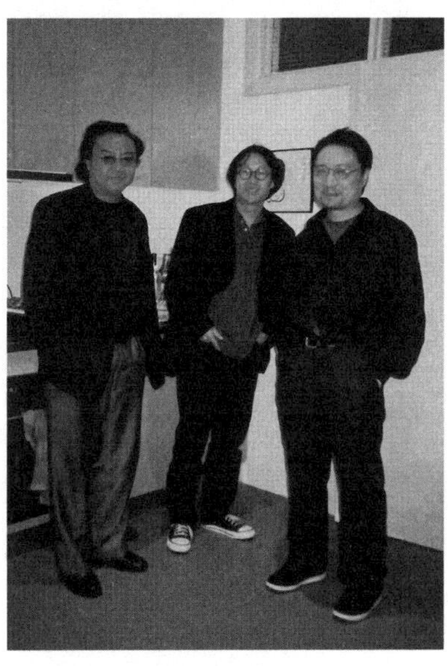

The artist in Jerusalem, 2005
Photograph by Kate Mizrahi

Left to right: Chen Zhen 陳箴, Xu Bing 徐冰, and the artist at the artist's home, Melbourne, 1999

facing page
Page from the artist's notebook (JYNB2007)

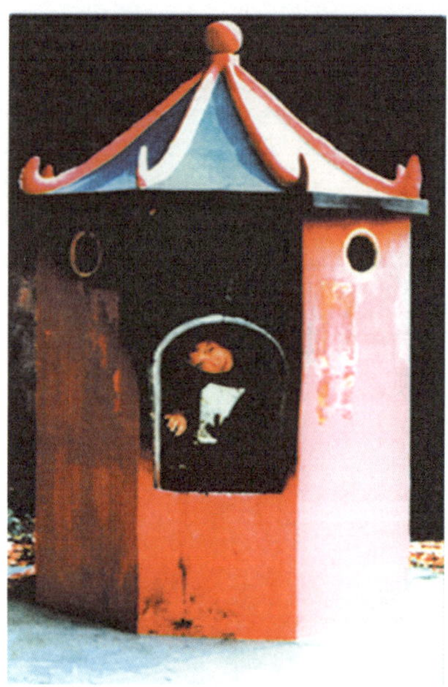

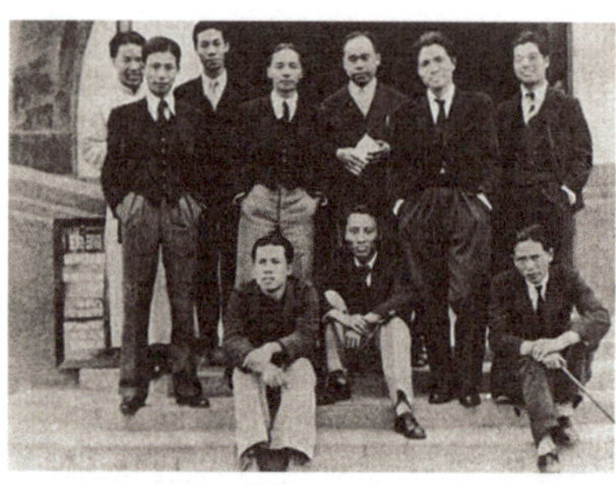

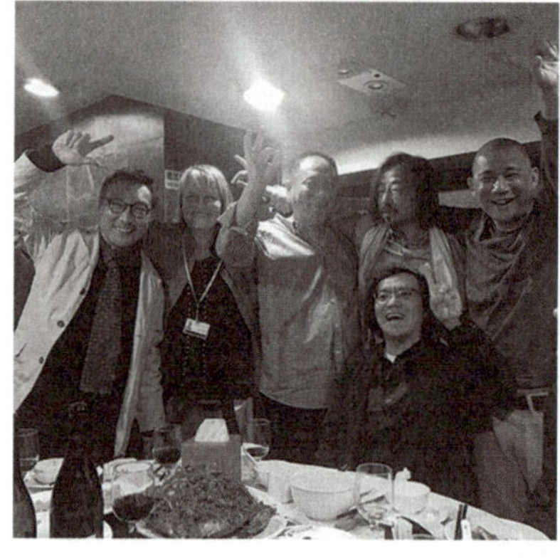

Invitation to the exhibition *Awful Backlash*,
Sherman Galleries, Sydney, 2000
Photograph by William Wright

The Storm Society (Juelanshe 決瀾社),
Shanghai, 1933
Artist's note: image presented by Ralph Croizier
at the conference convened by John Clark,
'Modernity and Postmodernism in Asian Art',
Australian National University, Canberra, 1991

Left to right: John Young, Katie de Tilly, friend
of the group, Huang Rui 黃銳, Fang Lijun
方力鈞, and Shi Guorui 史國瑞, Hong Kong, 2017

or Asia/Europe. Geopolitical and economic changes have inevitably challenged
the accepted theory of an art 'centre' dominated by Europe and North America,
leading to a reconceptualisation of global frameworks for art. Young's Asian heritage
is clearly important to his practice and his public expression, and he has explored
this quite extensively. He travelled to China in 1979, where he undertook a site-
specific conceptual work, *Manchurian Snow Walk*, partly to reconnect with his
Chinese heritage.[6] During the late 1990s, Young travelled to Hong Kong and to
Guangzhou on a number of occasions. Carolyn Barnes notes that this had the effect
of 'heightening his connections with Asia but also his awareness of being neither
Western nor Eastern'.[7] Not until he connected with the Chinese artists Chen Zhen,
Cai Guo-Qiang and Xu Bing, who were all at that time living outside China, did
he begin to identify as a Hong Kong Australian artist, 'reflecting the world's view
of him, even if it did not necessarily fit his own perception of himself'.[8]

John Young's concern is less about personal identity and more directly about questions
of cross-cultural perceptions and the ethical dimensions of transcultural experiences
and relations. His approach to art has been deeply informed by his background in
Western philosophy and literature.[9] He was trained in a period in Australia when
Euro-American modernism and postmodernism was the focus of artistic discussion,
and from the early 1980s he experimented with conceptual and minimal approaches.
He later engaged with newly emerging discourses, including postmodernism,
postcolonialism and globalisation and explored the complexities of transcultural
crossings through his art, through writing for seminal postmodern journals such as
Art and Text, and through his connections with other transcultural artists, particularly
Imants Tillers.[10]

The exploration of these issues by Young finds visual expression in the *Double Ground
Paintings* (1993–2005), a series of multimedia paintings, which begin with what
Young has called 'underbelly images'[11] —images he creates from painted generic
photographs. The backgrounds are drawn from secondary, often historical, sources,
and have no necessary reference to the foreground. Many of the images in the *Double
Ground Paintings* series deliberately reflect stereotyped and romantic projections
of the transcultural, and their backgrounds contain Asian or 'Oriental' elements,
including the work of the eighteenth-century Jesuit missionary Giuseppe Castiglioni,
and imagery from Persian art. The series also continued his investigation of the
formal structures of paintings, as well as ideas of historical resonance and of cultural
formations.[12] Young has produced several other key series related to Asia, including
1967Dispersion (2008), which commemorates the labour disputes in Hong Kong
during 1967 and the severe floods the city experienced that year; and *The Macau Days*
(2012), which explores the rich transcultural history of the oldest European settlement
in Asia.

In such ways, Young's work can be understood as addressing an East/West binary,
but this is not his core focus. Australian cultural studies scholar Jacqueline Lo
questions the way that much writing about Young's work identifies it 'as a signifier
of his Chinese-Australian identity', despite the fact that the artist has resisted such
categorisation.[13] Indeed, Lo makes the point that Young expresses 'unease with the
prevailing discourse of diaspora and racialised positions', seeing them as reflecting
'wider concerns in diaspora and critical race studies in Australia and in the USA'.[14]

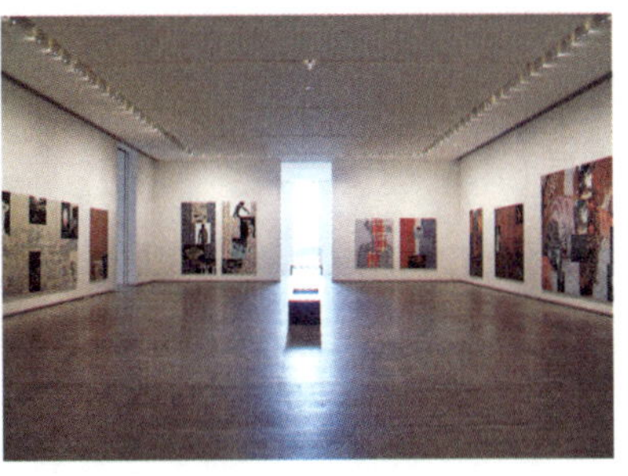

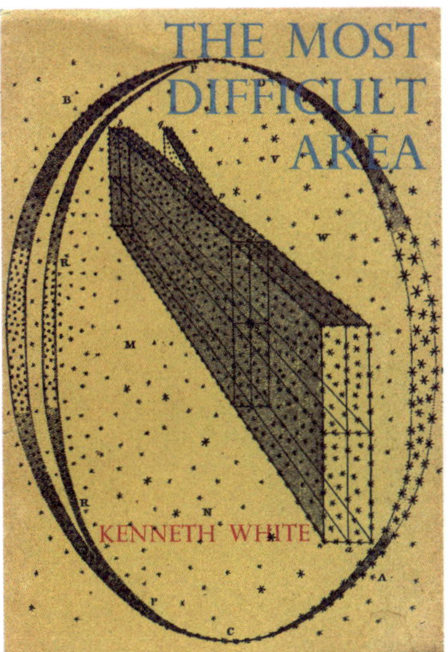

This is an issue of significant importance in the Asian region, given that so many artists are in fact transnational—living as members of a diaspora, or living in their home nation as one cultural group among many.

For Asian artists living in, say, Australia or the United States, who are often designated 'Asian-Australian' or 'Asian-American', there is a double bind: the choice seems to be either to identify with their Asian cultural background and be caught in what is often a ghettoised or restrictive identity, or to adopt the dominant identity and efface the important Asian cultural tradition they possess. Young has expressed his own concerns about this. His artistic oeuvre is essentially cross-cultural in its qualities, and, as he insists: 'All my projects today are transcultural, or at least had something to do with the condition of crossing cultures'.[15]

Young's later History Projects focus on the Chinese in Australia. In 2012 he was awarded a two-year Fellowship for Senior Artists, funded by the Australia Council for the Arts, to research the Chinese diaspora in Australia from 1850 to the present. This became part of a multi-year project that includes a number of creative outcomes. One significant work is the public art commission *Open Monument* (2015), a contribution to understanding the history of the Chinese in Ballarat, a gold-mining city that attracted many Chinese in the nineteenth century. Indeed, these more recent works on Chinese migrant experience in Australia since the nineteenth century are full of forgotten personal stories. These include the nineteenth-century life story of successful businessman Lowe Kong Meng, contrasted with that of illiterate miner Jong Ah Siug, who was placed in the Yarra Bend and Sunbury 'lunatic' asylums for over thirty years until his death.[16]

There are instances in this series of positive relations with 'White' Australia, which include the generosity and humanity demonstrated by farmer James Roberts, when he gave refuge to more than a thousand Chinese miners fleeing violent attacks on them at Lambing Flat in June 1831.[17] In the video *The Burrangong Affray* (2018), however, which forms part of this project, Young substitutes a redheaded white woman for the Chinese victims. According to Young, 'the reversal of identities between perpetrator and victim within this work is in order to imply a universal capacity (to violence, trauma, or benevolence), and to thereby make it more difficult for a viewer of the work to distance themselves from these histories on the basis of their own cultural background. The purposeful discomfort induced by this slippage reveals the significant role that cultural subjectivity plays in the retelling of histories'.[18]

Young is not in any simplistic sense a 'political artist' and his art is not essentially focused on individual identity. Rather, his art attends to deeper questions of the condition of humanity, and the role of art and the artist in society. Young is interested in moral and ethical dilemmas, including for those confronting catastrophic situations, and his art engages the ambiguities and uncertainties of the human condition and of history in an attempt to 'reawaken an intrinsic ethical impulse in the present'.[19] In many ways, his art also mirrors art historian Marsha Meskimmon's concept of the 'cosmopolitan imagination' as 'future-oriented and generative', and of the capacity of contemporary art to engage in empathetic intersubjective connections between people across cultural borders, 'transforming our relationship with/in the world'.[20]

Installation view, *Orient/Occident: John Young— A Survey of Works, 1978–2005* Tarrawarra Museum of Art, Victoria, 2005

Cover of Kenneth White, *The Most Difficult Area*, Cape Goliard Press, London, 1968

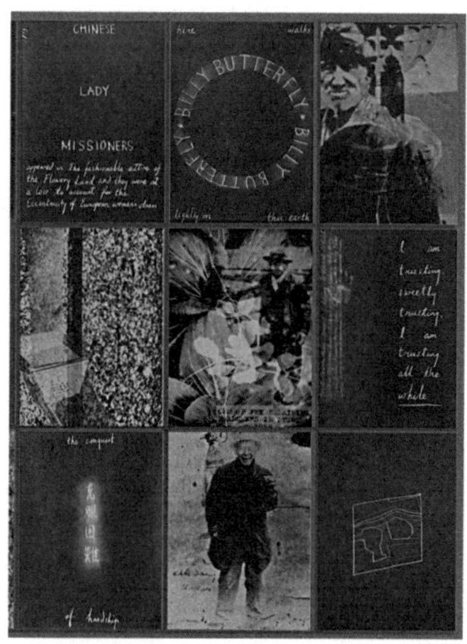

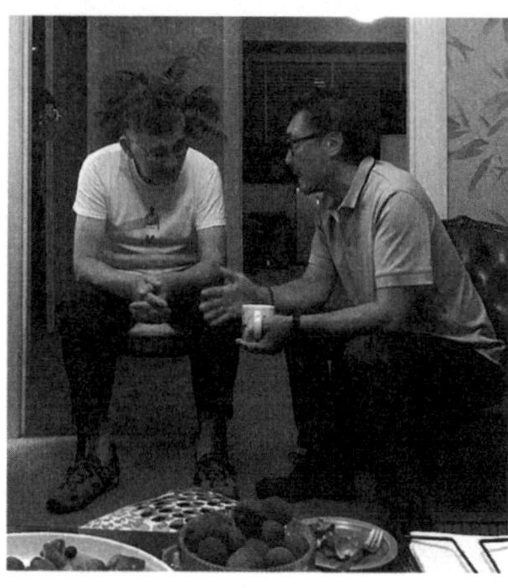

Detail of *Transculture*, part of *Open Monument* 2015

The artist in discussion with the late Senator Tsebin Tchen, the first Asian migrant and second Chinese–Australian elected to the Parliament of Australia, Melbourne, 2017

An important work that illustrates these concepts is John Young's installation *Bonhoeffer in Harlem* (2009). It commemorates the sixty-fourth anniversary of the execution of German Lutheran theologian, pastor and martyr, Dietrich Bonhoeffer. Originally designed for St Matthäus Church, Berlin, where Bonhoeffer was ordained, it is now permanently installed in the Erlöserkirche ('Church of the Redeemer') in Bamberg.[21] The title derives from the fact that Bonhoeffer travelled to the United States in 1930 to undertake postgraduate study at New York City's Union Theological Seminary. There he was introduced to the Abyssinian Baptist Church in Harlem, under Pastor Adam Clayton Powell Sr, a founder of the National Urban League and member of the NAACP (National Association for the Advancement of Colored People), who had made the church a vibrant centre for social justice in the African American community. Bonhoeffer became aware of the levels of discrimination against African Americans and also discovered the spirituality of gospel music. 'Through this experience', Young writes, 'Bonhoeffer returned to Germany with the understanding to defend the "marginalized, the vulnerable and the oppressed"'.[22] Bonhoeffer returned to his homeland in 1931 to find that extreme racial oppression, especially towards Jews, was about to be enforced as state policy. This led him to challenge the principles and practice of the Nazi regime, first openly, then undercover as a committed member of the resistance. He was eventually arrested by the Gestapo and hanged in 1945, just weeks before the camp where he had been incarcerated was liberated by American troops.

Young interpreted this history in a work that responds both to the story and to a stained-glass window in the Abyssinian Baptist Church in Harlem: its vivid purples and greens, initially 'felt very distant … It was a black aesthetic which was as alien as Chinese opera to Western ears'.[23] The glass, though, captures something of the vibrancy of local African American culture in the Harlem renaissance of the 1920s. Young has said that, in finding a way to engage with this effusion of floating colour, he is able to overcome his personal cultural boundaries as an artist, which is his response to Bonhoeffer's attempt 'to see the other. And not only to see the other, but to try to be the other. In other words, to make art not from the point of narcissism, but hopefully from empathy'.[24]

The work consists of three discrete parts. One is a series of chalk drawings on paper covered with blackboard paint. These include exhortations, some partly erased, such as 'Evil—oppose it directly', and Bonhoeffer's call to be 'eine Speiche im Rad des Staats' (a spoke in the wheel of the state). These 'chalkboard' works are accompanied by inkjet prints that contain biographical details about Bonhoeffer and include poignant images of Bonhoeffer as an adult, and as a young child with his twin sister. There is also an image of a thrush, a small bird that Bonhoeffer had seen and heard singing from his prison window, and had described in a letter to his fiancée. Young's innovative approach to 'history painting' in this work combines historical photographs with the impermanence and erasures of the chalk drawings to evoke a sense of the often-fragmented quality of history and memory.

In *Bonhoeffer in Harlem*, the other central element is a large silk tapestry that responds directly to the stained-glass window. This was a collaborative, transcultural project, which involved Young's concept being 'translated' by the German rug designer Jürgen Dahlmanns, and then produced in Nepal by the weaver Dolma Lob Sang, daughter of a Tibetan monk. The final element in the work is a pair of abstract paintings created through a computer manipulation of images, which the artist has then transferred in oil to canvas. Certainly this transcultural work—informed by African American sensibility, designed by a Hong Kong-born Australian of Chinese descent, and then woven by a Tibetan exile in Nepal—contrasts sharply with the monocultural Lutheran church and, as Young has suggested, significantly changes its cultural frame.[25]

Safety Zone (2010) again responds to a major instance of integrity, humanity and transcultural ethics. This is an installation of sixty works on paper—chalk drawings and digital prints—along with several paintings. For Berghuis, these works 'resemble historical reminiscences of human survival by linking experimental contemporary art with investigative visual reports, in historical photographs and documents'.[26] The installation grew out of research and interviews undertaken by Young in Nanjing, Berlin and Heidelberg, about the events that occurred when Japanese troops occupied the Chinese city of Nanjing in December 1937. Tens of thousands of civilians were killed and there was widespread rape of Chinese women. The Chinese authorities had abandoned the city, leaving an International Committee of fifteen Americans and Europeans to try to establish a safety zone for the protection of the Chinese civilians remaining in the city.[27]

Young treats this tragedy with empathy and with philosophical reflection. The images in his work are not so much about Japanese atrocities but rather what transcultural individuals did to try to prevent them. The representation of broken branches and shattered tree trunks in the paintings that comprise *The Crippled Tree*, for example, obviously symbolise the brutal violence inflicted on the Chinese victims. One of the paintings, however, *Flower Market (Nanjing 1936)*, deploys a more elusive poignancy. In this work, 'carefully painted spring flowers and bleached corals are superimposed over historical photographs taken in Nanjing a year prior to the massacre'—a reminder, perhaps, that there can be beauty and rebirth despite the horrors of history. [28]

Can art provide new models for cultural, social and political understanding in a globalising world, or for understanding historical, political and cultural identities? Historian Jörn Rüsen writes that 'aesthetics break [sic] through the practical constraints of historiography and liberates the audience in the way it relates to historical experience and its orientational potential in practical life … It introduces the chance of autonomy within the framework of historical determinism'.[29] Rüsen's focus is on historians writing history, but it applies equally to artists such as Young. Both modes of production provide ways of thinking about how the world is and how it might be, and both have the potential to be acts that are committed to human rights. As African American writer bell hooks observes, 'our living depends on our ability to conceptualize alternatives … Theorising about this experience aesthetically, critically is an agenda for radical cultural practice'.[30]

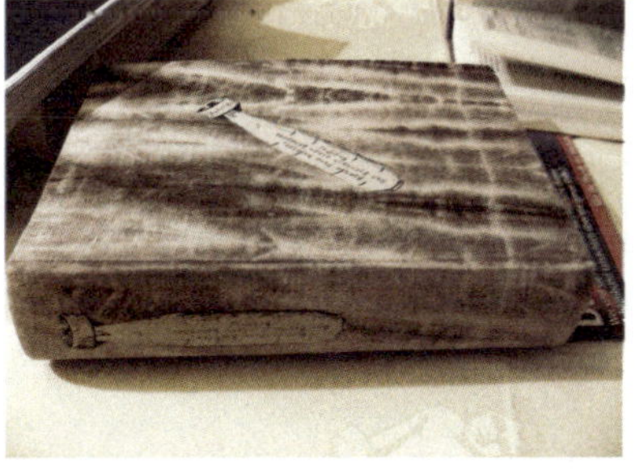

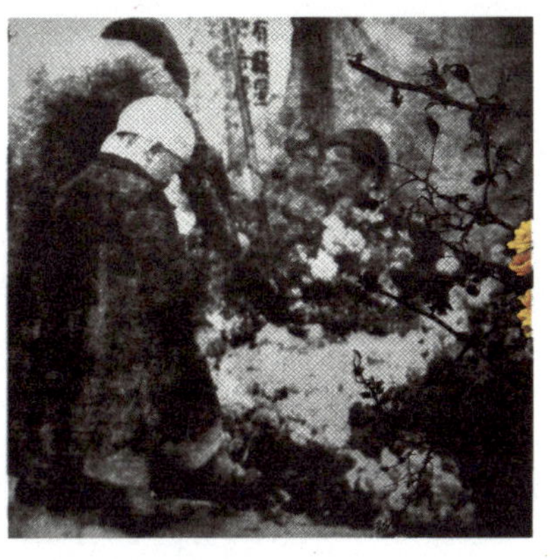

Internal page and cover of the diary
of John Rabe, c. 1937
Collection of Thomas Rabe Archive, Heidelberg

Flower Market (Nanjing 1936) #3 2010
Digital print and oil on linen, 240 × 240 cm

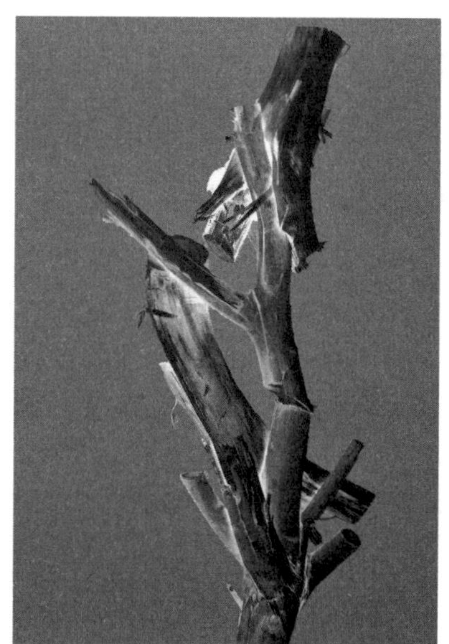

Cultural theorist Homi Bhabha has highlighted the ethical function of the right of interpretation among particular people in a particular time and place, writing:

> The universality of Rights lies less, I believe, in the value of the Individual as an end-in-itself. The value of Universality comes with our growing awareness that to fulfil our ends—of equality, freedom, well-being—, or to find a means to survive our fates—of pain, oppression, humiliation, failure—we need to belong to the solidarity and the community of Others, be they Neighbours or Strangers, and through their alterity derive a sense of agency.[31]

Young's art can be identified as part of an art practice that explores memory, identity and our ethical responsibilities, including to 'strangers', in our postcolonial and globalised world. Terry Smith has described contemporary art as 'truly an art *of* the world. It comes *from* the whole world, and frequently tries to imagine the world as a *differentiated yet inevitably connected whole*'.[32] Artists such as John Young possess a strong sense of art that is *of* the world, in Smith's terms, and the importance of interrogating notions of identity and conceptualising alternative visions for that world. Rather than attempting to impose a single way of seeing and being, or perceiving human culture in binary or bifurcated ways, artists such as Young are concerned with providing more nuanced accounts of the different ways in which we might understand ourselves and each other, and, in the process, how we might connect with others ethically, with a shared sense of humanity.

The Crippled Tree #1 2010
Oil on linen, 274 x 183 cm

1. This essay is based on a chapter of our book on art and human rights in which we include the art of John Young as a case study because his work exemplifies the issues we associated with the power of art, which is to mirror both the failures and the aspirations of humanity, and to highlight our common condition. Our definition of 'human rights', drawn from the United Nations Universal Declaration of Human Rights (1948), encompasses issues including poverty, social justice and the environment. See Caroline Turner and Jen Webb, *Art and Human Rights: Contemporary Asian Contexts*, Manchester University Press, Manchester, 2016, pp. 130–39.

2. Wang Gungwu, 'Foreword', in Caroline Turner (ed.), *Tradition and Change: Contemporary Art of Asia and the Pacific*, University of Queensland Press, Brisbane, 1993, p. vii.

3. Stuart Hall, 'Cultural Identity and Diaspora', in J. Rutherford (ed.), *Identity: Community, Culture, Difference*, Lawrence & Wishart, London, 1990, p. 225.

4. Chen Zhen, 'Transexperiences: A Conversation between Chen Zhen and Zhu Xian', in *Chen Zhen: Invocation of Washing Fire*, (transl.) William Y. Jiang, Gli Ori, Siena, Italy, 2003, p. 156.

5. Ibid.

6. It is important to note in this context Young's role in the 1990s in supporting opportunities for Asian Australian artists and developing 'Asian and Australian cultural relations' as one of the founders of the Asian Australian Artists' Association and its gallery, which is now the 4A Centre for Contemporary Asian Art in Sydney. See 'History', 4A Centre for Contemporary Asian Art, https://4a.com.au/about/#history.

7. Carolyn Barnes, 'Towards a Layered Imaginary', in Barnes, *John Young*, Craftsman House, Fishermans Bend, 2005, p. 61.

8. These artists came to Australia to participate in the Asia-Pacific Triennial of Contemporary Art at the Queensland Art Gallery in 1999. See also Barnes, in *John Young*, p. 61.

9. Young's academic and art training, and early career had a Western inflection. At the University of Sydney, he studied the philosophy of science and aesthetics and wrote a thesis on the Austrian British philosopher Ludwig Wittgenstein. Later, Young visited a house in Ireland where Wittgenstein had stayed to complete important writings.

10. Judith Blackall notes that Tillers' work *Tabula Rasa (for my father)* (2011) is 'a monumental work in acrylic paint and gouache on 288 canvas boards … It is the tenth and final piece in the *Diaspora* series, an important body of work that Tillers began in 1992 as a direct response to the disintegration of the Soviet Union in 1991 and the Baltic States' independence.' See Judith Blackall, 'Imants Tillers', *MCA Collection Handbook*, Museum of Contemporary Art Australia, https://www.mca.com.au/artists-works/artists/imants-tillers. Young's art has also had a strong focus on migration and displaced people, including his series *Refugee Patterns* (2003).

11. Andrew Frost, 'John Young: Ghost on Canvas', *Australian Art Collector*, no. 6, November 1998, pp. 40–44.

12. Young has indicated that attending John Clark's 1991 conference 'Modernism and Postmodernism in Asian Art' at the Australian National University, was an impetus in his own further explorations of Asian modernity. (John Young communication with the authors, 2014). See John Clark's introductory essay in this volume in which he discusses Young's work in terms of modernism and postmodernism in Asia, pp. 24–35.

13. Jacqueline Lo, 'Diaspora, Art and Empathy', in *John Young: The Bridge and the Fruit Tree*, Drill Hall Gallery, Australian National University, Canberra, 2013, pp. 19–43, republished in this volume with a new introduction, see pp. 137–47.

14. Lo, p. 23.

15. Cited in Sylvia D. Volz, 'John Young: Bonhoeffer in Harlem', in Alexander Ochs (ed.), *John Young: Bonhoeffer in Harlem*, St Matthäus Church, Berlin, 2009, p. 84. See Volz's expanded essay in this volume, pp. 92–95.

16. See Nadia Rhook, *1866: The Worlds of Lowe Kong Meng and Jong Ah Siug—Of Historical Imagination and Moral Relations*, in this volume, pp. 232–45.

17. See 'The Burrangong Affray', John Young, artist website, https://www.johnyoungstudio.com/w/the-burrangong-affray/5.

18. Ibid.

19. Thomas Berghuis, 'The Situational Ethics of John Young', *Art and Australia*, vol. 48, no. 3, Autumn 2011, republished in this volume, p. 134.

20. Marsha Meskimmon, *Contemporary Art and the Cosmopolitan Imagination*, Routledge, London, 2010, p. 8.

21. The site where, in 1934, members of the Confessing Church had resisted the consecration of this church by pro-fascist German Christians. Young was invited to re-create his installation *Bonhoeffer in Harlem* in Bamberg, as part of an exhibition entitled *Circles* with a number of international artists including Ai Weiwei and Micha Ullman.

22. Cited in Volz, p. 80.

23. Volz, p. 87.

24. Ibid.

25. John Young, communication with the authors, 2014.

26. Berghuis, 'Safety Zone: Resistance as an Act of Humanity'.

27. This group, which was able to provide some protection for Chinese in the city, included John Rabe, Minnie Vautrin, John Magee, and Robert Wilson—the only surgeon left in the Nanjing hospital. See Lo, 'Diaspora, Art and Empathy', 2013, republished in this volume with a new introduction, see pp. 137–47.

28. Thomas Berghuis, 'Safety Zone', Anna Schwartz Gallery, Melbourne, 2010, https://annaschwartzgallery.com/exhibition/safety-zone.

29. Jörn Rüsen, *History: Narration, Interpretation, Orientation*, Berghahn Books, Oxford, 2005, p. 52.

30. bell hooks, *Yearning: Race, Gender, and Cultural Politics*, South End Press, Boston, 1991, p. 149.

31. Homi K. Bhabha 'On Writing and Rights: Some Thoughts on the Culture of Human Rights', keynote speech at *Our Common Future* congress, Hanover, 2–6 November 2010, http://www.ourcommonfuture.de/fileadmin/user_upload/dateien/Reden/Bhabha_keynote_final.pdf.

32. Terry Smith, 'Worlds Pictured in Contemporary Art: Planes and Connectivities', *Humanities Research*, vol. 29, no. 2, 2013, p. 12.

BONHOEFFER IN HARLEM

2009

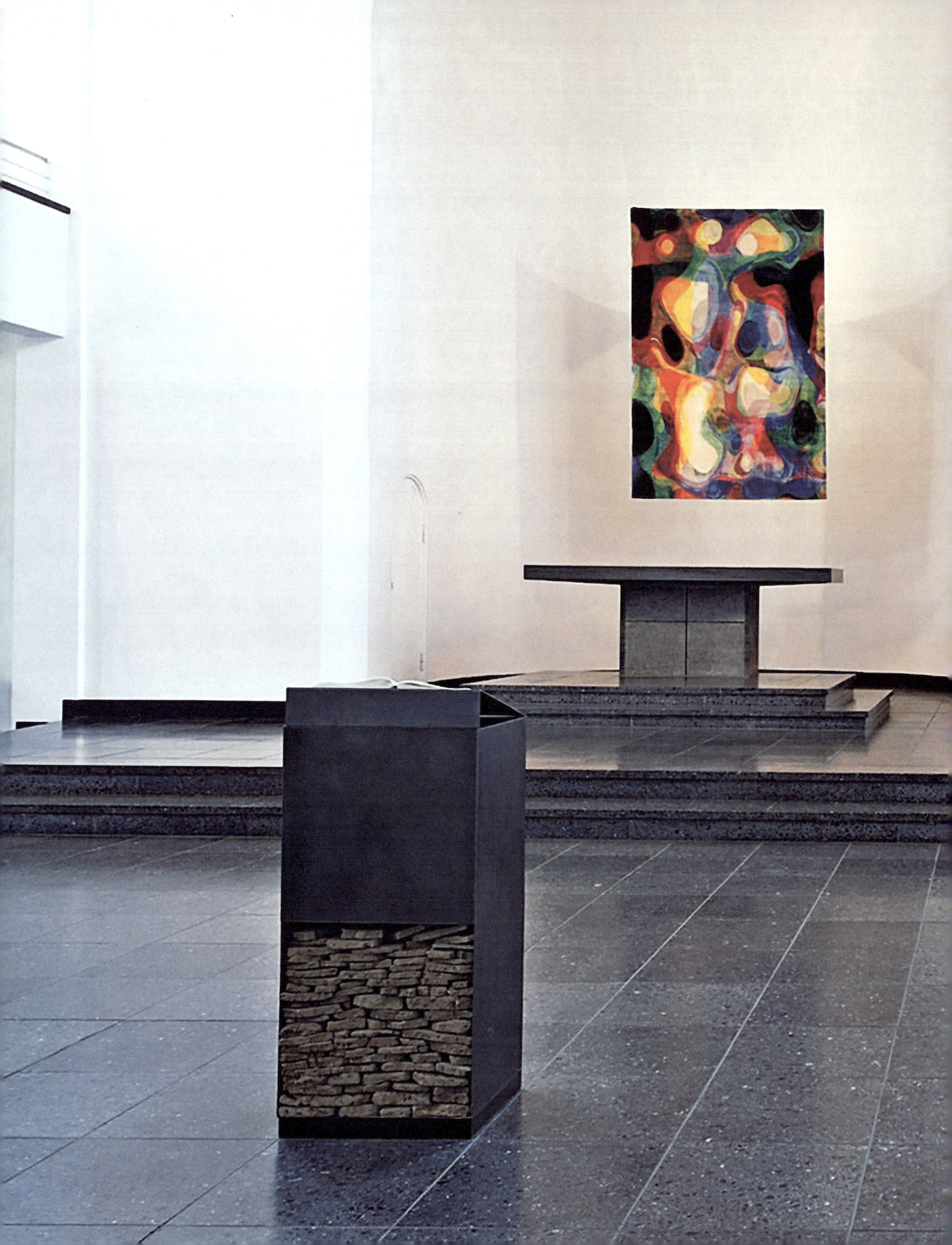

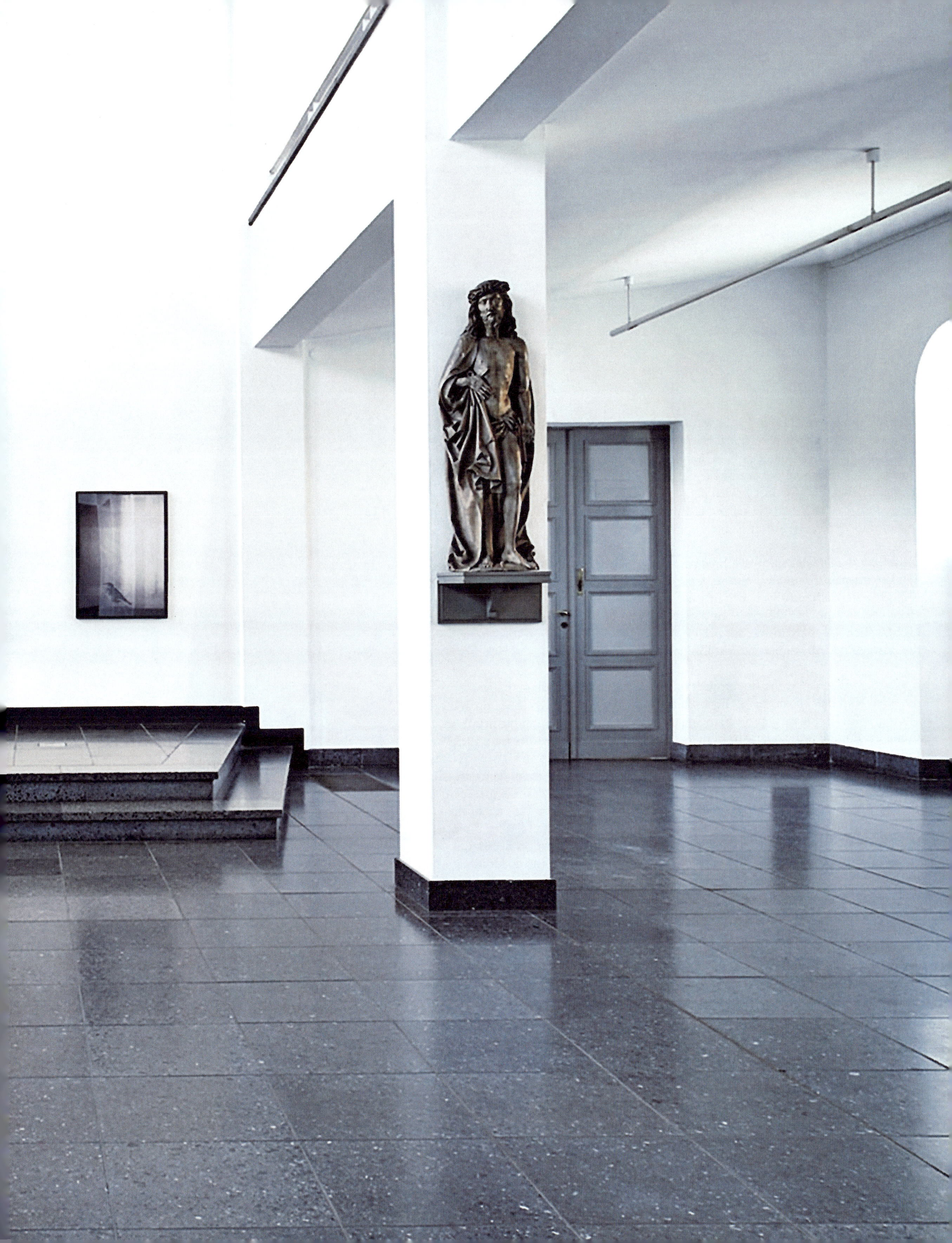

BONHOEFFER IN HARLEM

Dietrich Bonhoeffer (1906–1945) was a Lutheran pastor and theologian known for his resistance to German National Socialism. After spending time in Harlem, New York, with the Abyssinian Baptist Church, and its predominantly African American congregation, Bonhoeffer became deeply engaged by discrimination and social inequality, including against Jewish people in Nazi Germany. He was eventually hanged on 9 April 1945, during the last weeks of World War II, for his involvement in a plot to assassinate Adolf Hitler.

Bonhoeffer in Harlem comprises three parts: a series of eight chalk drawings on blackboard-painted archival cotton paper and three digital photographic prints (100 × 70 cm each); a handwoven, brightly coloured Chinese silk tapestry—also titled *Bonhoeffer in Harlem* (303 × 119 cm); and two paintings of oil on linen (190 × 150 cm each), which use the same colour palette as the tapestry, drawn from the stained-glass windows of the Abyssinian Baptist Church in Harlem.

Bonhoeffer in Harlem is the first project in which Young uses chalk on paper prepared with blackboard paint, in combination with digital prints based on archival photographs. In this early project, the chalk drawings and photographic prints are framed and hung individually or in pairs throughout the space, rather than the grid formation that visually defines the History Projects as a body of work. As with later projects, the chalkboard drawings make use of multilingual quotations, key dates, words, phrases and images gathered through the research process. These pieces of 'fact' are fragmented, obfuscated or effaced in the making process. The size of the individual panels (100 × 70 cm each) is consistent throughout the History Projects. It is also in this project that Young introduces a halftone dot filter on the digital prints of archival images as a rhetorical device which highlights the documentary truth claims of newsprint media and photojournalism.

There have been multiple presentations of *Bonhoeffer in Harlem*. The first, in 2009, was in St Matthäus Church, Berlin. Here the tapestry was installed as the church altarpiece and the chalk drawings and photographs were displayed in various white-walled spaces around the church. At the exhibition launch on 12 April 2009, a jazz singer from Queens, Jocelyn Smith, and the local 'Different Voices' choir for homeless Berliners, were invited to give musical performances. The second presentation, entitled *The Bonhoeffer Concept*, was shown in a white cube gallery space, at Alexander Ochs Gallery, Berlin, in 2011. There the tapestry was placed centrally on the floor, with chalk drawings and photographs hung around it on the wall. (Complementing this iteration was a proposal for a work titled *Steps* by Micha Ullman, for which Ullman intended to excavate a 2 × 2 × 1 metre space in the floor of the St Matthäus Church). In 2013, *Bonhoeffer in Harlem* was again exhibited in a sacred space, at Erlöserkirche (Church of the Redeemer), Bamberg, as part of the Circles festival (curated by Alexander Ochs), where it remains as a permanent installation. In this presentation, the tapestry is exhibited high inside the church, to the left of the altar, while the drawings are hung in a semicircle around the rotunda.

ARTIST STATEMENT

Excerpt from an interview with Sylvia D. Volz (December, 2008)

Alexander [Ochs] and I walked across the Tiergarten to St Matthäus;
we sat and talked quietly about the art projects that had been done in
this church and he explained to me the life of Bonhoeffer, who was
ordained in the church; but we also talked about many other topics.
He left it to me to decide what kind of project I would like to propose
to the church. I was not used to going into Lutheran churches, where
the interior was very sparse, not decorative at all like Catholic churches.
I remembered only two things in the church that stood out for me:
a yellow star hung from the ceiling for Christmas, and a modest bronze
plaque commemorating Dietrich Bonhoeffer. Later that day, I bought
a similar yellow star from a market stall, which I took back to Australia
for my children. I hung it in our house for Christmas. It was around that
time that I started to think about a project for the Church. I mentioned
Bonhoeffer to my partner Kate, who reminded me that our present
Prime Minister, Kevin Rudd, wrote a long article about his admiration
for Bonhoeffer, regarding faith and government. Rudd wrote this before
he became head honcho, then foregrounding the issue of the necessity
for our society to return towards an ethical life. It was around the time
when I was in Berlin that there was a change in government in Australia,
from nine years of conservative neoliberalist government toward a more
social-democratic model. I felt I needed to know more about Bonhoeffer.

Reflection (2022)

Now the language of politics has become repellent. Its economism is barely able
to acknowledge the richness of culture and value. We may wait and hope that
transcultural works and transcultural ethics can work as one, or indeed become
identical. To learn, as I have poorly tried, through becoming Bonhoeffer's values
via chalk and blackboards, in the way of Beuys and Steiner, though scribed not
as the teacher but the slow learner. And in the same way, transcultural works
listen and accept, and also force one to relinquish one's artistic will.

pages 88–89
Bonhoeffer in Harlem 2009
Installation view, St Matthäus Church,
Kulturforum, Berlin, 2009

JOHN YOUNG:
BONHOEFFER IN HARLEM

Sylvia Dominique Volz

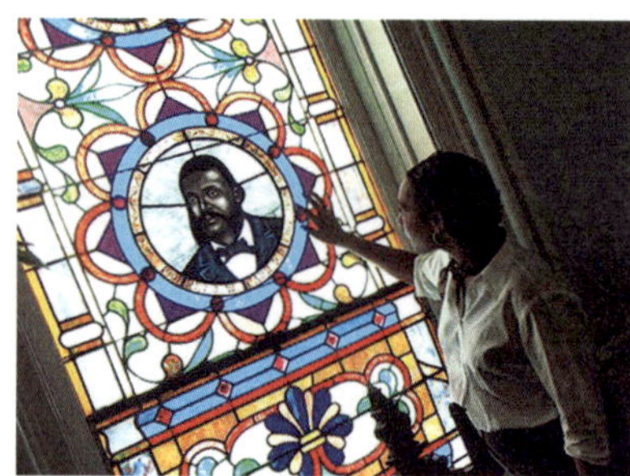

Stained-glass window depicting early pastors
First African Baptist Church, Savannah, Georgia

The 9th of April 2009 marked the sixty-fourth anniversary of Dietrich Bonhoeffer's execution by the Nazis. A few days later, on the 13th of April—Easter Sunday—the exhibition *Bonhoeffer in Harlem* opened in the very place Bonhoeffer was ordained a minister in 1931, the St Matthäus Church in Tiergarten, Berlin.

Dietrich Bonhoeffer, Lutheran theologian, proponent of ecumenism, peace activist, and one of the central figures in the German Resistance against Hitler and Nazism, was born as the sixth of eight children in Breslau on 4 February 1906. After his father, a professor of psychiatry and neurology, accepted a position at Charité hospital, the family moved to Berlin's Grunewald district in 1912. In 1923, Bonhoeffer began studying theology in Tübingen, and continued his studies in Berlin the following year. It was there that he first encountered the theology of Karl Barth, who, alongside Adolf von Harnack, would become one of his most influential teachers. He received his doctorate in 1927 with a dissertation entitled *Sanctorum Communio (The Communion of Saints)*. Despite a promising academic career, Bonhoeffer decided to train as a minister and spent 1928 as the vicar at the German evangelical-Lutheran church in Barcelona. After returning in 1929, he wrote his post-doctoral 'habilitation' thesis. The next year, still too young to be ordained, Bonhoeffer accepted a one-year fellowship at Union Theological Seminary in New York, on the advice of his church superior Max Diestel, a representative of the Protestant ecumenical movement, World Alliance.

In New York, Bonhoeffer experienced the impact of the Great Depression, racial issues, and, at Abyssinian Baptist Church, the open protestant movement of the Social Gospel, which left a deep impression upon him. This church, founded in 1808 and one of the oldest and largest African American congregations in the United States, had developed since the early twentieth century into an important religious, social, and political institution in the struggle against racism (and remains so today). Pastor Adam Clayton Powell, who led the church during the time of Bonhoeffer's stay in New York, played a key role in the expansion and organisation of the Abyssinian Baptist Church after assuming office in 1908. Bonhoeffer's experience of the social and political discrimination against Black Americans would form the basis for his later passionate struggle against Nazi ideology. During this period, Bonhoeffer also began to engage with ecumenism, towards which he previously had taken a rather critical stance. After his return, he was finally ordained at St Matthäus on 15 November 1931.[1]

The whole Bonhoeffer family was very disturbed when the Nazis came to power on 31 January 1933. In a radio lecture the next day for Berliner Funkstunde, a Berlin radio station, Dietrich Bonhoeffer formulated a clear critique of the Nazi principles of the *Führer* ('leader'), and as a result the broadcast was interrupted. His experience of anti-Jewish discrimination was also quite personal: his brother-in-law, Gerhard Leibholz, the husband of his twin sister Sabine, as well as his friend and colleague Franz Hildebrandt, were both of Jewish origin.

From the passing of the Non-Aryan Law of 7 April 1933 to his own execution, Bonhoeffer fought for the church to take a critical position and decisive ecumenical action against the violation of human rights under Nazism. He joined with Martin Niemöller, one of the founders of the Young Reformationist Movement

(Jungreformatorische Bewegung), and others to establish the Ministers' Emergency
Association for the Protection of Threatened Colleagues of Jewish Descent
(Pfarrernotbund zum Schutz der bedrohten Amtsbrüder jüdischer Herkunft).
Bonhoeffer also worked abroad to persuade Europe to take a more critical stance
towards Germany. For example, during his year and a half in London (1933–35)
he exchanged views about the situation in his homeland, particularly with his
friend George Bell, the Anglican Bishop of Chichester.

After his return in April 1935, Bonhoeffer took on the role of training ministers
for the Confessing Church *(Bekennende Kirche),* which emerged in 1934 as an
oppositional Protestant movement against the Nazi-controlled Evangelical Church
in Germany *(Deutsche Evangelische Kirche),* at Predigerseminar Zingsthof, later moving
to Finkenwalde (now Zdroje in Poland). In 1937, it was closed by the Gestapo,
but Bonhoeffer was able to continue his work in the form of an 'illegal seminary'
(Sammelvikariat) until March 1940, first in Groß Schlönwitz (Pol. Słonowice),
then, from 1939, at Sigurdshof, an estate in Tychow (Pol. Tychowo). At the start of
June 1939, he accepted an invitation to the United States of America, but ended his
stay prematurely after just a few days. Bonhoeffer returned to Berlin to stand by his
brothers and sisters in their struggle during difficult times. In the autumn of 1940,
Bonhoeffer joined the resistance circle around his brother-in-law Hans von Dohnanyi
(his sister Christine's husband), General Hans Oster, as well as Admiral Wilhelm
Canaris, using his international ecumenical connections. His participation caused
a profound conflict for Bonhoeffer, for he saw it as a fundamental violation of the
basic principles of his Christian faith. On the other hand, he felt inaction or failure
to take responsibility would implicate him in a guilt that would be impossible to undo.
This obligation to act is explored extensively in his posthumously published work
Ethics (1949). Officially working for Nazi counterespionage, he undertook trips across
Europe in 1941 and 1942, using his contacts to encourage the Allies to support the
German Resistance, of which he had become a part.

In January 1943, Bonhoeffer became engaged to Maria von Wedemeyer, only
months before two failed Resistance attacks against Hitler, on the 13th and 21st
of March. On 5 April, Bonhoeffer was arrested based on incriminating files found
in Dohnanyi's papers, and imprisoned in the army prison, in northwest Berlin's
Tegel district. Although escape was possible, he refused, in order to prevent further
endangering his family. On 8 October 1944, Bonhoeffer was moved to the Prinz-
Albrecht-Straße prison in central Berlin, then taken to Buchenwald Concentration
Camp on 7 February 1945. After the Gestapo found counterespionage papers in
Zossen, south of Berlin, Hitler finally condemned Bonhoeffer and other participants,
including his brother Klaus, to death. Three days later, Dietrich Bonhoeffer
was brought to Flossenbürg Concentration Camp, where he was executed
on 9 April 1945.

Artist John Young formed the idea behind *Bonhoeffer in Harlem* while visiting
St Matthäus Church with gallerist Alexander Ochs in late November 2007. In 2003,
when Ochs had presented Young's first solo show in Berlin, *Three Propositions*, he
invited Young to Berlin to do research for their next project together. This was to
become part of the exhibition series that Ochs developed, along with several Chinese
artists, entitled *Berlin Reflections*, which explored intercultural artistic engagement

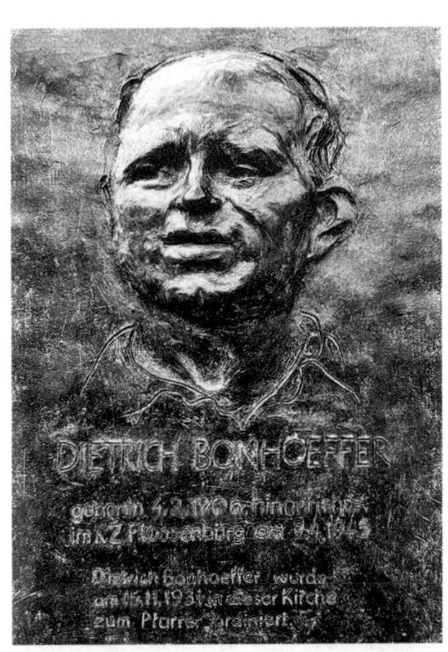

Johannes Grützke (1937–2017)
Memorial plaque of Dietrich Bonhoeffer 2006
St Matthäus Church, Kulturforum, Berlin
Engraved metal plaque, 60 × 40 cm
Photograph by the artist

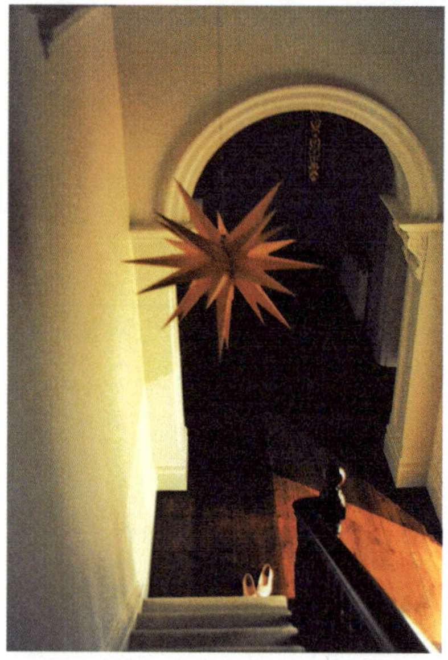

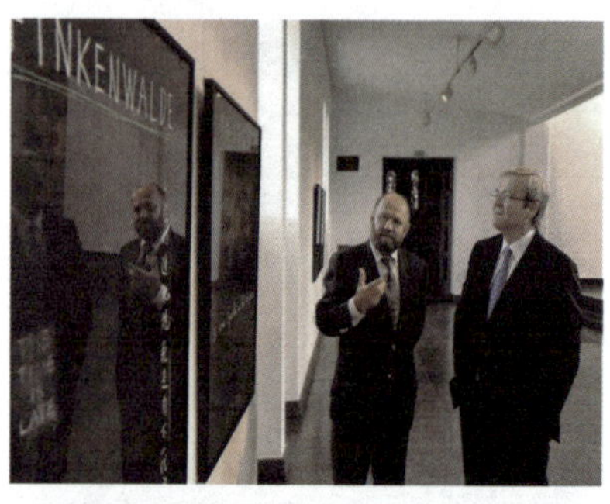

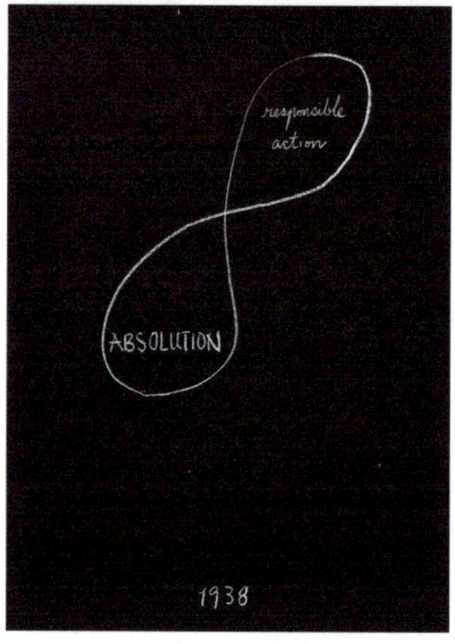

Yellow star in the artist's home, Melbourne, 2005

Left to right: Alexander Ochs and Kevin Rudd
Bonhoeffer in Harlem, St Matthäus Church,
Kulturforum, Berlin, 2009

Responsible Action/Absolution, 2008
Chalk on blackboard-painted archival cotton
paper, 100 × 70 cm

with Berlin and its history.[2] While visiting St Matthäus, the two spoke about Bonhoeffer, his ordination there, his life, his texts, his struggle and his fate:

> Alexander and I walked across the Tiergarten to St Matthäus; we sat and talked quietly about the art projects that had been done in this church and he explained to me the life of Bonhoeffer, who was ordained in the church; but we also talked about many other topics. He left it to me to decide what kind of project I would like to propose to the church. I was not used to going into Lutheran Churches, where the interior was very sparse, not decorative at all like Catholic Churches.[3]

Young was impressed by the simplicity and the balanced, clear structure of the church interior. Two additional things in front of the church's main portal also attracted his attention: on the one hand, the bronze Bonhoeffer memorial plaque by Berlin artist Johannes Grützke and on the other, a large yellow star that had been hung to announce the coming Christmas season. A smaller version of this star, which Young later purchased for his children at a Berlin Christmas market, would accompany him on his return to Australia, repeatedly reminding him of the image of St Matthäus and Bonhoeffer as a person. In the immediate wake of this visit, a desire grew in the artist to dedicate an exhibition to this outstanding figure and the church of his ordination.

Back in Australia, Young began to develop his concept. During his stay in Berlin, a decisive political transformation took place at home. After nine years in office, the conservative Liberal government was replaced by the more social-democratic Labor Party. Tellingly, just before taking office, the new Prime Minister Kevin Rudd, with whom Young was acquainted, wrote an extensive article entitled 'Faith in Politics', about the meaning of Dietrich Bonhoeffer for politics today.[4] In Bonhoeffer's spirit, Rudd argued for the need for contemporary society to return to a life based on ethics.

Young continued to engage with Bonhoeffer. He read about the time spent by the theologian with the residents of Harlem, about his deep sympathy for the people he came to know at Abyssinian Baptist Church. For Young, who comes from a bi-ethnic background, intercultural approaches have always played a central role in his artistic career. The loss of his cultural-ethnic identity and the problematic of grounding identity in transcultural contexts have been repeatedly thematised in his work. Young explains his close affinity to Bonhoeffer, saying:

> There is a theory that 'because he identified with the racial underclass in American society' on his return to Germany he was able to perceive the condition of the Jewish people. All my projects to today are transcultural, or at least had something to do with the condition of crossing cultures. The more I looked into them, the more I felt disowned by the original culture that one has crossed from, and the more futile I felt asking questions about identity in cross-cultural situations. Hence, I moved my questioning from identity to looking at people who had done tremendous good because they were in cross-cultural situations.[5]

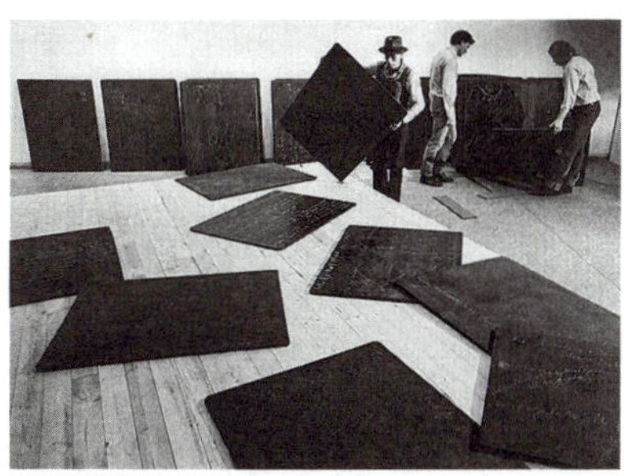

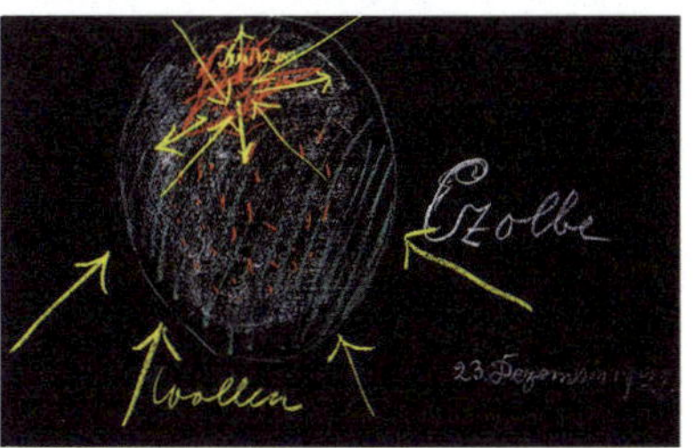

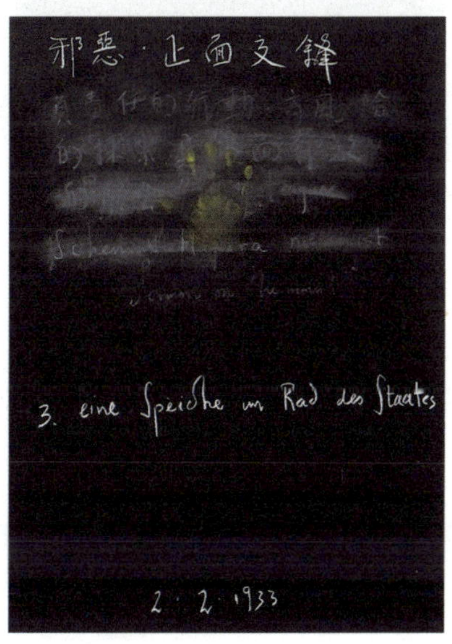

However, it is not only Bonhoeffer's experiences in Harlem that play a decisive role here. Young also emphasises the fact that Bonhoeffer curtailed his second stay in the United States to face his responsibility in Germany, as well as the deep discord that arose within him due to his participation in the Resistance.

In Young's view, this ethical conflict, in an abstract form, is equally applicable to problems resulting from the confrontation of very different cultural values:

> When you are crossing cultures, you are in the middle, and you can see both sides, so you are put in a conflictual or a paradoxical situation where something is right and wrong at the same time, depending on which cultural perspective you are looking from.[6]

The exhibition *Bonhoeffer in Harlem* consisted of three sections. The first was a portfolio of eleven conceptual works: eight of these are chalk drawings, the three remaining works are digital inkjet prints. The works located on the walls of the nave refer to Bonhoeffer's key biographical details and beliefs, starting with his birth, his childhood, his time in Harlem, the resistance up to his arrest, and his ultimate execution at Flossenbürg in April 1945.

It is initially surprising that the chalk drawings are actually works on paper, since they look like chalkboards, having been first painted with chalkboard paint. Using almost only white chalk, these drawings note significant dates, sites, and textual phrases, sometimes only vaguely legible because they have been smudged by hand. We can read faint words in German and in English, and Chinese characters also emerge from the matte black ground.

This material and aesthetic evokes an association with the chalkboard works of Joseph Beuys, with which he presented his *Directive Forces for a New Society (Richtkräfte einer neuen Gesellschaft)* between 1974 and 1977. But, like Beuys, Young is also referring to the earlier chalkboard drawings of the philosopher, anthroposophist and epistemologist Rudolf Steiner, who used chalkboards in his lectures to communicate his ideas and visions of social reform with the help of live, multi-coloured drawings. Beginning in 1919, on the suggestion of someone from the audience, the boards were covered with black cardboard before each lecture, in order to save the chalk drawings and texts for later generations.

Young values the didactic character of Steiner's 'works', dating from the years 1919 to 1924, of which around 1100 are still extant today. Although transferred to a different support, they evoke in the beholder the original context of the chalkboard and the schoolroom, and directly confer their didactic impact. Steiner used drawings to help articulate his highly complex thoughts and visions. In Young's view, the significance of Steiner's drawings lies in our need for a spiritual perspective amid today's materialistic world. As Young suggests, 'it was good that he used such a didactic medium, chalk on blackboard, to make you feel these values which he illustrated are emphatic and necessary',[7] The board becomes paper, and the paper, in turn, is visually elevated to the status of a chalkboard. This media transformation, which in Steiner's case grew out of a necessary act of conservation, becomes part of

Jürgen Müller-Schneck (1942–2020)
Joseph Beuys during his installation "Richtkräfte einer neuen Gesellschaft" in the Nationalgalerie 1977
Collection of bpk, Nationalgalerie SMB and Jürgen Müller-Schneck, © Joseph Beuys; image courtesy of Verwertungsgesellschaft Bild-Kunst/ Copyright Agency, 2023

Rudolf Steiner (1861–1925)
Blackboard drawing illustrating a lecture, c. 1919–24

Politics 2008
Chalk on blackboard-painted archival cotton paper, 100 × 70 cm

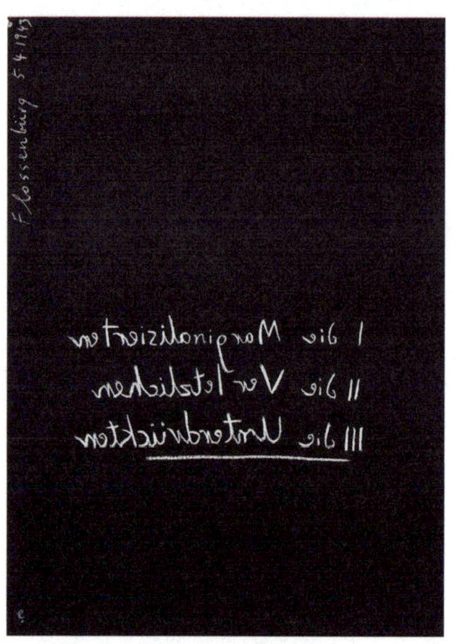

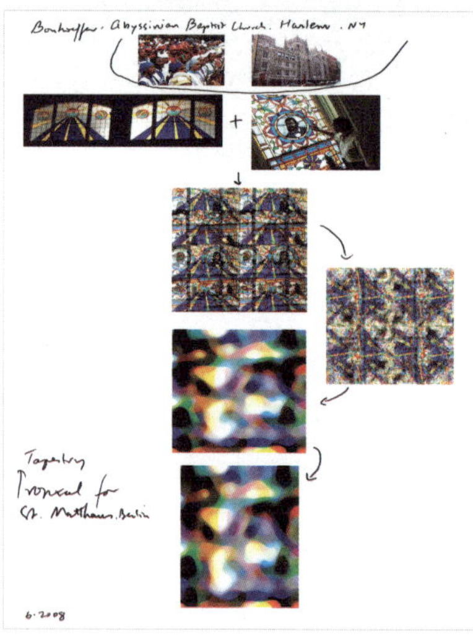

The Othered 2008
Chalk on blackboard-painted archival cotton
paper, 100 × 70 cm

Concept development notes for *Bonhoeffer
in Harlem*, 2008

the concept for both Beuys' and Young's own works. While Beuys also used blackened wooden boards that he inscribed with chalk, Young, more akin to Steiner, uses paper, though not industrially prefabricated cardboard. He undertakes the colouring of the paper itself, giving it a smooth surface, like the board, adding an element of illusion. As for Beuys, the works are not only a didactical means of communication but also autonomous works of art. By way of their character as boards, an immediacy is shared: the act of inscription is constantly present. At the same time, they evoke fugacity, especially where the writing is blurred, as in *Politics*, which is emblematised by the yellow handprint, or *The Othered* and *Prison*, where the name of Bonhoeffer's execution site, Flossenbürg, surfaces like an evil premonition from the dark.

But Young's access to the board pictures can also be explained from a very different context: as a child, his father had him learn the complex art of Chinese calligraphy. As is customary for children, he first practiced by using a brush and water on a smooth stone. Since the water quickly evaporates, the characters need not be erased. This technique is practiced until the written signs can be made perfectly. As Young recalls, 'you basically practice till you get the word right, then one deserves to write it with ink'.[8] This system, learned from his father, also lies at the foundation of these chalk drawings. The words can be erased and created anew, reassembled or changed, until the 'right tone is found'.[9] Using different words in three different languages and cultures, Young collects multiple voices and uses them to explore the transcultural approach: 'In these drawings, there are many voices, and these voices may be from different cultures, different passions—all trying to think around the life of Dietrich Bonhoeffer'.[10] In so doing, Young is expressly emphasising that he does not want to imitate Bonhoeffer's handwriting. Instead, it is Young's own writing that is used to lend the voices a form.

Even more closely linked to Bonhoeffer's period in Harlem is the large format silk tapestry, in myriad colours, that hangs in place of the crucifix as an altarpiece at the center of the church. This tapestry's process of conception and creation came to play a key role for the whole project. Young had already been thinking for some time about designing a tapestry that, in its colours and structure, would look like a church window. While developing the Bonhoeffer project, this idea took on concrete form. The execution of a design in tapestry in and of itself is not new to the artist—in 2007, he had a tapestry woven for his exhibition *Walden in China*, which was held at the state library in Nanjing.[11] But this earlier work is a more figurative representation, in the style of Young's realistic works. In contrast to this, the Bonhoeffer tapestry is more akin to the series of abstract paintings he has been making since 2005: *Naïve Sentimental Paintings* and *The Day after Tomorrow*.

As the foundation for the tapestry, the artist decided to use the windows of the Abyssinian Baptist Church, built in 1922—the place that had left such a lasting impression on Bonhoeffer during his one-year stay in New York. But Young's decision to use the windows of the church presented quite a different challenge:

> When I first saw the stained-glass colours, the purples and greens, I felt very distant from it. I couldn't imagine how I would design something with that palette. It was a Black aesthetic which was as alien as Chinese opera to Western ears. I could not affect the colour relationships, the taste of it, to make a design. I had to work against myself and what I was familiar with.[12]

Young saw himself confronted with an aesthetic that, in its colour composition, was foreign to his own familiar taste. In a metaphorical sense, it was difficult for him to overcome cultural boundaries on an artistic level; but this challenge led him directly back to Bonhoeffer. He saw the overcoming of precisely these kinds of limits as the theologian's message to him as an artist—his ethical call:

> It occurred to me that this was precisely what Bonhoeffer may have wanted me to do: to see the other. And not only to see the other but [also to] try to be the other. In other words, to make art not from the point of narcissism, but hopefully from empathy.

> Therein lies the meaning for me of this project: the process of transforming myself as an artist parallels the ethical transformation Bonhoeffer requires of people.[13]

Yet, we encounter the transcultural aspect in another sense as well. In a method of making that was initially prompted by the concerns of conceptual painting, an artwork, for Young, is often the product of several participants, never one alone. In this way, he makes no secret of the fact that he employs studio assistants who are responsible for a certain portion of the production; they are sometimes credited on the reverse of works they have assisted in painting, for example. In this sense of shared authorship, Bonhoeffer too can ultimately be understood as a co-author—especially in Young's chalk drawings. In the tapestry, this aspect is equally striking, for the execution of the artistic design required several 'co-producers'. Jürgen Dahlmanns, a rug designer and owner of the Berlin company Rug Star, had to examine Young's concept for its technical feasibility and develop a concrete blueprint for the weaver. He then sent this blueprint to his partner, the weaver Dolma Lob Sang in Nepal, who runs a small company with several employees. Interestingly, as we learned only later, she is the daughter of a Tibetan monk, and lives in exile in Nepal, cut off from her homeland, forming a certain parallel to Young's own story. At the end of a long production chain, she was finally responsible for the material realisation of the tapestry. In this way, the work combines very different cultural interpretations, from Young's original conception to its final execution.

In recent years, the work of contemporary artists using the medium of stained glass in sacred spaces has been a special focus of attention. After Markus Lüpertz' designs were realised in 2005 for St Andreas in Cologne, Gerhard Richter and Neo Rauch also worked in this medium. Richter's abstract, 113 square metre window in the southern nave of Cologne Cathedral, comprised of approximately 11,000 stained-glass squares (based on his painting 4096 Farben, 1974), and was dedicated in August 2007. At the end of that same year, in Naumburg Cathedral, three round arched windows showing figurative scenes on a red background were unveiled, based on designs by Neo Rauch.

In Young's tapestry, by contrast—and this is the decisive difference from the positions above—the medium of stained glass is subjected to a different kind of transformation. Just like Richter's windows, here too computer-generated abstract images serve as the foundation. But, for Young, the starting point is real objects, namely the windows of the Abyssinian Baptist Church. Young adopts the colour of the windows, in altered form, for his artistic design, which ultimately finds its expression in a medium that can hardly be any less like the original material of glass, instead picking up on the

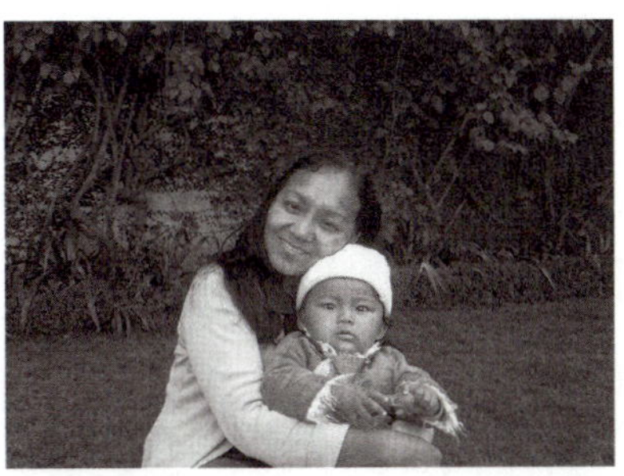

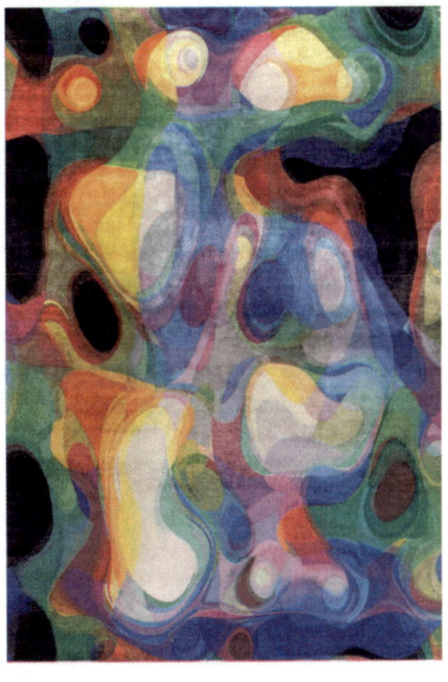

Weaver Dolma Lob Sang and her son
Nepal, 2009

Bonhoeffer in Harlem 2009
Chinese silk tapestry, 303 × 119 cm
Collection of Erlöserkirche, Bamberg

millennial tradition of tapestries. Tapestries are a firm part of artistic creation, not only in China but also in Europe—think of the tapestries from the Middle Ages and the Renaissance that played a significant role not least in a sacred context. In a startling way, Young's work succeeds in uniting two media that are quite opposite in character, yet they are both ancient crafts. In so doing, however, the two retain their original qualities: the tapestry is recognisable, but its technically impressive use of colour along with the silk's oscillating form, unmistakably echoes the glow and transparent materiality of the Harlem stained-glass windows.

The third section of this exhibition comprised two abstract oil paintings that visibly take up the motif of the tapestry. In technical and conceptual terms, they follow in the tradition of the abstract series that Young has been developing since 2005. Like the tapestry, these works are based on a complex technique which emerged from Young's reflection on the role that technology plays in our lives today. Each day, the artist compiles around 1000 digital images from various sources: usually the internet, but also CDs, his own photography, video images, and so on. A computer then transforms these into abstract images overnight, with the help of filters that Young has defined beforehand. He then selects from these newly generated images, enlarges them, and transfers them with oils onto canvas. As Young has suggested:

> This way of abstracting images is interesting to me. As with anything today, our sense of choice has gone exponential in the twenty-first century. Where people in the early twentieth century may have one thousand abstracted drawings that they make to paint from in a lifetime, we can produce this overnight. Hence it is our sense of possibility and choice that has changed in the process of art making.[14]

Young even catches himself seeking out patterns in the computer-generated images: 'I find that I still choose images out of the 1000 on the basis of my education. For example, my eye is drawn to images that are proximate to Western abstract paintings of the twentieth century ("this one looks like a Rothko"; "this one reminds me of a Richter"; "this one reminds me of a Kandinsky"), or abstract ink paintings from China ("this one reminds me of an abstract Sung Dynasty ink painting of rocks").' Such images remind Young of his upbringing and training as an artist. He concludes: 'We are at the moment looking at computer imagery still through the lens of photography, much like in the early twentieth century we looked at photography through the eyes of nineteenth-century genre painting'.[15]

The exhibition's two paintings, *Bonhoeffer in Harlem I* and *II*, were made using this technique. Young had his computer, as a kind of 'co-author', generate images based on photographs of the church windows that he took from the internet; he chose two of the resulting images and then transferred them to canvas. If we compare these pieces to earlier abstract works like *Walden I* and *Walden II* from 2006, we clearly notice an increased degree of abstraction. While the landscapes in these earlier works can still be glimpsed, the Harlem works seem to stand more strongly on their own. This is primarily due to the striking empty parts of the paintings—new in Young's oeuvre—where the visual support, the canvas, comes to the forefront. These parts were already cut out or covered in the computer image. If we consider the complete canvas images, we see that Young removes the illusory sculptural quality from the abstract images with the help of these voids, flattening them. In so doing, he tries to return the beholder to a feeling for the surface of the work, now again visible and graspable.

Despite the abstraction, the Harlem church windows are still present. According to Young, the materiality that is introduced with the unpainted raw canvas relativises the 'feeling of illusionism and transcendental quality from the original stained glass' to create a balance.[16]

In his works for *Bonhoeffer in Harlem*, John Young succeeds in spanning a great distance in both thematic and artistic terms. Starting with Dietrich Bonhoeffer, in whom central terms like transculturality, ethical commitment, and responsible action are combined, we are presented with political developments that begin in the Third Reich, continue through the history of Young's own identity, and end with the Nepalese exile of Tibetan weaver Dolma Lob Sang. This thematic complexity finds its artistic expression in three distinct groups of artworks, across which Young plays with various media and materialities, subjecting them to processes of transformation: paper becomes chalkboard, glass becomes silk or canvas, the digital image becomes oil painting. In this combination, we are presented with an iridescent image, a shifting between light and dark, opacity and transparence, earthliness and Christian spirituality. The chalkboard drawings emblematise repression and death, but the tapestry and the abstract paintings diffuse the severity of these works, and in so doing Young leads us back to light and hope.

1. All biographical information on Bonhoeffer is sourced from Eberhard Bethge, *Dietrich Bonhoeffer: In Selbstzeugnissen und Bilddokumenten (Bonhoeffer: An Illustrated Introduction in Documents and Photographs)*, Rowohlt Verlag, Hamburg, 1976.

2. *Berlin Reflections* was a project-based exhibition series initiated by Alexander Ochs in 2008. As part of the series, a number of Chinese artists were invited by Ochs to spend time in Berlin and then develop bodies of work based on their reflections about the city.

3. John Young, interviewed by the author, 10 December 2008.

4. Kevin Rudd, 'Faith in Politics', *The Monthly*, October 2006, pp. 22–30.

5. Young, interviewed by the author, 10 December 2008.

6. Young, interviewed by the author, 19 March 2009.

7. Ibid.

8. Young, interviewed by the author, 10 December 2008.

9. Ibid.

10. Ibid.

11. This was a commission from the Victorian government to commemorate the twenty-fifth anniversary of sister state ties between Victoria and Jiangsu prefecture, of which Nanjing is the provincial capital. See conversation about *Open World* in this volume, pp. 42–53.

12. Young, interviewed by the author, 10 December 2008.

13. Ibid.

14. Ibid.

15. Ibid.

16. Ibid.

DEAR GRANDMOTHER

Dietrich Bonhoeffer

Editor's note: The following translation of a letter written in German by Dietrich Bonhoeffer to his grandmother in 1931 reflects the language and idiom of the time.

600 West 122nd Street, New York
April 12, 1931

Dear Grandmother,

Over the last few weeks, I was rather busy with work, the results of which have hopefully reached you by now. Three weeks remain of my time here, and I will have to squeeze as much into them as possible. I want to read a lot of that which I know I won't get to once I'm home; I haven't finished all of what I had intended to finish, by far. …

… I stayed in New York over Easter. Good Friday is not a bank holiday here, everyone seems to work. As if to make up for that, everyone then seems to go to church on Easter Sunday, whoever is so inclined. Also, it seems to be the general consensus that Easter is celebrated as the beginning of the spring season; one sports one's spring dress in church. It is necessary therefore to secure tickets for the bigger churches well ahead of time. Since I hadn't known this, I was left to attend a service given by a very famous rabbi who speaks every Sunday in the biggest concert hall, filled to the brim, and who gave a rousing sermon on the spread of corruption in the state of New York; he also called on the Jews, who constitute a third of the city's population, to turn this city into the City of God, to which the Messiah might then truly come. In the afternoon, a local friend of mine and I sailed the coastal waters where ships from Europe were passing through.

On Easter Monday, I went on a jaunt with a group of negro kids. Some of them are already seniors in high school, some at a surprisingly young age—one graduated at the age of fifteen, another at sixteen—others are rather slow and have barely managed to advance beyond the first classes of primary school. The strange thing is that all of them have a striking sense of belonging to one another, as if coeval. That is of course positive in many ways, but it also shows that the intelligent negro can't keep company with intelligent whites and is dependent on those who share his race and age. Without doubt, this slows down his advancement; it probably also steels his strength. I just finished reading a brilliant novel written by a very young negro. In contrast to the otherwise generally cynical or sentimental American literature, I find in it a very productive strength and warmth, of the kind that prompts me to wish to meet the man himself. – Friday and Saturday saw a conference of the leading systematic theologians of America, to which professor Baillie, who was its president, had invited me. The discussions, however, were unsatisfying to such a degree, really almost like discussions of students in their first semesters, that I still feel dejected. There was so much self-indulgent confusion and vagueness. – These are the latest ongoings here. – I will probably leave on 2 May. … My exact itinerary isn't set yet. Anyway, Mexico is the destination. Since yesterday it is clear that spring has arrived in all its splendour. The crocuses are out and one longs to leave the city. …

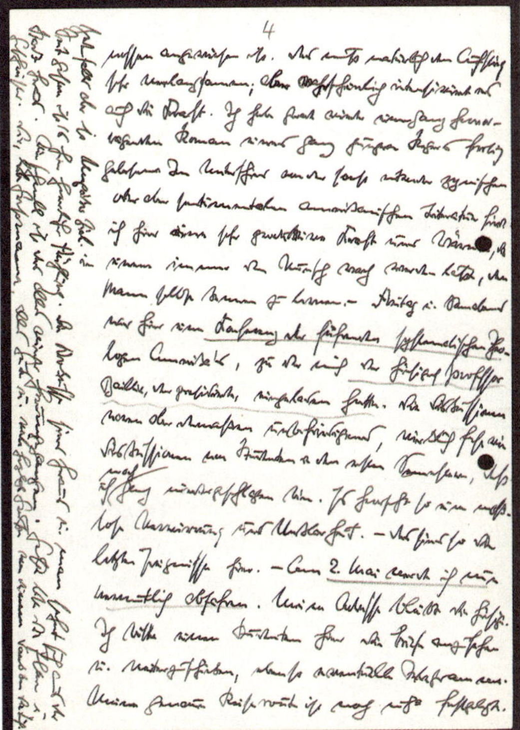

Letter from Dietrich Bonhoeffer to his
grandmother, New York, 12 April 1931
Collection of Staatsbibliothek zu Berlin
Image courtesy bpk and Staatsbibliothek zu,
Berlin

SPEECH FOR THE OPENING OF THE EXHIBITION *BONHOEFFER IN HARLEM*

Wolfgang Huber
Translated from German by Lea-Friederike Neubert

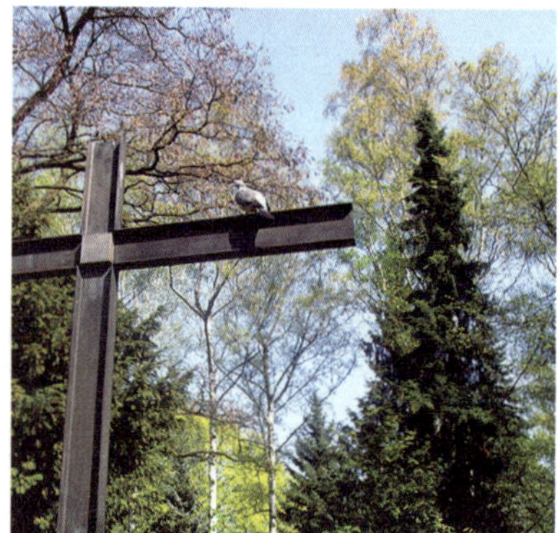

The memorial site of Dietrich Bonhoeffer
Dorotheenstaadtischer Friedhof, Berlin, 2008
Photograph by the artist

12 April 2009, St Matthäus Church, Berlin

What do the church of St Matthäus and Harlem have in common? They are both connected to Dietrich Bonhoeffer, and in a strange way at that. Dietrich Bonhoeffer visited St Matthäus on the occasion of his ordination on 15 November 1931—rather late, in fact. In his opinion, he should have been duly ordained already. Before he was, however, he came to live in Harlem.

The young and talented theologian Dietrich Bonhoeffer liked to take care of his matters as swiftly as possible. Thus, he earned his doctorate in theology in 1927 at the age of twenty-one and completed his first exam in theology soon thereafter. In 1930, he sat the second exam in theology, and several days later, on 18 July 1930, he was awarded his Habilitation (post-doctoral lecturing qualification). That's all well, but what was a university to do with a twenty-four-year-old lecturer in theology; he could surely not expect to be offered a professorship any time soon? And what was the Church to do with a twenty-four-year-old candidate of theology? He could not even be ordained, for he had not yet reached the required age of twenty-five. Bonhoeffer had to wait.

Nowadays, going travelling might appear to be an obvious solution; under the circumstances at the time, however, it was far from ordinary. Nevertheless, the young Bonhoeffer had undertaken extensive journeys to Rome and Morocco, and had worked as a curate in Barcelona. Without hesitation, he used the freedom his youth afforded him to embark on a study visit to the Union Theological Seminary in New York.

There, he forewent the opportunity to gain yet another academic title and instead spent a lot of his time encountering American reality. That was, at times, a sobering experience as perhaps exemplified by Bonhoeffer's indignation at a 'twelve-year-old girl being given a make-up box as a reward for regular attendance at a Methodist Sunday School and [at] the pastor being proud of this adaptation to the present'.

Yet, Bonhoeffer was also elated at what he encountered. Thus, his enthusiasm was ignited by the Abyssinian Baptist Church in Harlem:

> For more than six months, I went almost every Sunday at 2.30 to one of the large negro Baptist churches in Harlem, and together with my friend, or sometimes in his absence, I led a group of young negroes in Sunday School; I also led the negro women in Bible classes and at one time helped weekly in a weekday Sunday school … In a negro church, it is not difficult to notice when the interest of the parishioners is aroused and when it is not, because the terrific emotional intensity of the negroes keeps welling up in form of exclamations and interjections. It is undoubtedly clear, though, that whenever the gospels are addressed, participation peaks. … Whoever has heard and understood the negro spirituals, knows about the strange mixture of unexpended melancholy and erupting jubilance in the soul of the negro.

Bonhoeffer continues: When opposition against the circumstances 'will truly catch on, then White America will have to accept the blame for these Black masses having become godless. We are on the verge of a sea change here.'

A dramatic view of Harlem. Dietrich Bonhoeffer's older brother Karl Friedrich affirmed the judgement of the younger one, from his own experience. Indeed, race tensions in the United States seemed so dramatic to him that he uttered—in the summer of 1931!—that 'by all means, our Jewish question pales in comparison, there will be only very few who maintain that they would be oppressed here.' This was very soon to change fundamentally. The grievous oppression was to happen in Germany. Furthermore, several decades were to pass until the civil rights movement in the United States found its charismatic leader Martin Luther King, and until its dream of the indivisible dignity of man became manifest in the guarantee of equal rights. That this conviction has taken root in Germany, too, is symbolised—and more than just symbolised—by Bonhoeffer's stay in Harlem.

In order to keep this connection alive, we founded, as a joint American-German project, the Dietrich Bonhoeffer professorship at the Union Theological Seminary fifteen years ago. I sense just the same spirit in John Young's art project *Bonhoeffer in Harlem*. I am deeply grateful to all who made this project possible and who saw to it that it was given the right space here at St Matthäus.

As a matter of fact, Bonhoeffer went to Harlem a second time—only for one month, however, in June 1939. Friends intended to save him, a conscientious objector, from the fangs of Hitler and the impending war by offering him refuge in the United States. But Bonhoeffer was not capable of knowing himself safe, while in his own country the fight over justice and injustice was growing ever more acute. His decision was definite:

> To stay here while a catastrophe is unfolding is absolutely unthinkable,
> unless it could not be helped. But to be responsible for it myself, to have to
> blame myself for having left unnecessarily, would certainly be unbearable.

These are astonishingly decisive words. For, the alternative was crystal clear. 'In time of a catastrophe', Bonhoeffer sought to be where it was transpiring, namely in his own country. It was what was demanded of him by the gospel, which was received in the United States so much more passionately by the oppressed Black community than by the established bourgeois of the protestant churches, whom Bonhoeffer attested practised a 'Protestantism without reformation'. The African American Christians in Harlem were also purer and more passionate than the Christian majority in Germany; it was to this majority that Bonhoeffer returned, knowing that it would not support his path to conspiracy.

Bonhoeffer in Harlem is the Bonhoeffer who discovered the Sermon on the Mount and heeded it. This happened soon after the return from his first stay in New York, soon after the sixth month he spent in Harlem. In retrospect, Bonhoeffer described this turning point in 1936 as follows:

> I found the Bible for the first time. Now, that is upsetting to say. I had
> already given sermons frequently, I had already seen much of the Church,
> had spoken and written about it—and still, I had not yet become a
> Christian, had been fiercely and untameably my own master. …The Bible
> liberated me, and in particular the Sermon on the Mount. Since then,
> everything has changed.

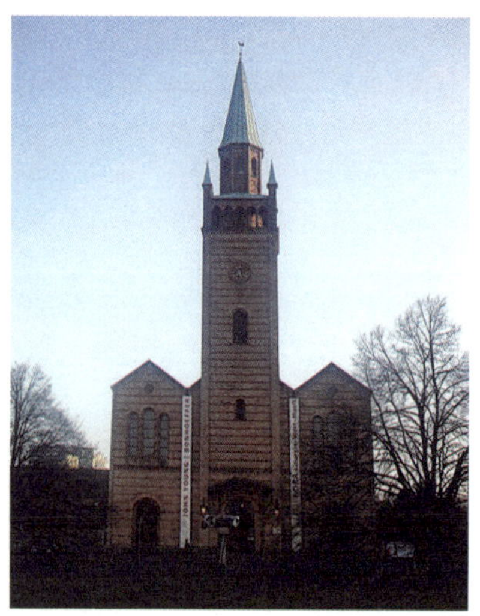

For a long time, these sentences—addressed to a friend in 1936—have been, for me, amongst the most important statements found in Dietrich Bonhoeffer's correspondence overall. How magnificent that someone thus professes his love for his own life, 'fiercely and untameably my own master'. Who would not wish to experience the decision for living in Christ this consciously! It is one of the remarkable strokes of fate in the twentieth century that a man experiences liberation through the Sermon on the Mount and that this experience leads him even to a conspiracy against Hitler. In this, Bonhoeffer's encounters in Harlem undoubtedly played a crucial role.

What then connects Harlem with the church of St Matthäus? Bonhoeffer's manuscripts, a treasure without comparison, are kept just across the street, in the Berlin State Library–Prussian Cultural Heritage, where they are given the by now considerable care and maintenance they need.

More direct even is the reference I related to earlier: the great freedom that allowed for Bonhoeffer's residence in New York, resulted from his early graduation. He could only be ordained once he had reached the age of twenty-five, but well before that he had passed all his exams in theology. Hence, he celebrated his twenty-fifth birthday in the US, and when he returned, no one was able to block his way to parochial office.

Bonhoeffer was thus ordained here in St Matthäus on 15 November 1931. It was a sober ceremony. After he had paid five Reichsmark 'as financial support for the costs of the ordination to be entrusted to the sexton', the general superintendent Vits administrated the required acts. Who would have imagined that a panel by Johannes Grützke would come to commemorate this event? Then, neither Bonhoeffer nor his family took the occasion very seriously. The freshly ordained pastor himself spent the afternoon with his friend Franz Hildebrandt in Schöneberg, where Hildebrandt gave a sermon on the occasion of Hegel's 100th day of death.

The Harlem-experienced Bonhoeffer quickly realised the seriousness of the situation in Germany. For one, he did not trust the self-proclaimed saviours offering ways out of the global economic crisis. He was not convinced of the Church's reaction to them, either; it remained too clearly in the realm of routine. On the eve of his ordination, Bonhoeffer posed this desperate question to a friend from his time in New York: 'Will our Church survive yet another catastrophe, will it not be over for good unless we radically change our ways of being, speaking, and living immediately?'

This, I think, is the question of Bonhoeffer in Harlem. His question asks us whether we duly counter the catastrophes of our time instead of just asking how we can weather them—be it the ways in which we imperil the climatic stability of the earth or be it the widening gap between rich and poor around the globe. We have to stand up to inquiries as to how we expect to justify our short-term crisis interventions to the next generation and whether we really aim to rectify the logic of near-sighted profit or whether we only seek to alleviate the most obvious of detriments that result from it.

When were such questions more topical than today? At what time and place would an exhibition be more appropriate than here, at the centre of Berlin, and now, in the middle of the most dramatic global financial crisis since the year in which Bonhoeffer called upon us 'to radically change our ways of being, speaking, and living?"

St Matthäus Church, Kulturforum, Berlin, 2009
Photograph by the artist

Editor's note: All quotes from Dietrich Bonhoeffer are sourced from Mary Bosanquet, *The Life and Death of Dietrich Bonhoeffer*, Harper & Row, New York, 1968.

A SPOKE IN THE WHEEL OF THE STATE

Pastor Anette Simojoki

Sunday, 21 July 2013

Dear congregants,

There is a picture from my youth that has been burned into my memory like no other. This event took place on 5 June, 1989. On the day before, demonstrations in Beijing's Tiananmen Square had been violently suppressed. Instead of protesting students, the streets were now controlled by tanks. So too was it on this day along Chang'an Avenue leading into the Forbidden City. Apparently unchallenged, the column of tanks drives down the empty street. Suddenly a man is standing there, slender, black trousers, a white shirt, two plastic bags in his hand. Standing tall in an almost military fashion, he faces the oncoming tanks—and manages to bring the column to a halt. They remain facing each other for an extended moment, man versus machine. Then the tank starts to move and tries to drive past the man in front of it. He immediately counters and blocks it again. It's like a silent dance. The tank moves forward and the man takes a small step back. Back to a standstill. Obviously at a loss, the tank driver comes to a stop and switches off the engine.

The unknown man climbs up and begins (though the pictures aren't very clear) to talk to the driver. Then he climbs down and takes up his position anew. The tank starts up, but the man stands his ground. Then four people rush out to him and hustle the suicidal man out of the way. After that, the column continues on its way.

For me there is no more impressive image that represents how a single person can stand up to an all-powerful system. We don't know what became of that man, but the images have remained. In April 1998, *Time* magazine named 'Tank Man' one of the 100 most influential people of the century.

The individual and the system: that is the topic of the panel, *Politics* (2008), which is up here. It is the fourth in our series of eleven panels that make up our exhibition. Following the two images and biographies of the siblings Dietrich and Sabine, came the topic of last week's sermon, the thought provoking image, *Harlem* (2008), recalling Bonhoeffer's time in Harlem, specifically at the Abyssinian Baptist Church. By this time the fight against racism was already well established and the argument-based justification for Bonhoeffer's return to Germany can be found on our panel for to.

Our image today looks like a notice on a blackboard. It reminds me of when I was in school. The blackboard was the main medium. It was constantly being written on, erased, and written on again. Occasionally something would remain if the board wasn't erased properly or too quickly. On John Young's panel, this feature has been used intentionally. Snippets of words, dates, and quotes have been brought together in various languages, some drawn clearly, some faded, and others erased.

2 February 1933. On this day Bonhoeffer gave a speech on the radio about the term *Führer* (leader). Adolf Hitler had but two days before been named Chancellor to much cheering and celebration. Dietrich Bonhoeffer called upon the responsibility a leader must bear in these days, and he warned against leaders slipping into archetypes. After the sentence 'leaders and offices who make themselves into God are mocking His …', the radio program was interrupted. The radio station simply switched the power off. Snippets of words, as if to clarify the ideas, are merely blurred images on the panel.

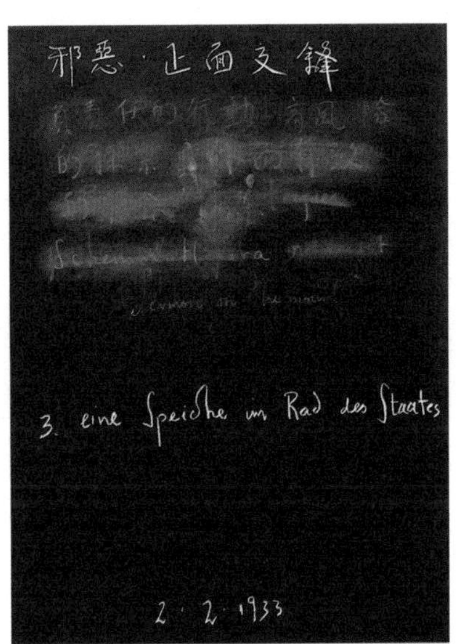

Politics 2008
Chalk on blackboard-painted archival cotton paper, 100 × 70 cm

Nonetheless, two titles of texts that are written on the drawing *Politics* can still be guessed.

'SchemmHapora' is one of them. *Vom SchemHamphoras (Of the Unknowable Name and the Generations of Christ)* is a book that the German Reformation leader Martin Luther wrote in 1543, in which he compares Jews to the devil and vilifies them using obscene language.

The second text on the panel is the so-called Sermon on the Mount. Whoever has read the well-known beatitudes carefully will notice something. The strongest motif is that of righteousness: 'Blessed are they that hunger and thirst after righteousness: for they shall be filled. Blessed are they that have been persecuted for righteousness' sake: for theirs is the kingdom of heaven.' Righteousness is a rather concrete thing and is constantly at stake. That's why this panel is not trying to hang onto and commemorate something from the past. It's about our actions in the here and now.

John Young expresses this in different ways. On one hand, he interprets Bonhoeffer's impulse in his own words. At the same time, we can find three sentences in Chinese and snippets of text on the panel. At the top, the summons 'Evil, resist it at once'. Underneath, almost completely erased, two other proverbs: 'Responsible deeds— a highly risky venture' and 'Act honestly, directly, and benevolently'.

The artist seems to want to tell us that the mark of faith is demonstrated in how we live and go about our lives. The Christian faith remains lifeless when it does not leave traces. That sounds plausible, but it can force the individual to make hard decisions. That's what the snippets of words in the middle of this picture are referring to. It alludes to a famous word of Bonhoeffer's, and that, in a way, leads us back to our final picture. After the Aryan paragraphs had been made into law, Bonhoeffer gave a speech in the same month, on 7 April 1933. There he took the side of the persecuted Jews with such clarity as was unprecedented from the Church at the time: 'The Church is in no uncertain terms responsible for the victims of this social order, even if they do not belong to our Christian community'. Bonhoeffer's words were not only addressing the totalitarian state but also the church, which was lacking in consequence at that time. Therefore, when push comes to shove, the church must be ready 'to not only bandage up those victims crushed by the wheel, but to stop the wheel from turning by jamming the spokes'.

There it is again, the question of the individual and the system, and with this point my sermon is coming to its end. Stopping the wheel by jamming the spokes does not always have to mean doing something heroic. The ability to stand in the face of tanks or to directly challenge evil, like Dietrich Bonhoeffer did, is given to very few of us. But we too face situations in our everyday lives in which it seems that the wheel cannot be stopped.

When a girl in our class is systematically bullied.
When an older colleague at work can't keep up with the ever-increasing workload.
When global competition pushes local businesses out of the market.
When behind the guise of a digital revolution hides a totalitarian surveillance system.

'Look carefully' is the message bravely emanating from this panel. It says, the gospel gives us an inner freedom as opposed to those systems in which we find ourselves. When these systems threaten to run us over, then it comes down to me. I have been asked to use my voice, my convictions, my direct actions, or as demonstrated on this panel, my own personal mark.

Amen.

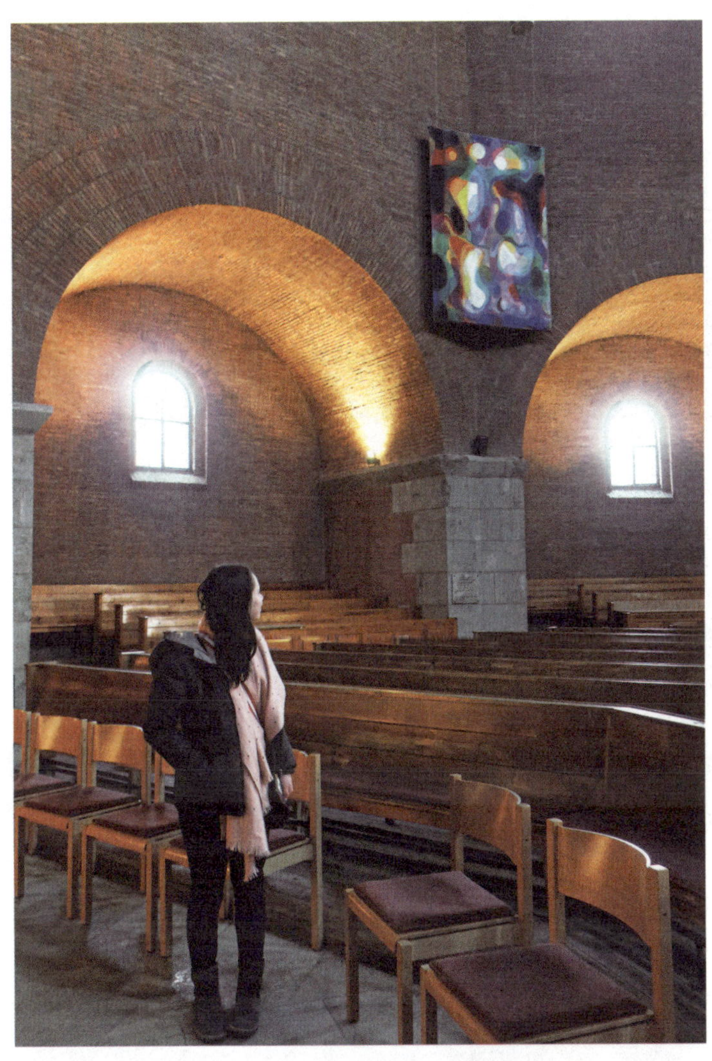

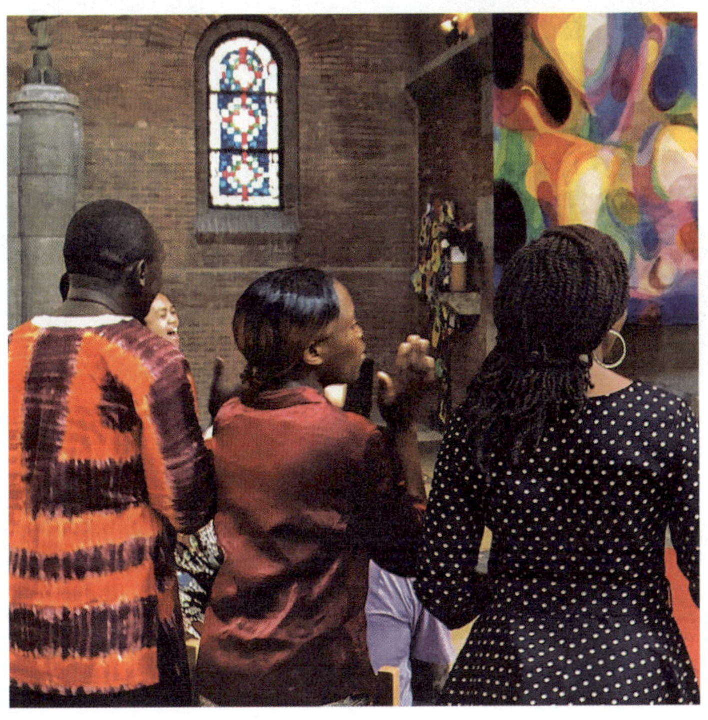

Bonhoeffer in Harlem 2009
Installation views, Erlöserkirche, Bamberg, 2013

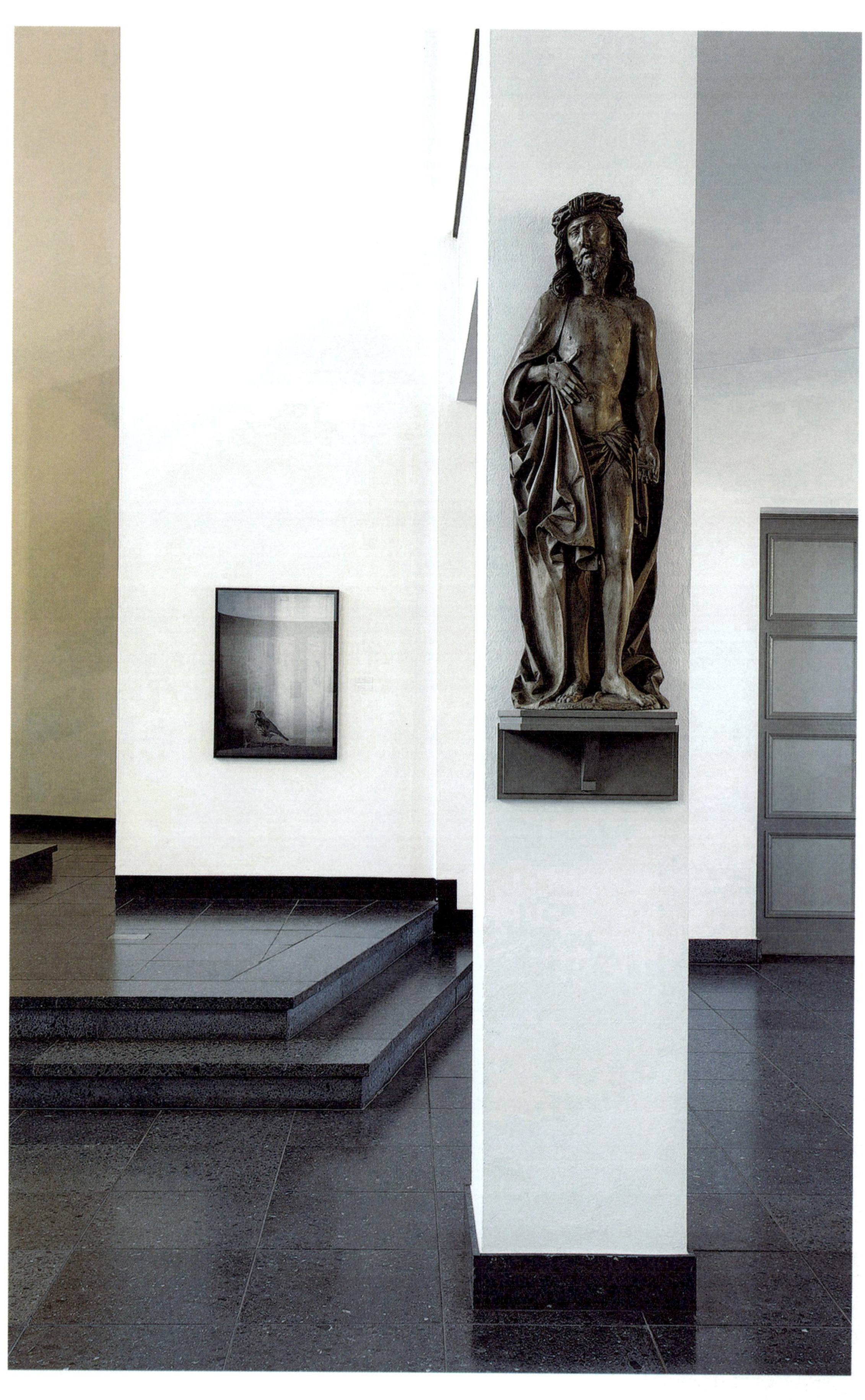

Bonhoeffer in Harlem 2009
Installation views, St Matthäus Church,
Kulturforum, Berlin, 2009

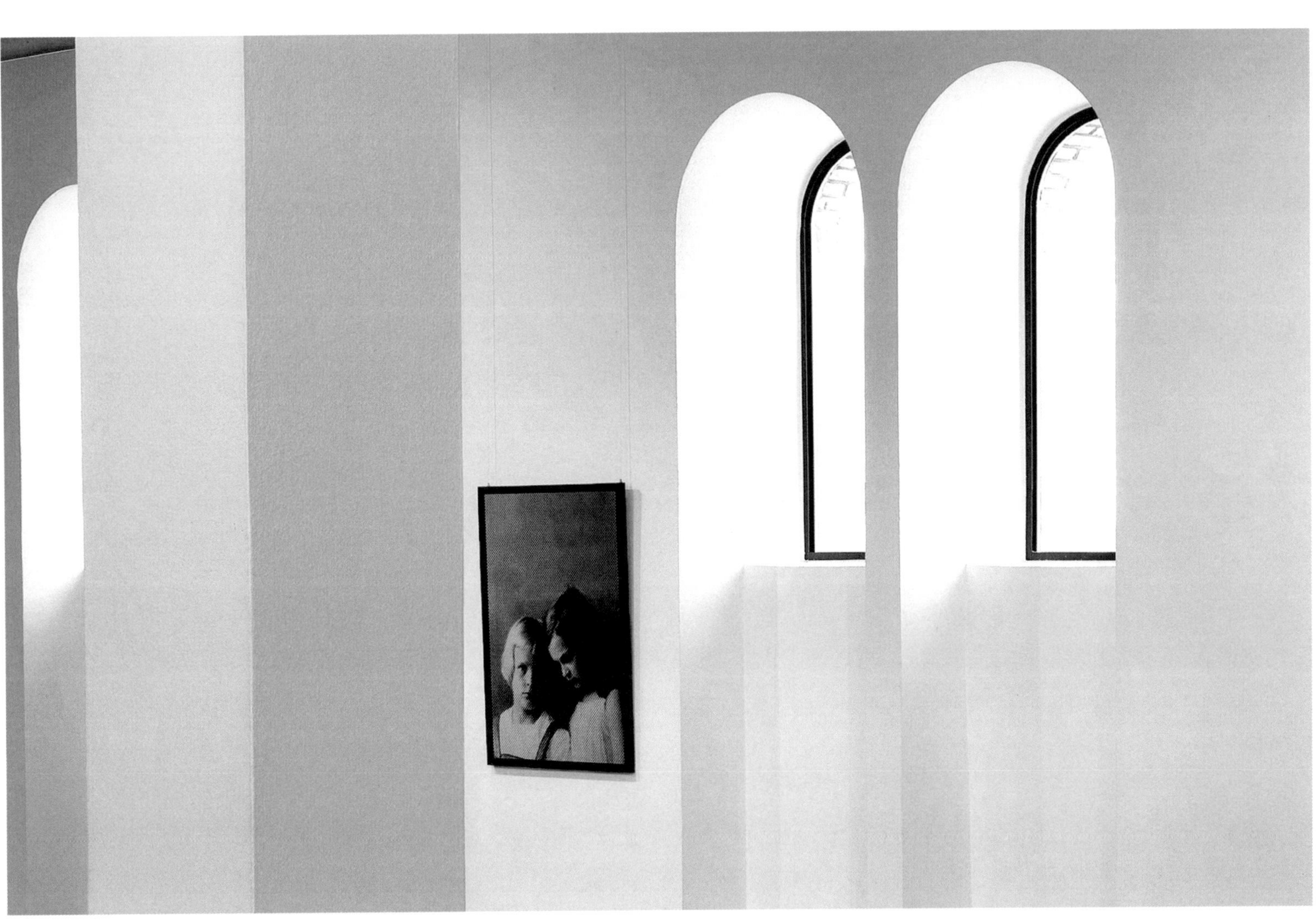

Bonhoeffer in Harlem 2009
Chinese silk tapestry, 303 × 119 cm
Installation view, St Matthäus Church,
Kulturforum, Berlin, 2009
Collection of Erlöserkirche, Bamberg

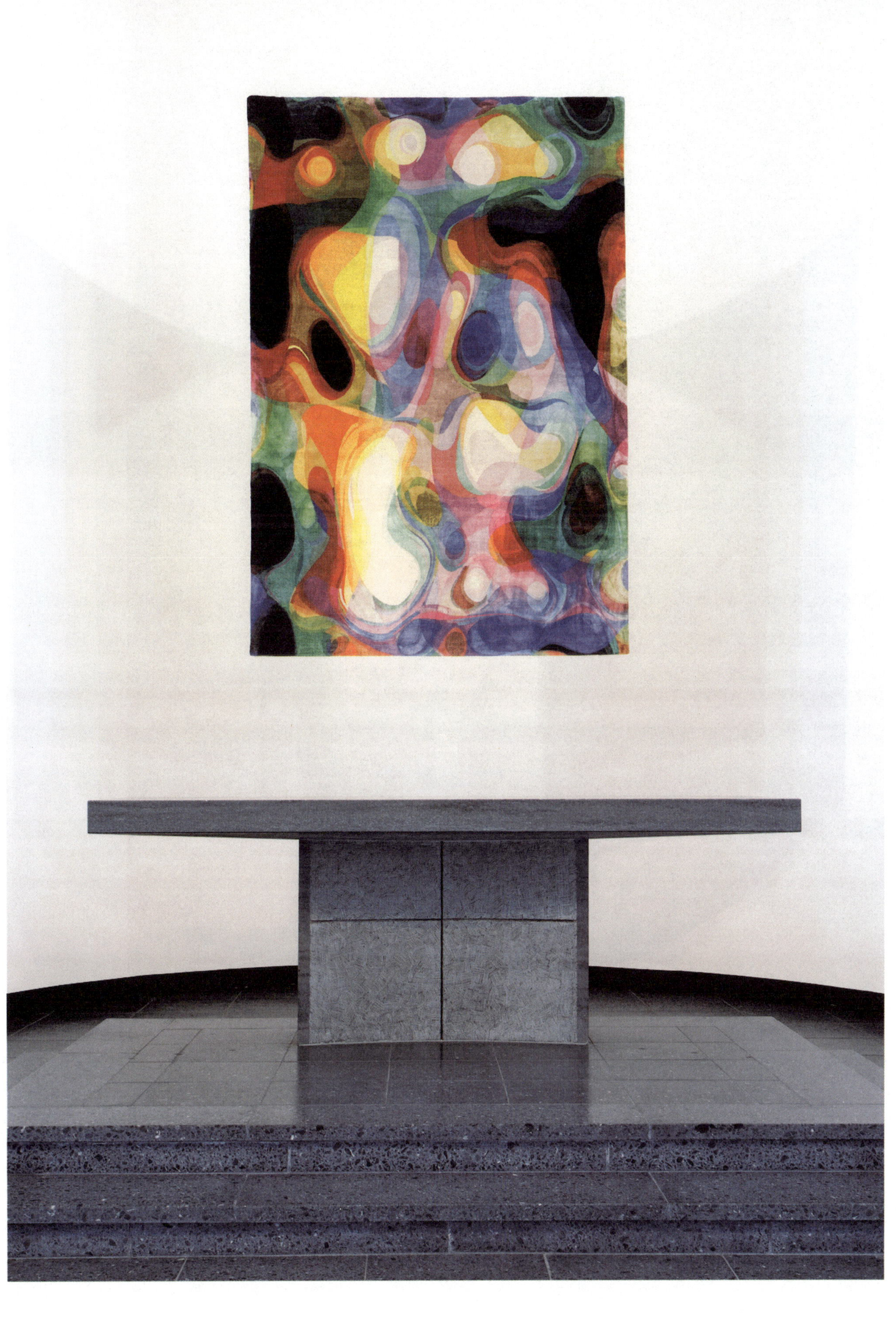

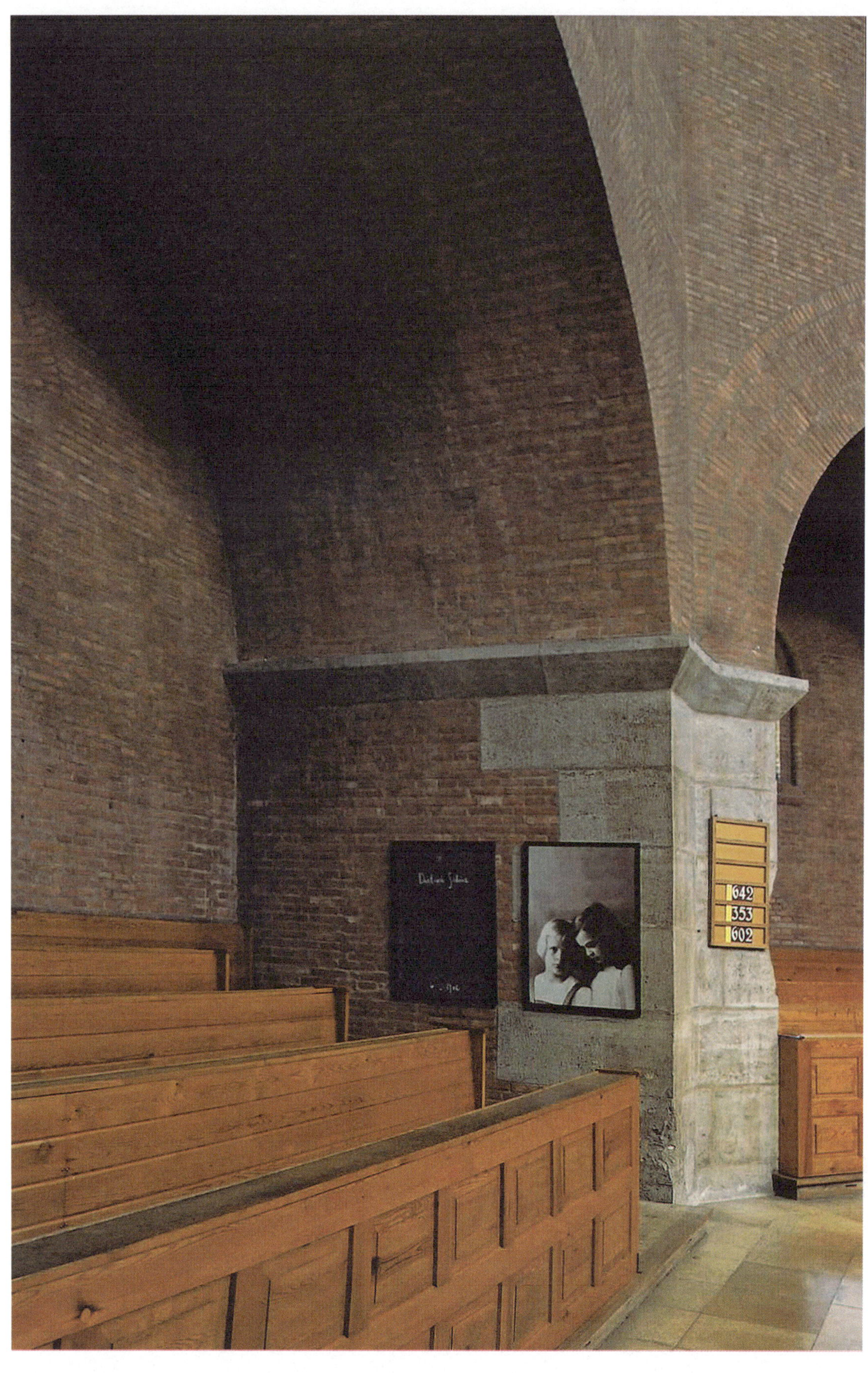

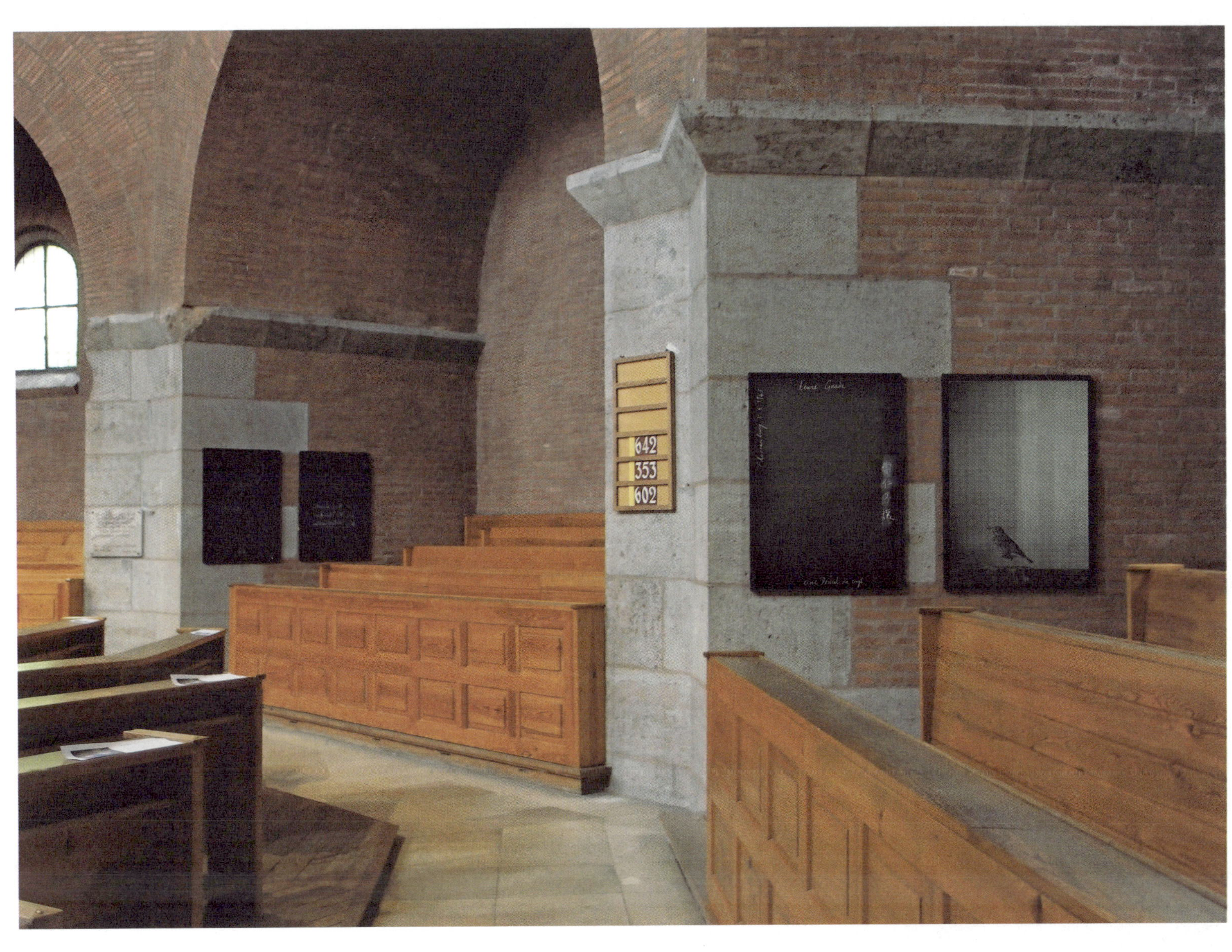

Bonhoeffer in Harlem 2009
Installation views, Erlöserkirche, Bamberg, 2013

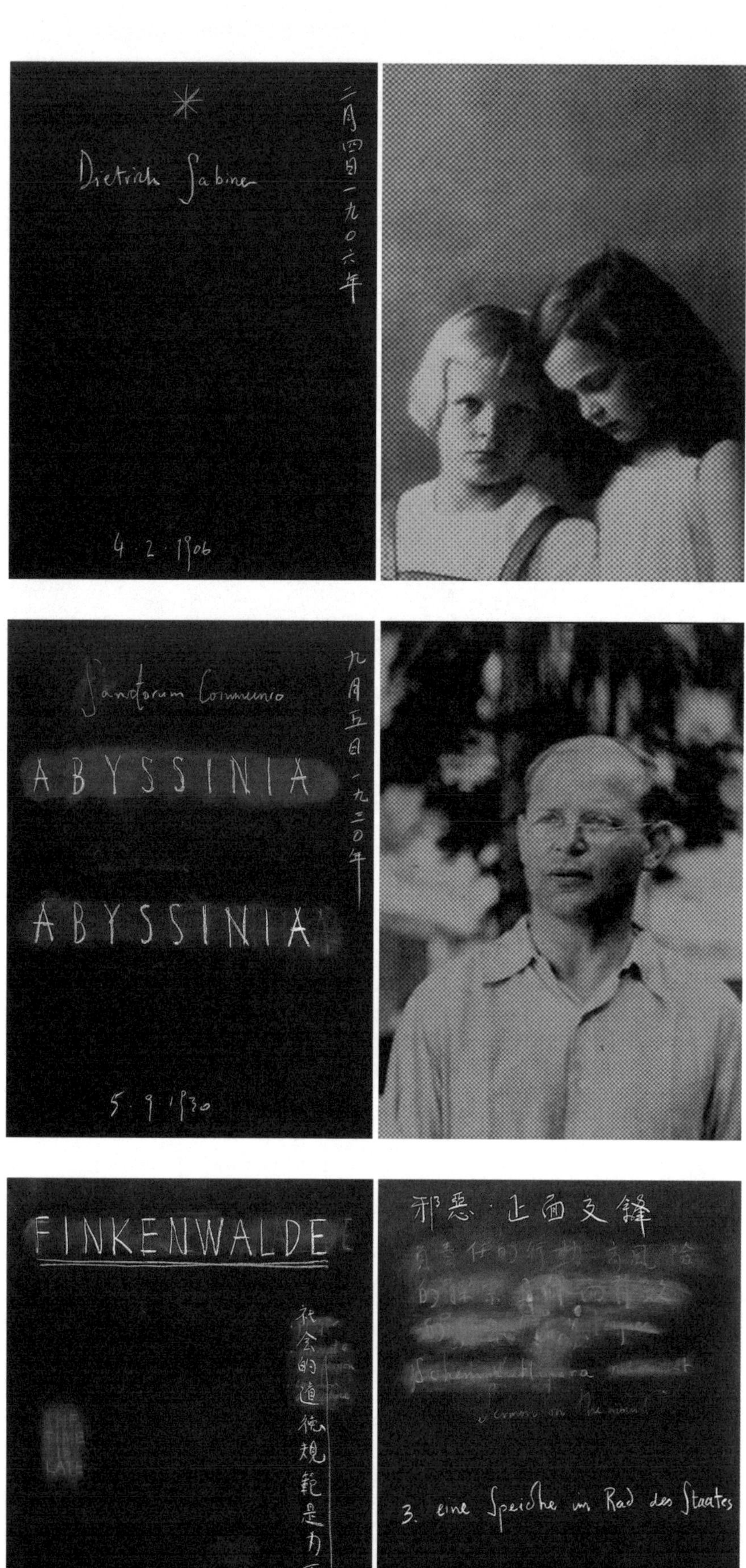

Birth; Children 2008
Harlem; Bonhoeffer 2008
Meditation; Politics 2008
Digital prints on photographic paper and
chalk on blackboard-painted archival cotton
paper, framed, 100 × 70 cm each
Collection of Erlöserkirche, Bamberg

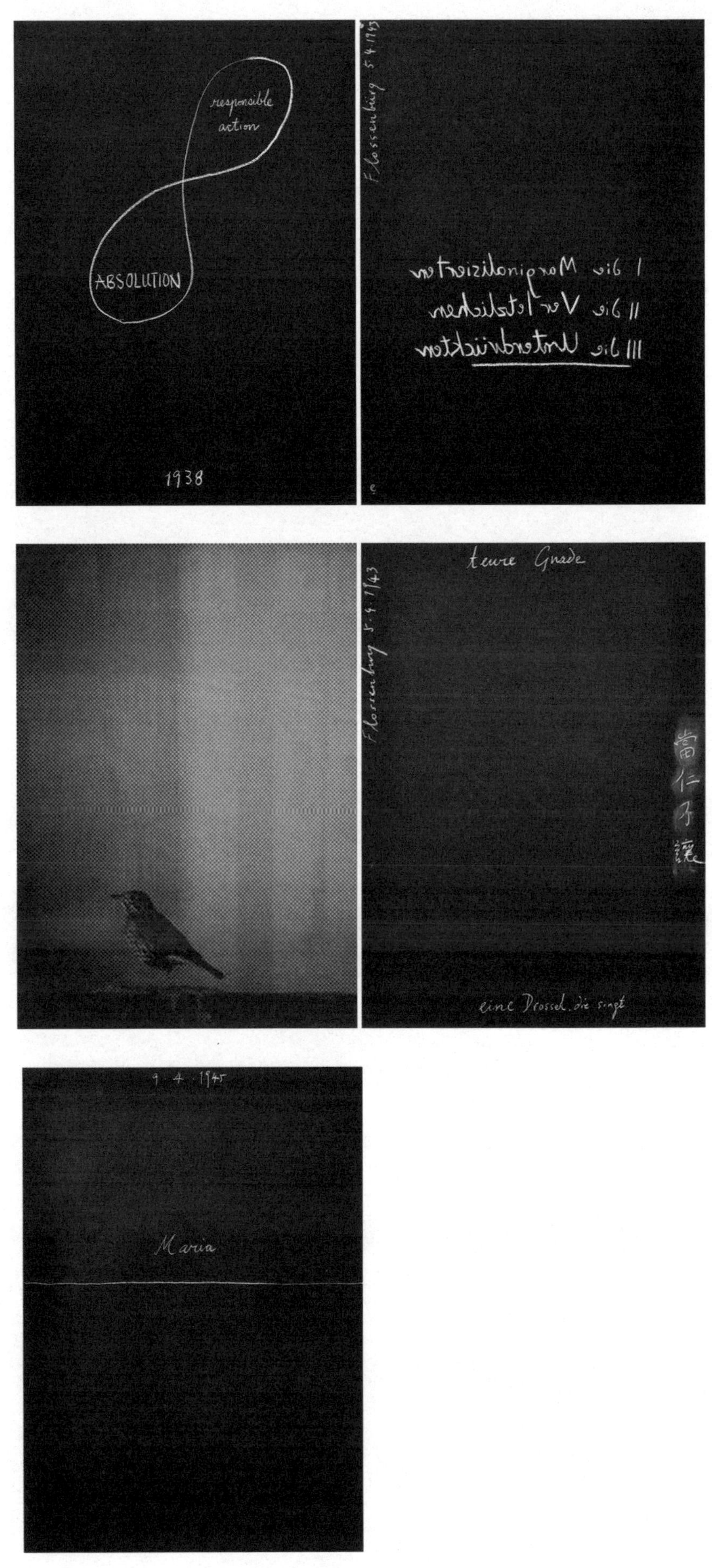

Responsible Action/Absolution; The Othered 2008
Thrush; Prison 2008
Death 2008
Digital prints on photographic paper and
chalk on blackboard-painted archival cotton
paper, framed, 100 × 70 cm each

SAFETY ZONE

2010

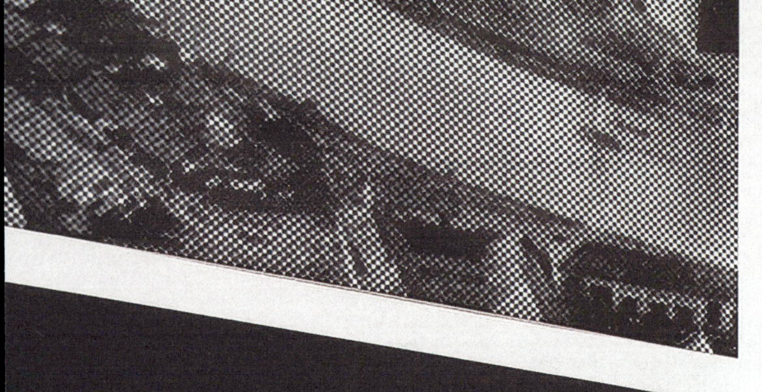

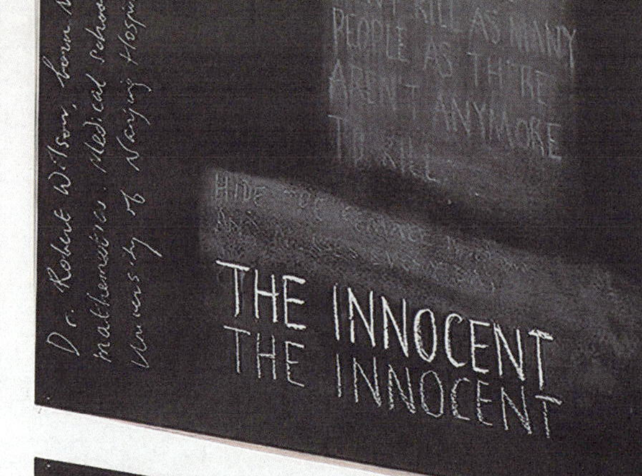

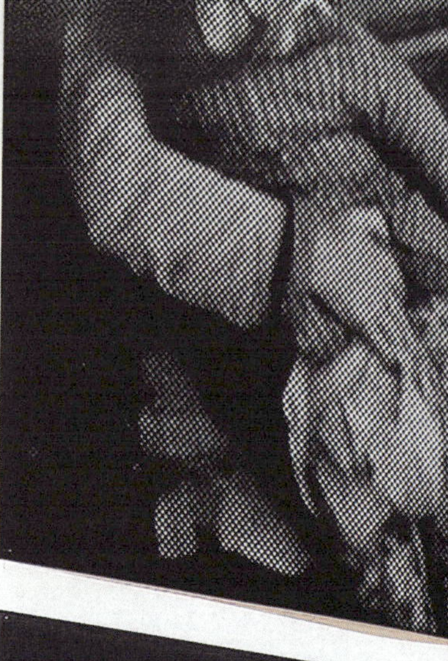

IVA HYNDS
HERBERT FORSTER
GEORGE FITCH
MINNIE VAUTRIN
GRACE BAUER
ROBERT ORY WILSON
JOHN GILLESPIE MAGEE
HUBERT LAFAYETTE SONE
WILSON PLUMMER MILLS
CLIFFORD SHARP TRIMMER
WILSON PLUMMER MILLS
NICOLAI PODSHIVOLOFF
CHARLES HENRY RIGGS
CHRISTIAN KRÖGER
AUGUSTE ZAUTIG
EDWARD SPERLING
JAMES McCALLUM
MINER SEARLE BATES
A. ZIAL
JOHN RABE
LEWIS SMYTHE

GIRLS

1. Cut your hair
2. Blacken your faces.
3. Wear men's clothes.

the refugee, the peddler,
the gardener, the carrier,
the mother, the daughter,
the child

DESERTED

BUDDHA'S
RAY

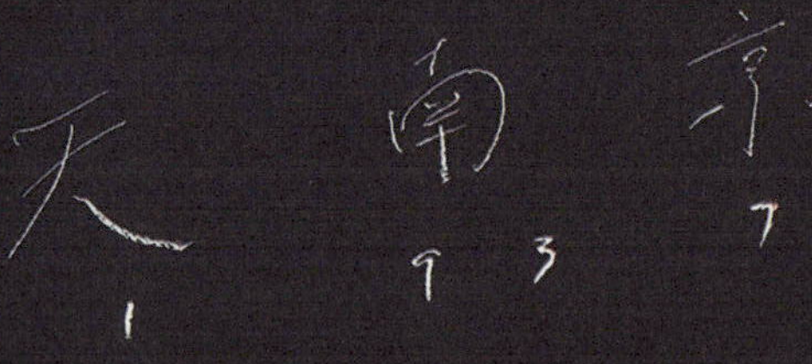

天　南　京
1　9　3　7

...in vertical holes, covered in the winter earth, for two and a half months.

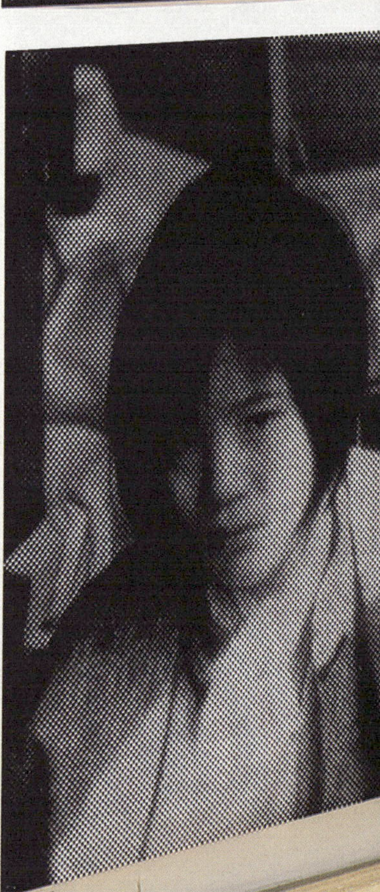

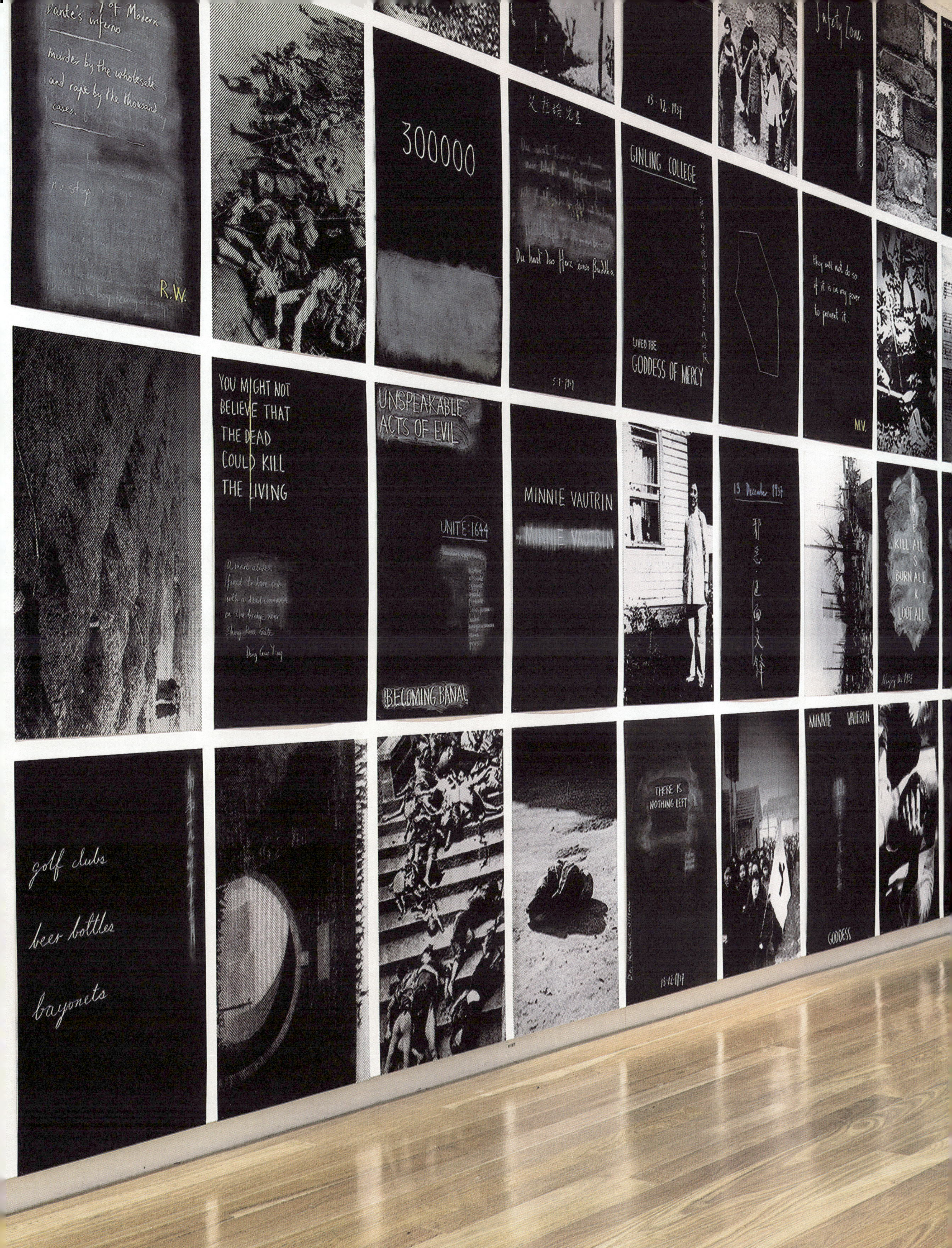
Dante's 1st Modern
murder by the wholesale
and rape by the thousand
cases.
no stop.
R.W.
300000
GINLING COLLEGE
LIVEB THE
GODDESS OF MERCY
M.V.
YOU MIGHT NOT
BELIEVE THAT
THE DEAD
COULD KILL
THE LIVING
UNSPEAKABLE
ACTS OF EVIL
UNITÉ:1644
MINNIE VAUTRIN
MINNIE VAUTRIN
13 December 1937
KILL ALL
S
BURN ALL
&
LOOT ALL
BECOMING BANAL
golf clubs
beer bottles
bayonets
THERE IS
NOTHING LEFT
MINNIE VAUTRIN
GODDESS

SAFETY ZONE

OUTLINE

Over a period of six weeks in 1937, during the second Sino-Japanese War (1937–45), Japanese Imperial troops murdered, raped and brutalised many thousands of Chinese civilians in an event known as the Rape of Nanjing. As the Japanese marched closer to Nanjing, Republican China's capital at the time, the Nationalist (Kuomintang) Government relocated inland, leaving the city's fate to an International Committee led by German businessman John Rabe. In a demonstration of great benevolence, fifteen Americans and Europeans stayed behind to establish a 3.85 square kilometre 'safety zone' to shelter local civilians, saving the lives of an estimated 200,000 Chinese people.

Young's *Safety Zone* (2010) project includes four series of work, often installed around a semi-enclosed space to create an intimate and reflective setting for the gravity of the historical event to which they refer. The centrepiece, also titled *Safety Zone*, is a monumental three-row grid installation of sixty chalkboard drawings and digital prints from archival photographs (320 × 1590 cm total). The largest of the History Projects, in one iteration it was presented, towering over the viewer, at four metres high.

Exhibited alongside this grid are three series of paintings: *Flower Market, Crippled Tree* and *St Francis of Assisi at Lao Tzu*. *Flower Market #1, #2,* and *#3* (240 × 331 cm each) combine a digitally printed background image of a flower market, photographed in Nanjing just one year prior to the massacre, with a foreground of hand-painted blossoms, tree branches and coral. Halftone dots, recalling newsprint images, are applied to the archival photographs that form the background. *Crippled Tree #1* and *#2* (274 × 183 cm each) depict the image of roughly-cut tree stumps and branches in negative colours, which are incongruously reassembled on raw linen. Finally, *St Francis of Assisi at Lao Tzu I* and *II* (320 × 151 cm each) are a pair of large-scale colour field abstracts. In these, deep tones of dark madder and brown form a sombre palette, with dimensions reminiscent of large hanging scrolls.

Reflection (2009/2022)

Synchronicity. This was how this work began. Prior to my departure for Berlin in 2008, I learnt about the story of John Rabe, the man who led the party of foreigners that harboured Chinese citizens in a 'safety zone' in Nanjing in 1937. Among the citizens that he saved, John Rabe was known as the 'Living Buddha' of China. On route to Berlin, I saw a perfectly round rainbow in the sky, a rare phenomenon that I recalled is known as 'Buddha's Ray' (佛光 *foguang*) in Chinese. This apparition prompted me to think of John Rabe, the 'Living Buddha of China'. On arrival in Berlin, this thought became all consuming, and my gallerist Alexander Ochs immediately bought me a return ticket to Heidelberg to visit Thomas Rabe, John Rabe's grandson, who holds his grandfather's archive.

For two years, the work left me emotionally threadbare. Confronted with the inadequateness and impossibility of representing this event, what was ultimately brought to the fore was the sublimity of empathy and atonement. To partake in the trauma felt by all those in the party of foreigners—who could only write about it in their diaries—I simply hoped to enter a shared space of sorrow by inscribing their words in chalk calligraphy.

The Nanjing Massacre, or the Rape of Nanjing, in 1937, was really the end point of several Chinese social historical processes. Historical events are rarely linear, cause-and-effect political directives. An event is often the culmination of ideological and historical premises set, developed, and interacted with by other forces that inevitably play out in reality. The event—the Rape of Nanjing—is witnessed in the present through its fragments; laid out in a grid, it becomes a corporeal confrontation. Yet the grid, with its ethereality, can barely be defined as an art object. It has a paradoxical quality, just like the relationship of the present to its past. The paintings that accompany the grid of drawings and photographs ripple out to form another experience, a corporeal and physical experience from a different a point of view.

TOWARDS A SITUATIONAL ETHICS:
A CORRESPONDENCE WITH
THOMAS BERGHUIS

Situational ethics was a concept developed by art historian and curator Thomas Berghuis while working on a range of projects involving artists and artist collectives whose practices not only crossed cultures and traditions, but also whose goals ultimately lay in fulfilling an ethical role for art in relation to society. For such artists, their practices constitute the social-aesthetic domain precisely by maintaining an autonomous perspective. Situational ethics was intended as an alternative or corrective to 'relational aesthetics' and challenge to the 'situational aesthetics' of 1960s conceptual art.[1]

Berghuis' essay 'The Situational Ethics of John Young' was published in *Art & Australia* in 2011. Below are edited excerpts of the email correspondence between Young and Berghuis that took place in 2010, prior to Young's solo exhibition *Safety Zone*, at Anna Schwartz Gallery in Melbourne later that year.[2]

From: JOHN YOUNG
Sent: 28 JULY 2010
To: THOMAS BERGHUIS

Hi Thomas,

I have framed a few questions (answer any of them you like!) to clear the table before we get into specifics about the *Bonhoeffer* and *Safety Zone* projects. As we agreed, it's very casual and it's between the two of us for the moment, before the actual article can be written, the only thing is that we have to leave a week or so before the deadline for the article to be edited/crafted by someone to our satisfaction before it goes to *Art and Australia*.

Cheers,
John

1. Looking at the prevalent condition of contemporary art in China—would you say that in general the notion of state resistance has moved to a co-optation of artistic practice by the state, or at least by late-capitalist forces? Do you feel this drift is moving in a more or less similar trajectory as Euro-America, or is it fast developing a radically different direction in China, even though globalised economic forces (of circulation, instantaneousness of information) are similar? Or, considering that in your book you articulated a difference between different media, that performance art would hold a different status to object-based works?

2. The authenticity in some contemporary performance art in China seems refreshing and effective compared with the 'radical superficiality' of late-capitalist art in liberal democratic states. Such 'radical superficiality' seems more than often driven by commoditisation, management and advertising discourses, and such discourses have seemingly exhausted their enquiry of the subject (of subjectivity, corporeality). Even an art investigation of the edges of consciousness, such as madness, neurosis, 'outsider's art' or other forms of social transgression, now becomes sub-cultural commodity. What seems to be left is postmodern terror (destruction of state power) and cloning (the destruction of subjectivity), and basically the disintegration of humanist values toward a posthuman condition. Within this apocalyptic, exhausted condition there have been calls for a revelatory, salvational or redemptive art practice—such as the works of Alfredo Jarr, or novels such as *The Road* by Cormac MacCarthy. What are your thoughts in response to this sentiment to recall primary 'human' values in the face of the dissolution of the ethical, since the ethical has been dissolved not through avant-gardism, but commoditisation?

3. In Australia, artists from the Chinese diaspora generally exploit icons of Chineseness to create a new space or identity for their practice. Yet if we think through transculturalism, there is a possibility that in fact the identity question vanishes, and what remains are not metaphysical Chinese values, but contradictions, paradoxes, humour.

4. In your book, you have described a trajectory in Chinese performance art whereby 'the human' as a question ceased to exist after June 4, that prior to June 4, the possibility of high art was impossible, yet after that time, performance art became the propellant to an 'art production constituting its own consumption and also capable of producing the destruction of its own utility'.[3] In other words a truly avant-garde activity which enables the destruction of iconic aesthetic values and public morals. My question to you is this: Even though this space is exceptionally useful and the activities challenge an authoritarian condition such as that in China, in the West, and specifically in Australia, we are faced with a condition where such challenges to 'assumed social morals' have become an institutional logic; that is, the avant-garde is now so institutionalised to the degree that almost everything is allowed (everything but the challenges to the institutional status quo). Can we sort of assume that a replay of universal human values now actually constitutes a challenge to the late-capitalist logic of consumption?

From: THOMAS BERGHUIS
Sent: 13 AUGUST 2010
To: JOHN YOUNG

Dear John,

Thanks for sending me these questions. First, I would like to stress the need for artists, and include the urgent need to look at individual artists and their works. In a world saturated with celebrity culture this almost seems like a paradoxical statement to make. Clearly, I don't want to highlight the celebrity status of individual artists, nor that of curators, writers, gallerists, and so on. Instead, I am hoping to point to the urgent need for art in terms of culture, society and everyday life.

Here the phrase 'urgent' may be a way of reflecting not only a form of 'insistence', but also a way of generating the 'criticality' of art—or perhaps these notions of 'urgency' and 'criticality' become even more important than art itself. For the latter (art) would inherently lead towards a return to aesthetics, whereas I feel that the 'criticality' is something that would indeed refer more to the disappearance (or as you mention 'dissolution') of the ethical. This may also relate to the prevalent condition of not only 'contemporary art in China', but also, more importantly, to contemporary society (not just in China, but elsewhere around the world as well).

In short, I would like to ask if we are starting the conversation by referring to a time of 'late capitalism' in which everything becomes a farcical evocation of something that used to be considered real history; or do we argue that tangible conditions (be it ethical, or aesthetic) can still be evoked (or provoked) by the work that we do (as artists, curators, writers, or even gallerists)? Does art still have a function? If so, what does art do? Does it prevent anything?

Next, I see how we can discuss the issue of identity, particularly as this concerns the self-invoked, or communally provoked cultural identities such as that of the Chinese artist, or Chinese Australian artist. I feel this topic is important to discuss, as it becomes used by so many to generate a 'hyphen' around something that could easily distract from some of the real issues—maybe similar to naming someone a 'political artist'. One of the real issues at stake here may be 'displacement', where cultures become displaced, but also individuals become displaced in society, especially in a global society like ours. Some of the 'grand narratives' would speak of 'melancholy', or of 'nostalgia', which can be juxtaposed by parody and cynicism, as a form of resistance. But, looking more closely, we are often left with 'recollecting', 'memory' (as well as 'amnesia')—a need to try to put some of the puzzle pieces back together, which we lose as we grow older and as time progresses too quickly. These ideas of 'displacement' and 'amnesia' can maybe also be linked to contemporary society, which tends to erase itself as it progresses towards a consumer culture.

Hence, 'displacement' and 'disappearance' may be some of the leitmotifs on which to build this conversation, and asking the question of what artists and writers can do to bring back some recollections that are needed to survive in the abyss of culture, society, and identity? Here, your pointing at the ethical dimension could be an important point for discussion, but perhaps the aesthetic dimension also needs to be put into play—how would the aesthetic dimension operate beyond Chineseness, as the exotic, the mysterious, the majestic? What about the ethical and aesthetic dimensions of realism in China?

Here, we can also look at the comment made by Mao in 1917, on the importance of physical education, which I refer to at the start of my book on performance art in China, when he postulated that 'in order to civilise the mind one must first make savage the body'.[4] This seems to be a pointing at a different aesthetic than the 'exotic' and indeed could point at the less exotic characteristics of Chinese modernity and aesthetics, including through looking at the work of Lu Xun. Also, on the level of personal experiences of having lived and worked in China, I also became interested in the concept of 忍 (ren3) endurance, sufferance, forbearance; next to 仁 (ren2) humaneness, benevolence, kindness. Maybe these are important concepts to bring into our conversation, do you think?

Okay, that is it for now. I am not sure if I actually answered your questions, although I have unconsciously been reflecting upon them. More important, I have aimed to keep an eye on some of the important points that we discussed previously, particularly in relation to *your* work.

Best regards,
Thomas

From: JOHN YOUNG
Sent: 13 AUGUST 2010
To: THOMAS BERGHUIS

[Editor's Note: Here Young responds in-line to points from Berghuis' earlier email.]

TB

Thanks for sending me these questions. First, I would like to stress the need for artists, and include the urgent need to look at individual artists and their works. In a world saturated with celebrity culture this almost seems like a paradoxical statement to make. Clearly, I don't want to highlight the celebrity status of individual artists, nor that of curators, writers, gallerists, and so on. Instead, I am hoping to point to the urgent need for art in terms of culture, society and everyday life.

Here the phrase 'urgent' may be a way of reflecting not only a form of 'insistence', but also a way of generating the 'criticality' of art—or perhaps these notions of 'urgency' and 'criticality' become even more important than art itself. For the latter (art) would inherently lead towards a return to aesthetics, whereas I feel that the 'criticality' is something that would indeed refer more to the disappearance (or as you mention 'dissolution') of the ethical. This may also relate to the prevalent condition of not only 'contemporary art in China', but also, more importantly, to contemporary society (not just in China, but elsewhere around the world as well).

In short, I would like to ask if we are starting the conversation by referring to a time of 'late capitalism' in which everything becomes a farcical evocation of something that used to be considered real history; or do we argue that tangible conditions (be it ethical, or aesthetic) can still be evoked (or provoked) by the work that we do (as artists, curators, writers, or even gallerists)? Does art still have a function? If so, what does art do? Does it prevent anything?

JY

Your notion of disappearance of the aesthetic and ethical realm is an interesting one. I recall that Wittgenstein, early in the twentieth century, in his dissertation *Tractatus Logico Philosophicus*, adhered strictly to Kant's tradition by claiming that ethics and aesthetics are one (as a matter of interest, this text was translated into Chinese very early on). In less than a century, the very disappearance of the backbone of Western culture seems imminent. [Jean] Baudrillard is not read but felt in our everyday negotiations. However, I do not now wish to take the position, much like a climate-change doomsayer, that the disappearance is inevitable, nor of course like a climate-change denier—but simply, that we can do something about it.

Both *Bonhoeffer in Harlem* and *Safety Zone*, although both based on historic evidence, were never constructed as documentaries. I merely utilised the didactic character of historic documents—like how the chalk drawings are didactic—to deliver a sort of timely lyric epic of horror. In doing so, it may evoke a redemptive will in us; not so much a deliverance from sin, but a protection from damnation (apocalypse). I am halfway a Westerner, so perhaps there is some fascination in me (still) that the Greeks considered the best content as tragedy, and when we think of the tragic, we think of catharsis.

TB

Next, I see how we can discuss the issue of identity, particularly as this concerns the self-invoked, or communally provoked cultural identities such as that of the Chinese artist, or Chinese Australian artist. I feel this topic is important to discuss, as it becomes used by so many to generate a 'hyphen' around something that could easily distract from some of the real issues—maybe similar to naming someone a 'political artist'.

JY

Well, in these two projects, I had absolutely NO intention of being political, or a political artist. I guess I am too doubtful about the capacity of the social sciences to take 'the social' or 'the everyday' seriously. An epoch's mood is more of interest (well, there has always been a *fin de siècle* mood that allowed many to put a bullet through their heads in Vienna). But I feel the mood of the present, at least in the art world, has been fuelled for many decades by Duchamp's cynicism, which has now been dovetailed with extreme consumerism. Both these aspects contribute towards an annihilation of feeling by sensation and the spectacle.

The contemporary icon, as W.J.T. Mitchell suggests, is the 9/11 World Trade Centre terrorist image—it is an image of an old icon (the skyscraper) being annihilated (plane crashing into it). I'm trying to suggest here that this image of annihilation is not so different to Duchamp's *LHOOQ* (1919).

> **TB**
>
> *One of the real issues at stake here may be 'displacement', where cultures become displaced, but also individuals become displaced in society, especially in a global society like ours. Some of the 'grand narratives' would speak of 'melancholy', or of 'nostalgia', which can be juxtaposed by parody and cynicism, as a form of resistance. But, looking more closely, we are often left with 'recollecting', 'memory' (as well as 'amnesia')—a need to try to put some of the puzzle pieces back together, which we lose as we grow older and as time progresses too quickly. These ideas of 'displacement' and 'amnesia' can maybe also be linked to contemporary society, which tends to erase itself as it progresses towards a consumer culture.*

JY

The amnesia seems like the logic of consumer culture, but don't forget it's also the logic of the avant-garde! Yet one asks us to change for the better, and the other just asks us to buy.

> **TB**
>
> *Hence, 'displacement' and 'disappearance' may be some of the leitmotifs on which to build this conversation, and asking the question of what artists and writers can do to bring back some recollections that are needed to survive in the abyss of culture, society, and identity? Here, your pointing at the ethical dimension could be an important point for discussion, but perhaps the aesthetic dimension also needs to be put into play—how would the aesthetic dimension operate beyond Chineseness, as the exotic, the mysterious, the majestic. What about the ethical and aesthetic dimensions of realism in China?*

JY

Very, very interesting.

> **TB**
>
> *Here, we can also look at the comment made by Mao in 1917 on the importance of physical education, which I refer to at the start of my book on performance art in China, when he postulated that 'in order to civilise the mind one must first make savage the body'. This seems to be pointing to a different aesthetic than the 'exotic' and indeed could point at the less exotic characteristics of Chinese modernity and aesthetics—including through looking at the work of Lu Xun. Also on the level of personal experiences of having lived and worked in China...*

JY

Funny, I have also been thinking of Lu Xun; give me a day or so to reply to this aspect. I need to think about this one, and also the following concepts you introduce may be a great way to short circuit the 'apocalyptic–disappearance' impasse.

Cheers,
John

From: JOHN YOUNG
Sent: 18 AUGUST 2010
To: THOMAS BERGHUIS

Hi Thomas,

How is your *Third Text* paper going?

On your arrival back to Sydney on the 23rd, I guess there is about at most two weeks before we have to submit the 1300 words. I am selecting the images and having them recomposed for the article this week and next, and will send them to you and see which ones you would definitely like in.

Just a few notes for the essay—

1. I hope at the beginning, I'm sure you have to give a few lines of description of the two projects, it is possible to also say that the initial premise and impetus for these two projects was to explore an ethical dimension—with events that have enabled people to act in ethical ways when they cross culture. This came with my growing scepticism towards the discourse of transcultural identity. Whilst the melancholia associated with cross-cultural existence is indeed poignant, both intellectually and emotionally (as identified in my many years of interest following the geopoetic writings of Kenneth White), there was a need to search for an active principle, which I believe I have found in these projects.

2. It was the gallerist Alexander Ochs who encouraged me to look at Bonhoeffer, and it was also a series of synchronic events and apparitions that edged me more and more towards looking at the Nanjing event in 1937. (For your reference: Sylvia Volz's essay in the *Bonhoeffer in Harlem* book, attached below, and Ulrike Muenter's essay in the *Asia Pacific Times*, also attached below).[5]

3a. *Bonhoeffer in Harlem* was life changing for me, as this work was done outside the conventional art frame or context. It was held at St Matthäus, at the Kulturforum, where, historically, Albert Speer was to build Germania. So, the introduction of a completely cross-cultural work (Afro–Abyssinian–Chinese–Tibetan–Australian) and event (we flew in a Harlem jazz singer and the school of hard knocks (homeless) choir of Berlin) within a monocultural context of this Bach-singing Lutheran church shifted the cultural frame of this site significantly.

3b. *Safety Zone*, initially conceived as an account of cross-cultural heroism, became a show regarding our new Dada—desertion, amnesia, disappearance and apocalypse!—in a wider sense of modernity's disappearance and the apocalypse of art as we know it. Even the *pinghua* [6] of Lu Xun is barely possible, perhaps what may be possible is Lu Xun's 'appropriationism'[7], this time to appropriate concepts such as *ren3* [忍] and *ren2* [仁], as you suggest, or even *shi* [勢] (from Francois Jullien's *The Propensity of Things*), which apparently indicates 'a kind of potential that originates not in the human initiative but instead results from the very disposition of things … instead of always imposing our own longing for meaning on reality, let us open ourselves to this immanent force and learn to seize it'.[8]

Hope this is OK …
Cheers,
John

From: THOMAS BERGHUIS
Sent: 28 AUGUST 2010
To: JOHN YOUNG

Dear John,

Good to hear Carolyn Barnes will assist us with copyediting the piece. It is a bit of a shame that we didn't have more time for the conversation—I should maybe travel to Melbourne. For now, I hope you allow me to shoot off some questions that I feel would add some important context to the text.

The project outlines look fine, and I have got a good insight into the aspects of the two projects that can be drawn out in the text. However, I am starting to become interested in the way you perceive these projects in the larger context of contemporary art today, and what type of role you perceive artists to undertake?

The contemporary art world is a strange and interesting phenomenon. On the one hand, there is a lot of writing (including curatorial) on engagement, collaboration, process, and extending art into a public function. In my essay for *Third Text*, I am also looking at how the art world frequently talks about making worlds out of art, but there doesn't seem to be much spoken about making art out of the world.[9] How would you perceive your work in relation to the art world vis-à-vis, let's say, the role of the artist in producing art?

Is there a particular way in which the world of contemporary art offers new ways of producing art, and extending it into other areas—social, historical, political, aesthetic? What is the role of the gallery, museum, exhibition vis-à-vis other platforms (including sites outside the art institution)? Is it important for these projects to connect to these sites? What about public engagement and the broader social function of art? The historicity of art in relation to society would also be a point about which I would be interested in hearing some of your thoughts.

I am sure that you would also have some views about other artists and projects that you feel are providing important examples in making people aware of some of the important issues relating to contemporary art. I recall in an earlier email you mentioned one or two, but I can't recall which ones. Could you elaborate a bit on where you feel artists around the world are making a clear difference and in what way? What about the role of curators in working with artists? Also, what type of platforms do artists need to work? I am hoping you can draw out examples on an international level, but also reflect a bit on Australia and whether you feel the art world here is taking enough opportunity to link itself to developments elsewhere, or whether (following comments made by some in the past) Australia may be too parochial to deal meaningfully with culture or too provincial (also see my reflection on this comment in *Broadsheet*, 'Becoming Australia(n)').[10]

It would also be interesting to read your ideas about the role of collaboration? Finally, what about the role and position of the studio, including the way you move your work as an artist into working within the context of the contemporary artist studio (which may be different from the modern concept of the atelier)? Besides working with assistants, is there an extended role of the studio, in terms of collaboration? I am also interested in looking at your role as an educator and the way you work with students?

By covering some of these questions I am hoping that we can draw out a bit more understanding of the process behind works such as *Bonhoeffer* and *Safety Zone*, in order to bring better understanding to these projects and the conceptual thinking behind them. Here it would also be useful to elaborate a bit more on the ethical dimension (below). Do we relate this to Badiou as well? Or in deliberation to the role of art in relation to aesthetics, going back to Schiller and Kant?

In the past I have also hinted at linking the proposition of 'relational aesthetics' ([Nicolas] Bourriaud reinventing the idea that art needs to be communicative) to 'situational ethics'. I still need to work this out, but maybe it means something like what happens if art crosses into culture, society and everyday life and the politics, reality and truth of human interaction? Besides art producing the world, can the world produce art? Can art solve ethical questions that concern culture, society, politics and history? Can artists draw from the past to re-envision a better future and make

people aware in the present, and in their present encounter of the work? How do artists move the demand for the immediacy
of encounter (which may entail the demand from audiences for something spectacular) to establishing a more intimate, durable experience in which audiences reflect on a multiplicity of layering behind the work, its process and extension into the time of reflection when it is exhibited?

Sorry John, I realise these are many questions to consider, but I would find it interesting if we could incorporate some reflections on these, where the 1300-word essay for *A&A* could be treated as a starting point to continue writing a much bigger piece that can be used elsewhere. This I would find interesting, as it would allow us to position your work in art history.

Best regards,
Thomas

From: JOHN YOUNG
Sent: 31 AUGUST 2010
To: THOMAS BERGHUIS

Hi Thomas,

So here it is, some answers to your questions. I appreciate that you asked me these questions to clarify my philosophical position. How I've answered you may lead to lots of other questions, but at least it will give you an idea of the philosophical grounding and perspective to the two projects.

I still feel it is very important to describe the two projects first, as nobody in Australia (except Kevin Rudd!) has seen *Bonhoeffer in Harlem*. Secondly, these projects are a new departure from my previous works up until 2005. As you will see, my philosophical position, especially on the art world and its mechanisms, is essentially pessimistic, so it's up to you how you interplay these two projects with my general philosophical position.

For convenience, the points I feel are important to describe initially … (these are the points I've already sent you)

At the beginning, I'm sure you have to give a few lines of description of the two projects; is it possible to also say that the initial premise and impetus for these two projects was to explore an ethical dimension, with events which have enabled people to act in ethical ways when they cross culture […]

[Editor's Note: Here, Young reiterates the key points (1, 2, 3a, 3b) presented in the earlier message of 18 August.]

Now for some answers to your questions regarding my overall views of contemporary art.

TB
The project outlines look fine, and I have got a good insight into the aspects of the two projects that can be drawn out in the text. However, I am starting to become interested in the way you perceive these projects in the larger context of contemporary art today, and what type of role you perceive artists to undertake?

The contemporary art world is a strange and interesting phenomenon. On the one hand there is a lot of writing (including curatorial) on engagement, collaboration, process, and extending art into a public function. In my essay for Third Text *I am also looking at how the art world frequently talks about making worlds out of art, but there doesn't seem to be much spoken about making art out of the world. How would you perceive your work in relation to the art world vis-à-vis, let's say the role of the artist in producing art?*

JY
I find much talk about engagement, collaboration, process, and so on, in the art and curatorial world often finally comes down to one word: management. In a wider perspective, talk about making worlds out of art (presumably the art world or practice) is a rather quaint modernist ideal. In Western modernism, worlds have always been triumphantly made out of art—from Constructivism to Surrealism. Yet through our discussion, I feel the conditions now have really changed, especially when you also brought up the subject of disappearance. In 1981, I wrote an essay for *Art & Text* journal titled 'On Some Alternatives to the Code in the Age of Hyperreality'.[11] This essay was one of the earlier introductions to Baudrillard's notion of indifference and disappearance of values, and the essay introduced this to the Australian art world.[12] This was almost thirty years ago! Yet the era of indifference, disappearance and speed surely has not simply gone away.

If anything, we can now say that since speed ([Paul] Virilio)[13] has exploded values, as well as time, in our era, what is at stake in this age of indifference and speed is a politics of melancholy. By that I mean a melancholy for bygone stories, memories for bygone allegories and values. My position is to make art out of a world of forgotten stories, discarded objects, earlier memories, so to speak. Making art means to remember these stories and values in an era of techno indifference and impoverished irresponsibility. That is why I'm a great admirer of Cormac McCarthy's fable *The Road* [2006]—a simple resistance, a passive endurance in an apocalyptic era.

At present, to honestly answer your question about my work's relation to the art world—from the widest philosophical perspective (of course not in the practical professional context)—I find I can't really see my work in relation to the art world, since in many senses, this world has in fact disappeared (rather than say, 'expanded' or 'globalised'). That is, the art world of cultural values and aesthetic ideals, the world you so aptly characterised as of Kant and Schiller, maybe even down to Sartre.

> **TB**
>
> *Is there a particular way in which the world of contemporary art offers new ways of producing art, and extending it into other areas—social, historical, political, aesthetic? What is the role of the gallery, museum, exhibition vis-à-vis other platforms (including sites outside the art institution)? Is it important for these projects to connect to these sites? What about public engagement and the broader social function of art? The historicity of art in relation to society would also be a point about which I would be interested in hearing some of your thoughts.*

JY

I do not wish to answer you with arrogance, and of course, for example with the *Bonhoeffer in Harlem* project, I felt great elation in the fact that it worked outside the conventional museum world, that it actually changed the cultural frame of a critically symbolic monocultural site, but then the introduction of a totally cross cultural work really felt like a bit of a triumph in terms of broadening art's social function.

Yet, against this is a background of my feelings and comprehension about contemporary art, which is actually a lot more pessimistic, especially when you look at contemporary art practice in relation to biotechnology and info-technology. I really feel that contemporary art is made up of 'dis-organisations' that interpenetrate many other areas, yet it tends to innovate, much like other techno-disciplines, like design or architecture, with a politics of irresponsibility. Within the era of speed (Virilio) these art projects' very rationale is indeed not values, but interconnectivity to other sites, and with accelerating speed. This is the apocalyptic social function of what is considered as contemporary art practice: to make value, time, memory disappear through speed and connectivity. Connectivity between bio-techs and info-techs, between 'humans' and non-humans.

> **TB**
>
> *I am sure that you would also have some views about other artists and projects that you feel are providing important examples in making people aware of some of the important issues relating to contemporary art. I recall in an earlier email you mentioned one or two, but I can't recall which ones. Could you elaborate a bit on where you feel artists around the world are making a clear difference and in what way?*

JY

I really empathise with the work of Alfredo Jarr; there was a truly felt, ethical dimension, especially with the works regarding South American gold-mining slavery.[14] Also the work of the architect [Daniel] Libeskind, even when I don't necessarily always agree with his politics.

I'm not too sure if the art will ever make people aware of some important issue. Perhaps the only thing I hope to do is to retell some old stories—stories and values that have always been around up until now ... Both *Bonhoeffer in Harlem* and *Safety Zone* recall existential heroes; these heroes belonged to the era of time and value. Their ethical values are noble politics, are the good life, not dissimilar to the values *ren3* [忍] and *ren2* [仁]. Now, in the era of indifference, disappearance and speed, my attempts at the recounting of these stories—stories of existential heroes—is merely a melancholic inability to forget certain values. But it may turn out to be an important inability.

In *The Road*, the survivors of the apocalypse—a father and his son, pushing a trolly—spell out only one crucial value making them different from the others, who are cannibals. The son says to the father:

We wouldn't ever eat anybody, would we?
No. Of course not.
Even if we were starving?
We're starving now.
You said we weren't.
I said we weren't dying. I didn't say we weren't starving.
But we wouldn't.
No. We wouldn't.
No matter what.
No. No matter what.
Because we're the good guys.
Yes.
And we're carrying the fire.
And we're carrying the fire. Yes.
Okay.[15]

That's it, that's all!

> **TB**
> *What about the role of curators in working with artists? Also, what type of platforms do
> artists need to work? Here I am hoping you can draw out examples on an international
> level, but also reflect a bit on Australia and whether you feel the art world here is taking
> enough opportunity to link itself to developments elsewhere, or whether (following
> comments made by some in the past) Australia may be too parochial to deal meaningfully
> with culture or too provincial (also see my reflection on this comment in Broadsheet,
> 'Becoming Australia(n)').*

JY
In the 80s, artist [Francesco] Clemente already said the curators are the artists of today … If you look at the exercise of new ideas and dissemination of cultural effects, yes—the curator is far more efficient an artist than the old sort of artist. Yet, we remember, the role of an artist traditionally was one of resistance, not of the exercise of power and dissemination.

Australia is still dealing with its recent, gigantic colonial past. It seemed like just yesterday the country formulated its myth of colonial invasion—'terra nullius', the inhospitable outback ([Sidney] Nolan, [Albert] Tucker). The art world here is still finding their natural white artists who have an *a priori* feel for the land (and thus of sovereignty). The AGNSW's major thematic for collecting paintings of Australian artists is still 'the figure in the landscape', why landscape? Because it finally means—symbolic sovereignty of the land. Yet, virtually every single Indigenous painting is a landscape, but they are put under a different category—this is an issue of the legal and of power, not of the aesthetic.

John

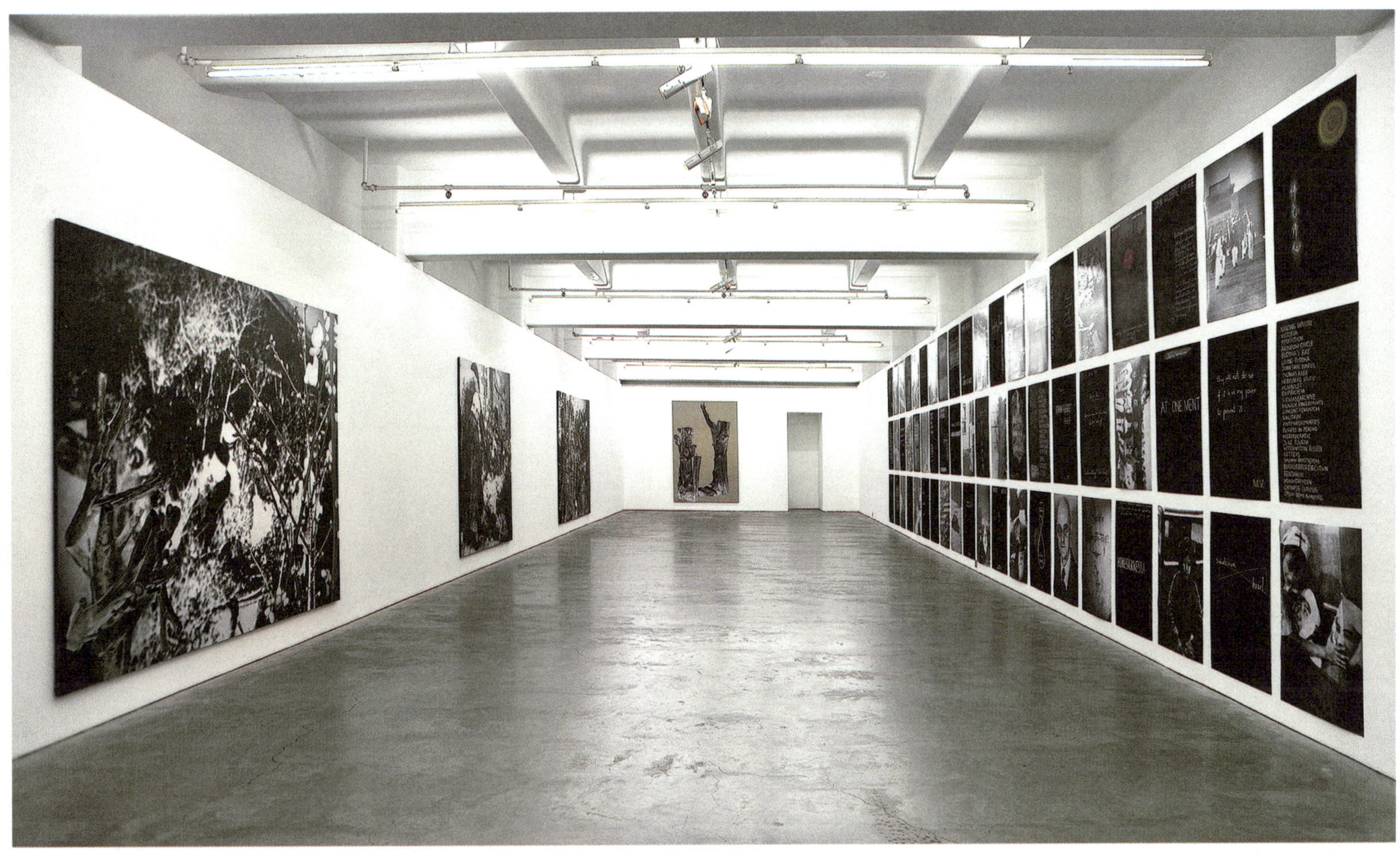

1. See Nicolas Bourriaud, *Relational Aesthetics*, trans. Simon Pleasance and Fronza Woods, Les Presses du Réel, Dijon, [1998] 2002; and Victor Burgin, 'Situational Aesthetics', *Studio International*, vol. 178, no. 915, October 1969, pp. 118–21.

2. Thomas Berghuis, 'The Situational Ethics of John Young', *Art and Australia*, vol. 48, no. 3, Autumn 2011, pp. 440–43.

3. Thomas Berghuis, *Performance Art in China*, Timezone 8, Hong Kong, 2006, p. 9.

4. Mao Zedong, 'A Study of Physical Education', originally published in the April 1917 issue of *New Youth* (Xin Qingnian) magazine; see Stuart Schram (ed.), *Mao's Road to Power: Revolutionary Writings, 1912–1949*, M. E. Sharpe, New York, 1992, volume 1, p. 119.

5. See Volz's expanded essay in this volume, pp. 92–99.

6. 平話 *(pinghua)*, literally 'common speech', refers here to the more vernacular or spoken style of written Chinese for which Chinese writer Lu Xun (1881–1936) was well known.

7. A reference to the title of a famous 1934 essay by Lu Xun, titled 拿來主義 *(nalaizhuyi)*, sometimes translated as 'Grabism', a phrase coined by Lu to humorously describe the selective appropriation of useful foreign ideas and practices in China.

8. François Jullien, *The Propensity of Things: Toward a History of Efficacy in China*, Janet Lloyd (transl.), Zone Books, New York, 1999, p. 13.

9. Thomas Berghuis, 'ruangrupa: What could be "Art to Come"', *Third Text*, vol. 25, no. 4, 2011, pp. 395–407.

10. Thomas Berghuis, 'to become Australia(n)', *Broadsheet: Contemporary Visual Arts + Culture*, vol. 37, no. 3, 2008, pp. 188–91.

11. John Young and Terry Blake, 'On Some Alternatives to the Code in the Age of Hyperreality: The hermit and the city dweller', *Art + Text*, issue 2, Winter 1981, pp. 4–17.

12. Primarily in reference to Jean Baudrillard, *L'Effet Beaubourg: Implosion et dissuasion (*The Beaubourg Effect: Implosion and Deterrence*),* Éditions Galilée, Paris, 1977.

13. A reference to Paul Virilio's work, such as *Speed and Politics* (first published in French, 1977, and in English translation, 1986).

14. See for example Alfredo Jarr, *1+1+1* (1987), installation of three silver dye transparencies, three light boxes, gilded frames and mirrors, 127 × 487.7 × 182.9 cm, collection of the Art Institute of Chicago. https://www.artic.edu/artworks/146911/1-1-1.

15. Cormac McCarthy, *The Road*, Knopf, New York, 2006, pp. 128–29.

Safety Zone 2010
Installation view, Anna Schwartz Gallery, Melbourne, 2010

THE SITUATIONAL ETHICS OF JOHN YOUNG (2011)[1]

Thomas Berghuis

The role of an artist should ideally incorporate that of a teacher. At the very least, when confronting ceaseless change in society, it is important that an artist's work should include a didactic dimension. Some people today might fail to notice the shared past that stares at us from history's rear-view mirror, and its reflection on our present life may be much closer than we think.

In John Young's work, ethical systems generate the object and materials of art making through time and space. More than transcultural, the recent works of Young are, in fact, transhistorical. They link objects in real time and space to transhistorical time and space, essentially allowing the viewer to time-travel. For Young, the speed brought about by globalisation can generate a sense of ethical indifference. Alternatively, it can lead to an explosion of values and sentiments, leaving a 'politics of melancholy' in its wake.[2] Young sees a role for art in linking the present to 'a world of forgotten stories, discarded objects, and memories'. As he explains, 'making art not only means to recollect stories, but to reawaken an intrinsic ethical impulse in the present'. This ethical impulse generates a sensory experience across time and space.

Two of Young's earlier projects, *Bonhoeffer in Harlem* (2009) and *Safety Zone* (2010), reflect Young's growing skepticism towards the discourse of transcultural identity and highlight this important new impulse at play in his work. This shift in the artist's practice has prompted an exploration of stories that 'situate ethics and moral judgment within the context of crossing from one culture into another', articulating an important notion of situational ethics that is dependent on the crossings of different cultures rather than on a universal moral code.

As a Hong Kong Australian artist, Young has experienced the state of melancholy associated with cross-cultural existence, which he feels is 'indeed poignant, both intellectually and emotionally'. His experience draws him to literary sources such as the geopoetic writings of Kenneth White, which he has read over many years. Yet Young is also conscious of the need to move beyond such a state of loss and 'search for an active principle' in engaging the ethical dimension of cross-cultural exchange for individuals, groups and societies. Young believes he has found this active principle in his two most recent projects.

Young conceived *Bonhoeffer in Harlem* while speaking with his German gallerist Alexander Ochs, during a 2007 visit to Berlin. Young recalls how Ochs encouraged him to look at the case of Dietrich Bonhoeffer (1906–1945), a Lutheran pastor and the chief protagonist in a lost story of the Second World War. Before his 1931 ordination in Berlin, Bonhoeffer spent a year in New York, teaching Bible studies to local African American women while assisting at Harlem's Abyssinian

Baptist Church. Here Bonhoeffer wrote about the need for strong opposition to racial divisions in the United States of America and, on returning to Germany, further revealed his strong moral conviction by defying Hitler's rise to power. When the Second World War broke out, Bonhoeffer remained to work for the German Resistance until his arrest in 1943. He was sent to Flossenbürg Concentration Camp and executed on 9 April 1945.

Preparing for the 2009 exhibition (which was staged at Berlin's St Matthäus Church where Bonhoeffer was ordained and which now forms part of the city's cultural precinct, Kulturforum) was a life-changing experience for Young, pointing in particular to ways of working in art 'outside of the conventional art frame or context'. In delving into Bonhoeffer's life, what unfolded for Young was a series of synchronistic events and apparitions that led him to discover another lost story—this time to do with the Japanese invasion of the Chinese city of Nanjing in 1937. In the six weeks following the 13 December invasion, Japanese troops killed an estimated 250,000 Chinese citizens in what has become known as the Nanjing Massacre.

In the resulting exhibition *Safety Zone* (presented at Anna Schwartz Gallery, Melbourne, in 2010), Young explored the intrinsic 'ethical dimension' behind the forgotten story of another German figure, John Rabe (1882–1950). A member of the Nazi Party who was stationed on business in Nanjing in 1937, Rabe, together with the American missionary Minnie Vautrin, led a group of around twenty foreigners who attempted to create a safety zone to protect the city's citizens from the Japanese.

Bonhoeffer in Harlem and *Safety Zone* both feature a series of chalk drawings on blackboard paint-covered paper. Here Young makes a reference to the 1970s blackboard drawings of Joseph Beuys and Rudolf Steiner's blackboard lectures following the First World War – a connection already made by Allison Holland's exhibition at Melbourne's National Gallery of Victoria, *Imagination, Inspiration, Intuition: Joseph Beuys & George Steiner* (2007–08).

Once an important tool for teaching, the blackboard underscores the vital didactic dimension of Young's recent work. Presented with texts in Chinese, English and German, most viewers would experience nostalgia towards a vanishing medium now largely replaced by digital media. The blackboard was arguably the primary didactic medium of the twentieth century—it is impossible to calculate the number of important ideas that would have been worked out and shared on this medium during this time. Furthermore, blackboard and chalk bring together writing and drawing, allowing quick erasure and thus offering an ideal metaphor for Young's recent explorations on the theme of disappearance and loss.

In both projects, *Safety Zone* and *Bonhoeffer in Harlem*, Young combines blackboard drawings with digital inkjet prints and painting or tapestry. Each visual element evokes the search for a 'principle' in the process of recollecting and retracing lost memories. The combination of these media relates the artist's inherently pessimistic view of the contemporary interconnectivity of art, medium and technology. As Young explains:

> *Safety Zone* was initially conceived as an account of cross-cultural heroism, but it became a project that can be related to our contemporary dada— linked to desertion, amnesia, disappearance and the apocalypse; including in a wider sense modernity's disappearance and the apocalypse of art as we know it.

With *Bonhoeffer in Harlem* and *Safety Zone*, Young offers a valuable insight to the art world, particularly as it looks for ways to link itself to the world at large. Contemporary art's recent focus on relational aesthetics provides little real function to art except to highlight the role of art as a medium for communication. To identify an actual role for an art grounded in communication, Young suggests, artists need to take on a more didactic approach. This includes exploring the important ethical dimension in forgotten stories and resituating these within the present. Witnessed by Young's projects, the act of crossing culture could be seen as a crucial vehicle in exploring our ethical impulse through the active principle of art.

Starting in 2015, John Young has taken on forgotten histories of Chinese in Australia as the main subject of his History Projects, comprising works such as *1866: The Worlds of Lowe Kong Meng and Jong Ah Siug* (2015), *Open Monument* (2015) for the City of Ballarat, and *The Burrangong Affray* (2018). These works continue part of the situational ethics described in relation to the earlier history projects in 2009 and 2010. However, these more recent projects come to link a cross-cultural experience that is more country specific and less transhistorical and transcultural.

1. This essay is a republication of Thomas Berghuis, 'The Situational Ethics of John Young', *Art and Australia*, vol. 48, no. 3, Autumn 2011, pp. 440–3.

2. John Young, email correspondence with the author, 31 August 2010. All quotes in the article are from this correspondence. Some of the longer correspondence between Young and Berghuis is edited and published for the first time in this volume, see pp. 122–32.

A NEW INTRODUCTION TO 'DIASPORA, ART & EMPATHY' (2013)

Jacqueline Lo

Diasporas emerge through losses that have happened but that also define the future. Drawing on Homi Bhabha's concept of the unhomely, Lily Cho describes the state of diasporic consciousness thus:

> To live in diaspora is to be haunted by histories that sit uncomfortably out of joint, ambivalently ahead of their time and yet behind it too. It is to feel a small tingle on the skin at the back of your neck and know that something is not quite right about where you are now, but to know also that you cannot leave. To be un-homed is a process. To be unhomely is a state of diasporic consciousness.[1]

Diasporic subjectivity is thus marked by a specific ambivalent temporality characterised by being out of joint, neither before nor after an event, haunted by the pastness of the future. The orthodox narrative about diaspora emphasises loss, and especially the loss of homeland, language and culture. However, as many scholars including Marc Nichanian assert, the elemental diasporic loss is the relationship to history, rather than land or territory.[2]

John Young's History Projects are an exemplary meditation on unhomeliness and the search for a cosmopolitan ethics. Young's approach to history is highly nuanced and self-reflexive. The History Projects are not an attempt to correct the ledger books by recuperating what has been broken, ignored, erased or neglected, nor are they preoccupied with a narrative of victimisation and wounding. Rather, the History Projects challenge us to engage with history in a way that brings the past into our present to consider what can be done differently for our world-making future.

This expansive series of works focuses on a kind of ethical cosmopolitanism that necessitates an engagement with alterity beyond the interest of the self and, following Kant, to not consider oneself as the world but merely as a citizen of the world. John Young describes this as a form of 'world-feeling', activated by an 'empathic reaching out to the other, as you find a way to bring the other to a proximity to oneself that makes sense … the conjoining of the head and the heart chakra'.[3]

As my 2012 essay explores below, Young's practice has been deeply informed by his diasporic experience as an Asian Australian of Hong Kong Chinese ancestry. The essay, reproduced in its entirety as a historical artefact, was written in response to the opening chapters of the History Projects at a time when the political elite in Australia was attempting to engage with the so-called Asian Century. Then, and more so now, Rising Asia was conflated with Rising China, and the challenges for Asian Australians and especially for those with Chinese heritage have not abated. The History Projects are indeed timely, in these interesting times. Young's work is both provocative and profound, challenging us to reach those moments of ethical clarity from which acts of hope and benevolence stem.

AUGUST 2022

DIASPORA, ART AND EMPATHY (2013)[4]

Jacqueline Lo

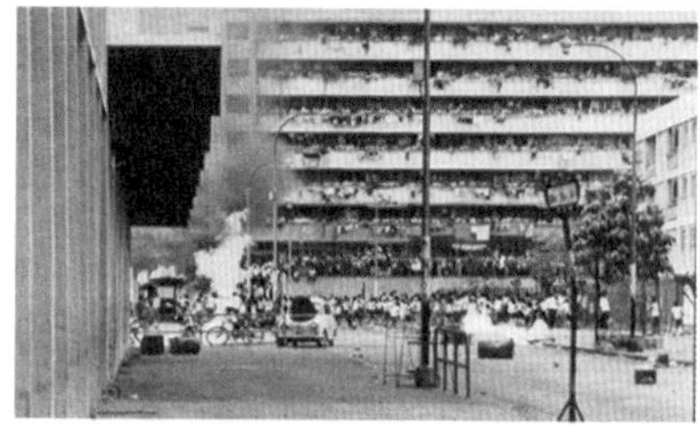

The 2013 deposed (Labor-led) Australian Government released its 'Australia in the Asian Century' white paper in October 2012.[5] The document has been the subject of public and academic scrutiny both within Australia and in the region. There was praise for the document's emphasis on education to develop Australia's 'Asia-relevant capabilities', even while the issue of how the Asia-turn is to be implemented and funded remained unaddressed. The *Jakarta Post* gave an insight into the region's response to the white paper:

> [B]efore a nation can become a competitive force, it must have an accepted place in the region. On this key strategy, the white paper does little more than make a 'rally call' to Australians to come out and make it happen. … Though Australia has some deeply historical links with many parts of the region due to some heroic actions of troops during World War II, tragically these opportunities to further develop relationships were not capitalized upon … It's not about learning Asian languages but about understanding different points of view, approaches, and 'mindsets'. Austro-centrism must take a back seat in relationships around the region for Australia to be seriously considered a member of the region.[6]

At the point of writing, the new Coalition government headed by Prime Minister Tony Abbott has just been formalised. While the fate of this white paper remains uncertain, there are already signs that the new government is similarly keen to capitalise on 'Rising Asia' as the source of Australia's continuing prosperity. The 'Australia in the Asian Century White Paper', for now at least, is indexical of the policy-imaginary of contemporary Australia.[7]

It should be noted that the white paper is a domestic economic policy and, as such, does not develop a nuanced approach to foreign relations, specifically through the articulation of modes of relating to Asia beyond a trade and productivity centred model founded on the notion of 'opportunity'. Nevertheless, even within this paradigm, it fails to account for the ways in which Australia is already 'Asianised'. For all the attention on Asia and Asians, there is a remarkable absence of discussion about the role of Asian Australians in the document. As Tim Soutphommasane asserts:

> Some of us seem to believe that Asia is something out there, wholly apart from us. In fact there is already a lot of Asia in Australia … That is because so much of our Asian-ness … is currently invisible. With one or two exceptions, Asian-Australians aren't in the room when it matters. Where are they represented in our ministerial cabinets, our corporate boardrooms and our editorial offices? Will they be represented in such settings soon?[8]

Detail from *Riot* 2008
Digital print and oil on linen, two panels,
170 × 125 cm
Collection of M+, Hong Kong

Within such a landscape, what are the implications of rising Asia for cultural studies
at large, and for Asian Australian Studies, specifically? What does it mean to be
an Asian Australian in the face of so much polemic? The discourse of rising Asia
is frequently conflated with rising China, which produces specific challenges as well
as opportunities for Australians of Chinese descent. John Young's story illustrates
as well as problematises the politics and poetics of diaspora.

JOHN YOUNG ZERUNGE

John Young was born in Hong Kong in 1956, the youngest of a Westernised Catholic
family. His parents sent him to a Sydney boarding school in 1967 to remove him
from the immediate consequences of China's Great Proletarian Cultural Revolution.
Aside from annual trips back to Hong Kong, Young has made Australia his home.

Young belongs to what might be considered the first wave of Chinese Australian artists
that include Lindy Lee and William Yang—these Chinese Australians grew up and
began their professional careers at a time when the White Australia policy was still
in place and there was little cultural space for notions of diasporic or hybrid identities.
Although the work of all three artists investigates, in different ways, their Chinese
cultural heritage, this was not always the case: their early works are underscored by
modernist and postmodernist Euro-American precepts.

Young's intellectual and artistic education is resolutely Western; he studied the
philosophy of science and aesthetics at the University of Sydney and studied sculpture
and painting with European-trained artists at the Sydney College of the Arts. His
formative art training was in European and American modernism, and he maintains
a strong interest in European philosophy, especially the works of Walter Benjamin and
Ludwig Wittgenstein. Despite this, Young's work has been read through conventional
diasporic frameworks, particularly in the 1990s when contemporary Asian art gained
increasing currency in the international arts market. While the dominant multicultural
paradigm operating at the time created new spaces for non-Anglo artists to present
their works, the interpretation of the works tends to be subsumed under simplistic
identity discourses of hybridity and fusion.

Young's work is consistently interpreted as a signifier of his Chinese Australian identity.
His *Double Ground Paintings* series that began in 1993 developed his technique of
painting over layered digital photographic prints on canvas to create a single plane
of vision that is segmented and palimpsestic. The images that he draws on come from
diverse sources including gardening books, catalogues, landscapes, nude photography
and movie stills.

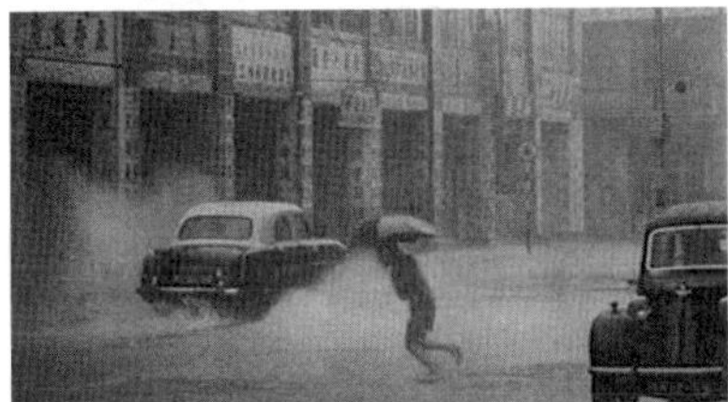

Hong Kong storm, 1968
South China Morning Post

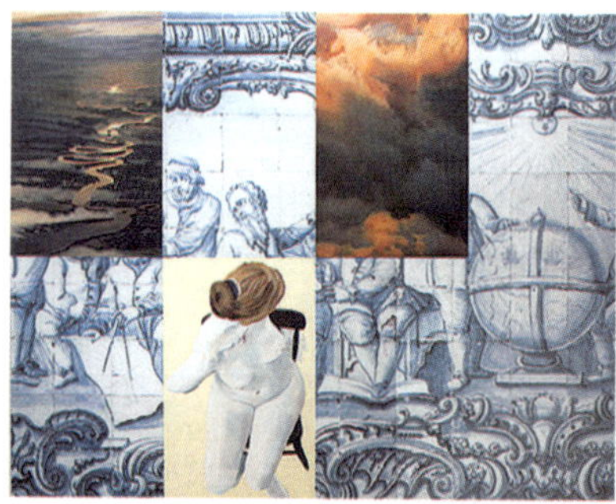
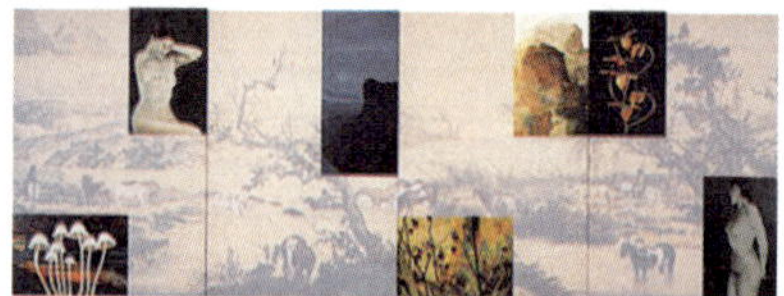

The Comprador's Mirror #3 1998
Digital print and oil on canvas, 183 × 223.5 cm
Collection of Museum of Contemporary Art
Australia, Sydney

The Bridge 1994–95
Digital print, oil and synthetic polymer paint
on canvas, 219.5 × 576 cm
Private collection, Vancouver

The Comprador's Mirror #3 (1998) is a large work composed of juxtaposed images of an ancient Roman relief, a female nude and aerial landscapes. According to Carolyn Barnes, by juxtaposing these diverse images on the same picture plane, the artist resists forming a singular narrative or core meaning. He did not want to be seen as simply an 'ethnic' artist charged with the weight of representing a social or cultural group: 'Rather, he saw the primary value of being positioned both within and outside the structures of Western thought and culture as enabling him to meet the idea of difference head on'.[9]

The double ground trope refers not only to the layering of images and the unstable plane of sight but also to the ways it speaks to different kinds of audiences—from the West and Asia. Yet despite some critical attempts to theorise the processual and intertextual aspects of the paintings, Young's work has largely been interpreted as representing the tensions between these separate cultures. The visual distinction between Asian and Western references in the works, as well as his technique of merging painting with digital imaging technology are interpreted as signifiers of Young's own contested and hybrid cultural identity.

The orthodox multicultural paradigm operating at the time led to a tendency to over-emphasise the biographical and ethnic identification of Asian Australian artists as the primary means of elucidating the artworks. The institutionalisation of such practices within academia and the arts market has the unfortunate consequence of delimiting Asian Australian artworks as ethnographic testimonials of racial difference, thereby reinforcing the location of the works at the fringes of mainstream Australian culture.

In 1996 Young led a team of artists to establish Gallery 4A, Australia's first exhibition space for Asian Australian artists. Now the 4A Centre for Contemporary Asian Art, Sydney, 4A is the shorthand for Asian Australian Artists' Association. He became the Founding President of the association in 1997 when it formally launched its role of public advocacy for Asian Australian art. This was in the heyday of the so-called Asianisation of Australian arts, when the Australia Council for the Arts had a designated budget for developing relations with Asia, and local Asian Australian artists, theatre practitioners and writers were making some inroads into mainstream institutions. Young was heavily involved in the activities of 4A for the next few years but, in early 1999, he resigned from the presidency after moving to Melbourne. He was starting to have doubts about the impact of the Asianisation push. He perceived a destructive cycle emerging that racialised artists fell into when trying to assert their identity and transcend stereotypes.[10]

By the late 90s, multiculturalism as government policy was on the wane. The idea of the Asian Australian artist, while a factual reality, became increasingly problematic from the perspective of policy-makers and funding bodies. The decision to express cultural allegiance outside a performative Australianness was perceived as lacking identification with the nation while encouraging, in some factions, a kind of cultural cannibalisation or excessive production and consumption of ethnic and racial Otherness. 4A's commitment to the specificities of Asian Australian identity and, in particular, its distinction from the fixed notion of Australianness often resulted in the delimiting of ways to find common ground with mainstream culture as well as overlooking the diversity within Asian Australian cultural practices.

The challenges faced by 4A and Young's unease with the prevailing discourses of diaspora and racialised positions offered by the hyphenated Asian/Chinese-Australian category reflects wider concerns in diaspora and critical race studies in Australia and

in the United States. As someone who is thoroughly implicated in this period of
Asian Australian politicisation, and who remains engaged with the project of Asian
Australia, I do not wish to come across as disavowing the efforts to create and sustain
organisations such as 4A, but it is equally important to critique foundational concepts
and challenge their political efficacy in the face of changing social conditions.

THE CHALLENGE OF 'POST-RACE'

The term post-race entered popular discourse when Barack Obama became the
first African American President of the United States. Simplistic notions of post-
race assume that race no longer matters: racism is 'over' with the instatement of a
coloured man in the country's top job. For others, the term post-race is used with
more subtlety as a political challenge and intellectual problematic. Post-race in this
context signifies a turn from essentialist views about race as a biological 'fact' and the
search to find a framework that offers political agency to critique new forms of racism
informed by cultural differences rather than notions of race as biological heredity.

This form of neo-racism—what Etienne Balibar calls 'racism without races'—'does
not postulate the superiority of certain groups or peoples in relation to others but
"only" the harmfulness of abolishing frontiers, the incompatibility of lifestyles and
traditions'.[11] Neo-racism 'presents itself as having drawn the lessons from the conflict
between racism and anti-racism'[12] and argues that if you want to avoid racism,
you must maintain cultural differences and, 'in accordance with the postulate that
individuals are the exclusive heirs and bearers of a single culture'[13], keep collectivities
separate. As the increasing visibility of far-right anti-immigration and anti-Islam
groups in the United States, Europe and to a lesser extent in Australia evidence, the
social purchase of 'race' and the effects of 'racism' are still prevalent. For Young, the
post-race challenge is to find ways of engaging critically with race-consciousness
by working paradoxically with *and* against the conceptual tools that we have yet
to replace.

Young's recent work is instructive in this respect. Rather than focusing on issues of
racial or transcultural identity, his interest has turned instead to the question of how
people act in cross-cultural situations. Globalisation has had a profound impact on
the international arts market, opening new opportunities across national borders.
There has been a surge of interest in contemporary Chinese art since the 1980s with
the likes of Cai Guo-Qiang, Wenda Gu and Xu Bing becoming major figures in
festival circuits. Although the international art world is now a diffuse network of
institutions and circuits of collaboration, production and exchange, Young maintains
that the works of these Chinese artists are still required to perform racialised roles
and deal with Chinese issues in order to maintain currency. He also sees international
curators adopting a deterritorialised approach to the works themselves, specialising
in the thematic manipulation of artworks drawn from diverse locations with little
attention to the historical contexts that support the artworks.[14]

For Young, the speed of globalisation has exacerbated this sense of ethical
indifference in the constant search for the next 'hot' commodity. He sees a role for art
in linking the present to 'a world of forgotten stories, discarded objects, and memories
… Making art not only means to recollect stories, but to reawaken an intrinsic ethical
impulse in the present'.[15] This shift to 'situate ethics and moral judgment within
the context of crossing from one culture to another'[16] began with his exhibition,
Bonhoeffer in Harlem, staged at the St Matthäus Church in Berlin's Kulturforum.[17]

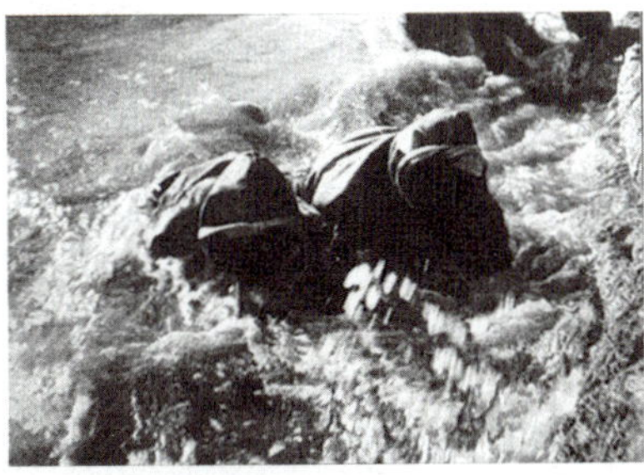

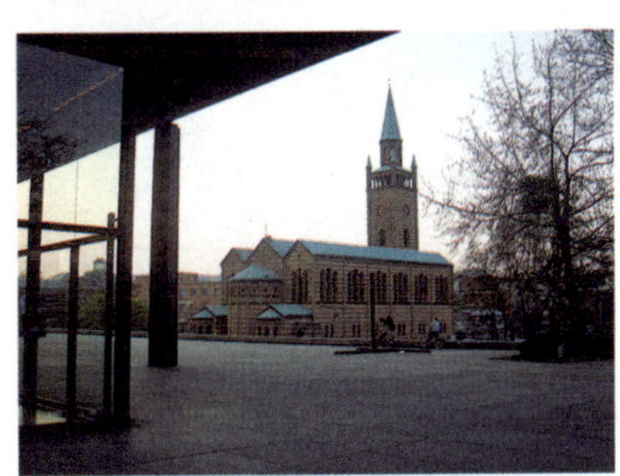

Detail of *Folks* 2008
Digital print and oil on linen, two panels,
169 × 118 cm

St Matthäus Church, Kulturforum, Berlin, 2009
Photograph by the artist

ART AND ETHICS

Dietrich Bonhoeffer was a German Lutheran pastor and theologian who became known for his resistance to the Nazi dictatorship, and specifically to the genocide against the Jews. He was also involved in plans by members of the *Abwehr* (German Military Intelligence Office) to assassinate Adolf Hitler. He was arrested in April 1943 by the Gestapo and executed by hanging in Flossenbürg in April 1945, a mere twenty-three days before the Nazis surrendered.

Bonhoeffer received his doctorate in theology at the tender age of twenty-one; he returned to Berlin in 1929 to work on his Habilitation thesis, which was conferred a year later. As he was considered too young to be ordained, Bonhoeffer went to the United States in 1930 for postgraduate study on a teaching fellowship at New York City's Union Theological Seminary. While the American seminary did not live up to his expectations, he was exposed to a very different way of life. He met Frank Fisher, a Black fellow seminarian who introduced him to the Abyssinian Baptist Church in Harlem, where Bonhoeffer taught Sunday school and formed a lifelong love for African-American music. He heard Adam Clayton Powell, Sr. preach the Gospel of Social Justice and became aware of issues of discrimination and social inequity wrought not only by the authorities and mainstream society, but also of the Church's own ineffectiveness to improve the situation. It has been suggested this period abroad played a crucial role in his intellectual and spiritual development, where Bonhoeffer 'turned from phraseology to reality'.[18] The Harlem experience made him a sensitive critic of American racism and deepened his resistance to German anti-Semitism. He returned to Berlin in 1931 with a clear conviction to fight against racist ideologies. He was ordained at St Matthäus Church on 15 November 1931.

There are many memorials to Bonhoeffer including a bronze torso by the Zion Church in Berlin and its replica in Breslau/Wroclaw, and a statue in Westminster Abbey. What distinguishes Young's artwork is that it is not a static memorial but an installation that stages a process of remembering with particular sensitivity to issues of race and dispossession. While most monuments commemorate Bonhoeffer's undoubted heroism and sacrifice, Young's installation explores his connections with the Harlem community, a community that understood all too well the trauma that an ideology of racial supremacy is capable of generating.

Young took inspiration from the stained glass from the Abbysinian Baptist Church in Harlem and translated it, firstly into an oil painting of swirling Afro-American colours capturing the vivacity and joy of the church community that so inspired Bonhoeffer. The painting was then interpreted into a tapestry woven with Chinese silk in Nepal by Dolma Lob Sang, who comes from a family of Tibetan exiles. The tapestry hung as the centrepiece in St Matthäus, and in the words of Young, it was 'like listening to Black gospel music".[19]

The series of chalk-drawings on blackboard paint-covered paper are a reference to the 1970s blackboard drawings of Joseph Beuys and Rudolf Steiner's blackboard lectures on social reform following the First World War. As a tool for teaching, the blackboard underscores the more didactic aspects of Young's recent work. Written in German, English and Chinese, the works revisit his earlier concept of double ground and the effort and losses of crossing cultures, languages, and media. The visibly erased text in some of the works haunt and elude totalising epistemological capture—the chalky residue visible reminds us of lives lost, stories untold and the nagging presence of pain and loss.

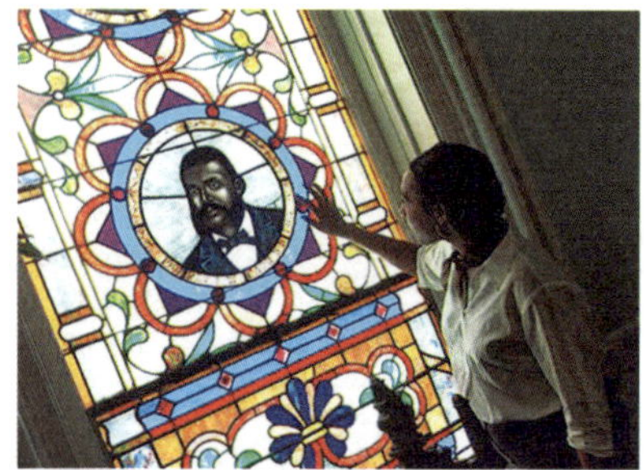

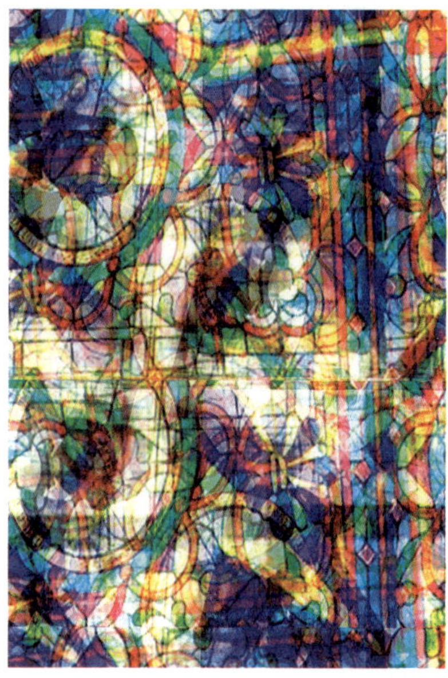

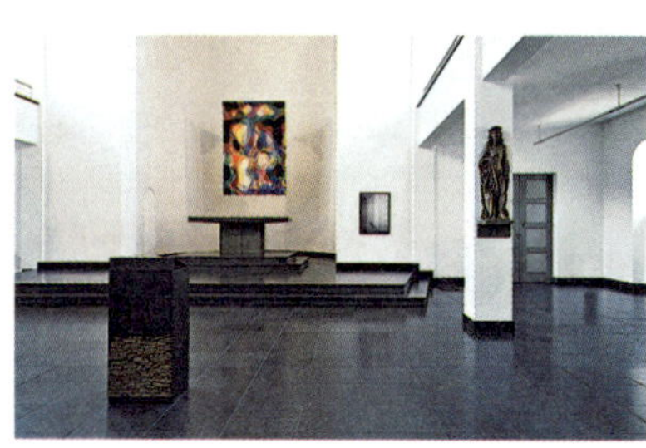

Stained-glass window depicting early pastors
First African Baptist Church, Savannah, Georgia

Composite drawing of stained-glass window, 2009

Bonhoeffer in Harlem 2009
Installation view, St Matthäus Church, Kulturforum, Berlin

While appearing deceptively simple, the chalk drawings communicate the weight of history in three different languages: Chinese, German and English. The inscribed words '*Sanctorum Communio*' (Communion of Saints) is a reference to the title of Bonhoeffer's thesis, while the date 9 May 1930 denotes the date he arrives in New York. Also written in Chinese is the injunction 'Evil—oppose it directly'.

'Eine speiche im rad des Staats' is German for 'a spoke in the wheel of the State'. Bonhoeffer believed that in the face of an illegitimate State, the Church had a role to be a disruptive force: to jam a spoke in the wheel of that State. February 2, 1933, denotes the date when Bonhoeffer, on his return to Berlin from the United States, spoke on radio against the rise of Nazism. The authorities abruptly terminated the broadcast. The erased writings resemble a palimpsestic struggle of religious and moral ideologies. The Chinese characters proclaim 'real concrete social action', while the German 'Schem Hamphoras' is a reference to the controversial anti-Jewish text *Vom Schem Hamphoras und vom Geschlecht Christi (Of the Unknowable Name and the Generations of Christ)*, by Martin Luther, published in 1543. Also written in English is 'Sermon on the Mount', the collection of teachings by Jesus about morality found in the Gospel According to Matthew. There are also visible signs of another erased text in Chinese characters denoting 'responsible action, a highly risky action'. The overlay markings of a small handprint—perhaps of a child—adds to the poignancy of the work.

The chalk drawings are sometimes paired with digital inkjet prints from photographs, for example of Bonhoeffer in his prime. The combination of digital technology and chalk drawings underscore the passing of time, drawing attention to the ways by which memories are stored, mediated and re-presented. In *Meditations* (2008), Finkelwalde refers to the location of the seminary that Bonhoeffer led from 1935 to 1937 for the Confessing Church, a church established in opposition to the Nazi-controlled German Evangelical Church. Written in Chinese is the phrase: 'The test of the morality of a society is what it does for its children'.

The paired images that denote the final years of Bonhoeffer's life are stark yet poetic. In *Prison* (2008), '8.4.1945' marks the date when Bonhoeffer was hanged in the concentration camp at Flossenbürg. 'Teure Gnade' means costly grace in German. Also written in German is 'Eine Drossel, die singt' ('a thrush that sings'). During his incarceration, Boenhoffer would sometimes hear a bird sing through the bars of his window. He wrote about this in a letter just before his death to his fiancée Maria von Wedemeyer. Also written in Chinese: 'Action springs not from thought but from a readiness for responsibility'. The sheer simplicity and beauty of the inkject image of the thrush stands as a strong contrast to what we know happened in the camps.

Bonhoeffer in Harlem is an artistic tour de force. Young plays with various media and materialities so that glass becomes silk or canvas, paper becomes blackboard, and what is dark and forgotten comes to light once again. Working on Bonhoeffer's story also led Young to another cluster of lost stories of humanitarian action: this time about foreigners who stayed behind to assist the Chinese during what became known as the Nanjing Massacre. This led to the development of *Safety Zone*. This work comprised sixty blackboard drawings and digital images, three large paintings entitled *Flower Market (Nanjing 1936) #1–3* (2010), and two vertical oil on raw linen paintings entitled *The Crippled Tree #1* and *#2* (2010). The exhibition premiered at Anna Schwartz Gallery in 2010 and was restaged at the University of Queensland Art Museum in 2011.

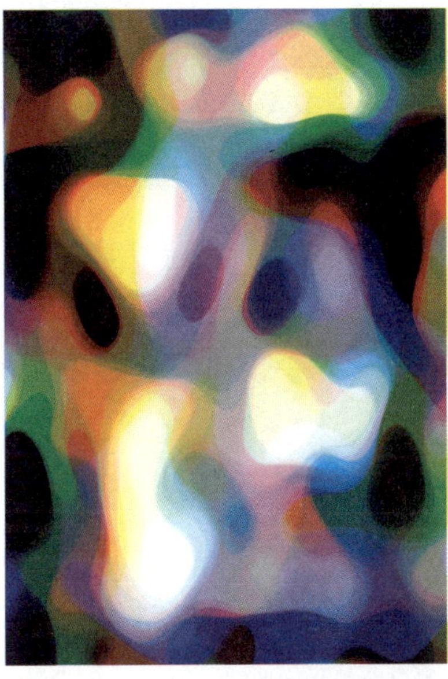

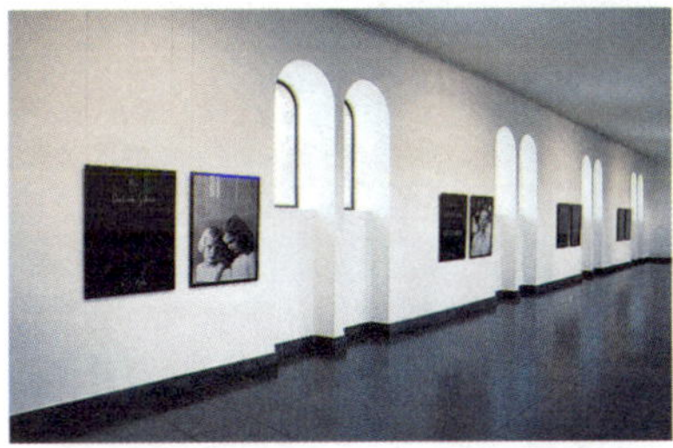

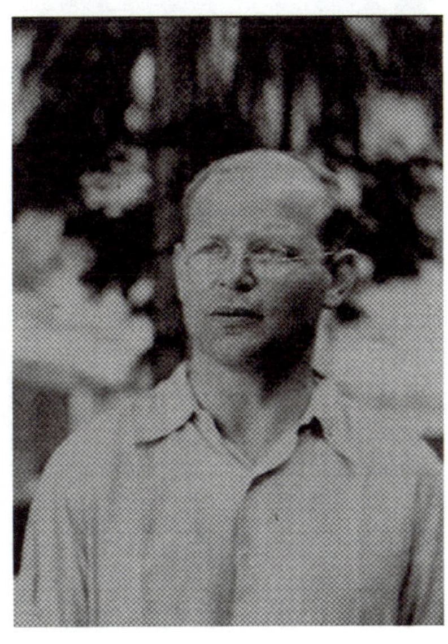

Final rendering for *Bonhoeffer in Harlem* 2009

Bonhoeffer in Harlem 2009
Installation view, St Matthäus Church,
Kulturforum, Berlin

Dietrich Bonhoeffer 2008
Digital print on photographic paper,
100 × 70 cm
Collection of Erlöserkirche, Bamberg

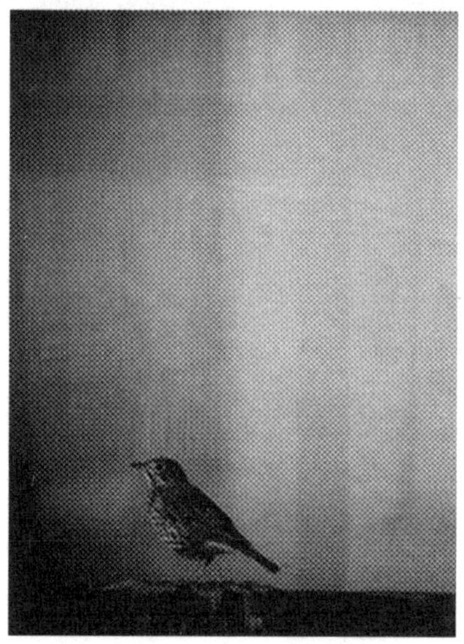

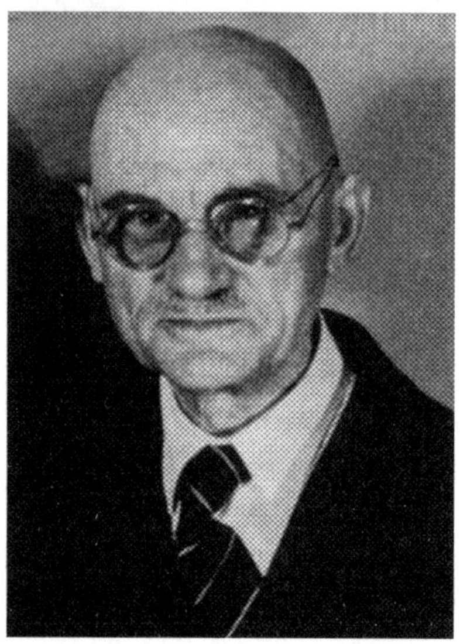

Prison 2008
Chalk on blackboard-painted archival cotton
paper, 100 × 70 cm
Collection of Erlöserkirche, Bamberg

Thrush 2008
Chalk on blackboard-painted archival cotton
paper, 100 × 70 cm
Collection of Erlöserkirche, Bamberg

John Rabe 2010
Digital print on photographic paper,
100 × 70 cm

The Crippled Tree paintings are Young's highly personal reflections about this historic event. The chopped off limbs and vestiges of violence marking both surface and inner core of the tree recall some of the untold brutalities inflicted by the Japanese assailants. While undertaking research for this essay, I came across a number of photographic documents including John Magee's work (one of the members of the International Committee who photographed the brutalities of the Japanese soldiers in an effort to prove the reality of the violence to the international community). One of the most horrific photos I came across was of a female corpse profaned by a large tree branch inserted into her vagina.

As in *Bonhoeffer in Harlem*, Young also uses a series of chalk-drawings on blackboard painted paper interspersed with inkjet prints from archival images for the *Safety Zone* panels. Most of these images focus on the atrocities.

As the Japanese marched closer to Nanjing in 1931, most foreigners left the city except for twenty-one Americans and Europeans, who stayed behind and formed the International Committee to protect the Chinese. They set up a 'safety zone' of some 3.85 square kilometers. At the height of the Nanjing invasion, the International Committee protected some 200,000 civilian Chinese. Among many individuals acknowledged in Young's work are John Magee, mentioned earlier, and Robert Wilson, the only surgeon left in the Nanjing Hospital. In this essay I focus on two other foreigners whose stories resonated with Young..

John Rabe was a businessman working for the German electronic and engineering company, Siemens. He was appointed leader of the International Committee largely because he was a member of the Nazi Party. This afforded him some negotiating capacity as the Germans were allies with the Japanese at the time, as part of the Anti-Commintern Pact. When the safety zone was disestablished in 1938, Rabe was sent back to Berlin. After Hitler's reign however, he and his family encountered great hardship because of his Nazi association; he was first held by the Gestapo and then after the war, by the Soviet NKVD (The People's Commissariat for Internal Affairs) and, later, by the British Army. He was forced to undergo an arduous de-Nazification process and lost his job at Siemens. He and his family lived in poverty to the point of starvation until the citizens of Nanjing heard about his situation. They sent money and later monthly food packages to help the family. Rabe died in 1950 in pitiful circumstances.

In *You have the heart of a Buddha* (in German, 'Du hast das Herz einer Buddha'), the interplay of two languages operates dialogically. Written in Chinese is 'This is a drawing for John Rabe'. Text under erasure denotes: 'You have saved thousands of poor people from danger and want', which is juxtaposed against Rabe's own writing— 'Everyone thinks I am a hero and that can be very annoying. I can see nothing heroic about me or within me'. Then, in Chinese, 'for Mr. Rabe'.

The other person of note is Minnie Vautrin, an American who established the Ginling Girls' College and saved hundreds from rape and worse fates. But even Vautrin could not prevent numerous incursions by the Japanese soldiers, who came into the College and raped girls as young as three, as well as their mothers and grandmothers. Vautrin was sent home along with other foreigners in 1938 when the safety zone was disestablished after the Japanese army claimed formal control of the city. Traumatised by the events she had witnessed and feeling responsible for the lives she could not protect, Minnie committed suicide by turning on the gas stove in her apartment in Indianapolis in 1940.

The inkjet portrait of girls from Ginling Girls' College innocently playing in the safety zone compound are identified by the caption of Ginling College, then we find, once again, Bonhoeffer's quote used by Young in the *Bonhoeffer in Harlem* show, reproduced here in Chinese: 'The test of the morality of a society is what it does for its children'. For me these words seem all the more chilling, when accompanied by the visual image of youth.

Girl depicts the only full-face portrait of a Chinese subject in Young's panel, and thus, an important assertion of embodied Chinese agency and resistance to the violence at the time. It is likely that this young girl was the victim of rape and a patient of the only foreign doctor who stayed behind at the University of Nanking Hospital, Dr Robert Wilson.

The image, with the caption 'Unspeakable acts of Evil', also includes a reference to Unit Ei-1644, the Japanese unit that undertook biological and chemical experimentation on captive human subjects. The erased text denotes 'human experiments, acetone, arsenate, cyanide, nitrate, prussiate, cobra poison, habu, amagasa venom, germs, gases'. 'Unspeakable Acts of Evil, Becoming Banal' was mentioned many times in the witness records at the Nanjing War Crimes Tribunal. This quote is attributed to George Ashmore Fitch, the Director of International Committee who kept a diary and filmed some of the events during his time in Nanjing.

Pheng Cheah reminds us that 'the globe is not the world'. Globe thinking focuses on geo-economic relationships informing, among other things, the thinking behind the 'Australia in the Asian Century White Paper'. World-thinking on the other hand, is about how humans relate to each other and their environment in time and space.

> The globe … [is] the totality produced by processes of globalization, … a bounded object or entity in Mercatorian space. When we say "map of the world", we really mean "map of the globe". It is assumed that the spatial diffusion and extensiveness achieved through global media and markets give rise to a sense of belonging to a shared world, when one might argue that such developments lead instead to greater polarization and division of nations and regions. … By contrast, "The world is a form of relating or being-with".[20]

Histories of war and trauma are powerful world-making forces. More specifically, war and trauma make powerful national memories. The memories of the Holocaust and the Nanjing massacre have been contested and deployed by the states of Germany, Israel, China and Japan at different times towards different (and sometimes similar) ends.

In contrast to these official memory projects, Young's work reimagines the events from a diasporic perspective, focusing on ordinary people who find themselves caught up in extraordinary circumstances that require moral decisions to be made and sustained. I believe that it is possible to argue for these works as instances of postmemory, following the work of Marianne Hirsch who defines postmemory as:

> [T]he relationship that the generation after those who witnessed cultural or collective trauma bears to the experiences of those who came before, experiences that they 'remember' only by means of the stories, images, and behaviors among which they grew up. But these experiences were transmitted to them so deeply and affectively as to seem to constitute memories in their own right. Postmemory's connection to the past is thus not actually mediated by recall but by imaginative investment, projection, and creation.[21]

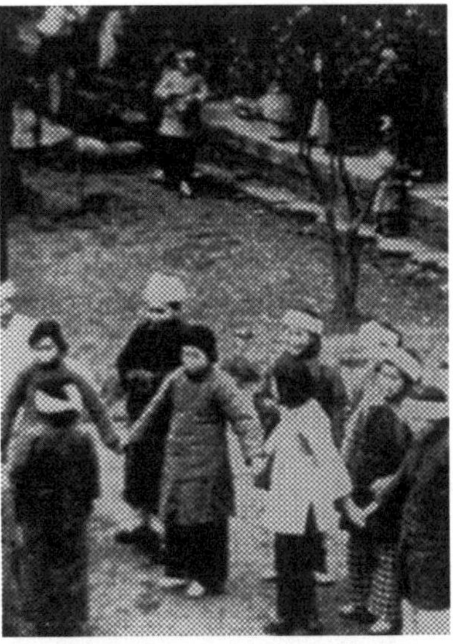

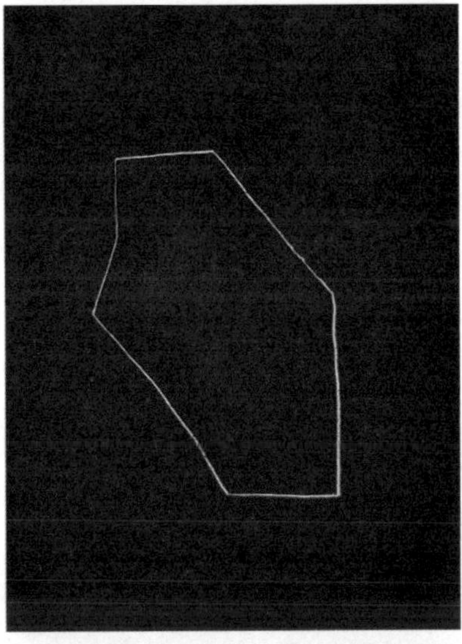

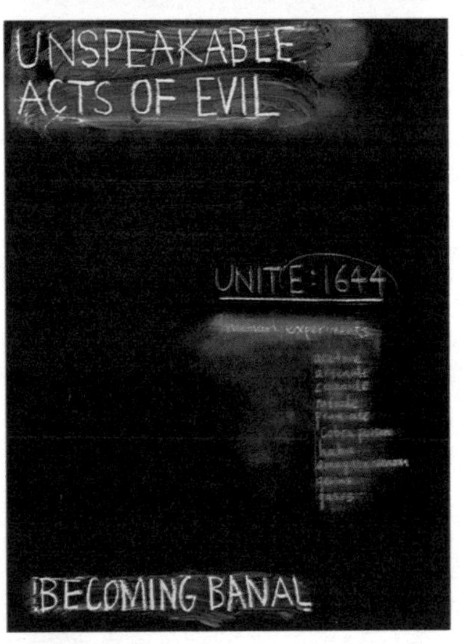

Ginling 2010
Digital print on photographic paper,
100 × 70 cm

Zone 2010
Chalk on blackboard-painted archival
cotton paper, 100 × 70 cm

Unspeakable Acts of Evil 2010
Chalk on blackboard-painted archival
cotton paper, 100 × 70 cm

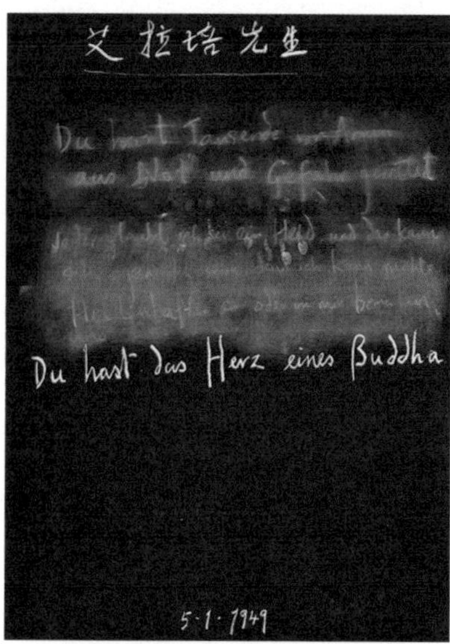

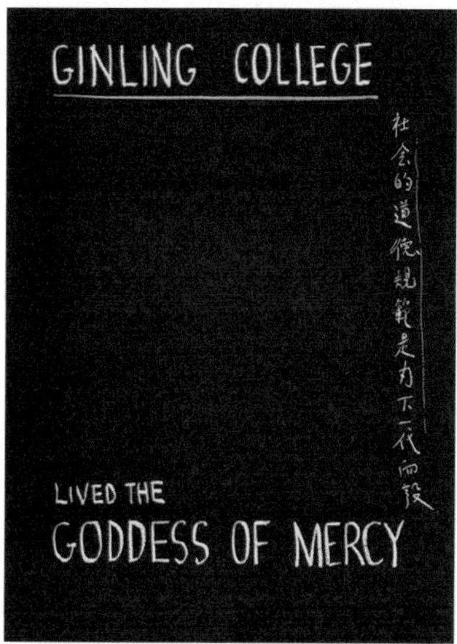

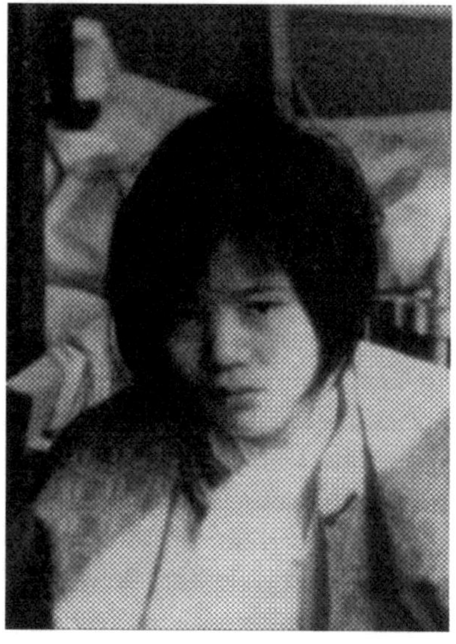

Heart 2010
Chalk on blackboard-painted archival
cotton paper, 100 × 70 cm

Goddess of Mercy 2010
Chalk on blackboard-painted archival
cotton paper, 100 × 70 cm

Girl 2010
Digital print on photographic paper,
100 × 70 cm

What is striking about Young's work is that this postmemory was not bequeathed to him as a member of the German, American or Nanjing Chinese communities per se. Rather, his work demonstrates the ways in which the transnational memory of both Bonhoeffer and Nanjing has been memorialised from an inter-diasporic perspective. Young's memory-making is not conventionally postmemory in the sense of a memory that has been bequeathed to the artist. However, I assert that a convincing case can be made on the grounds of affective communication. Postmemory is less about veracity—typified by debates about how many Chinese or Jews were actually murdered—but rather about the structures of feeling that the memory-making inspires, and the ways in which this memory-making echoes something of the ethics and history of the memory-maker.

I believe that while the transmission of pain, loss and displacement in the aforementioned works echoes something of Young's own history and desires, nonetheless that is not the primary objective of the works. These works are not concerned with the vertical pronoun—the 'I'—but a search for mutuality and reciprocity with an 'Other'. As a creative act, the artworks bridge personal and collective memories, producing new narratives of social belonging, new affective capacities across diasporas and challenges us to rethink collective responsibility.

Young's memorial works are as acts of minor transnationalism that engage with the past with a political and ethical imperative that Tessa Morris Suzuki conceptualises as 'implication':

> 'Implication' means the existence of a conscious connection to the past, but also the reality of being (in a legal sense) 'an accessory after the fact'. It is the status of those who have not stolen land from others, but who live on stolen land; the status of those who have not participated in massacres, but have participated in the process by which the memory of those massacres has been obliterated; the status of those who have not injured others, but allow the consequences of past injury to go unaddressed … We who live in the present did not create the violence and hatred of the past. But the violence and hatred of the past, to some degree, created us. It formed the material world and the ideas with which we live, and will continue to do so unless we take active steps to unmake their consequences.[22]

These are important lessons for Asian Australian Studies, which has been founded on the discourse of racial wounding: of racism, discrimination and political marginalisation by mainstream culture and the State. John Young's work offers a way to grieve for this history from a position of alterity, not to reify a victim discourse or promote cultural chauvinism but rather to reimagine, reengage and co-exist with others with compassion and empathy.

1.   Lily Cho, 'The Turn to Diaspora', *Topia* 17, Spring 2007, p. 19.

2.   Cho, p. 16.

3.   John Young, as quoted in Cher Tan, 'Interview #115', *Liminal Magazine*, September 2019.

4.   This essay was first published as: Jacqueline Lo, 'Diaspora, Art and Empathy', *John Young: The Bridge and the Fruit Tree*, Drill Hall Gallery, Australian National University, 2013, pp. 19–43.

5.   Julia Gillard and Australia in the Asian Century Task Force, 'Australia in the Asian Century White Paper', Australian Government, Canberra, 2012, https://trove.nla.gov.au/work/174416664.

6.   Murray Hunter, 'White Paper: "Australia in the Asian Century" or Lost in Asia?', *Jakarta Post*, 30 October 2012, http://www.thejakartapost.com/news/2012/10/30/white-paper-australiaasian-century-or-lost-asia.html.

7.   The 'Australia in the Asian Century White Paper' is, of course, not the first of its kind. The 'Asian-turn' in Australia's policy framework occurred in the late 1980s and early 1990s and is most often associated with the government of former Prime Minister Paul Keating, who advocated the privileging of Australia's geographic location in the region over our historical connections with Europe. The Keating years have become the yardstick for the promotion of 'Asia-literacy' and of changes introduced not only to foreign policy but also in the domestic education and cultural sectors.

8.   Tim Soutphommasane, 'Australia's Asian-Ness Is Barely Visible', *The Sydney Morning Herald*, 5 November 2012, https://www.smh.com.au/politics/federal/australias-asian-ness-is-barely-visible-20121104-28ryq.html.

9.   Carolyn Barnes, 'Towards a Layered Imaginary', in Barnes, *John Young*, Craftsman House, Fishermans Bend, Victoria, 2005, p. 61.

10. Barnes, p. 60.

11. Etienne Balibar and Immanuel Wallerstein, *Race, Nation, Class: Ambiguous Identities*, Verso, London and New York, 1991, p. 21.

12. Ibid., p. 22.

13. Ibid., pp. 22–23.

14. Barnes, 'Towards a Layered Imaginary', p. 61.

15. John Young, in Thomas Berghuis, 'John Young: Situational Ethics', originally published in *Art & Australia*, vol. 48, no. 3, 2011, p. 440. Republished in this volume, p. 134.

16. Berghuis, p. 440. And in this volume, p. 134.

17. St Matthäus Church today is still a predominantly 'White' monocultural congregation. At the opening of the installation, a Black jazz singer from Harlem, Jocelyn B. Smith, and the Berlin Choir of Hard Knocks performed, which made a strong contrast to its usual performance repertoire.

18. Quote from Dietrich Bonhoeffer, *Letters and Papers from Prison*, MacMillan, New York, 1973, p. 275, and cited by Clifford J. Green, *Bonhoeffer: A Theology of Sociality*, Wm. B. Eerdmans Publishing, Michigan, 1999, pp. 105–6. See also David F. Ford, *The Modern Theologians: An Introduction to Christian Theology in the Twentieth Century*, Blackwell, Oxford, 1997.

19. Alexander Ochs and Christhard-Georg Neuber (eds), *John Young: Bonhoeffer in Harlem*, St Matthäus Church, Berlin, 2008, p. 80.

20. Peang Cheah, 'World Literature as World-Making Activity', *Daedalus*, Summer 2008, p. 30.

21. Marianne Hirsch, 'The Generation of Postmemory', *Poetics Today*, vol. 29, no. 1, Spring 2008, pp. 106–07.

22. Tessa Morris-Suzuki, from the unpublished English manuscript to her Japanese book *Hihanteki Souzouryoku no Tameni: Guro-baruka Jidai no Nippon* (For Critical Imagination: Japan in the Era of Globalisation), Heibon-sha, 2002, pp. 57–85; quoted in Minoru Hokari, 'Globalising Aboriginal Reconciliation: Indigenous Australian and Asian (Japanese) Migrants', *Cultural Studies Review*, vol. 9, no. 2, 2003, pp. 97–98.

MEMORISING/THINKING IN SPACES: JOHN YOUNG'S NEGOTIATION OF IMAGE, SPACE AND TRAUMA

Marc Glöde

> What is aura? A peculiar web of space and time: the unique manifestation of a distance, however near it may be.
>
> Walter Benjamin,
> *A Short History of Photography* (1931)

> The trace is not a presence but is rather the simulacrum of a presence that dislocates, displaces, and refers beyond itself. The trace has, properly speaking, no place, for effacement belongs to the very structure of the trace. […] In this way the metaphysical text is understood; it is still readable, and remains read.
>
> Jacques Derrida,
> *Speech and Phenomena* (1973)

> Thus the life of someone whose existence has somewhat preceded our own encloses in its particularity the very tension of History, its division. History is hysterical: it is constituted only if we consider it, only if we look at it – and in order to look at it, we must be excluded from it. As a living soul, I am the very contrary of History, I am what belies it, destroys it for the sake of my own history (impossible for me to believe in "witnesses"; impossible, at least, to be one) …
>
> Roland Barthes,
> *Camera Lucida* (1980)

OCCURRENCES

Something has happened. Something profound; a long time ago. Something that, when it happened, was in many ways impossible to process, then later too difficult to forget. And it seems that no matter how long it has been since then, no matter how much time has passed, no matter how many attempts there have been to forget—what happened was so impactful that it still resonates today. It is a past that is stubbornly present. But its manifestations are split into thousands of traces in individuals, families, books, seminars, shared memories, images, texts, or artworks; distributed, scattered, to a point that what occurred in the past, though still present in such manifestations, becomes more and more ungraspable. It has become a reference point without location, communally internalised, pushed into a state of common knowledge through a process whereby the disintegrated 'fragments that we perceive as though through a peephole' are now composed into 'an image of the whole, mediated through this partial view, according to our own emotional capacities and needs for comfort'.[1] Yet, as Saul Friedlander has pointed out with reference to the Holocaust: 'Three decades have increased our knowledge of the events as such, but not our understanding of them. There is no clearer perspective today, no deeper comprehension than immediately after the war'.[2]

Facing this difference between knowing and understanding, as well as acknowledging how we tend to make sense of the surrounding fragments, forces us to understand how 'memorising' is always an activity that happens in the present.[3] It is an activity that needs to be continued, but also carefully reflected on; not just as a general process, but similarly and more specifically in relation to the narratives, images or spaces that are used for this process. How do we negotiate the fictional in relation to the factual? To what extent are certain artistic perspectives constructed and what can we see in the process of memorising through and with them? What is at stake; what new chances lie within these frames? And with these reflections, a more profound question emerges: What are we actually seeing and understanding? Friedlander, and later Gertrud Koch, point out that these new narratives, in popular representations in film or art, might be better described as 'focusing on certain "phantasms" rather than on historical knowledge'.[4] But, as such, they impact our ways of memorising and so impact the ways in which we think about that past and even our capacity to do so.

Many of John Young's works touch on exactly this dilemma. His History Projects lead into a field that negotiates memory and remembering, aesthetics and ethics, through his use of images and the oscillating dynamics between image and space that he employs. These works raise questions about how image, body and space are connected in a process of memorisation. By understanding what the artist invites us to experience and how, I seek to open a discussion that echoes Georges Didi-Huberman's discussion of the 'oppressive imaginable' in his influential book *Images in Spite of All* (2008):

> In order to know, we must *imagine* for ourselves. … Let us not invoke the unimaginable. Let us not shelter ourselves by saying that we cannot, that we could not by any means, imagine it to the very end. *We are obliged* to that oppressive imaginable. It is a response that we must offer, as a debt to the words and images that certain prisoners snatched, for us, from the harrowing Real of their experience. So let us not invoke the unimaginable.[5]

THEMATIC ECHO CHAMBERS

John Young's History Projects focus on such fragments of history, these split-up traces, like memories that are dislocated yet internalised. 'He sees', as Jacqueline Lo has emphasised, 'a role for art in linking the present to a "world of forgotten stories, discarded objects, and memories … Making art not only means to recollect stories, but to reawaken an intrinsic ethical impulse in the present"'.[6] Hence, in his History Projects, Young circles around those moments in time that are akin to open wounds, like the Nanjing Massacre, the death walks of Chinese migrant labourers through the Australian desert or the Holocaust. These are deeply traumatic historical realities that often, when addressed through images, texts or artworks, engender controversial discussions about the representation of violence and trauma.[7] Such discussions— including Didi-Huberman's analysis of Auschwitz photographs, or debates around films such as Steven Spielberg's *Schindler's List* (1993), or Art Spiegelman's graphic novel *Maus* (1986)—revolve around questions of a negotiation between aesthetics and ethics, fiction and documentary, and with that address the challenging relation the depiction of atrocities has to voyeurism and spectacle.[8] These controversies might be a continuation of a broader philosophical dilemma that stems from the late eighteenth century, when 'the view took hold that the aesthetic realm and the ethical realm are each absolutely autonomous from the other'.[9] As a result, we see stark contrasting positions, as Ulrich Baer has described regarding the approaches of Claude Lanzmann and Jean-Luc Godard:

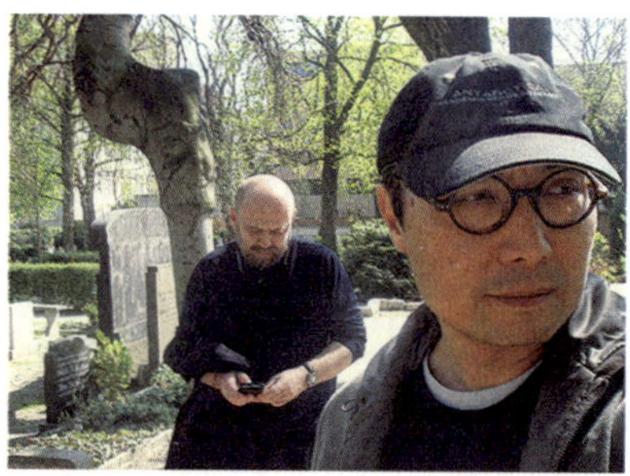

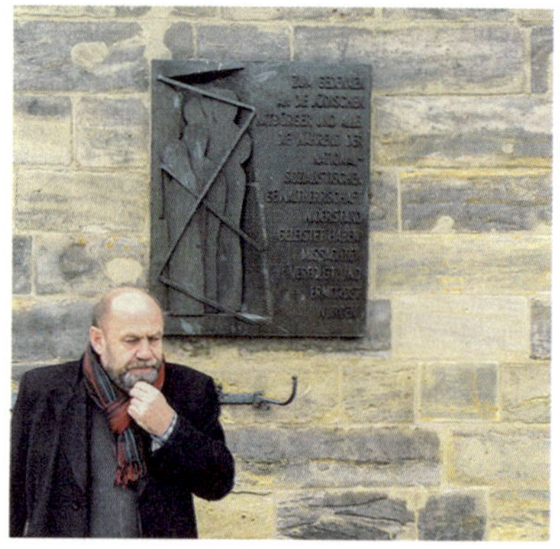

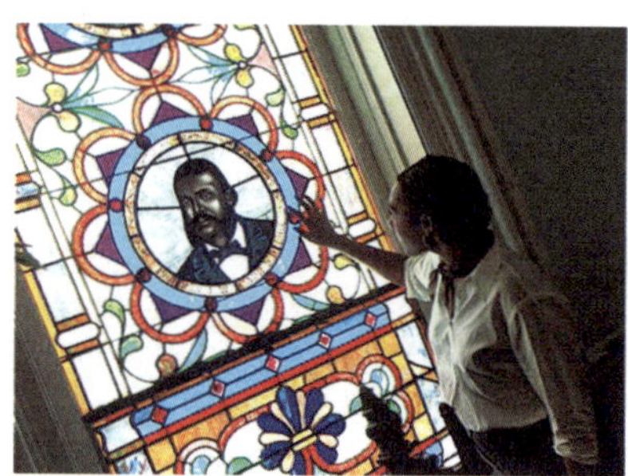

Left to right: Alexander Ochs and the artist
Dorotheestädtuscher Friedhof, Berlin, 2008
Photograph by the artist

Alexander Ochs at the memorial site
of Dietrich Bonhoeffer
Dorotheestädtuscher Friedhof, Berlin, 2008
Photograph by the artist

Stained-glass window depicting early pastors
First African Baptist Church, Savannah, Georgia

Lanzmann's polemical position is that no archival footage of the Holocaust explains anything. We must ignore or even destroy the archives and seek to present the event in our present time in order to approach it as something that has yet to be understood. This purist position is largely in keeping with a Freudian understanding of trauma as an event that cannot be adequately understood at the time of its occurrence and by definition must await expression or resolution at a later point. Godard's position, in contrast, seeks to show how memories and even actual images of the Holocaust haunt the postwar imagination and must be activated in our culture's image repertoire. [10]

John Young's position in this context seems closer to Godard's approach of 'activation', a shift that dates from his 2009 exhibition *Bonhoeffer in Harlem*, held at St Matthäus Church, Berlin.

Bonhoeffer in Harlem (2009)

The name Dietrich Bonhoeffer is closely connected with the resistance towards the atrocities of Nazi Germany. Mentioning the name Bonhoeffer in Germany—*if* people remember it—usually evokes an association with values of morality and ethics. The reason being that Bonhoeffer, a German Lutheran pastor, member of the Confessing Church and theologian, is known for his resistance to the Nazi government (including his involvement in plans to assassinate Adolf Hitler), and his strong opposition to the genocide of Jewish people. These attitudes, combined with the tragic circumstances of his execution in the Flossenbürg concentration camp during the last days of World War II, have made him a key figure in the memory of ethical resistance to Nazism. Less well known is the fact that his travels—specifically his encounter with the Abyssinian Baptist Church in Harlem during a sojourn to the United States of America in the early 1930s—inspired him to become an outspoken critic of what he considered to be a dysfunctional church:

> It has been suggested this period abroad played a crucial role in his intellectual and spiritual development, where Bonhoeffer 'turned from phraseology to reality'. The Harlem experience made him a sensitive critic of American racism and deepened his resistance to German anti-Semitism. He returned to Berlin in 1931 with a clear conviction to fight against racist ideologies. He was ordained at St Matthäus Church on 15 November 1931.[11]

Significantly, when Young began developing his project on Bonhoeffer, he not only returned to the same Berlin church that was so important for the pastor (where Bonhoeffer was ordained in 1931), he also connected Bonhoeffer's name not with the common narrative of resistance to dictatorship, but rather with Bonhoeffer's transcultural experience in New York, that to many might have been unknown. In 2009, when Young described key aspects of the project he had started, he highlighted why it was so important for him to focus on this aspect of Bonhoeffer's life and how it would be addressed—particularly in a large hanging tapestry based on the colourful stained-glass windows of the Abyssinian Baptist Church. However, though the large silk tapestry played a crucial role, it is important to understand this exhibition project as multifaceted, consisting of three corresponding segments.

The first segment was the prominent colourful tapestry, which was positioned in the centre of the church. Designed as an altar piece, it hung where the crucifix would usually be; a central point for the audience or community to see. On the one hand, its positioning resonates with a tradition of stained-glass windows that for centuries have created an experience of colourful, transcendental light around the altar space.[12] On the other, by exchanging material, from glass to silk, Young combines this medium with traditional tapestry weaving, which in this case (if we understand the tapestry as what Michel Foucault referred to as heterotopic) similarly creates a form of transcendental space.[13] Rooted in the actual space of St Matthäus Church in Berlin, and in the windows of the Harlem Gospel Church, the work invites the audience into a state of immersion and contemplation.

As a stark contrast to this colourful, meditative experience, the second part of the work consists of eleven more conceptual pieces: eight chalk drawings on blackboard-painted paper and three inkjet prints, distributed along the side aisles of the church. This segment creates a darker tone, an atmosphere that with its regular rhythm forms a strong opposition to the colourful space in the nave. Yet it is not only through its colour that this segment produces such gravity. What we can see written in chalk on the blackboard-paper is a combination of names, central ideas, theories and biographical data related to the life of Bonhoeffer. These are highly charged with meaning for those who know about the life of the central figure and can therefore decode the words; they are also undecipherable fragments to those who are not familiar with the history, and for whom the works may only be reminiscent of educational tools that invite or challenge the observer to 'do their homework' and learn about this unknown (hi)story. Even though a number of scholars have noted how these works seem to resonate with the (art) historical works of German artist Joseph Beuys or the anthroposophical philosopher Rudolf Steiner, to those who don't know these histories it will not be art history that resonates.[14] Instead, it is a grim dark form that speaks from these boards.

However, these eight works are also combined with a set of black-and-white inkjet images. These depict a portrait of Bonhoeffer, two children and an image of a bird, specifically a thrush. Compared to the dark panels these images strike a different chord and attract. They are different in that they are approachable, and in a way nostalgic—in a literal sense, from the Greek *nostos algos*, meaning 'open wound'. If we apply this idea to the impact of the images, it seems that specifically through them we can grasp something of that open wound of the past, of the pain that is in the past. This highlights the different modes of memorising by language-based information and images; as Gertrud Koch has noted, 'Pictorial representations evoke special interest because they serve our need to unveil the unseen (including the past we were not part of). Images activate different sites of memory from those activated by language'.[15]

In terms of Young's installation, this means that an audience can move back and forth between images and language, between two modes of memorising, and with each oscillation dig deeper into Bonhoeffer's history. Until, that is, the visitor leaves the side aisles of the church and encounters the third segment: two colourful abstract paintings. These seem to pick up the audience, lead back into a lighter atmosphere and reconnect the audience with their initial experience of the central altarpiece. The installation becomes a physical experience that an audience is drawn into. An experience that requests not only understanding but also even more spatial action and empathy.

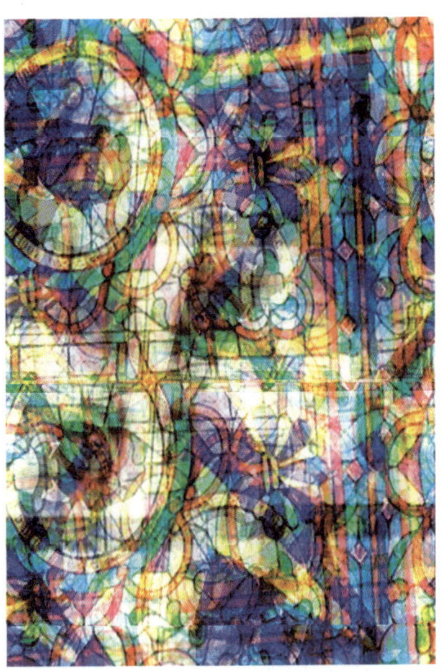

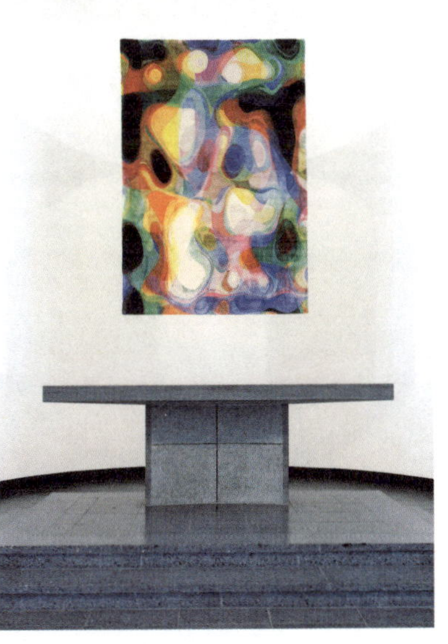

Composite drawing of stained-glass window, 2009

Bonhoeffer in Harlem 2009
Chinese silk tapestry, 303 × 119 cm
Installation view, St Matthäus Church,
Kulturforum, Berlin, 2009
Collection of Erlöserkirche, Bamberg

In a way Young's work here resonates with the philosophy of Bonhoeffer himself, who wrote: 'Mere waiting and looking on is not Christian behavior. Christians are called to compassion *and* to action'.[16]

Schindler (2016)

There are three outstanding formal aspects that closely connect *Bonhoeffer in Harlem*, with Young's *Schindler* project, realised seven years later in the same city. The first is the fact that again, at the centre of the project, we find a seminal figure that holds a special position in the history of the Holocaust. The second similarity is that Young again realised the project in a space of utmost significance to Germany's historical experience during fascism: the New Synagogue, Berlin-Centrum Judaicum. Since its construction, the New Synagogue has been the biggest synagogue in Berlin, and even though it was attacked by a Nazi mob during the November Pogrom of 1938 and bombed during the air raids of World War II, it has survived and stands today as one of the most important places of Jewish worship in Germany. Finally, the third correspondence is Young's use of the blackboard paper form—but in contrast to his earlier work, this time Young does not use colourful works that would alternate with this somber tone.

Despite these similarities it is important to point out one significant difference to the Bonhoeffer work: *Schindler* was not presented as a solo exhibition but was part of the group show *The Repetition of the Good. The Repetition of the Bad*, curated by Alexander Ochs. This means that the work was not standing by itself developing its qualities, instead it was put into a thematic frame with works by other artists.

Young contributed his *Schindler* installation in one of the main spaces of the Synagogue, the circular Repräsentantensaal (representational hall). Thematically, this work circles around the figure of Oskar Schindler, the German industrialist and member of the Nazi Party, who by strategically employing 1200 Jews saved their lives and is therefore acknowledged by the State of Israel as a 'Righteous among the Nations'. He is a particularly interesting person in the frame of this analysis, since his name is not only connected to the actions he took during the National Socialist period, but also because he later became the famous subject of a novel (Thomas Keneally's *Schindler's Ark*, 1982) and its movie adaption (*Schindler's List*, 1993) by Steven Spielberg. Spielberg's film engendered a heated and many layered debate, but one of the most critical takes on it came from director and scholar Claude Lanzmann, who saw it as a 'kitschy melodrama' and a 'deformation of truth'.[17] I think it is important to lay out some of his arguments against Spielberg's film in more detail since he raises questions that are also relevant, though in a different way, to Young's works.

Lanzmann writes:

> Spielberg will see himself confronted with a dilemma. He cannot tell the story about Schindler without also telling what the holocaust has been. But how can he tell what the holocaust was, if he is telling the story of a German who saved 1300 jews, while the overwhelming majority of the Jews was not saved? Even when he shows the moment of the deportation to the Cracau ghetto, or the camp officer shooting at the deported, how can he do justice, even then, to the normalcy of the procedure of murder, the machinery of the extermination? It did not go like that for everyone. In Treblinka, or in Auschwitz, the possibility of salvation was inconceivable.

He further explains:

> The whole film is attached to the personal story of Schindler: Schindler
> and women, Schindler and sex, Schindler and money, Schindler who is
> a gambler of sorts. That appeals; it is a bit like *Raiders of the Lost Arc*. Yet,
> when you see Schindler at work, having dinner with German officers or SS-
> people to implicate them in the story, these figures certainly appear corrupt,
> but at the same time, they are not wholly unsympathetic in their beautiful
> uniforms. This is, exactly, the problem of the image, of the picture.[18]

Indeed—we must understand what it means to shift perspectives when the history
of the Holocaust is addressed through the 'peephole' perspective of a German figure.
Even though in Young's work we don't see the Holocaust through the eyes of Schindler
(as we partially do in Spielberg's film), we do *think* the Holocaust through this figure.
It is a shift of perspective, which in Young's case shows an approach that steps away
from the general categories of good and bad (echoing the exhibition title) and complicates
the narrative towards a position that searches for the ethical good in the bad.

For *Schindler*, Young quite intentionally does not include photographic images as
in the Bonhoeffer work, and with that embraces what Lanzmann had pointed out
as problematic: the storytelling image that is the starting point of a revisionist history.
Young here instead favours the written information and the blackboard paintings,
which in this case are placed in pairs between columns and in line with the circular
architecture of the hall. They are rhythmically grouped and suspended in mid-air, which
creates the visual effect that they seem to float strangely in space, even though they
appear heavy through their blackness—almost like a mixture of tombstones and the
portentous monolithic block in Stanley Kubrick's film *2001: A Space Odyssey* (1968).

Looking at the individual works of this group we again find hand-written fragments
that relate to the protagonist's life (such as 'Emalia', which relates to Schindler's
enamelware factory). Furthermore, we see words like 'atonement', which invite the
audience to a more general reflection of what these words might mean to us. Finally,
we see that the addressing of the audience goes even further, turning into a more direct
and individual exchange when, on one of the works, we read the words 'you – ou –
near'. It is a moment when the reflection and construction of history, the process of
remembering, turns into a question for the now. How do we as an audience in this art
installation, and in this very moment in time, think about being near? Where is the
other? Where are you next to me?

These questions address us and make us think about compassion, about care for the
other, or in religious terms the love of one's neighbor, which means that these works
challenge our understanding and our capacity to relate, even when the traces and the
fragments we are confronted with seem almost completely erased. Some of Young's
blackboard paintings look like they have been freshly wiped with a sponge. Fog-like,
chalk smeared, no information is left, no words are decodable anymore.

For Young, it seems other connections start to appear out of these clouds; connections
that tie this investigation of the artist back to other frames of the History Projects.
This means that we can not only see a formal correspondence between the *Schindler*
and *Bonhoeffer* projects, but also that we find one of the original Bonhoeffer blackboard
paintings (Abyssinia) included in the *Schindler* work. By transferring this segment, the

Schindler 2016
Chalk on blackboard-painted archival cotton
paper, 100 x 70 cm

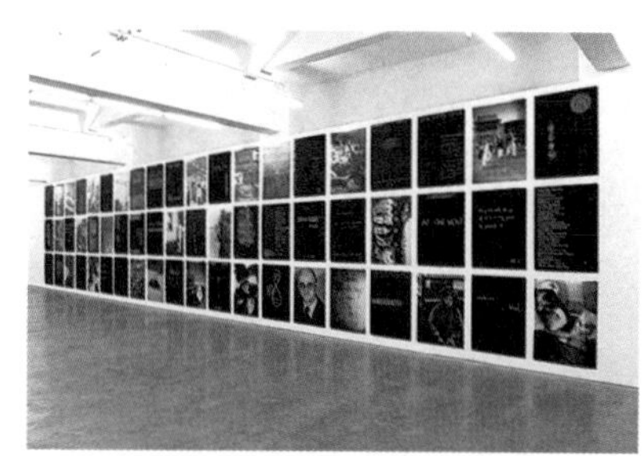

artist increasingly steps away from a story that relates to the actual historic events and develops a different strategy, looking into the question of a meta-narrative about ethical behavior; and that creates a connection between Bonhoeffer, Schindler and—since Young includes another blackboard painting from his *Safety Zone* work in *Schindler* as well—John Rabe.

Safety Zone (2010)

In *Safety Zone*, Young turns his focus to the Chinese city of Nanjing. In December 1937, the city was captured by Japanese Imperial Forces and in the following weeks they committed war crimes including rape, torture and unjustified executions on an unimaginable scale. Almost a quarter of a million Chinese citizens were killed, according to the late American writer Iris Chang, who called it the 'forgotten holocaust of World War II'. In her book *The Rape of Nanking* (1991), apart from the massacre and atrocities, a different story is brought to light. She presents a collection of documents and memoirs that highlight how a group of expatriates living in Nanjing had created a 'safety zone' that made it possible to protect a large number of Chinese citizens from the Japanese troops.

As pointed out above, in this work Young zooms in on this unknown history. And here again, we find one protagonist (John Rabe) who, like Schindler, is German and a member of the National Socialist Party, with conflicted connections to the atrocities of the Holocaust, and so stands out. But in *Safety Zone*, it is not only the cross-cultural ethical action of an individual that is addressed. Rather, it concerns the activities of fifteen American and European missionaries and businesspeople in Nanjing at the time, saving some 200,000 Chinese citizens from the advancing Japanese army—and this is an important shift. Even though the figure of John Rabe is very relevant for the work, instead of centralising the ethical question around one protagonist, here Young highlights the communal aspect of their efforts. This work does not narrate a superior ethical individual to produce a heroic monumentalism to which the audience can only bow in reverence. Instead, we see that this act of resistance is realised by very different individuals, adding a variety of layers to this history. Young has commented on this shift away from individual heroism, saying: '*Safety Zone* was initially conceived as an account of cross-cultural heroism, but it became a project that can be related to our contemporary dada—linked to desertion, amnesia, disappearance and the apocalypse; including in a wider sense modernity's disappearance and the apocalypse of art as we know it'.[19] Therefore, with *Safety Zone*, the artist produces less of a salvation story—the work offers a far more complex narrative. It delivers a quality that in relation to other works of art (that deal with historic atrocities) has been subsumed as:

> [A] wider range of emotions, affects and aesthetically induced expressive reactions, for it does not focus only on moral feelings such as pity, righteousness, ritual mourning, and so forth. By accepting normatively less valued emotions such as pain, despair, sadness and rage, it avoids sinking into a morality tale and expresses the more complex subjectivity contained in aesthetic representation.[20]

And as with Young's other installations, *Safety Zone* is also a very spatial experience that shows his strong interest in the architectural layout. In this case the audience enters a long rectangular space where the works are placed in a very rigid manner. On the right, we can see a long wall almost completely covered by three rows of Young's blackboard paintings mixed with digital prints from archival images. These images

Safety Zone 2010
Installation view, Anna Schwartz Gallery, Melbourne, 2010

154

include portraits of some of the key figures of the group of foreigners (Dr Robert Wilson, John Rabe), or images of schoolgirls from the Ginling Girls' College, which was established by the American Minnie Vautrin, and was for a long time a safe haven for Chinese girls. Interspersed on the blackboard paintings we can read again, written in chalk, messages like: 'Unspeakable acts of Evil', 'This is a drawing for John Rabe'; or 'Du hast das Herz eines Buddha' (You have the heart of a Buddha). And we once more see the 'Atonement' painting—the element that literally connects all three installations. With artworks covering almost its full length and height, this dark wall appears massive and leaves a palpable physical impression on the audience.

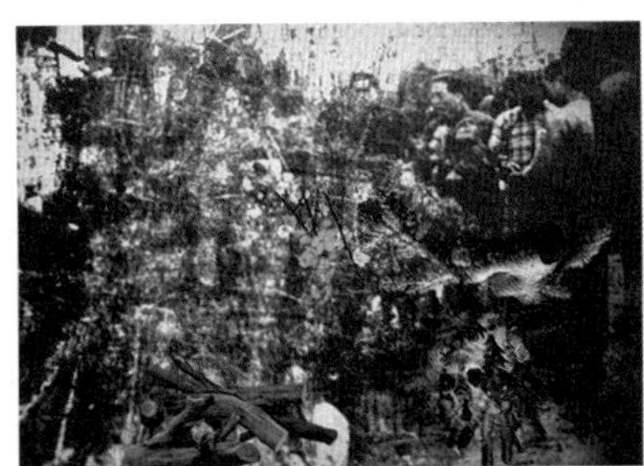

Opposite this wall, on the left, we see three bigger works distributed more generously. At first glance, and from a distance, these works look like archival photos. A few figures can be seen, but generally these images are hard to decode. Even after looking for a while, they appear more like visual undergrowth, difficult to penetrate. But when we get closer, we discover different layers: the archival photo that is digitally printed, and another layer painted in oil. While one cannot fully decipher the images—even though the figures and the aesthetics of these three works suggest a connection to the images on the other side of the room, and to the tree paintings at either end of the gallery—these works begin to develop a completely different conversation: one that is less about targeting the questions of 'What do I see?' and 'How useful are certain images in the process of remembering?'. Here, Young seems increasingly interested in enquiries such as how reliable the photo or painting is as a mediation of reality and history, or how to navigate the question of ethics and aesthetics in the dynamic tensions between analogue and digital spheres. Young leads us to negotiate between these fields and demonstrates that the question of how to represent atrocities needs to be taken absolutely seriously in relation to these discourses: 'Otherwise there is a danger of ending up either with the reductionism of postmodern historiography (all stories are possible and all historiography is nothing more than telling stories) or with morality tales'.[21]

SPATIAL CONFIGURATIONS

> Here are we, one magical movement from Kether to Malkhuth
> There are you, you drive like a demon from station to station.
>> David Bowie,
>> *Station to Station* (1976)

> Bergson's warning about the temptations of spatializing thought remain current in … an era of urban dissolution and re-ghettoization, in which we might be tempted to think that the social can be mapped that way, by following across a map insurance red lines and the electrified borders of private police and surveillance forces. Both images are, however, only caricatures of the mode of production itself (most often called late capitalism) whose mechanisms and dynamics are not visible in that sense, cannot be detected on the surfaces scanned by satellites, and therefore stand as a fundamental representational problem – indeed a problem of a historically new and original type.
>> Frederic Jameson,
>> *The Geopolitical Aesthetic* (1992)

After taking a closer look at aspects like depiction, narratives, language, materiality or formal correspondences between works, I lastly turn to the question of space and how

Flower Market (Nanjing 1936) #1 2010
Digital print and oil on linen, 240 × 331 cm

it impacts all of Young's works analysed above. By that I don't mean to return to an analysis of the specific symbolic gravity that some of these historic spaces themselves contain. Instead, I would like to highlight how Young's works use certain socio-spatial structures embedded in these architectures. It has been important to critically reflect on how images, texts and themes raise questions and configure our understanding and thinking. But if we don't consider the impact of the spatial frames and dynamics in which we experience them we might miss a crucial point that not only impacts our thought processes but also forms a profound aspect of Young's work in general. As Jungmin Lee has emphasised, 'installation is always contained within a frame, whether it be a site, spatial location, or cultural context'.[22] This aspect might become clearer now, at a historical distance—since we are no longer immersed in the here and now of these installations we are able to see more clearly how the works' different spatial formations add to them a very specific dimension. Comparing these History Projects as installations thus allows us to understand how these different works are also an investigation into the way space shapes our processes of remembering.

The Church

We have seen how space is a crucial element in Young's *Bonhoeffer* project. Placing an art installation in a church is by no means entering neutral territory. In this space, each part of the installation is charged with meaning that is connected to certain processes and rituals. Young is very aware of this, as we see in the way he uses a clear spatial division in the placement of the various groups of works. He creates a form that follows the distinct architectural features of the church, producing a specific narrative. While the central piece, for example, is located in the sanctum over the altar, between the usual location of the cross and the apse, Young's other works can be found spread throughout the side aisles. This placement, combined with the fact that we find fourteen works in this cycle, gives a strong indication of the kind of spatial layout and narrative being followed: the Way of the Cross. Since the seventeenth century, this has been a distinct feature of almost all Catholic churches. Architecturally, the fourteen stations of the cross are spread out along the side aisles. Devotees move from station to station, saying their prayers, honoring the passion of Christ and strengthening their belief by contemplating his sufferings. This path—a spatialised narrative—constitutes a form of sacred conversation. Since early Christianity, this sacred conversation has not necessarily come from the content of the images, such as the depiction of Mary being overwhelmed by the pain of her son (mimesis). Instead, the idea shifts towards a form in which images create the feeling of being overwhelmed directly, allowing the observer to feel the impact the experience might have had on her.

If we recognise this Catholic ritual, including the role of images, and connect this to the experience of Young's work, we understand that the artist creates a very specific environment. It could be interpreted along the lines of Christian philosophy: 'In the combination, we are presented with an iridescent image, a shifting between light and dark, opacity and transparence, being earthly and Christian spirituality. The board drawings emblematise repression and death, but the tapestry as well as both abstract works disperse the severity of these works, and in so doing Young leads us back to light and hope.'[23] Yet a different path of interpretation might well be possible when we, as observers, experience Young's installation as a struggle in which neither the words nor the images gain the upper hand, an experience similar to that described by Didi-Huberman:

> Before this image, all of a sudden, our present may see itself stopped in its tracks and simultaneously born in the experience of the gaze. … Before

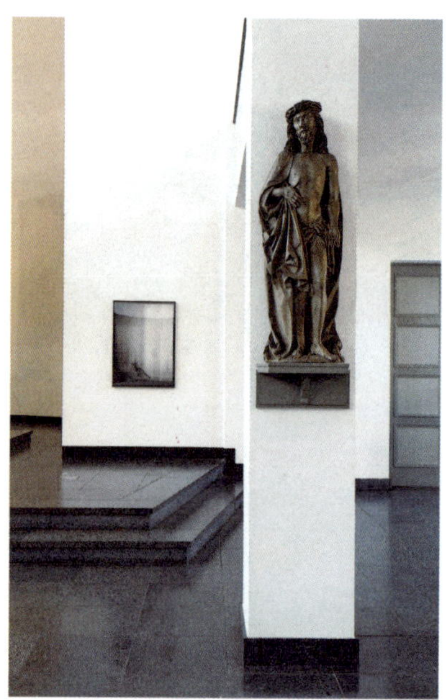

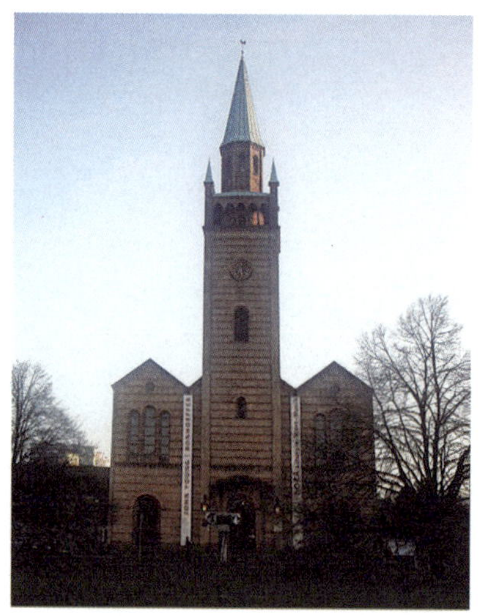

Bonhoeffer in Harlem 2009
Installation view, St Matthäus Church,
Kulturforum, Berlin, 2009

St Matthäus Church, Kulturforum, Berlin, 2009

an image, however old it may be, the present never ceases to reshape,
provided that the dispossession of the gaze has not entirely given way to
the vain complacency of the 'specialist'. Before an image, however recent,
however contemporary it may be, the past never ceases to reshape, since
this image only becomes thinkable in a construction of the memory, if not
of the obsession. Before an image, finally, we have to humbly recognize
this fact: that it will probably outlive us, that before it we are the fragile
element, the transient element, and that before us it is the element of the
future, the element of permanence. The image often has more memory
and more future than the being who contemplates it.[24]

For Young's installation this means that we, placed in a specific situation like this,
not only become aware of a certain history in time, but furthermore we understand
through this setting the impact of images and even more importantly our own
involvement—how we are a crucial and active part of this texture.

The Synagogue

One of the significant features of Young's *Schindler* installation is its location in the
rotunda of the Berlin Synagogue. The rotunda structure leads us back to one of the
matrices of circular architecture: the Pantheon. A roman temple structure that was
built in the second century as a place of worship for the gods—Πάνθειον *(Pantheion)*,
meaning 'relating to, or common to all the gods'—its iconic structure influenced
architectural sites not just for centuries, but millennia.[25] This impact, architecturally
and spiritually, can be found again, for example, in the Parisian Church of Sainte
Geneviève, which, during the French Revolution, was turned into the secular
monument named the Panthéon of Paris. Here, as well as in other sites, architecturally
the rotunda structure was not necessarily kept intact. Instead, the name Panthéon
became a more general term used to indicate buildings to bury or honour the dead.
And specifically in Paris, the Marquis de Villette suggested that this designation,
following the model of the Pantheon in Rome, should even be a temple in honor
of liberty: 'Let us install statues of our great men and lay their ashes to rest in its
underground recesses'.[26] In April 1791 it was decided 'that this religious church
become a temple of the nation, that the tomb of a great man become the altar of
liberty', and the assembly approved a new entrance text that reads: 'A grateful nation
honors its great men.'[27]

When John Young actively positioned his project in the Berlin Synagogue's rotunda,
he was not simply choosing an iconic space for the display of his work—he was
placing his work in a 2000-year-old architectural concept, closely linked since the
French Revolution to the idea of the memorial. Furthermore, it is noteworthy that
just three years before Young installed his work in that rotunda, a plaque had been
installed in the Panthéon of Paris by then French president Jacques Chirac honoring
2600 people who had been recognised as Righteous among the Nations by the
Yad Vashem memorial in Israel for saving Jewish lives. The plaque reads:

> Under the cloak of hatred and darkness that spread over France during
> the years of [Nazi] occupation, thousands of lights refused to be
> extinguished. Named as 'Righteous among the Nations' or remaining
> anonymous, women and men, of all backgrounds and social classes, saved
> Jews from anti-Semitic persecution and the extermination camps. Braving
> the risks involved, they embodied the honour of France, and its values
> of justice, tolerance and humanity.[28]

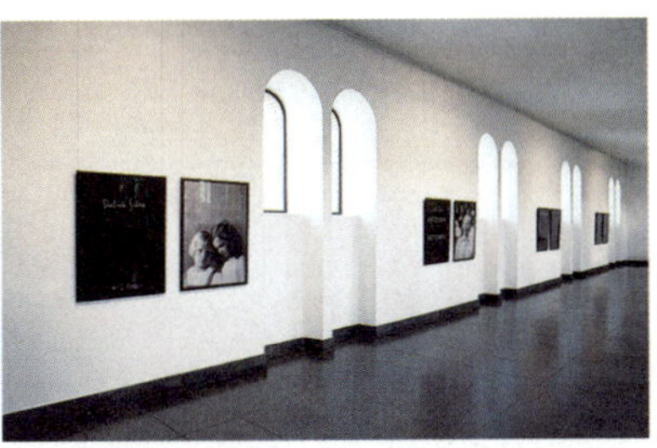

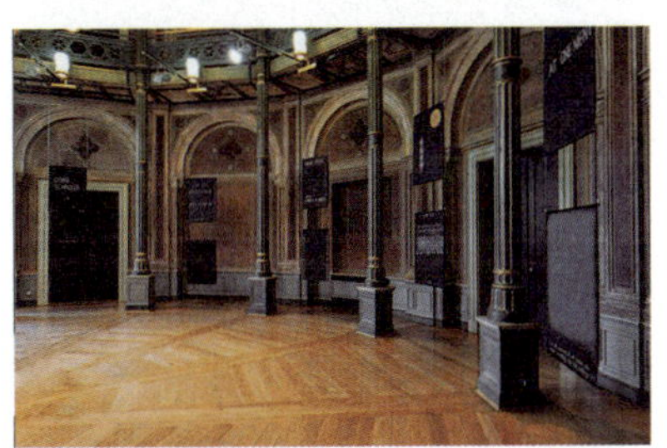

The *Schindler* work in the rotunda in Berlin thus creates an echo between these spaces. What we can grasp here is how the tradition of remembering has manifested in the physical architecture of the Pantheon and crosses and spreads between nations, cultures and times—and this is something in which Young has been profoundly interested throughout the History Projects.

But beyond this historic layer, there is something interesting about the specific physical experience of the rotunda: the circular structure clearly departs from the dominant architecture of rectangular spaces in the everyday.[29] While rectangular spaces usually create a dynamic in which we can find a certain directionality, and a more linear orientation, the rotunda does not. On the contrary, it is an architecture in which we are given no lines of orientation and therefore often feel strangely disoriented. Finding our way through, or reorienting ourselves in this space, requires us to step away from our usual behavior and enter into a circular movement that oscillates between centrifugal and centripetal forces. A strange dance unfolds, which can be experienced either as a virtuous *or* vicious circle—one that is deeply positive or devastatingly negative. This disorienting dynamic, this moment of divisiveness within one place, again seems to be in sync with the artist's interest in 'in-between-states'.

As such, the space of experience may be as impactful as the images and information that we are directly confronted with in Young's work. This offers the audience two things. Firstly, the chance to immerse oneself in a circular movement can increase to a spin into layers and repetitions of history. This can in turn create an opportunity to see history in a completely new way or lead to the feeling of losing oneself— creating a double-bind. In both cases we can detect that, as Paul Watzlawick has diagnosed, 'virtually all these cases of pathological communication … are vicious circles that cannot be broken unless and until communication itself becomes the subject of communication, in other words, until the communicants are able to metacommunicate. But to do this they have to step outside the circle'.[30] In other words, Young installs a situation in which, no matter if the experience is positive or negative, we have to step out of the frame in order to grasp the full scope of the work.

Secondly, given the location of the space in the Synagogue, it connects the audience to another important cultural tradition of repetition: repetition in the Jewish religion. The repetition we find, for example, in the concept of *Midah Mishnah* (learning by repetition), the Jewish liturgical prayer, or in the celebration of Yom Kippur, The Day of Atonement.[31] And Yom Kippur, specifically, seems to be very significant in the context of this work. Since to atone does not mean to atone only on one day. As Rabbi Dusty Klass explains:

> 'Yom Kippur' is really a misnomer—for we do not atone merely on this
> day. Rather, we spend the entire month leading up to Rosh Hashanah
> and then even more intensely in these ten days between Rosh Hashanah
> and Yom Kippur making t'shuva, making space in us to forgive and
> asking for forgiveness from others. T'shuva, the act of returning, is all
> about repetition. We circle back to ourselves, looking inward to find those
> moments in which we missed the mark. We circle back to those we have
> hurt and we apologize. Maimonides teaches that we have only made true
> and complete t'shuva when we find ourselves in a repeat situation—only
> when we are faced with the same opportunity to transgress and refrain
> have we made full repentance.[32]

Young adapts this process of repetition; and connects it, as Carolyn Barnes has observed in relation to his paintings, 'to Deleuze's idea from *Difference and Repetition* that for the past to achieve its full potential as a basis for understanding and action in the present, it must be represented as a 'pure' form while simultaneously retaining certain 'surface intensities' that reflect its specificity'.[33] It is important to highlight here again that Young primarily accomplishes this mode, not through the individual works themselves, but by creating a complex structure in which the installed works collaborate with the specific architectural form of the location.

The Gallery

For the final part of our journey through Young's installation spaces we return to *Safety Zone*, in its first manifestation, in 2010.[34] Above, I described how the layout leaves its mark on the audience: specifically, the wall on the right, with its intense configuration of digitised archival photo prints and blackboard paintings, creates a kind of gravity. Filling the length and breadth of the wall, its dark tones have an almost visceral impact. And even though, in this case, the space itself is architecturally not as symbolically loaded as the Berlin installations, the density of this gridded wall of dark rectangles resonates with memorial architecture. This form is reminiscent of the columbarium: structures that for centuries have featured walls with rows of grid-like niches for the cremated ashes of the dead. In comparison to individual tombs that have often been a privilege of the elites, the columbarium, in its simple form, has closer ties to the poorer or non-elite members of society. And instead of the representational and typically public character that is likewise associated with individual tombs, the niche of a columbarium offers a more personal, individual form of commemoration.[35]

Thinking of Young's installation with this in mind, it is not difficult to see how the spatial idea of commemoration in the columbarium is quite apt. But, of course, in the gallery we don't stand in front of a particular niche to which we have personal ties. We are not going to one specific spot in order to exclusively pay our respects. This means that in contrast to the columbarium, here we walk among and relate to the whole series of images. And with an awareness for this movement through the space another aspect becomes graspable: depending on how the audience is approaching the wall, this work offers different modes of perception. For example, if the audience stays closer to the wall the work slowly unfolds image by image, painting by painting—an experience that has been described as cinematic:

> In *Safety Zone*, reproductions of historical photographs and drawings on chalk blackboard paint comprise a quasi-cinematic language of reference and representation, especially in regard to the role of characters as bearers of narrative and embodiments of values and meanings. The sum effect evokes memory as a montage of elements, some fully wrought, others fleeting in form—a text whose countless potential connections are open to exploration.[36]

However, if the observer is further away from the wall, the perception shifts more towards a non-filmic mode. The more distanced we are from the wall the more we can see the grid in its totality, more as a collage. But this wider perspective, this 'overview', comes with a price: the further we are away from the actual works, the more the individual works begin to blur. The further we move, the more the blur of the images and paintings intensifies. This creates not only a visually, but a psychologically

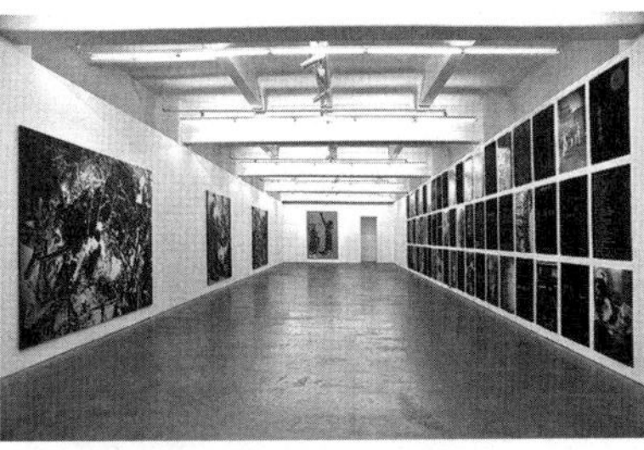

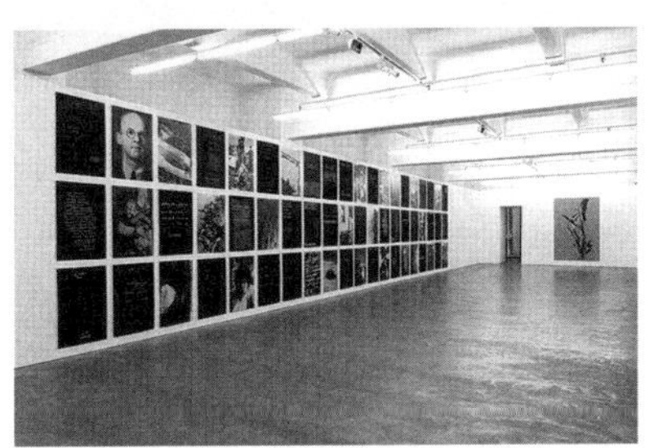

uncomfortable situation. While the installations in the church and in the synagogue offered spatial frames in which the process of thinking and commemorating was taking place, in the gallery it seems the installation does not offer such structures. Instead, the works are installed in such a way that the audience is constantly thrown back on itself. There is no safety here—the work throws the observer back into a grey zone in which no rituals for historical digestion are preconfigured. Nevertheless, with that, 'John Young's work offers a way to grieve for this history from a position of alterity, not to reify a victim discourse or promote cultural chauvinism but rather to reimagine, reengage and co-exist with others with compassion and empathy'.[37]

Moreover, caught in this in-between space, in this state of blurring, a more painterly resonance can also emerge, like the work of Gerhard Richter. Both Richter and Young use blurring as a tool to challenge our visual approach to our surroundings and with that our approach to our histories:

> In phenomenological terms, it can be conceived of as a mental state
> in which the relation to the world of objects blurs and the act of
> blurring causes that world to appear particularly threatening—to
> appear as an impenetrable presence. And against the background of a
> phenomenological description of vertigo as a way of relating to the object
> world, some of the motifs that recur in Richter's pictures, photographs,
> and paintings take shape as embodiments of a conscious preference for
> the out-of-focus, for the blurred. It is not simply a case of imprecision;
> rather, it is the capture of a sliding glance.[38]

If we recognise the same 'sliding glance' in Young's work, the question for us as an audience becomes: How do we work with these forms? How do we relate or engage with them? Genevieve Trail has highlighted how the History Projects 'are driven by the search for a temporally and spatially specific ethic, one that eschews the vagaries associated with the collapse into a universal moral code and relies instead on a didactic communicative principle in order to reground art's function, while retaining its autonomy as an aesthetic domain'.[39] Yet, besides this ever-present discourse in Young's projects, if we step away from the specific narratives and frames of each individual work, then we can understand Young's whole cycle of History Projects as an even more radical and critical investigation into the hidden impact of spatial frames and can grasp how our 'understandings of the spatiality of memory have developed'.[40]

1. Gertrud Koch, '"Against All Odds" or the Will to Survive: Moral Conclusions from Narrative Closure', *History and Memory*, vol. 9, no. 1 and 2, p. 397.

2. Saul Friedlander, 'Some Aspects of the Historical Significance of the Holocaust', *Jerusalem Quarterly*, issue 1, 1976, p. 137.

3. Here I use memorising not in the sense of remembering/preserving a certain aspect by fixing it, or learning by heart. Instead, I understand it more as a process of continuous renegotiation, in which we have to rethink and reconsider the idea of a certain history, again and again.

4. Koch, p. 398. See as well: Saul Friedlander, *Reflections of Nazism: An Essay on Kitsch and Death*, Harper & Row, New York, 1984.

5. Georges Didi-Huberman, 'Four Pieces of Film Snatched from Hell' in *Images in Spite of All: Four Photographs from Auschwitz*, University of Chicago, Chicago, 2008, p. 3.

6. Jacqueline Lo, 'Diaspora, Art and Empathy', originally published in *John Young: The Bridge and the Fruit Tree*, Drill Hall Gallery, Australian National University, 2013, and republished in this volume with a new introduction, see pp. 137–47.

7. An overview of the complex debate since Adorno can be found in Saul Friedlander (ed.), *Probing the Limits of Representation: Nazism and the 'Final Solution'*, Harvard University Press, Cambridge, MA, 1992. For the more recent debate see: Bruno Chaouat, 'In the Image of Auschwitz', *Diacritics*, vol. 36, no. 1, 2006, pp. 86–96; Karoline Feyertag, 'The Art of Vision and the Ethics of Gaze', *Transversal Texts*, (trans.) Camilla Nielsen, April 2008, https://transversal.at/transversal/0408/feyertag/en.

8. For an analysis of these debates, see Noël Carroll, 'Art and Ethical Criticism: An Overview of Recent Directions of Research', *Ethics*, vol. 110, no. 2, January 2000, pp. 350–87.

9. Ibid., p. 350.

10. Ulrich Baer, 'Images in Spite of All: Four Photographs from Auschwitz', *Visual Resources*, vol. 26, no. 2, 2010, p. 183.

11. Lo, pp. 25–26.

12. I addressed this question of immersion and thinking through colour, light and space perception in my dissertation: Marc Glöde, 'Farbige Lichträume: Manifestationen einer Veränderung des Bild-Raumdenkens' ('Coloured Light Spaces: Manifestations of a change in image-making'), Wilhelm Fink Verlag, 2014.

13. Michel Foucault, 'Of Other Spaces', *Diacritics*, vol. 16, no. 1, Spring 1986, pp. 22–27.

14. The list includes Allison Holland, Thomas Berghuis, Sylvia D. Volz and Jacqueline Lo, to name the most prominent scholars.

15. Koch, p. 399.

16. Dietrich Bonhoeffer, *Letters and Papers from Prison*, 'After Ten Years: A Reckoning made at the New Year 1943', Macmillan, New York, 1972, p. 17.

17. Claude Lanzmann, '*Schindler's List* is an impossible story', 1994, archived version, Rob van Gerwen (trans.), University College Utrecht, 26 March 2018, https://www.phil.uu.nl/~rob/lanzmannschindler.shtml.

18. Ibid.

19. Young quoted in Thomas Berghuis, 'John Young: Situational Ethics', originally in *Art & Australia*, vol. 48, no. 3, 2011, pp. 440–43, republished in this volume. See p. 134.

20. Koch, p. 405.

21. Ibid., pp. 405–06.

22. Jungmin Lee, 'Modes of Exhibition as Mediated Space: Projection Installation as Spectatorial Frame', *Art & Education*, nd, http://www.artandeducation.net/ paper/modes-of-exhibition-as-mediated-space-projection-installation-as-spectatorial-frame/.

23. Sylvia D. Volz, 'John Young/Bonhoeffer in Harlem', in Alexander Ochs (ed.), *John Young: Bonhoeffer in Harlem*, St Matthäus Church, Berlin, 2009. See the expanded version of Volz's essay in this volume, pp. 92–99.

24. Georges Didi-Huberman, 'Before the Image, Before Time: The Sovereignty of Anachronism', in Claire Farago (ed.), *Compelling Visuality: The Work of Art In and Out of History*, University of Minnesota Press, Minneapolis, 2003, pp. 31–33.

25. I am aware that similar connections to other architectural influences can be drawn here, like the dakhma (Tower of Silence) in Zoroastrian culture. However, in contrast to the Pantheon, the rationale behind this is not the idea of a place for commemoration, but strictly for the containment of the dead.

26. Alexia Lebeurre, *The Pantheon: Temple of the Nation*, Éditions du Patrimoine, Paris, 2000, p. 16.

27. Ibid.

28. See *Wikipedia's* entry on the Panthéon: https://en.wikipedia.org/wiki/Panthéon.

29. The right-wing art historian and former Nazi Party member Hans Sedlmayr believed circular architecture was crucially connected with the French Revolution and therefore the beginning of what he considered the 'downfall of modern culture'. See Hans Sedlmayr, *Art in Crisis: The Lost Center*, Routledge, London, 2006.

30. Paul Watzlawick, Janet Helmick Beavin and Don D. Jackson, *Pragmatics of Human Communication*, Norton, New York, 1967, pp. 95–96.

31. Here we see that Young's blackboard painting with the word 'atonement' has taken a completely different connotation than in the *Bonhoeffer* installation before.

32. Rabbi Dusty Klass, 'Return Again: Finding Meaning in Repetition and Repentance', *Temple Beth El*, October 6 2016, https://templebethel.org/return-finding-meaning-repetition-repentance-rabbi-dusty-klass/.

33. Barnes, p. 61.

34. 'Safety Zone' was first exhibited at Anna Schwartz Gallery, Melbourne, 15 April–22 May 2010.

35. See Dorian Borbonus, *Columbarium Tombs and Collective Identity in Augustan Rome*, Cambridge University Press, Cambridge, 2014.

36. Barnes, p. 62.

37. Lo, p. 43.

38. Gertrud Koch, 'The Richter-Scale of Blur', *October*, vol. 62, Autumn 1992, p. 136.

39. Genevieve Trail, 'Plurality of Memory: History Projects, Diaspora and Nationalism', *Di'van Art Journal*, Issue 8, September 2020, p. 98.

40. David Atkinson, 'Kitsch Geographies and the Everyday Spaces of Social Memory', *Environment and Planning*, vol. 39, 2007, p. 522.

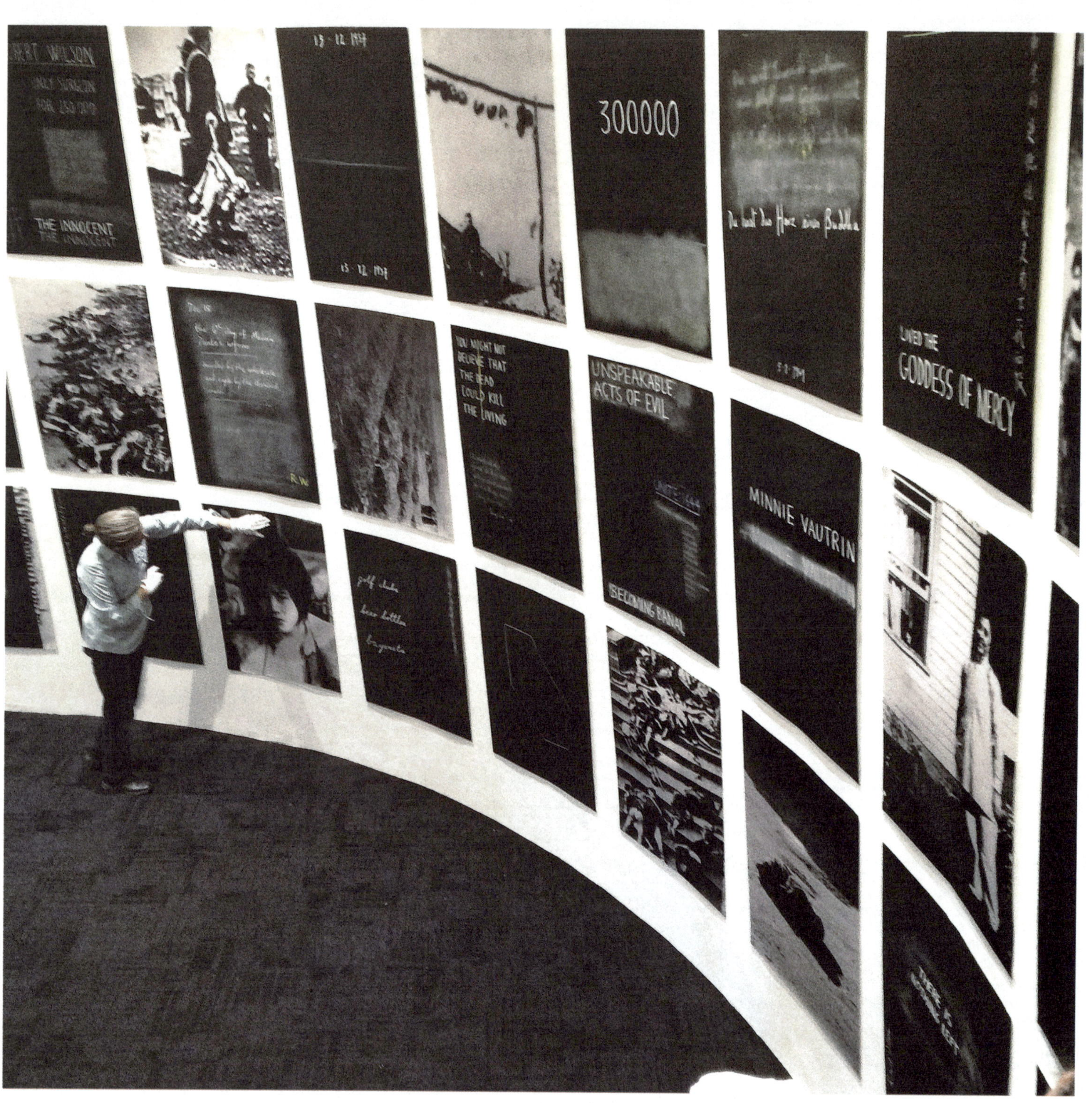

Safety Zone 2010
Installation view, Museum of Australian
Democracy at Eureka, Ballarat, 2014

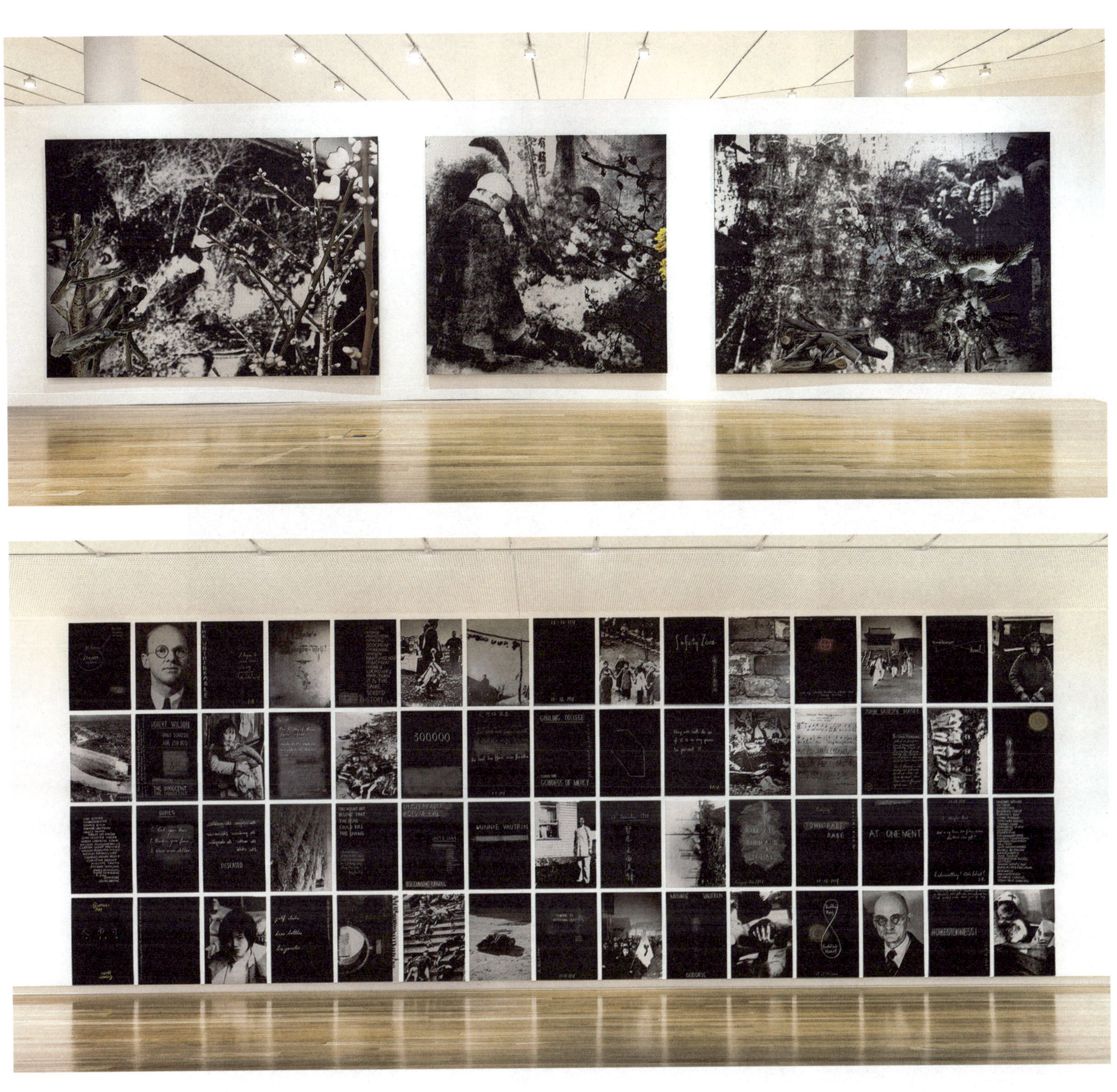

*Flower Market (Nanjing 1936) #2, #3
and #1* 2010
Installation view, *John Young: Diaspora, Psyche,*
Bunjil Place, Narre Warren, 2021

Safety Zone 2010
Installation view, *John Young: Diaspora, Psyche,*
Bunjil Place, Narre Warren, 2021

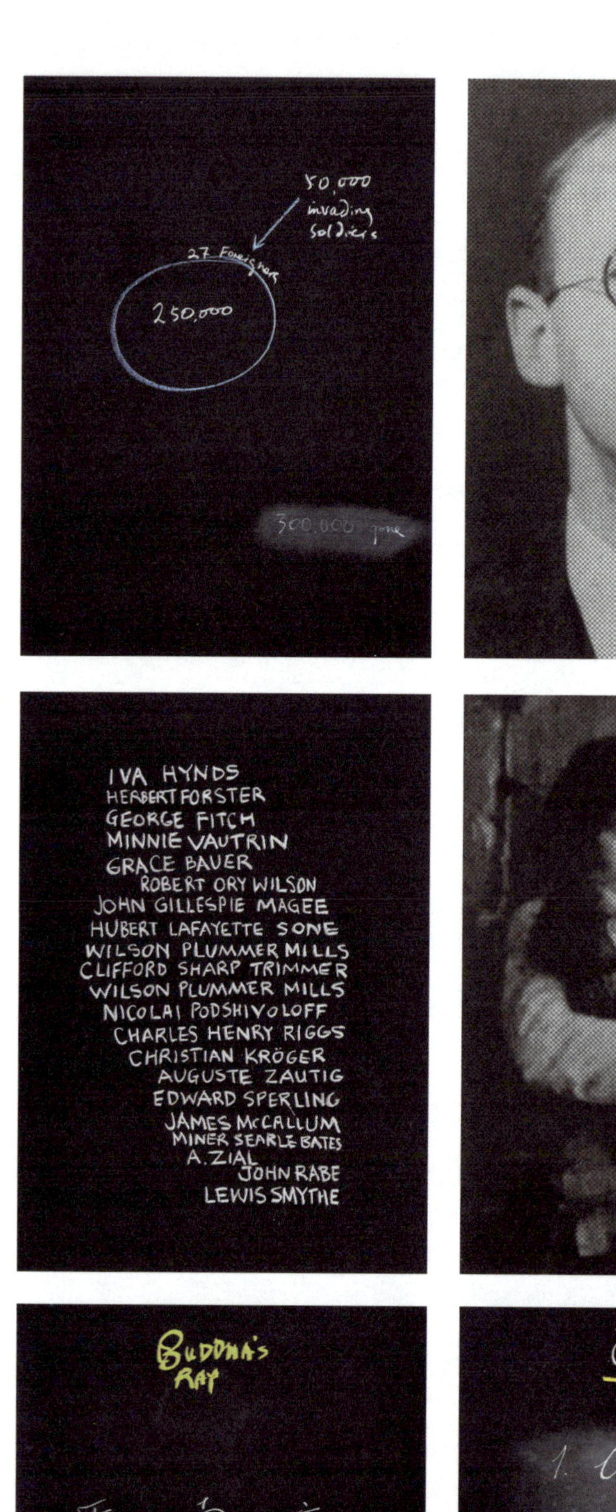

50,000 invading soldiers
27 Foreigners
250,000
300,000 ???
IVA HYNDS
HERBERT FORSTER
GEORGE FITCH
MINNIE VAUTRIN
GRACE BAUER
ROBERT ORY WILSON
JOHN GILLESPIE MAGEE
HUBERT LAFAYETTE SONE
WILSON PLUMMER MILLS
CLIFFORD SHARP TRIMMER
WILSON PLUMMER MILLS
NICOLAI PODSHIVOLOFF
CHARLES HENRY RIGGS
CHRISTIAN KRÖGER
AUGUSTE ZAUTIG
EDWARD SPERLING
JAMES McCALLUM
MINER SEARLE BATES
A. ZIAL
JOHN RABE
LEWIS SMYTHE
BUDDHA'S RAY
天　南　京
1　9　3　7
BUDDHA'S HEART

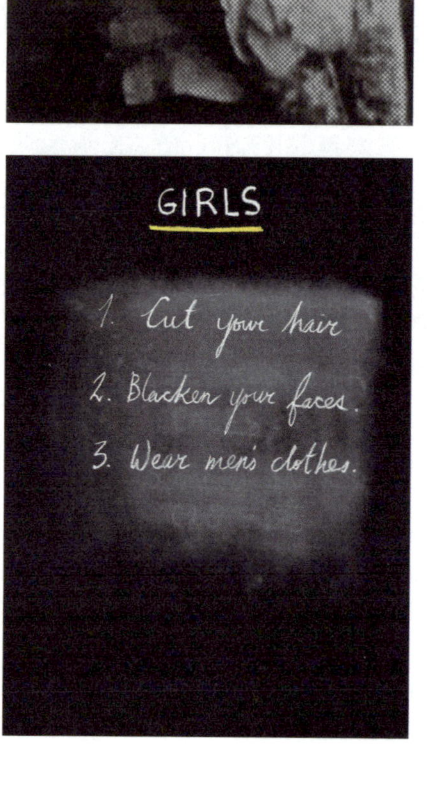

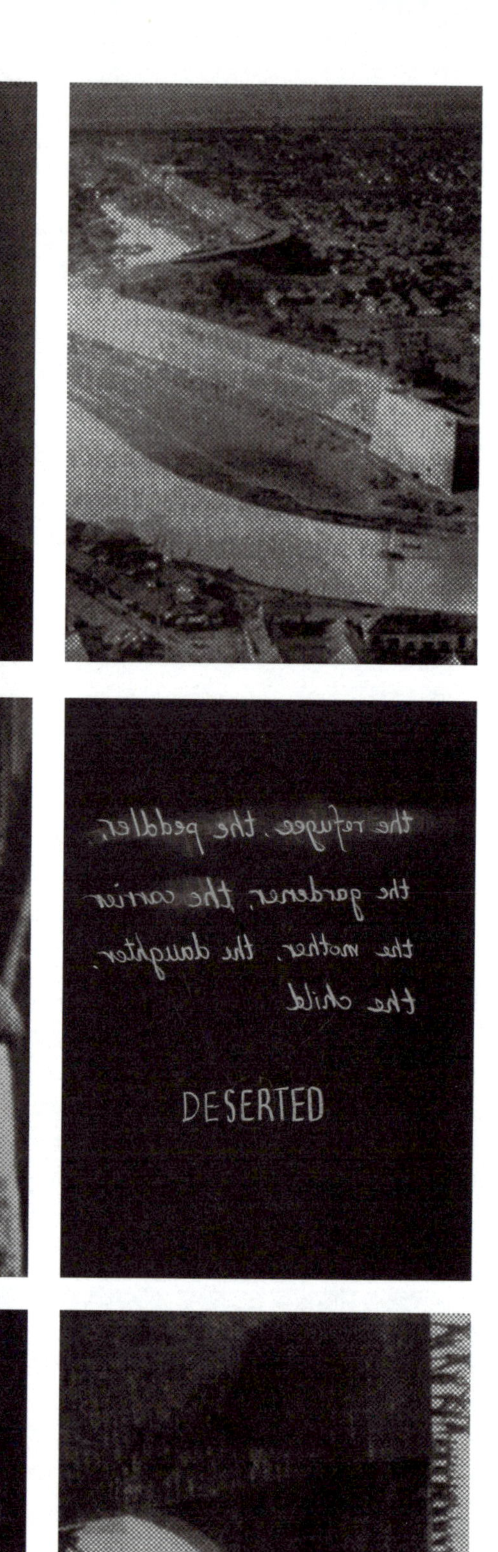

the refugee, the peddler,
the gardener, the carrier,
the mother, the daughter,
the child

DESERTED

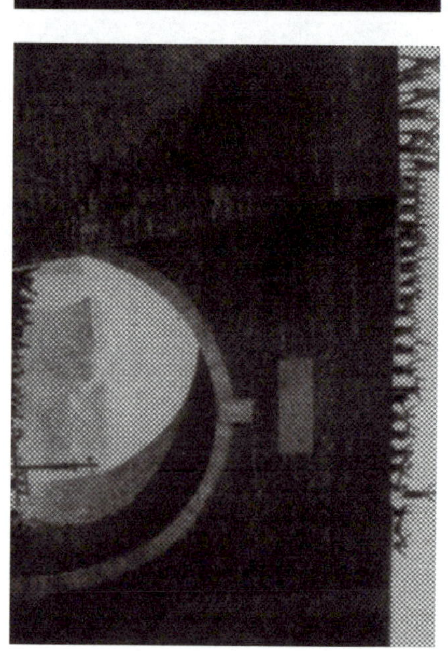

GIRLS
1. Cut your hair
2. Blacken your faces.
3. Wear men's clothes.

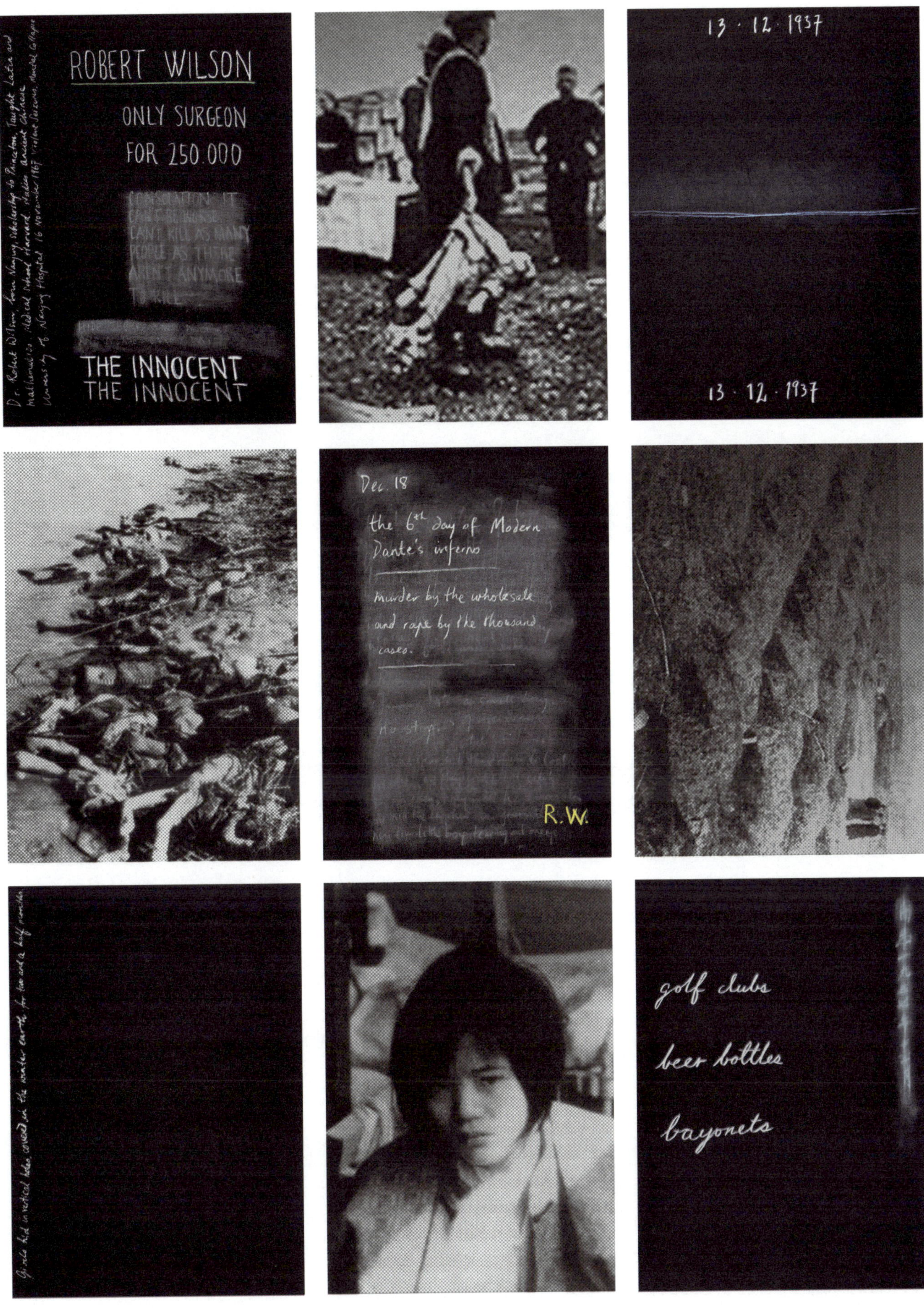
ROBERT WILSON
ONLY SURGEON
FOR 250.000
THE INNOCENT
THE INNOCENT
Dr. Robert Wilson, born Nanjing, Scholarship to Princeton, Taught Latin and Mathematics. Medical School Harvard. Studies Ancient Chinese University. To Nanjing Hospital 16 November 1967 Violent Seizures. Mantel Gallager
13 · 12 · 1937
13 · 12 · 1937
Dec. 18
the 6th day of Modern
Dante's inferno
murder by the wholesale
and rape by the thousand
cases.
R.W.
golf clubs
beer bottles
bayonets

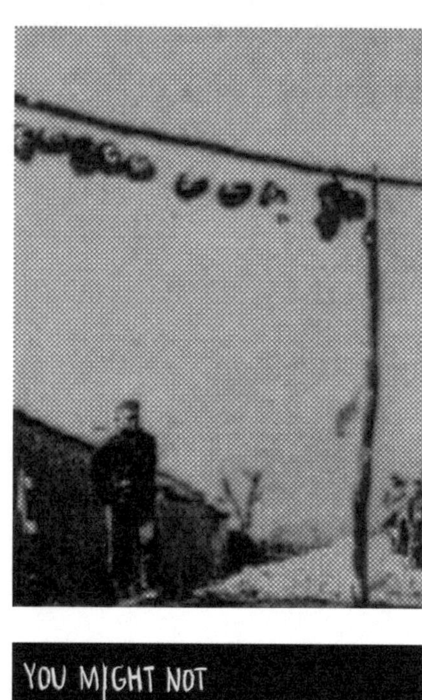

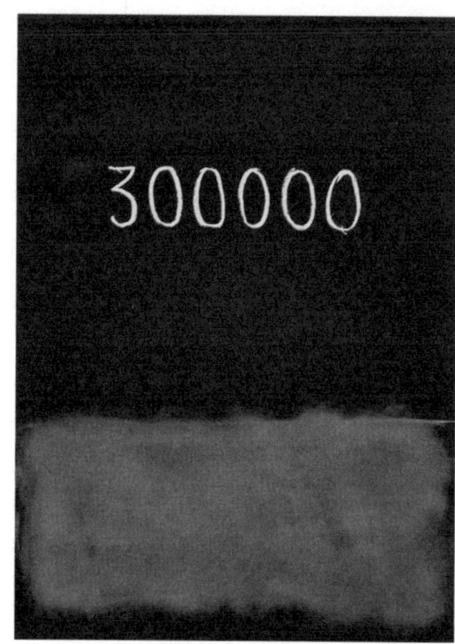
300000

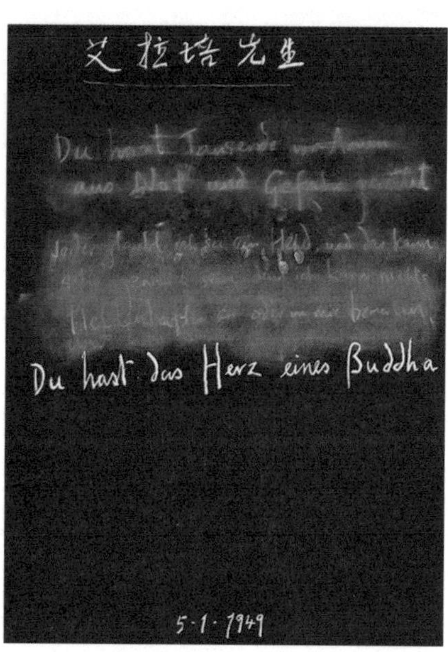
艾拉培先生
Du hast das Herz eines Buddha
5·1·1949

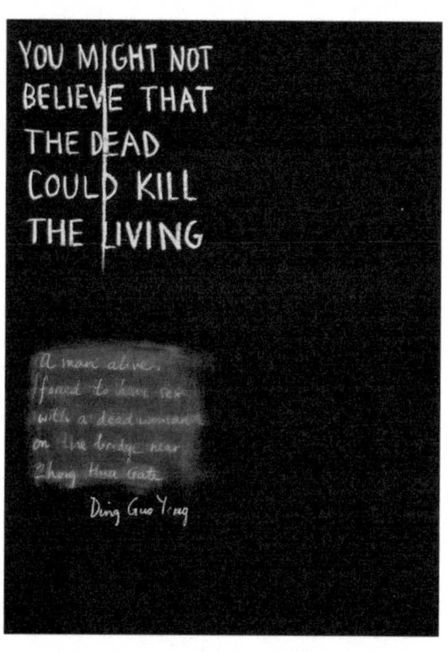
YOU MIGHT NOT
BELIEVE THAT
THE DEAD
COULD KILL
THE LIVING
Ding Guo Yong

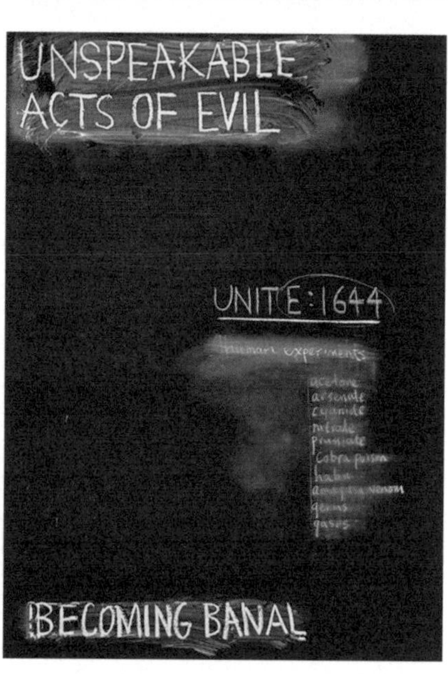
UNSPEAKABLE
ACTS OF EVIL
UNIT E: 1644
BECOMING BANAL

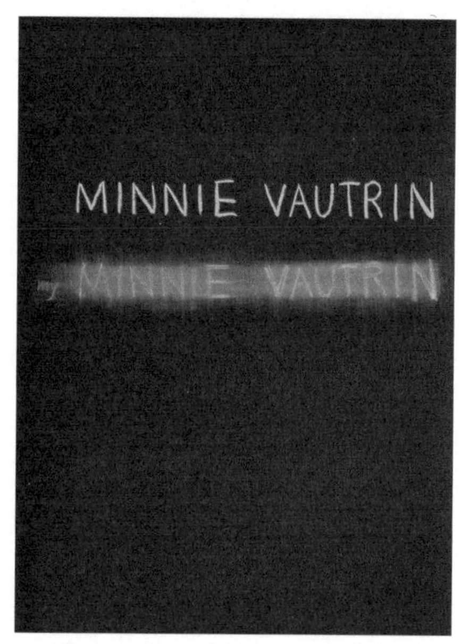
MINNIE VAUTRIN
MINNIE VAUTRIN

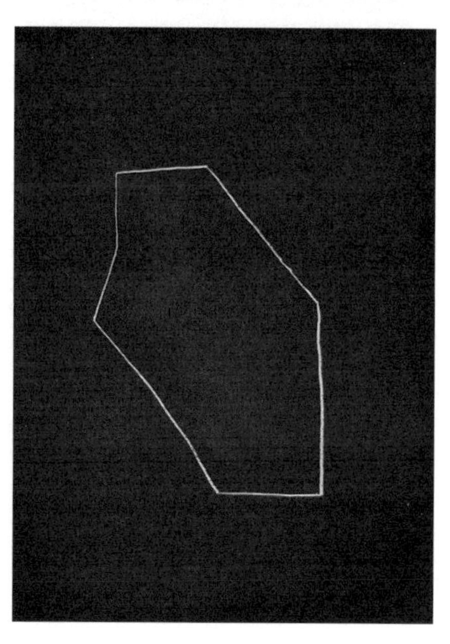

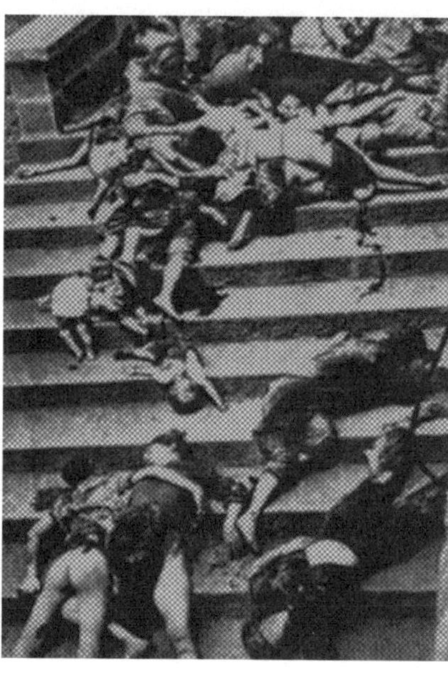

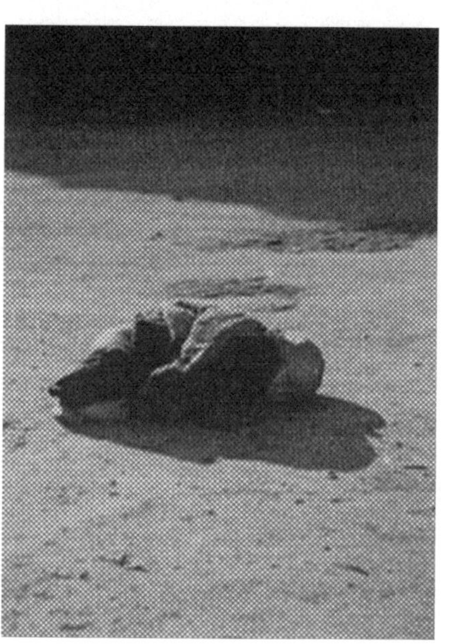

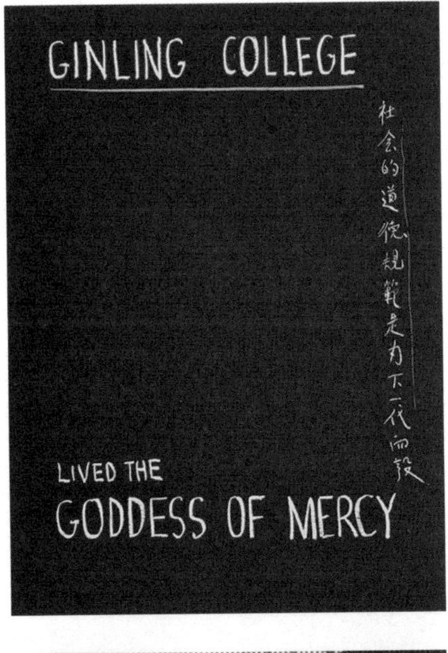

GINLING COLLEGE

社会的道德规范是为下一代而设

LIVED THE
GODDESS OF MERCY

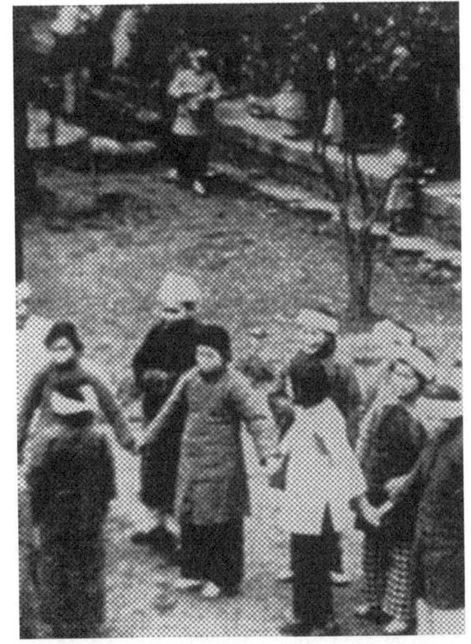

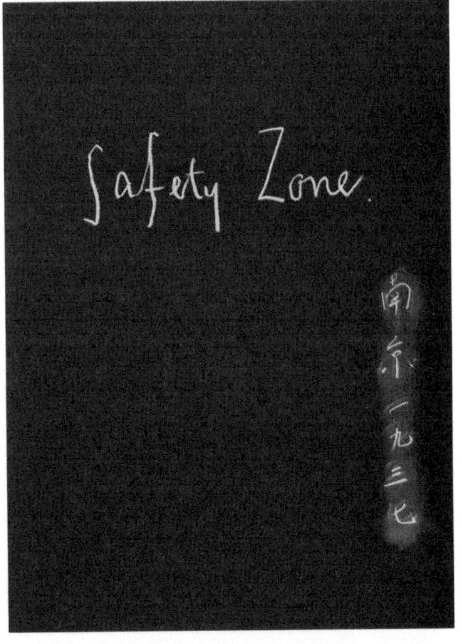

Safety Zone.

南京一九三七

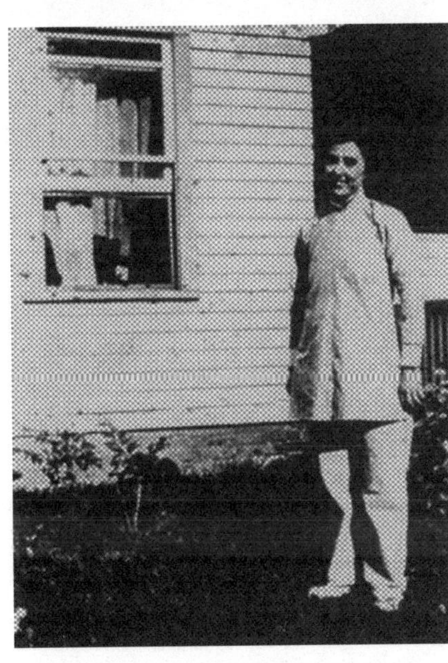

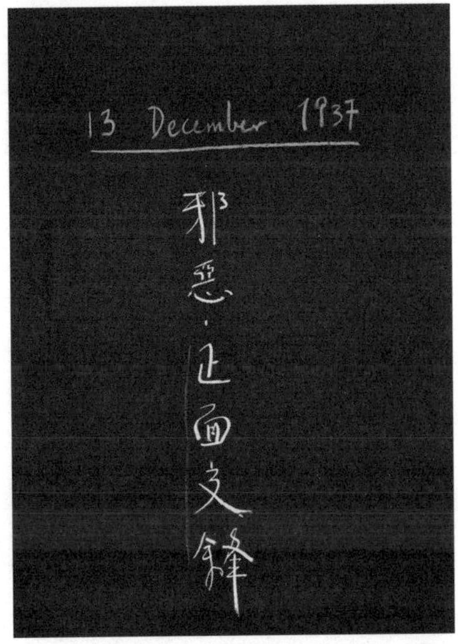

13 December 1937

邪恶·正面交锋

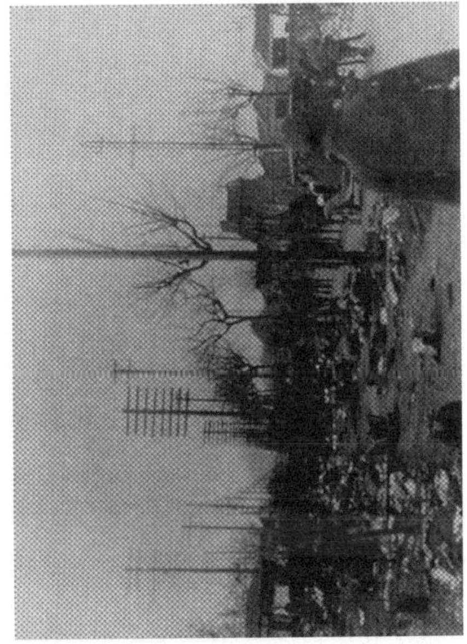

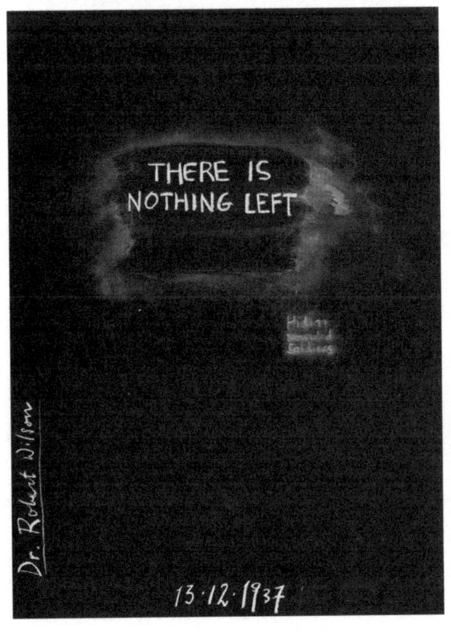

THERE IS
NOTHING LEFT

Dr. Robert Wilson

13·12·1937

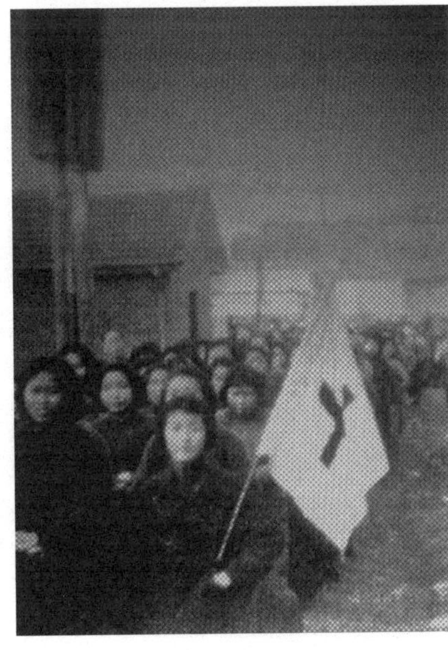

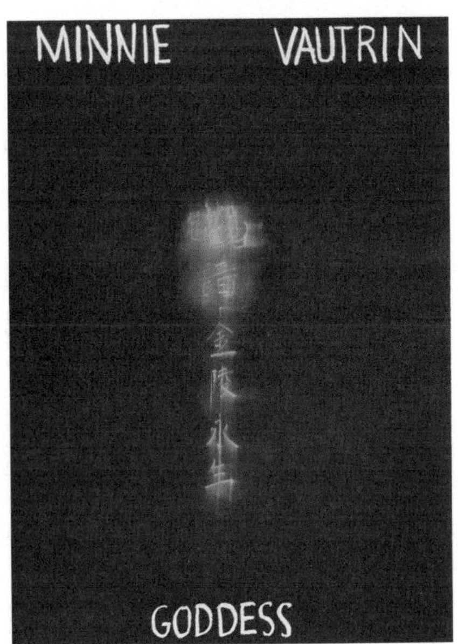

MINNIE   VAUTRIN

金陵永生

GODDESS

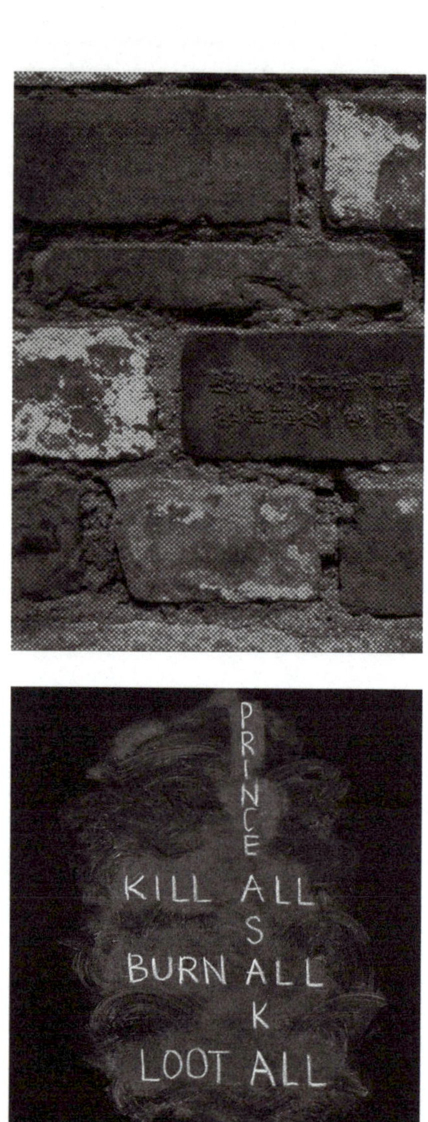

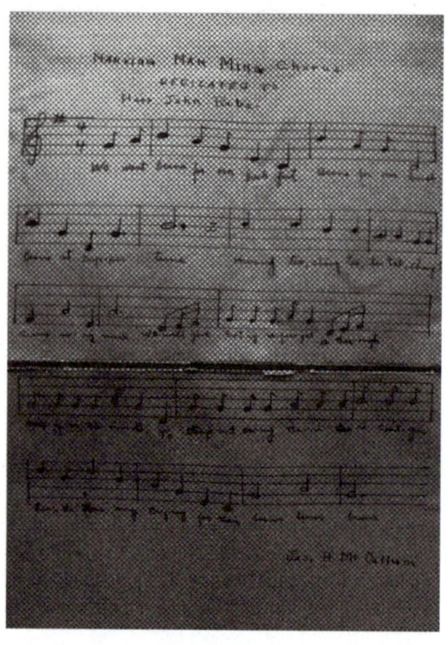

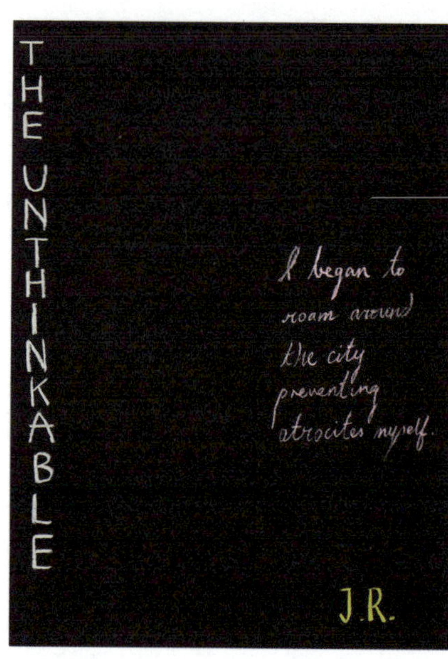
THE UNTHINKABLE
I began to roam around the city preventing atrocities myself.
J.R.

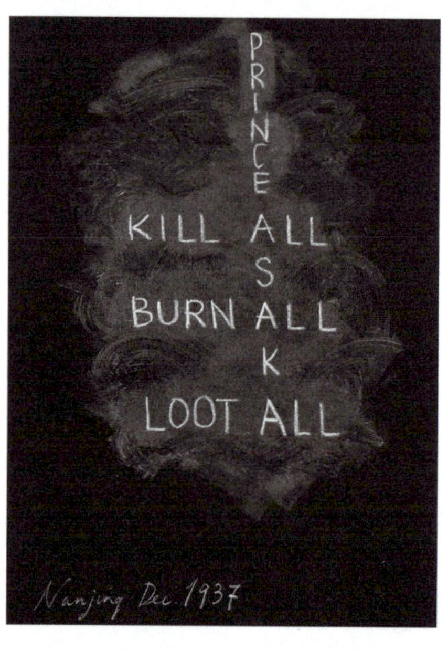
PRINCE
KILL ALL
S
K
BURN ALL
LOOT ALL
Nanjing Dec. 1937

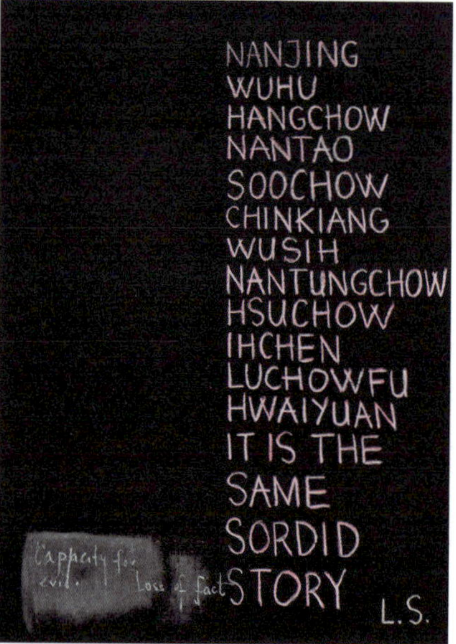
NANJING
WUHU
HANGCHOW
NANTAO
SOOCHOW
CHINKIANG
WUSIH
NANTUNGCHOW
HSUCHOW
IHCHEN
LUCHOWFU
HWAIYUAN
IT IS THE
SAME
SORDID
STORY
L.S.

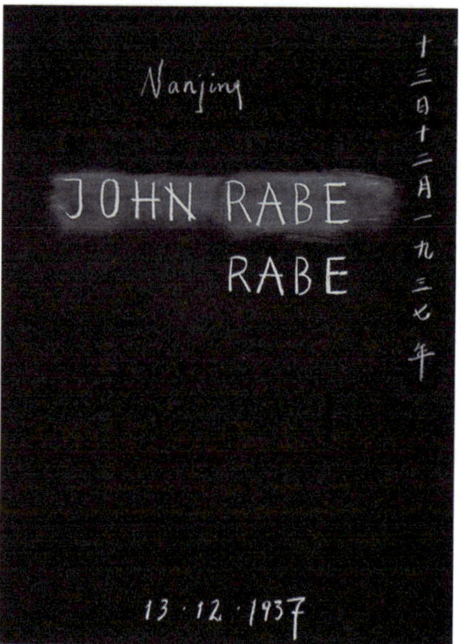
Nanjing
JOHN RABE
RABE
13·12·1937

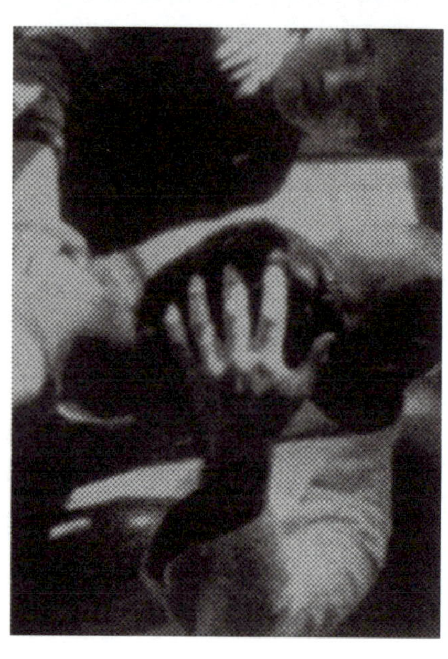

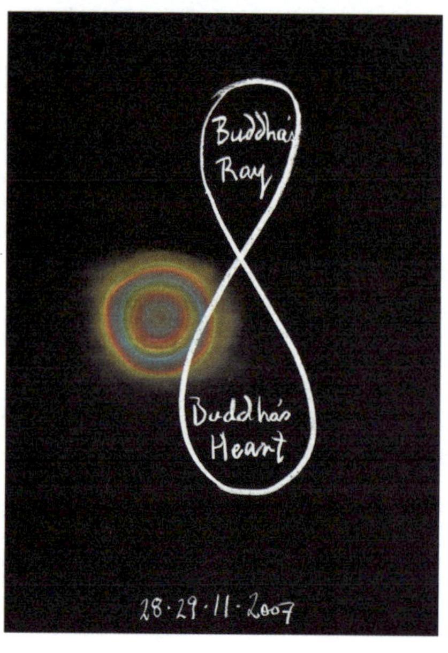
Buddha's
Ray
Buddha's
Heart
28·29·11·2007

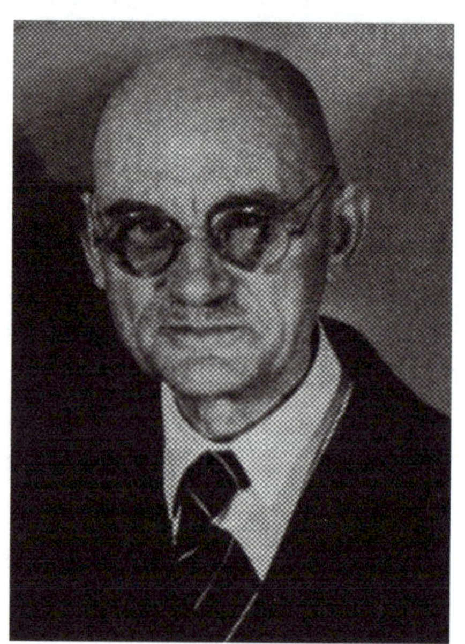

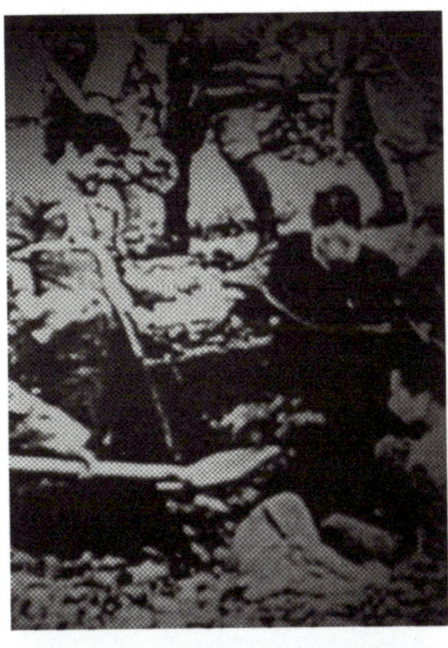

MINNIE   VAUTRIN
Last days Mental Breakdown, Electro-shock
therapy 14.5.1941
Suicide

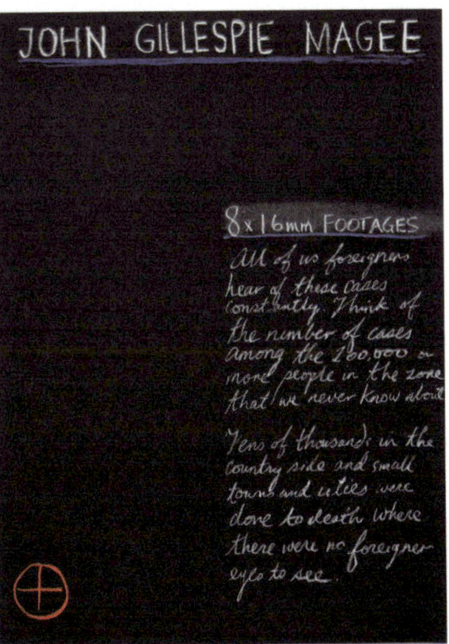
JOHN GILLESPIE MAGEE
8 x 16mm FOOTAGES
All of us foreigners
hear of these cases
constantly. Think of
the number of cases
among the 260,000 or
more people in the zone
that we never know about.

Tens of thousands in the
country side and small
towns and cities were
done to death where
there were no foreigner-
eyes to see.

JOHN RABE
last days
Arrested by gestapo, the Soviets, the British. malnutrition
skin diseases. lived on acorn flour soup and stinging nettle
1948 Chinese raised US $2000 for Rabe. posted
bundles of food each month from Nanjing 28.1.1949

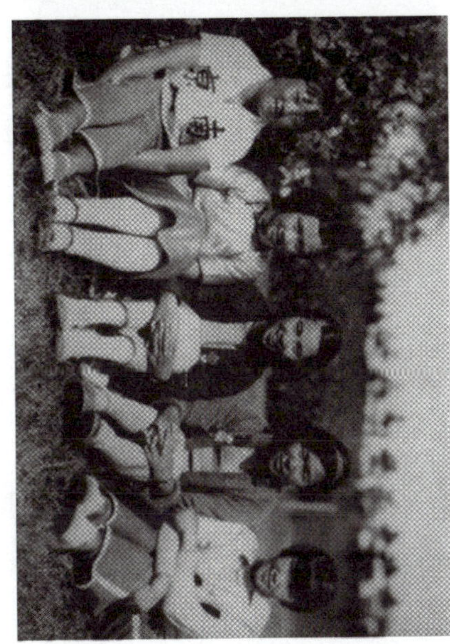

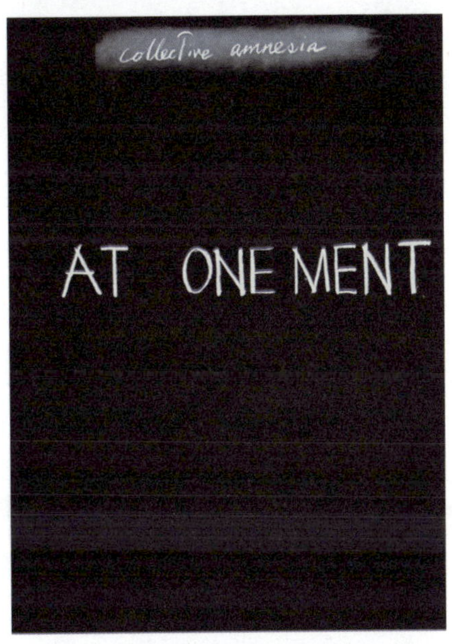
collective amnesia
AT ONE MENT

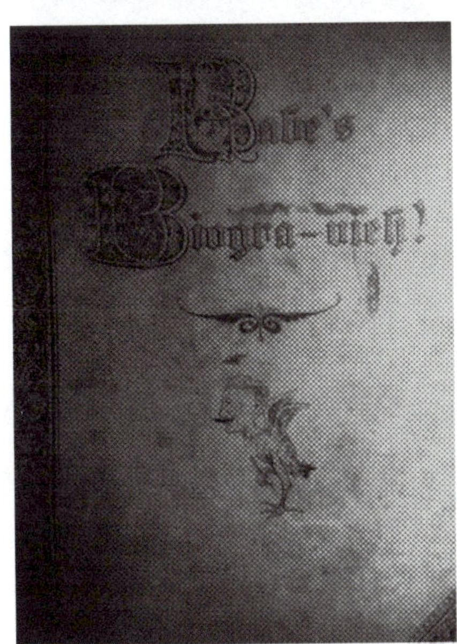
Rabe's
Biogra-phy!

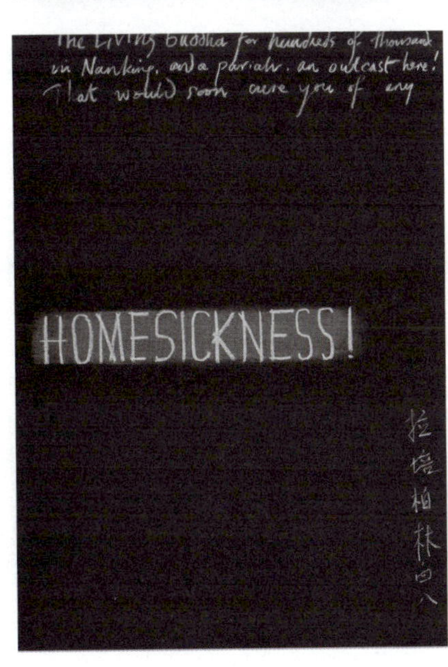
The Living Buddha for hundreds of thousand
in Nanking, and a pariah. an outcast here!
That would soon cure you of any
HOMESICKNESS!

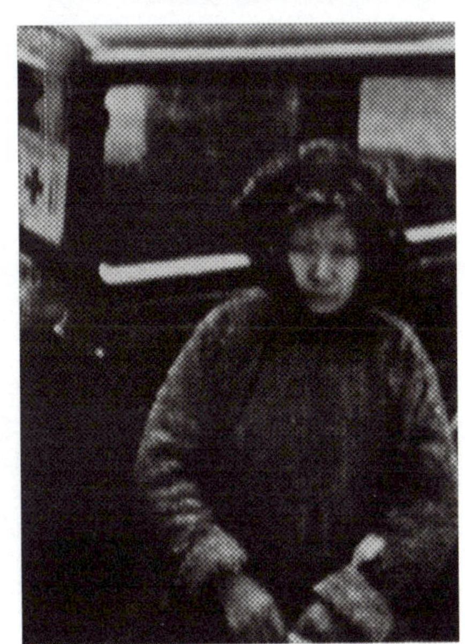

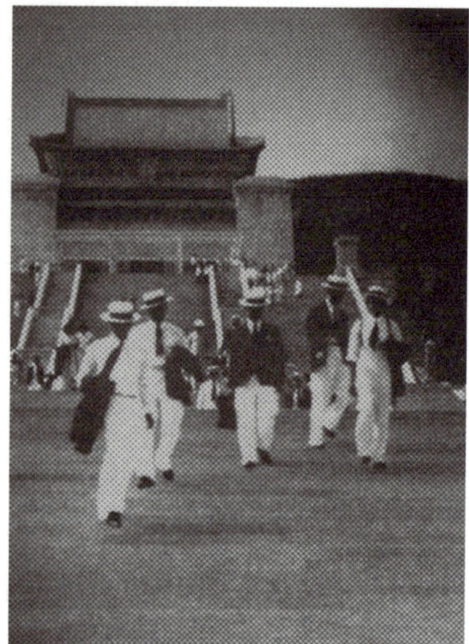
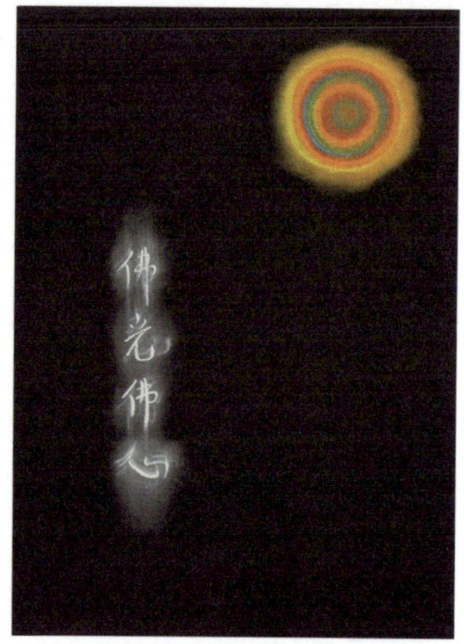

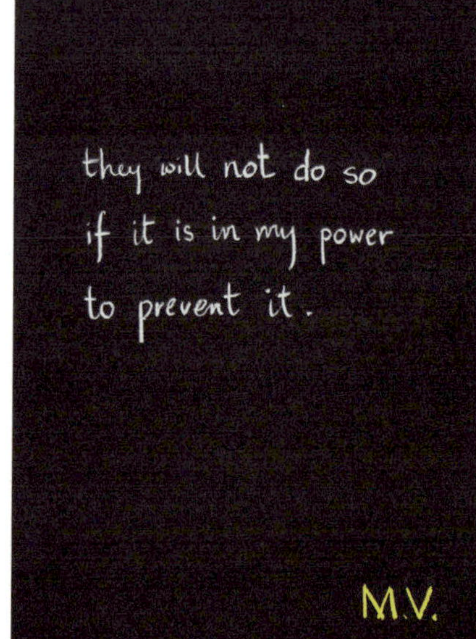

NANJING TAPESTRY
VICTORIA
APPARITION
RAINBOW CIRCLE
BUDDHA'S RAY
LIVING BUDDHA
JOHN RABE DIARIES
THOMAS RABE
HEIDELBERG STUDIO
HUMBOLDT
EMPIRICISM
SIEMANSARCHIVE
MUNICH FINGERPRINTS
GINLING FEMINISM
VAUTRIN
ANTI-MISSIONARIES
RUSSELL IN PEKING
MERITOCRATIC
JUNE FOURTH
WITTGENSTEIN RUSSELL
LETTERS
SHOWN MYSTICISM
BONHOEFFER EXECUTION
BENJAMIN
MUMMEREHLEN
CHINESE CURIOUS
OPIUM DENS NANJING

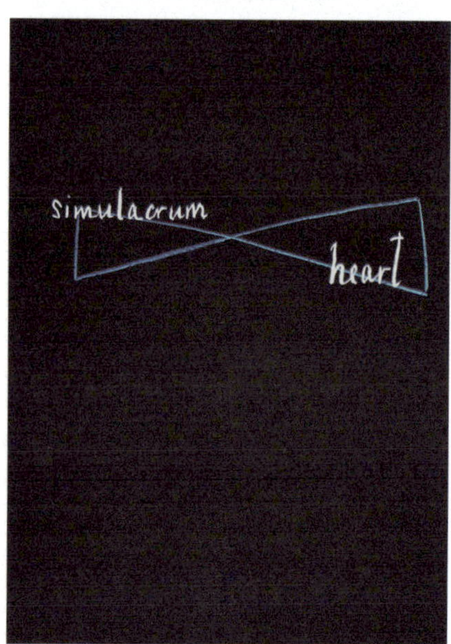

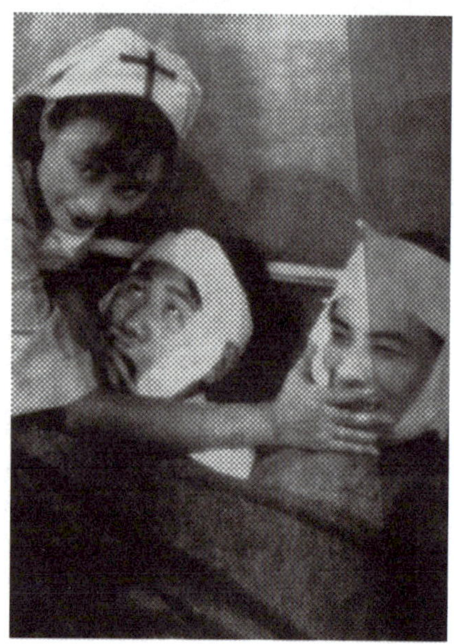

pages 162–70

Safety Zone 2010
Digital print on photographic paper and chalk
on blackboard-painted archival cotton paper,
60 units, 320 × 1590 cm

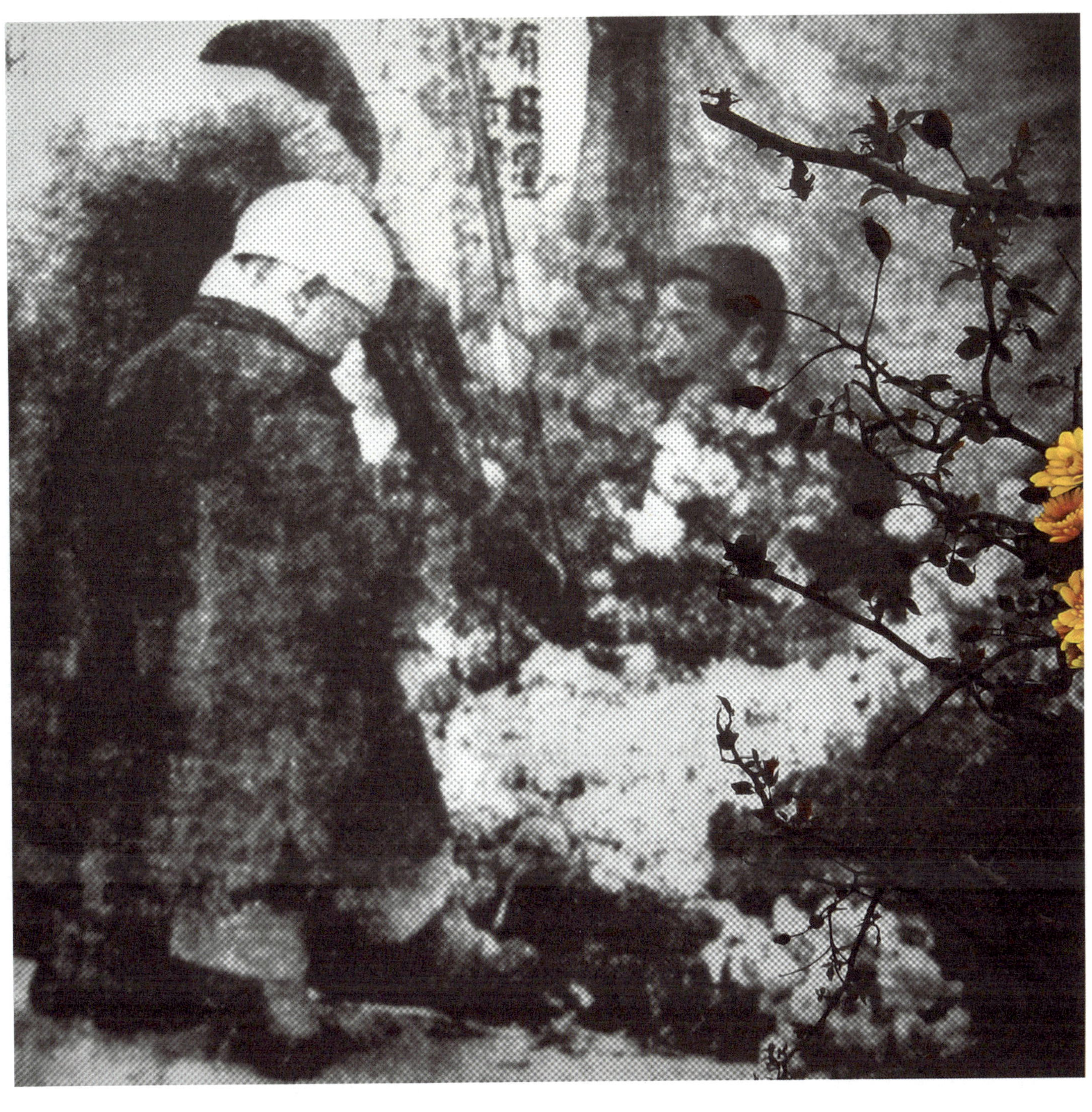

Flower Market (Nanjing 1936) #3 2010
Digital print and oil on linen, 240 × 240 cm

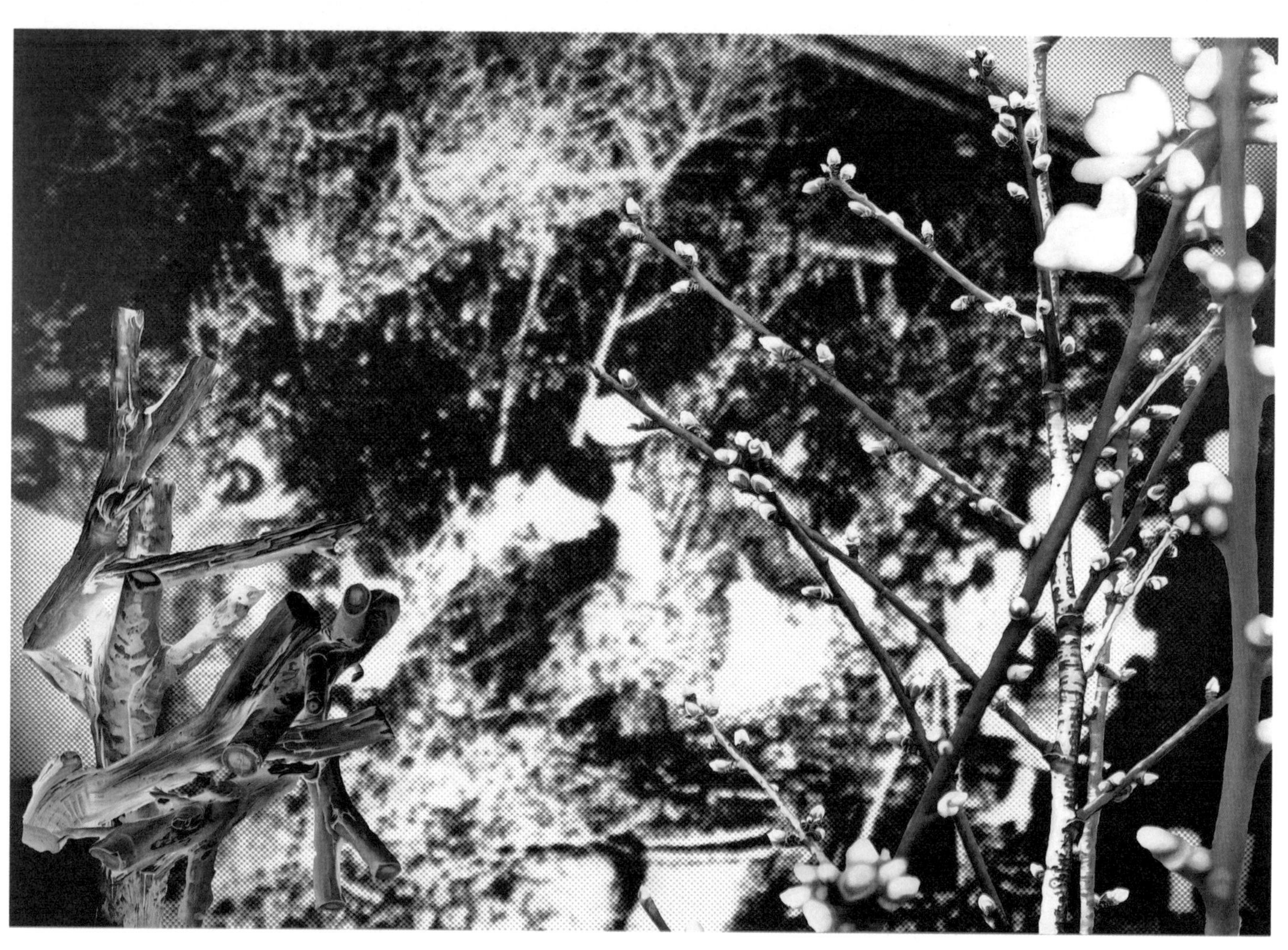

Flower Market (Nanjing 1936) #2 2010
Digital print and oil on linen, 240 × 331 cm

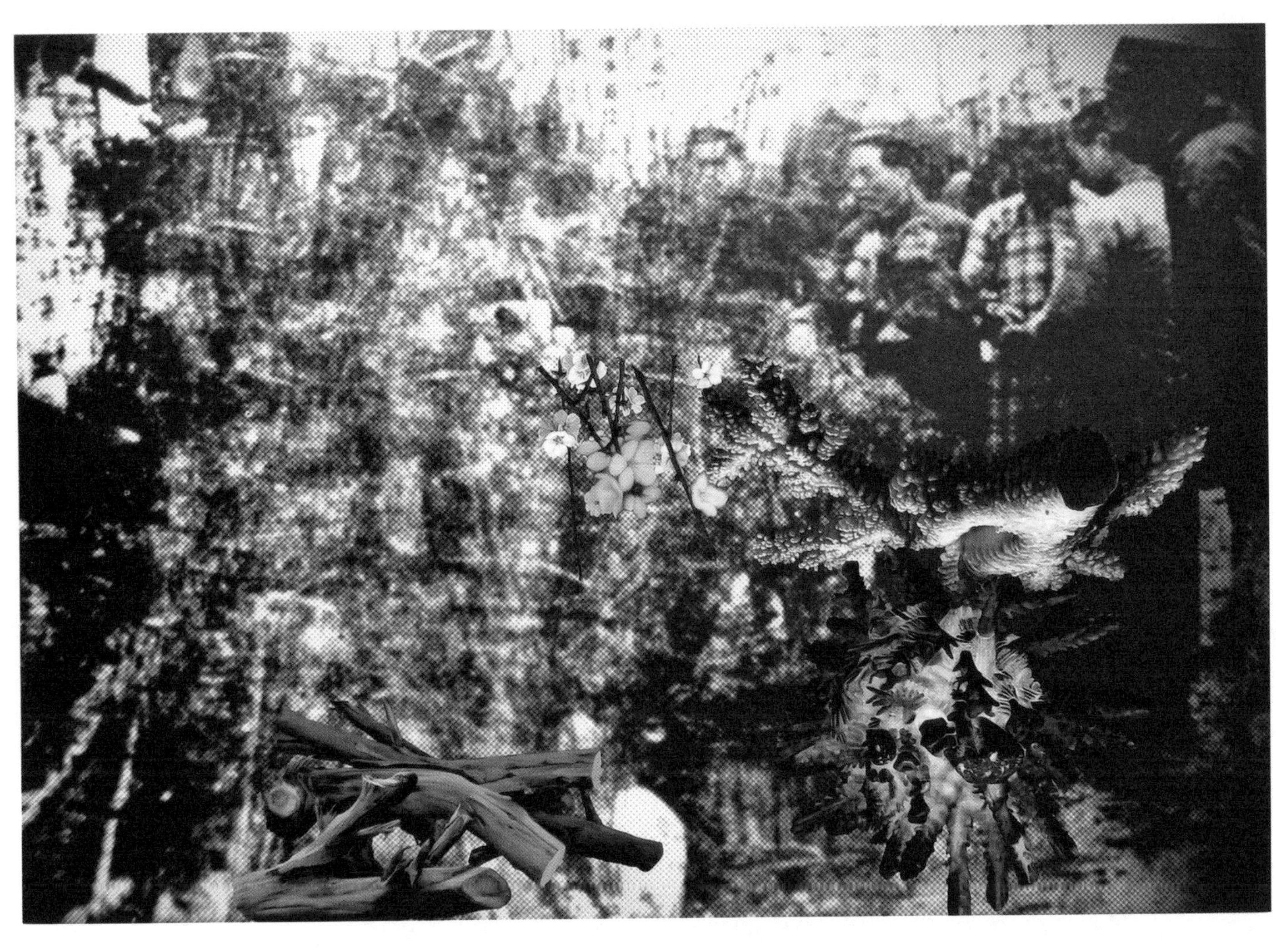

Flower Market (Nanjing 1936) #1 2010
Digital print and oil on linen, 240 x 331 cm

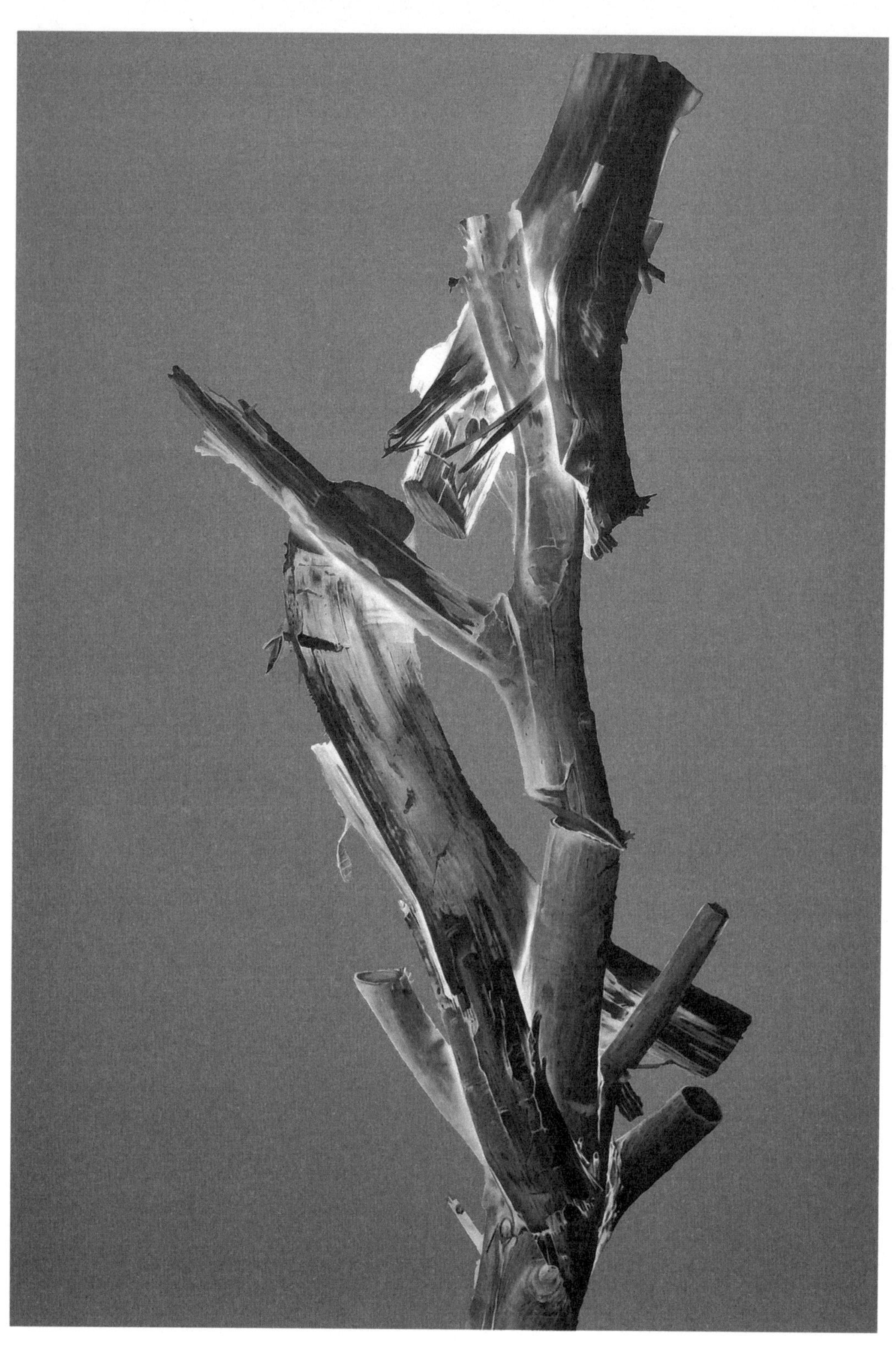

The Crippled Tree #1 2010
Oil on Belgian linen, 274 x 183 cm

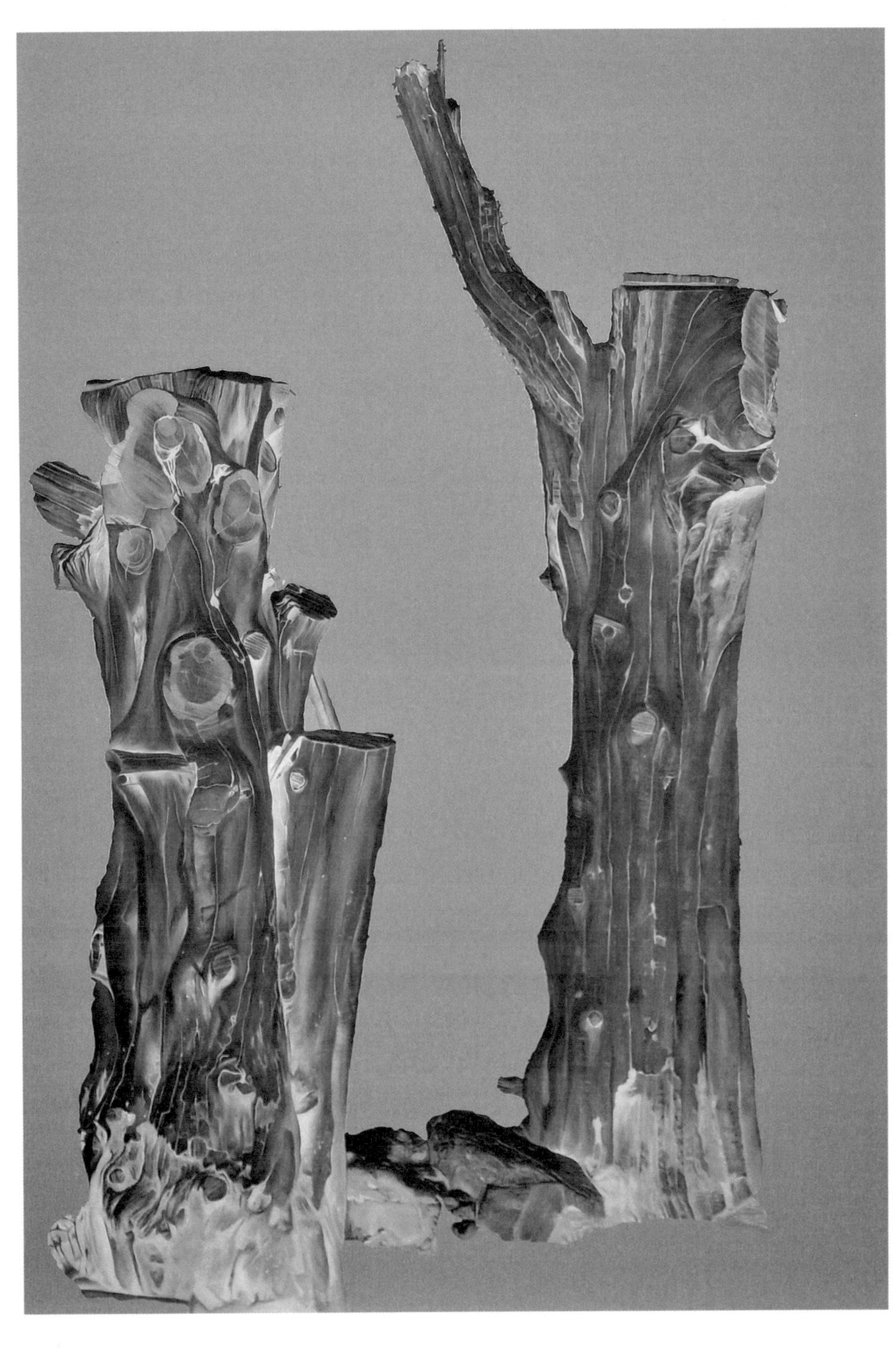

The Crippled Tree #2 2010
Oil on Belgian linen, 274 x 183 cm

St Francis of Assisi at Lao Tzu's I 2012
Oil on canvas, 320 x 151 cm

PART TWO

THE MACAU DAYS

2012–2017

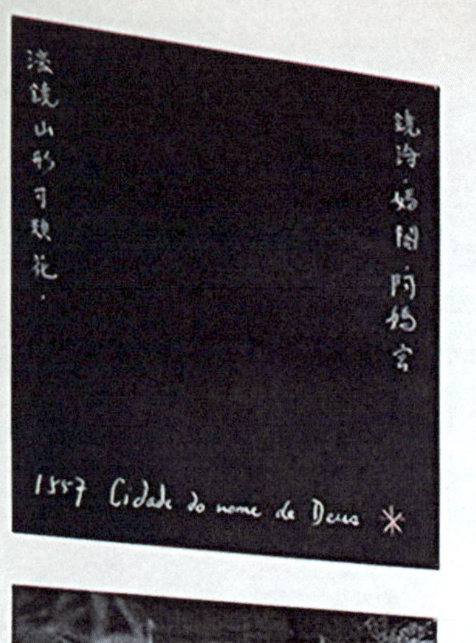
1557 Cidade do nome de Deus
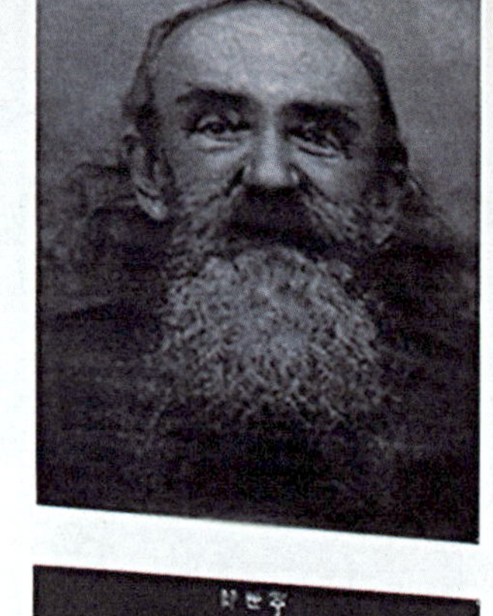
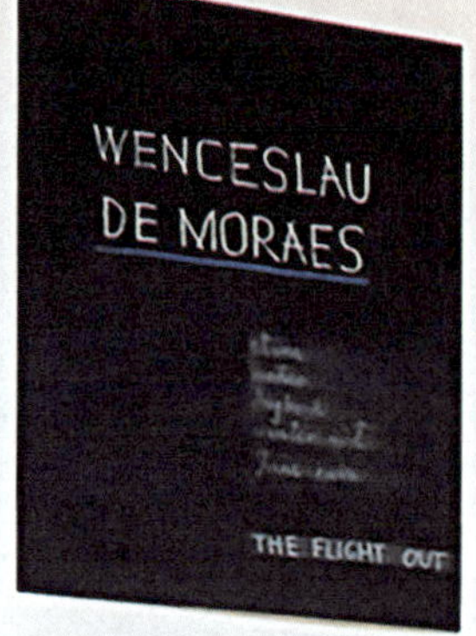
WENCESLAU
DE MORAES

THE FLIGHT OUT
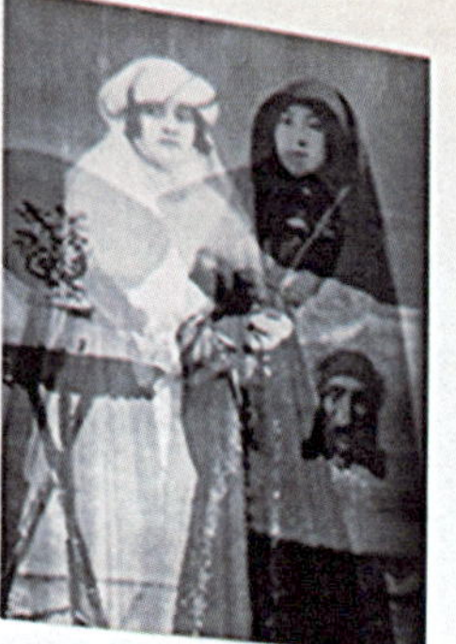
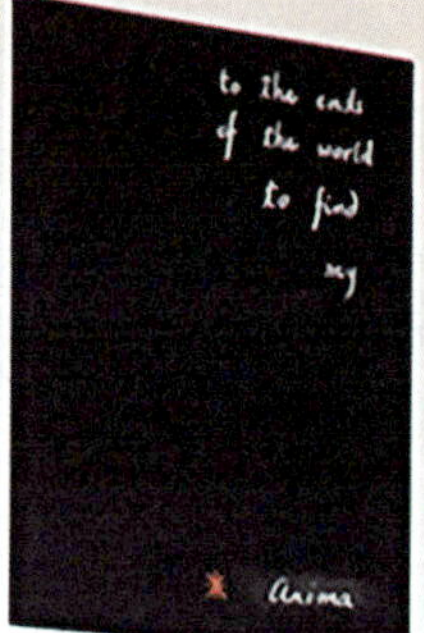
to the ends
of the world
to find
my
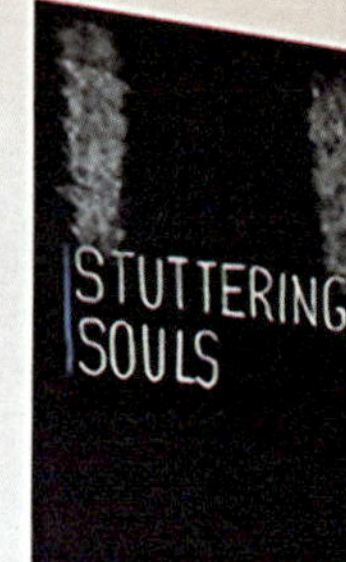
STUTTERING
SOULS
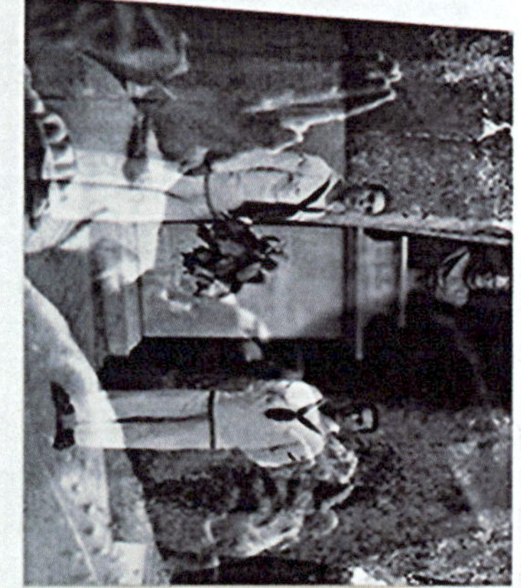
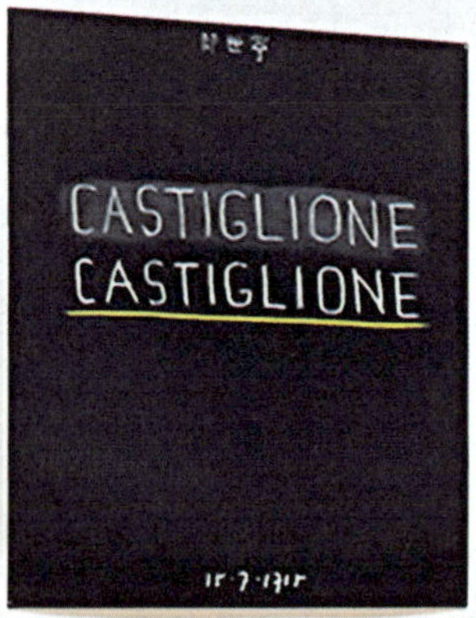
CASTIGLIONE
CASTIGLIONE
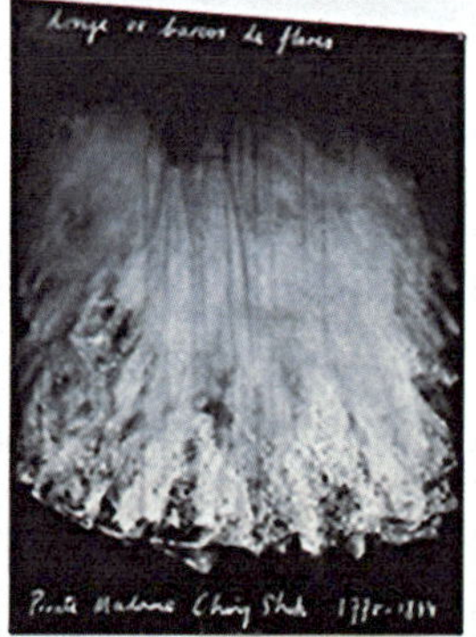
longe os barcos de flores
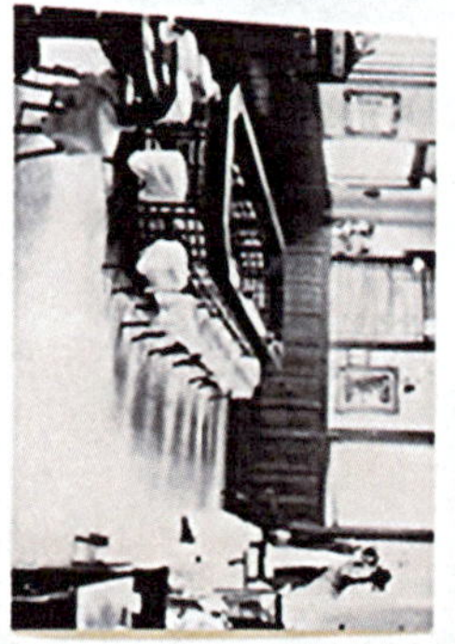
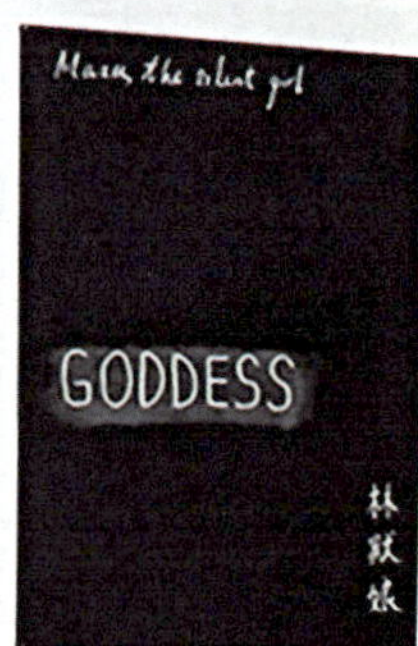
GODDESS
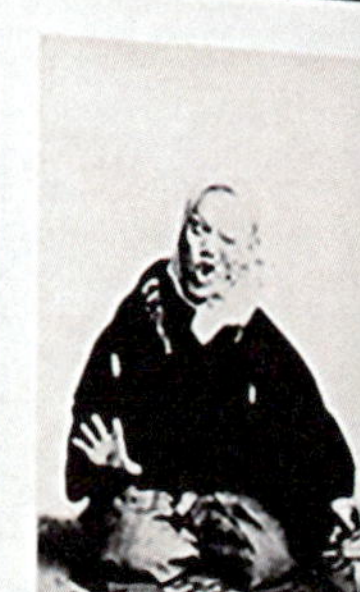
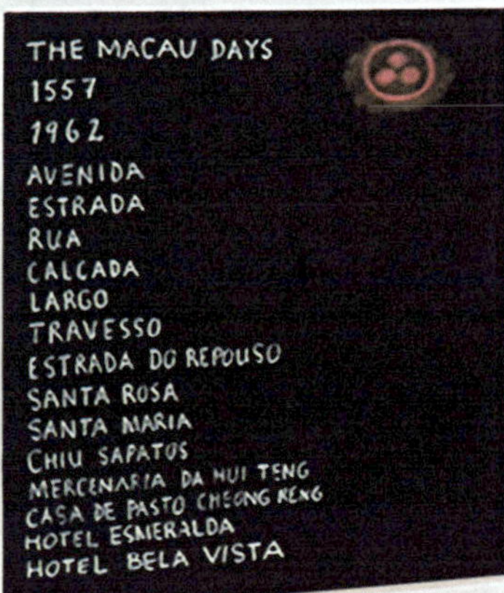
THE MACAU DAYS
1557
1962
AVENIDA
ESTRADA
RUA
CALCADA
LARGO
TRAVESSO
ESTRADA DO REPOUSO
SANTA ROSA
SANTA MARIA
CHIU SAPATOS
MERCENARIA DA HUI TENG
CASA DE PASTO CHEONG KENG
HOTEL ESMERALDA
HOTEL BELA VISTA
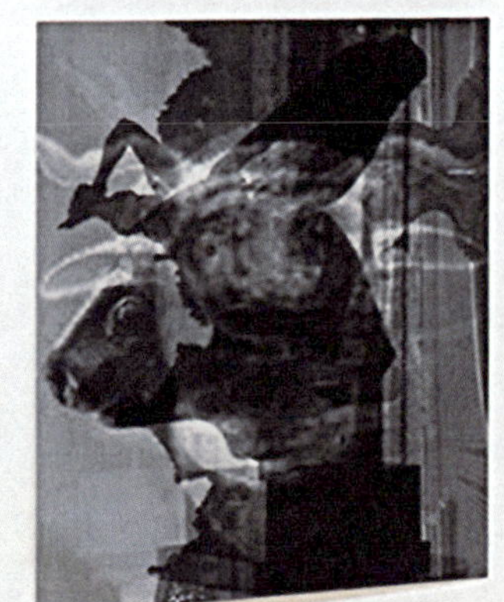
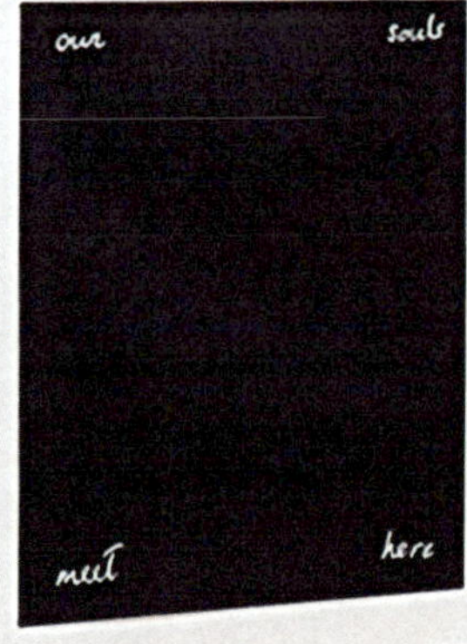
our   souls

meet   here
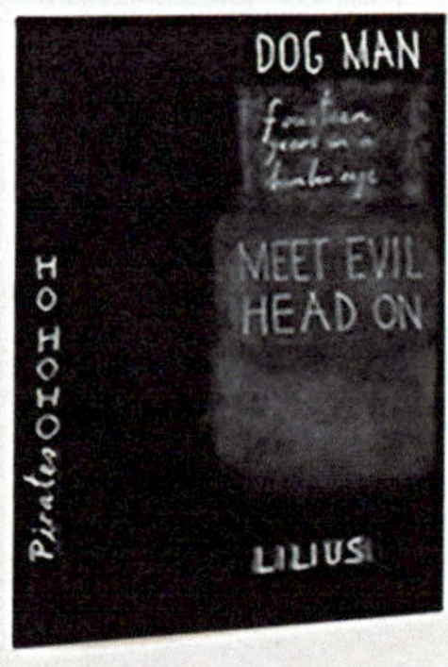
DOG MAN

MEET EVIL
HEAD ON

LILIUS
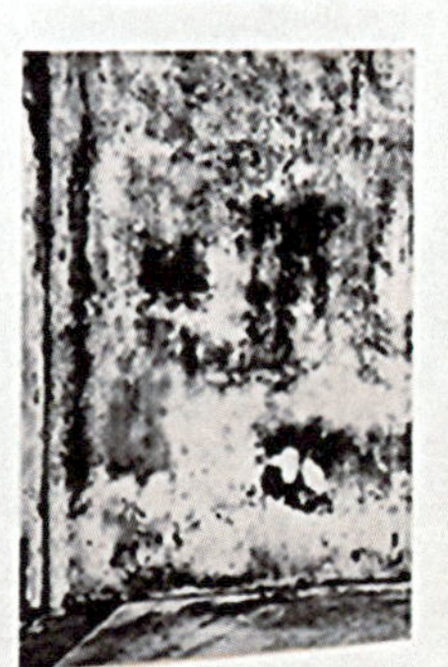
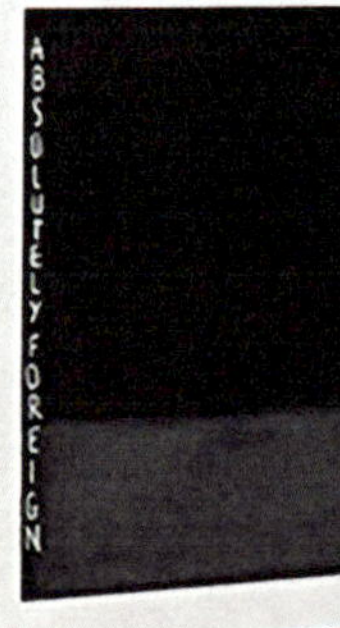
ABSOLUTELY FOREIGN

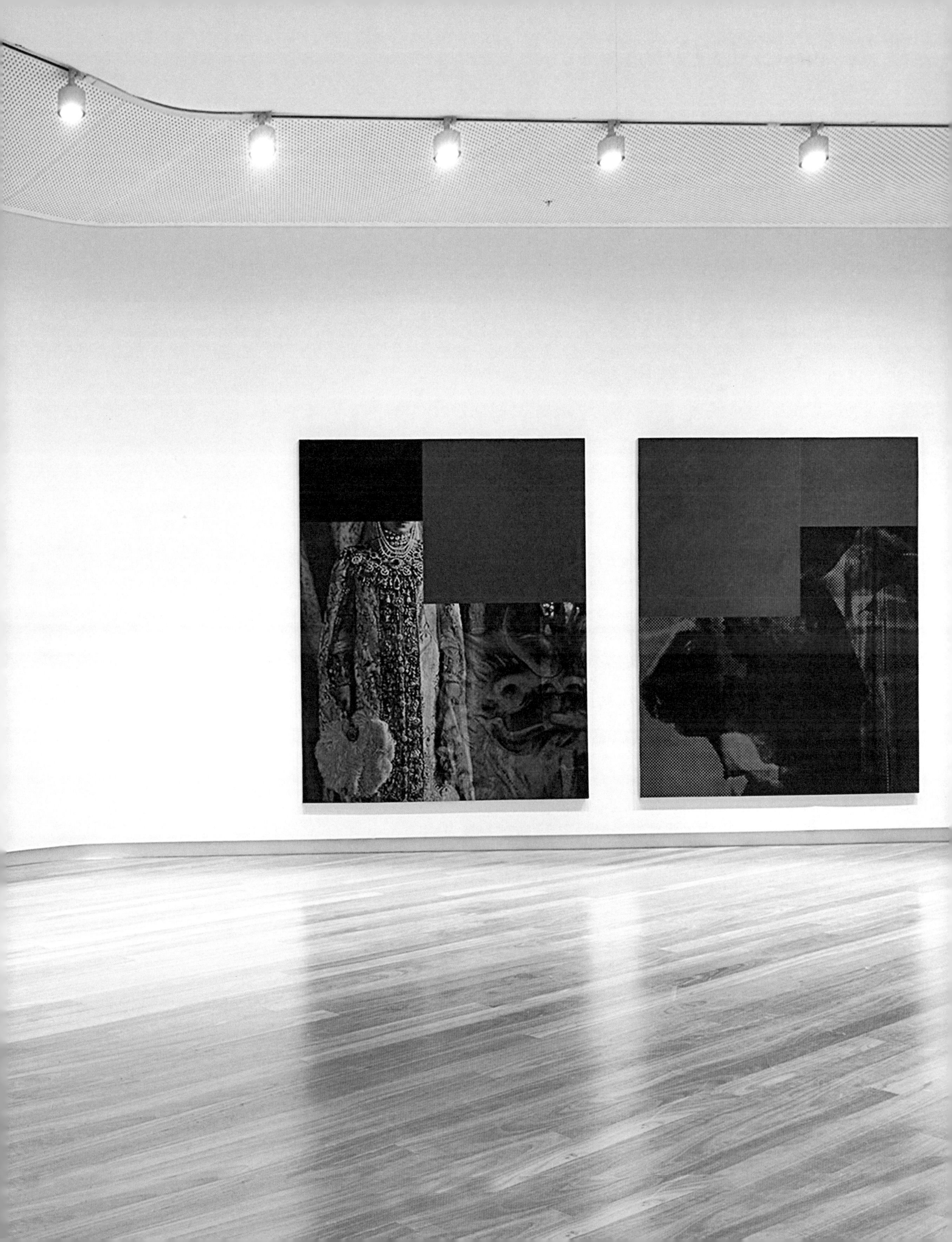

THE MACAU DAYS

The Macau Days consists of a central installation of chalkboard drawings and digital prints based on archival photographs, and three groups of paintings: *Mazu, Goddess of the Sea; Macau;* and *Marienbad*. Later presentations of this project have also included a new series of photographic prints titled *I Sailed with Women Pirates* (2017).

The central installation, also titled *The Macau Days* (2012), comprises 15 works arranged in a three-row grid (320 × 390 cm total). It offers fragmented visions of Macau's transcultural history: the ruins of St Paul's church; a portrait of the Portuguese sailor, consul and writer Wenceslau de Moraes; opaque references to the Jesuit priest turned Qing court painter Guiseppe Castiglione (known in Chinese as Lang Shining); and the zodiac animals of his design that once adorned Beijing's Old Summer Palace, the Yuanming Yuan 圓明園.

Mazu, Goddess of the Sea is a series of three figurative paintings (190 × 145 cm each), in which translucent bodies float on raw linen amongst antique cast bronze Qing dynasty zodiac heads. These heads, once looted by French and British troops during an attack on Beijing in 1860, were purchased by Macau's casino magnate Stanley Ho in the 2000s. The series title references the goddess Mazu 媽祖, who in Chinese mythology is believed to protect sailors, fishermen and travellers.

The other two groups of paintings, *Marienbad Macau (pink), (yellow), (amber),* and *Macau I–V*, combine backgrounds showing the interior of Macanese intellectual and art collector José Vicente Jorge's home, rendered with a halftone dot filter, overlaid with blossoms, coral and 'dismembered' tree branches painted in oils. The title *Marienbad* refers to the 1961 French New Wave film, *Last Year at Marienbad*, directed by Alain Resnais.

Subsequent iterations of this project—such as the 2017 publication *Macau Days*, made in collaboration with novelist Brian Castro, and a presentation in the 2020 survey exhibition *Diaspora, Psyche* held at Bunjil Place gallery, Victoria—include the additional photographic series *I Sailed with Woman Pirates*. This series of eleven intensely coloured duo-tone digital prints depicts some of the female pirates who terrorised the South China seas in the late eighteenth and nineteenth centuries. Their exploits were documented in a first-hand account by Finnish American journalist and photographer Aleko E. Lilius in *I Sailed with Chinese Pirates* (1931).

ARTIST STATEMENT

Artist statement for 'The Macau Days' exhibition,
10 Chancery Lane Gallery, Hong Kong (2012)

> This is an homage to the flight out, for all those whose lives were
> lived transformations: Wenceslau de Moraes, who left Portugal,
> sojourned in Macau and spent the rest of his years in Tokushima,
> but introduced to the West the first haiku … A-ma, who was
> and still is the guardian goddess of seafarers in Macau, yet she
> drowned saving others, so the story goes. Guiseppe Castiglione,
> who brought to China trompe l'oeil, who conceived the 'Western
> Mansions' or the 'Chinese Versailles' at Yuan Ming Yuan and who
> left Italy, travelled via Goa to stay in Macau to master Chinese,
> then to Beijing, never to see Milan again. Or Wu Li, the poet
> who dedicated his time at St Paul's to understanding the Western
> spirit. For more than five centuries, the days spent in Macau have
> inspired and nourished those on the bird's path, the flight out,
> those who have given their lives to the great transformation. This
> exhibition is for those people, and their days spent in Macau.

Reflection (June 2022)

Above all, *The Macau Days* was a melancholic project. I think my friend and
collaborator Brian Castro may well agree. The initial impulse was the sense of loss,
of the place and the treasured moments from decades back; the loss of a transcultural
jewel that had survived almost half a millennium. Those from a diaspora often have
this acute sense of loss, of place, of values, of rituals and most importantly in relation
to Macau, the loss of a sense of living cultural plurality, a xenophilia of sorts. Macau
was never simply a colony. The Portuguese made it a province of Portugal; the
citizens had political and civil rights. But it was its disappearance that was the impulse
for the first exhibition in Hong Kong in 2012—and not just its disappearance, but
also its transformation into a vulgar, xenophobic casino city (cities that we all now
share globally). Perhaps it was a premonition, a sort of Zeitgeist, in which we saw
the disappearance about to happen in neighbouring Hong Kong—first with the
'Umbrella Revolution' (2014), and then in the brutal quashing of the now unspeakable
'Revolution of Our Times' (2019–20).

The second iteration of *The Macau Days* was fortunately recast with the novelist
Brian Castro, himself from the old Macau, in 'The Script Road—Macau Literary
Festival' (2017). This iteration was still a sort of parallel concern: Castro's important
novels were featured, such as *The Bird's Passage* (1999) and *Shanghai Dancing* (2003),
both of which anchor consciously and poetically the diasporan's plight; and my
installation was also exhibited as part of the festival. Yet it was not until the third
iteration, in 2017, in the form of a book, that we collaboratively decided on printed
matter, through poetry and visual presentation. The book is a tri-lingual articulation in
English, Chinese and Portuguese, cunningly realised by the design of John Warwicker.
In the fourth iteration, *The Macau Days* installation was elaborated with sound pieces
by Luke Harrald, who provided a purely imaginary dimension to the work and the
times. The unfolding over four iterations felt seamless, with no apparent loss of focus,
only a continual enriching, a continual re-imagining.

pages 180–81
Installation view, *John Young: Diaspora, Psyche*
Bunjil Place, Narre Warren, 2021

SELECTED POEMS FROM
MACAU DAYS (2017)

Brian Castro

The following poems are selected from the collection 'Macau Days: or six characters in search of a dish', published in the book *Macau Days* (A+a Publishing, 2017) by Brian Castro and John Young. This was the second major outcome of Young's project *The Macau Days*, the first being an exhibition held at 10 Chancery Lane, Hong Kong in 2012. The *Macau Days* book was published with all texts in three languages—Chinese, English and Portuguese—bringing Castro's poems and Young's paintings and photographs into a dialogue around their shared histories with Macau.

ENTRÉE

So what was eaten and what talked
was as natural as night and day
when wine and forgetting, grief uncorked,
tasted briefly of Proust's Combray.
Our childhood rosary
sung at Sunday dusk
used to echo over the Praia Grande,
mingling smells of kitchen and musk
with recipes of how
we used to live in old Macau
dining on bittersweet memory.

MAINS

I
A-Ma or Mazu (born circa 960)
or how Macau got named.

Let's begin with a goddess.
It's how Macau gets its name –
but like all Chinese etymology,
there is a mixture of myth and practicality.
Originally it was called Aomen
or the inlet gates to the bay.
But that is too literal a level
with which to play on what to say.
They reverted to the A-Ma temple
of the sea-goddess Mazu,
and Ma became not just *mother* but
someone heavenly and spiritual.
Then arrived the homophonic Portuguese
who loved confusion, mixing in Lusitanian
and Chinese – A-Ma Gao, they called it,
rendering it less alien,
half-punning on the word *Guia*,
Our Lady of Guidance,
giving Catholicism its proper salience.

A-Ma was a goddess who saved sea-faring souls,
propped shipwrecked sailors on wooden spars
her apparition swirling in silken robes
now among the stars, then along the shoals.
It was sex that saved them on the point of death
– we are told that an orgasm lasts longer
when submerged beneath water –
or according to the ancient Chinese,
willful retention led to longevity.
So she went under with them,
always dressed in red,
held their hands,
calmed them below the waves,
fishing for men,
riding clouds across the ocean
in an Ang Lee film,
a crouching tiger, hidden dragon,
arriving just in time to deal with climate change,
with advanced weather reports
for those still about to embark.

Hark!
If you were drowning and called her name
she would come immediately,
but if you were virtuous and extolled her
deity
praying to her as the Empress of Heaven,
she would repair to her rooms,
put on her make-up,
lay out her silks,
perfume her feet,
even take out her looms
to weave another pattern
in life's menagerie,
or in this case, doom's imaginary.

WENCESLAU DE MORAES (BORN 1854)
...AND ANGEL HAIR

Angel hair, called in Portuguese *fios de ovos* ('egg threads') is a traditional Portuguese sweet food made of eggs (chiefly yolks) drawn into thin strands and boiled in sugar syrup. They are a traditional element in Portuguese and Brazilian cuisine, both in desserts and as side dishes. Like other egg-based Portuguese sweets, *fios de ovos* is believed to have been created by Portuguese nuns around the fourteenth or fifteenth century. Laundry was a common service performed by convents and monasteries, and their use of egg whites for 'starching' clothes created a large surplus of yolks. (Wikipedia, 2017).

You liked sweets as most children did,
and your mother starched your collars for school
like the general's daughter that she was;
you all had fine literary sensibilities
which guaranteed your solitude.
They had named you Wenceslau
like the good Bohemian king
you thought you were, believing
you were giving alms
when you bought your wife Atchan
while deputy harbour-master of Macau
on a very good wage.
But we all knew your mother
was strong inside your heart
and you couldn't help
falling in love
everywhere in the East
because the feminine side was strong
and the East was a woman
but the barbarian from the West was
passionate, and with many faults.
You wrote the landscapes and cultures
of China and Japan, a painter
with an eagle's eye watching the invasions
of the industrial West and
the destruction of the environment
whose plants and animals spoke to you
and then fell silent as your garden
iced over with frost black as gunpowder,
and in the spring the new grass rising
of feminism.

Your dream came true.
A better posting in Japan was promised;
you told me you were leaving,
assuming that I, Atchan, would follow.
But I, the girl who thought our blood
would mingle unto dust at the end,
was now a woman with children
and Japan sounded sorrowful,
wind through the strings of a samisen,
luring you from my keening.
The crickets in the Camões garden
deafen me to your words.
I grow without you.

You wrote many books in Portuguese,
you married again and lost your job
and lost your wife in Tokushima.
You married her niece and were
the talk of the town in murderous terms;
she had betrayed you with another's child
and tuberculosis claimed her like her aunt.
Unlucky, you could have said, so many deaths,
but life is selfish and always takes away
something as it gives.

The village on Coloane is still the same;
I know you found it dirty,
but you must still be the Bohemian king
with no friends save your dog;
they sing your praises now and
the Dogman is your nickname,
high up there on a clean Japanese mountain
where the snow falls lightly
like angel-hair.
If you return this way
I will be waiting
with fios de ovos
which I know you like,
its sweet swirls of floss tasting of
the time your mother starched your collar
readying you for other worlds.

CIGARS

A saudade for John Young (born 1956)

Macau does not exist anymore for me,
glossed in hyper-reality,
postmodern madness,
building upon rebuilding
and filling in and dumping
and clearing and faking up
all kinds of sadness.

In the Marienbad Casino
next to the Venetian,
Woman A is being courted
by Man X, who mercilessly beats
the woman's Husband M
in games.
It is a labyrinth of disorientation
in a room full of rhizomes,
lies, deceptions, flowers and fine arts.
Outside there are gondolas afloat
in a fake lagoon
and by the tables the women swoon
their men in tuxedos offering placebos –
"At the end of the spin the lucky ball will fall
with a huge big deal for our next of kin."

As in your art
Macau is now a city
of forgetting
searching for memory.
When deciphered through
chalk on slate or a photographic plate,
or through your tapestries
woven with the histories
of exotic countries,
flesh on silk, ink on linen,
the names we stole are captured
in cloth you've unfurled
to reveal so much more than just
the gambling centre of the world.

Having studied Ludwig Wittgenstein
you know that culture determines
the way we see; that a person's name
is, has to be, the picture of a situation.
Doubled and tripled, we crossed borders
easily, but now the paranoia of ignorance
has folded up your tapestry
and it's a DNA test for ancestry
which supposedly clarifies how
humanity runs in generations
alongside insanity
depending on the periodic flood
that brings on the clash of blood.

O, but to harbour an after-taste
for a salty, hazy sea
where others have ventured before,
gambling with a past in a convex mirror
which shaped a world that didn't last
and didn't deliver glory
but ended in a sabotage of fantasy,
an untranslatable melancholy,
a *saudade*.

That determines the way we see.

We don't have to depart right now
or long for returning by indulging in dreams.
There's enough of the real
in the smell of *chau-chau*,
the flavours of Macau,
in a glare of liquid days, mirage
of home-going not home-coming,
strolling from room to room
listening for the dinner chime.
It's good your images beckon first –
I reckon we can enter here –
our reason is that they rhyme
with a fragrancy sublime.
Let's start then, on this ancient journey.

HISTORY AND POIESIS:
A CONVERSATION WITH BRIAN CASTRO

Moderated by Jennifer Mackenzie

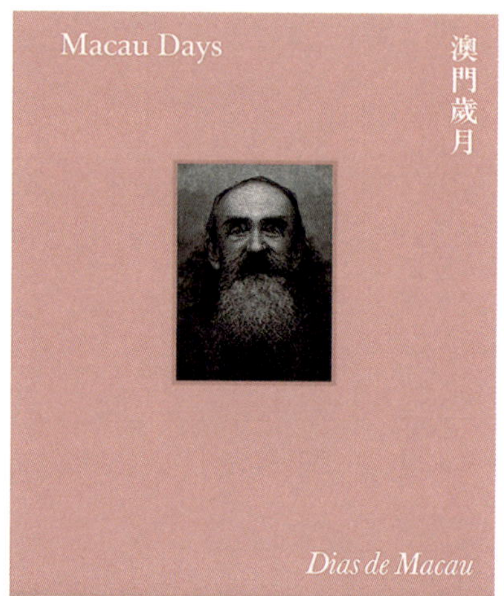

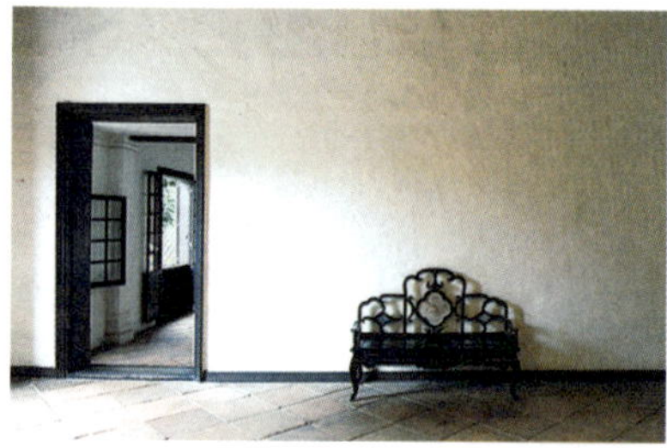

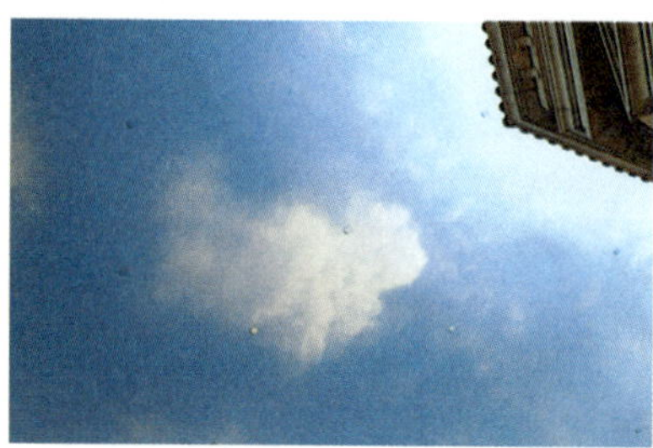

Cover of John Young and Brian Castro,
Macau Days, 2017
Art + Australia, Melbourne

'The Mandarin's House', residence of
Zheng Guanying (Cheng Kuan-ying 鄭觀應,
1842–1922)
São Lourenço, Macau, 2017
Photograph by the artist

Ceiling with sky graphic and downlights
Third floor, The Venetian Macao, Macau, 2017
Photograph by the artist

The following conversation was moderated by Jennifer Mackenzie via email between February and March 2022. It revisits the collaboration between John Young and writer Brian Castro for their book project *Macau Days* (2017). The conversation raises issues relevant to the broader History Projects, including the role of collaboration and a poetic, creative engagement with history.

Jennifer Mackenzie: John and Brian, in my review of *Macau Days* (2017) for the Hong Kong journal, *Cha*, in 2019, I described the trilingual book accompanying the exhibition as 'both a literary amplification of the exhibition and a transformation of its spatial presence into a physical object, a keepsake of its phantasmagorical content'.[1] I was interested in what I sensed as a transfer or connection between Luke Harrald's soundscape in the exhibition and John Warwicker's design and typography for the book. Could you comment on these observations, and perhaps amplify how they may relate to or influence your collaboration, and how you see your work in the dynamics of collaborative practice in this project?

John Young: In proposing this radical collaboration, Brian and the [J. M.] Coetzee Centre liberated my conception of creativity from the siloed medium of the visual arts. The conjunction of all these disciplines produced a multifaceted contemplation of an idea, *Macau Days*, or of differing ideas, imaginings and recollections. What emerged from this collaboration were precious moments of contemplation within friendship, rather than the quagmire of spectacle that neoliberal institutions demand today. From the initial instance when I made the exhibition, what was of most interest to me was the transition from the old Macau to today's casino 'colony' based on speculation. Of course, this transition might be an analogy for many situations that we are living with. However, the collaboration in this project really revealed the limits and strengths of different media in the articulation of memory and imaginings; how truly multifaceted and lyrical human experience can be. For example, the way in which visual works may affect with an immediate gestalt, or the strength of literature, especially in the use of trilingual translations, to reveal the liminal spaces between cultures.

By the end of the project, such works, via different media, had become fruitful keepsakes (in your words) of phenomenological approaches towards memory and imagination. At the same time this conjunction made evident the politics associated with the spaces that different media are allowed to inhabit in neoliberal societies, whether it be painting, literature, gastronomy, sound or design.

Brian Castro: I think John's phrase 'contemplation within friendship' is very apt and is the key to any collaboration. I could add the fact that real friendship comes from a lot of sharing: of backgrounds, language, experiences and finally, of a history. Both Hong Kong and Macau were colonial experiences, the former more so than the latter. In many ways, growing up in these places brought the insider knowledge of working with cultural miscegenation; how to deal, as it were, with interpretation, reconciliation and compromise. Both John and I grew up in families whose skills were honed on shared values and deals. In my case—to use the Portuguese word—my father was a 'comprador', a go-between in business, straddling trade, cultures and languages. Thus was implanted in my DNA a curiosity about a more expansive (under)world. Unlike many Western systems, parliamentary and otherwise, the adversarial position in this practice was the least trodden path. The teahouse was where history was made. So, to put it simply, collaboration was always an excellent fit between us: hand in glove; like ducks to water. Combined with a long friendship, it was always going to be inevitable. Added to this, our different media practices gave us an entrée into unleashing creativities beyond isolated purviews. I might also add that critique, other than self-critique, didn't enter the equation. The pleasure was in the pursuit of always being astonished by each other's art forms.

JM: I do like the way you have focused on friendship as the core of both influence and transformation in the creation of *Macau Days*. I also like the way this collaboration can act as a subversive undercurrent to received ideas of artistic production. When reflecting on my recent work, the joy and wonder of it is the number of writers and artists that inhabit the stream of the work through both influence and friendship. What do you think of collaboration, across cultures or otherwise, when it is set up through institutions?

BC: I think collaboration can work across cultures, but sometimes the gap can be too great; not so much in cultural differences but in the formation of a particular art form peculiar to that culture, which may hamper the understanding of each creator. I have never found any collaboration set up *prima facie* by an institution to be workable, since the institutional infrastructure is by nature either competitive between different institutions or siloed within departments. Creative centres, however, do work well. The J. M. Coetzee Centre,[2] for example, acts as a coordinator for collaboration, mainly through assisted funding between art forms and finding outside industry partners. Once such a structure is in place, ideas and events tend to happen, because venues can be found and funding can be facilitated.

JM: John, you have written that 'for more than five centuries, the days spent in Macau have inspired and nourished those on the bird's path, the flight out, those who have given their lives to the great transformation'[3] Could I ask you both how the historical opening of trade and cultural routes, which can be viewed as an expansion of mind to the crucial awareness of the periphery, of the here and now, has given impetus to your work?

BC: In my case at least, impetus often stems from a besieged mentality because the perception by mainstream Australia is always a categorisation, stereotypical and comfortable, with knowns rather than unknowns. I was pleasantly surprised in Los Angeles to discover that many Asian American writers denounced being classified as Chinese or Korean or Japanese, for example, because those labels are generations old, replete with racist assumptions. In particular, Asian Americans who are either third or fourth generation or more, and born in the United States of America, see themselves as something different, not only incorporating their ancestry but also creating a centrality for themselves, a movement with a different and dynamic way forward.

JY: Working in Australia, I often take solace in what Kenneth White once said; I recall it was something like 'Real work goes on at the periphery, not at the noisy congested centre. And what begins as a margin is often in the history of culture, what allows humanity to turn a page'.[4]

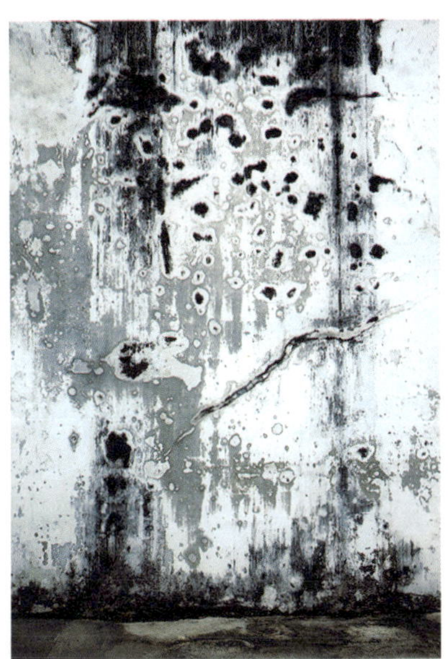

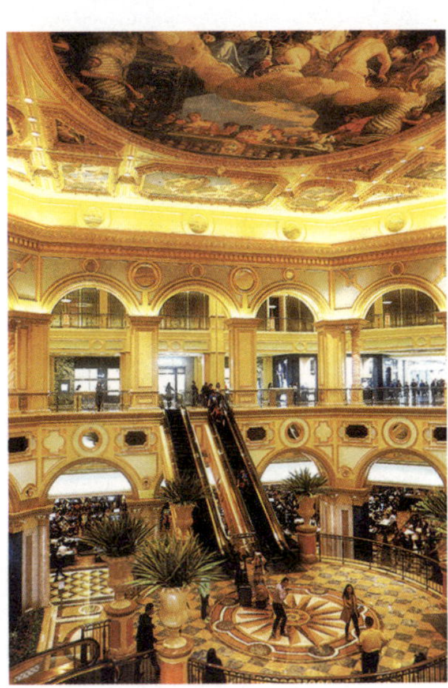

Garden wall, 'The Mandarin's House', residence of Zheng Guanying (Cheng Kuan-ying 鄭觀應, 1842–1922) São Lourenço, Macau, 2017
Photograph by the artist

Interior view of The Venetian Macao, Macau, 2017
Photograph by the artist

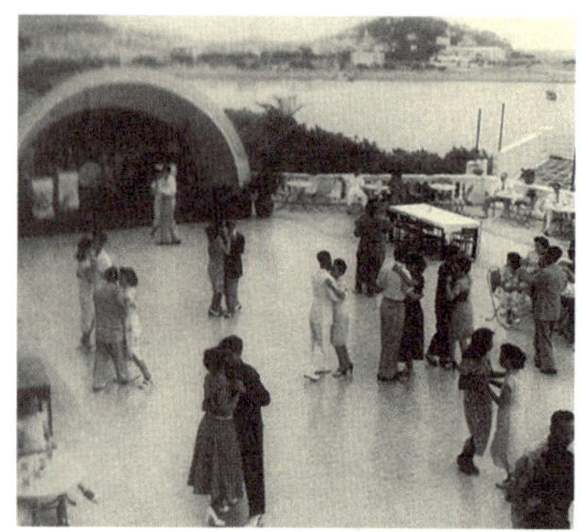

We now have generations of different diasporans in Australia and, in a sense, this is an opening of cultural routes. The current condition is such that there is a certain possibility for our acceptance and transformation of different modes of existence drawing from these various diasporic cultures, and to do so with density and resonance. In other words, a mature form of cultural pluralism, especially in terms of our comprehension of values and duration. The trading or proliferation of cultural routes often happens on the periphery, as the centre tends to have an obsession with maintaining identity, producing a stasis around where one's being may belong. Yet at the periphery, becoming is our belonging. And it is the clarity, acceptance and awareness of this changing process of becoming in the present that I hope for. I feel that this is part and parcel of individuation. The counterforces to this—the colonial, the cliches of national identity, the herd—which are predicated on power and ownership, often require stasis, a sort of thoughtlessness that is disguised as natural, and thus they have no generative potential to push at the margins of thinking, creativity, plurality, and art making. This may be a total oversimplification, but I can certainly say that the counterforces of cultural stasis stand in direct opposition to imagination, desire and the potential incarnation of values from different diasporas. Currently, I see a potential folding in; I have the sense that the periphery is starting, within Australia, to inhabit the centre.

BC: I think I can speak for writing as a test of time. Most often a writer takes many decades to produce an oeuvre that captures critical attention. There are many one-book-wonders, but few who can run long-distance. As John said earlier, the herd mentality is about consolidating identity, so every new kid on the block who taps into any of the available clichés becomes a brick in the national monument. This monument does not provide a telescope on its rooftop to view the periphery or the horizon. If I could name one Ukrainian Australian writer, for example, working with ideas of the periphery, it would be Maria Tumarkin. She fuses forms and crosses boundaries and borders, all the while revolting against the disappearance of the past by highlighting the traumas of the present.

JM: Yes, I agree that creative work coming out of an awareness of the periphery can be an exceptionally fruitful direction to take. As you've said John, it is often the ready-made work which fits right into ideas of cultural identity that are given most prominence but aren't necessarily the most innovative.

As someone who engages with history in my writing practice, I am intensely engaged with the question of what constitutes a historical image in art. How does the image form out of historical material? What are the poetics/aesthetics involved in lifting, almost tweezering the image, as in the developing of a photograph, to make, out of the ether, a compelling and aesthetically satisfying form?

JY: In the History Projects, the 'historical image' is always a ruse. Historical material, at least within the disciplines of European history and archiving can never detach itself from notions of truth and justice. Metaphysical truths, the factual and the judicial are planted so deeply within a context of empirical material. But you can also see, in other cultural contexts, truths that are more located within, say, analogy. With this position, however, remains your question of transforming a historical image into a compelling form. It may very well be that the manner of transformation is where ethics and aesthetics become one.

Often, my aesthetic/poetic preoccupation in 'tweezering the image', as you put it, is to use formal devices of cropping, layering and scale to alter the historical photograph in order to change the agency of the work. This shift in agency might be from locating the individual who was historically constituted as an abject object of

Macau, c. 1965
Photograph from the artist's research archive
for *The Macau Days*, 2012

a colonial gaze toward a layered introspective view, an internal dialogue in the mind
of the individual—a sort of apparent psychological selfie! This kind of updating of
historical material also makes obvious that the past is not placed spatially prior to the
present but is really co-existent with the present, which is a very important existential
expression of those who live in diaspora. For diasporans—the notion of memory and
its daily presence is fundamental, more so than spatial relocations.

BC: Absolutely. For me, the past, the photographs which capture it, are not stills,
but moving images and unreeling narratives. The 'psychological selfie' is indeed
another apposite phrase! I might also suggest a kind of synaesthesia comes into play:
involuntary memory—sight, sound, taste, and so on—constitutes a nervous impulse
which re-assembles fragments of memory and imagination, all of which form a
counter-narrative to official historical documentation: a new 'affective cartography.'

JM: Brian, I was very interested in what you had to say in the *Macau Days* book
about the connection between style and taste. I enjoyed the appreciation of a kind of
Rabelaisian excess, particularly in relation to [Luís Vaz de] Camões[5], and the portrait
of your father and his recipes. Would you care to comment on this in relation to your
own literary style? Also, could I ask you both more generally about your relationship
to biography/autobiography—how crucial, tangential, or minor is it?

BC: Yes, well, a synaesthesia of sorts. A baroque play of excess initiated by the
oyster's irritation, ending hopefully in a pearl! I guess this irritation is in assimilating
biography and autobiography into the imagination, in not being pinned by one form
or other, which would constrict play and enchantment to a master-narrative from
mother-countries. In *Macau Days* there is no one fit between image and text, in the
same way that style and taste are never quite equivalent to their representation. I think
that is why, in my humble opinion, collaboration works to create a new environment.
Having said that, one's taste is a formation of childhood—I have yet to meet a
Westerner who could appreciate stinky tofu. But apart from the literal, taste forms
style, which is an appreciation of literary upbringings, readings, and layer upon layer
of intertextualities, influences and strivings beyond the ordinary.

JY: Following on from your remarks Brian, on style and the density of style, I recall
a few years back, you felt that you'd like the reader to work at reading your texts.
This actually struck a chord with me then, in taking on a position with my work in
relation with the viewer, specifically regarding the History Projects. Instead of
a seamless consuming of reading and viewing, the reader and viewer is positioned
at a threshold when confronted with the written text or artwork—whether it be
an ethical or aesthetic threshold—where they have to commit in order to go down
a new, perhaps deeper path with the text or artwork. Obviously, crossing this threshold
does not undermine one's sense of play and enchantment in the reader/viewer;
depth and enchantment are not mutually exclusive. I'm interested in what your
position of hoping for the reader to work is now, or is it dependent on the text that
you are writing?

BC: That's an interesting question, John. Perhaps subconsciously I'm asking the
reader to do some work, to participate in the creative project, to do creative reading.
Quite honestly, I'm probably incapable of writing blandly with lots of plot and action
made for the consumer to buy the book and skim-read for the ending. It's not in my
DNA, and I don't sell at airports. As you say, 'depth and enchantment are not mutually
exclusive.' What is required from the reader/viewer is slowness. Slowness allows one
to think with the emotions and feel with the mind. I remember putting that into
practice when I first viewed your paintings for *The Macau Days*.

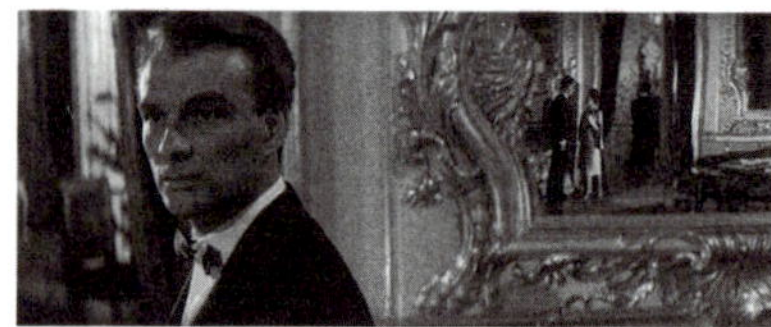

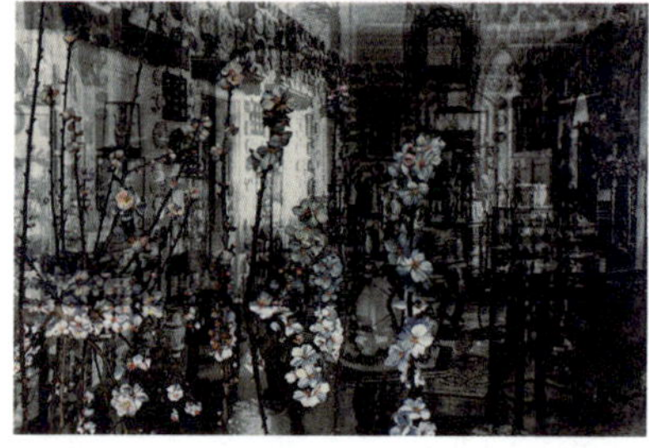

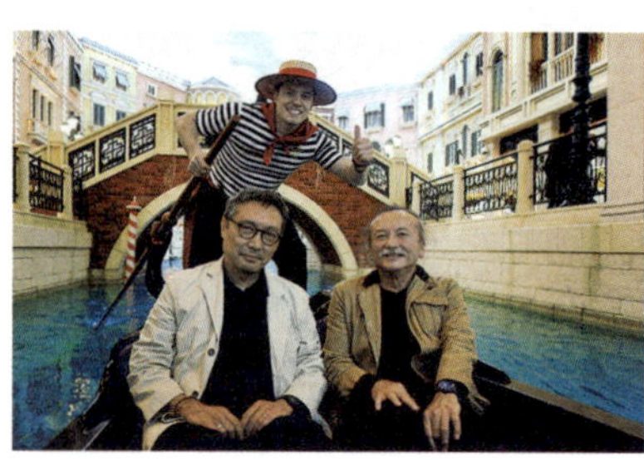

Still from the film *The Last Year at Marienbad*, 1961, directed by Alain Resnais

Marienbad 2012
Digital print and oil on canvas, 185 × 270 cm

left to right, seated: the artist and Brian Castro
A gondolier navigates the indoor canal, third floor, The Venetian Macao, Macau, 2017

JM: Since writing the review of *Macau Days* I've had the opportunity to visit Macau for a conference and that experience made me appreciate more the connections you both draw between the historical image, the nostalgic component, and the fakery so amplified by the casinos. Could you say something about those connections, and perhaps the predominant political/aesthetic phenomena of fakery in our contemporary world?

BC: I don't think there is greater fakery than that exhibited in many of China's so-called 'historical' sites. Indeed, the Cultural Revolution demolished many of the originals, so now there are re-builds and reconstructions in quite a few historical locations. In a way, this is the postmodern moment *par excellence*, when fragments are re-constituted, where history sits side by side with the hyper-real, creating a new site of feeling, somewhat like Hollywood. In Macau, seventeenth-century churches and cathedral façades sit next to imitation Venetian canals atop casinos, setting up a dialogue between religion, a history of colonisation and an exotic wonderland. But there you have it: the comprador spirit is alive and well, albeit obtusely. The theme park, though, demonstrates it cannot do without history

JY: The postmodern theme park, as Brian described it, reminded me so much of [Alain] Resnais' film *Last Year at Marienbad* (1961), which led me to make the painting *Marienbad* for the exhibition. Prior to making the book, Brian and I travelled in Macau and somewhat reluctantly boarded a gondola on the San Luca canal, on the third floor of the Venetian Hotel and Casino, together with an Italian gondolier serenading in Mandarin. Amongst all the questions that defined that presence, all I could think of at that stage was [Thomas] Mann and to a certain extent [Luchino] Visconte's *Death in Venice* (1971), where the notion of passion as confusion and degradation was (as I later discovered) inspired by Goethe's *Marienbad Elegy*.[6] Sitting in that gondola for me, the passion for the authentic and for resonating memory was brought into crisis—the sense of loss of this passion only to be cruelly serenaded in a sweet kitsch song by the Italian gondolier, in Mandarin!

Going back to the creation of sites of feeling away from the authentic, Brian's observation of the role of synaesthesia in our collaboration was apt—the cross media, dissociative experience is, hopefully, liberating. It is a refuge that frees us from an insistent identity constructed through image and sight. Synaesthesia pluralises the way diasporic experiences, such as memory, can be experienced.

1. Jennifer Mackenzie, 'A Trilingual History of Benevolence', *Cha: An Asian Literary Journal*, 2019, https://www.asiancha.com/wp/article/macau-days/.

2. The J. M. Coetzee Centre for Creative Practice, at the University of Adelaide.

3. See Young's artist statement for *The Macau Days* project in this volume, p. 183.

4. Kenneth White, *Coast to Coast. Interviews and Conversations, 1985–1995*, Open World in Association with Mythic Horse Press, Glasgow, 1996, p. 46.

5. Luís Vaz de Camões (c.1524–1580) is considered Portugal's greatest historical poet; his epic poem *Lusíadas* or *The Lusiads (The Portuguese)*, written in 1572, describes explorer Vasco da Gama's completion of a sea route from Europe to India, via southern and eastern Africa, between 1497 and 1499.

6. Here Young refers to Thomas Mann's novella *Death in Venice* (1912), Luchino Visconte's 1971 eponymous film, and a poem by German writer Johann Wolfgang von Goethe written in 1823.

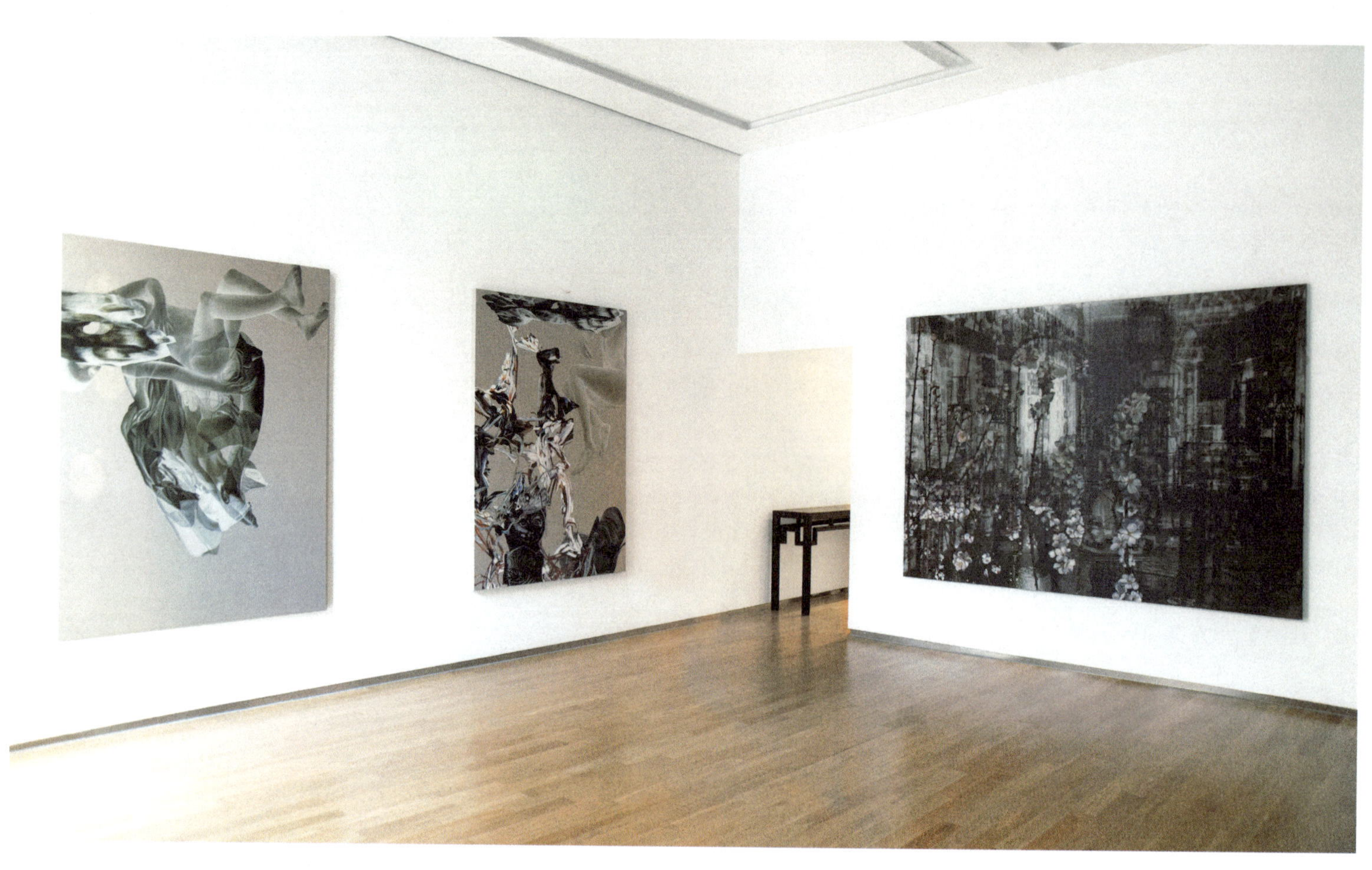

The Macau Days 2012
Installation view, 10 Chancery Lane Gallery,
Hong Kong, 2012

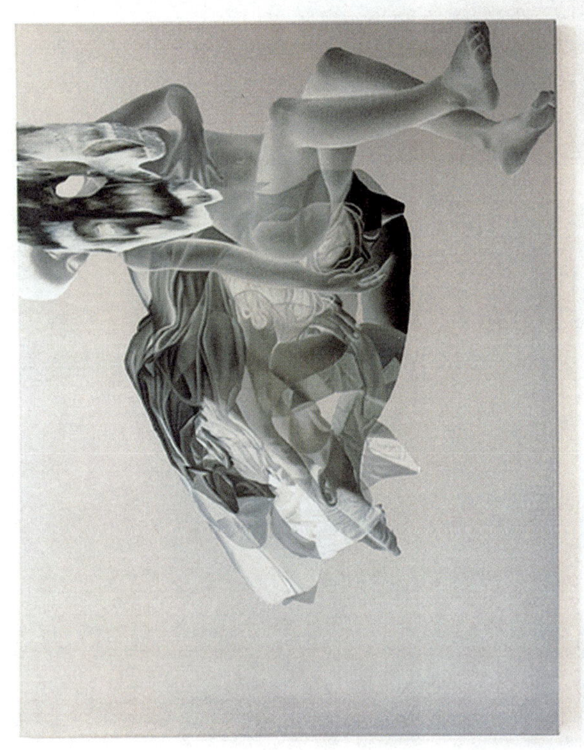

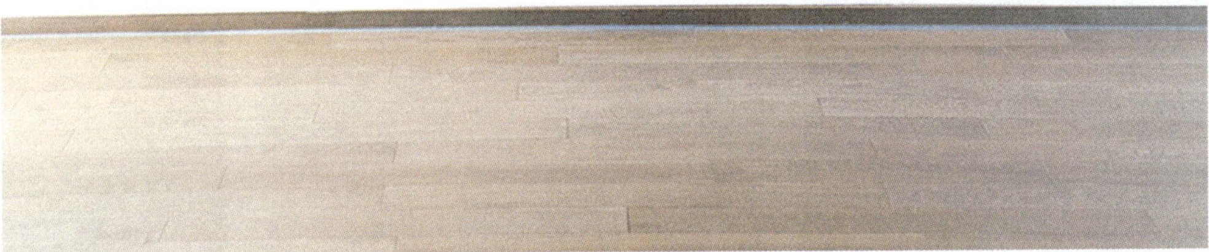

Mazu, Goddess of the Sea II
(The Drowning of Mazu) 2012
Oil on linen, 190 × 144 cm
Installation view, 10 Chancery Lane Gallery,
Hong Kong, 2012

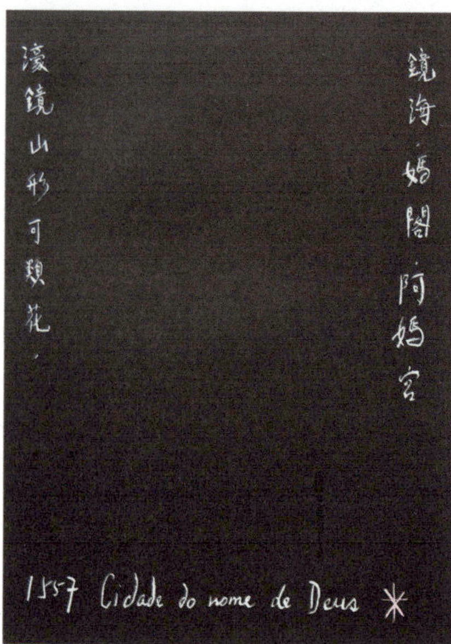

淺鏡山形可類花
鏡海・媽閣・阿媽宮
1557 Cidade do nome de Deus ✳

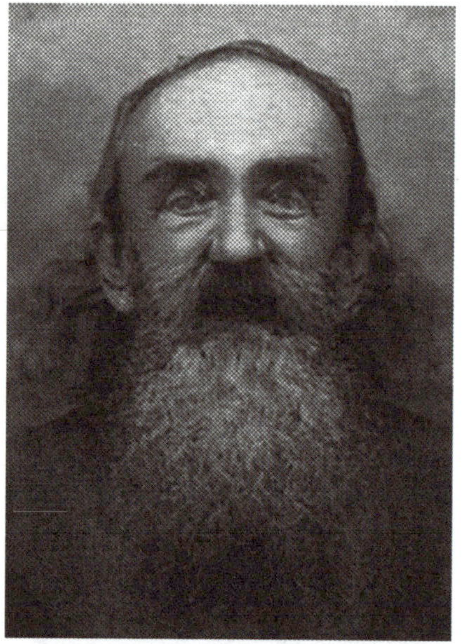

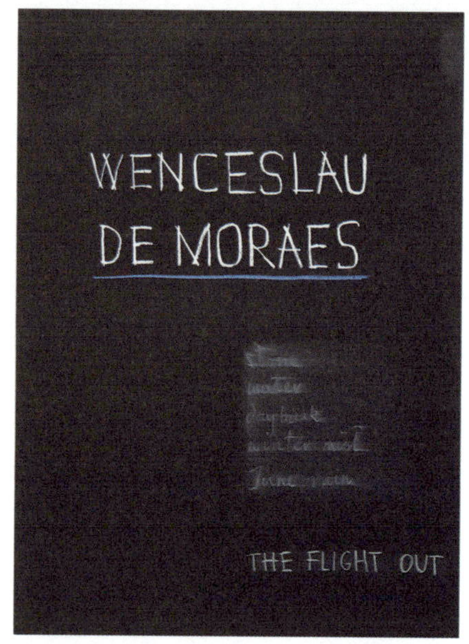

WENCESLAU
DE MORAES
THE FLIGHT OUT

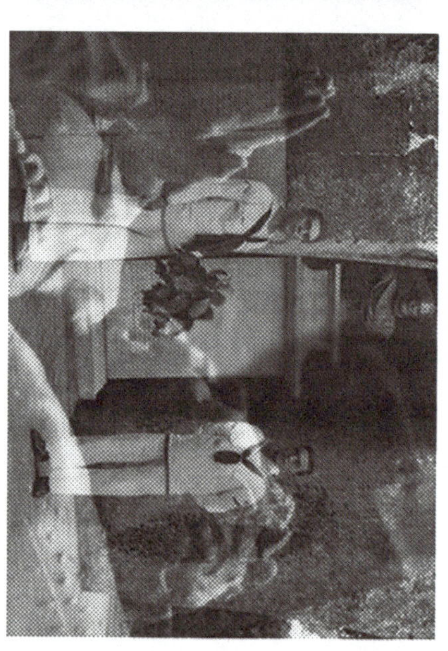

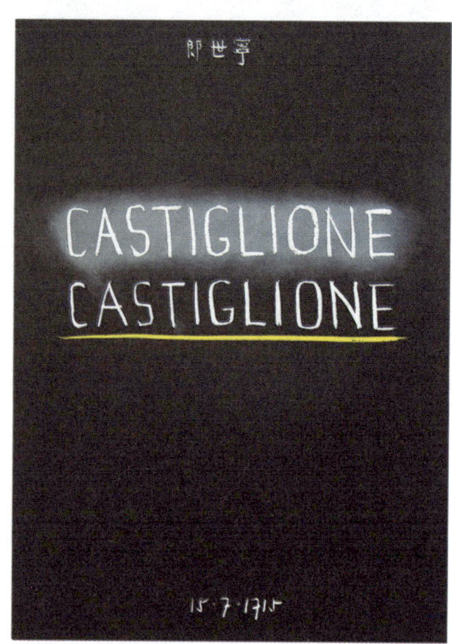

郎世寧
CASTIGLIONE
CASTIGLIONE
15·7·1715

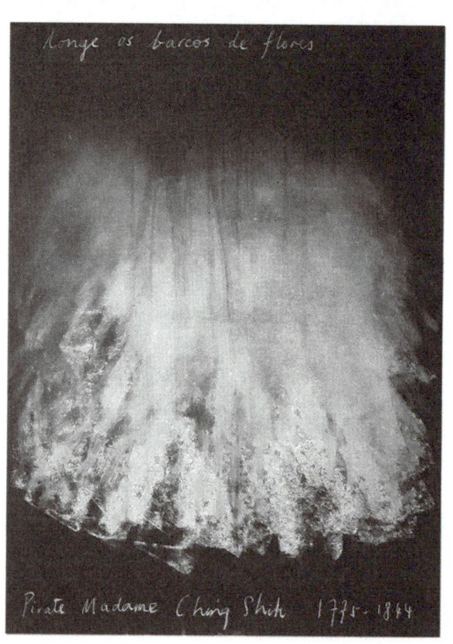

Longe os barcos de flores
Pirate Madame Cheng Shih 1775-1844

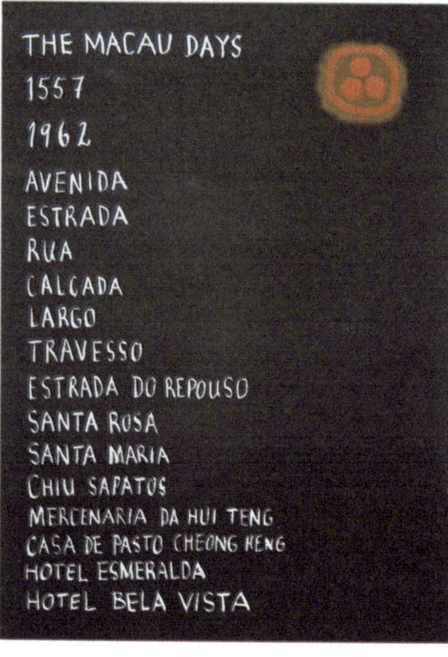

THE MACAU DAYS
1557
1962
AVENIDA
ESTRADA
RUA
CALCADA
LARGO
TRAVESSO
ESTRADA DO REPOUSO
SANTA ROSA
SANTA MARIA
CHIU SAPATOS
MERCENARIA DA HUI TENG
CASA DE PASTO CHEONG HENG
HOTEL ESMERALDA
HOTEL BELA VISTA

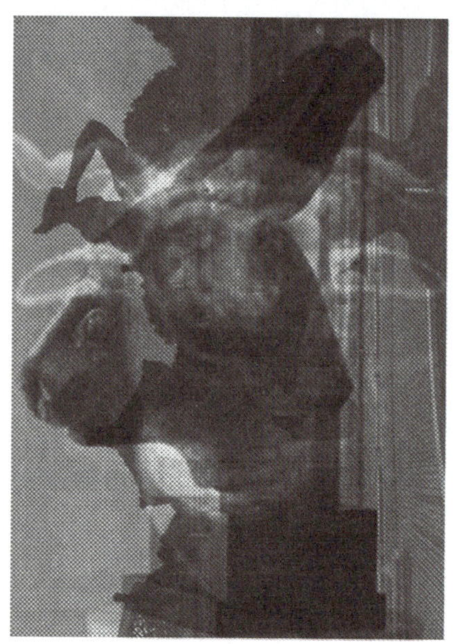

our   souls
meet   here

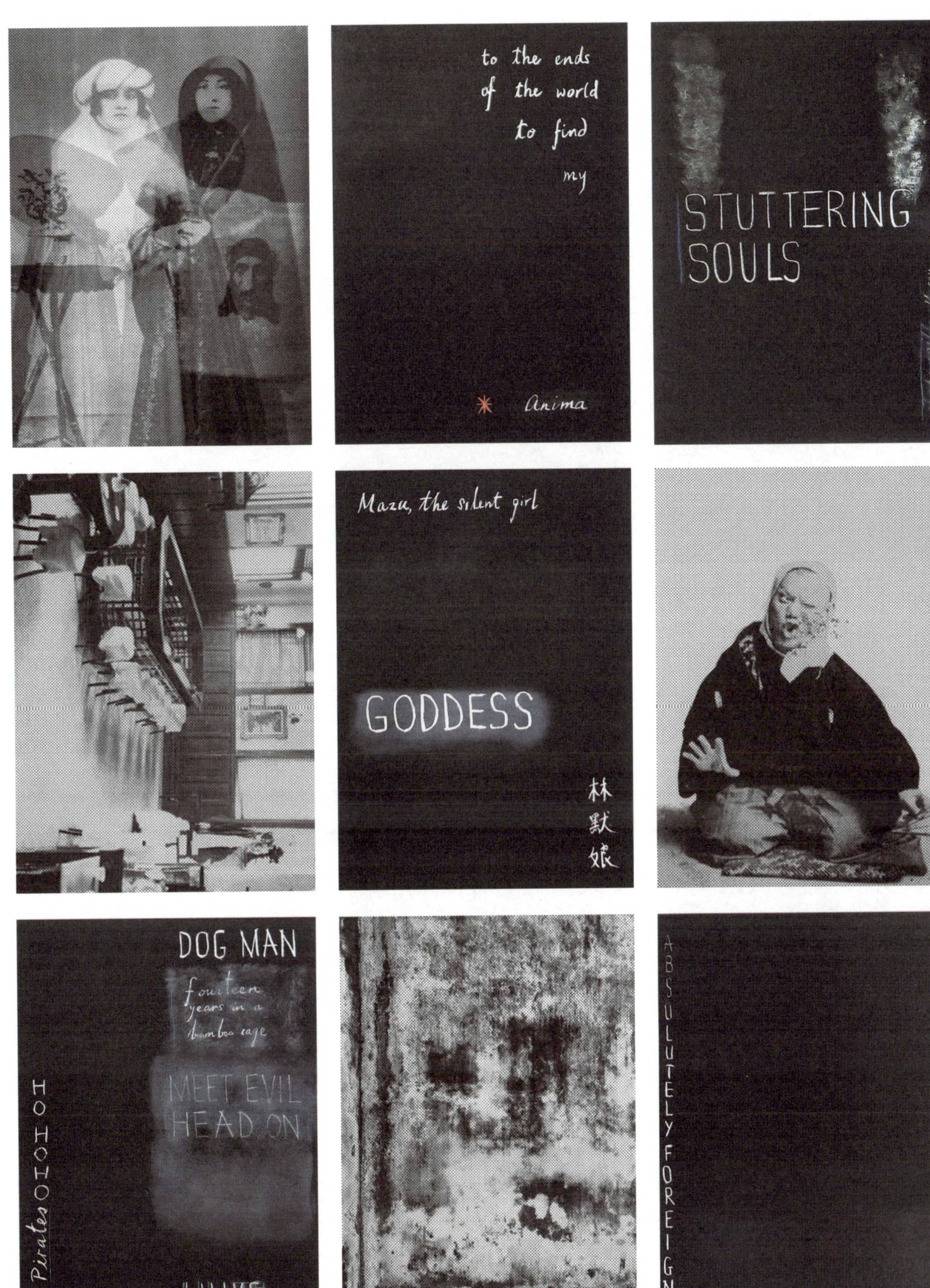

The Macau Days 2012
Digital print on photographic paper and chalk on blackboard-painted cotton archival paper, 15 units, 320 × 390 cm

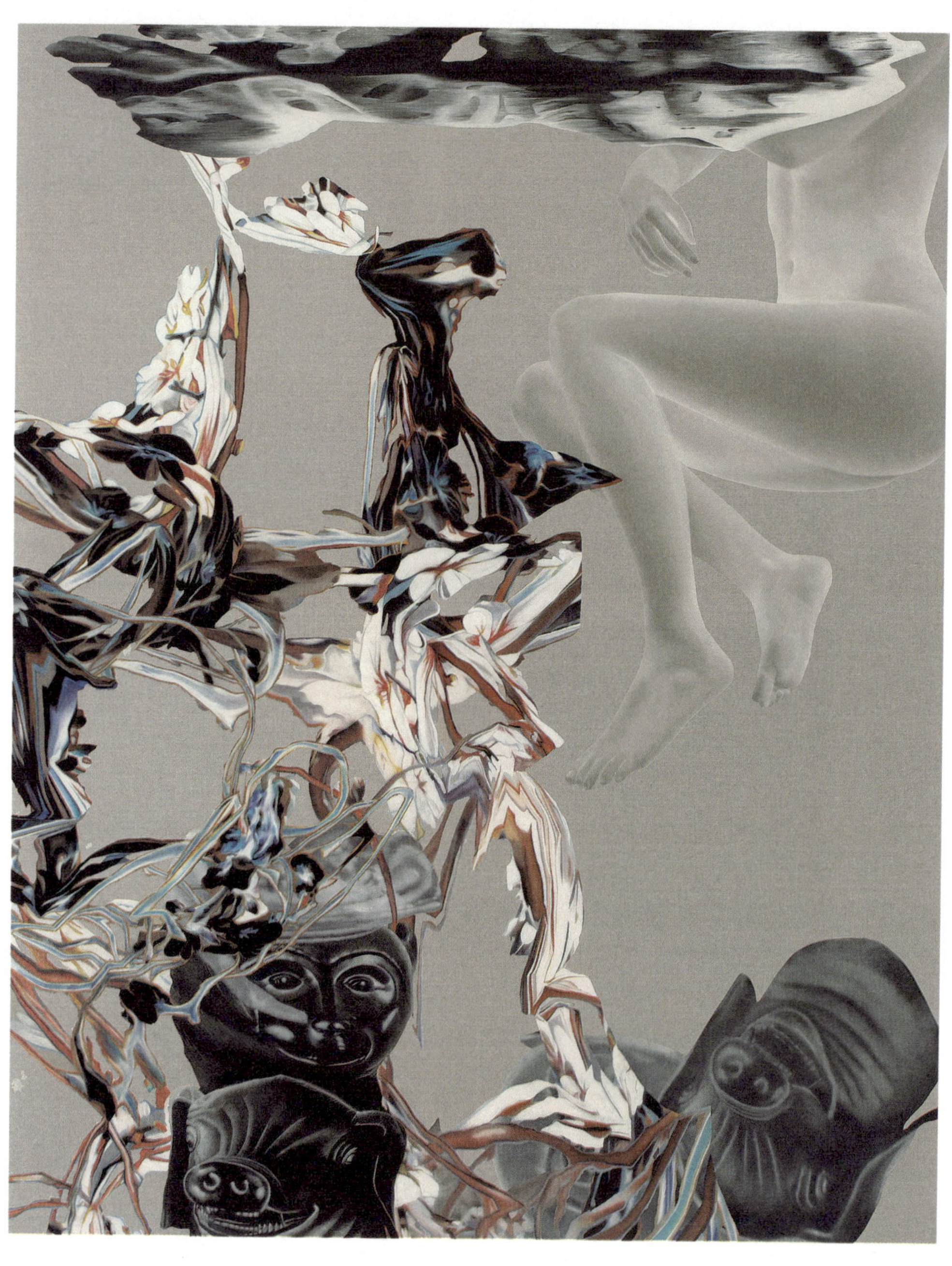

*Mazu, Goddess of the Sea III (Mazu Swimming
Amongst the Pantheon of Idiots)* 2012
Oil on linen, 190 x 145 cm

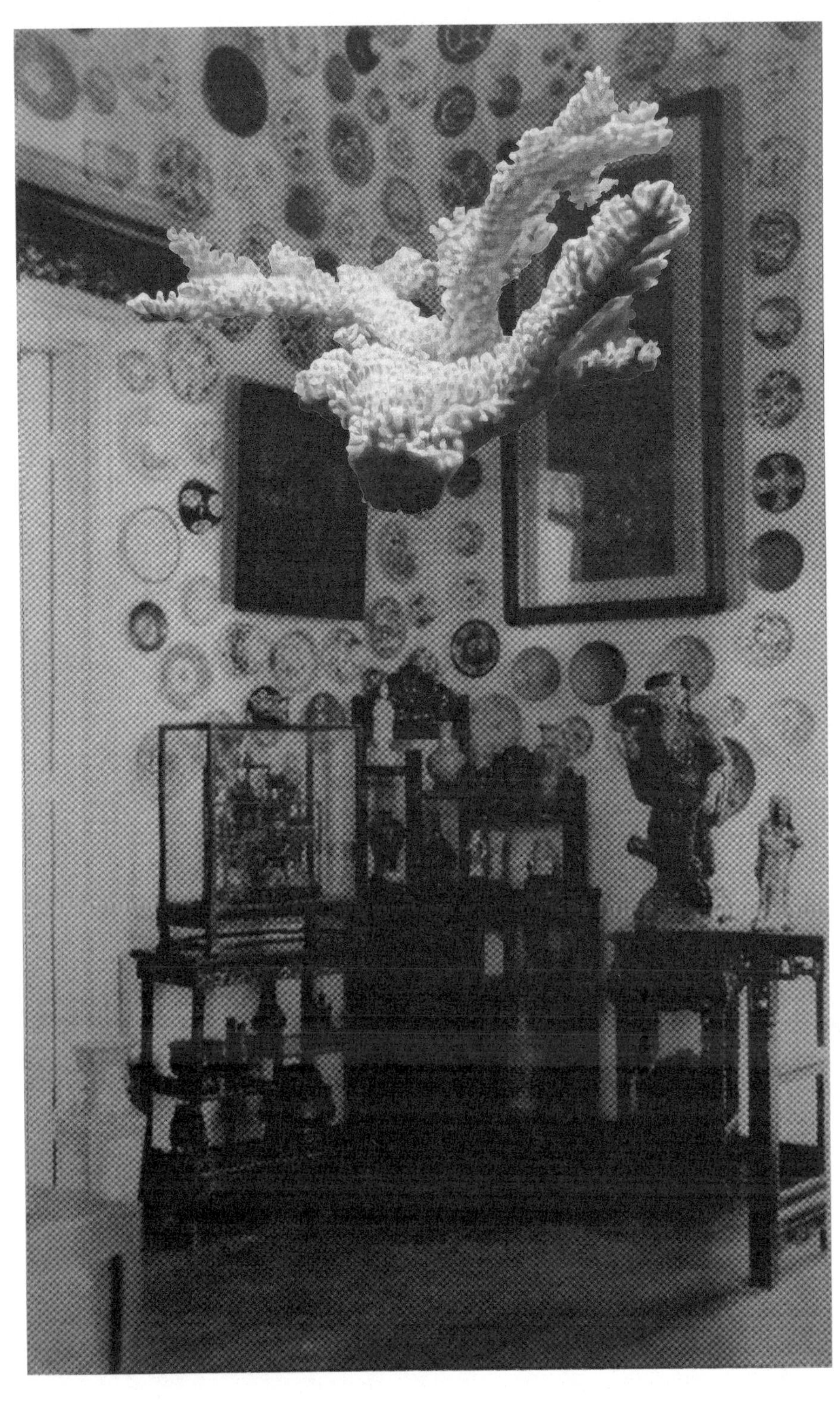

Macau IV 2012
Digital print and oil on canvas, 115 × 68.5 cm

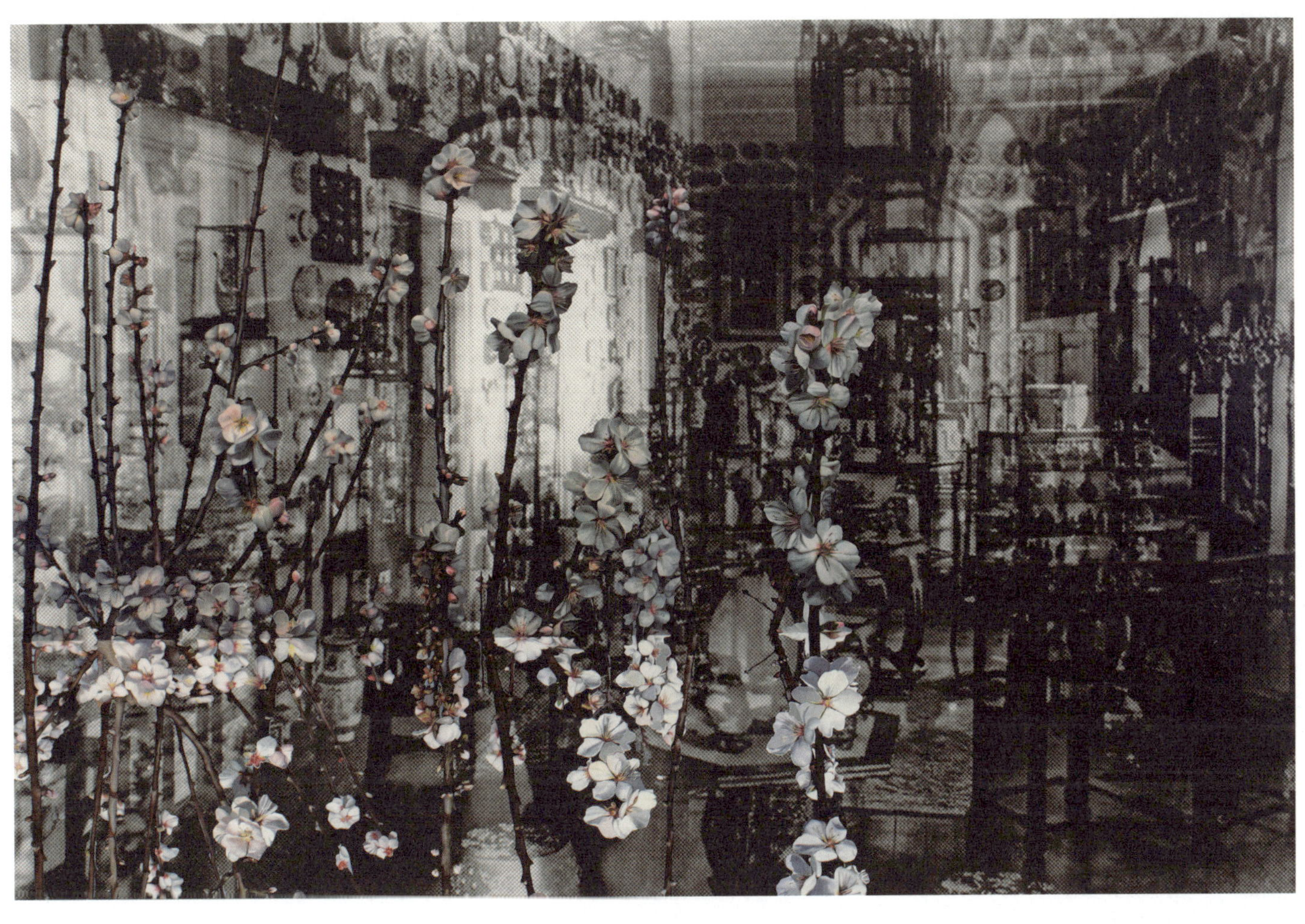

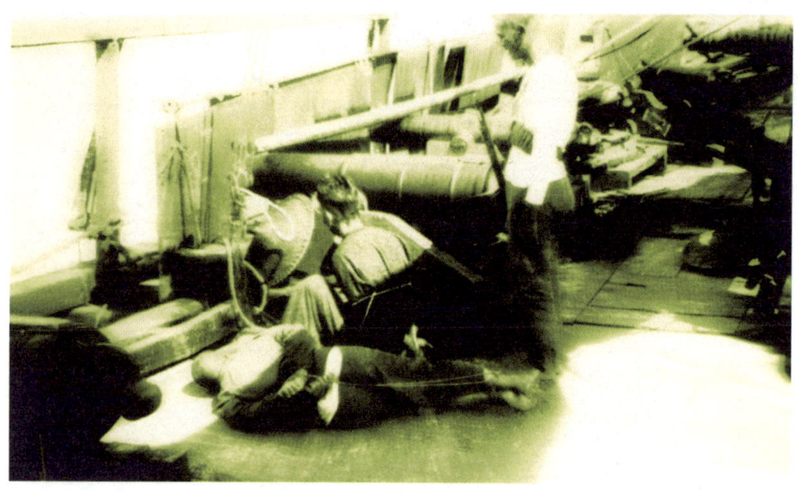

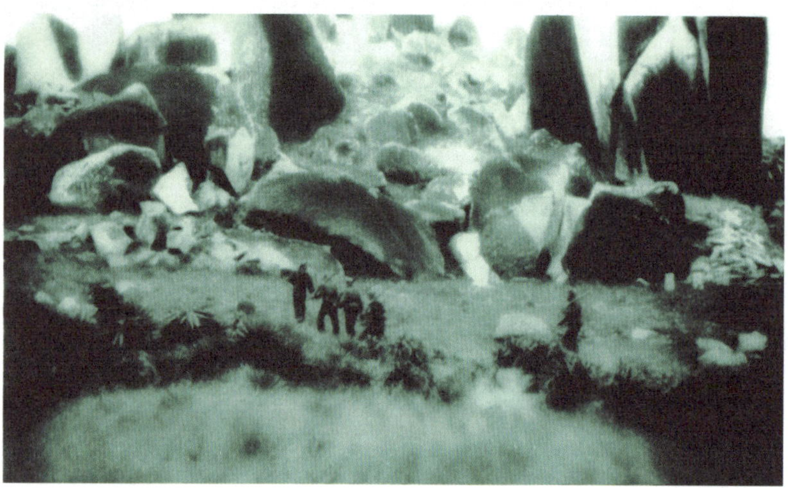

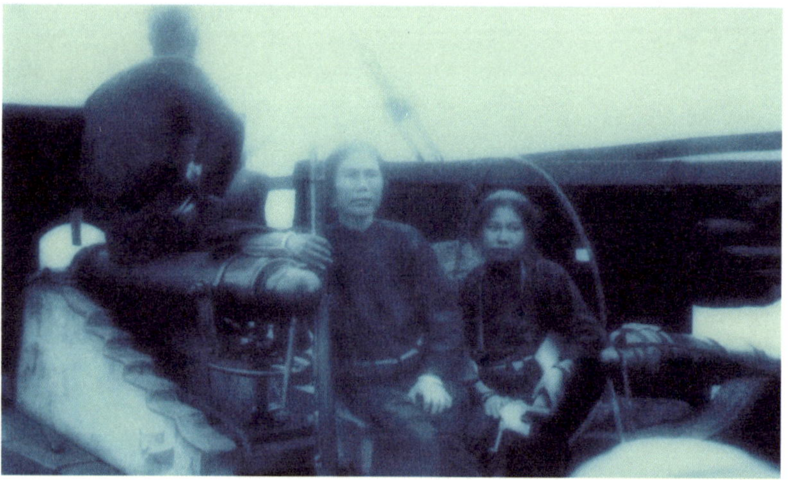

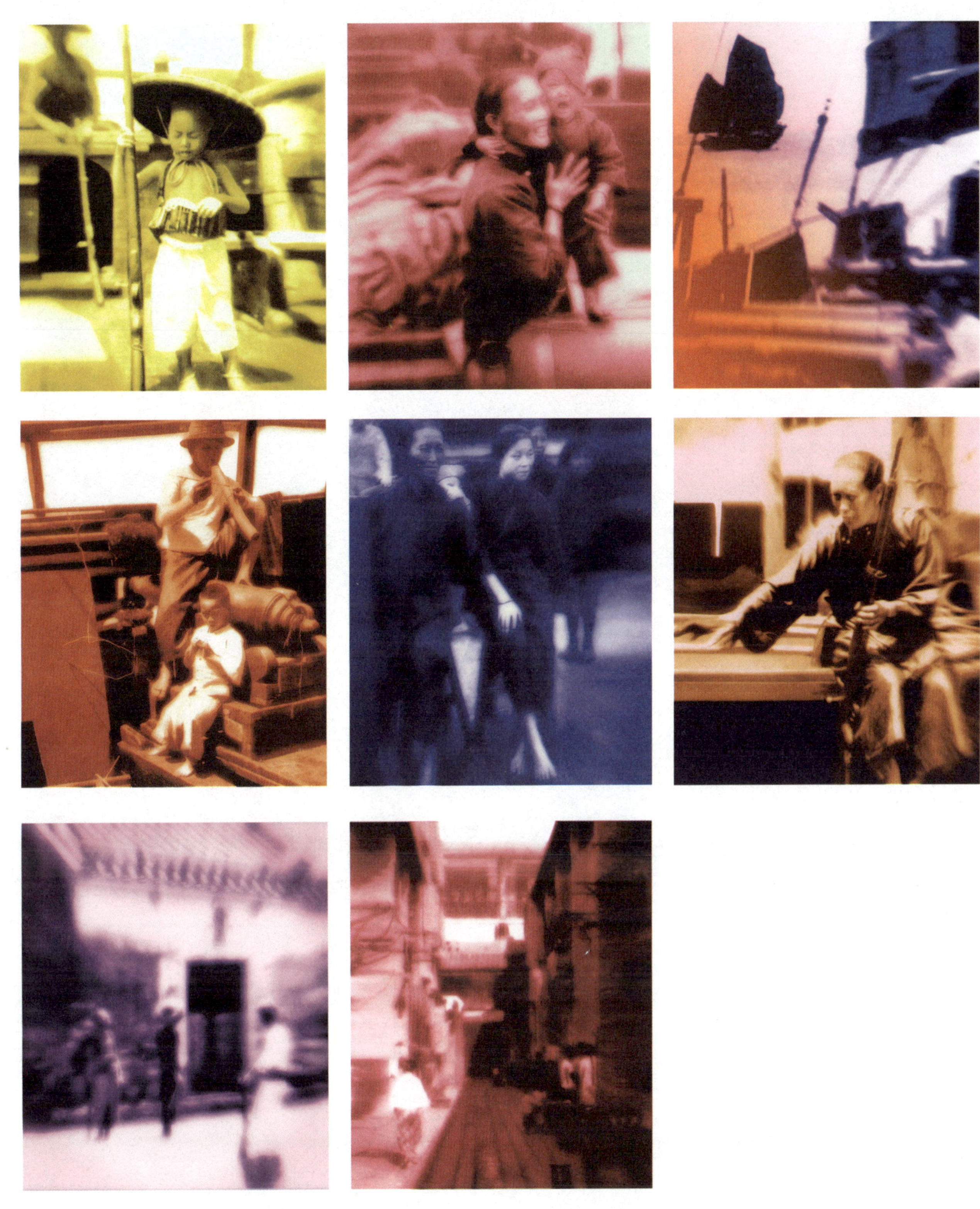

I Sailed with Women Pirates 2017
Digital print on photographic paper, 14 units,
74 × 90 cm (each)
Private collection and collection of the artist

THE NEW
WOLF OF ROME

2012

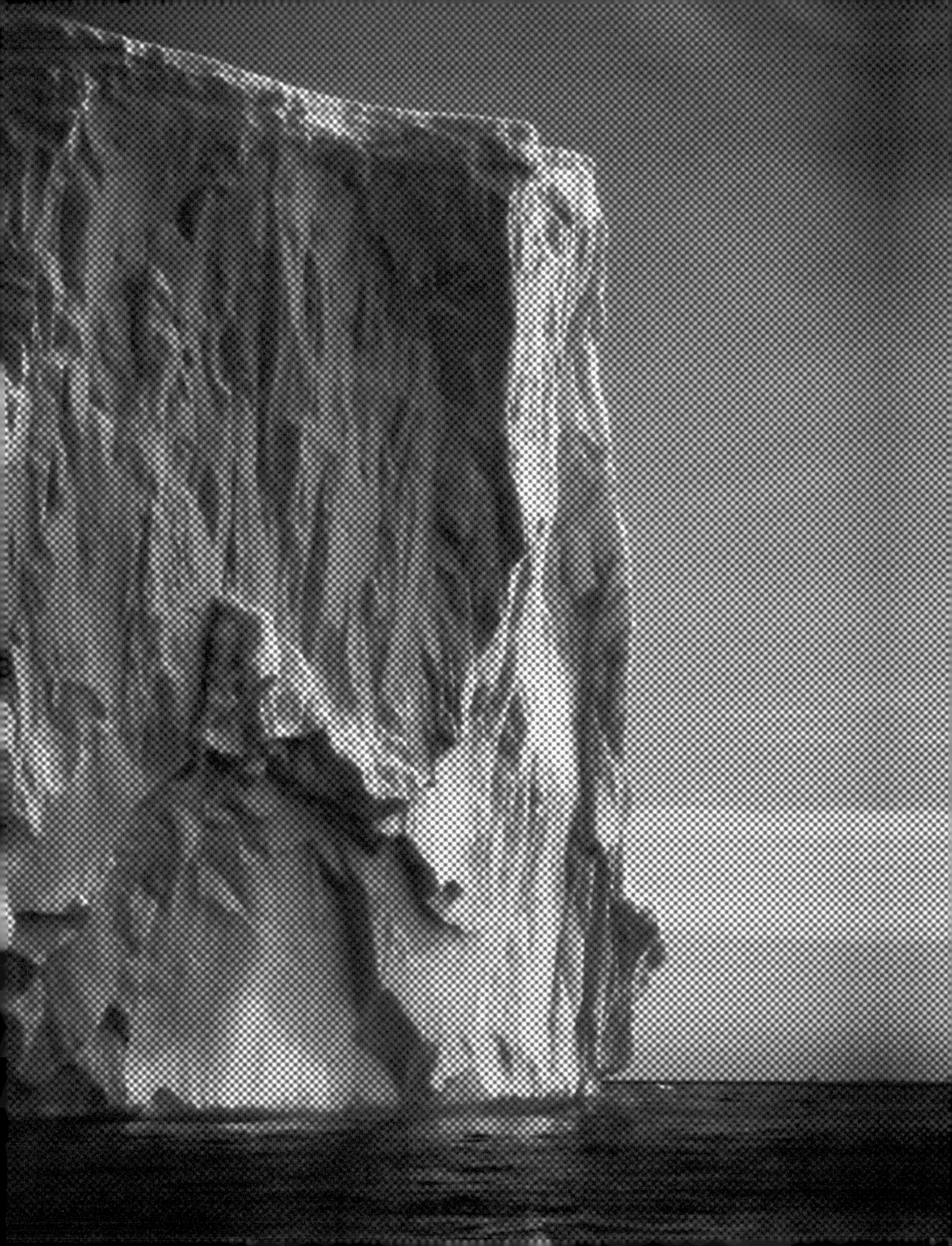

ANCIENT
WATERS

THE NEW WOLF OF ROME

The New Wolf of Rome is a new allegory that revisits the Roman founding myth
of *Lupa Capitolina*—the 'Capitoline Wolf'. In the original, the she-wolf finds the
abandoned infant twins Romulus and Remus by the banks of the Tiber River. She
suckles and cares for them until they are found by a shepherd, Faustulus. In time,
Romulus becomes the founder of a new capital, Rome.

This project consists of two groups of works. *Through the Eyes of the Wolf* (2012) is
a series of six pairs of digital photographic prints and chalkboard drawings (100 × 150
cm each). Unlike in the majority of History Projects, this series pairs a single vision
of an ancient landscape—a crystalline river, a hermit's hut, a towering iceberg, cloud-
like jellyfish—with its poetic double in a chalkboard drawing. Phrases from the nature
poems of Tang Dynasty poets Li Bai 李白 (701–762) and Du Fu 杜甫 (712–770) are
scribed in Chinese and English, alongside chalk drawings of alchemical and Jungian
symbols. Each pair of images forms a meditation on myth, nature and eternal forms.

Like the *Mazu* series, the collection of five paintings depict timeless, partially nude
figures delicately painted in negative colours with oil on raw linen. The figures,
shrouded in ancient-looking robes, are often layered over one another and appear
seated or sometimes falling, accompanied by wolves, plum blossoms or icebergs. The
image of monumental vistas of ice in works such as *Born from Ice* (2012) are from
photographs made by Young on a field trip to Antarctica between 2008 and 2009.

ARTIST STATEMENT

Excerpt from exhibition catalogue *The New Wolf of Rome*, Philip Bacon Galleries,
Brisbane (2012)

From the ancient founding myth, a new allegory is presented here; the wolf, blessed with
values of the human and nature, is born from ice. She finds the crowd and she feeds and
cares for it. In time, the crowd, who only recognises itself and the literal, devours her. Figures
and slippages abound in this cycle of works, but what is also present is a set of visions,
drawings and images on paper. They are primal and mysterious yet embellished with ancient
Chinese nature poems and alchemic symbols; the visions and imaginings of the world
through the eyes of the she-wolf.

HISTORIC VISIONS, COMPELLING PRESENCES

Claire Hielscher

The gradual phasing out of the historically alienating elements of the postmodern artistic idiom left open a space for a new form of artistic engagement. A generation of artists have emerged in contemporary practice that choose to abandon the largely impersonal postmodern precepts of deconstruction and pastiche in favour of 'aesth-ethical' notions of reconstruction, myth, and pragmatic idealism. Put simply, individual empathy has once again become essential to understanding history as being formed by generations, and the present as an often-fractured recounting of events, places and perspectives.

For the artist operating in this time, the challenge is how to work with such complexity in a way that responds intelligently to what has come before and not slip into self-referentiality without feeling. To push beyond the need for easy hybridity, often associated with postmodernity, art has needed to find a new sense of contemporaneity, one that could acknowledge and defy the heavy pull of multiple grounds; grounds that now have to be simultaneously visual, historical, cultural, and fantastical. Forming a recognisable route through these shifting spaces, times and planes of existence is no easy task for the individual, let alone for a culture on the precipice of immense change or upheaval. Throughout history, we have used maps to situate, orient and direct us to our new destination. But if there is no longer a singular, solid ground for us to cling to or a linear narrative of history to trace, the question of recognition—of culture, of past and of self—becomes exceedingly complicated. With the slow weakening of the once implacable nation state narrative, traditional concepts of history have increasingly made way for the recording of the multiplicity experienced by the mobile subject, both in the representation of experience and in the effort of finding a place within contemporaneity. In the face of an identity that does not fit or appropriately contend with the old or the new, in sense of time or space, the requirement becomes an opening of a completely new space; one that we all have to cross.

Operating within these new measures for contemporary understanding in an alienating globalism, and a historic comprehension in a hyper-technical present is John Young. Young's arrival to a new space after the 1967 Riots in Hong Kong (echoing China's Cultural Revolution) was the nexus for a subsequent career-long visual exploration into an oscillating 'figure' and 'ground'. Much of Young's oeuvre can be seen as constantly moving, amassing and redefining space, both in terms of historical rhetoric and aesthetic choice. These oscillations have formed multiple series of history-laden works that are complex and intricately layered. Inevitably, this movement also results in many recurring tension points evident throughout the different phases of Young's artistic exploration; tensions between realism and abstraction, idealism and historic brutality, past and present, as well as between grand and individual narratives.

pages 206–07
Ancient Waters 2012
Digital print on photographic paper and chalk
on blackboard-painted archival cotton paper,
100 × 150 cm

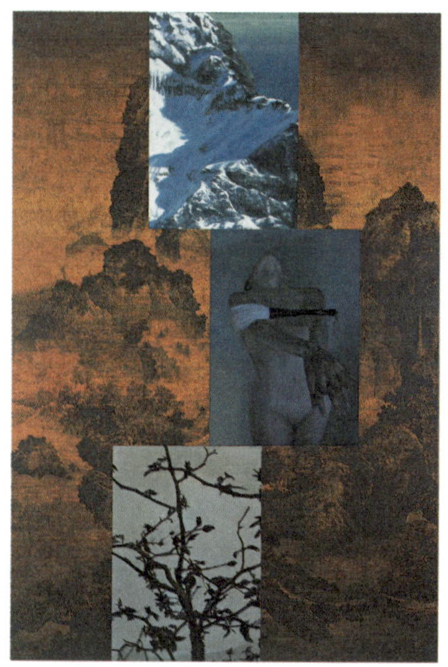

Nest (Version II) 2003
Digital print and oil on linen, 231 × 151 cm
Private collection, Berlin

This text explores a group of Young's works that contend with these tensions and oscillations of identities and histories, beginning with the *Silhouette Paintings* (1986–89), *Polychrome Paintings* (1989–93) and *Double Ground Paintings* series (1993–2005), which explored the syntax of painting, in order to re-evaluate the fracturing nature of the postmodern idiom and its relationship to aspects of Young's later History Projects. For Young, the act of painting itself is an attempt to disrupt the notion that the artist is a disillusioned witness acting from their own clear conception of linear time and defined place. Instead, Young challenges the skepticism and irony often associated with postmodern ideas by reigniting a dilemma that still troubles much of postmodern discourse around what art, and the artist, can and should do. Where postmodernism insists upon disillusionment and a seemingly haphazard hybridity, Young responds with a different vision: a simple conclusion evades us all, we are each continually peeling back layers of cultural memory, historical memory, and the negotiation of meaning in-between.

At the height of his earlier periods of experimentation, Young's aesthetic choices synthesised his version of postmodernism and postcolonialism; elements of a cultural and critical make-up that highlighted the seemingly irreconcilable notions of temporal alienation, cultural difference, and the fracturing of the spaces in-between. These works deal with the artist's concept of self, time and identity; however, as Carolyn Barnes has argued, 'while Young's cultural ancestry provides a background for the *Double Ground Paintings*, this series is not only limited to his personal experience'.[1] As these works exemplify, Young has little use for strict concepts of 'identity' that serve to limit artists to specific thematic and analytical problems.[2] Instead, Young seems to insist that the question of what it means to revisit history and the narratives we build for ourselves goes far beyond the individual's often inconsistent recall of an experience. Ideally, the contemporary gaze is one that sees through the cracks it creates and celebrates what passes through the resulting spaces and fractures.

Similarly, in later bodies of work from the History Projects—including *The New Wolf of Rome* and *The Macau Days*—Young's intention is to stretch the limitations of historical memory and collective emotional recall by investigating what it means to move past a definitive deconstruction of time, place and fact for our own comprehension of the ostensibly solid ground beneath our feet. By highlighting how painting can be explored beyond a contained system or historical canon, Young now seeks to explore the medium more as a conversation between different notions of nature, the human body, myth, and history, operating in differing and shifting cultural spheres, in terms of both time and place.

When considered in tandem with his earlier, less figurative works, Young's later explorations emerge as a natural progression of the culmination of decades of practice. It is a practice that is born of multiple tongues and origins, of slowly revealing gazes of a greater whole, and of the roles that absence and presence play in his hauntingly beautiful aesthetic. Young's work speaks to the enduring issues of contemporaneity—of being both in and out of time, place and self, and what it means to address these elements without aiming to resolve any tension or misalignment bubbling beneath the surface. For Young, the power of the artist lies in this ability to continually play with such pressure and interact with what emerges from the abyss of the forgotten, the embellished, and the misremembered.

Throughout Young's body of work, there is a gentle confrontation with this part of the human condition and its need for certainty, both as an exploration of time either compounded or released in a work, or as a transitory joining of previously unmeshed cultural boundaries. Young's work occupies a space seemingly divined for the intercultural, migratory artist; a space bordered by questions that tease out whether living in a place makes it one's own, and how revisiting its past can engender it with disquiet, acceptance and newness in equal measure, especially if we float in the uncomfortableness for long enough. As Terry Smith insists, in our contemporary time, world-picturing, place-making and connectivity can take many forms in art. It can tend in many directions and operate in many dimensions, but it keeps circling back to four main artistic preoccupations: the changing sense of what it is to be in time, to be located or on the move, to find freedom within mediation, and to piece together a sense of self from the fragmented strangeness that is all around us.[3]

If we take on board Smith's analysis, it is possible to say that the issues that serve to complicate traditional linear art history are two-fold—they are both spatial and temporal. The traditional art-historical relationship that acts to incorporate the defined space of a national or historical identity with the linearity of time, between experience and representation, can no longer contend with the multiple temporalities that construct contemporary experience. Further to this, the subsequent cultural phenomena of the postmodern accompanies a sense of distrust and the consequent desertion of meta-narratives, amid the emergence of late capitalism, the fading of historicism, and in turn the waning of affect.

It is to this point that Young keeps returning piece by piece, layer by layer: empathy for what and who has come before is often more important for our shared humanity than precise historical recall and documentation. Or at the very least for many postmodernists, a synergistic blending of duelling ideologies and times. As Young emphatically states: 'To connote things and to turn things into stories in the simplest form is one way to deepen the experience of looking at a work beyond the momentary and the literal.'[4] Young can be seen as an artist resisting the fall into self-interested perspectives. Instead, the space created by painting is a prospective, intermediary one where varied attitudes, values and ideas are experienced at an immanent level through the condition of subjectivity, and ultimately achieved at the level of the aesthetic process.

In the case of *The New Wolf of Rome* series (2012), Young describes the entire collection and aesthetic treatment as 'an allegory'. If we are to take this description in a literal sense, the symbolic narrative Young provides is one that represents an abstract or spiritual meaning through certain concrete or material forms; a figurative treatment of his subject under the guise of another. In a set of six main canvases and smaller drawings—complicated in construction both as individual images and as a collection— Young revisits the Roman founding myth centred on the interaction between the natural and civilised worlds, a line of thought that he carries through from the progression away from innocence and a regression toward eventual destruction.

Born from ice and destroyed by one another, the crowd that Young draws together is semi-corporeal, cloaked, and evasive. The inhabitable world seems removed from the lushness of the natural; it is ungrounded in empty space. The she-wolf or lupa, represented in exquisite detail in *The Wolf Feeds the Crowd* and *Repose*, engages the viewer to see her influence at the centre of the circling images of quiet destruction. In a set of smaller chalk text and photographic pieces, such as *Through the Eyes of the Wolf: Ancient Waters* and *Through the Eyes of the Wolf: Deep Solitude*, Young directs the gaze of the wolf to focus on ancient mantras, classical Chinese nature poems and mythology.

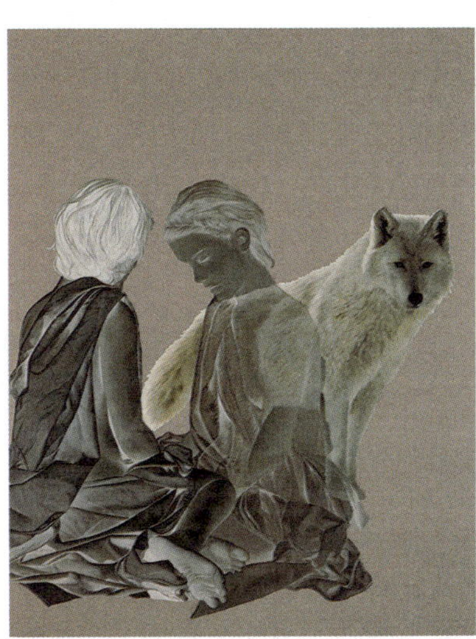

Repose 2012
Oil on linen, 190 × 144 cm

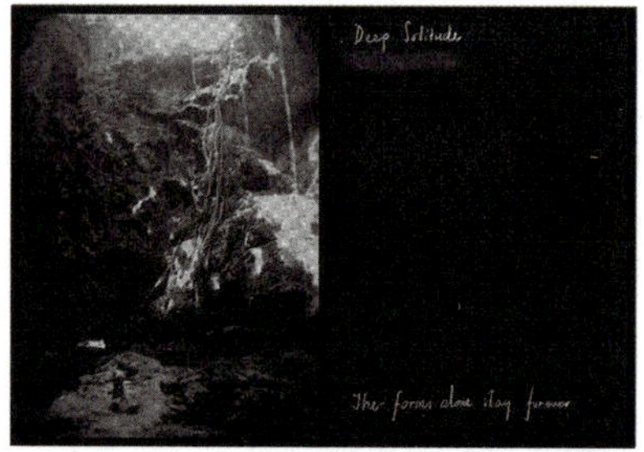

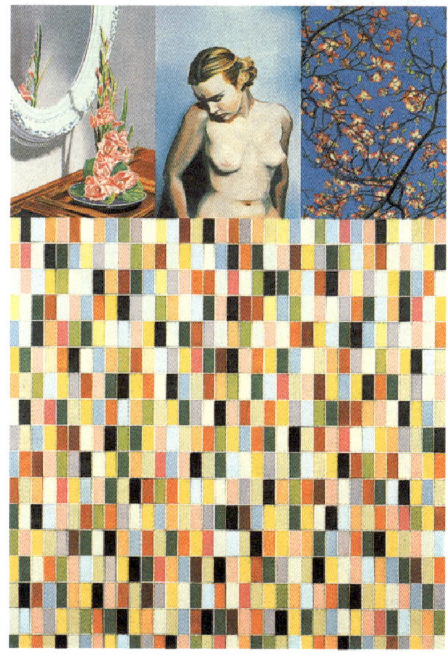

Ancient Waters 2012
Digital print on photographic paper and chalk
on blackboard-painted archival cotton paper,
100 × 150 cm

S Painting, 1992
Oil on canvas, 274 × 183 cm

This gaze is drawn backward yet it is still distinctly interested in the progression forward. The wheel of life continues to turn in Young's constructed world, but it is shifting, unsure and unstable.

In terms of the application of elements to create such imagery, Young engages in a layering act of medium, subject matter and meaning. Through a complex process of painstakingly applied oils, the nature of such a multi-focused aesthetic draws together the visual elements of the transparent personage of the crowd, the natural world, clear and stark in its detail, and the empty space amid these simultaneously active presences. The allegorical nature of Young's work resides in both the treatment of his subjects and their specific combinations. The foundation-myth of the main subjects of Romulus and Remus is pivotal to understanding the interconnecting elements of Young's carefully constructed viewpoint throughout *The New Wolf of Rome*. The joining of old and new worlds, the creation and continuation of a society, along with the many contradictory and uncertain elements that constitute and continue to fuel the myth, all hold steadfast at the centre of this body of work. By revisiting the Roman founding myth of Lupa Capitolina, Young's allegory touches upon the very nature of the mystical city-state; a city that is founded on embattled destruction and a clamouring for a clarity that continues to evade it.

In *Rome* (2011), Robert Hughes traces the foundations and myths that still permeate the Rome of today and yesterday. For Hughes, Rome is a city born on an uncertain date and raised by a myth centred around 'ambition, parricide, fratricide, betrayal and obsessive ambition'.[5] Seemingly destined by its origin myth and material grandeur to be a city enduring beyond comprehended time, the imperial ideals that form the very foundation of the Roman empire are deftly explored through the materiality Young employs in *The New Wolf of Rome*. Throughout the now ancient city there still resides the lilting presence of figures crafted from white or luna marble, which was prized for its brilliant translucency, rivalling the luminescent qualities of the moon, from which it took its name.[6] Chosen by early artisans for its capacity to hold form against internal veins and cracks, the marbled remnants of ancient Rome have still, inevitably, transformed over time. By construction and design, Rome itself is a city that is melded with nature; it is a city and an empire continually moving between the apexes of Nature and Culture.

As Young's figures move through the natural expanses in *The New Wolf of Rome*, they emulate Rome's early artists' evocation of the ancient, sculpted figures and the directed movement of the city. As Hughes notes of these early divine figurations, 'you notice them, you see them as exceptions to the surfaces of stone or brick, but it seems that they are to be breathed, not just seen'.[7] Young's choice to represent his figures as semi-corporeal beings, flesh-like and touchable, yet still oddly removed from their earthy surrounds, is reminiscent of the nature of such classical Roman sculpture. Just as the marbled appeal of ancient Rome connected, and elevated, its subjects from their daily surroundings, so too does Young's work seek to connect to and distance itself from a world normally outside of reality and surface consideration. Through Young's aesthetic choices, a fantastical and distant sense of history is brought closer and made clearer, even as it remains vaguely transparent and poignantly fragile when scrutinised.

Hughes follows the breaking relationship between Romulus and Remus through to its bloody end. Abandoned at birth and raised from destitution by the she-wolf, the twin brothers eventually overthrow the usurpers of their kingdom to found a new settlement that will become Rome. During a vigorous argument over boundaries, power and the shape of the city, Romulus murders his brother. As Hughes notes, history does not tell how Romulus may have felt about slaying his only brother over a perceived threat to his sovereignty. But what the myth does offer is a partial glimpse into the past to better comprehend the complicated and shifting elements that interact in the act of creation—whether it be of a city, an empire, a civilisation, or a history. As a contemporary artist concerned with the artist's role as a visual synthesiser of histories, Young's work around such a myth seeks to tackle the manifold, coincidental and tangled nature of determinations in society now, in order to provide insight into the structural foundations and historical dimensions of meaning that continue to guide our understanding of the past.

This continual act of looking backwards to move forward, of harvesting and foraging in the natural and historical world, has defined much of Young's practice. Directing this gaze along the lines of form as well as subject, previous works have also heralded to earlier times while maintaining a firm grasp on the power inherent in the act of remembering in the present. In the *Double Ground Paintings* series, which stressed the visual and cultural alternation between figure and field, the act of painting places selected images on top of a digitally mediated surface, underlining the shift in modes of representation. The projection of meaning is accomplished through nature and the human body operating in differing and shifting cultural spheres, in terms of both time and place. Pre-empting this thought, even the *Polychrome Paintings* series focused on the fractalised surfaces represented by the contemporary screen-based, accelerated society. In works from that series, such as *Survival Spirit* and *S Painting* (both Summer 1992), Young utilises the supposed clarity of the grid to complicate the understanding of space and time in identity creation. The gridded nature of Young's work has always offered a glance of a whole, but it still denies a complete, non-fractured image to which the viewer might more easily relate.

By contrasting the gridded structures against forms that evoke figures, far horizons, the domestic and natural, and the barely remembered past, Young purposefully continues to disrupt linear time and clearly distanced space, maintaining the incomplete and repetitive notion of a previous narrative as one that is reiterated, but still distanced, from simple conclusions. It is Young's ability to balance closeness and distance, presence and absence, figure and field, the grand and the individual, that draws many of his works together. As a development of the layering of culture and nature in the *Double Ground Paintings,* the elements of *The New Wolf of Rome* additionally indicate a renewed fascination with grander—classical or mythical—ways of understanding an increasingly complex world and its systems of change. According to Young's treatment, the stimulations that traditionally accompany our concept of sublimity are not only found in the face of grand stimuli such as a snow-capped mountain, a thunderstorm or a gaping chasm. Instead, sublimity can be found in glimpses and flashes of recognition we find when we can sit with what we know and what we think we know in one moment, extending our concept of self beyond what we believe we've experienced alone.

In *New Wolf of Rome*, a universal image of youth, vitality and innocence abounds in one canvas, *The Offering*. Within *The Offering*, the treatment of the natural world is strikingly reminiscent of works in the earlier *Polychrome Paintings* series. The image of nature, represented in the floral suspension which covers both figures in the pale space, is not denied any detail by the artist. Despite this close and careful treatment, the vine which connects them does not descend from a root branch, just as the mother and child figures seem out of context in empty space. In the same breath, Young's subjects

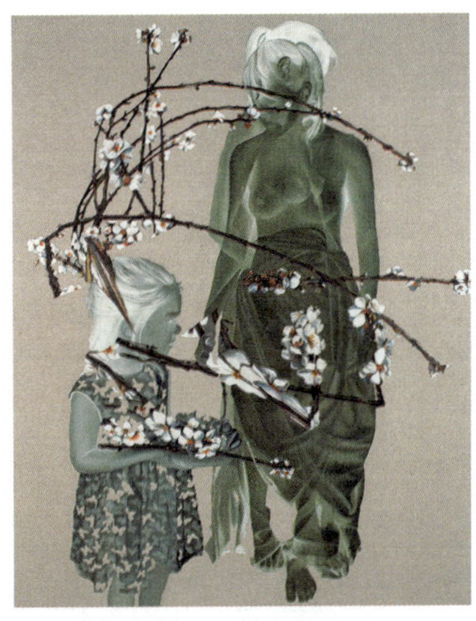

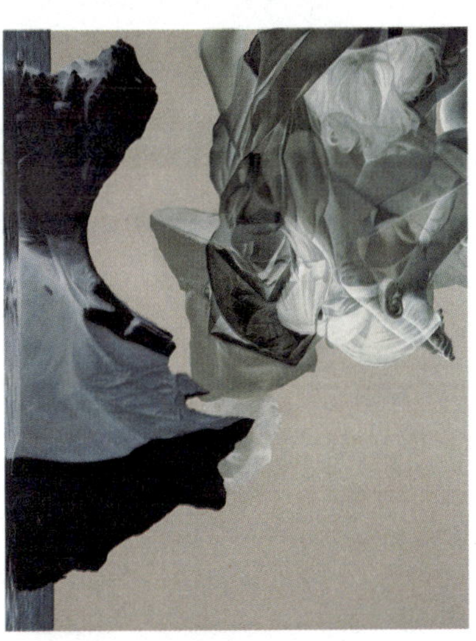

The Offering 2011
Oil on linen, 190 × 144 cm
Private collection, Brisbane

The Crowd's Arrival 2012
Oil on linen, 190 × 144 cm
Private collection, Melbourne

move on to the freezing natural space, as seen in *Born from Ice* and *The Crowd's Arrival*. The polar caps, emerging steadily from a calm sea, are joined by the descending single vision of an effortlessly cloaked figure in *Born from Ice*. Almost embodying classical sculpture in its form, the figure sits poised and removed from its freezing, uninhabitable surroundings, yet it also seems to be at one with the landscape itself. Assisted by Young's tonal application of colour and the similarly delicate rendering of the icecaps and subject's clothing, the figure melds with the seascape, while also appearing above and beyond it. In *The Crowd's Arrival*, the descending crowd seems to fall in slow motion past the ice caps beside them. As the world is spun on its side, the crowd that follows descends, entangled and multi-layered, their bodies and fates decidedly connected in motion. Suspended outside of the real world, the layered, marble-like figures of Young's shift between solid, icy rock and liquid air; they are neither completely a part of the world that Young's mythic vision has created, nor are they ever too far away from it.

Similarly, on the surface at least, the *Silhouette* series of paintings exude classical modernist harmony, but underlying this rhetoric of perfection and control there lies a deconstructive ambivalence. In doing so, they lead the viewer away from any simple dialogue or conclusion.[8] In earlier yet similarly ethereal works to those in *The New Wolf of Rome*, such as the triptych *Floating World* (1988), Young conducts an experiment into the death of linear time and the disjointed division of space.[9] Focusing upon the integration of the incomplete natural and bodily worlds, *Floating World* introduces the grid as a series of vertical divisions that function as a metaphor for linear time—this non-diverging linearity representing, for Young, a form of imprisonment.[10] The panoramic canvas is split vertically, separating the barely distinguishable human figure from the more clearly articulated nature motifs. Young references this image as a 'field of vision which entombs us'.[11] As with his later works, these earlier explorations are not simply a recovering or resurfacing to unveil a particular truth either forgotten or ignored. It is not Young's intention to lead the viewer towards a simple dialogue or conclusion.

In *The New Wolf of Rome*, history and myth are joined, not only to challenge postmodernism's aversion to the historically informative nature of the past but also modernism's insistence on surface clarity. The layering within the series serves to better answer previous aversions to nuanced considerations of change and diversion. It allows the 'unrepresentable' to emerge, in this case with the assistance from the grand narrative foundation myth of the benevolent nature of the she-wolf, and the inherently violent nature of the crowd in motion. According to Young's artistic assessment, the violence of the crowd isn't punctuated by a singular, dramatic blow or traumatic remembering; it is layered, gradual, individual and, eventually, overwhelming. Numerous figures fall gracefully yet forcefully towards the earth, tumbling towards an icy, viscous and unknown void below. For Young, the tumbling fate of humanity expressed in *The New Wolf of Rome* can be seen as a return to the original Fall at the centre of Christian faith. While the notion of the Christian Fall may have waned in strength in a more secular, globalised worldview, the 'Fall' now is that of the traditions that once drew us together, and shifted us apart, and of the waning safety and surety of our natural, living world in the face of gradual destruction.

When considered as a development of the *Double Ground Paintings'* layering treatment of culture and nature, the elements of *The New Wolf of Rome* indicate a renewed fascination with grander ways of understanding an increasingly complex world, and its systems of change. It is in this space that the figures in *The Crowd Devours the Wolf*—

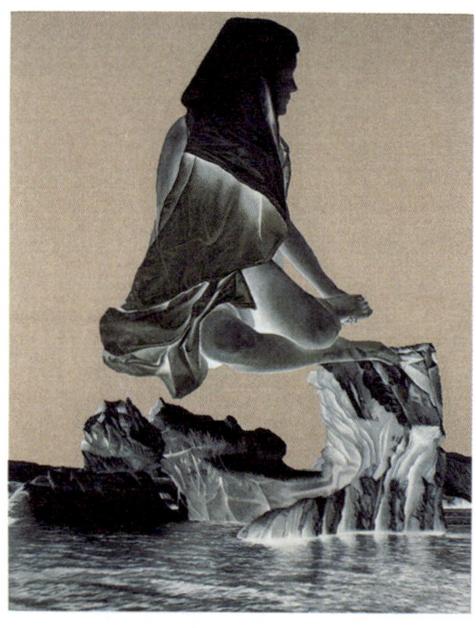

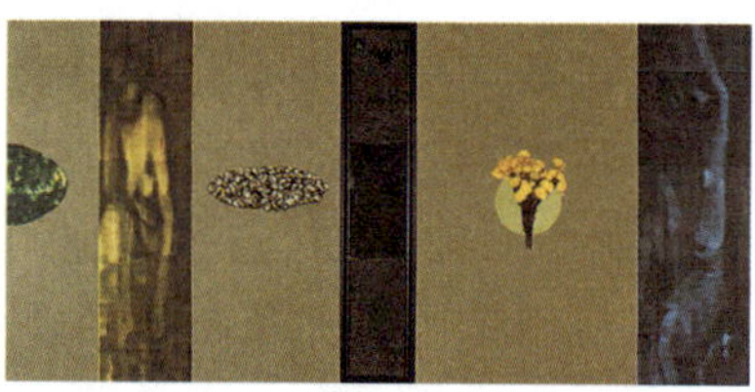

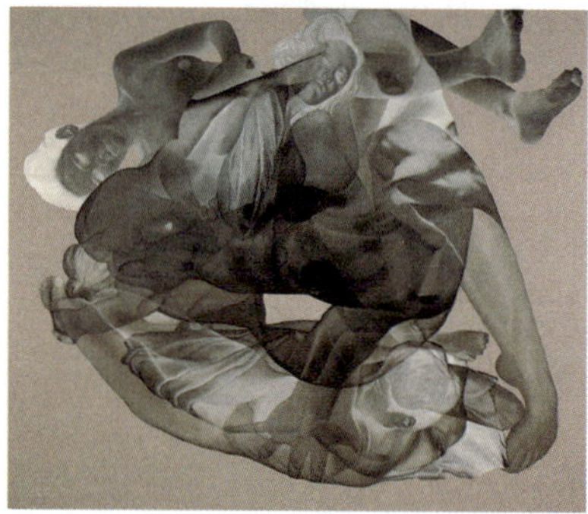

Born from Ice 2012
Oil on linen, 190 × 144 cm

The Floating World 1998
Oil on linen, 183 × 372 cm
Collection of The Art Gallery of Western
Australia, Perth

The Crowd Devours the Wolf 2012
Oil on linen, 190 × 217 cm

silent, swirling, and devouring in the open gaze of history and the devastation
it leaves behind—pivot against the original hopeful image that civilisation was
designed to be in the presence of the wolf. In terms of what Romulus and Remus
can represent for a modern audience, Young seems to insist that cultural meaning,
regardless of the distance, never truly leaves historical memory. In this sense, only
by paying equal attention to the interposed yet separate layers between the past
and present can the viewer foster an understanding of these works.

The Macau Days series (2012/2017) can also be seen as the culmination of a
historically bound rhetoric that has developed to formulate the core of much of
Young's exploration throughout the History Projects. Just as Young's exploration of
the allegorical founding of Rome in *The New Wolf of Rome* sought to comment on the
development of art, criticism, and greater notions of civilisation, his focus on the city
of Macau raises questions around how a distinct blurring of the real and the possible,
the solid and the transparent, the present and the absent, can lead to the re-discovery
of new territories—especially on ground that is heavily interconnected, layered, and
indeed saturated, in terms of space, time and place. Macau is now a gambling and
tourist playground largely for Mainland China's populace, but Young instead focuses
upon the precious days that Macau once hosted—a Macau of vibrant cultural cross-
pollination. This Macau is a place of paradoxical cultural exchange, including those
seeking 'the flight out'. As Young states, 'this is a homage to the flight out, for all those
whose lives were lived transformations – [to] Wenceslau de Moraes, who left Portugal,
sojourned in Macau and spent the rest of his years in Tokushima, but introduced to the
West the first haiku …'.[12] For Young, the Macau in these images is one that fosters the
importance of cross-cultural exchange and metamorphosis. Young's own past is one of
these cross-cultural interchanges and historical linkages, and his own work emphasises
the importance of shared beauty and experience, without stressing the alienating
aspects of unnecessary abstraction or disconnect.

Macau did not develop a major settlement until the Portuguese arrived in the sixteenth
century. It stands now as the first and last European colony in Asia. In works such
as *Marienbad* and *Macau III*, Young brings together this cultural exchange of organised,
Sino-European sophistication with hyper-natural layers of floral wreathing. The spirit
of *Last Year at Marienbad* (1961, dir. Alain Resnais), an enigmatic film that focuses on
the partitioned, maze-like nature of high powered, wealthy living, is integrated into
the overall atmosphere of *The Macau Days*. This maze becomes a visual slip into an
old man-made world, and a world of idealised nature. The colour washes of gold and
vermillion in paintings *Macau (yellow)* and *Macau (pink)* act as a kind of visual screen
to the stylised backdrop of sophistication, one that begs to be stepped through. The
past here is made more dramatic in its connection with the natural floral foreground.
To seek the way forward into the image, to find a way back, is to step into the natural
world. Young makes the journey to understanding these images a cyclical one, defying
the linear and the literal, and a simplistic sense of past and present.

Acting as a visual and allegorical recollection of a transcultural period, now largely
eclipsed by the wealth and greed represented by present-day Macau, Young's work
is able to figuratively comprehend a dramatically colourful past—Macau as a place
at once entrenched in the pull of Western modernity, yet momentarily balanced in
a courtship of Chinese and Portuguese history. The consideration in these paintings
converses with the imagined days of a Macau that experienced transcultural exchange
and intermarriage between the Portuguese, Chinese and British. Young creates a still
space of transformation and integration in this series, typifying an idealised past that

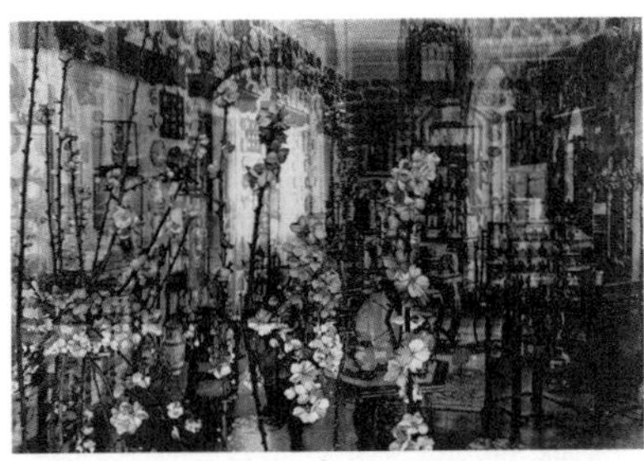

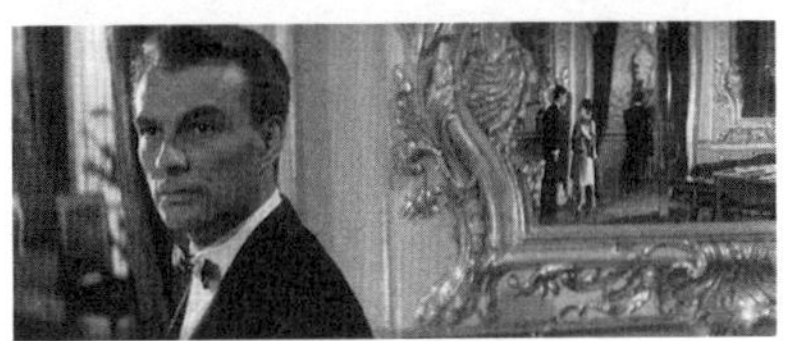

Marienbad 2012
Digital print and oil on canvas, 185 × 270 cm

Still from the film *The Last Year at Marienbad*
1961, directed by Alain Resnais

perhaps once was, yet may never be again. In opposition to the hyperreality of Macau today, with its gambling and tourism, Young's paintings speak to a past as pictorial reality that he dictates; one that is more concerned with the transient nature of history.

For Young, interacting with history is not so much an interjection, but rather an ever-developing dialogue punctuated by pauses, codas and thoughtful returns. Throughout the History Projects, Young's impulse is to embrace the position of artist as a counterpoint to the often devastatingly alienating positioning of postmodernism. This includes the exploration of forgotten stories, and the re-situation of these within the present. In doing so, Young seems to insist that cultural meaning, regardless of distance, never truly leaves historical memory. Whether it be Young's revisitation of the violent realities and narratives that feature throughout *Safety Zone* (2010), or the humanising re-telling of a seemingly distant city creation myth in *The New Wolf of Rome*, he insists on initiating a conversation between times and places beyond the factual nature of pure historicism. His re-visitings fundamentally involve individual narratives, those made up equally of reason and feeling, and the effect that their continual presence, yet undeniable absence, has upon our own consideration of history.

Throughout Young's own narrative self-exploration, such as in the *1967Dispersion* series (2008), the return of the past is achieved with tangible links to the flesh-bound present. Young recognises his early relationship with art as follows: 'I left Hong Kong, as a child, with a C-class British passport … I was told these stories about people who had run away from disasters, who would roll up their paintings and take them with them. That was my image of what art was'.[13] This image of art, as an act of creation after a period of violence and confusion, speaks of Young's version of diaspora: '[For] those from a diaspora—more often than not, their reasons for leaving were abject. The year of 1967 in Hong Kong was no exception.'[14] Young's own dispersion from Hong Kong folds into a larger definition of a people's experience with diaspora. In order to relate to a new sense of a whole, Young integrates photographic documentation with hyper-coloured abstracts. Similar to other aesthetic treatments, such as those seen in *The New Wolf of Rome*, these images are meticulously painted in oils, but originally generated out of thousands of images technologically. The discourses of time, history, and diaspora are melded throughout the works, creating rhetoric between them where the multiple perspectives that accompany the elements of history are glimpsed as uncertain realities, combined in disjunctive forms.

According to Homi K. Bhabha's reading of Fredric Jameson, it is through the phenomenon of diaspora that the architecture of the new historical subject emerges at the limits of representation itself. As originally posited by Jameson, the notion of 'cognitive mapping' enables 'a situational representation on the part of the individual to that vaster and unrepresentable totality which is the ensemble of society's structures as a whole'.[15] For Jameson, the concept of cognitive mapping is an explanation of the main task of the postmodern subject: to make sense of our place in the global system. For Bhabha, this task of understanding can only be achieved in the 'in-between'; it is only through the splitting and displacement—'the fragmented and schizophrenic decentring [of the Self]' (Jameson)—that the new historical subject emerges at the limit of representation itself.[16] The two ends of diaspora are here elegantly expressed by Bhabha: the violence at the origins, followed by a dispersion to new lands, will ideally result in a cross-cultural conversation between the old and the new. For the diasporic artist, this physical sense of displacement or loss, transient restlessness, 'un-at-homeness' or groundlessness, can be abstracted and layered in representation—but the new that emerges speaks to the task of sense-making with positivity, and with hope.

These shifting borders between nature, the figure, myth, and historicism continue
to fascinate Young. Through his aesthetic choices, as in *The Macau Days*, a fantastical
and distant sense of history is brought closer and made clearer, yet it is still vaguely
transparent and evocatively fragile. When viewed as a complete vision, Young's subtly
layered aesthetic speaks to a collective phenomenon and challenge that extends
beyond the strictures and borders of postmodernity and the wide-eyed assumptions of
globalism. Through the use of grids, fragments, half-seen visions and a shifting 'double
ground' of the historical, mythical, cultural and fantastical, Young's work insists that
we are all in a constant process of negotiation: with language, sentiment, visual
memory, history and cultural boundaries.

By partly exposing these shaded places with precision and originality, Young has
developed a vision which seeks to both rearrange and free the individual from the
experiences, landscapes and historical ties that previously bound them. For Young, by
acknowledging humanity's inconsistent procession through different times and spaces,
we can clearly see our own sublime and changing fragility in the present. In this flux,
a luminosity can be witnessed. The transparent, ghostly figures and abstracted visions
of Young's individual and collective series gently pass through and surround the
viewer, serving to both comfort and confront them in a manner that at once
transcends history and compels our own presence.

1. Carolyn Barnes, 'John Young's Double Ground Paintings – Integral
   Histories', *Art and Australia*, Autumn 2006, p. 427.

2. Ibid.

3. Terry Smith, *What Is Contemporary Art?*, University of Chicago Press,
   Chicago, 2009, p. 235.

4. Personal correspondence with the artist, 2016.

5. Robert Hughes, *Rome*, Weidenfeld & Nicolson, London, 2011, p. 15.

6. Ibid., pp. 101–02.

7. Ibid., p. 9.

8. Graham Coulter-Smith, 'Ecstasy and Administration: John Young's
   Major Work's 1979–1992', in *John Young Silhouettes and Polychromes
   1979–1992*, Schwartz City, Melbourne, 1993, p. 34.

9. Ibid., p. 35.

10. Ibid.

11. Young quoted in A. D. S. Donaldson, 'John Young: Super-occupancy
    and Entombment', interview, *Tension*, no. 15, 1989, p. 32.

12. Press release for 'The Macau Days: John Young', 10 Chancery Lane
    Gallery, Hong Kong, 25 August 2012,
    http://www.10chancerylanegallery.com/exhibitions/2012/The_
    Macau_Days/press_release_en/.

13. John Young, 'Artist Statement', *1967Dispersion*, 10 Chancery Lane
    Gallery, Hong Kong, 2008.

14. Ibid.

15. Frederic Jameson, as quoted in Homi K. Bhabha, *The Location of
    Culture*, Routledge, London, 1994, p. 217.

16. Homi K. Bhabha paraphrasing Jameson, ibid., p. 216.

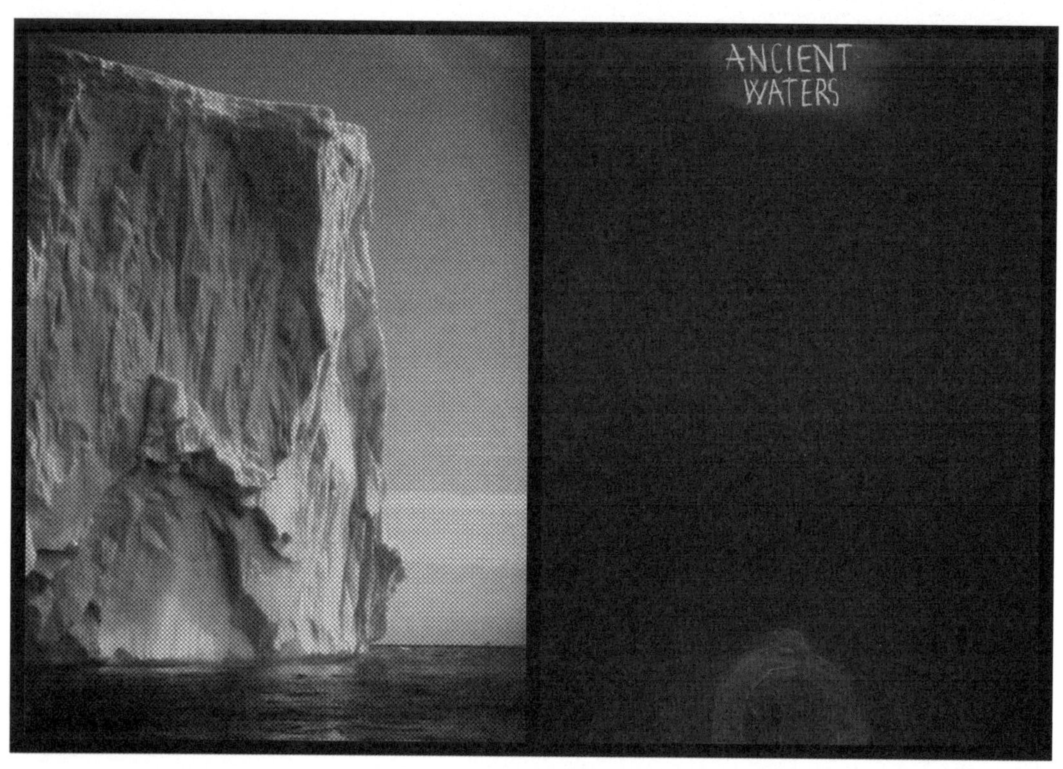

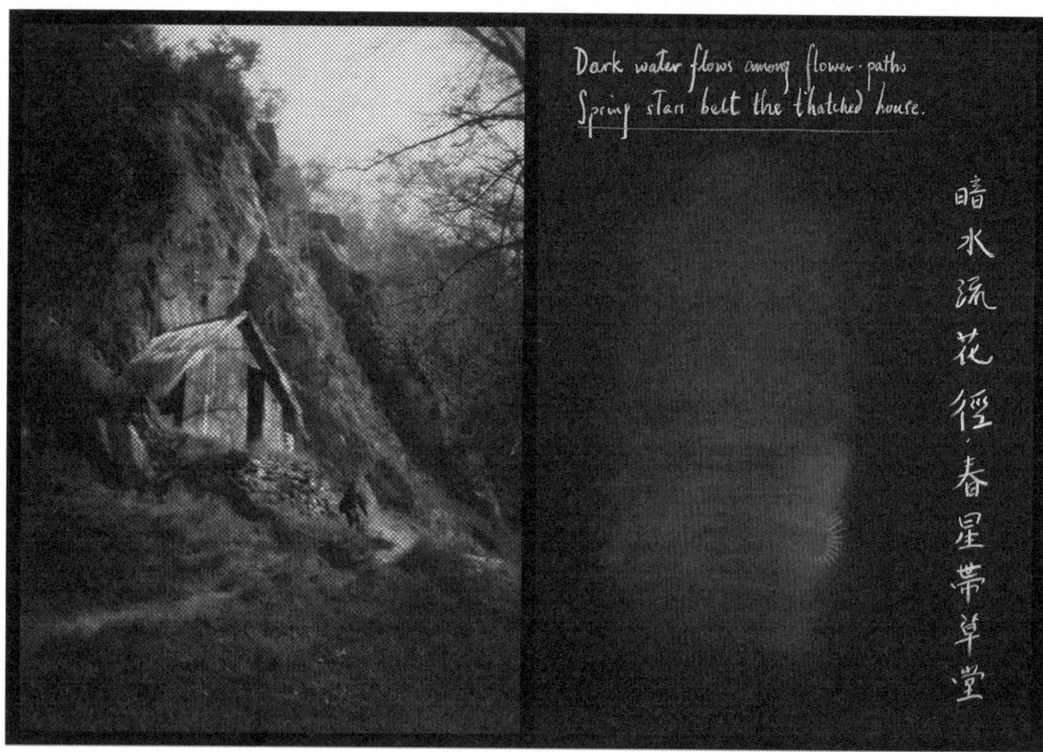

Ancient Waters 2012
Digital print on photographic paper and chalk
on blackboard-painted archival cotton paper,
145.2 × 102.4 cm

Dark Waters 2012
Digital print on photographic paper and chalk
on blackboard-painted archival cotton paper,
145.2 × 102.4 cm

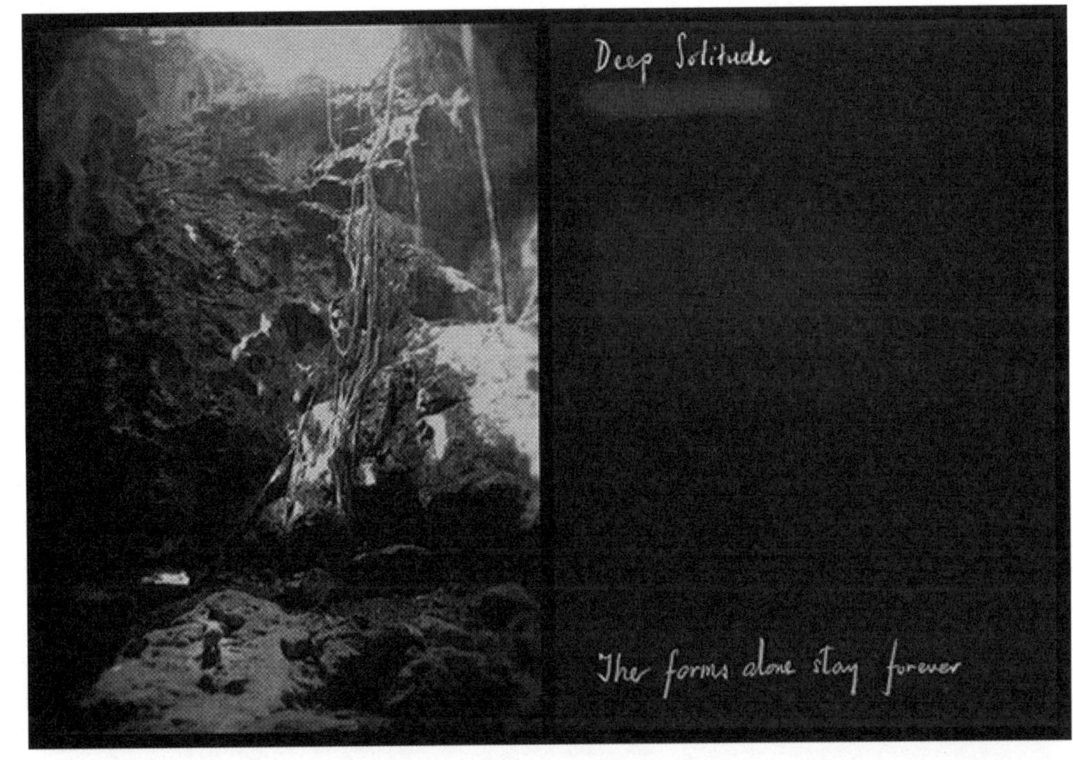

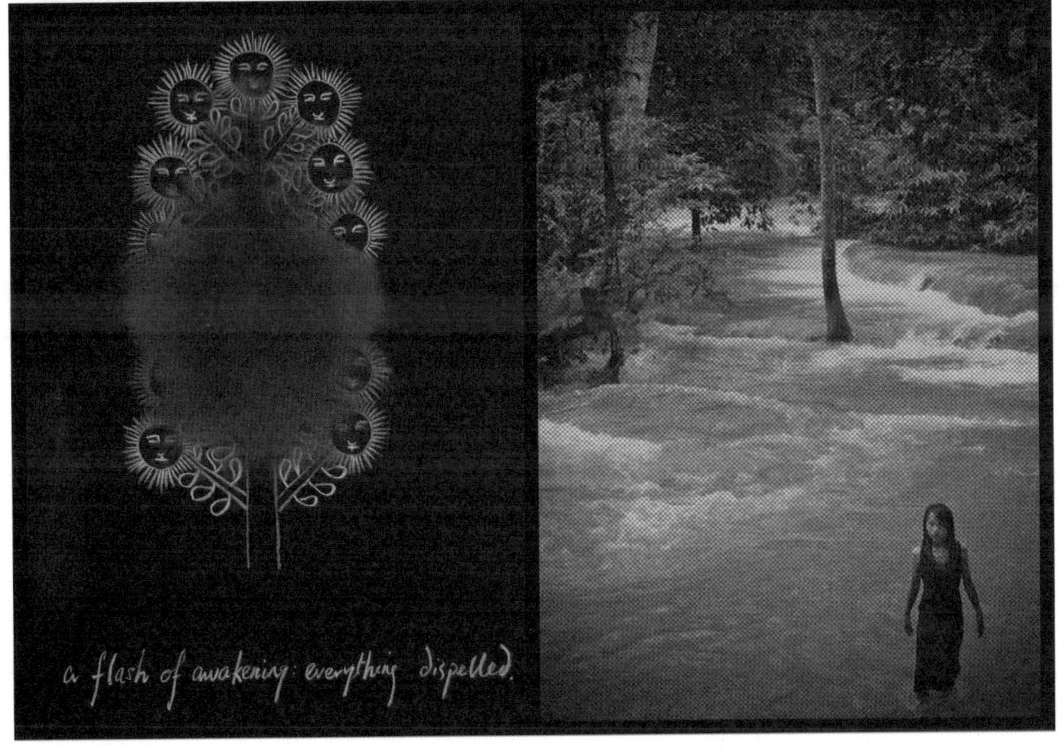

Deep Solitude 2012
Digital print on photographic paper and chalk
on blackboard-painted archival cotton paper,
145.2 x 102.4 cm

Awakening 2012
Digital print on photographic paper and chalk
on blackboard-painted archival cotton paper,
145.2 x 102.4 cm

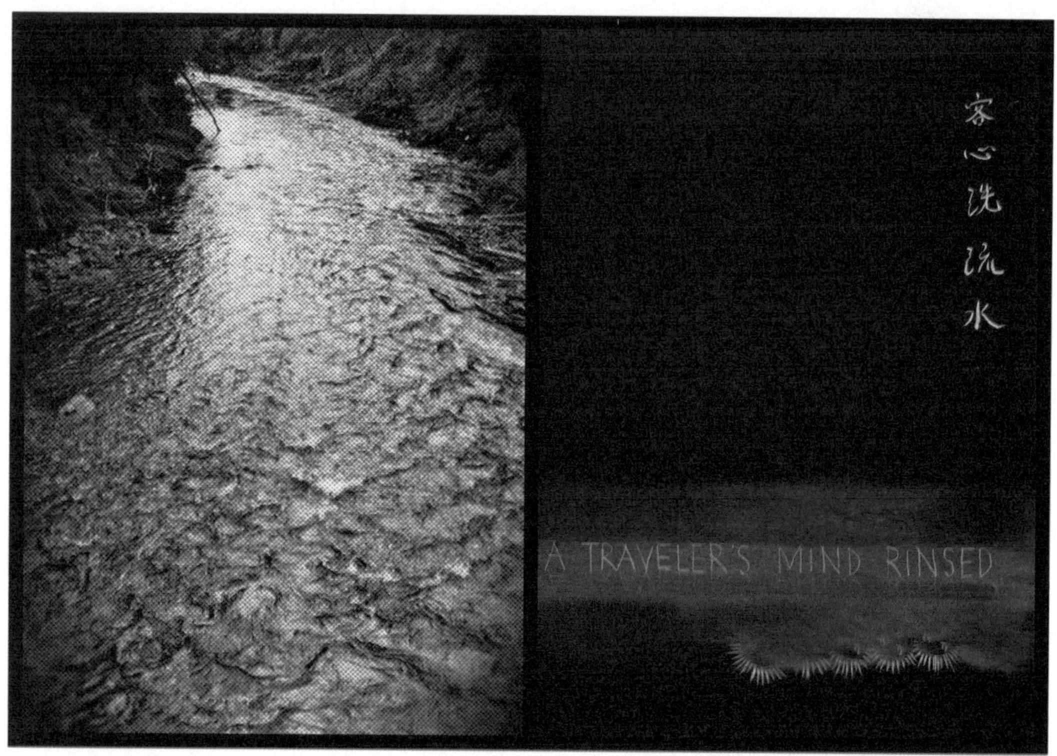

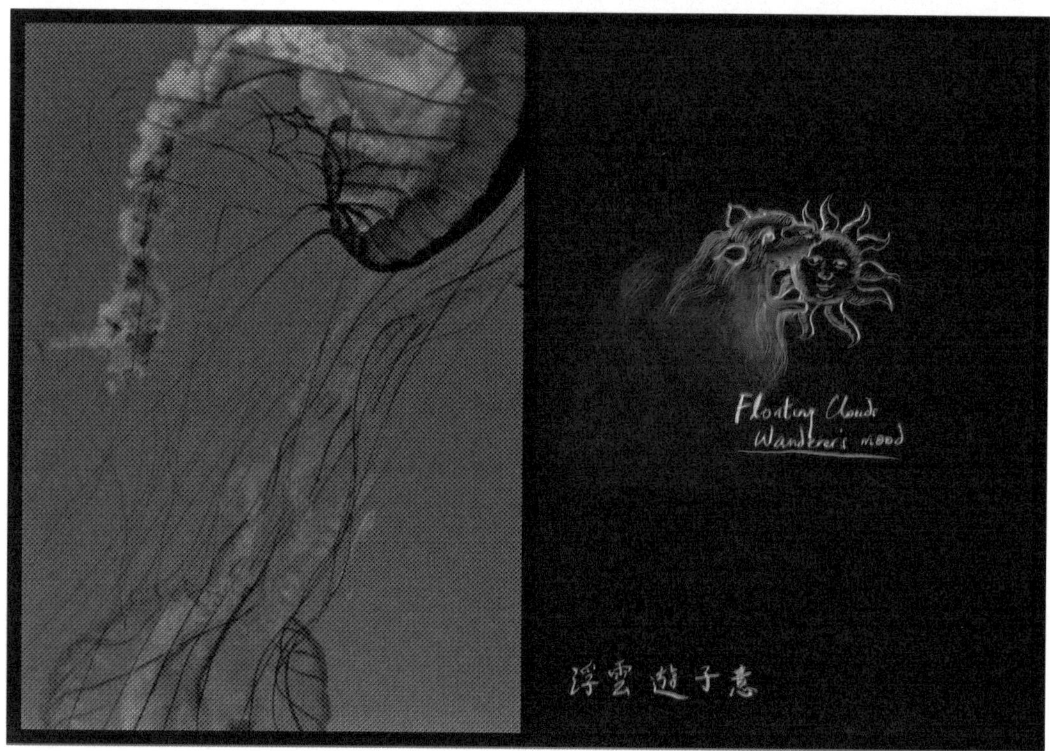

A Traveller's Mind Rinsed 2012
Digital print on photographic paper and chalk
on blackboard-painted archival cotton paper,
145.2 × 102.4 cm

Floating Clouds 2012
Digital print on photographic paper and chalk
on blackboard-painted archival cotton paper,
145.2 × 102.4 cm

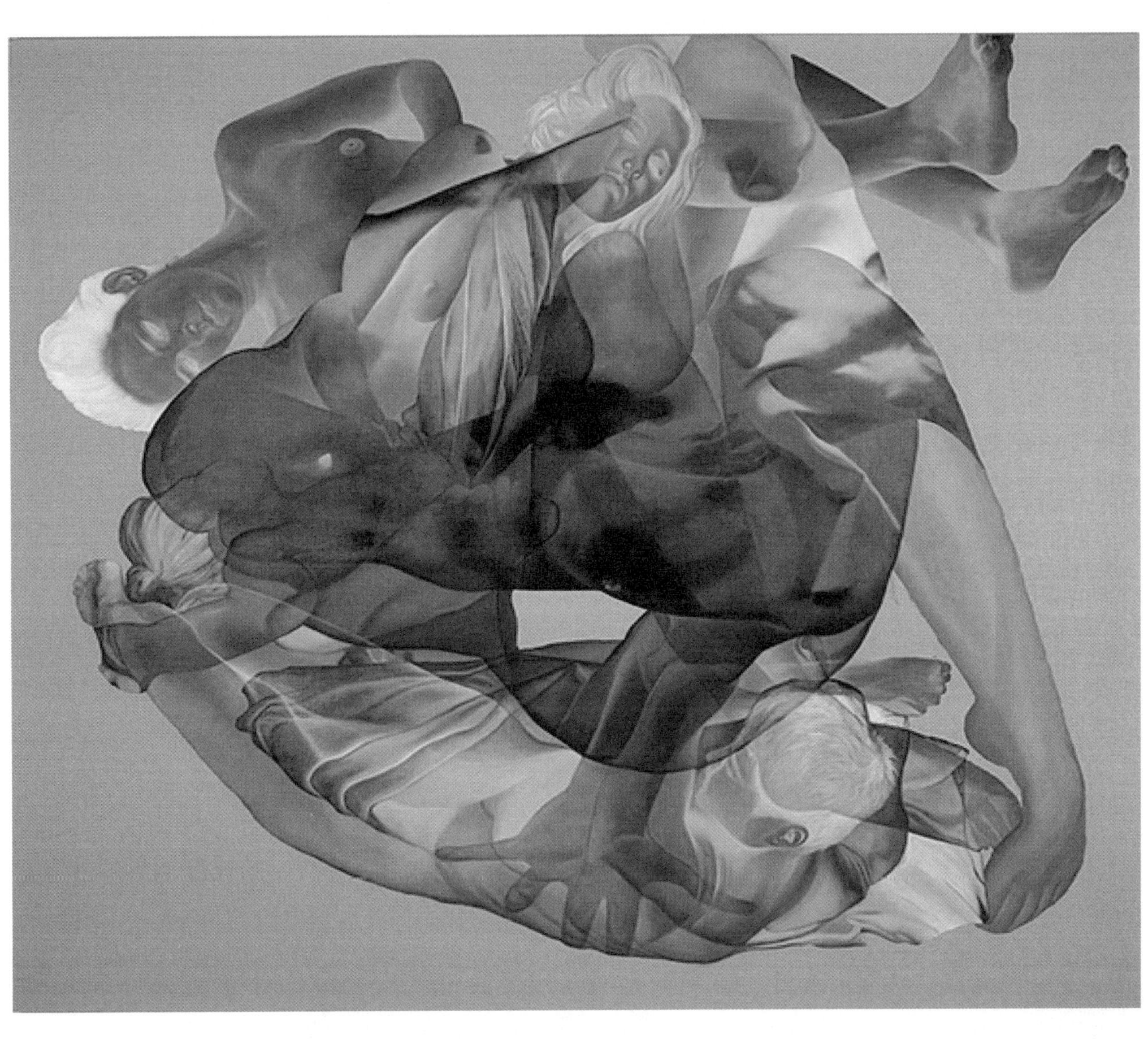

The Crowd Devours the Wolf 2012
Oil on linen, 190 × 217 cm

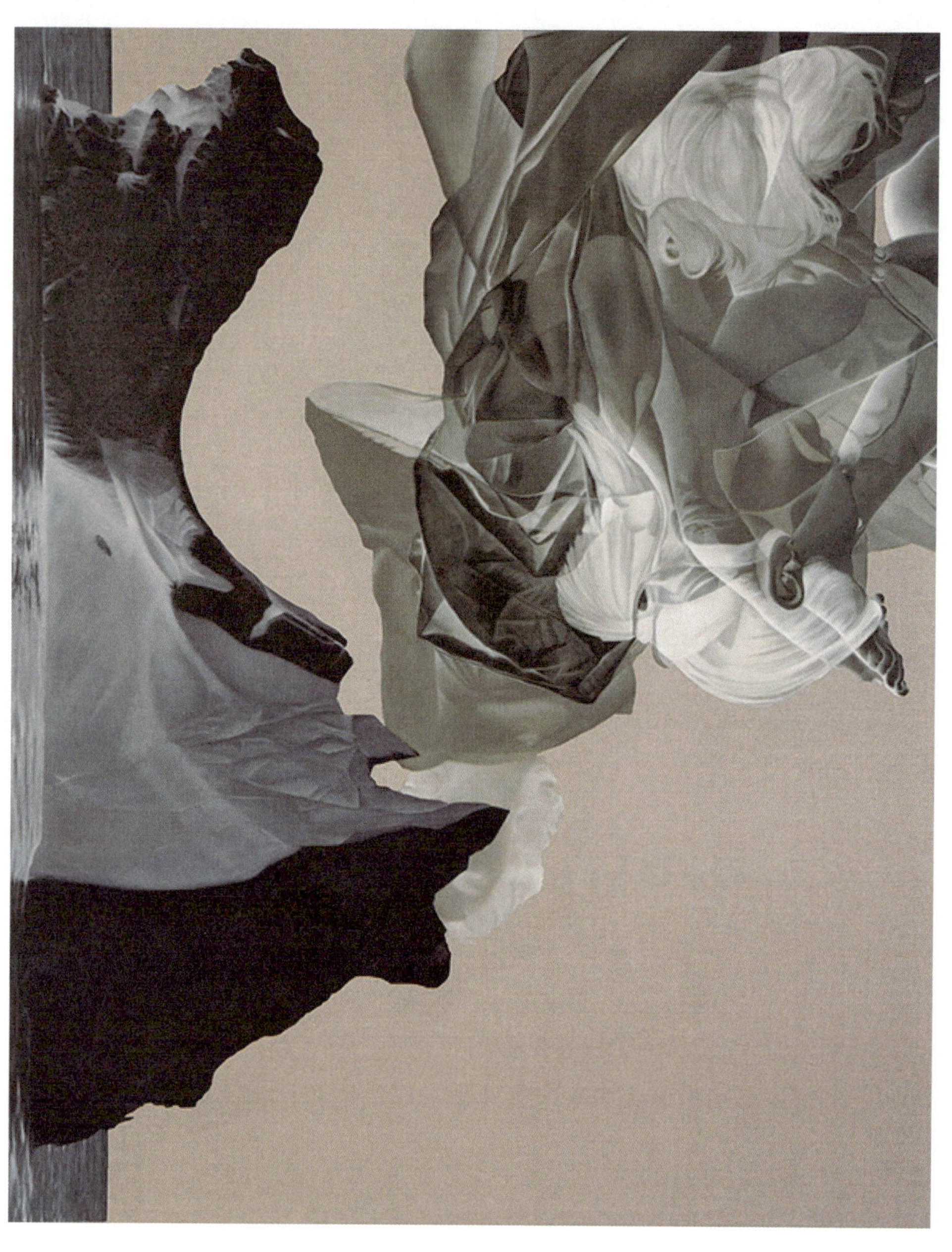

The Crowd's Arrival 2012
Oil on linen, 190 x 144 cm
Private collection, Melbourne

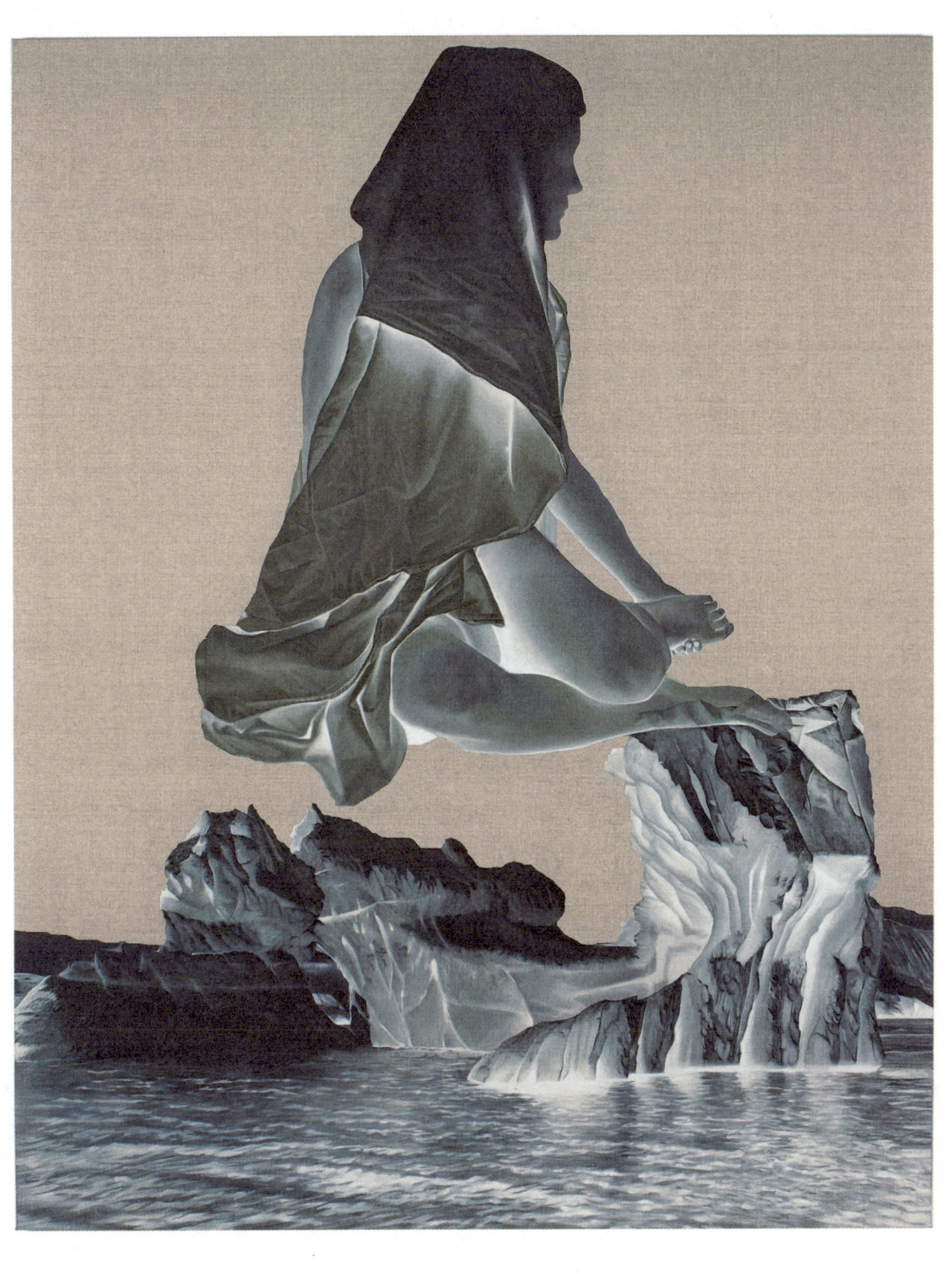

Born from Ice 2012
Oil on linen, 190 x 144 cm

1866: THE WORLDS OF LOWE KONG MENG AND JONG AH SIUG

2015

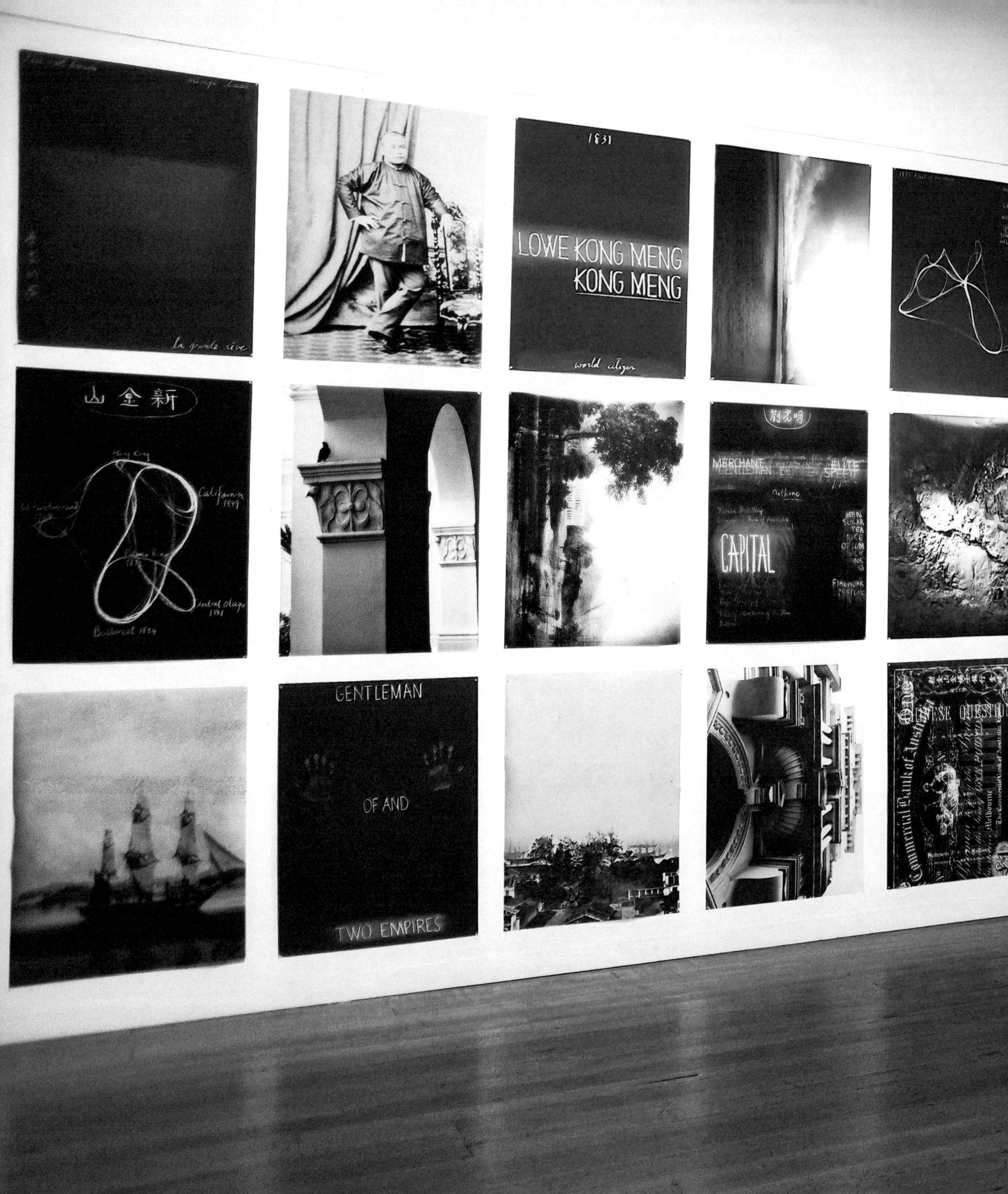
La grande rêve
1831
LOWE KONG MENG
KONG MENG
world citizen
山金新
Hong Kong
California
1849
Central Otago
1861
Ballarat 1854
明老刘
MERCHANT
GENTLEMAN
ELITE
CAPITAL
MEN
SUGAR
TEA
RICE
OPIUM
FIREWORK
PERFUME
GENTLEMAN
OF AND
TWO EMPIRES
Chinese Question
Commercial Bank of Australia
Melbourne

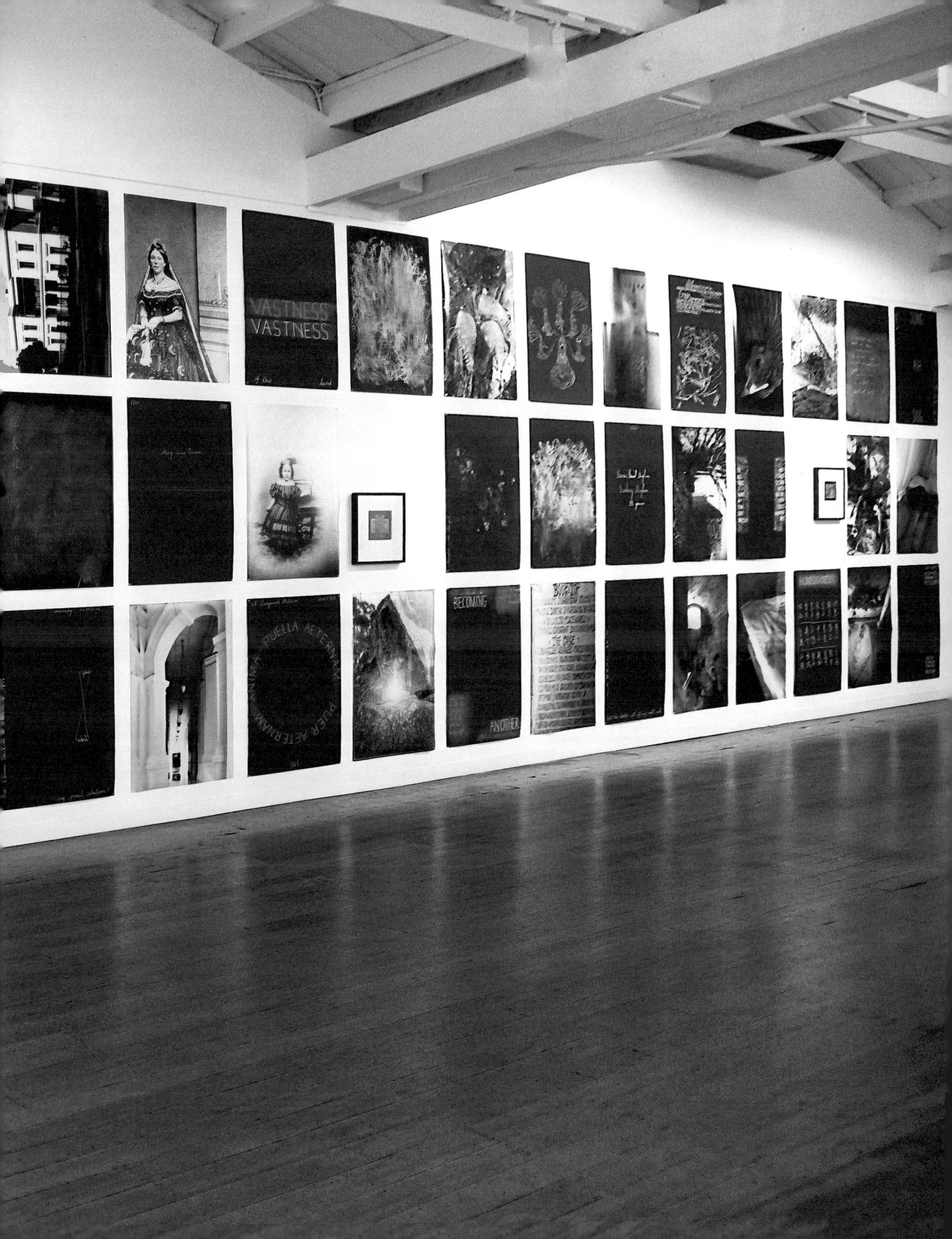

1866: THE WORLDS OF LOWE KONG MENG AND JONG AH SIUG

OUTLINE

In the mid-1800s, two young men arrived in the colony of Victoria to seek their fortune on the goldfields. Lowe Kong Meng (Liu Guangming 劉光明, 1831–1888) was an educated Malaysian Chinese merchant from Penang who, at twenty-two years of age, arrived speaking four languages. Jong Ah Siug (possibly Zhang Yasheng 張亞聖, c. 1837–1900; his brother was Zhang Luoyuan 張絡元) was an illiterate miner who landed aged eighteen, following an arduous boat journey from the southern Chinese city of Zhongshan.

By 1866 the paths of these two migrants had diverged dramatically. Lowe had become a colonial elite: he owned a fleet of trading ships, was active in Australian politics and was a board member of the Commercial Bank of Australia (now Westpac), all while remaining connected to the Qing government as a prominent overseas Chinese. By contrast, in 1867 Jong was tried for 'malicious wounding' following an altercation with a fellow miner. Though found not guilty due to 'insanity', he was sent to the Yarra Bend and Sunbury lunatic asylums. In time, he learnt some English and documented his plight in a palm-sized diary, apparently in an attempt to plead his innocence to the visiting Duke of Edinburgh, but he remained incarcerated for over thirty years until his death in 1900, despite repeated attempts at self-exoneration.

The first of the History Projects to focus on Australian historical subjects, *1866: The Worlds of Lowe Kong Meng and Jong Ah Siug* (2015) comprises five significant groups of work.

The first, *The Worlds of Lowe Kong Meng and Jong Ah Siug*, is an installation of forty nine chalkboard drawings and digital prints from archival photographs arranged in a three-row grid (320 × 1350 cm total). In it, the stories of these two Chinese Australian men are represented through imagery of the Yarra Bend Asylum where Jong was incarcerated, the colonial architecture of Lowe's elegant home, quotations from Jong's diary, as well as key dates and events from their lives.

This installation is accompanied by two intricate single-thread silk embroideries, *Cochran Town* and *The Meeting*, which have sometimes been incorporated into the grid installation. Both embroideries include reproductions of pages from Jong's diary. *Cochran Town* features a map that Jong drew based on recollections of his local mining area. *The Meeting* combines one of Jong's diary pages with an image of Australia's first bilingual (English and Chinese) one-pound note, printed by the Commercial Bank of Australia, of which Lowe was a founding shareholder.

The work also includes three painting series: *LKM, The Illustrious Fleet of Lowe Kong Meng,* and *The Days of Jong Ah Siug*. The first, *LKM (Blue), LKM (Gold),* and *LKM (Pink)* are three abstract paintings in burnished blue, gold and pink (156 × 126 cm each). *The Illustrious Fleet of Lowe Kong Meng* (250.5 × 175 cm) and *Lowe Kong Meng and The Eternal* (320 × 151 cm) combine digitally printed background images of Lowe, his family and his fleet, all treated with halftone dots, with geometric overlays of yellow felt. Finally, *The Days of Jong Ah Siug I* and *II* (156 × 126 cm each) are two abstract colour field paintings which, in contrast to the *LKM* series, are in a muted, sombre palette of deep madder and browns.

ARTIST STATEMENT

Reflection (2022)

Here the History Projects start to see the Chinese in Australia. And the question
is: How to find ways to engage visually with people and the events that surrounded
them over a century and a half ago? There is a distance now. I hoped to engage
with these historical narratives stripped of their original frames of national pride
or shame, ethnic identity or justice, and to instead present the broken yet resonating
narratives of these flickering characters: their dealings, their survivals and their
sufferings from the demands of the empire of their time in this land of Australia
(1840–1960). Or, better still, to see those who drifted—the Chinese diaspora to be—
from Canton, Macau and Hong Kong, to San Francisco, to Ballarat, to Arrowtown,
to Palmer River, as well as to Witwatersrand. Australian visual history has never
really been only Ned Kelly and the cops in the landscape, as much as the virtuoso
Nolan may like us to believe. Perhaps becoming a visionary like Lowe Kong Meng
or a madman like Jong Ah Siug can also bookend a vision of us and for us too,
as Australians.

THE GREETING[*]

Nadia Rhook

a labourer met a merchant and now sense lives in
a capacious wood-split frame

Commercial Bank of [The [Murder] Case] Australasia

right angled souls, the insanity of capital, this
diary lightly conquers that banknote; pens fire, and ink's
unfurled from grainy words to characters, firm, in silken thrum

Cantonese dances with halcyon English and
meanings are unhinged, by pounds, and history's odd limbs

Jong Ah Siug never shook Lowe Kong Meng's hand so in this world
triumph translates into the daily timbre, of prison, & Pidgin, as if carved words
flew to be cut by razored ears, as if when

nothing's level loss is telling stories like they're only one

two men, clear in open sunlight beyond a graves' lines and muddy amalgam, deposit
perpendicular pains, & pride, but

even after all tongues are untied
some walls remain more soundproof than others

don't be fooled; it's neither competition nor some hapless union
but a greeting, to incense the border's gilded innocence

*   'The Greeting' was previously published at: Nadia Rhook,
'The Greeting', *Mascara Literary Review*, Issue 22, 2018.
https://www.mascarareview.com/nadia-rhook/

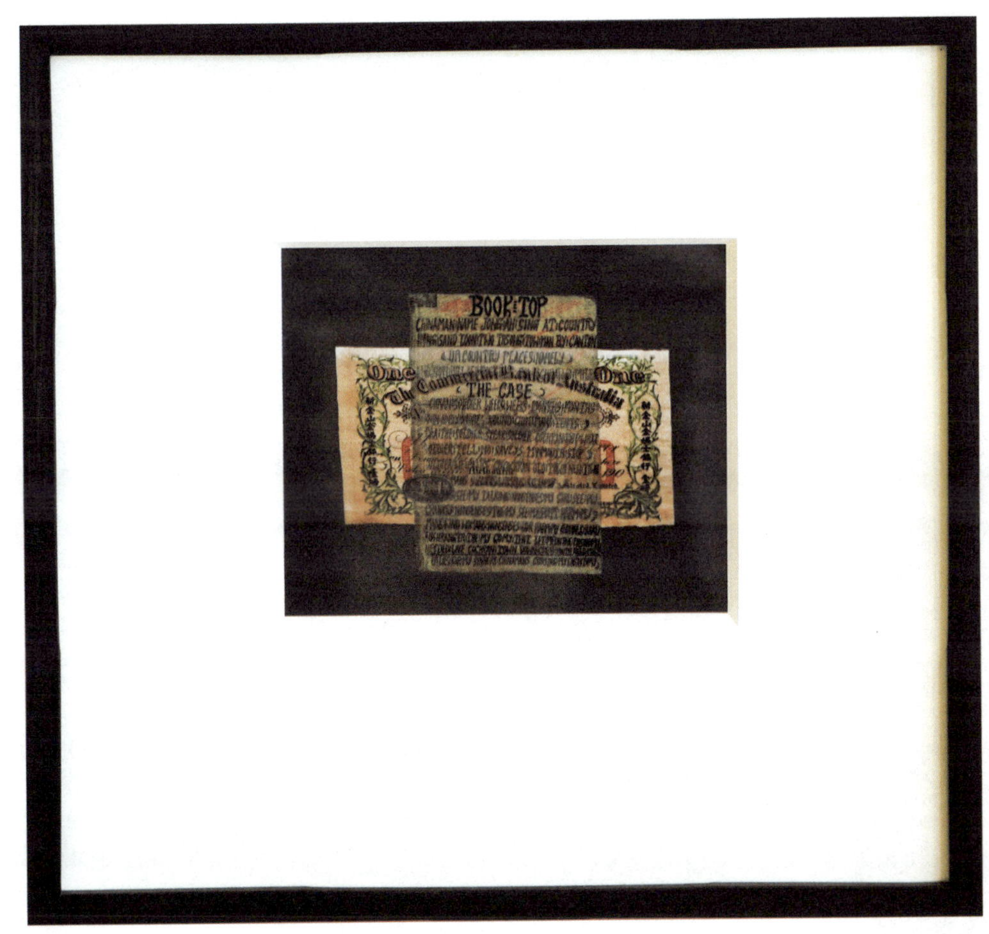

The Meeting 2015
Single thread hand-sewn embroidery, framed,
41 x 42 cm
Collection of Town Hall Gallery, Boroondara
City Council, Melbourne

1866: THE WORLDS OF LOWE KONG MENG AND JONG AH SIUG: OF HISTORICAL IMAGINATION AND MORAL RELATIONS

Nadia Rhook

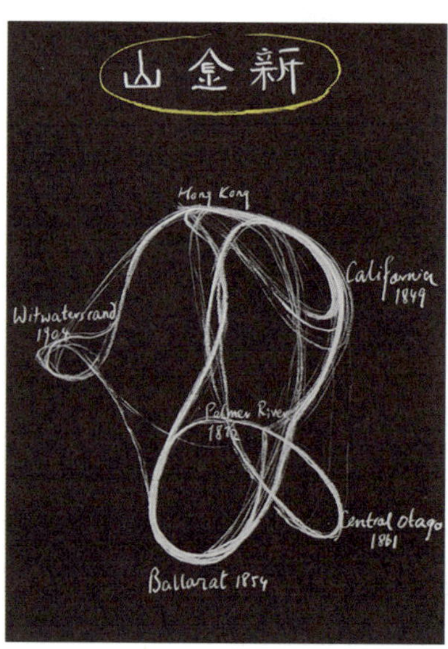

New Gold Mountain 2018
Chalk on blackboard-painted
archival cotton paper, 100 × 70 cm

In his exhibition *1866: The Worlds of Lowe Kong Meng and Jong Ah Siug*, held at ARC ONE gallery in Melbourne in 2015, artist John Young Zerunge brought two historical lives into conversation.[1] On the left side of the installation, Young's chalk drawings and printed images tell the story of a prominent nineteenth-century merchant and political leader, Lowe Kong Meng; to the right, that of an institutionalised labourer, Jong Ah Siug. The work explores these contrasting lives around the temporal pivot of its namesake year, '1866'—a year when, Young imagines, the two men may have crossed paths in Victoria.

1866 is an exploration of two masculine worlds sculpted by the heady winds that propelled migration and imperial mobility. An estimated 60,000 to 80,000 Chinese people migrated to Australia during the mid to late nineteenth century, the majority being men, with lesser numbers of women. Coming from southern provinces of Canton (Guangdong), as well as Hong Kong and the Straits Settlement (current day Malaysia), their lives became enmeshed in the daily life of settler colonial cities, towns and rural landscapes, while often retaining links to home provinces.[2] Jong and Lowe disembarked in Port Melbourne, Victoria in 1855 and 1853 respectively. In doing so, they moved onto Indigenous land that had for two decades been a meeting ground for subjects of the Chinese and British Empires. Heeding this global context of imperial and oceanic migration, *1866* directs viewers to the local intricacies of two personal stories in the emerging Chinese Pacific Rim diaspora.[3]

As a historian viewing Young's *1866*, I was compelled to ask questions that connect with debates old and yet current: for example, what kinds of engagement with history does art permit that scholarly 'history' still steers readers away from? As this essay will explore, the scaffolding of historical imagination through visual encounters with archival records is key. *1866* is valuable not only for its ability to communicate history but also for showing how Jong and Lowes' lives—and by extension, history—are more than the sum of their textual and material traces. In this essay, I wish to respond to *1866* by drawing on the ideas of historians Ross Gibson and Inga Clendinnen to suggest that Young opens up a 'space of imagination' that enables a viewer to come into a subjective, under-determined, and moral relationship with the past. This 'space' is not formed through an unchecked freedom to imagine history in any which way the artist wishes, but rather through a concern for empathy and its relationalities.

DIASPORIC (HI)STORIES

Approaching Australia from the north, Chinese people began arriving in Victoria
in their hundreds soon after gold was discovered. Some came as temporary sojourners,
some moved through circular routes and regular village returns, and others, like
Lowe and Jong came and stayed, as settlers.[4] Jong was born in the southern Chinese
city of Zhongshan, and moved to Victoria from the age of sixteen. He lived in the
regional town of Bealiba before he became caught up in a series of legal trials; first,
for allegedly creating spurious gold and then for conflict with fellow Chinese miners.
Jong was held in Maryborough Gaol, in central Victoria, for two months before the
charge was dismissed. A few years later he had an altercation with another Chinese
gold digger over an Irish woman and was charged with malicious wounding. The
authorities interpreted Jong's own injury as self-inflicted and deemed him insane.
Jong spent the next twenty-three years incarcerated in the Sunbury Lunatic Asylum.
Previously illiterate, he taught himself a mixture of English and Chinese by which
he penned his diary in an attempt to demonstrate his legal innocence.

Jong's story indexes the many instances of cultural mistranslation and
miscommunication that shaped Chinese diasporic engagement with British-
dominated colonial society, law and institutions. If Jong's story is one that evokes
the experience of physical labour and confinement and their attendant mental and
physical challenges, then Lowe's indexes the class privileges of linguistic, physical
and economic mobility, for his was a struggle of political and geographic expanse.
He was a trader whose life and influence spanned oceans and urban and regional
centres; 'a man of two empires', so Young observes. Fluent in four languages,
Lowe 'came to Australia with a fleet of boats … and ended up as part of the elite
of Melbourne'.[5] Here, he grew his Chinese and European networks to become
a member on the board of the Commercial Bank of Australia, now Westpac.
'[H]e convinced the bank to make bank notes bilingual, so there were Chinese
and English in the original one pound, five-pound, twenty-pound notes'.[6]

The power differential between the two men hinged along multiple axes—class,
occupation and language ability and literacy, most vitally—and these asymmetries
are reflected in the historiography. Lowe's story has been observed and analysed
by numerous Australian historians. Marilyn Lake and Henry Reynolds have told
the story of Lowe's migration to Victoria as one of modern cosmopolitan mobility,
describing how, in his work as a trader, he effectively supplied materials to support
an ongoing settler project to colonise Indigenous lands.[7] Paul Macgregor has written
that Lowe was 'no ordinary merchant', for he had influence in both the European
and Chinese political worlds of colonial Melbourne.[8] Indeed, Lowe negotiated his
way to occupy an exceptionally powerful position, a middleman who succeeded in
brokering power in the commercial, banking and mining spheres. In the property-
booming metropolis that was mid-to-late nineteenth-century Melbourne, his
influence was spatially and urbanely manifest; it spanned and connected the self-
important European dominated Collins Street and Little Bourke Street, the emergent
center of Chinese civil life in Melbourne. As a mediator between Chinese and
European communities, Lowe also played a major role in Victorian colonial politics.
He co-wrote *The Chinese Question in Australia, 1878-79* (1879) with missionary
Cheok Cheong Hong and solicitor Louis Ah Mouy, which drew on Confucian
values to vehemently contest white settler discrimination, and Lowe subsequently
shaped the outcomes of the 1880 Victorian election. Jong's story and diary have
been the subject of two scholarly works, yet his story remains relatively marginal
in the steadily growing field of Chinese Australian history.[9]

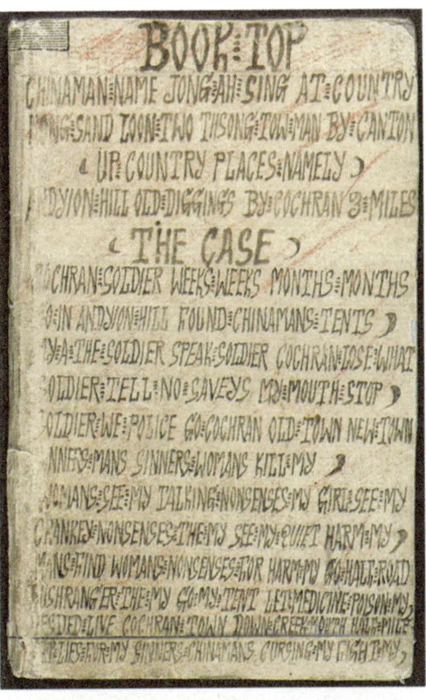

Page from Jong Ah Siug's diary, c. 1869
Collection of State Library Victoria, Melbourne

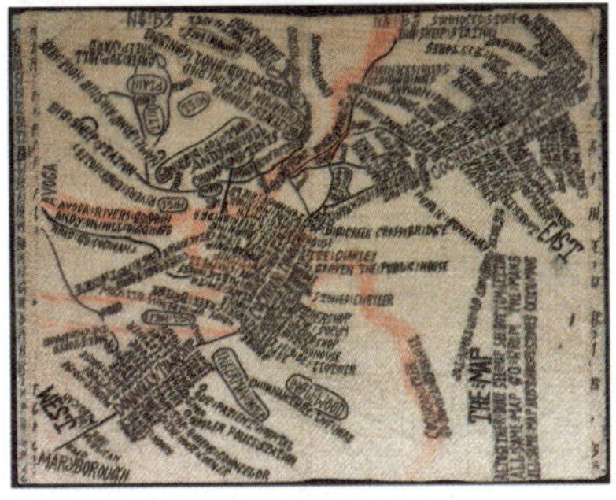

Hand-drawn map of Cochran Town in Jong
Ah Siug's diary, c. 1869
Collection of State Library Victoria, Melbourne

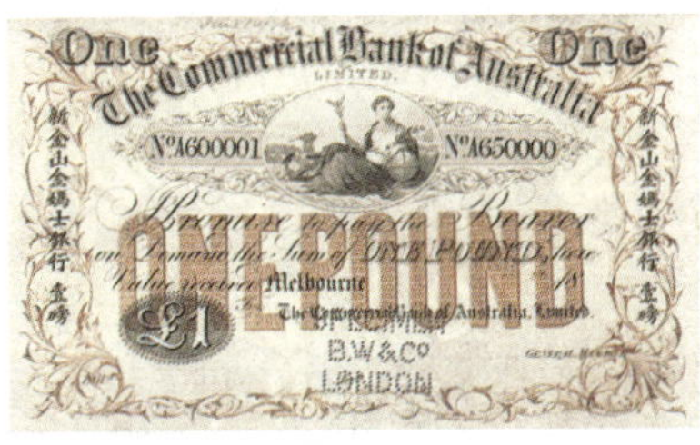

The Commercial Bank of Australia, bilingual
one pound note, 1909
Westpac Long Gallery, Sydney
Collection of Australian Museum, Sydney

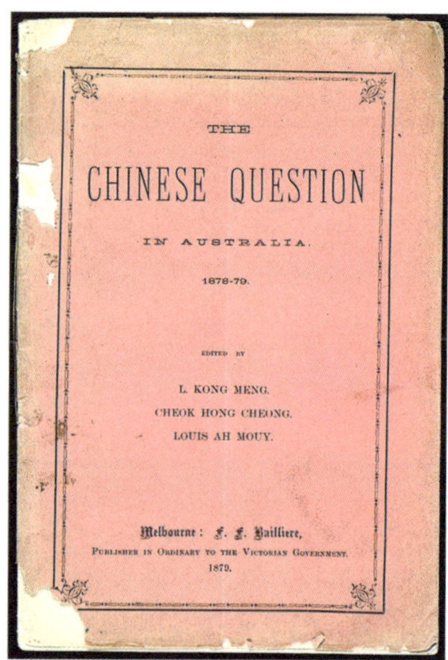

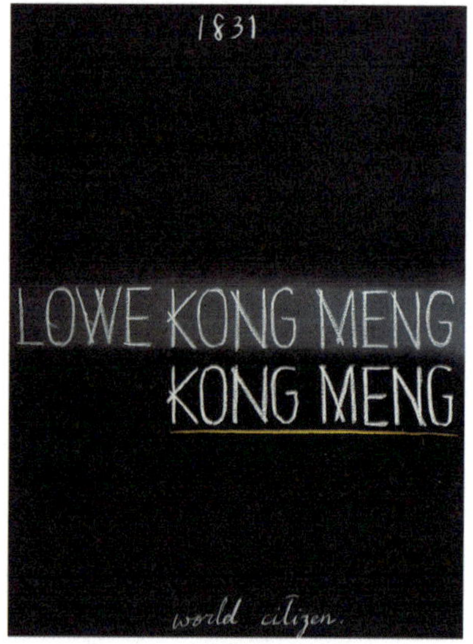

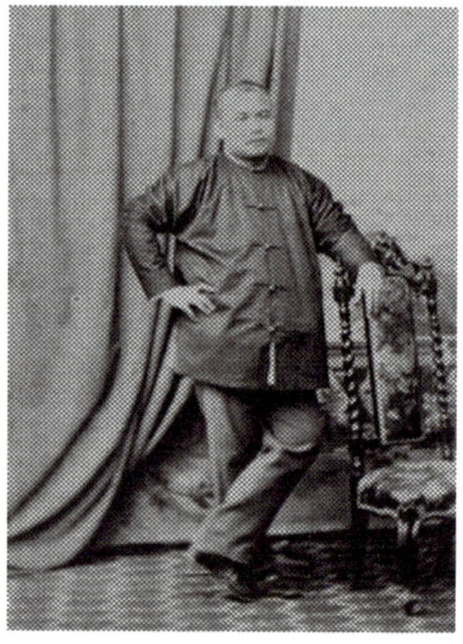

Book cover of *The Chinese Question in Australia,
1878–79*, 1879
Lowe Kong Meng, Cheok Hong Cheong
and Louis Ah Mouy (eds.), published by
F. F. Bailliere, Melbourne. Collection of National
Library of Australia, Canberra

Kong Meng 2015
Chalk on blackboard-painted archival
cotton paper, 100 × 70 cm

Lowe Kong Meng 2015
Digital print on photographic paper,
100 × 70 cm

1866 introduces audiences to these two men and their contrasting experiences of
migration and social mobility within the racial milieu of nineteenth-century Victoria.
Young's exhibition moves, left to right, from Lowe's economic success among the
bluestone-lined streets of Melbourne to Jong's struggles with the colonial legal system
and the straitjackets of the Sunbury Asylum. In focusing on these two men, *1866*
strongly reflects Young's concerns across the History Projects to create works that
respond to diasporic or cross-cultural figures and their histories. This is a concerted
move away from his previous explorations of questions of the relationship between
people and technology, and a continuation of the problematic of bicultural perspectives
and identities that informs his earlier practice. *1866* presents tangible narratives firmly
located in history and place.[10] Young and a team of researchers undertook extensive
research in the creation of this work, consulting and collating archives, images and
objects to narrate Lowe and Jong's Antipodean lives through a rich visual collage that
evokes the material and embodied stuff of 1860s life: the gold and the opium, the
wooden huts and bluestone colonial institutions, the banks and asylum cells, and the
'sweethearts' who 'pay visit'.[11]

This body of work is hence the product of a concerted labour of collection and
selection, and one that links the past with the present. In taking new images of relevant
historic sites, Young has engaged with the localities where this history played out. He
has also reframed extant archival materials—cropping and layering them—to remake
colonial objects into living repositories of diasporic meaning and stories. Doing so,
Young directs the audience to the many local places and moments that constituted
large lives, locating the two men and their dynamic movements across place and time.
One panel, for instance, writ in large chalk text, references Lowe's global mobility
and his related ethic and political subjectivity as a citizen of the world:

> *1831*
> *LOWE KONG MENG*
> *KONG MENG*
> *world citizen*

Another panel references Ah Siug's homemaking in the town of Cochrane,
on Indigenous Dja Dja Wurrung country:

> *1855-1866*
> *MY HOME TOWN*
> *COCHRANE*
> *HUT 6 x 3 YARDS*
>
> *DJA DJA WURRUNG*
> *TUAGGRA*
> *BEA LI BA*

As these works indicate, the exhibition moves easily and unapologetically between
different geographic scales, mapping the way that global, imperial and local forces
shape the men's world, and the men in turn made these worlds.

BINARIES AND DUALITIES

The selection of these two opposite lives sees Young walk a tightrope of colonial tropes.
Historians have shown that European settlers held positive attitudes toward so-called
'coloured' elites at the very same time they derided the mass of workers.[12] There is
much aesthetic gratification to be found in the symmetry and apparent polarity of

Lowe and Jong's experiences. Yet in the choice of these subjects, the work is at risk of reifying binaries: poor/wealthy, literate/illiterate, immobile/mobile, outcast/respectable. Indeed, Young chose these two lives in part for their very oppositeness. But at the same time as *1866* engages with this trope, so does it upend it: neither of these men is presented as neatly representative of their class. The particularities of their stories offer an alluring glimpse into their personalities, not only in their ways of navigating and resisting colonial institutions but also their styles of expression and communication. The representation of these two individual lives thus equivocally avoids collapsing the history of the Chinese diaspora in Australia into a singular 'Chinese Australian' experience. Nigerian writer Chimamanda Ngozi Adichie has spoken about the danger of the single story: 'The single story creates stereotypes, and the problem with stereotypes is not that they are untrue, but that they are incomplete. They make one story become the only story'.[13]

Mapping the polar ends of Chinese experiences of a settler colony evokes a spectrum, thereby illustrating the falseness of binaries. As curator Joanna Bayndran has alluded, Young's works implicitly evoke all the lives that are not represented within them, pointing to the complexity and nuance of individual experience.[14] The text within the work is instructive, revealing expressions/experiences of marginality in power, and power in marginality. Lowe faced limits and challenges, even though he had linguistic abilities and wealth. Jong broke boundaries of grammar and left a record that enables him to be remembered, even though, or more accurately because, he was trapped in the asylum.

The asylum appears as a place of pain, but also as a place of creativity driven by dire and coercive necessity; a place where Jong attempted to stretch his language abilities toward his attempt to prove his innocence, and hence exercised an attenuated mode of power. One of the chalkboard panels, with a wide blank black space in the middle, quotes Jong's diary at its margins. Here Jong tells a story of trying to perform surgery on himself when ill (evidently suffering from medical negligence in the Asylum) and it reads as poetry, practical and poignant:

> *'I tried to cure*
> *myself by cutting*
> *my stomach'*
> *'When I was*
> *in bed I saw Jinny? pictured*
> *in the Sky*
> *God Taa*
> *To Tomi Light'*
> *1868 B ward Yarra Bend*

In the settler colonies of Australia, where legal and social discrimination have been in play since the 1850s, the power of stereotypes has long been deployed as a strategy of denigration and justification for exclusionary policies. Historical images of such racial stereotypes have filtered down to popular consciousness through state-sponsored representations, school curricula and textbooks, so that in responding to the 2017 *Chinese Fortunes* exhibition at the Ballarat Museum of Democracy, writer Alice Pung reflected that:

> The first Chinese face I saw in a school history textbook had no body attached. Instead, eight tentacles emanated from his chin, each clutching prohibited goods such as opium and white women, or carrying nefarious ills like 'smallpox' and 'customs robbery'.[15]

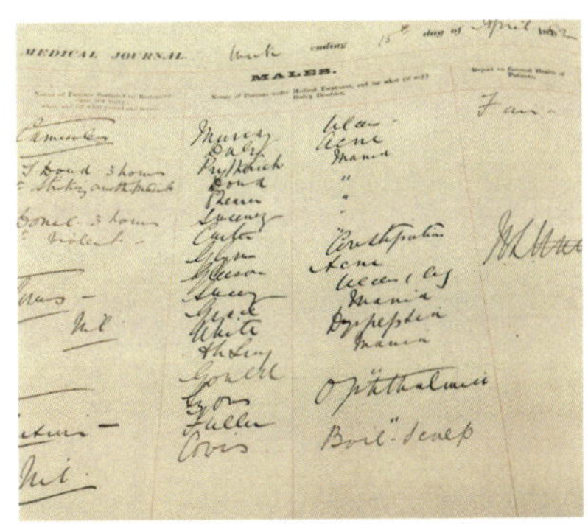

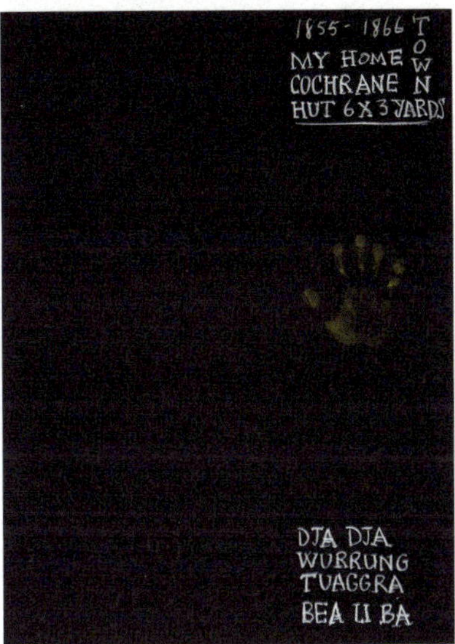

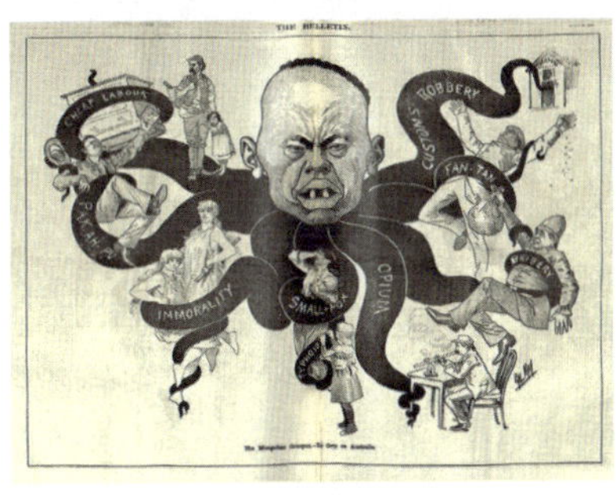

Asylum records of Jong Ah Siug, c. 1882

My Home Town 2015
Chalk on blackboard-painted archival cotton paper, 100 × 70 cm

Phil May, 'The Mongolian Octopus — Its Grip on Australia', *The Bulletin*, 21 August 1886
Collection of National Library of Australia, Canberra

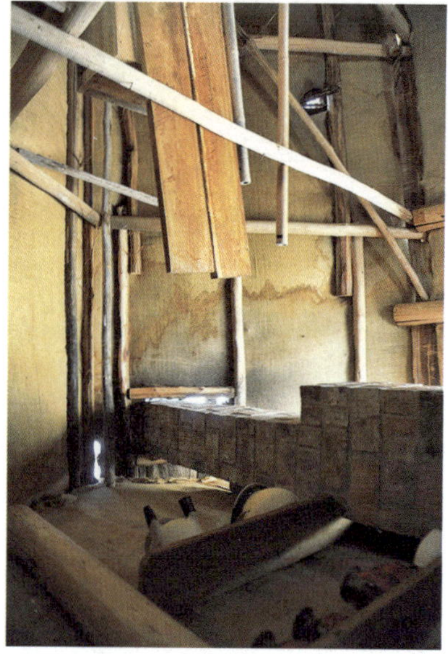

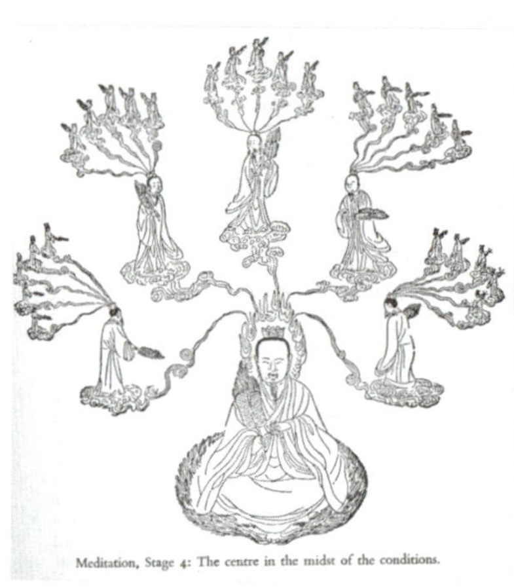

Meditation, Stage 4: The centre in the midst of the conditions.

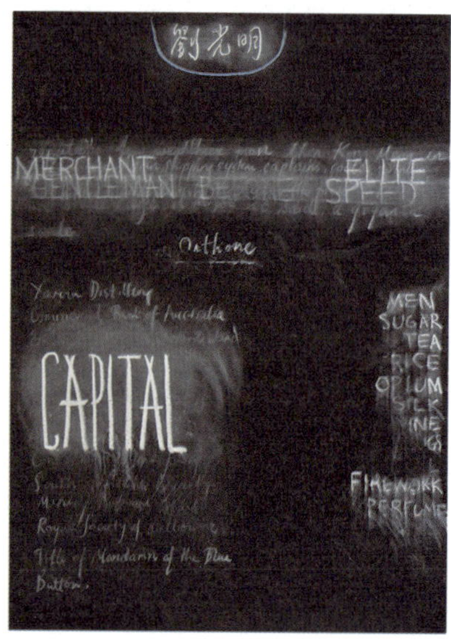

Interior view of a recreated goldminer's tent,
Sovereign Hill, Ballarat, 2015
Photograph by the artist

Illustration of Taoist meditation techniques from
Richard Wilhelm, *The Secret of the Golden Flower:
A Chinese Book of Life*, 1970

Capital 2015
Chalk on blackboard-painted archival
cotton paper, 100 × 70 cm

Given that academia—and the discipline of history manifestly—remains dominated by (self-consciously) white scholars, the inversion of authority in *1866* is of profound ethical and political importance.[16] It represents a challenge to the perpetual hum of white noise in academia, and, by a similar token, the sound of the enduring (re) creation of 'safe white spaces' in the Australian arts.[17] As historian and museum expert Karen Schamberger has observed, curators in contemporary Australia have been wont to confront audiences with the grossest expressions of white settler racism against Chinese, as if settlers might be shocked into a more humane position.[18] In contrast, *1866* is an engagement with imagination and with archives that takes Chinese agency and individuality for granted. Given the gross historic trope of Chinese Australian representation, there is something unsettling about the way that Young has placed these two lives in conversation. It offers an antidote to representations of white racism and violence which, as Pung's reflections instruct us, have been designed to gratify white rather than Chinese Australian or Asian audiences. Young implicitly calls attention to the spectrum of experiences that lies between wealth and poverty, entitlement and disenfranchisement.

The partiality of these life stories is significant. Not only does it mirror the partiality of public historical consciousness about the Chinese diasporic experience, but it also gives a feeling of the many loose ends in these life stories which may never be neatly tied up. An example is *Capital* (2015), on which 'CAPITAL' is writ large on the right of the panel, with a list of items in smaller font on the left: 'Men, Sugar, Tea, Rice, Opium, Silk, Wine, Rugs, Oil, Firework, Perfume'. Parts of the words 'Wine', 'Rugs' and 'Oil' are faded and barely legible, having been rubbed out. This visible erasure evokes the ways that texts are subject to destruction and disappearance, and, acutely, so are historical records. The list of words seems to invite viewers to undertake something like an imaginative 'join-the-dots' activity, as a subjective rather than definitive reconstruction of history.

INTELLIGIBILITY, LANGUAGE AND REFUSAL

Jong and Lowe's different possibilities to speak and be heard in Victorian society orients viewers to the ways that language matters. Language cuts to the heart of the colonial condition, for language differences both make and constitute asymmetrical power relations. This is not least because during and since the eighteenth century, the languages spoken by colonisers have been defined, and constructed, as superior and correct against other language varieties, such as Pidgin Englishes, which were frequently construed as inferior and infantile.[19]

In nineteenth-century Australian government and legal discourse, immigrants and settlers from disparate parts of Canton, Hong Kong and the Straits Settlements were described as speaking 'the Chinese language'. This generic label, however, covered a number of Cantonese (and other) 'Chinese' language varieties, only some of which were mutually intelligible.[20] An estimated 90 percent of Chinese in Victoria spoke a Sze Yap dialect, notable numbers spoke a Sam Yap dialect, and a small number spoke Hokkien (a variety of southern Min Chinese language).[21] A minority of the Chinese who immigrated to Victoria spoke English fluently. Members of the Chinese merchant elite had been educated in the Straits Settlements or British Hong Kong. Other Chinese studied at the English classes of the Chinese Mission on Little Bourke Street, and others learned English in Victorian schools.[22]

For many Chinese migrants, language barriers were part and parcel of daily life. Here, Young presents Chinese text without translations. As such, he risks repeating the colonial phenomenon where Europeans read and treated Chinese script as an

unintelligible object, rather than as a potent medium of communication. But along
with historical accuracy, there is a strong de-colonial rationale to present Chinese
script here. Within the prevailing monolingual anglophone culture of the Australian
art world and society at large, presenting and representing the historical power of
Chinese language is an inherently political act. As Young articulated in 2017 'there
is still an enormous resistance [to using multiple languages] in contemporary art'. [23]
For Young, then, who is Hong Kong-born and a Cantonese speaker, working in two
or more languages is part of his code of ethics:

> I only have one basic principle now in my artworks if I had to use texts,
> which is that if I work in a language, I always write it in Chinese and
> English, sometimes, you know, also in German, so I always have multi-
> languages in my work.[24]

The exhibition of *1866*, at ARC ONE Gallery (2015) and the Melbourne City
Library (2016), has constituted a rare public space in which Chinese script—and
its historical efficacy—can speak for itself. Departing from the colonial legacy that
posits anglophones as the normative, privileged reader of art, here, Chinese script
is written without apology for its unintelligibility to non-Chinese speakers such
as me. In this way, the art reflects the linguistic worlds of members of the Chinese
diaspora, where Chinese language often resounded in the same spaces as English,
and sometimes, as in the case of Jong's use of Pidgin, were hybridised.

Working alongside this expression of linguistic unintelligibility, is the cultural
misunderstanding/mistranslation/incommensurability of epistemes that emerges
through Jong's diary. Jong, Young tells us:

> wrote this diary, in English words and a sort of Chinese grammar, with
> observations from the Chinese world view or episteme—full of references
> to spiritual deities—land[ing] him the tag of madness. This is a testament
> to the difficulties that he faced whilst he was incarcerated. Whilst
> Jong was in the insane asylum there were reports of him seeing ghosts.
> Nowadays we would say that he was hallucinating. And judging by the
> names he attributed to these ghosts, they were known Chinese deities.[25]

In this way, Jong's inner world was unintelligible and largely misinterpreted by
the colonial authorities who watched him. The authorities thought that Jong was
hallucinating, but Young has suggested that Jong was acting in accordance with
his contemporary Chinese episteme. '[I]n fact', he notes, 'these sorts of things were
common even with the last generation of Chinese people like my grandparents;
so ghosts are considered part and parcel of life really'.[26] The violence the colonial
system inflicted on Jong was hence double: first that of his institutionalisation, and
then that of misinterpreting his visions as insanity rather than as a part of life—
according to Young's interpretation, as an expression of his cultural health, even,
his cultural normality.

The method of leaving some things unexplained, and unintelligible to a non-Chinese
audience, appears to be Young's intention. For as much as the work reaches for four-
dimensional, metaphysical and linguistic fullness, so does it commit to a narrative
partiality. It is possible that observers of *1866* would leave the exhibit without fully
comprehending the impact of these men or the colonial world they navigated.
As a historian invested in bringing the marginal(ised) lives of Asian migrants to public
knowledge, there is something about the artwork that, at first viewing, made me wish
for a fuller and more explicit telling of these men's lives, so that they might equivocally

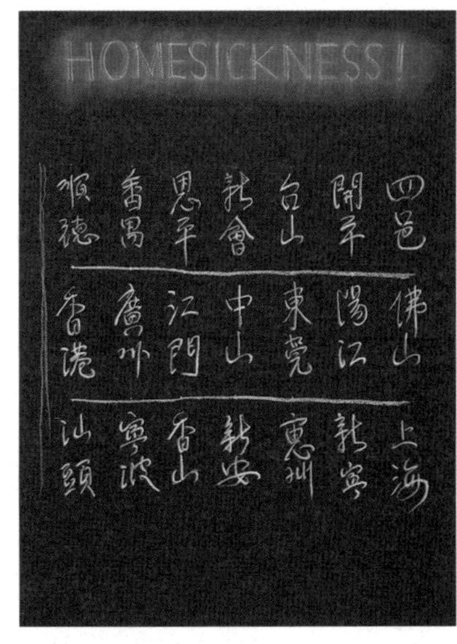

Homesickness 2015
Chalk on blackboard-painted archival
cotton paper, 100 × 70 cm

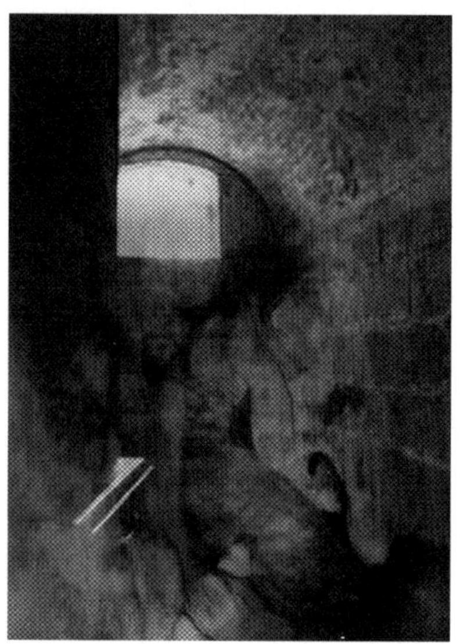

enter into the mainstream historical imaginary. On further reflection, what I wanted was to see these lives writ in the certainty of anglophone, textual narratives. It is, though, the visuality and partiality of the telling that is potentially liberatory. It invites a viewing of two life worlds, without pertaining to either of them. As follows, the 'worlds' of *1866* gain their vividness through silence in the historical record, as much as through presence.

TOWARDS IMAGINATION

In his essay that grapples with understanding the complex frontier relationship between Eora woman Patyegarang and lieutenant-turned critic of colonialism James Dawes, Ross Gibson similarly calls for us to enter a more radical 'space of imagination'.[27] He asks us to resist the grooves of colonial narratives that would have us readily sexualise their relationship, and instead imagine conversations that were curious and intimate.

In *1866* the matrix of chalk-board panels—blending and alternating text and images—activate a viewer's imagination. On the above-mentioned panel, the word 'Capital' is also imposed on top of a list of places that ends with a title: 'Tarra Distillery, Commercial Bank of Australia, Royal Society of Melbourne, Title of Mandarin of the Blue Button'. This layering appears to suggest that capital is an umbrella term for the various forms of social and economic capital that Lowe accrued during his time in Victoria – forms of settler colonial capital that contributed to the honours given him by the Chinese empire. But what went on behind the scenes to reach these distinguishments? The space around capital, the absence of text, indicates as much about the process of piecing together history as does its presence. History here is treated not as a canvas with gaps to be filled but as necessarily incomplete. In honouring the incompleteness of records of the past, rather than attempting to fill them in, Young's work resonates with the theory of historical fiction writer Natalie Kon-yu. On the challenges of writing women's history, Kon-yu explains how 'writing a fiction that simply filled in the gaps would perpetuate the idea that information about women's history can be easily recovered. Instead, I wanted to write a fiction that would not gloss over the difficulties in finding information about a woman from the past'.[28]

This sense of incompleteness is also evident in *Cell* (2015), in which an image of the asylum cell is pixelated with a blurring effect, giving a sense of ease and softness to the hard, confining walls. The presentation of fragments of language and image is true to the fragmentation of Lowe and Jong's lives in the archival record. While the story is presented in moments and dangling phrases, there is also a feeling of a life's completeness, and a spiritual fullness that we, as readers, might sense, if not know. Paradoxically, in leaving space around the historical materials he curates and reworks, Young presents stories that are more than—fuller than—the sum of their parts.

The use of blackboards as the central medium to carry the stories enables Young to place layers of text on top of each other, giving the impression that every word written threatens to replace an existing one; the impression that language—as history—can be a messy site of production and place-making as well as of destruction and replacement. Blackboards, used for teaching in India since the eleventh century, offer a powerful metaphor in relation with history. The blackboard is an educational device and is used with chalk, an erasable writing tool that is desirably ephemeral. Hence, in the use of blackboards, Young effectively displays a story that is susceptible to being overwritten. And yet, Young has fixed these chalk markings in place—perhaps to respect the way versions of history can be overwritten but making versions permanent enough to be seen again in the future. As with settler colonialism, this work signals a dynamic

Cell 2015
Digital print on photographic paper, 100 × 70 cm

project of erasure and replacement, where bodies and histories are placed on Indigenous land, threatening to overwrite existing culture and peoples. The chalkboards of *1866* appear ephemeral and yet they endure, mirroring the way that a life is fleeting and yet has effects that far outlast its embodiment and—whether or not they enter history's annals—cannot be erased.

PASTS BEYOND DISCIPLINE: ART, ARCHIVES AND AUTHORITY

Young's collaborative and imagination-activating engagement with archives, as well as with place, reflects and supports a larger trend among Australian artists. In performing de- and postcolonial imperatives, Indigenous, migrant and settler artists have in the last decade been interpreting archives in ways that both reproduce and challenge their power.[29] Yawuru and Noongar scholar of human rights Elfie Shiosaki has suggested, in relation to colonial archives that register her Noongar family's history, 'the archive is a site of justice. Breaking silences by amplifying ghosted voices within the archive, relocates marginalised groups from the periphery of history to its centre'.[30] In a similar vein, Narungga scholar Natalie Harkin has written poetry inspired by time spent researching her family history in state archives, and discusses the emotional labour of engaging with an archive that reflects the violence of racism and settler state policy and power.[31] Closer to Young's practice, visual and performance artist Eugenia Lim has explored her history as a second-generation migrant in works such as *Yellow Peril* (2015), described as a '[d]ialogue between place and performance'.[32] Lim engages with public representations of the history of Chinese migration to Victoria, notably those found in the recreation gold rush town of Sovereign Hill, Ballarat.

Comprising video, sculpture and digital prints, *Yellow Peril* considered socio-economic interconnections between Australia and China, linking local histories of mining in the Victorian goldfields with personal searches for wealth more globally. In the video, Lim poses in various locations within the goldrush village-cum-theme-park that is Sovereign Hill, panning by a stream, for example, and in a photographic studio. Clothed in a golden suit, Lim interrupts this historical stage—overwhelmingly dominated by white actors dressed in Victorian fashion—with her embodied Chinese-ness and present-ness. As Ulanda Blair insightfully notes, 'the intermeshing of different time-periods confuses the linear clock-time inscribed within the Sovereign Hill experience, whose own history lessons are tethered to concepts of progress and chronological succession'.[33] In 2019, and on the other side of so-called 'Australia', artists Gabby Loo and Gok-Lim Finch curated the State Library of Western Australia exhibition *Imagined Migrant Futures*. In doing so, they engaged Asian Australian artists to tell their stories through various creative media, using the literal space of the archive to speak back to its authority and its historic and contemporary practices of racial categorisation and exclusion.[34] For these and other artists, the archives of texts, as much as those of the landscape and the built environment, are simultaneously sources of authority, of imagination and of modes of resistance to historic and contemporary racism.

Young's work with his mentee, artist Jason Phu, who is of Vietnamese Chinese heritage, has adopted similar history-focused methods, drawing on archival research into Chinese Australian and other non-white bushrangers undertaken by white historian Meg Foster. Notably, Phu's series 'A MERCHANT, A MINER AND A BUSHRANGER WALK INTO A PUB' is an irreverent take on Chinese diasporic history that joyfully upends racial stereotypes.[35] Here, Phu engages with masculine figures that loom large in nineteenth-century history. In drawing attention to a historical bushranger of Chinese descent, Phu unsettles the racial mappings of these figures, which both his and Foster's research have shown to be historically inaccurate, and connected to racial violence

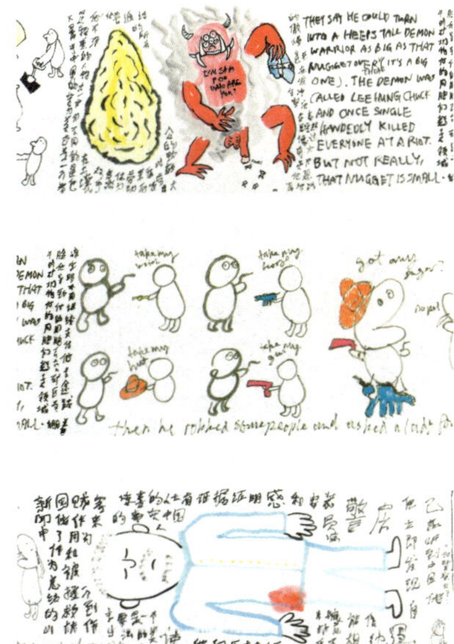

Jason Phu
Details from *The Ballad of The Widely Loved and Revered Aussie Bushranger Sammy "Pooey" Pu: The Successful Great Revolt Against the Southern Crossers by L.H.C., The Shooting Death of S.C.J.W. by a Chinaman, The Great Chase and Final Showdown at Barney's Reef, The Trial of The Mute, The Execution by Hanging of Sam Poo* 2015
Ink, texta, coloured pencil on Chinese paper, 1050 × 60 cm
Bathurst Regional Art Gallery commission
Courtesy the artist; photograph: Document Photography

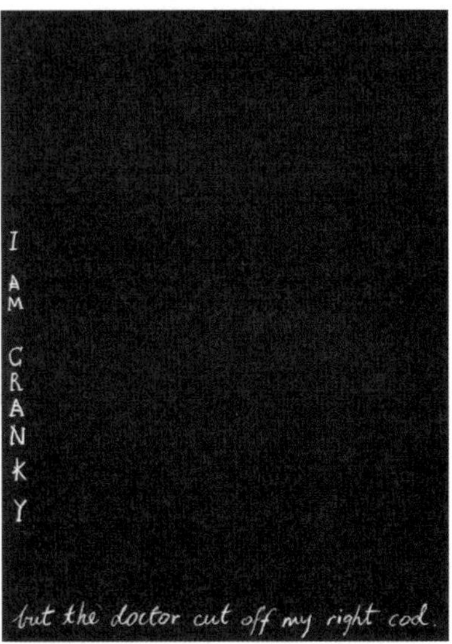

Cranky 2015
Chalk on blackboard-painted archival
cotton paper, 100 × 70 cm

and injustice. After he was alleged to have shot a police officer, white settlers chased down the bushranger Sam Poo, and in 1865 he was imprisoned and hanged in the old Bathurst jail. Phu also uses a 'non-linear approach to narrative, which, with its deliberate inaccuracies, obvious gaps, elements of fiction and humour speaks to the lack of historical records available, not only about Poo but the thousands of other Chinese sojourners in the Central West at the time, whose stories remain untold'.[36] Such art—like poetry—offers versions of the past beyond the scholarly discipline of history, which, debatably, remains wedded to empiricism and to temporal linearity.

Young's *1866* is thus part of a trend towards critical engagements with archives that are inspiring new narratives, which both respond to and simultaneously destabilise the authority of archives through acts of creativity and imagination. The conventions of academic history mean that historians generally speculate with intense caution, and often resist filling in or bridging narrative gaps, no matter how far we are immersed in archival materials. Indeed, the boundaries and liberties of the historians' imagination has, for over three decades, been a source of debate in the field.[37] For many historians, part of 'the discipline' of history is to make modest inferences, and to err on the side of empiricism rather than imagination.

The artist's freedom from conventional textual forms of history enables truths to be carried —including the truth that there is no absolutely complete version of history and, relatedly, that the inner lives of historical subjects are never entirely knowable. Young, for instance, places a statement of emotion 'I AM CRANKY' running vertically down one panel. The open space around this phrase appears to reflect the space around the emotional lives of Jong, a historical actor whose inner world was no doubt more lively—more lived—than is conveyed both in the archival records and the histories spun from him. Was Jong cranky about the injustice of his situation? About the living conditions in the asylum? About the state of his love life? About being contained so far from his first home? About all of these?

Through honouring the fragmentation of records and narratives that enable us to relate with the stories of Lowe and Jong, Young scaffolds a relation with the past and its injustices. This is a relation that knows the complex simultaneity of power and victimhood, and avoids trampling on the tenuous forms of self-authorship that Lowe and Jong—and other people of Chinese descent—fought for and asserted in a white-dominated colony. *1866* invites viewers to dwell in the reality that there is no singular 'Chinese Australian' history, that there is more than one trace of dignity and agency retained by people too often cast as colonial casualties. It is toward unpacking this moral relation with the past that the remainder of this essay turns.

HISTORICAL IMAGINATION, RACE, AND MORAL RELATIONS

In discussing the work of Indigenous artist Brook Andrew, Kate MacNeill has suggested that 'the archive is dangerous territory', since its images 'form an integral component of the project of colonialism itself'.[38] While this also rings true for the Chinese diaspora in Australia, for *1866*, Young selected archives that place colonial institutions and settler racism at the edges of the story. In particular, the bank note and the diary were living objects before they were archived; and were in part or full created by Lowe and Jong themselves. The bilingual banknote, currently the property of Westpac Bank, references Lowe's position as a founding member of the Bank of

Australasia. Jong wrote the diary during his time in the Sunbury Asylum to attempt to prove his legal innocence, and it later came to be stored in the State Library of Victoria. Curators have described Jong's diary as 'a curious historical document', but it is more profoundly significant for being an archival source of the Chinese working class that is not produced for and by European colonial authorities and bureaucracy; a text where Jong speaks for himself through a new vocabulary gleaned from his fellow inmates, as he struggles to find a language by which to effectively communicate with the asylum and legal authorities.[39]

The fact that these material artefacts evidence Chinese historical agency, speaks to the highly classed and often contradictory relationships forged by people of Chinese descent in the settler society of Victoria; a society structured on the displacement of Indigenous people from their land, and the contradiction between white desires for cheap Asian labour and trade, and European settlers' impossible dreams of creating a purely white society.[40] The existence of these self-narrations relate to Chinese privilege, as the largest non-European group in the colony. The chalkboard panels witness rather than judge this often heated and sometimes violent history. Some panels make explicit references to moments of Lowe and Jong's lives, such as '1854 Fleet of six ships. Mauritius Bombay Ceylon Calcutta Fuzhou Hong Kong Macau Penang Singapore Melbourne Robe Otago'. Others reflect the incompleteness of the archives, and call on imagination to fill gaps, such as the panel that lifts from Jong's diary: 'I AM CRANKY But the doctor cut off my right cod'. Each panel thus reflects an ongoing conversation between Young and historical sources and artefacts, a dialectic between the present and the past, and between historical truth and imagination.

When it comes to narrating colonial history in so-called Australia, the license of imagination taken by narrators who occupy positions of institutional and racial power still remains contentious. And rightly so. As Indigenous Australian writer and lawyer Larissa Behrendt has observed, historical narration by non-Indigenous historians and artists has often taken licence to imagine the pasts of Indigenous people in ways that constitute a (re)colonising practice, and the politics of this densely plays out in frontier contexts.[41] In the 1990s, non-Indigenous historian Greg Dening and others passionately engaged with the question of the role imagination can take in historical practice—a question that goes to the boundaries of what we can know about the past, and how we relate to it. Dening drew on the ocean as an alternative temporality or knowledge framework; a place that itself does not respect the boundaries between waters and lands that historians, thinking through the prism of the nation-state, might be seduced by. For Dening, however, empowering the imagination was important because it enabled historians 'to hear the absent things, the silences'.[42]

The trajectory of scholarly historical work to take imagination seriously was, however, interrupted by protracted debates—mostly between white historians—about the precise number of murders of Indigenous peoples by settlers; debates that came to be named 'the History Wars'. Tom Griffiths has observed that the History Wars brought a focus on imagination out of fashion, leading to a sacrifice of 'meaning for accountability—and countability'.[43] It was too dangerous, possibly too indulgent, to empower new imaginations of the past when what was at stake was the need to prove the scale and reality of colonial violence using archives, those produced by colonists most pervasively and vehemently. In these debates, writer Keith Windschuttle represented another extreme, a viciously denialist mode of engaging with frontier

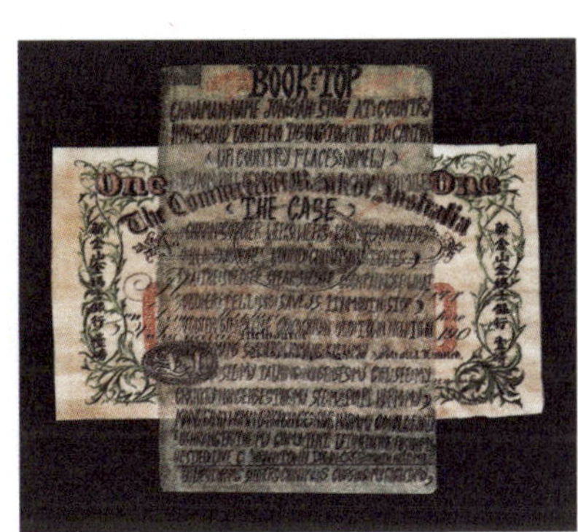

The Meeting 2015
Single thread hand-sewn embroidery, framed, 41 × 42 cm
Collection of Town Hall Gallery, Boroondara City Council, Melbourne

history and violence. His allegations of fabrication have left a legacy of concern for empiricism and hyper-vigilant referencing that continues to shape the ways in which non-Indigenous people relate to colonialism—in both its past and present incarnations and power structures—and generated a nervousness about the use of imagination as a resource to understand the past with.

It was in this context that historian Inga Clendinnen influentially suggested that 'the largest difference between History and Fiction is the moral relationships each establishes between writer and subjects, and writer and reader'.[44] Writing in the context of narrating the history of the Spanish Inquisition, Clendinnen noted: 'Reading the records of past actuality I am not free to refuse painful engagement of emotions and imagination, because I have entered into a moral relationship with the persons enclosed in the documents—which means, of course, not only the victims, but the torturers, too'.[45] This meant remaining faithful to written records and connecting a narrative with its original sources through footnotes. But Clendinnen's medium was the written word, and she did not dwell—as artists, writers, poets and scholars have since discussed and documented so thoroughly—on the ways that records are skewed, many reflecting and constituting a colonial lens. Young's work thus effectively—intentionally or not—offers a model for ethically engaging with the past from the present that historians might heed.

When reflecting on the History Projects and his hopes for his 2019 exhibition *The Lives of Celestials*, Young has said: 'Stories about the past bring out a sense of empathy and identification with us in the present. … My hope is not necessarily that people get a very succinct historical objective narratives about all these events. I hope the audience come away with this sense that it is possible to imagine a sense of benevolence when we approach the other, rather than shutting people out.'[46]

In focusing on the quality of one's relationship with the past rather than its facticity—and privileging the meaning drawn from a story over a fidelity to extant archives—Young circumvents the question of how much license an artist or writer can take with the historical record. This is a praxis. Respecting moral relations when engaging with the past means restraining the impulse to reclaim a 'truer' history solely from the archive. This sense is often promoted—that the 'true' history of Australia is multi-racial, and once this plurality is known Australia will be a more just place. But knowing historical truths does not guarantee that one knows humanity. *1866* offers a way of reading sources that understands that the quality of our connection with the past matters; it has implications for the structures and actions that one deems benevolent or violent, just or unjust, and hence, for the repetition of such structures and actions. Young's work orients viewers to the moral implications of history, while also leaving space for the viewer to respond to colonial racism and inequality in their own ways. The viewer must navigate the history on display with their own moral sensibility. This sensibility will likely be challenged by the stories and lives (re)presented, yet there are no simple judgements to be found here. Considered on a macro level, *1866* reads as an open invitation to enter into an ethically aware and humane engagement with the past.

1866: The Lives of Lowe Kong Meng and John Ah Siug does not merely combine art and history. It sits uncomfortably and productively between them. In its sustained engagement with Chinese diasporic agency and the archives in which such agency is registered, *1866* is an understated challenge to historians engaging with diasporic communities and their pasts. Like the figures whose lives it explores, *1866* undertakes the work of mediation—between the past and the present, between

Chinese and non-Chinese people and communities, and between Lowe and Jong themselves. It teaches us that there are still more Chinese Australian diasporic stories to be (re)cognised; stories that arrest and interrupt the pre-worn and, too often, Anglo-writ grooves of historical imagination. Young's work shows the possibility for art to be a place where history is an undetermined relation of morality as well as one of knowledge; a place where both artists and audiences exercise their imaginations to reckon with the colonial past. In this and other works, Young is impressive for working with the sensibility of a historian—exercising a respect for archives and sources and the processes of their production—as well as that of a fiction writer, creatively representing and responding to sources to enliven and nourish the imagination. Young's artistic method respects the specificities and materiality of historical archives, all while inviting viewers to engage with the past in ways that transgress the limits of conventional disciplinary modes of historical knowledge. *1866* leaves a lasting impression of the ways that lives are always more than the sum of the records that might appear to hold them.

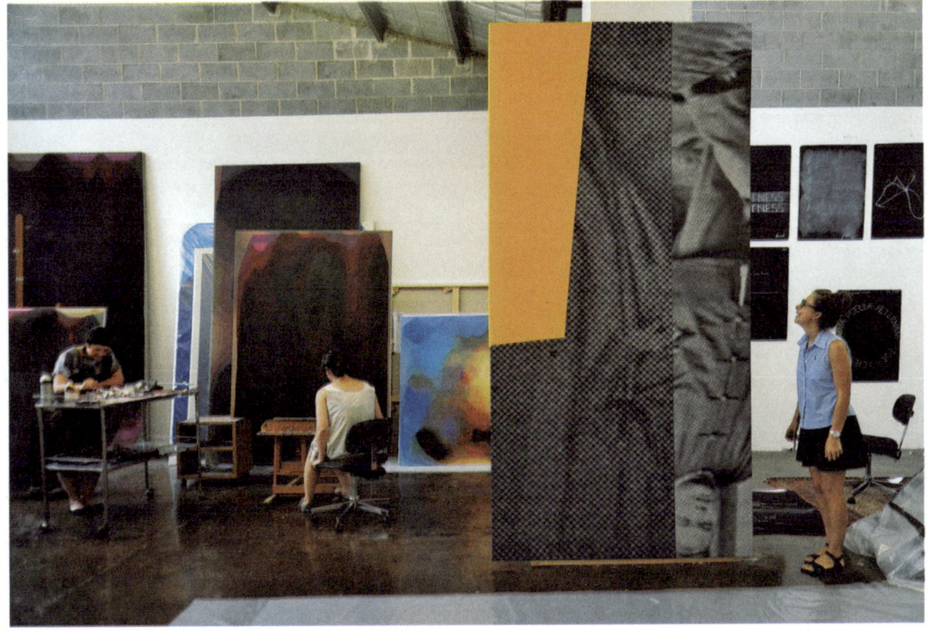

Left to right: Colleen Ahern, Kirsty Budge, and Ashlee Baldwin
Studio preparation for *1866: The Worlds of Lowe Kong Meng and Jong Ah Siug*, 2015
Northcote studio, Melbourne, 2015

1. John Young, *1866: The Worlds of Lowe Kong Meng and Jong Ah Siug*, Boroondara City Council Collection, held at Arc ONE Gallery, Melbourne, 11 March–11 April 2015.

2. Alister Bowen, 'The Merchants: Chinese Social Organisation in Colonial Australia', *Australian Historical Studies*, vol. 42, no. 1, p. 31.

3. In October of 1866 the *Intercolonial Exhibition of Australasia* opened in Melbourne and the Australian colonies came together for the first time, with exhibits from Victoria, New South Wales, Queensland, South Australia, Tasmania, Western Australia, as well as from New Zealand, New Caledonia, Mauritius and Netherlands-India. This exhibition brought together exhibits to assist in the selection of items to be forwarded to Paris for the 1867 Exposition Universelle.

4. See Keir Reeves, 'Sojourners or a New Diaspora? Economic Implications of the Movement of Chinese Miners to the South-West Pacific Goldfields', *Australia Economic History Review*, vol. 50, no. 2, 2010, pp. 178–92.

5. John Young, 'Talking About Translation: History, Art and Language', *Peril: Asian Australian Arts and Culture Magazine*, 1 March 2017. https://peril.com.au/topics/activism/talking-about-translation-history-art-and-language-1/.

6. Ibid.

7. Marilyn Lake and Henry Reynolds, *Drawing the Global Colour Line*, pp. 15–18; Paul Macgregor, 'Chinese Political Values in Colonial Victoria', p. 137.

8. Paul Macgregor, 'Chinese Political Values in Colonial Victoria: Lowe Kong Meng and the Legacy of the July 1880 Election', *Journal of Chinese Overseas*, vol. 9, 2013, p. 137.

9. Ruth Moore and John Tully, *A Difficult Case by Jong Ah Siug: An Autobiography of a Chinese Miner on the Central Victorian Goldfields*, Jim Crow Press, Daylesford, 2000.

10. For a discussion of the move toward artistic uses of archives in recent years see Martyn Jolly, 'Big Archives and Small Collections: Remarks on the Archival Mode in Contemporary Australian Art and Visual Culture', *Public History Review*, vol. 21, 2014, pp. 60–80. For a creative-ethical approach to responding to colonial archives see Natalie Harkin, 'The Poetics of (Re) Mapping Archives: Memory in the Blood', *Journal of the Association for the Study of Australian Literature*, vol. 14, no. 3, 2014, pp. 1–14.

11. This is a quote from one of the installation panels, drawn from Jong Ah Siug's diary.

12. Sascha Auerbach has observed this of European attitudes towards Chinese across the British imperial world in 'Margaret Tart, Lao She, and the Opium-Master's Wife: Race and Class among Chinese Commercial Immigrants in London and Australia, 1866-1929', *Comparative Studies in Society and History*, vol. 55, no. 1, 2013, pp. 35–64.

13. Chimamanda Ngozi Adichie, 'The Danger of Single Story', *TEDGlobal*, 2009, https://www.ted.com/talks/chimamanda_adichie_the_danger_of_a_single_story/transcript.

14. Andy Butler, 'Safe White Spaces', *Runway: Australian Experimental Art*, issue 35, 2017, http://runway.org.au/safe-white-spaces/.

15. Alice Pung, 'Chinese Fortunes Exhibition Charts Untold Tales of Wealth and Prejudice', *The Sydney Morning Herald*, 19 January 2017, http://www.smh.com.au/entertainment/chinese-fortunes-exhibition-charts-untold-tale-of-wealth-and-prejudice-20170119-gtugzg.html.

16. For discussion of the contemporary 'white hegemony' in the discipline of history in Australia, see Jordana Silverstein, 'Intersectionality, resistance, and history-making: A conversation between Carolyn D'Cruz, Ruth Desouza, Samia Khatun, and Crystal McKinnon', *Lilith*, issue 23, 2017, pp. 15–22; Larissa Behrendt, *Finding Eliza: Power and Colonial Storytelling*, University of Queensland Press, St Lucia, 2016, p. 93. To observe the operation of white hegemony is by no means to suggest it is total. Historians of Chinese descent are transforming and contesting white-made (hi)stories. See for instance: Mei-Fen Kuo, *Making Chinese Australia: Urban Elites, Newspapers and the Formation of Chinese-Australian Identity, 1892–1912*,

Monash University Press, Clayton, 2013; Natalie Fong, 'The Significance of the Northern Territory in the Formulation of "White Australia" Policies, 1880–1901', *Australian Historical Studies*, vol. 49, no. 4, 2018, pp. 527–45; Alanna Kamp, *Intersectional Lives: Chinese Australian Women in White Australia*, Routledge, London, 2022.

17. Butler, 'Safe White Spaces'.

18. Karen Schamberger, 'Gold, market gardens and race: Chinese Australian stories in museums', Dragon Tails Conference Paper, convened by Grace Gassin, Leigh McKinnon and Nadia Rhook, Bendigo, November 2017.

19. Quoted in Tracey Banivanua-Mar, *Violence and Colonial Dialogue: The Australian-Pacific Indentured Labour Trade*, University of Hawaii Press, Honolulu, 2007, pp. 2–3.

20. Court interpreter Ah Jack, testified to this diversity in *Depositions, The Queen v Mow Tan*, Supreme Court, Melbourne, 17 April 1895, Public Record Office of Victoria (PROV), VPRS30/P0, Unit 1013, Case 141.

21. The majority of Chinese came from the Sze Yap region (四邑 lit. 'four counties'), south of Canton/Guangzhou city and west of the Pearl River (Sunwui/Xinhui 新會, Toisan/Taishan 泰山, Hoiping/Kaiping 開平, Enping/Yanping 延平). Some migrated from Sam Yap (三邑, 'three counties'), the historical metropolitan area of Canton/Guangzhou (Shuntack/Shunde 順德, Punyu/Panyu 番禺 and Namhoi/Nanhai 南海), while others also came from nearby Zungsaan/Zhongshan (中山). See Charles Price, 'Restrictive Immigration to North America and Australasia, 1836–1888', Australian National University Press, Canberra, 1974, pp. 219–20

22. On the limited access of Chinese people to an English language education in colonial Australia, see Kate Bagnall, 'Across the threshold: White women and Chinese hawkers in the white colonial imaginary', *Hecate*, vol. 28, no. 2, 2002, p. 11. For more on the language-scape of colonial Victoria, see Nadia Rhook, "The Chief Chinese Interpreter", Charles Hodges: mapping the aurality of race and governance in colonial Melbourne', *Postcolonial Studies*, vol. 18, no. 1, 2015, pp. 1–18.

23. Young, 'Talking About Translation: History, Art and Language', https://peril.com.au/topics/activism/talking-about-translation-history-art-and-language-1/.

24. Ibid.

25. Ibid.

26. Ibid.

27. See Ross Gibson, 'Patyegarang and William Dawes: The Space of Imagination', in Banivanua Mar and Edmonds (eds), *Making Settler Colonial Space: Perspectives on Race, Place and Identity*, Palgrave Macmillan, London, 2010, p. 245.

28. Natalie Kon-yu, 'Letting go of the truth: researching and writing the other side of silence in women's lives', *TEXT*, vol. 14, no. 2, 2010, pp. 1–11.

29. Kate MacNeill, 'Undoing the Colonial Gaze: Ambiguity in the Art of Brook Andrew', *The Australian and New Zealand Journal of Art*, vol. 6/7, no. 2, 2006, pp. 179–94.

30. Elfie Shiosaki, 'Writing from the Heart', *Westerly*, vol. 61, no. 1, 2018, p. 85.

31. Harkin's work is extensive. See Natalie Harkin, 'Weaving the Colonial Archive: A Basket to Lighten the Load', *Journal of Australian Studies*, vol. 44, no. 2, 2020, pp.154–66; *Archival-Poetics*, Vagabond Press, Sydney, 2019.

32. Eugenia Lim, *Yellow Peril*, Bus Projects, Melbourne, 8–25 April 2015, https://busprojects.org.au/program/yellow-peril.

33. Ulanda Blair, 'Eugenia Lim: Yellow Peril', exhibition catalogue, Artereal Gallery, Sydney, 2016, http://www.sun-streaming-studio.com/eugeniadev/wp-content/uploads/2019/11/Eugenia_Lim_Yellow_Peril_PDF.02.pdf.

34. Gabby Loo and Gok-Lim Finch, *Seasons, Histories, and Hopes: Imagined Migrant Futures*, State Library of Western Australia, Perth, April 2019.

35. Joanna Bayndrian, 'A Merchant, A Miner and A Bushranger Walk into a Pub: John Young Zerunge and Jason Phu', *Runway*

Journal, issue 34, 2017, http://runway.org.au/a-merchant-a-miner-and-a-bushranger-walk-into-a-pub-john-young-zerunge-and-jason-phu/.

36. Ibid.

37. The broad contours of these debates can be traced in Kiera Lindsay, 'Deliberate freedom': using speculation and imagination in historical biography', *TEXT Special Issue, Life Narrative in Troubled Times*, no. 50, 2018; Tom Griffiths, 'History and the Creative Imagination', *History Australia*, 6:3, 74.1(74), 2009, pp. 1–16; Tony Birch, 'Footnote to a "History War" (Archive Box No. 2)', *Meanjin*, 2002; Greg Dening, 'Empowering Imaginations', *The Contemporary Pacific*, 9(2), 1997, pp. 419–29.

38. MacNeill, 'Undoing the Colonial Gaze: Ambiguity in the Art of Brook Andrew, *ANZJA journal*, volume 7, number 1, 2006, p.179.

39. Valerie Lovejoy, 'The Things that Unite: Inquests into Chinese deaths on the Bendigo Goldfields 1854–65 ', *Provenance: The Journal of Public Record Office Victoria*, no. 6, 2007, p. 10.

40. For discussion of 'White Australia' as an 'impossible' project see 'A Social Talk: A Drab Coloured Australia', *Examiner*, Launceston, Tasmania, 10 October 1903, p. 9.

41. See Behrendt, *Finding Eliza*.

42. Greg Dening, 'Empowering Imaginations', p. 421.

43. Tom Griffiths, 'History and the Creative Imagination', p. 5.

44. Inga Clendinnen, 'Fellow Sufferers: History and Imagination, *Australian Humanities Review*, September 1996, http://australianhumanitiesreview.org/1996/09/01/fellow-sufferers-history-and-imagination.

45. Ibid.

46. *The Lives of Celestials: John Young Zerunge* was held at Town Hall Gallery, Hawthorn Arts Centre, Boroondara, 31 August–20 October 2019. See 'John Young Zerunge prepares for The Lives of Celestials', 2019, https://www.boroondara.vic.gov.au/recreation-arts/boroondara-arts/discover-art/online-exhibitions/john-young-zerunge-lives-celestials.

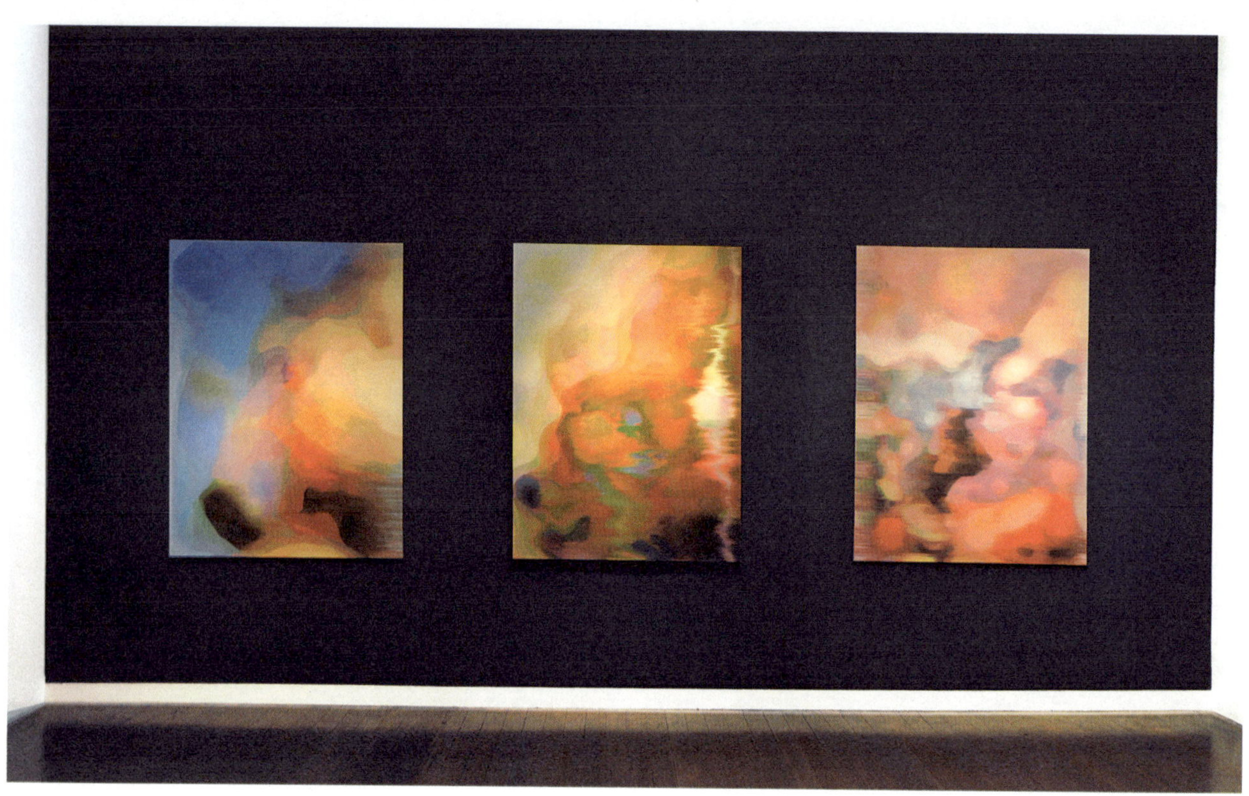

LKM (Blue, Gold, Pink) 2015
Installation view, ARC ONE Gallery,
Melbourne, 2015

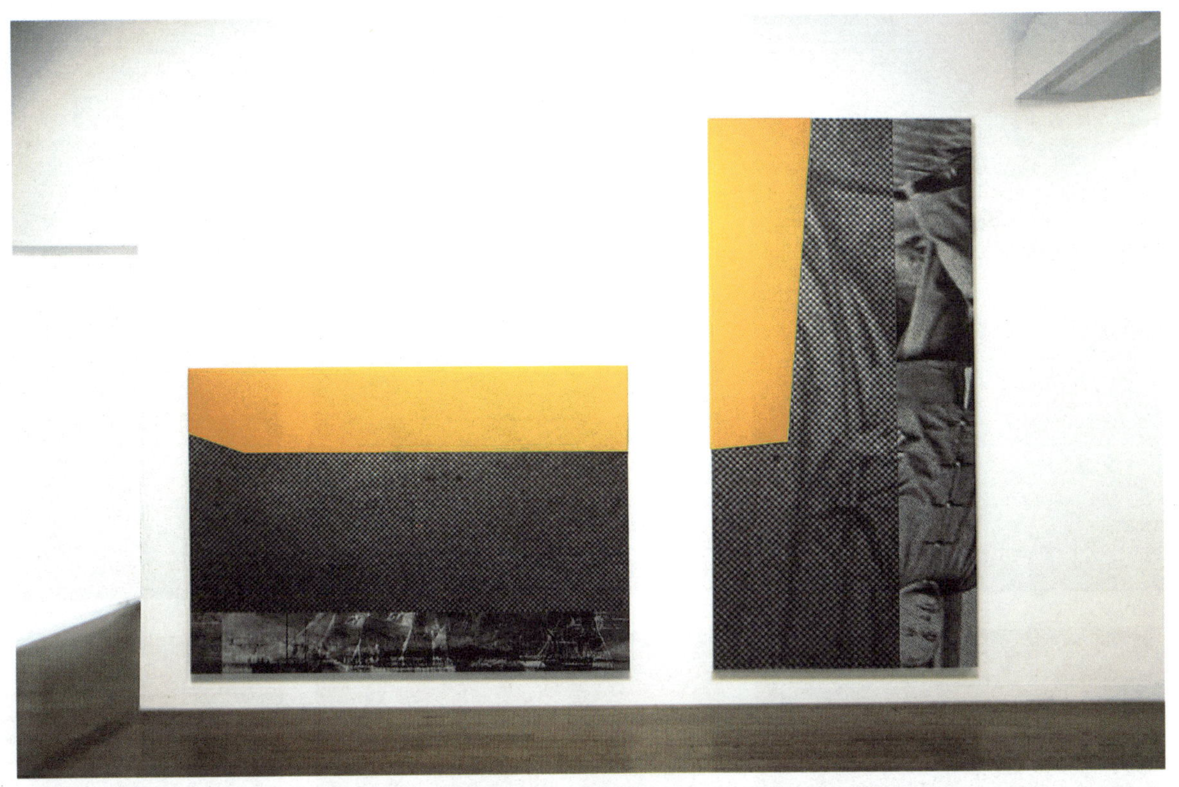

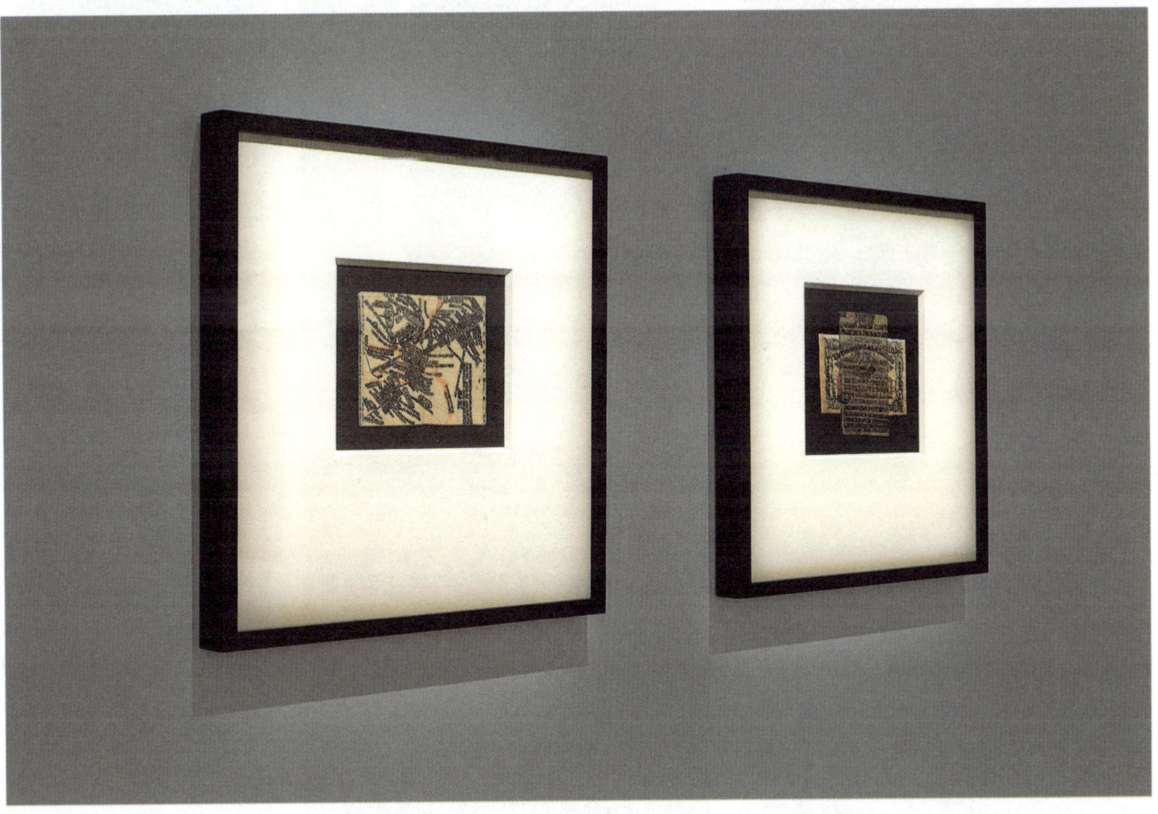

The Illustrious Fleet of Lowe Kong Meng
and *Lowe Kong Meng* 2015
Installation view, ARC ONE Gallery,
Melbourne, 2015

Cochran Town and *The Meeting* 2015
Installation view, Hawthorn Arts Centre,
Boroondara Arts, Melbourne, 2019

the vast dream
mimpi luas
唐末的夢
La grande rêve

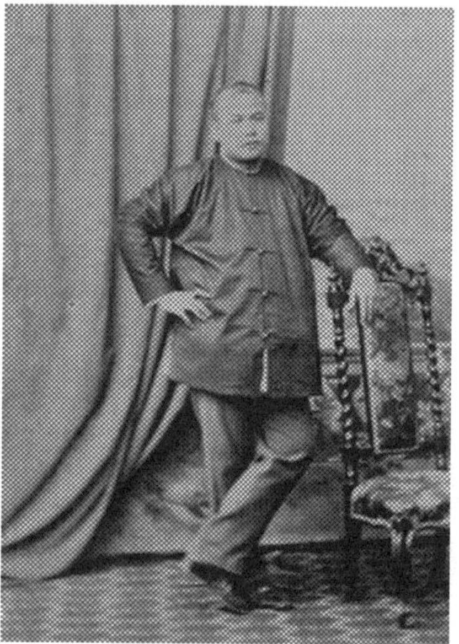

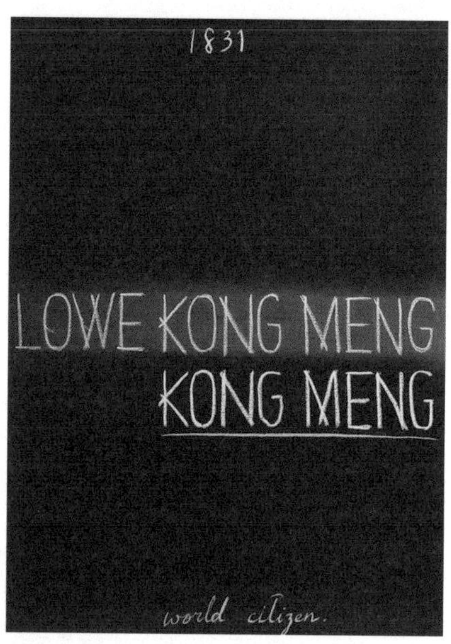
1831
LOWE KONG MENG
KONG MENG
world citizen.

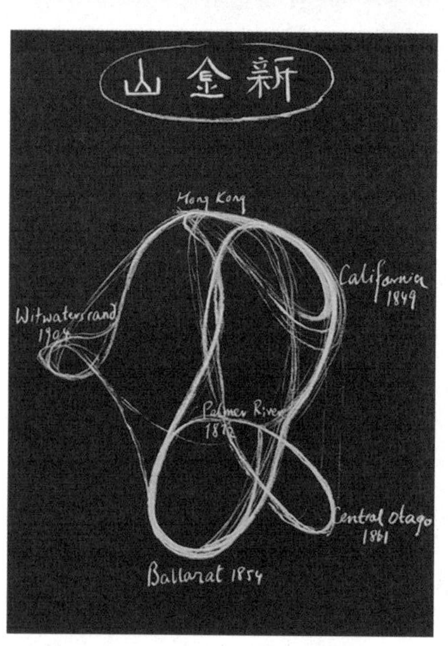
山金新
Hong Kong
California 1849
Witwatersrand 1904
Palmer River 1873
Central Otago 1861
Ballarat 1854
the vast dream mimpi luas

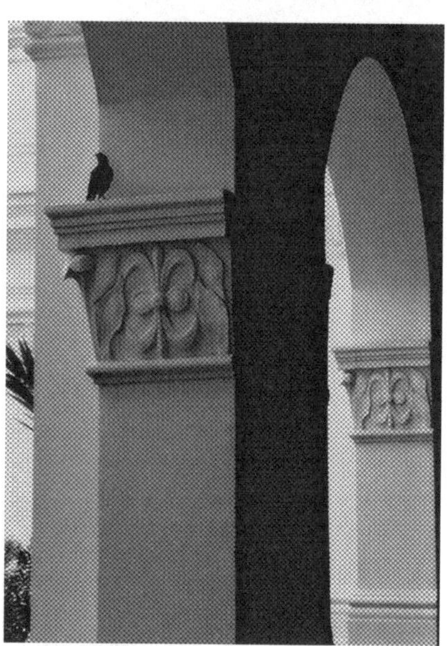

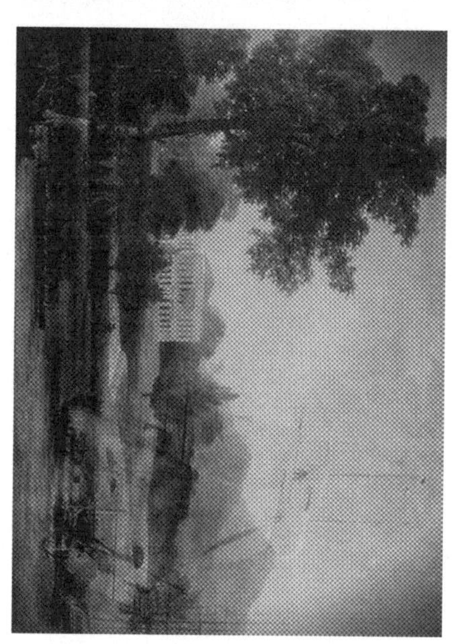

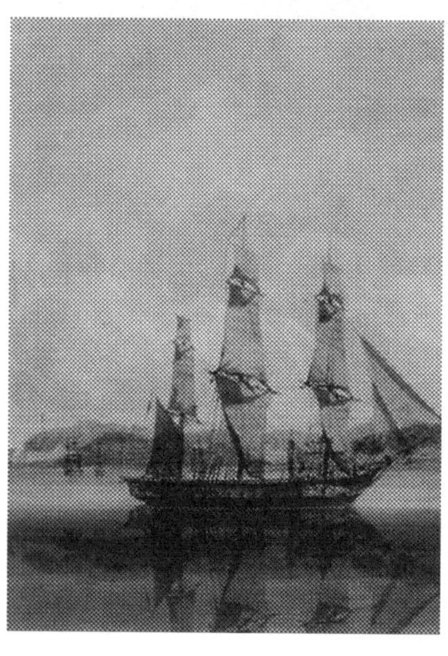

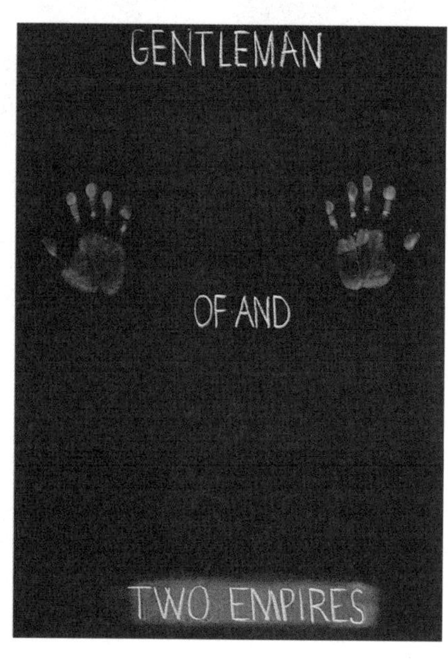
GENTLEMAN
OF AND
TWO EMPIRES

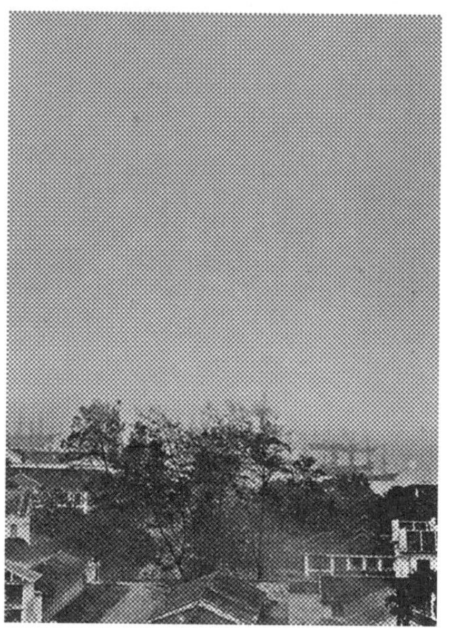

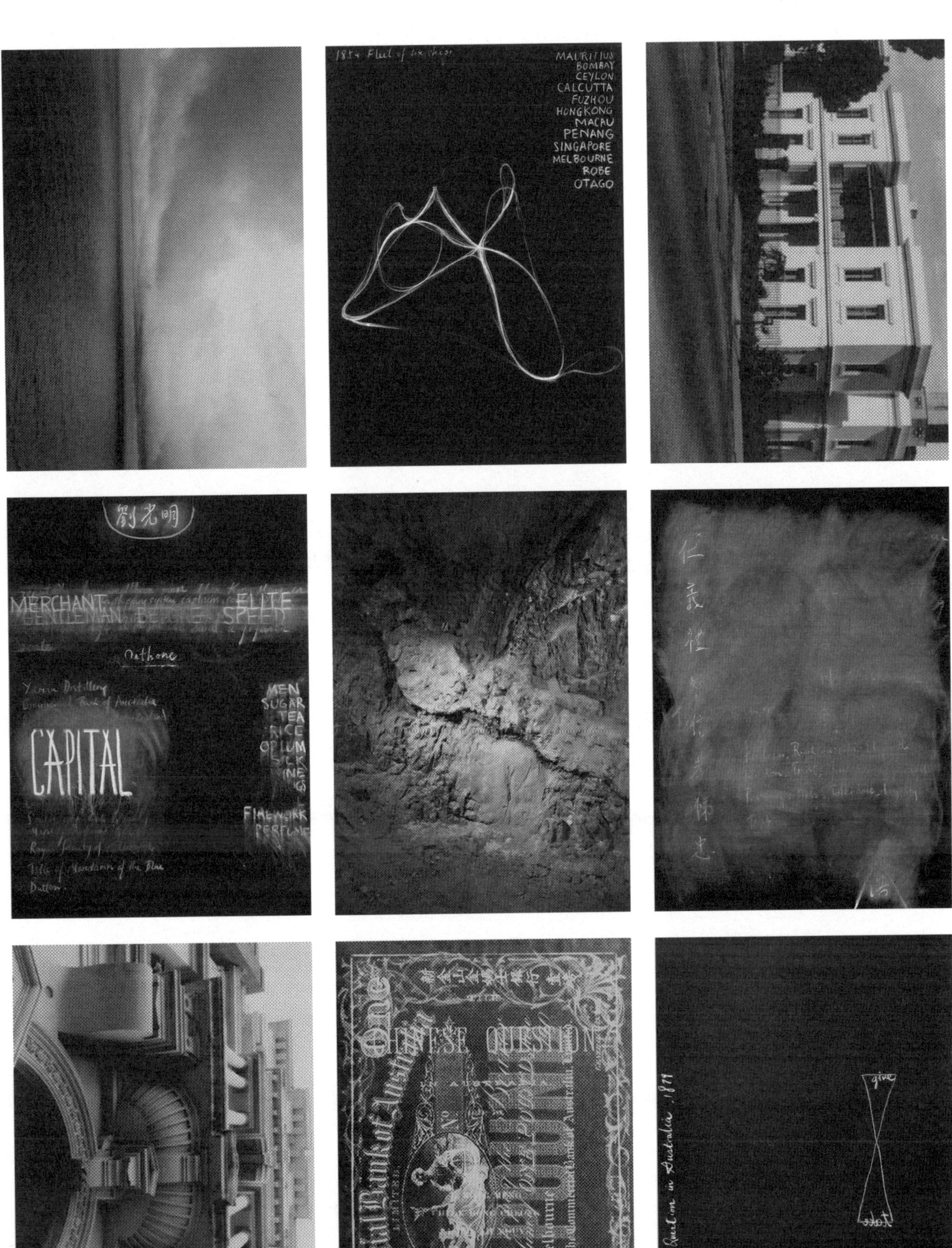

1854 Fleet of six ships
MAURITIUS
BOMBAY
CEYLON
CALCUTTA
FUZHOU
HONGKONG
MACAU
PENANG
SINGAPORE
MELBOURNE
KOBE
OTAGO
MERCHANT
GENTLEMAN
ELITE
SPEED
BEAUTY
Nathone
MEN
SUGAR
TEA
RICE
OPIUM
SILK
WINE
CAPITAL
FIREWORK
PERFUME
CHINESE QUESTION
One
Commercial Bank of Australia
The Chinese Question in Australia 1879
give
take

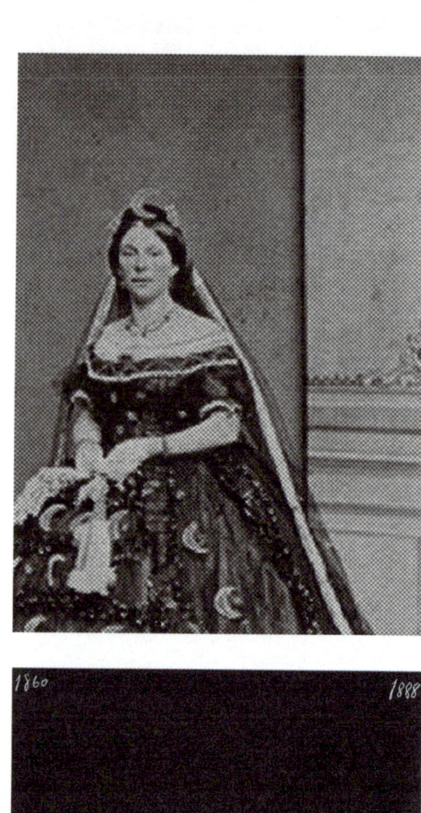

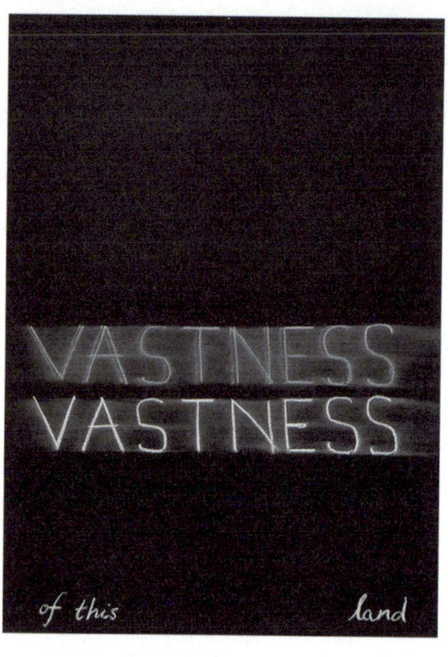
VASTNESS
VASTNESS
of this   land

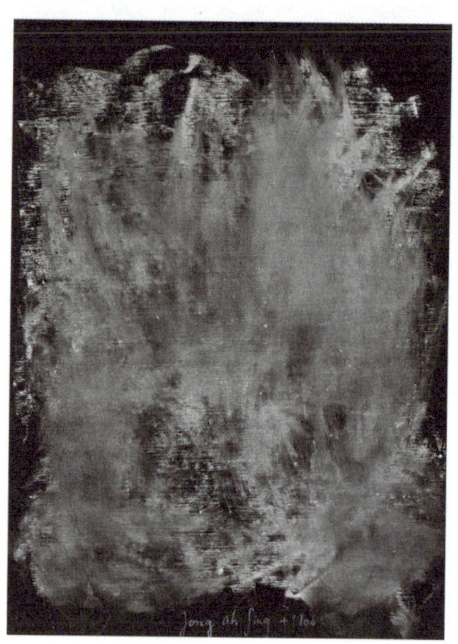
Jong ah Sing + Loo

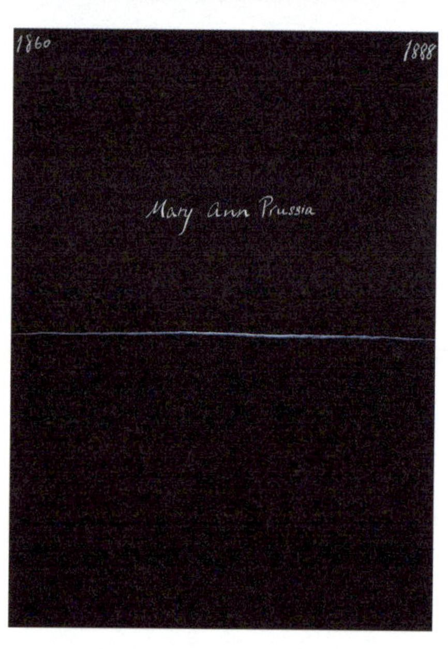
1860   1888
Mary Ann Prussia

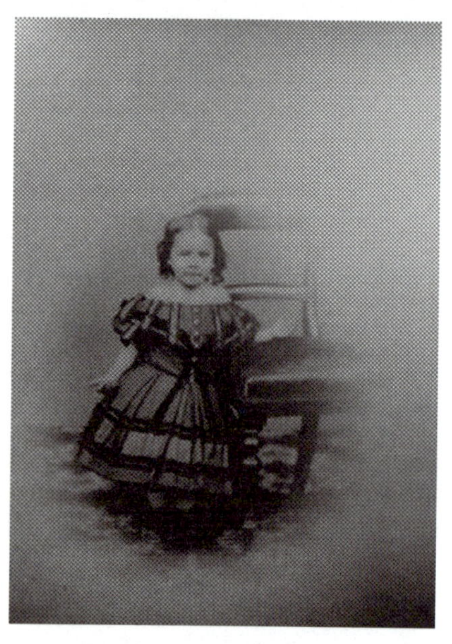

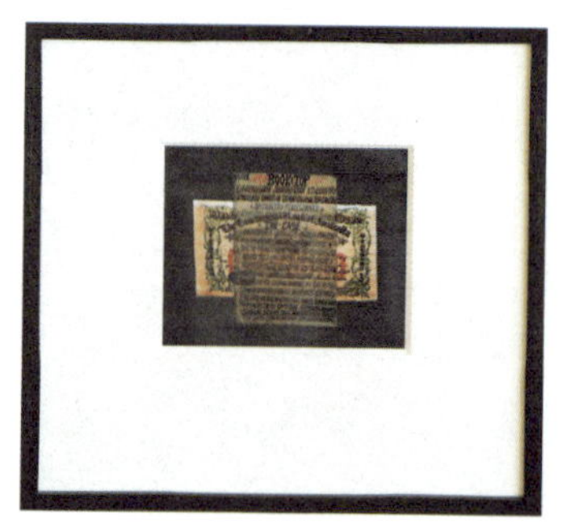

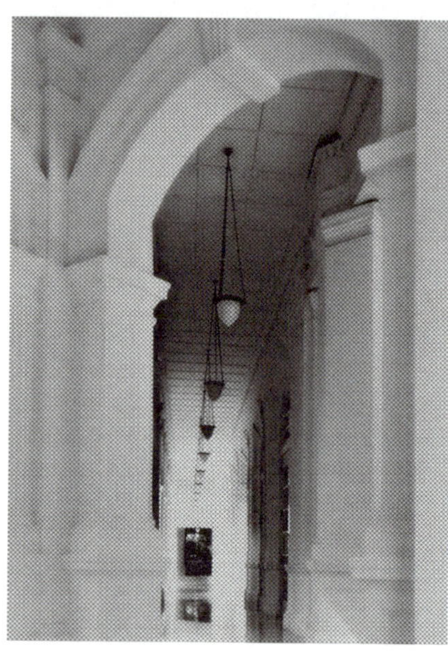

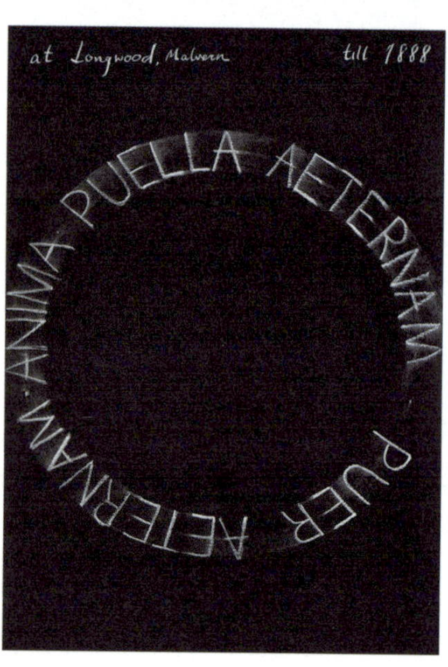
at Longwood, Malvern   till 1888
ANIMA · PUELLA AETERNAM · PUER AETERNAM ·

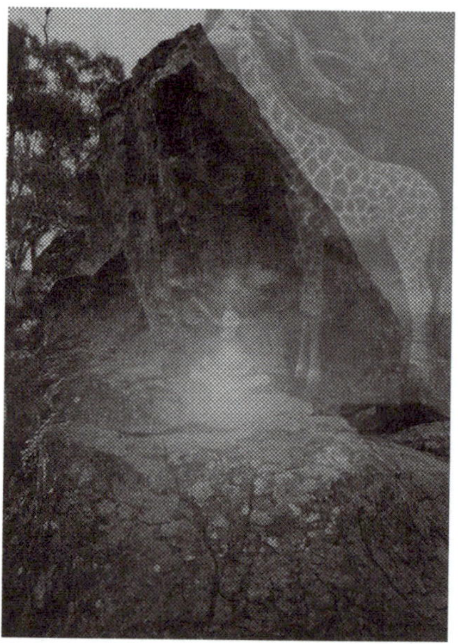

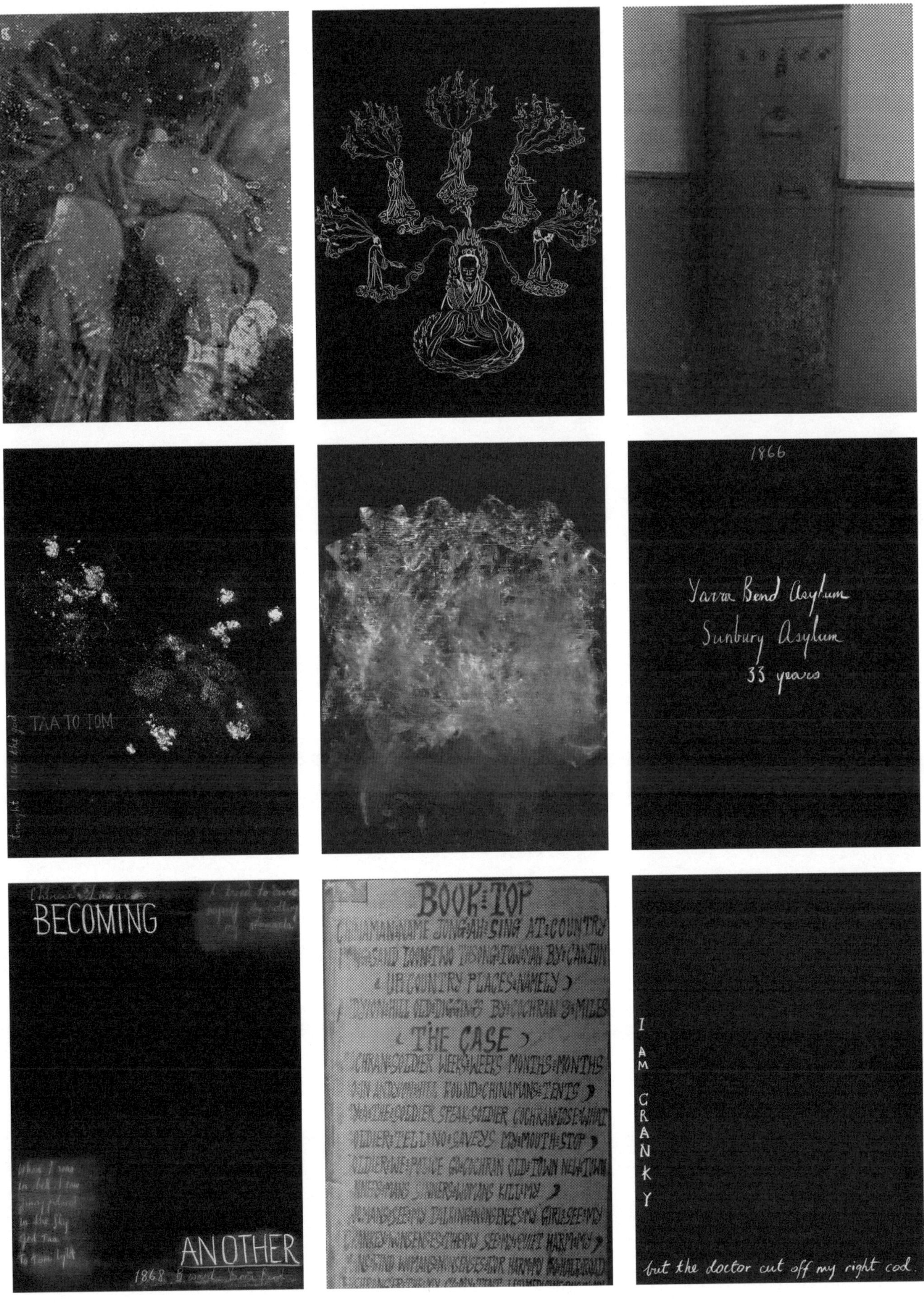
1866
TAA TO TOM
Yarra Bend Asylum
Sunbury Asylum
33 years
BECOMING
ANOTHER
BOOK TOP
THE CASE
I AM CRANKY
but the doctor cut off my right cod.

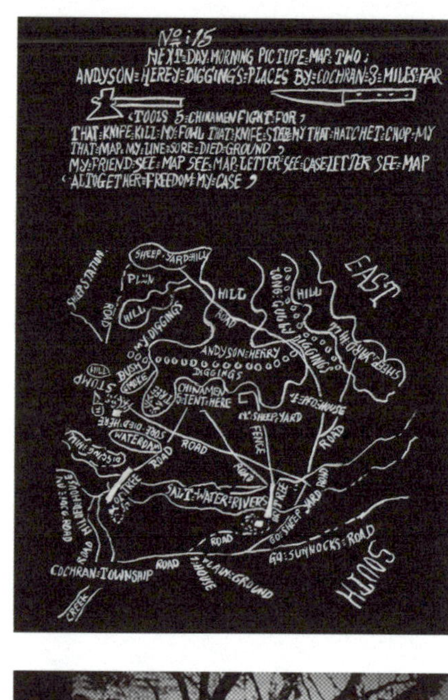

N°: 15
NEXT DAY MORNING PICTUPE MAP TWO;
ANDYSON HEREJ DIGGING'S PLACES BY COCHRAN 3 MILES FAR
‹ TOOLS 5 CHINAMEN FIGHT FOR ›
THAT KNIFE KILL NO FOWL THAT KNIFE STAB MY THAT HATCHET CHOP MY
THAT MAP MY LINE SORE DIED GROUND,
MY FRIEND SEE MAP SEE MAP LETTER SEE CASE LETTER SEE MAP
‹ ALTOGETHER FREEDOM MY CASE ›
SHEEP STATION
SHEEP YARD HILL
PLAN
ROAD
HILL
DIGGINGS
ANDYSON HERE
 DIGGINGS
HILL
ROAD
LONG GULLY
HILL
EAST
SHELLS
ORIENT HERE
FENCE
WATERHOLE
TEN PACE YARD
ROAD
THREE ROAD
ALT WATER RIVERS
PACE
ROAD
COCHRAN TOWNSHIP ROAD
WATER GROUND
SUMNOCKS ROAD
SOUTH

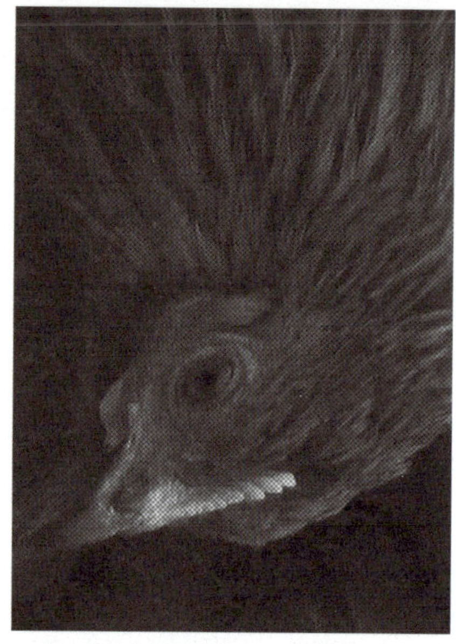

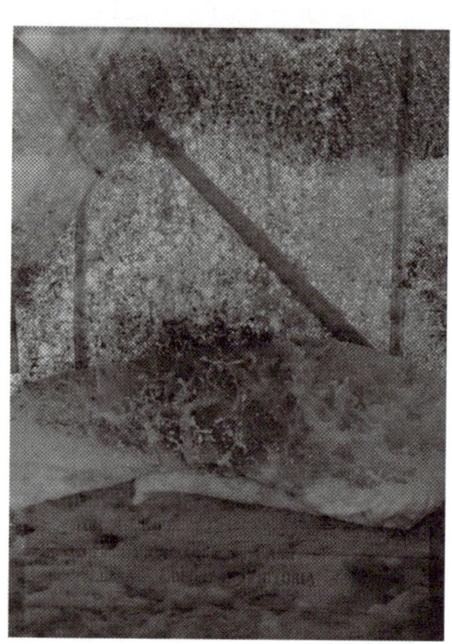

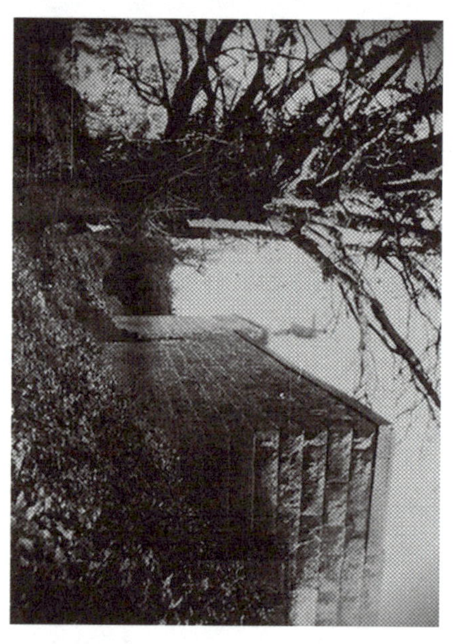

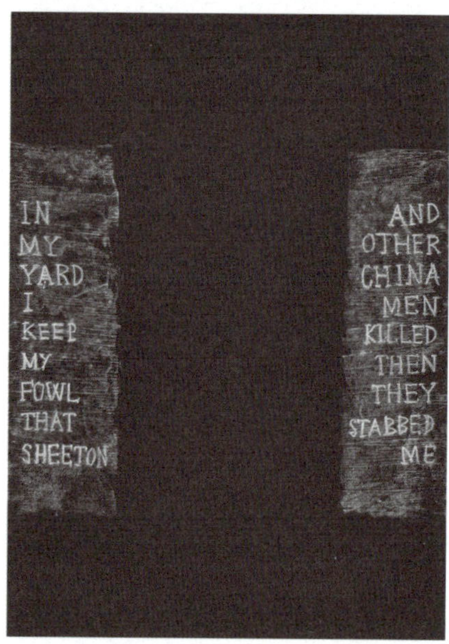

IN
MY
YARD
I
KEEP
MY
FOWL
THAT
SHEETON

AND
OTHER
CHINA
MEN
KILLED
THEN
THEY
STABBED
ME

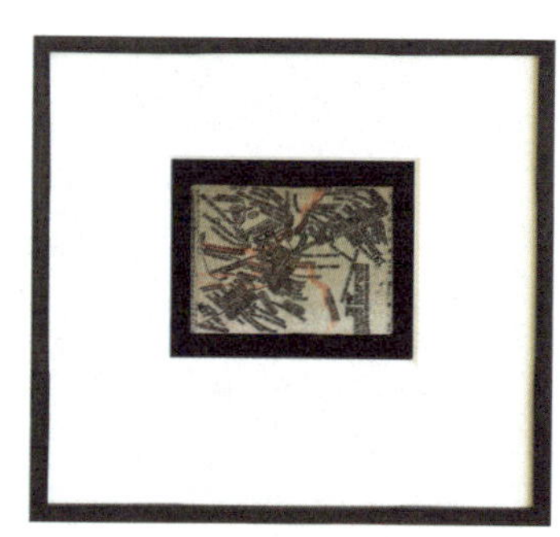

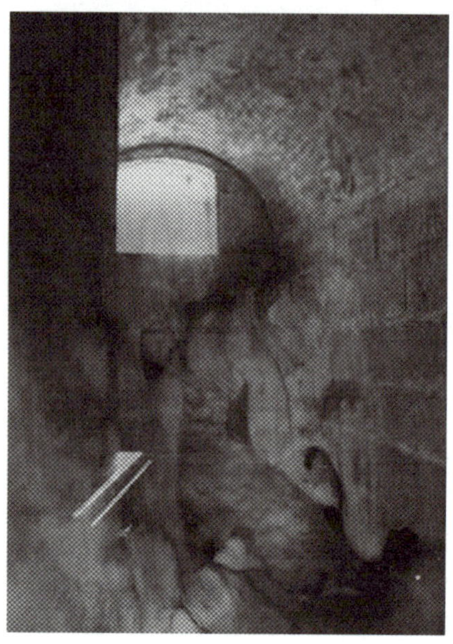

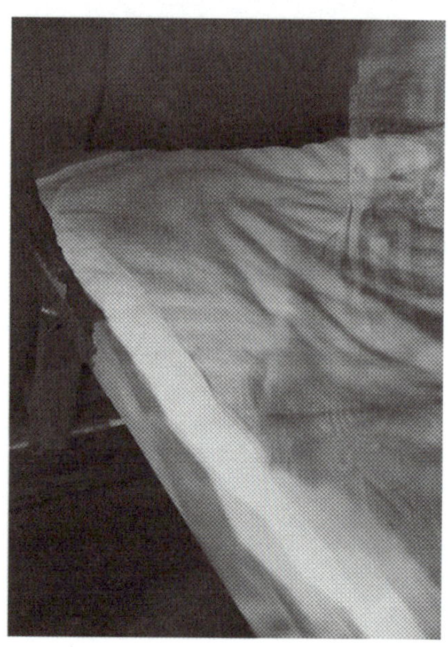

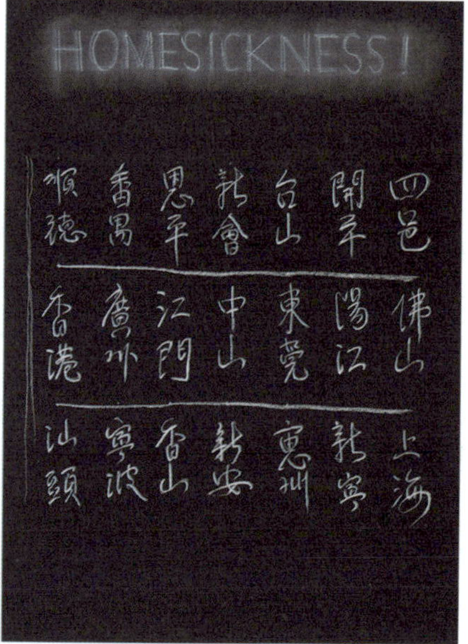

HOMESICKNESS !
四邑　開平　台山　新會　恩平　香邑　順德
佛山　陽江　東莞　中山　江門　廣州　香港
上海　新寧　惠州　新安　香山　寧波　汕頭

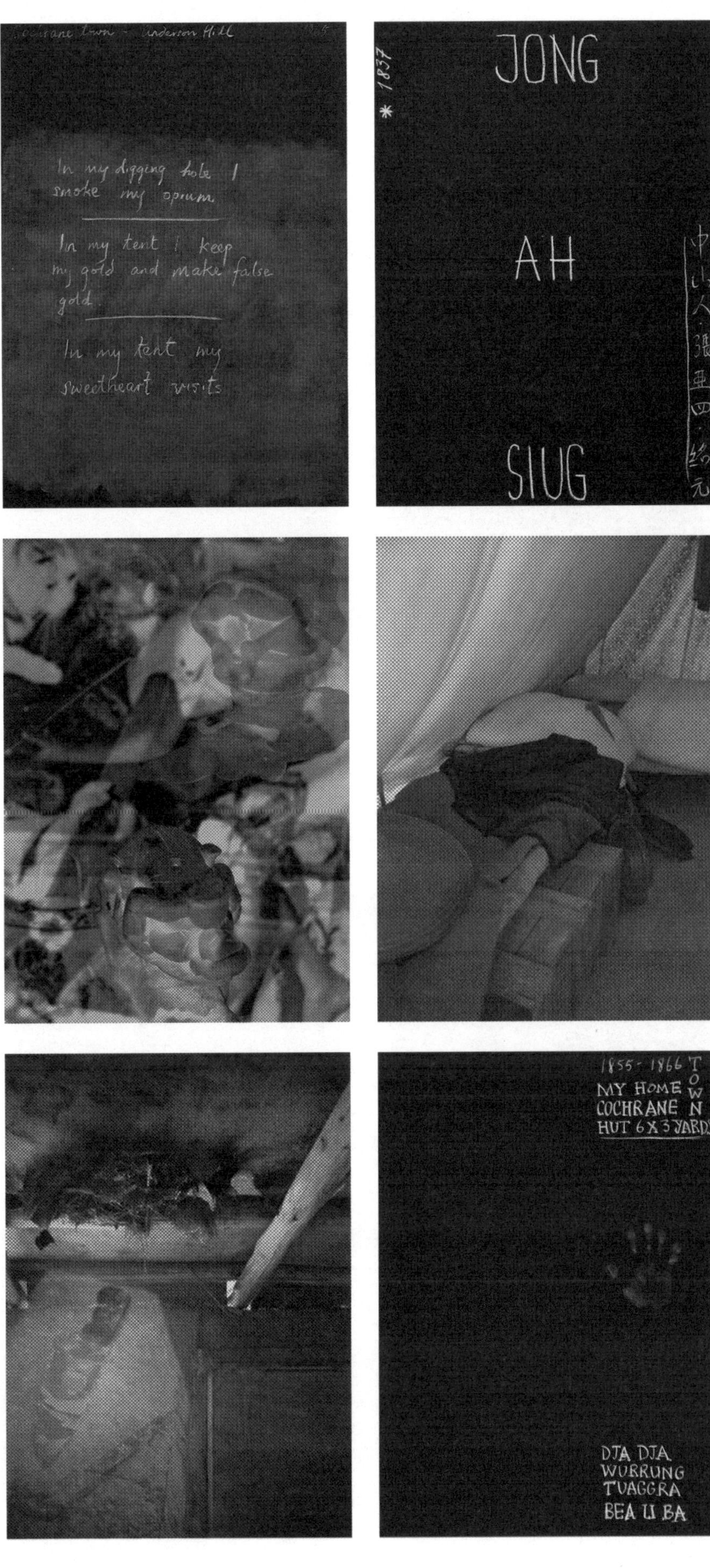

pages **248–53**
*The Worlds of Lowe Kong Meng and
Jong Ah Siug* 2015
Digital print on photographic paper and chalk
on blackboard-painted archival cotton paper;
49 units, 320 × 1350 cm
Collection of Town Hall Gallery, Boroondara
City Council, Melbourne

The Meeting (p. 250) and *Cochran Town*
(p. 252) 2015
Single thread hand-sewn embroidery,
framed, two units, 41 × 42 cm each
Collection of Town Hall Gallery, Boroondara
City Council, Melbourne

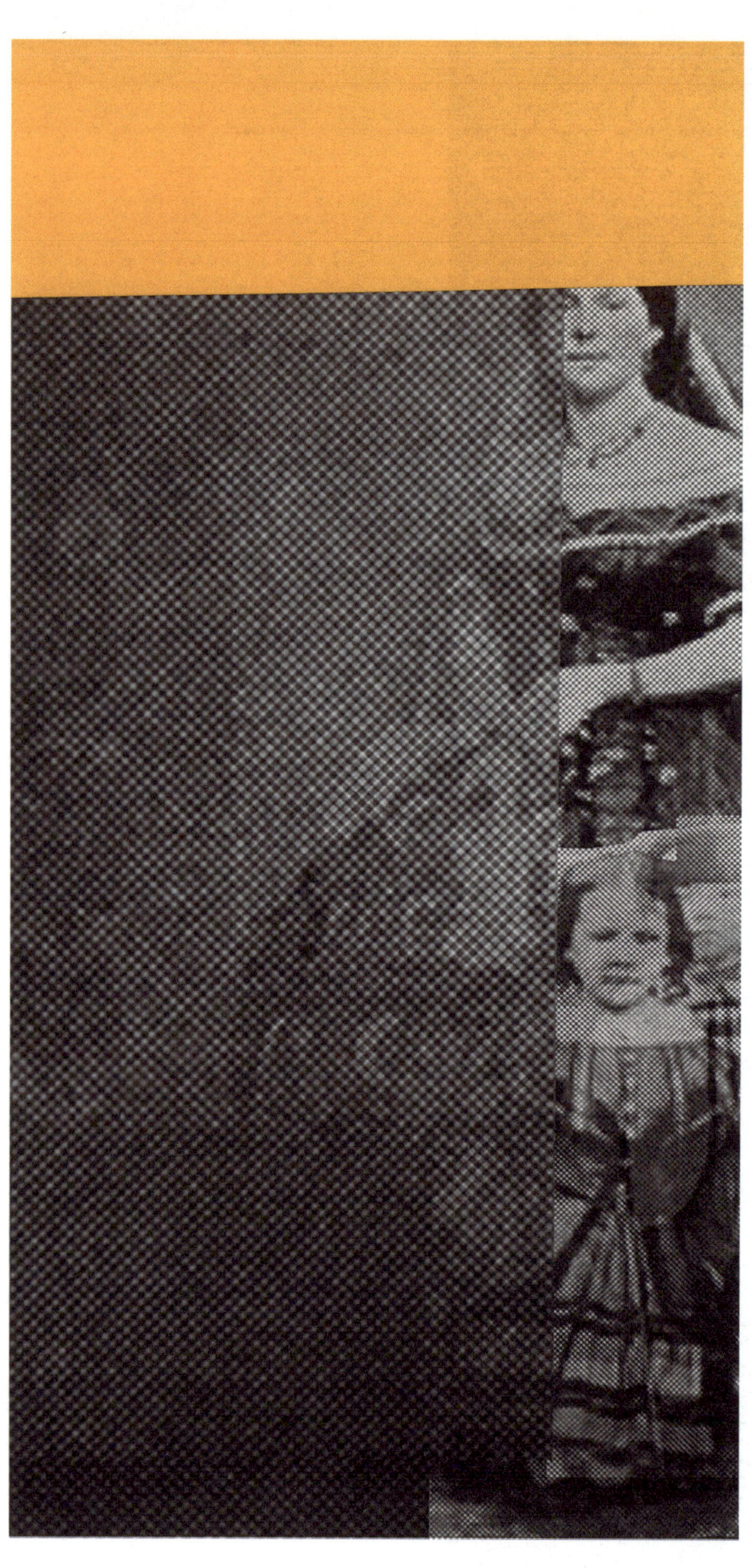

The Eternal 2015
Digital print and felt on canvas, 320 × 151 cm

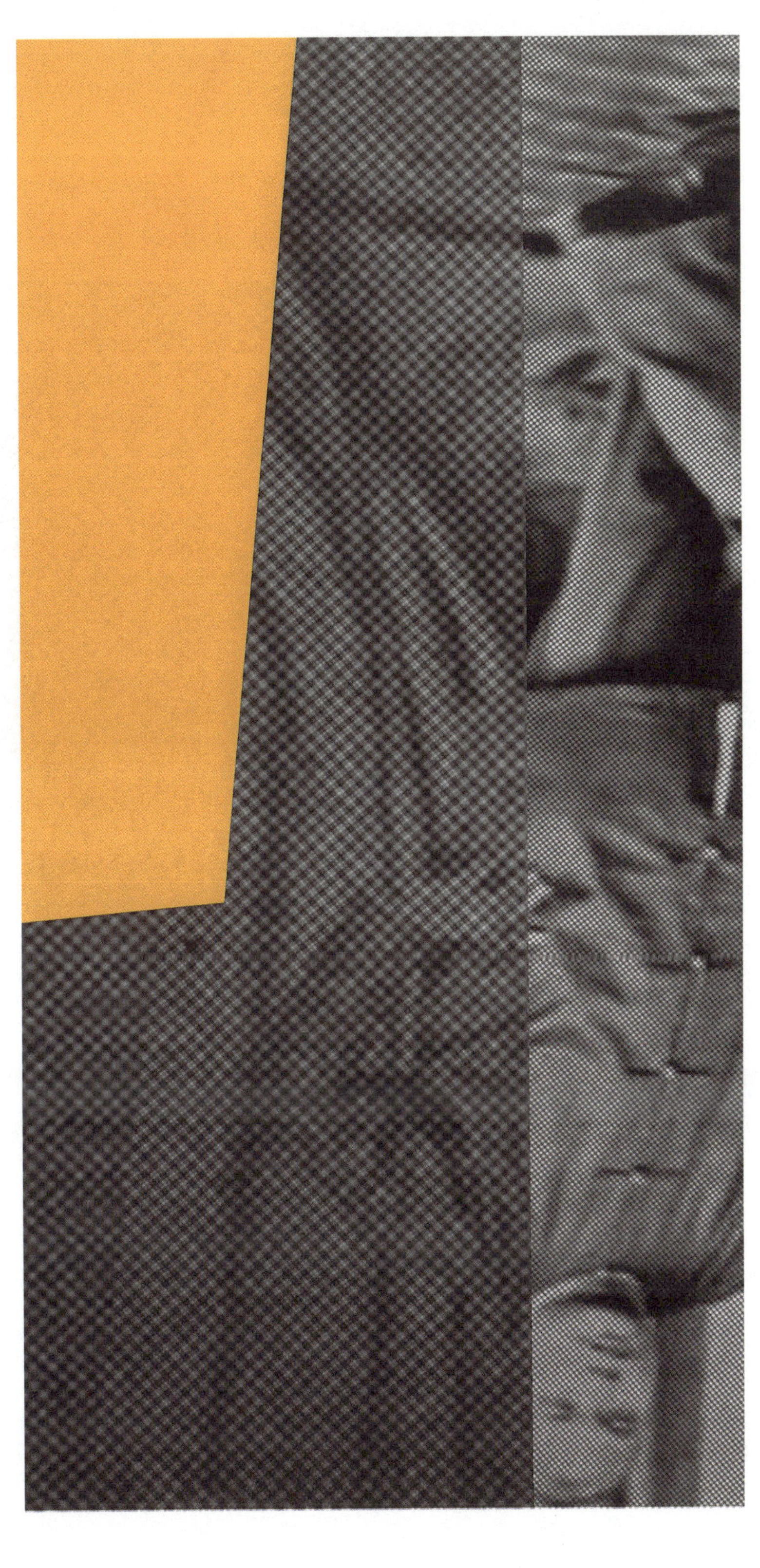

Lowe Kong Meng 2015
Digital print and felt on canvas, 320 × 151 cm

The Illustrious Fleet of Lowe Kong Meng, 2015
Digital print and felt on canvas, 250.5 × 175 cm

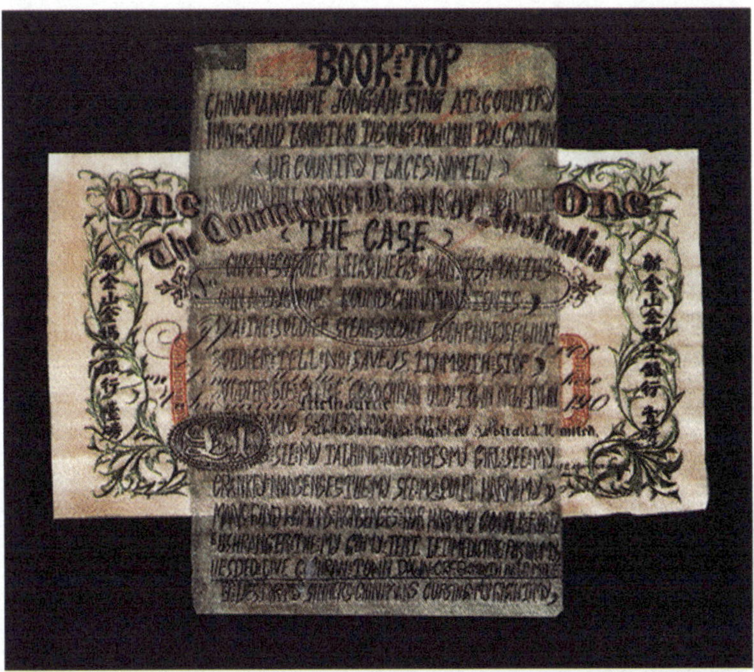

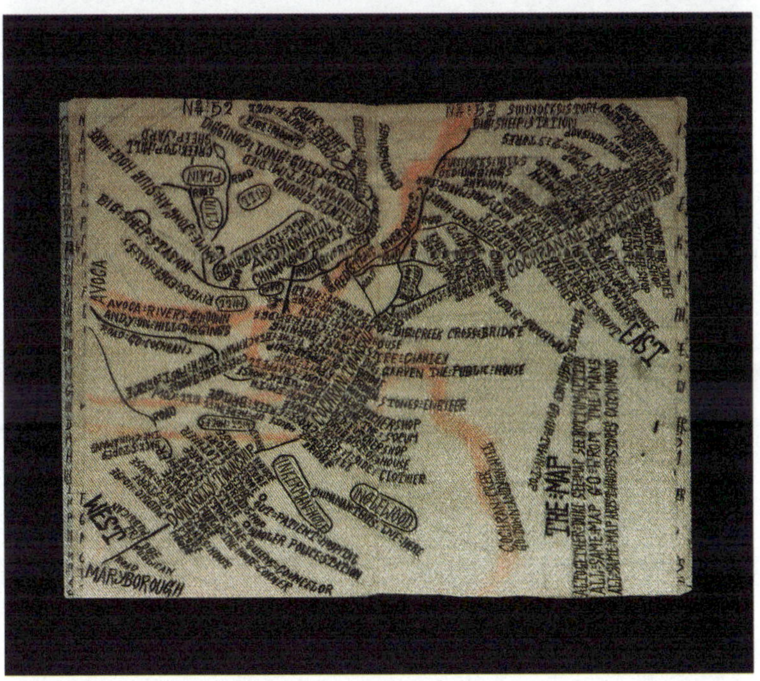

The Meeting 2015
Single thread hand-sewn embroidery,
framed, 41 × 42 cm
Collection of Town Hall Gallery, Boroondara
City Council, Melbourne

Cochran Town 2015
Single thread hand-sewn embroidery,
framed, 41 × 42 cm
Collection of Town Hall Gallery, Boroondara
City Council, Melbourne

OPEN MONUMENT

2015

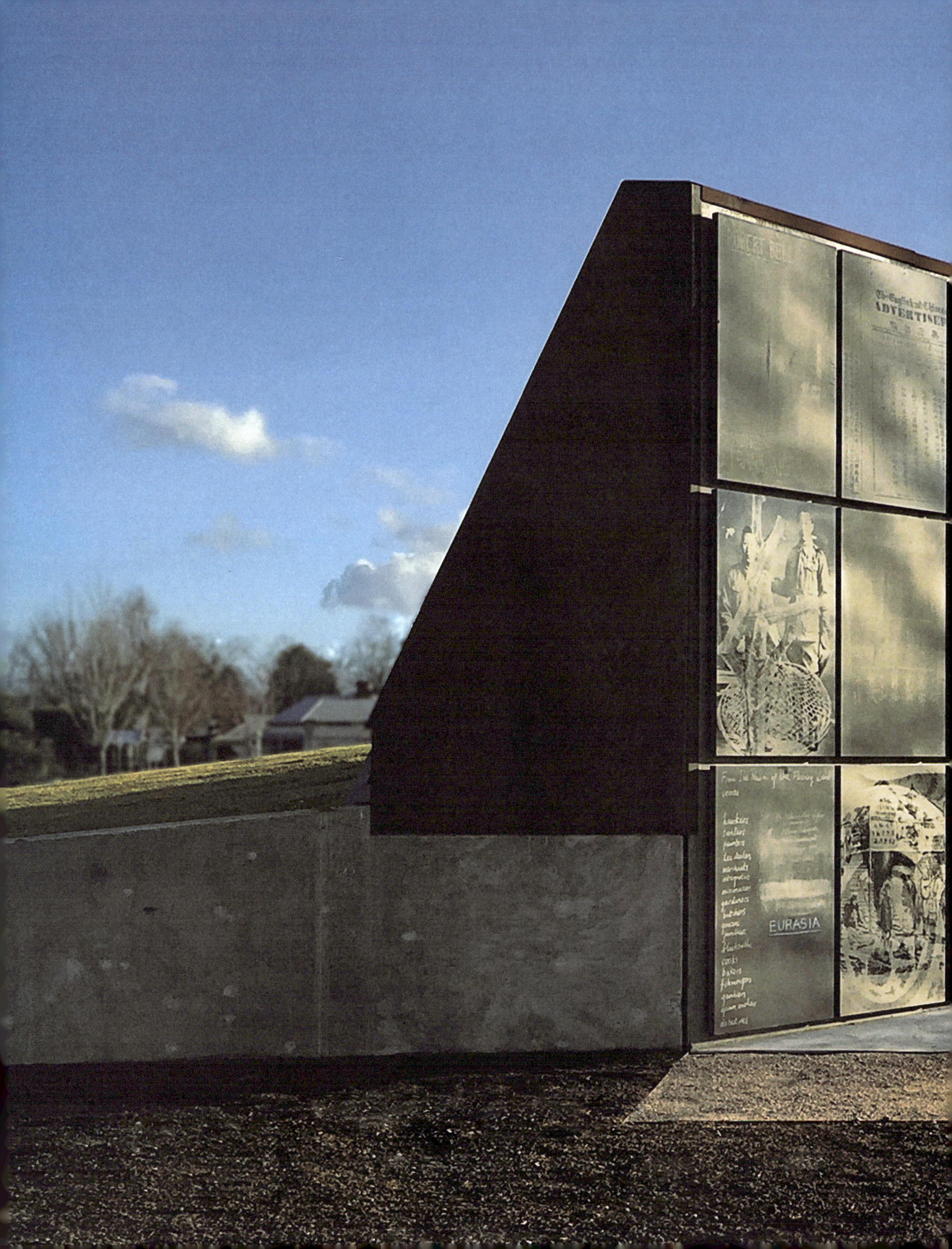
ALBERT PARK
The English and Chinese
ADVERTISER
From the History of the Mining Laws
hawkers
tinkers
tailors
tea dealers
merchants
interpreters
missionaries
gardeners
butchers
grocers
furniture
cabinetmakers
cooks
bakers
fishmongers
jewellers
storekeepers
and last of all
EURASIA

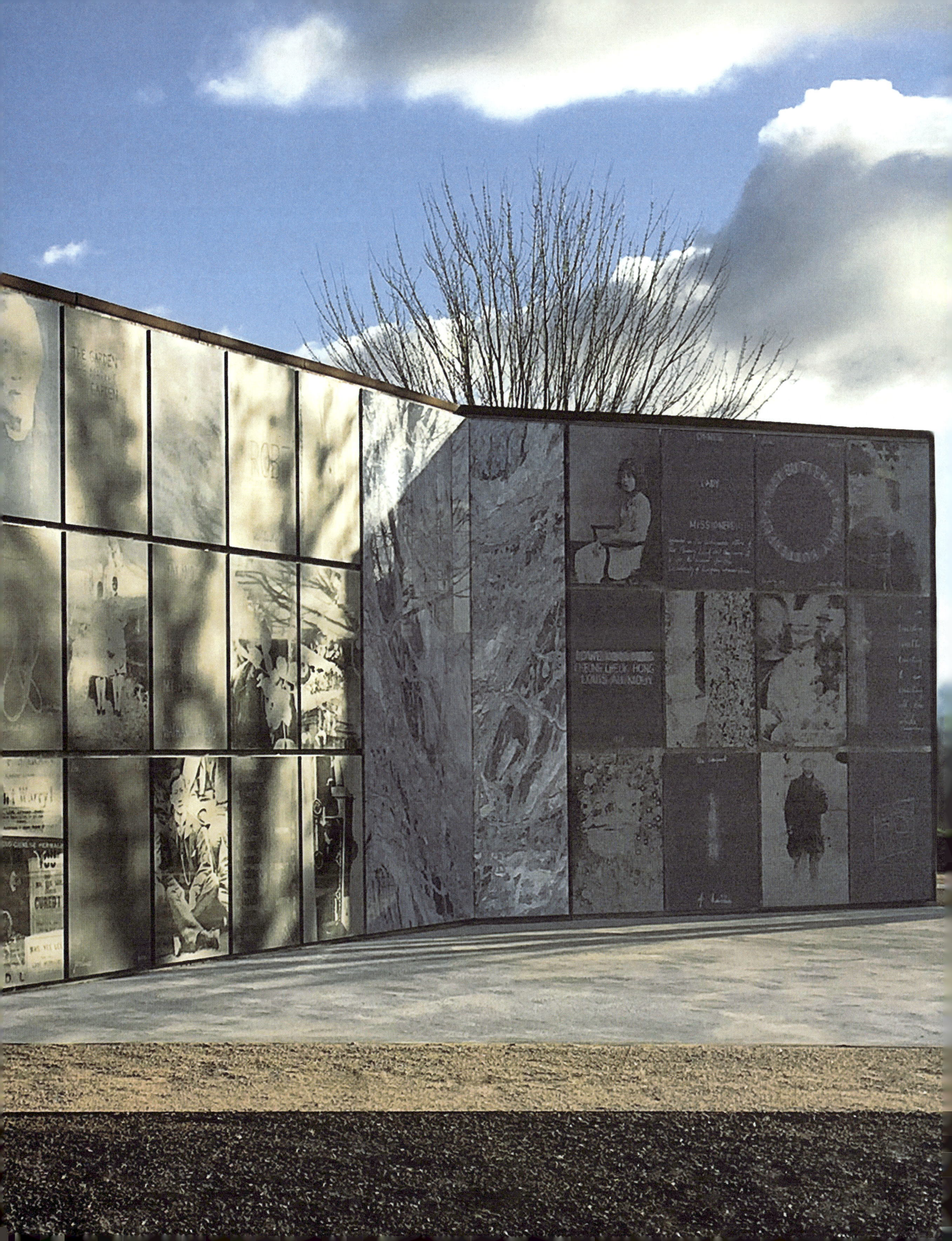

OPEN MONUMENT

The discovery of gold in Ballarat in 1851 sparked an influx of people within
days. Between 1851 and 1853, Ballarat was the world's richest alluvial goldfield,
attracting Chinese miners alongside prospectors from the United Kingdom, Europe
and the United States of America. By 1861, some 43,657 Chinese had entered the
colony of Victoria, predominantly from the southern regions of China. Many of
them stayed, making Ballarat and surrounds their home.

Open Monument (2015) is a public art commission comprising two artworks
permanently installed in Ballarat. The first, *Transculture*, consists of 33 laser-etched
granite panels, which are formally consistent with the chalkboard drawings and
archival images of other History Projects. The panels are divided into two banks,
which extend outwards from two large bilaterally symmetrical marble planes to
form a 'folding' wall. From the rear, *Transculture* resembles a shovel embedded
in a large grassy mound, referring to Ballarat's gold mining history. The second
artwork, *Timeline*, consists of 33 etched stone panels installed in the ground, which
extend over 40 metres, chronicling the major contributions of Ballarat's Chinese
community in every decade from 1850 to the present. The timeline folds out with
blank panels anticipating the year 2170, thus leaving the monument 'open' to
future records.

The drawings and photographs in *Open Monument* feature a range of stories and
images, including: a series of Chinese diasporic networks of gold miners that
connect southern China, California, Victoria, Central Otago and Witwatersrand;
pioneer translators; the walk that Chinese miners made from Robe to Ballarat
in the 1800s to avoid the Victorian poll tax; Ballarat's Joss House and Red Lion
Hotel; Australia's earliest bilingual newspapers; Chinese swagmen and middle-
class leisure activities; texts and precepts from Chinese secret societies such as the
Tiandihui 天地會 ('Heaven and Earth Society', also known as hung mun 洪門);
market gardens; Chinese-Australian soldiers bound for World War II; and life
on the goldfields.

The project was developed by The City of Ballarat's Public Art Advisory
Committee and was commissioned by Sovereign Hill in association with the City
of Ballarat and members of the Ballarat and Melbourne Chinese communities.

ARTIST STATEMENT

Studio notes (2015)

During our period of concept development and research I was moved by the
enthusiasm and spontaneous help we received from so many local residents. They
shared with us many inspirational lessons. To give just some examples: a father
and son's walk from Robe; a family who took care of the last swagman of Ballarat,
William Lung, alias Billy Butterfly, and held him in their hands till he took his last
breath; the reconstruction of the Ballarat Chinese cemetery; as well as historians
who have given so much to shape this chapter of Ballarat's history. Yet, historical
epochs are never final, each generation comes along and joins the dots differently,
and that is why this work is named *Open Monument*. Most important, though,
is that a memory is present, and that this memory calls for our empathy.

Reflection (2022)

Of all the projects, *Open Monument* reaches deep within the social function of the
History Projects. The social ramifications of introducing Chinese Australian history
were indeed immediate to this city, but the project was also structured to allow for
generations to come to configure the meaning of Ballarat history in their own way.
Yet, most importantly, by bringing these narratives into the forefront of Ballarat
history, it facilitated a sense of agency over that history for the Chinese community
that I had never imagined possible. It really brought home the importance of
visual-cultural actualisation, and the devastation of invisibility and silence that has
been rendered in Australian history and cultural history in the past. The becoming
of Australian visual-cultural history will only be possible if active imaginings
are allowed and invited—it is in a culture of hospitality, not one of defence nor
authority, that this becoming may perhaps be possible.

ACKNOWLEDGEMENTS

For their contribution towards realising *Open Monument*, John Young would like
to especially acknowledge: John Young Studio, Times Two Architects, the City of
Ballarat and its Public Art Advisory Committee, Ballarat Chinese Community
Association Inc, Chinese Australian Cultural Society Ballarat Inc, The Ballarat
China Community Committee, DJ Projects, Vivid Civil, Pyrenees Quarries, Butler
Excavations, Charles Zhang, Shirley Doon, Jim Quinn and many community
members who shared their stories. John also thanks the Mayor of the City of
Ballarat, the Honourable Joshua Morris, for the ground-breaking ceremony; council
members Julie Collins and Daniel Henderson; the Sovereign Hill Museums Trust
Board; Emeritus Professor Terry Lloyd, and Jeremy Johnson; as well as the financial
donors through the good work of patron and Golden Crown Restaurant owner,
Henry Thai.

The artist would also like to acknowledge that *Open Monument* stands on the
unceded lands of the Wadawurrung and Dja Dja Wurrung people.

pages 260–61
Open Monument 2015
Architectural monument, 430 sq m
Len T. Fraser Reserve, Ballarat
Collection of Ballarat City Council

OPEN MONUMENT: IN CONVERSATION WITH VENITA POBLOCKI

Venita Poblocki

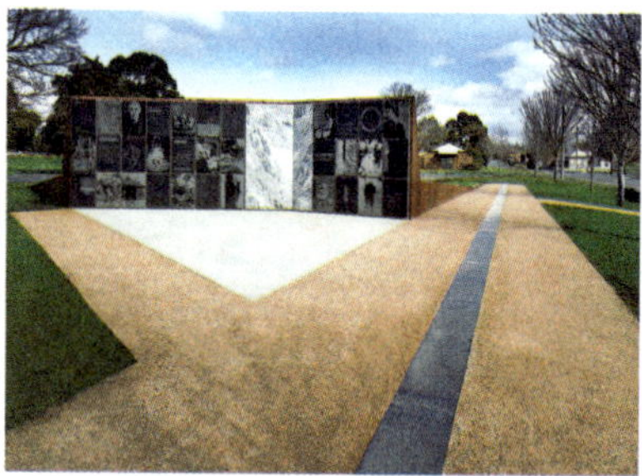

The following interview occurred over email between September and November, 2020.

Venita Poblocki: Your first public monument, titled *Open Monument*, came to fruition after your concept was selected in a competition initiated by the Ballarat Council in 2012. The intention of the monument was to commemorate the important history of the Chinese in the area. When conceptualising the monument, did you feel a greater sense of historic responsibility than you would in an impermanent exhibition context?

John Young: In a sense, my responsibility lies with the community who are still in Ballarat. My original thinking process was that, given the monument was to be a permanent work, people of different generations in the future would come along and construct their own version of history or engage with the narratives presented, based on their contemporaneous life needs and social context. I still believe this to be the case. Hence, I understood my job to be only the provision of some signposts or parameters to spark engagement. As for the images and words, I was aware that their meaning would change based on the context in which they were seen over time. There's a linguistic divide between this way of looking at the meaning of image and text, in contrast with a more 'verificationist' view within the discipline of academic history.

Yet, because of the generally under-recognised nature of the Australian histories that this monument is dealing with, even the generic signposts of these narratives that I was working with were not generally acknowledged or known publicly until they were made visible on the monument. In general, a monument and its accompanying rhetoric has a sense of finality and an indelible quality that I ultimately find problematic. There is a responsibility to put in slippages and ambiguities, so we all consider our ethical relation to the narratives as they are presented differently over time. As with the other History Projects, it is the rhetorical framework that invites people to take on an ethical attitude that is most important, especially in these transformative times when human consciousness is merging with the cybernetic.

VP: In 2012, you began your research with a wide-reaching team into the Chinese Diaspora in Australia from the Gold Rush onwards, funded by your Fellowship grant from the Australia Council (2012–14). In this research, you and your team resurrected many historical narratives—such as the Sam Family, whose five sons served in the Australian Imperial Force during World War I,[1] or Ah Hong, who brought his three Chinese Indigenous children back to Southern China after their mother, Western Arrernte woman Ranjika, passed away in childbirth.[2] Was there a level of community consultation in seeking these histories? If so, did you feel an onus to preserve their memories?

JY: This sort of research could not have happened without community consultation. In fact, people still guard their family histories dearly; you find them kept in piles of notepapers in shoe boxes, carefully preserved. Some narratives are guarded out of pride, others shame, or even a sense of vulnerability, yet they are inevitably treasured. I'm not a historian, so it was not within my capabilities to preserve or analyse individual or family memories in a wider societal context. It was, however, my duty to respect the community's generosity and the risk they feel in their telling.

Open Monument 2015
Architectural monument, 430 sq m
Len T. Fraser Reserve, Ballarat
Collection of Ballarat City Council

Yet, always, at the back of my mind, I felt that much of this history Australia had, at one point, not wanted to know, nor for it to exist, and it was this sense of muffling that I felt occasionally present in the fear of people who guarded their histories. As if, were it made wholly or partially public, they could still be vilified for making Chinese Australian narratives come alive in the public imagination. This is how deep and subtle racist pushback, and its mechanisms of historical denialism, can be. That encourages an artist, I believe, to exercise the responsibility to awaken these stories, to push past the first gate of barbaric cultural muffling at least, so that there is a hope that one day we can connect with the vitality of these narratives.

In fact, just last year there was a conference on Chinese Australian and New Zealand history in Wellington, and a paper was given regarding the Ballarat community suggesting that since the monument was erected in 2015, a lot of the anxious disagreements amongst the different Chinese groups have dissipated, due, I suspect, to the fact that fragments of their past can now be heard.[3] I hope this is true, for then the monument would have done something important. But ultimately, how different ethnic groups connect with this land, over time, is a critical thing for Australians to understand in our capacity to live in and connect with this place.

VP: Despite extensive research, due to the passing of time and lack of record keeping, there must have been many narrative gaps too. Typically, in your exhibitions this opens a way to incorporate creative re-imaginings. Was this public monument a place where you felt there was room to incorporate levels of fiction or imaginative truths, or did it demand not straying from the facts that were uncovered?

JY: In fact, there were so many narratives—the history is so unbelievably rich with evocative and heart-wrenching narratives—that there was barely any space nor need to fictionalise. You are talking about a whole community, through time, who have been here since 1840. You sort of become part of this community as you hear the stories and as you reimagine them, and it is so wonderful to look at it from the molecular level and stay there in their powerfully instructive presence. There is an awe and sublimity when you confront all these narratives; they are lives lived and to be lived again [through the work].

VP: And to this point, did you at times, feel like you had an ethical responsibility to work in direct opposition to the White Australia Policy and the historical realities it had attempted to erase?

JY: Yep. And with later projects, like *The Burrangong Affray*, it became very obvious how that primitive erasure is still very much alive, thank you. The pushback that you receive for bringing even the most innocent narratives to light; the silence, implied rage, the political dog whistling or out-and-out slander directed from certain insecure quarters was very, very surprising.[4] I thought I was living in a civil society; then I realised that I live in a very protected, civil, educated and generous cultural bubble in this young country. Defensive, nineteenth-century colonialism loves to erase difference, or at least turn difference into an object of subjugation, and to continue to propagate the mythic colonial narrative of heroic monoculturalism in the public imagination. This is not a question of occupation of land and power, because we ultimately need diverse narratives to generate a thorough understanding of the

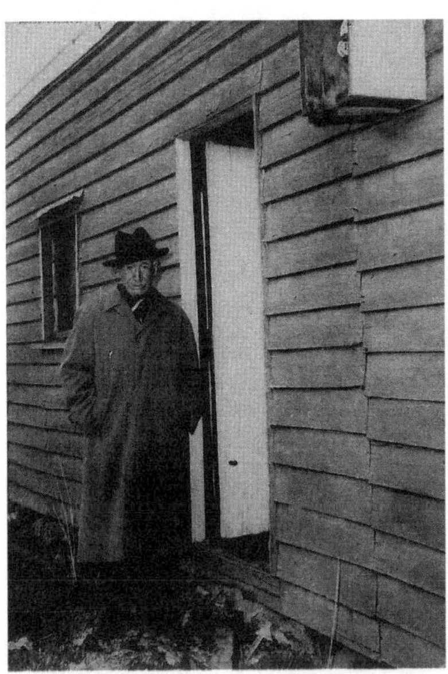

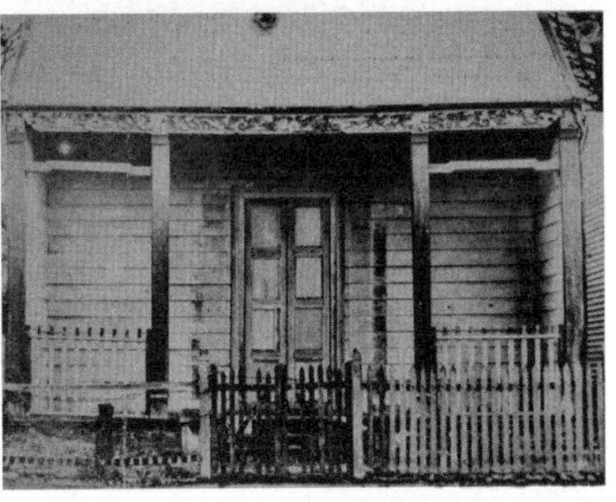

Billy Butterfly (born Willian Leung), a Chinese swagman, outside his house in Ballarat

The first Chinese Joss House in Ballarat, c. 1800s
On the present site of *Open Monument* 2015
Ballarat Historical Society Photograph Collection

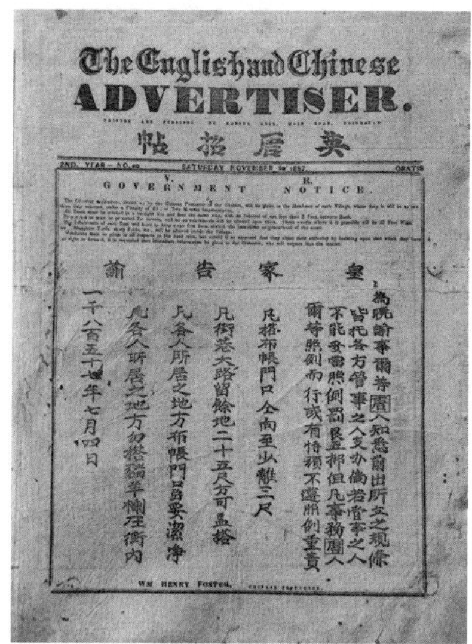

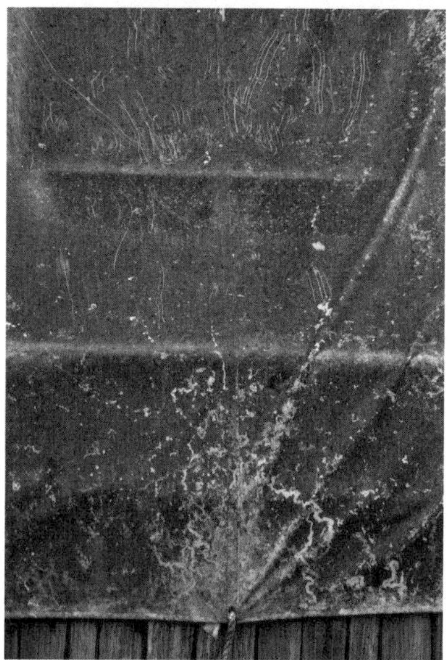

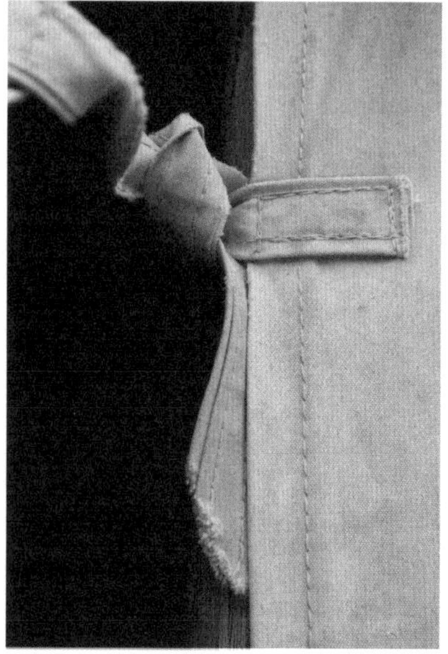

The English and Chinese Advertiser (1856–58),
28 November 1857, Ballarat, Victoria
The earliest bilingual Chinese–English newspaper
in Australia, published in Ballarat every Saturday
by Robert Bell, with a circulation of 400.
Victorian Collections

Exterior details of recreated goldminers' tents,
Sovereign Hill, Ballarat, 2015
Photograph by the artist

land—which aspects of a culture work for this land, and which aspects don't, with
a perceivable resolution in the distant future. The defensive mindset of Sidney Nolan's
Ned Kelly in a hostile landscape, which is a wonderful and accurate description
of the old condition, has to give way to a radical pluralism. We need to find methods
to live in harmony with the natural world here, we can't ravage it as human beings;
otherwise, as Paul Virilio warns, nature can answer back, and show us a thing or two.

VP: The monument is an experiential image bank. The dynamic range of historic
photographs incorporated in *Open Monument* spans the better-known histories of
the Chinese as early gold miners through to, in many cases, their transition to market
gardening, yet it also challenges the viewers' preconceptions with many lesser-known
histories. We see striking images of the early Chinese involvement in academic
circles, as soldiers bound for World War II, their leadership as Christian Ministers,
or as upper middle-class families engaging in fashionable leisure activities. I am sure
for many people the monument offers a level of re-evaluation and education. Was
it a challenge to source suitable historical images? Were there methodologies you
engaged to edit and select the final images used?

JY: I can only try to describe this to you in retrospect, and the activity is
ultimately difficult to put into words because it's a very personal, sympathetic and
phenomenological connection you have with the image. The intellect is only one
facet; it's also a bodily and psychic relation. If we talk about the process of choosing,
one has to be attentive to the image—what it offers and what possible latitude of
meaning people may read into it. It was important that images had a certain quality
of emotional engagement and ambiguity; a uniqueness and depth that resisted the
usual dismissive method we bring to things when we use them as mere representation.
Then in terms of the context of the monument, a 'permanent' installation is something
that has several temporal horizons. One needs to be aware that these exist, otherwise
the work fails. The info-media asks us to come to the end of time every day, to live
in an endless present of forgettable news cycles; yet our bodies do grow old and
mature with linear time and carry memories with them. Time passes, but we also
change as viewers. It isn't to do with an experience that we want with or from images,
rather it is a care that we need to meet images with, and in time our connection
with these images may enrich us.

VP: I'm interested in the word 'open', which you have used in two of your major
artworks that also happen to be interdisciplinary. Open World (2005)—a tapestry
made in collaboration with the pioneering Australian Tapestry Workshop, and then
Open Monument. Can you elaborate on this title and how it's implied in the physical
monument?

JY: *Open World* is the title of a book of poems by the Scottish poet Kenneth White,
who, amid all his nomadism, has carried plural cultural and intellectual history to
any location—be it the Atlantic Pyrenees, the Basho trail or Hong Kong. As I said,
I find the notion of 'monumentalising' problematic because it usually forces a
permanent, iconic finality. So perhaps the title *Open Monument*, albeit a seemingly
paradoxical term, may make people question these assumptions, and consider
long-term installation structures differently.

VP: You worked with Richard and Michelle Black from Times Two Architects
to develop the structure. You must have had a preconception of what form you
wanted the monument to take, but did this evolve once you were working with
the architects?

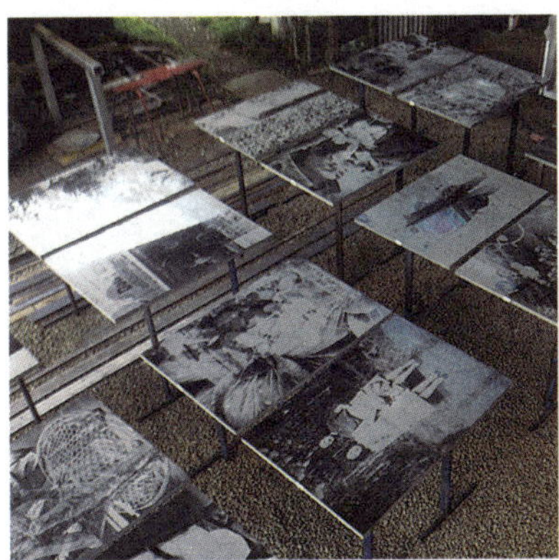

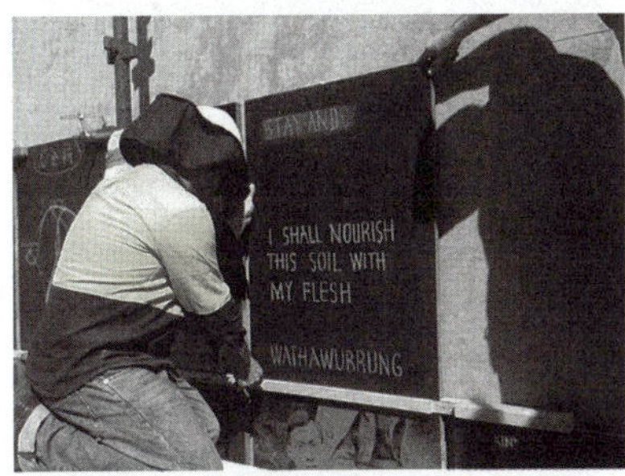

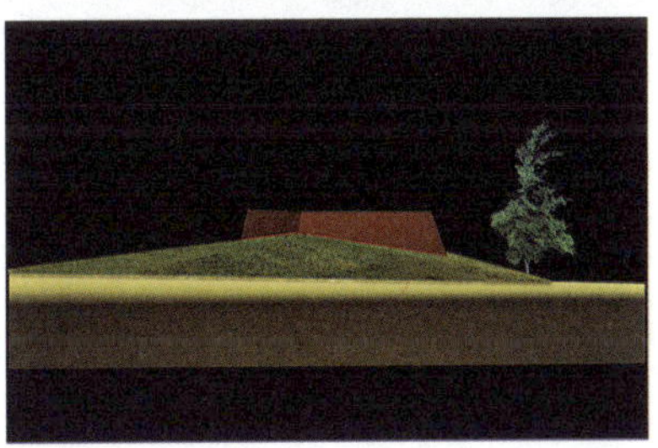

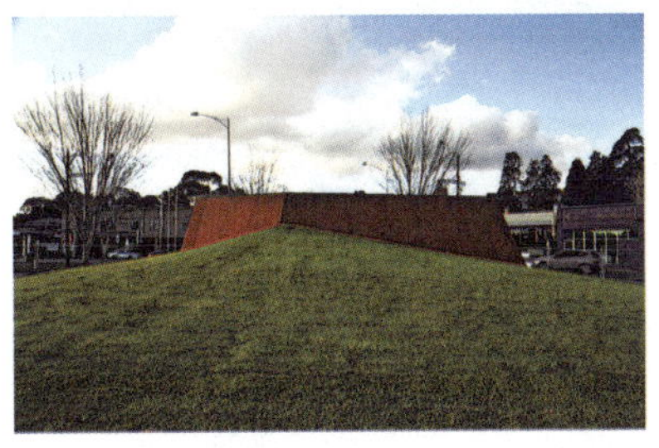

JY: Believe it or not, my initial impulse was to make this gigantic [Claes] Oldenburg-like shovel in a mound of earth! That populist impulse went very quickly, thank goodness, since we already have many big fixations in the country, like the Big Lobster, the Big Ned Kelly, the Big Banana—to name a few! So, there were these areas of address that grounded the conceptualisation of the work: the narratives, the history, and the signpost. The shovel-signpost idea is now the steel back of the monument, which is actually embedded into a large mound. This mound can also function as a place of public gathering or recreation. The narratives, which form a section of the work called *Transculture*, are a bank of laser-etched granite and marble slabs in a grid that is situated at the front of the monument, but the grid is folded so that it takes on a physicality rather than a screen-like look. Finally, this structure is flanked by a 30-odd-meter long timeline in the ground, which is a conceptual work that covers every decade since 1850 till 2010, and then folds out to the year 2170. Each decade, the community can inscribe the significant events that have taken place in Ballarat on the corresponding pavement stone in the timeline. This is the third time I have tried to make a timeline, once in Hong Kong (which failed because the history was censored) and on Melbourne's Chapel Street (a project that was unrealised). Times Two Architects came up with this wonderful structure, which is able to accommodate these three different aspects of the monument. I think they conceptually resolved it exceptionally well.

VP: Okay, so you had the conceptual elements and they designed the structure based upon them? Can you elaborate—it looks almost like a shovel has been taken to the ground, is that intentional?

JY: There were the three conceptual elements which were the givens, and which I spoke of earlier, but the important additional perspective that the architects brought to the project was an awareness of the civic-utilitarian context. This is not a sculpture on a plinth, nor is it strictly land art. It's more a sort of assemblage of architectural, environmental and artistic experiences. The physical aspects of the monument guide the public towards these experiences. Richard [Black] and I had good dialogues a long time ago about transitional spaces: these spaces, because they are not strictly utilitarian, can address extra-architectural elements, such as narration, care in craftsmanship, and so on.

I think the monument functions more like a town-centre transitional space than it does as something symbolic, like a conventional object sculpture or utilitarian architectural structure. It invites people to have certain experiences with it, but it's not a spectacle experience. It offers a sort of considered engagement; it's a new form of life. I think people may wonder why it exists on that site, but somehow, at the same time, feel it is necessary there! So, we started by thinking through what forms of life we were to address through the work, namely a considered engagement with the narratives and with locating history in an open space, and then we made something physical to allow this form of life to happen. That's the politics behind building something like *Open Monument*, it is actually anti-symbolic.

VP: When creating the work, did you feel like there was some tension between the strategies of transience, fragmentation and erasure by which you normally approach the retelling of history within your chalk drawings, and the inherent durability and permanence of a material like granite?

JY: I thought about this often. What gives me the right to cast writing in stone? Initially, the chalk drawings were made with an attitude of transience, and for a mostly

Laser-etched granite panels and documentation of thier installation for *Open Monument* 2015

Architectural prototype sketch of 'the shovel', 2014, for *Open Monument* 2015

View of 'the shovel', *Open Monument* 2015
Architectural monument, 430 sq m
Len T. Fraser Reserve, Ballarat, 2015

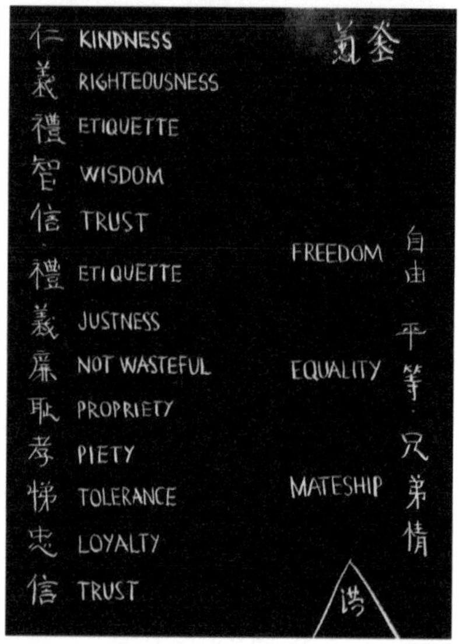

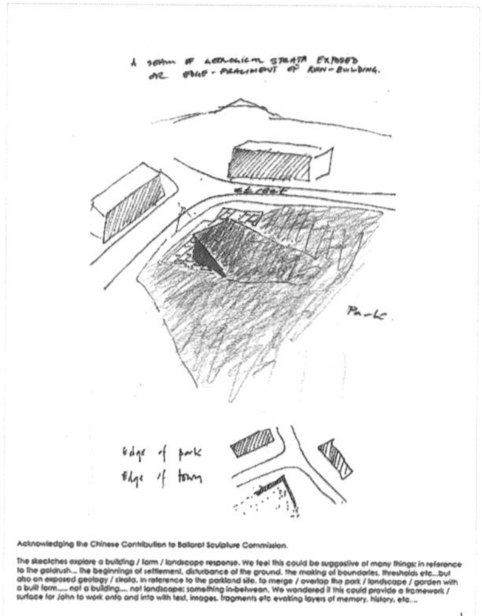

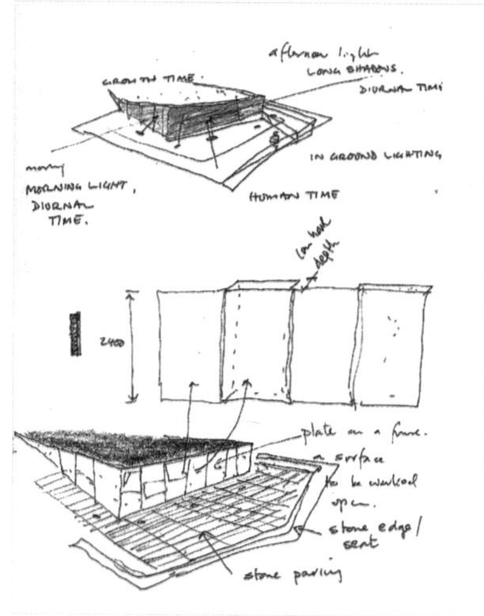

Freedom, Equality, Mateship 2015
Chalk on blackboard-painted archival
cotton paper, 100 × 70 cm

Concept drawings for *Open Monument* 2015
Times Two Architects, Richard Black and
Michelle Black

auto-didactic purpose. For me, it was a way of learning the values and feelings from resonating historical narratives or voices. The constant erasure and retracing that chalk allows was a way to hone in on what was important from those voices, so that the feelings and values, through a correct scribing, could etch themselves into my psyche. It is a medium-like process, where the voices from the past are so engaging that particular words insist on coming into being. Thus, those resonating historical values and feelings were not my voice. One can look at [Joseph] Beuys' *Directive Forces for a New Society* (1974–77) or Rudolf Steiner's pedagogical chalk drawings from the Goetheanum. They feel mediumistic because, firstly, the altruism of the dialogue overrides a subjective intent, and secondly, you can tell that the calligraphy of Beuys and Steiner has a similar, non-subjective quality to that of Daoist incantations (Cant. *fu luk* 符籙).

On the issue of symbolic permanence: even from the point of view of reception, it is as if the scribe and the viewer are sharing and re-imagining the discourse from the past. In that sense, there is no tension between what needs to be transiently written in chalk and what needs to be permanently there; since it is an indeterminate process, the scribe and the viewer both generate the new historic narrative. The meaning of the narrative comes first and foremost from how the images and the texts are strung together, and that is dependent on the context, the era. The grid in which *Transculture* is presented has no figure on a ground, it has no narrational linearity or hierarchy. This process of sharing the discourse from the past is not, I hope, a question of subjective expression seeking immortality.

Regarding text on granite, the tradition of chiselled text on stone has a long and interesting history in China. Not only were philosophical or poetic texts carved into stone, but these were then communicated down the ages, with generations taking paper rubbings from these stone texts. In fact, I was hoping to replicate this practice, taking some select stones in the monument, located at the lowest row of the grid, and directing them towards children's use and play in a similar fashion. For example, the panel which places side by side the two sets of ethical precepts and eight virtues upheld by secret Chinese societies (hung mun 洪門), and the Australian values of freedom, equality and mateship. Alas, the budget did not allow for this.

VP: What is the importance of this kind of memorialisation? What role do public monuments play in social consciousness? What is their significance in terms of collective memory?

JY: First of all, you cannot leave this question to the politicians. The politician's temporal horizon is quite different to that of the cultural worker. More often than not, a politician's horizon in facilitating changes in social consciousness is contingent on the short to mid-term future—for example, the election cycle. So, they try to facilitate changes functionally and specifically—through policy or propaganda. Cultural workers try to facilitate changes in social consciousness through and with aspects that are less tangible, quantifiable and literal. As the art historian John Clark points out, a work may not be allowed to have visibility or meaning in certain hegemons, and in another time, it takes on immense meaning, thus facilitating changes in social consciousness in the long term.[5]

We have been in this postmodern era of distraction and the spectacle for several decades, and now we are entering a new cyber-human phase of augmented reality. The collective social memory, then, is a composite, incorporating qualities that were important to old Enlightenment ideals and culminated in universal human rights, and simultaneously, new values that are emerging from technology and augmentation. Values cannot be memorialised to remain in a fixed symbolic framework, their frame needs to be elastic in order to accommodate the changes that are occurring in this era, and to give access to a mode of becoming. This becoming needs to be able to draw from societal and existential values not only of the present, but also re-imaginings and poeticising from the past, and from many cultures, particularly those that never held Western Enlightenment ideals of the human subject as part of their episteme.

When thinking about memorialisation in relation to collective memory and social consciousness, the 'right' of other cultures to have a position in the Australian context is only one part of it. We need to think of the past in relation to the future. What is more important is for the act of memorialisation to make present and living the values and images from plural worldviews, so that we have a chance for a meaningful, poetic coupling with this land, and to find modes of becoming with this land, rather than just relying upon the poverty of a denuded, literal mindset of the so-called techno-future, of scientism.

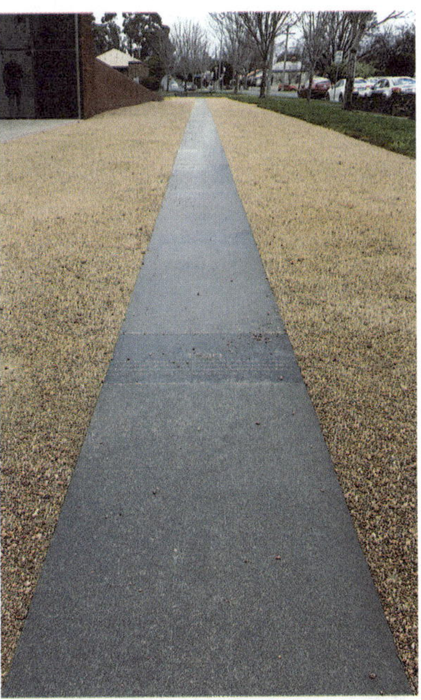

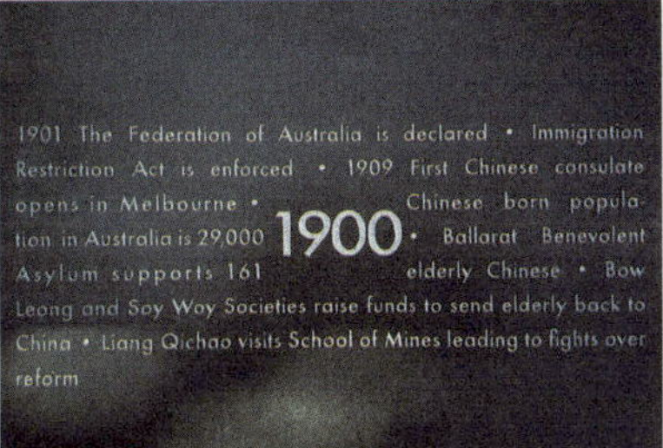

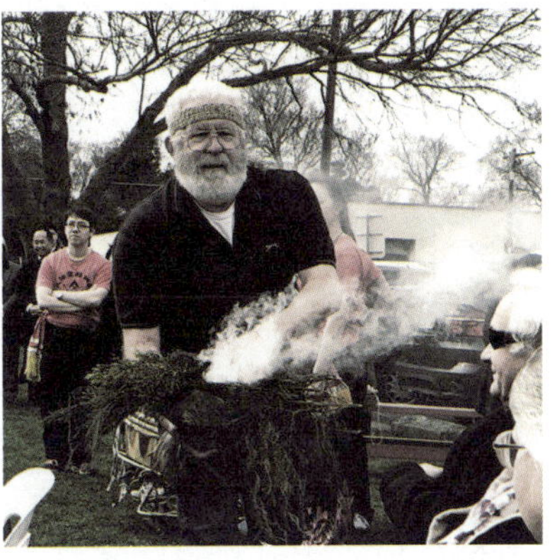

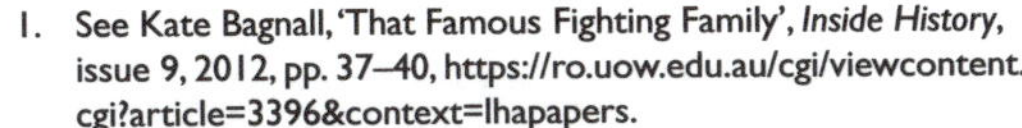

1. See Kate Bagnall, 'That Famous Fighting Family', *Inside History*, issue 9, 2012, pp. 37–40, https://ro.uow.edu.au/cgi/viewcontent.cgi?article=3396&context=lhapapers.

2. See Peta Stephenson, *The Outsiders Within: Telling Australia's Indigenous-Asian Story*, UNSW Press, Sydney, 2007 and Gloria Ouida Lee's oral history in Diana Giese, *Astronauts, Lost Souls & Dragons: Voices of today's Chinese Australians*, University of Queensland Press, Brisbane, 1997.

3. Yvonne Horsfield, 'A Tale of Two Cities: Ballarat and Bendigo Chinese-Cultural Contrasts and Transformations', presented at *Translation and Transformation*, Dragon Tails Conference, Victoria University of Wellington, 20–23 November 2019. The conference was convened by Grace Gassin and Karen Schamberger.

4. In response to the exhibition *The Burrangong Affray*, held at the 4A Centre for Contemporary Asian Art, Sydney in 2018, Young and others involved in the exhibition, including artist Jason Phu, were the target of racist vitriol published online by the Australia First Party. See James Hood, 'Two Dis-Oriented Chinamen Jason Phu and John Zerunge Hold Anti-Digger Hate Expo in Chinatown', *Australia First Party*, 25 August 2018, https://australiafirstparty.net/two-disoriented-chinamen-jason-phu-and-john-zerunge-stage-anti-digger-hate-expo-in-chinatown. See Mikala Tai's essay on the project in this volume, p. 328.

5. See John Clark's essay in this volume, p. 24.

Timeline (1850–2010–2170) from *Open Monument* 2015
Bluestone and 34 laser-etched granite panels embedded in ground, 4000 x 42 cm
Len T. Fraser Reserve, Ballarat
Collection of Ballarat City Council

Details of *Timeline (1850–2010–2170)* from *Open Monument* 2015

Wathaurung Elder Uncle Bryon Powell conducting a smoking ceremony at the launch of *Open Monument*, Len T. Fraser Reserve, Ballarat, 2015

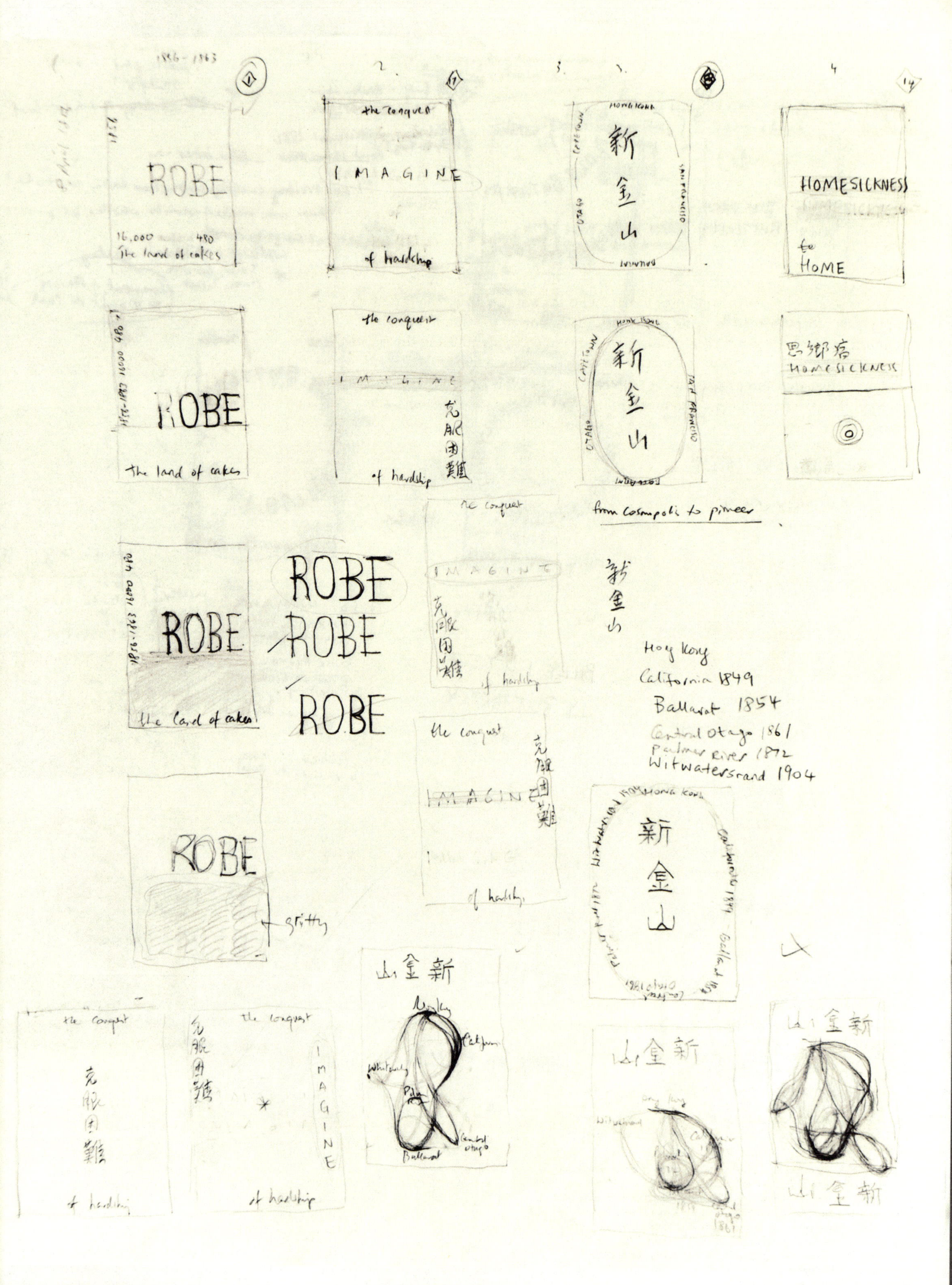

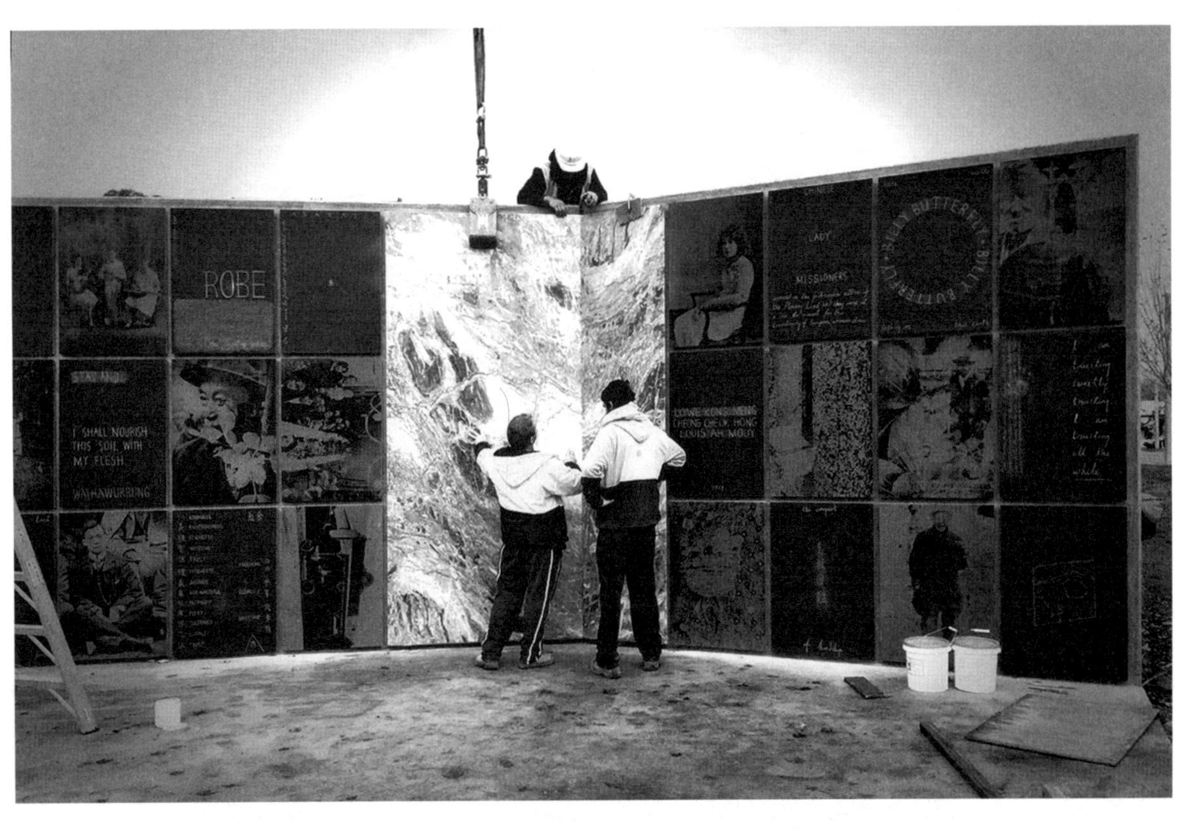

facing page
Page from the artist's notebook
(JYNB2012-14)

above
Construction of *Open Monument*,
Len T. Fraser Reserve, Ballarat, 2015

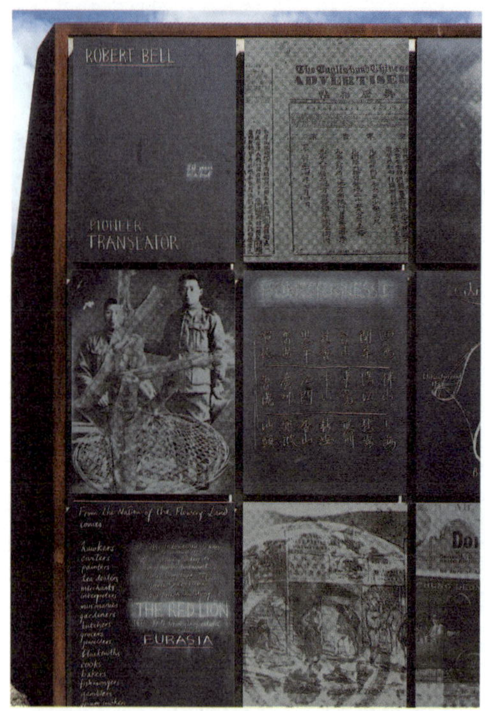

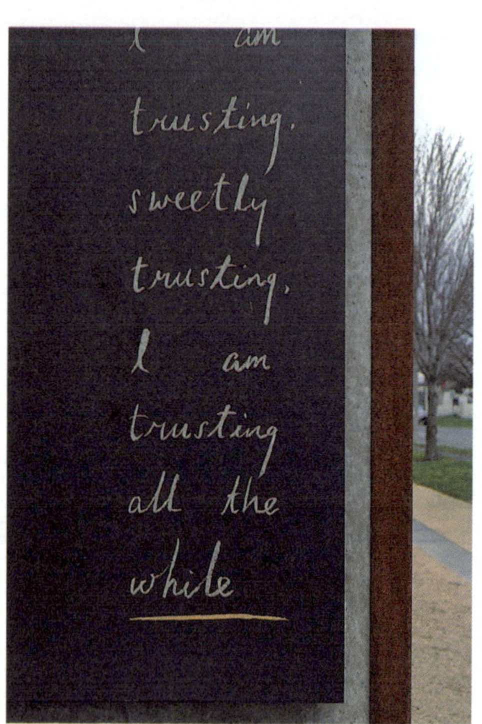

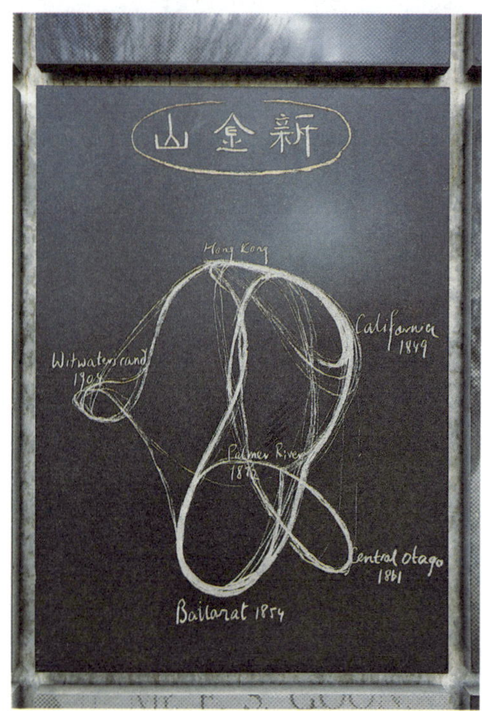

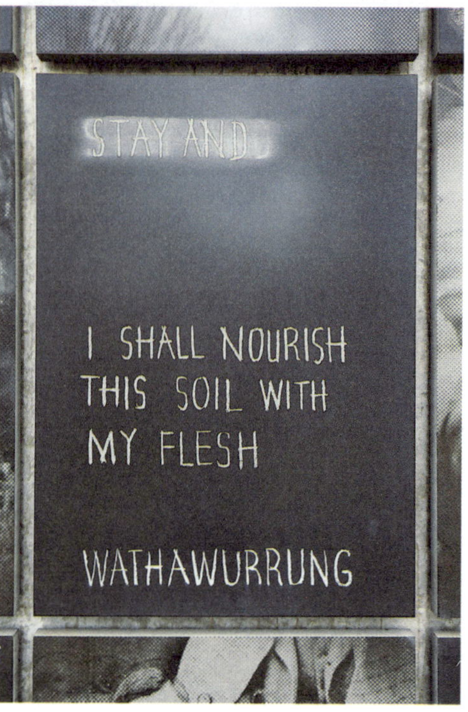

Details of *Transculture* from *Open Monument* 2015
Collection of Ballarat City Council

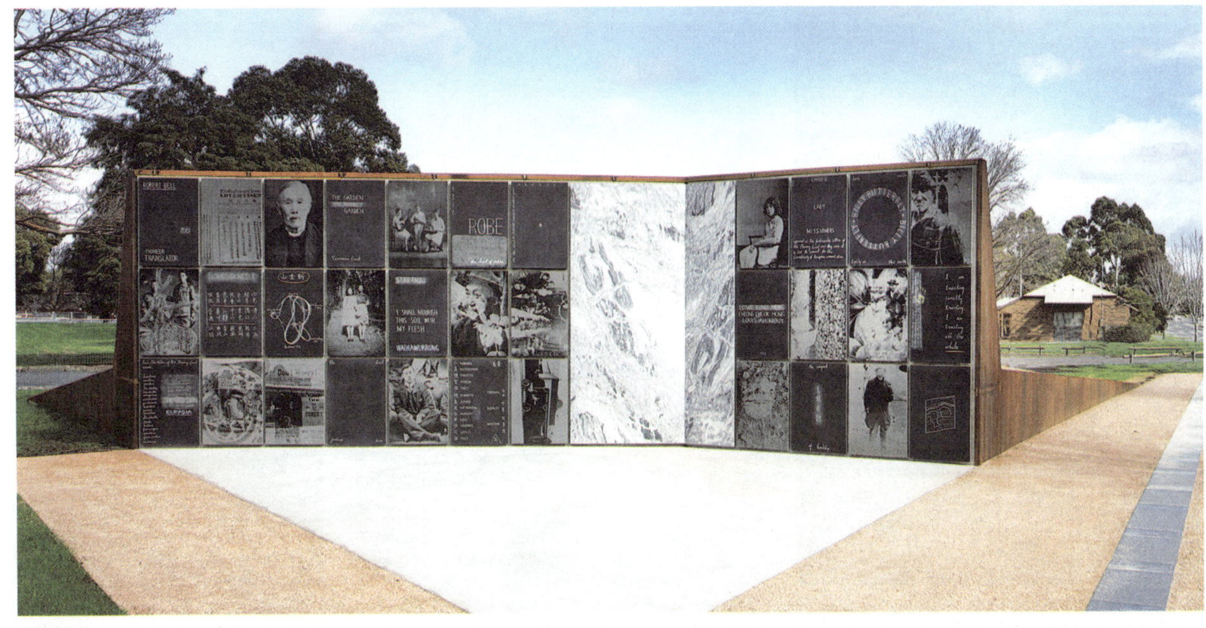

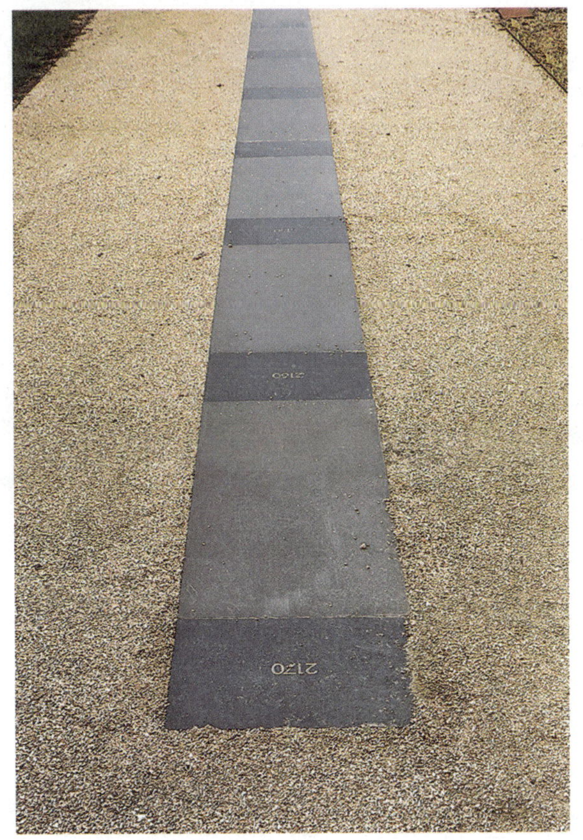

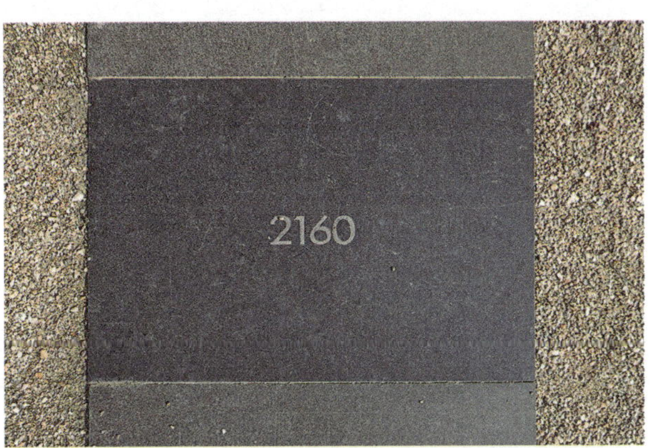

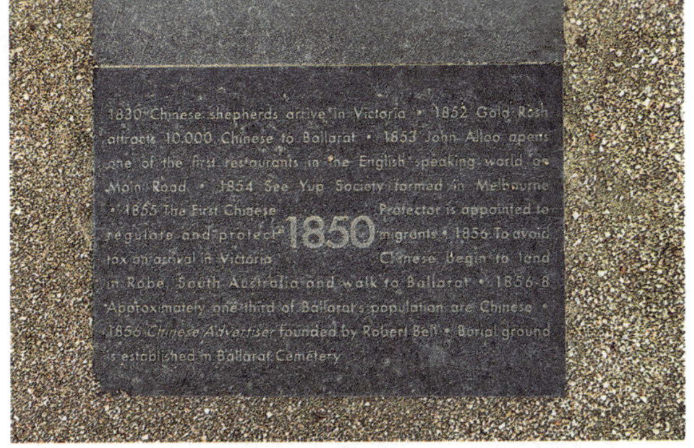

Open Monument 2015
Architectural monument, 430 sq m
Len T. Fraser Reserve, Ballarat
Collection of Ballarat City Council

Timeline (1850–2010–2170) from *Open
Monument* 2015
Bluestone and 34 laser-etched granite panels
embedded in ground, 4000 × 42 cm
Len T. Fraser Reserve, Ballarat
Collection of Ballarat City Council

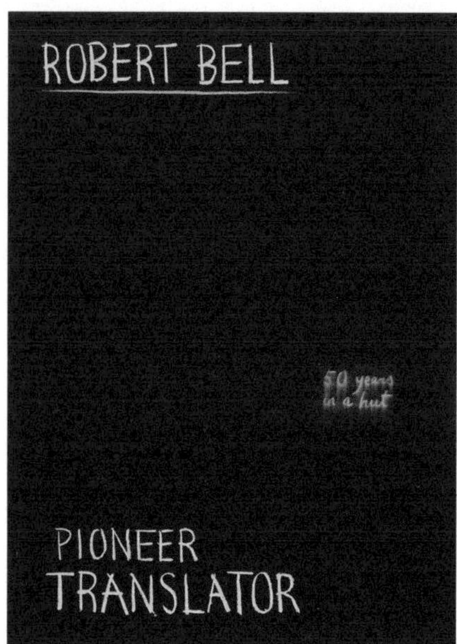

ROBERT BELL
50 years in a hut
PIONEER TRANSLATOR

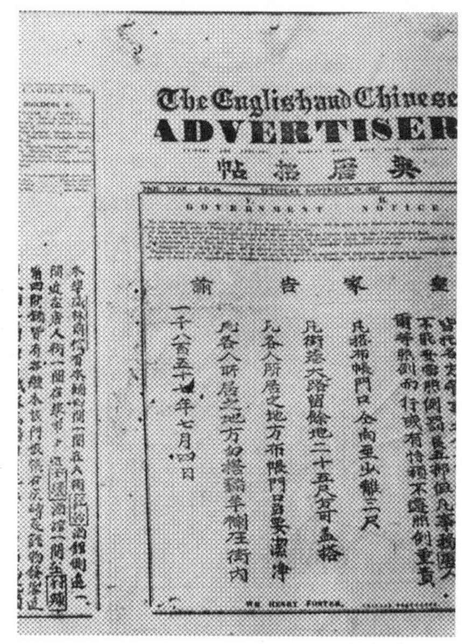

The English and Chinese
ADVERTISER

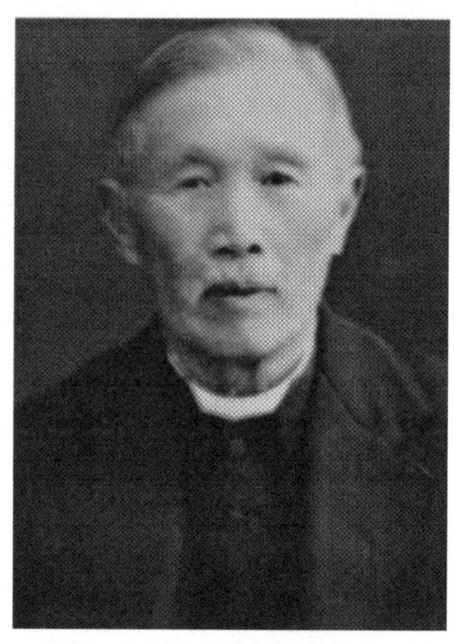

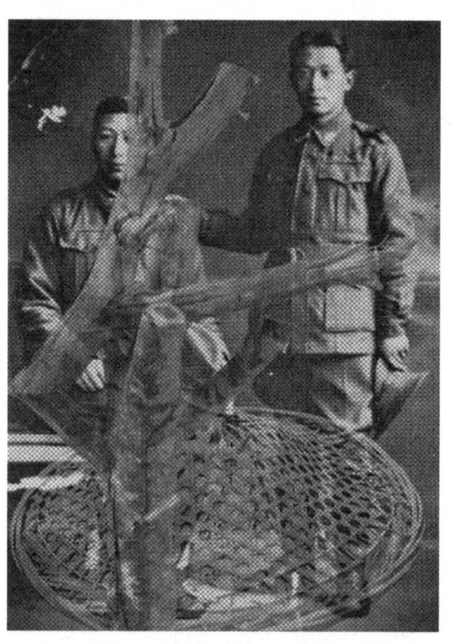

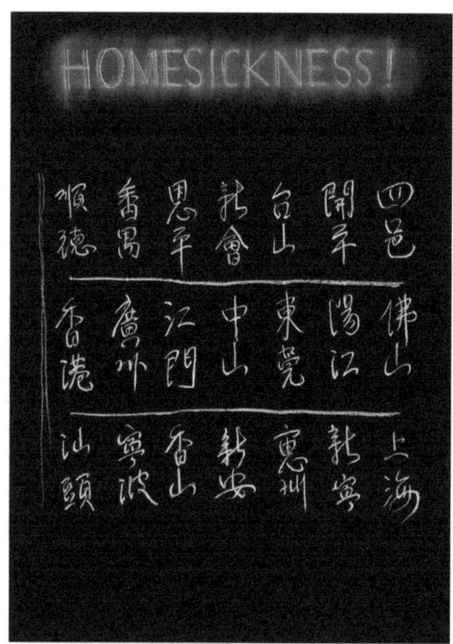

HOMESICKNESS !
四邑
佛山
開平
台山
新會
恩平
香寓
順德
湯江
東莞
廣州
中山
江門
香港
上海
新寧
惠州
新安
寶波
香山
汕頭

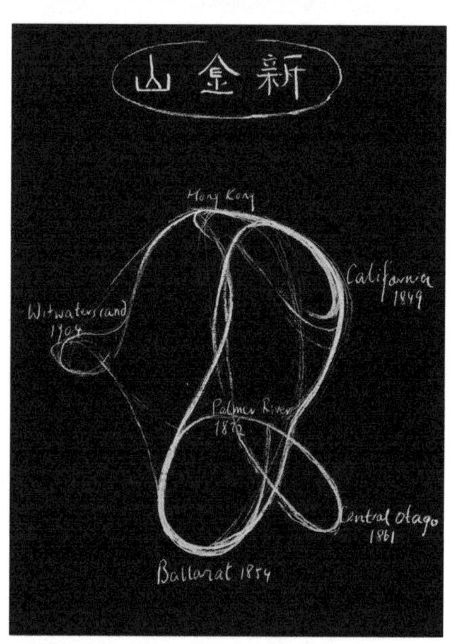

新金山
Hong Kong
Witwatersrand 1907
California 1849
Palmer River 1872
Central Otago 1861
Ballarat 1854

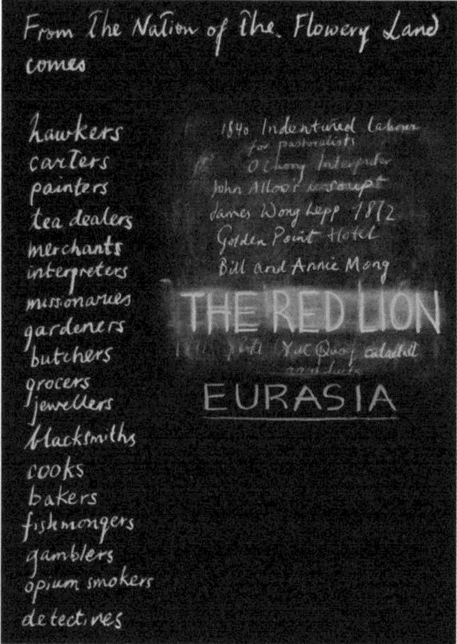

From The Nation of the Flowery Land comes
hawkers
carters
painters
tea dealers
merchants
interpreters
missionaries
gardeners
butchers
grocers
jewellers
blacksmiths
cooks
bakers
fishmongers
gamblers
opium smokers
detectives
1840 Indentured labour for pastoralists
O Cheong Interpreter
John Alloo's script
James Wong Lepp 1872
Golden Point Hotel
Bill and Annie Mong
THE RED LION
Yut Quoy
EURASIA

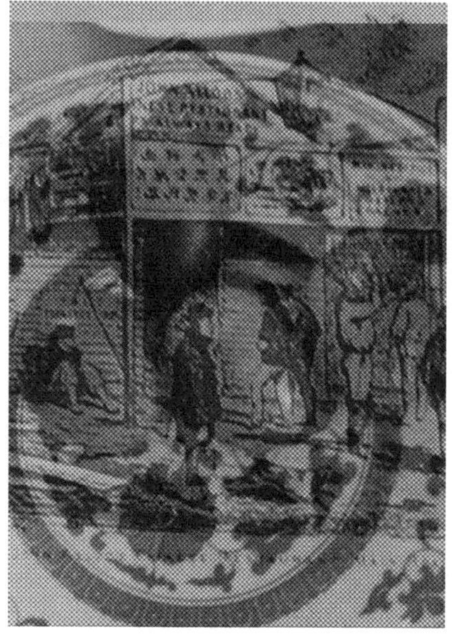

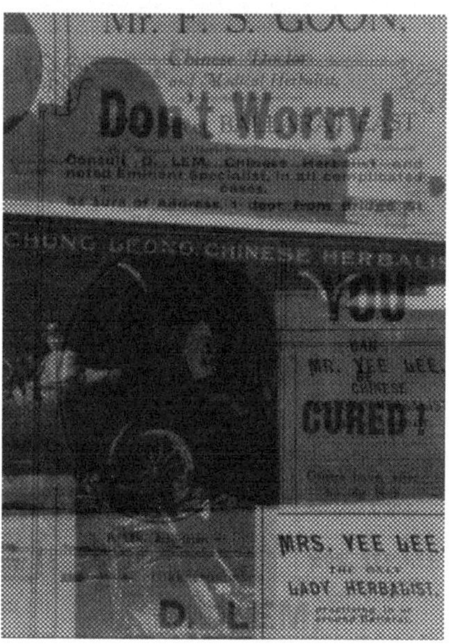

Mr. P. S. GOON
Chinese Herbalist
Don't Worry !
Consult D. LEM, Chinese Herbalist
noted Eminent Specialist in all complicated cases.
CHUNG GEONG CHINESE HERBALIST
YOU
CAN
MR. YEE LEE
CHINESE
CURED !
MRS. YEE LEE
THE ONLY
LADY HERBALIST

THE GARDEN
THE MARKET
GARDEN

Yarrowee Creek

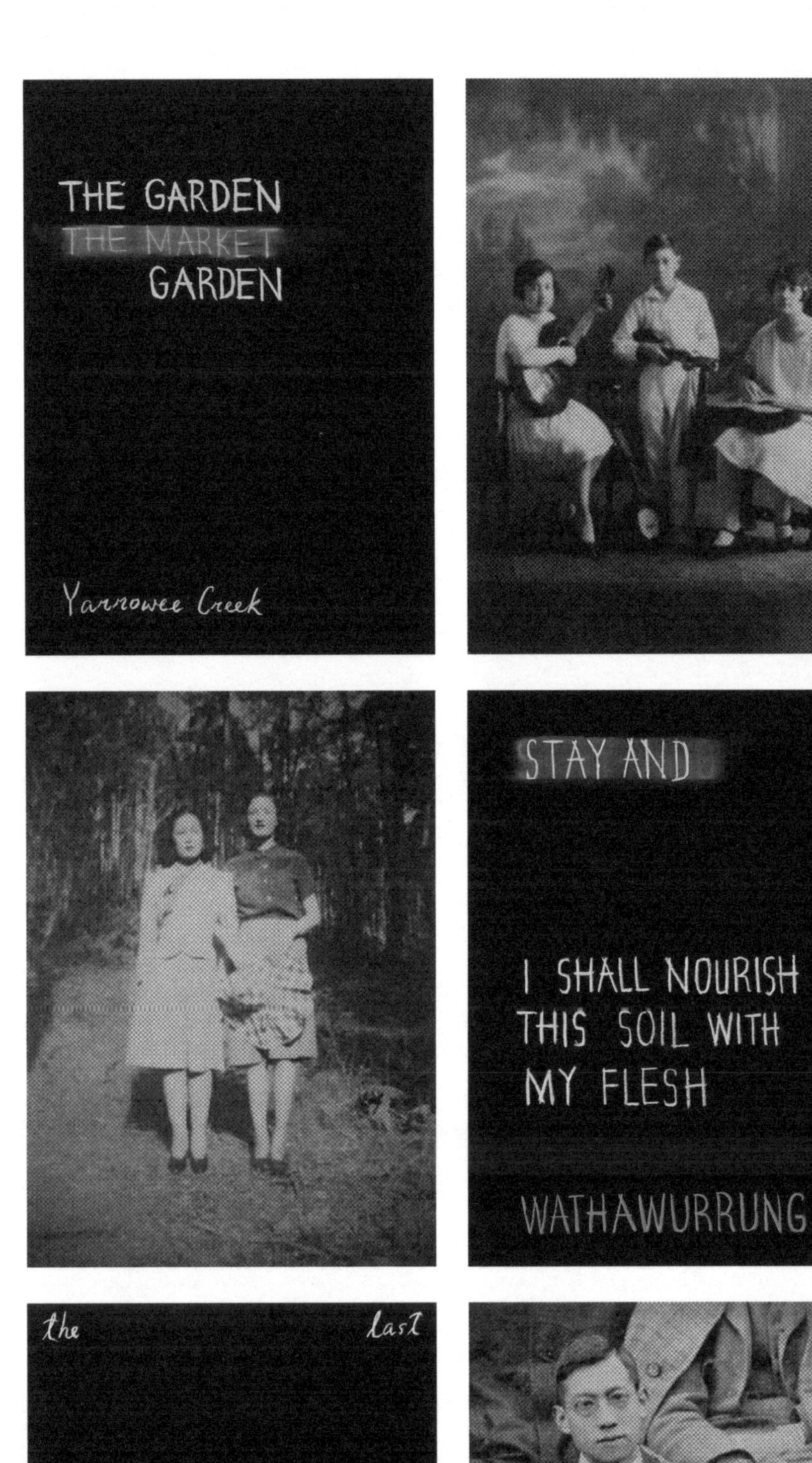

1856 – 1863   16,000 · 480

ROBE

the land of cakes

STAY AND

I SHALL NOURISH
THIS SOIL WITH
MY FLESH

WATHAWURRUNG

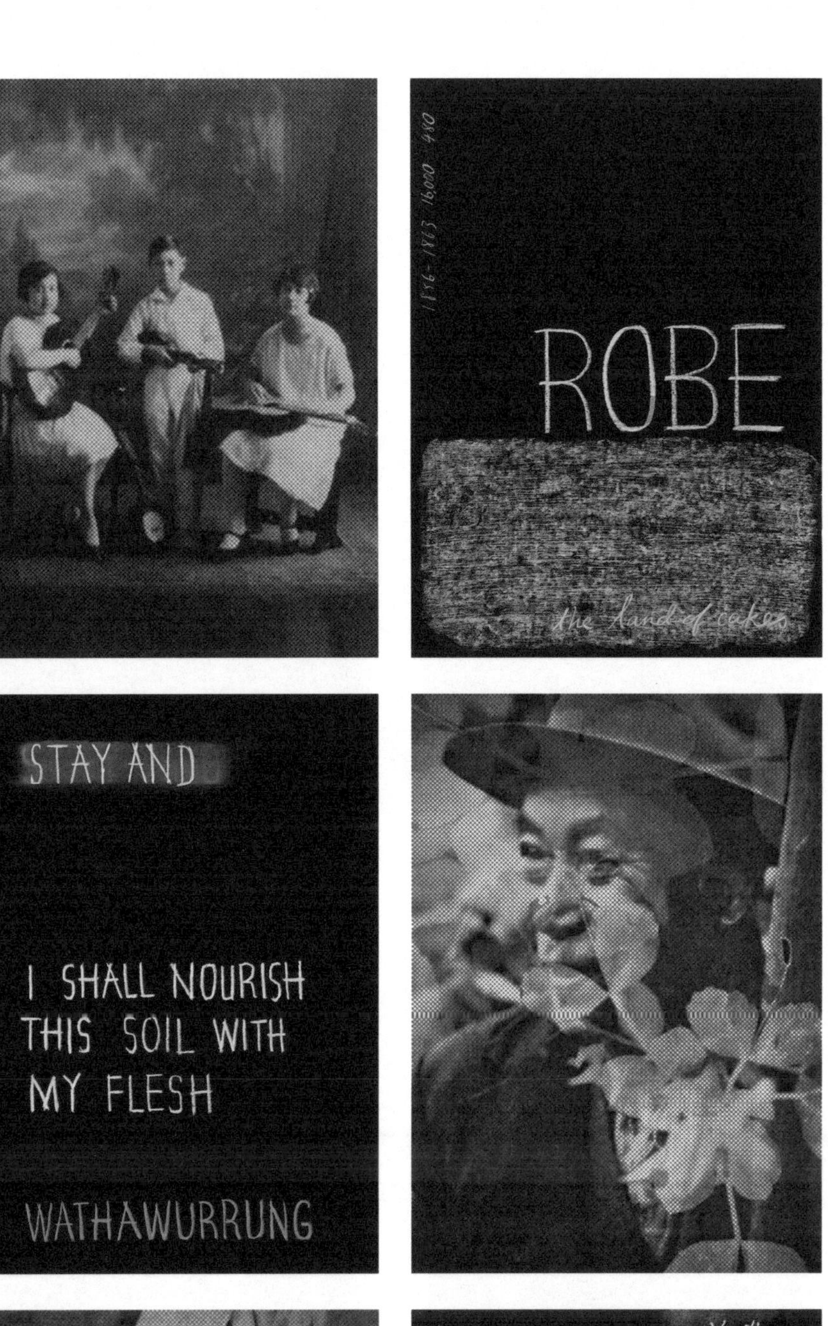

the   last

josshouse   here

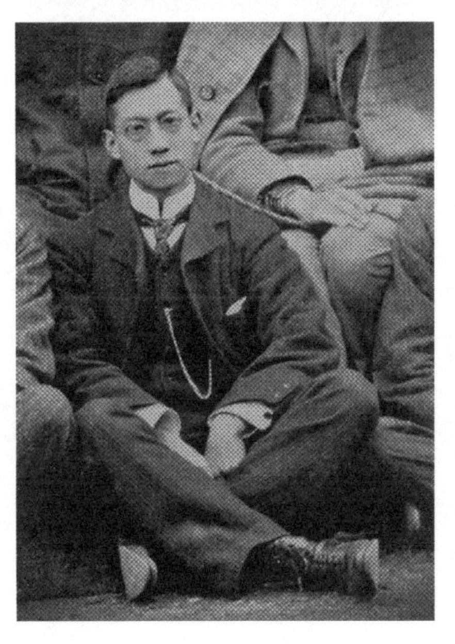

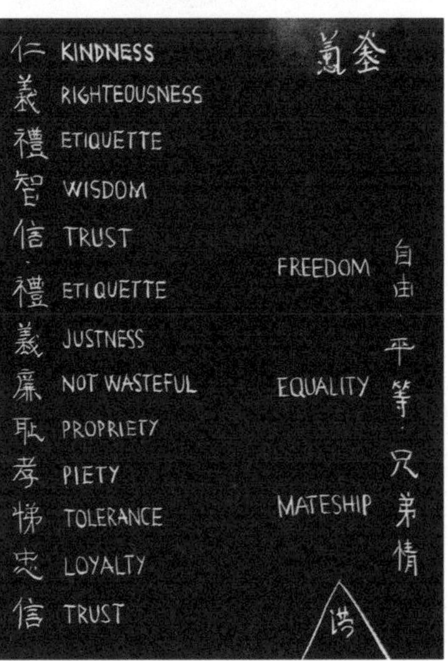

仁 KINDNESS   蒻釜
義 RIGHTEOUSNESS
禮 ETIQUETTE
智 WISDOM
信 TRUST
禮 ETIQUETTE   FREEDOM   自由
義 JUSTNESS
廉 NOT WASTEFUL   EQUALITY   平等
恥 PROPRIETY
孝 PIETY   兄弟
悌 TOLERANCE   MATESHIP
忠 LOYALTY
信 TRUST   洪

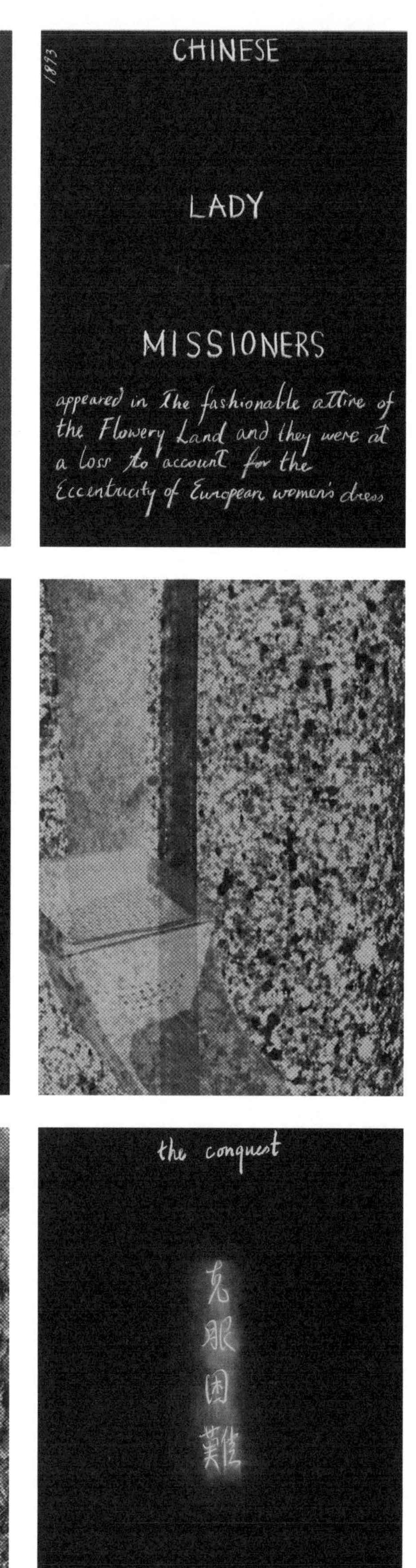

ARARAT
On the road to Ballarat, Celestials stumbled upon
CHINESE
LADY
MISSIONERS
appeared in the fashionable attire of
the Flowery Land and they were at
a loss to account for the
Eccentricity of European women's dress 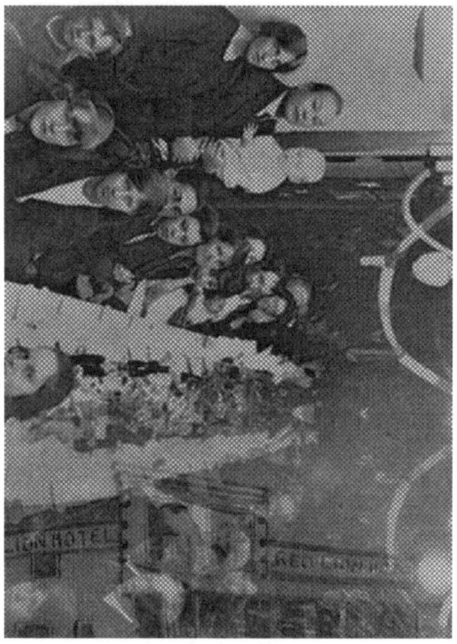 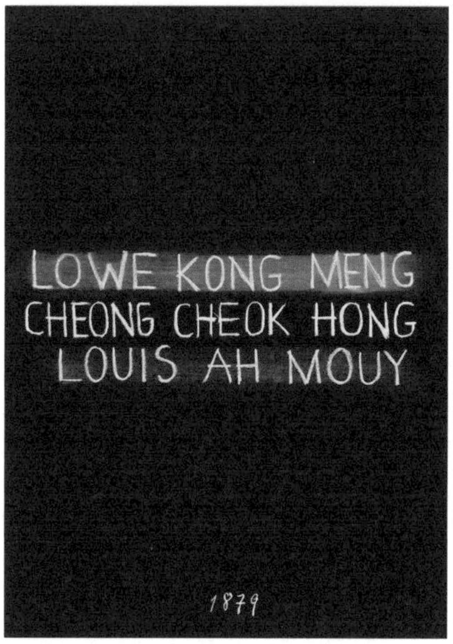
1893
LOWE KONG MENG
CHEONG CHEOK HONG
LOUIS AH MOUY
1879
J. CHUNG JEONG CHINESE HERBALIST 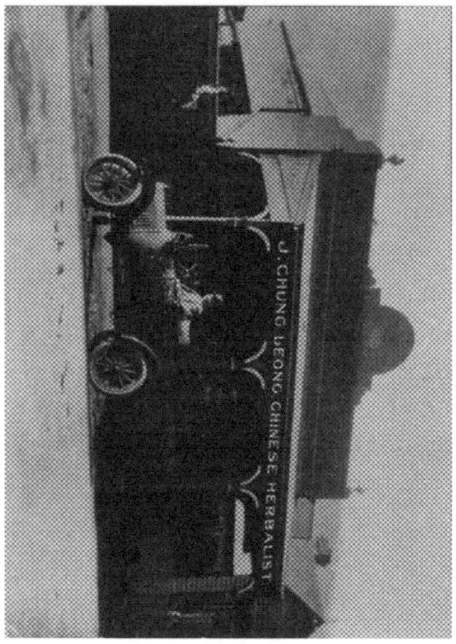 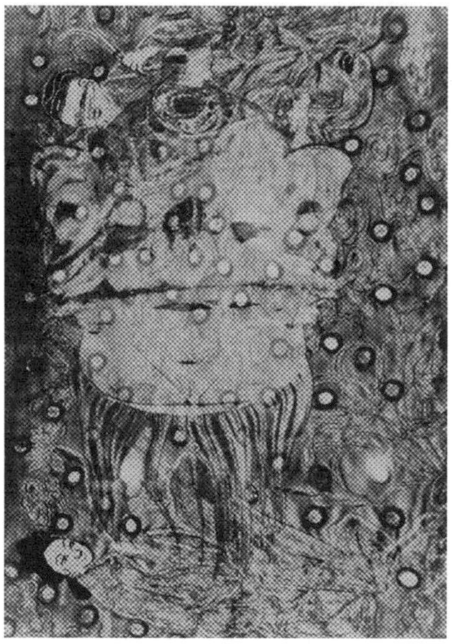
the conquest
of hardship

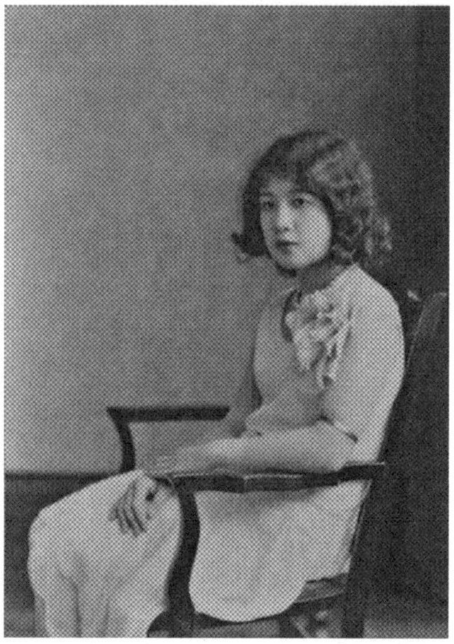

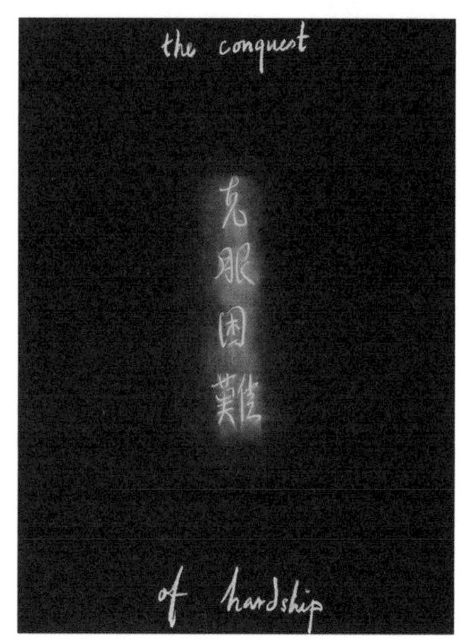

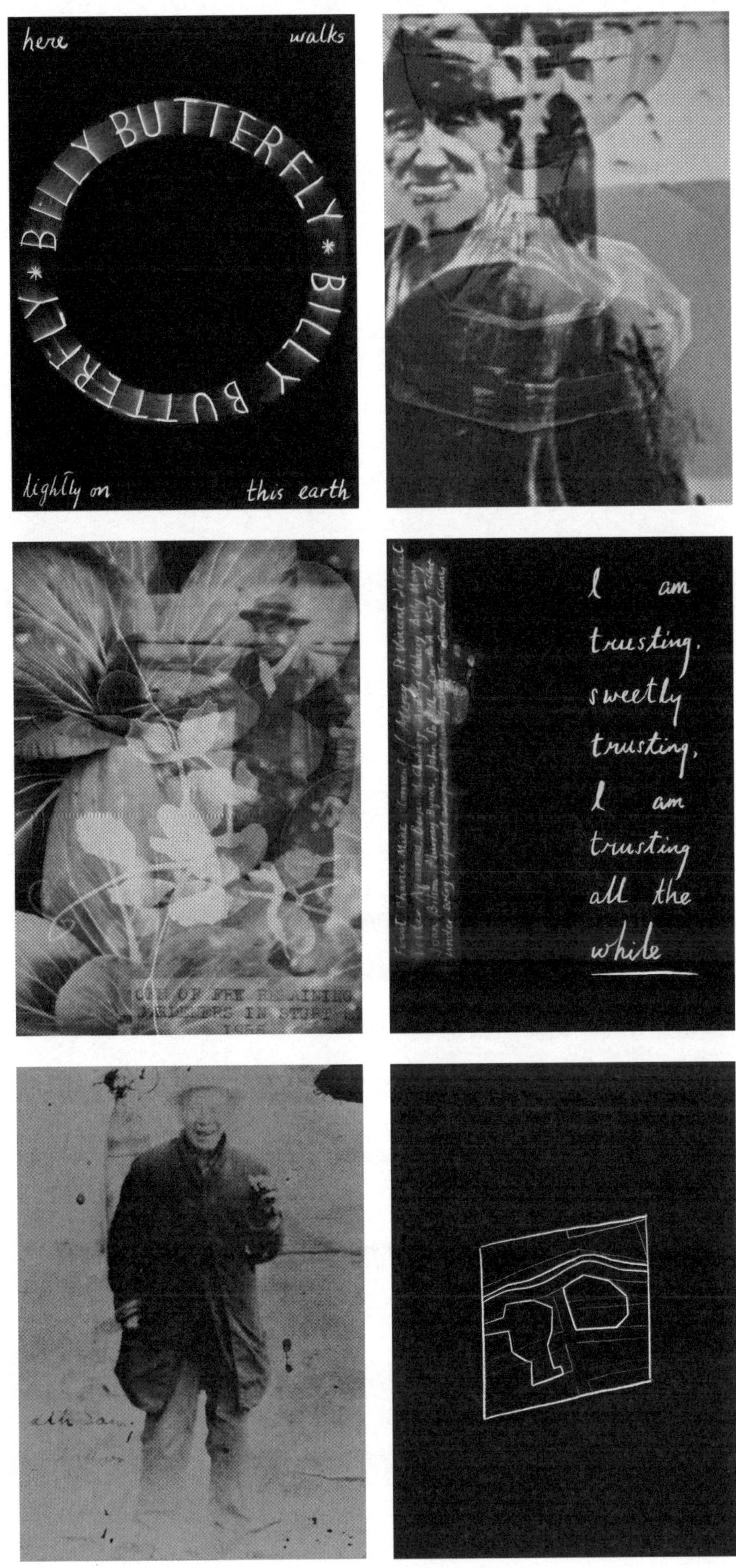

pages 274–77
Drawings and digital prints for *Transculture*
from *Open Monument* 2015
Laser-etched granite, 33 panels
Collection of Ballarat City Council

MODERNITY'S END:
HALF THE SKY

2016

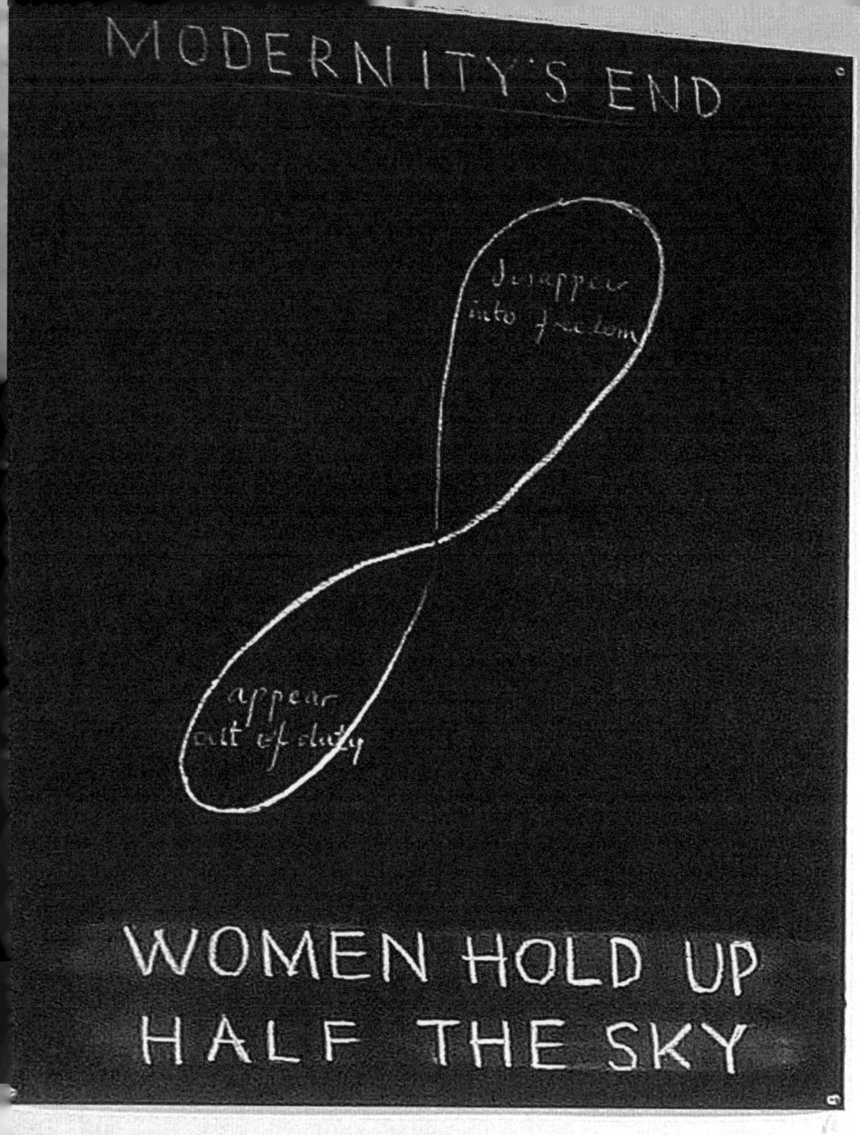

MODERNITY'S END
disappear into factory
reappear out of duty
WOMEN HOLD UP
HALF THE SKY

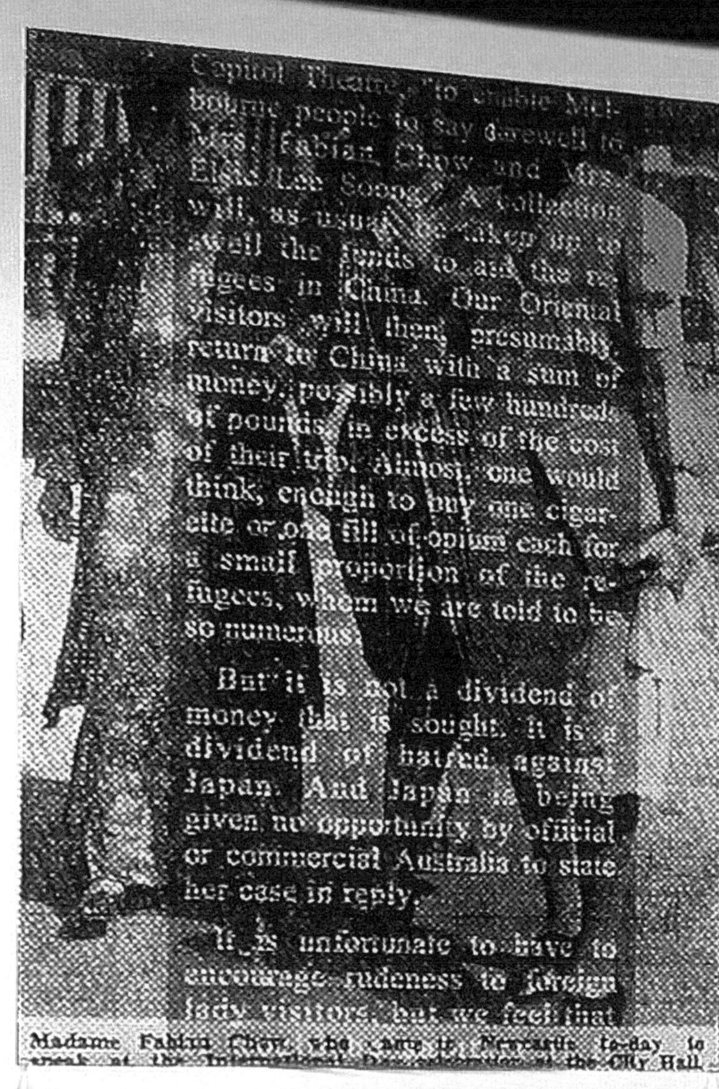

Capital Theatre, to enable Melbourne people to say farewell to
Mrs. Fabian Chow and Mrs.
Elsie Lee Soong. A collection
will, as usual, be taken up to
swell the funds to aid the refugees in China. Our Oriental
visitors will then, presumably,
return to China with a sum of
money, possibly a few hundred
of pounds in excess of the cost
of their trip. Almost, one would
think, enough to buy one cigar-
ette or one fill of opium each for
a small proportion of the refugees, whom we are told to be
so numerous.

But it is not a dividend of
money that is sought. It is a
dividend of hatred against
Japan. And Japan is being
given no opportunity by official
or commercial Australia to state
her case in reply.

It is unfortunate to have to
encourage rudeness to foreign
lady visitors, but we feel that

Madame Fabian Chow, who came to Newcastle to-day to
speak at the International Association at the City Hall.

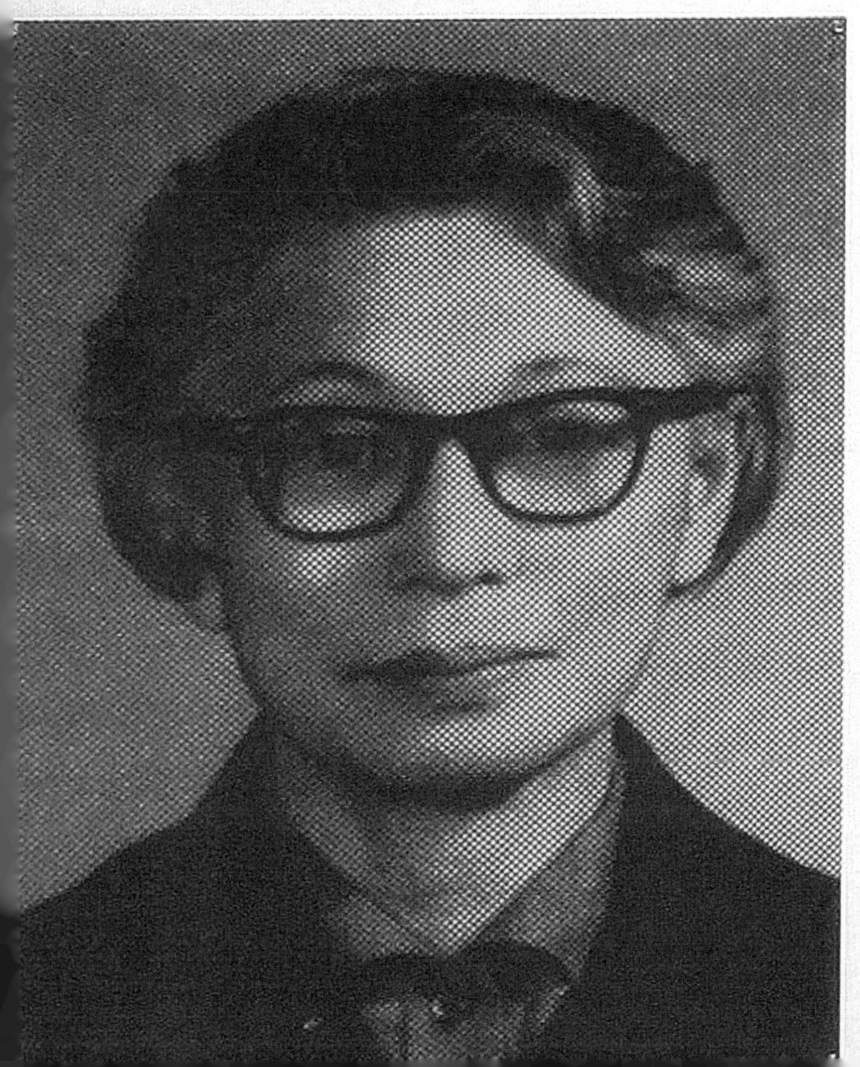

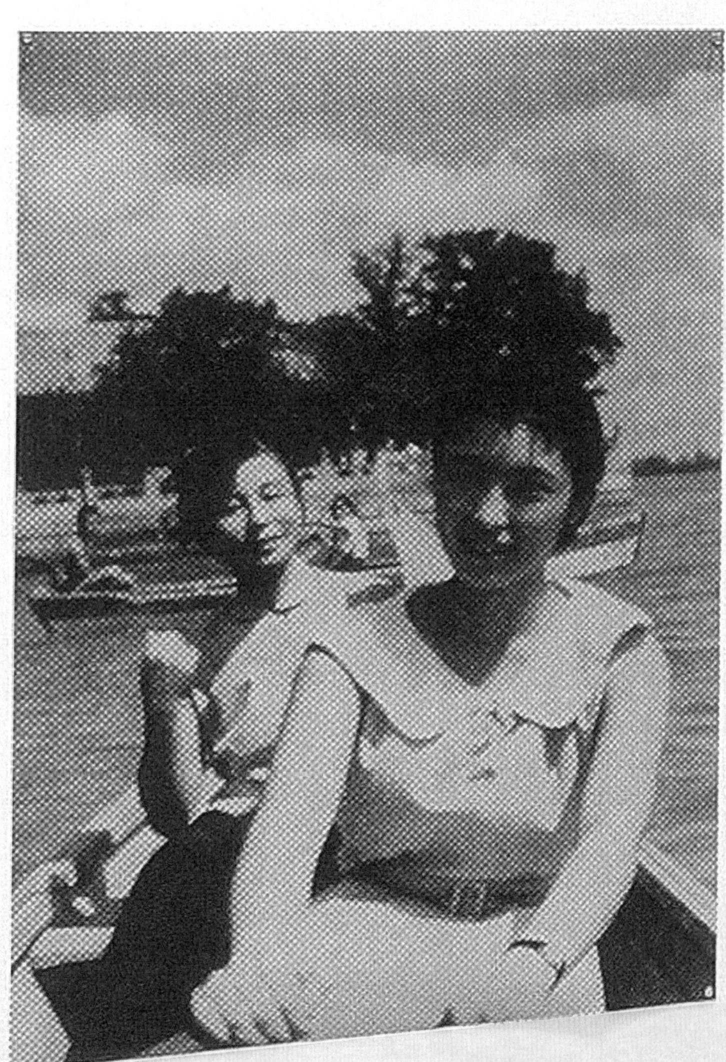

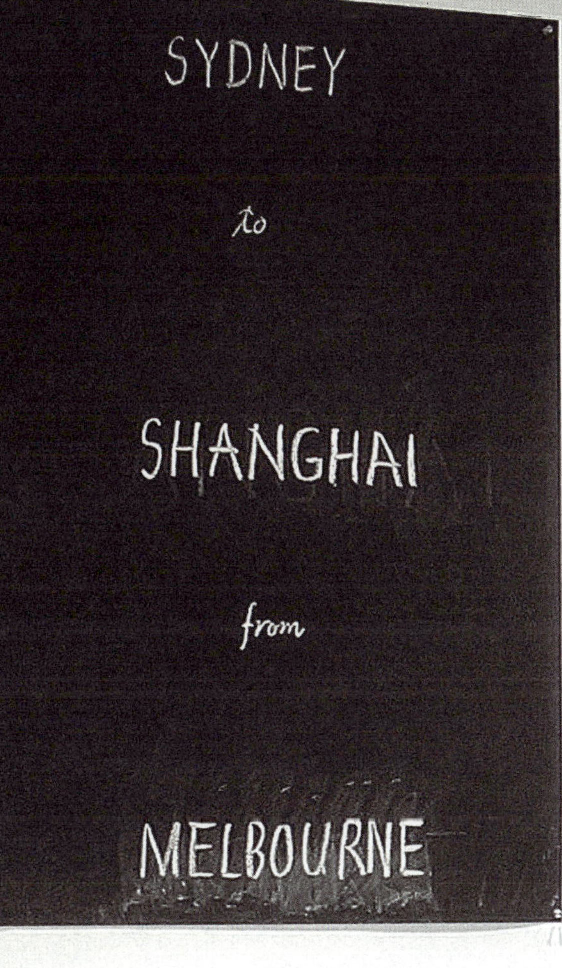

SYDNEY
to
SHANGHAI
from
MELBOURNE

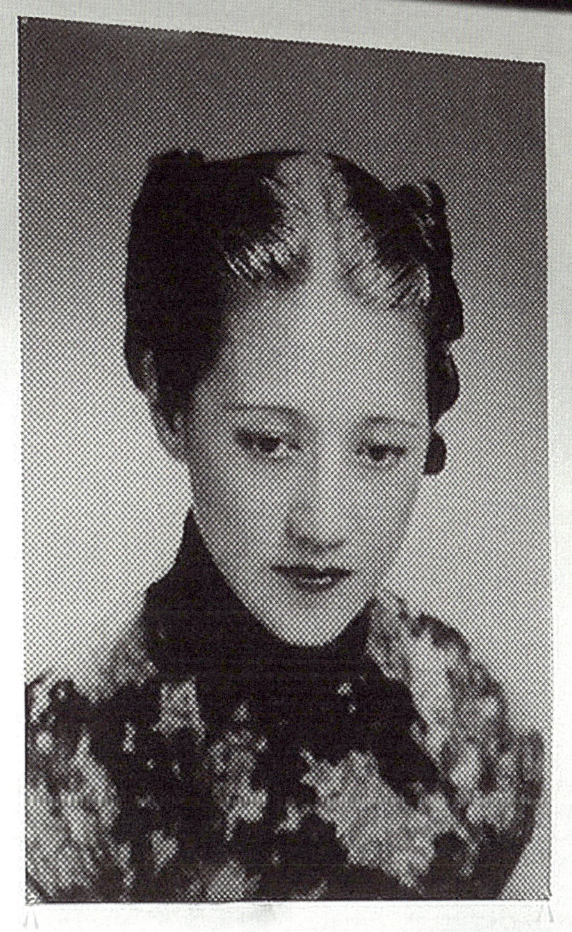

ALICE   LIM KEE
of Rutherglen, 1900

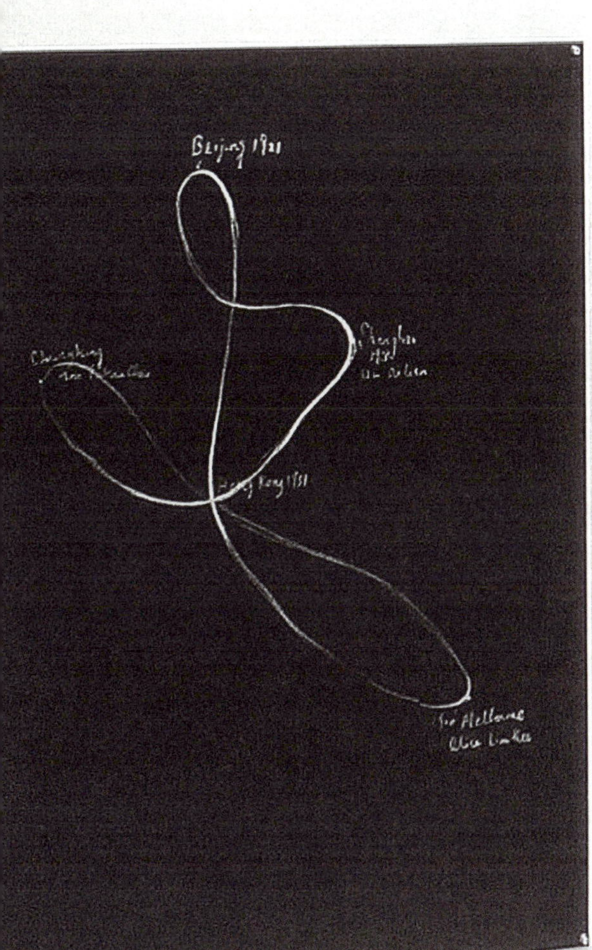

Beijing 1921
Shanghai 1936 the Artist
Chungking the Poet Matters
Hong Kong 1938
for Melbourne Alice Lim Kee

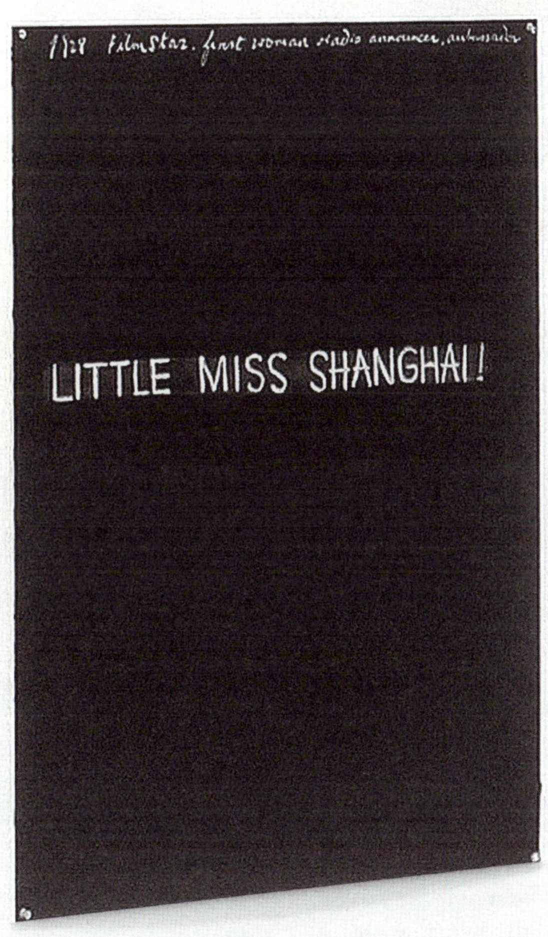

1928 film star, first woman radio announcer, ambassador
LITTLE MISS SHANGHAI!

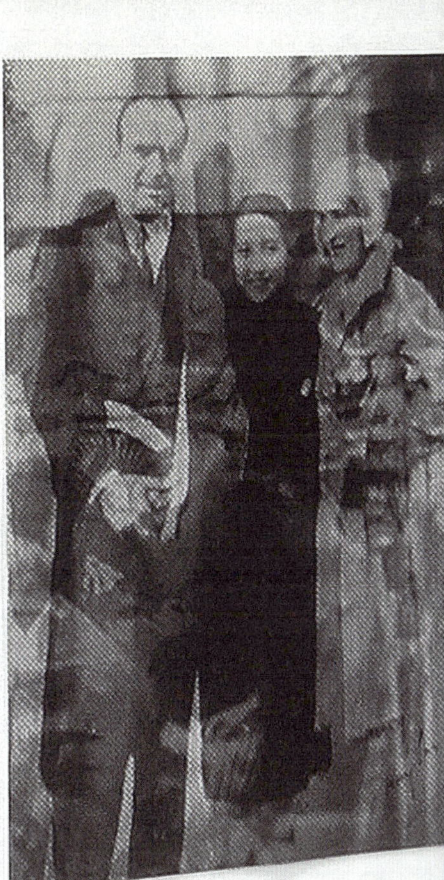

MODERNITY'S END: HALF THE SKY

OUTLINE

Modernity's End: Half the Sky (2016) reflects on the lives of Alice Lim Kee (伍愛蓮, 1900–unknown) and Daisy Kwok (郭婉瑩, 1909–1998), two Australian-born Chinese women who grew up in Australia before the women's liberation movement, and during the White Australia Policy (1901–73). Alice and Daisy migrated to Shanghai at the height of interwar modernity, rising to prominent positions in Shanghai society prior to the Japanese invasion and occupation in 1937. Alice became an actress and the first woman radio announcer in Shanghai's media industry, and, later, a journalist for the English-language *North-China Daily News*; she was also an ardent feminist. Daisy, through her family's ties to the luxurious Wing On Department store, was a member of Shanghai's vanguard elite, one of the first women in Shanghai to own and drive her own car.

Alice escaped the Japanese occupation and travelled back to Australia, then on to the United States of America, spending many years lecturing and advocating for the Chinese nation and Chinese refugees. Daisy chose to remain in Shanghai. Following persecution during the Communist takeover in 1949, she became a Chinese Australian historian, assisting the Australian consulate when it reopened in Shanghai in 1987, by translating documents and teaching the English language. She was an embodiment of the longer history of China-Australia connections prior to the cutting of diplomatic ties in the 1950s, dying in Shanghai in 1998, as an Australian citizen.

The exhibition installation of *Modernity's End: Half the Sky* featured two series of archival images and chalk drawings. One series focused on Alice Lim Kee and featured twelve works (210 × 470 cm), while the other focused on Daisy, in sixteen works (210 × 630 cm), each presented in a tight grid. In both these series, fragments from the women's diaries and layered historical photographs recall idyllic childhoods spent in Australia, cosmopolitan lives as socialites in modern Shanghai, and personal suffering under China's Cultural Revolution (1966–76).

For the original exhibition, at Incinerator Art Space, Sydney, in 2016, Young also invited artists Cyrus Tang and Pei Pei He to create works responding to the life stories of these remarkable Chinese Australian women. Tang's *The Final Cast Off (Alice Lim Kee and Daisy Kwok)* (2016) is a two-channel video installation, comprising looping video portraits of Alice and Daisy respectively, projected onto hanging rice-paper scrolls. The portraits are based on the archival images of the young women used in Young's installations, but in Tang's work they are made from incense ash floating on water, which slowly swirls, abstracting their faces in a poetic cycle.

Pei Pei He's *Eras in Daisy Kwok's Life (1920s –1940s)* and *(1960s–1980s)* are a pair of oil paintings (42 × 66 cm each), depicting blurred snapshots of Shanghai during two key periods of modern Chinese history through which Daisy lived. The tumult of this personal history is implied through the stark historical changes that can be perceived between these two paintings, despite their subtle abstraction, and reflects the artist's own recollections of growing up in Shanghai.

In the exhibition, a small, framed embroidery entitled *Modernity's End* (41 × 42 cm, 2016), designed by Young and sewn in Suzhou, accompanied Tang and He's works. The design of this textile—with its layered geometric graphics, typography and women's portraits—emulates modern pictorial magazines from 1930s Shanghai, such as *Liangyou/The Young Companion*, in which the modern woman, with her new social roles, was a central archetype. Images of a young Alice in a fashionable qipao, and an older Daisy with a standard Cultural Revolution-era portrait, are overlaid on the right with a phrase in modernist Chinese typography: *Shidai Funu* 時代婦女 or 'Women of the Times' (as in, 'Modern Women').

ACKNOWLEDGEMENT

John Young especially acknowledges Paul McGregor and Kate Bagnall for their early groundbreaking research on these two women's lives.

pages 280–81
Detail of *Modernity's End: Half the Sky* 2016
Installation view, Incinerator Art Space,
Willoughby City Council, Sydney, 2016

There were Chinese men in Australia, but there were also Chinese women from Australia. Two Australian women of Chinese heritage returned to China in the 1930s. Yet, a return to a point of origin is often found to be a new destination. The Queenslander, Daisy Kwok, and the lass born in Rutherglen, Alice Lim Kee, left for China in the 30s. The modern era of 1930s Australia was a time of the White Australia Policy. For those of Chinese heritage, life was better found outside of Australia. That included those working in the service of culture. The circumstances were such that neither woman returned.

Yet, despite such historically significant connections to their stories, as listed above, my voice in the work was never the most important. It was far more meaningful that this reflection be made by Chinese Australian women—especially women of culture with an acute sense of agency and reflection—through the works of Cyrus Tang and Pei Pei He. I could not have had a better reply when an invitation was extended to them to help create this project.

CYRUS TANG, ARTIST STATEMENT, 2022

The Final Cast Off (2016) is a video about two Chinese Australian women, Alice Lim Kee and Daisy Kwok. Alice and Daisy represented the new Chinese elite who decided to have their own professional careers rather than being housewives and following their husband's lives. They stood up for themselves and confronted traditional expectations of their behaviour as Chinese wives, daughters and women. Both women also reflect the complexities of Chinese Australian history, especially the history of women, children and family.

Incense has long been used in Chinese Buddhist and Taoist worship. It is reputed to be a method of purifying the surroundings, bringing forth an assembly of Buddhas, gods, demons and the like. *Jingxiang* 敬香 ('to respectfully offer incense') is a ritual of offering incense accompanied by tea and/or fruits in Chinese traditional religion. I used incense ash mixed with charcoal to create the images of both Alice and Daisy. It is a gesture of worship for these two incredible Chinese women who stood up for their own wishes. In the video, the images of Alice and Daisy, made out of ash on milky water, slowly swirl and disperse as they interact with my breath. To me, this breathing is the same as the ritual of offering incense to someone we respect.

Eras in Daisy Kwok's Life

非常感谢John Young邀请我参与他的艺术项目Modernity's End: Half the Sky，
让我有机会重温两位出生在澳大利亚但生活在上海的华裔女性跌宕起伏的人
生经历，其中我对Daisy Kwok的印象尤为深刻，那是因为Kwok家族的永安公
司伴随了许多我幼年的记忆。

我出生于上海，至今仍清楚记得在我成长过程中对永安公司的印象。永安公
司是当时上海最大的百货公司之一，也是最具标志性的建筑之一。拥有如此
庞大的商业大厦，毋庸置疑彰显着 Kwok家族当时在上海的社会地位。

然而数世代屡经巨大的社会动荡颠覆了中国，历次政治运动使Kwok家族饱受
摧残，财富散尽，尝尽人生的悲欢离合。让我无限感慨的是，Daisy Kwok能
始终保持着她的雍容优雅，坦然面对苦难，我相信, 这是一种内在的高贵精
神！

我想以两幅模糊的画面留住那个时代的记忆。第一幅画面中我隐隐感觉到
Daisy Kwok与永安公司的内在呼应，那个她曾经美好的少女时代的象征；第
二幅画面似乎隐喻着属于Kwok家族的风光不再，曾经的荣耀已被淹没在文化
大革命的洪流之中，此情此景Daisy Kwok以及她的家族犹如茫茫阴霾中岌岌
可危飘荡着的一粒尘埃。

A huge thanks to John Young for inviting me to participate in *Modernity's End:
Half the Sky,* which gave me an opportunity to review the life experience of two
Australian-born but Shanghai-based Chinese women. I was particularly impressed
by Daisy Kwok, because the Kwok family's Yong An (永安 Wing On) Department
Store accompanied many of my childhood memories.

I was born in Shanghai, and still clearly remember being impressed by the Yong
An Department Store when I was growing up. Yong An was one of the largest
department stores in Shanghai and also one of the most iconic buildings at that
time. It undoubtedly showed the Kwok family's high social status during this period.

Tragically, in the few decades between the 1920s and 1970s, social turmoil
overturned China tremendously. Successive political movements caused the
Kwok family to encounter numerous disasters and taste the sorrows of life. What
impresses me deeply is that Daisy Kwok always maintained her grace and elegance,
and faced hardships calmly. I believe it is her innate noble spirit.

I attempt to preserve the memory of these eras with two blurry paintings. In the
first painting, I faintly feel the connection and echo between Daisy Kwok and the
Yong An building—the symbol of her once beautiful girlhood. The second painting
seems to be a metaphor. The glory that once belonged to the Kwok family has been
submerged in the torrent of the Cultural Revolution (1966–76); Daisy and her
family are like specks of dust floating in the vast haze.

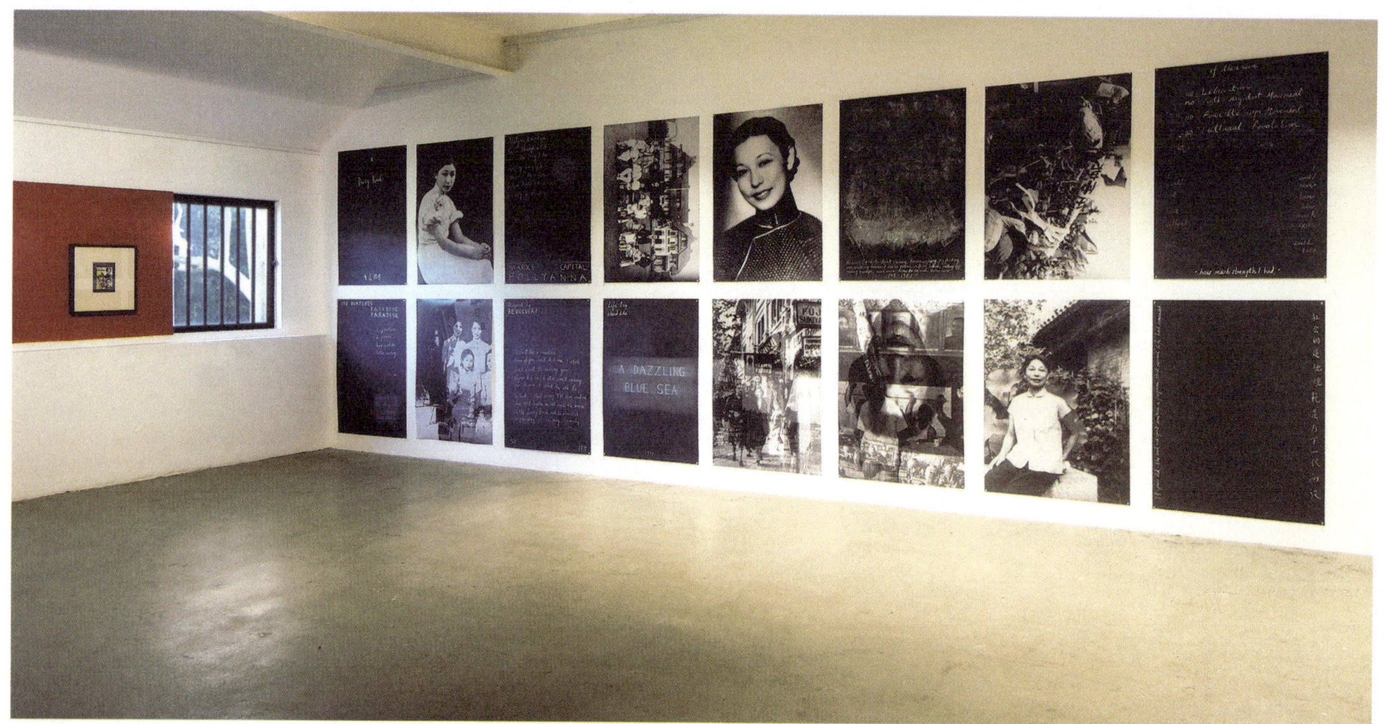

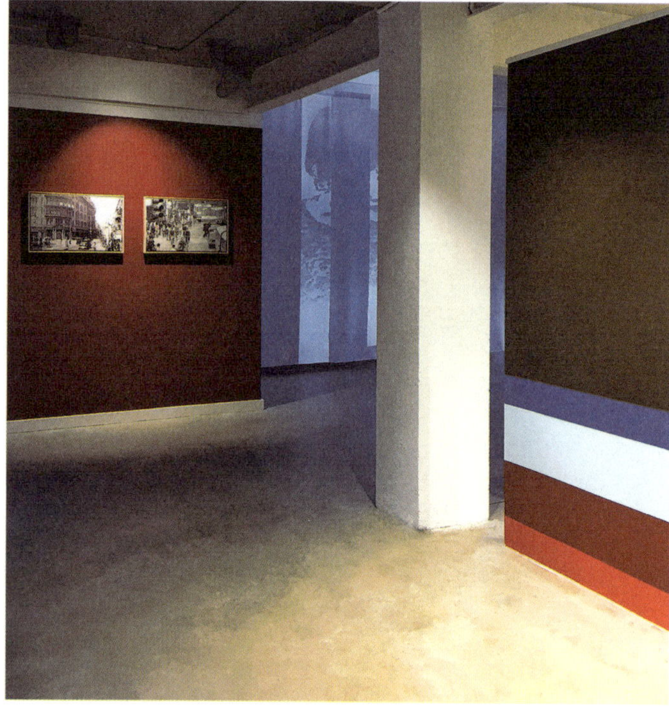

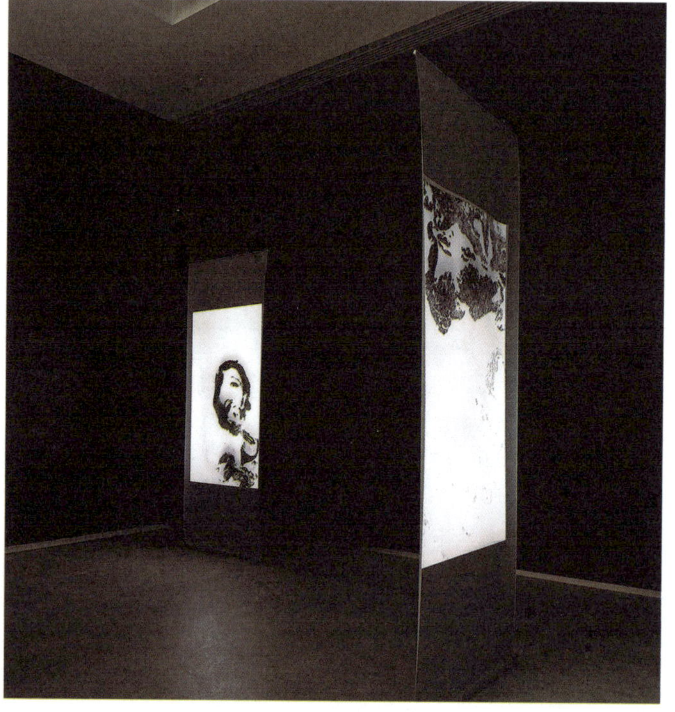

top
Modernity's End: Half the Sky 2016
Installation view, Incinerator Art Space,
Willoughby City Council, Sydney, 2016

bottom left
Modernity's End: Half the Sky, with:
Pei Pei He (1954–)
Era in Daisy Kwok's Life 2016
Oil on canvas, two panels, 42 × 66 cm each
Installation view, Incinerator Art Space,
Willoughby City Council, Sydney, 2016

bottom right
Cyrus Tang (1969–)
The Final Cast Off 2016–17
Dual-channel video projection on Chinese
paper scroll, dimensions variable, 16 min. 11 sec.
Image courtesy of the artist

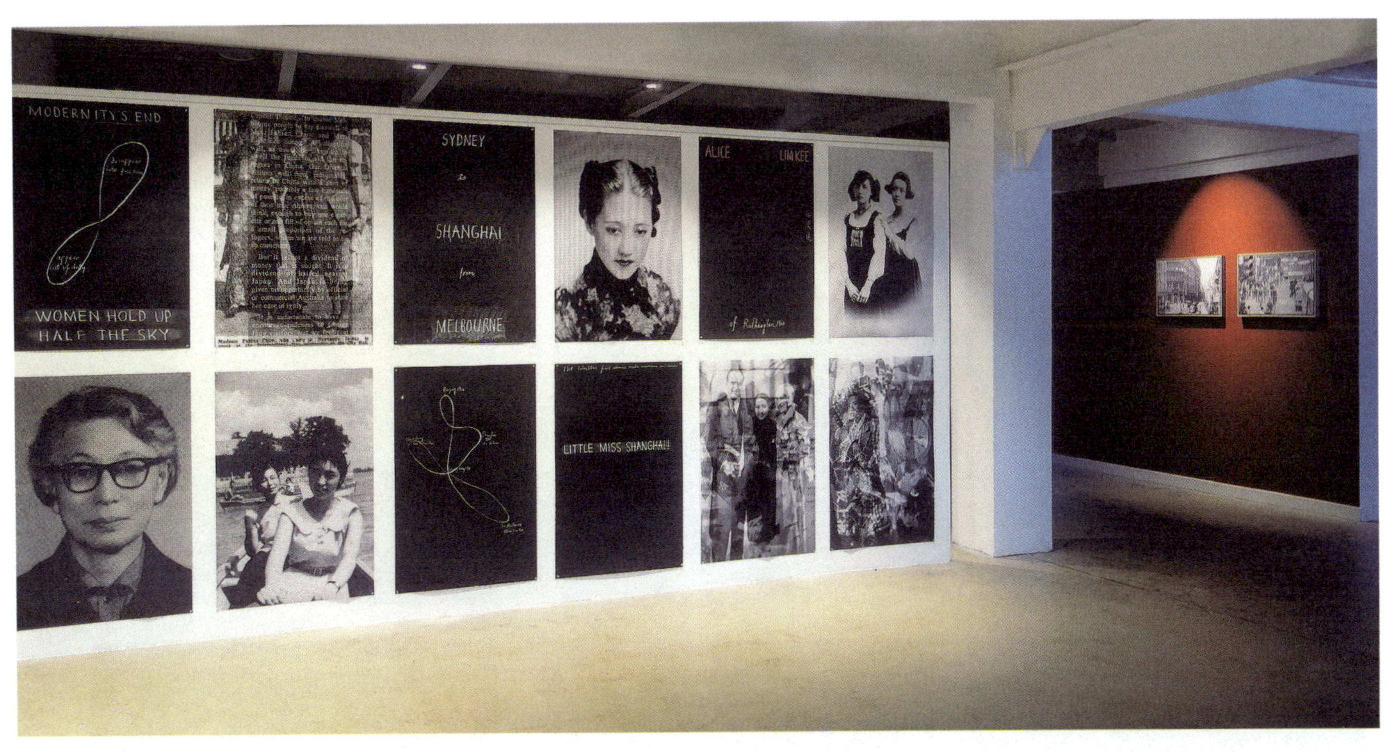

Modernity's End: Half the Sky 2016
Installation view, Incinerator Art Space,
Willoughby City Council, Sydney, 2016

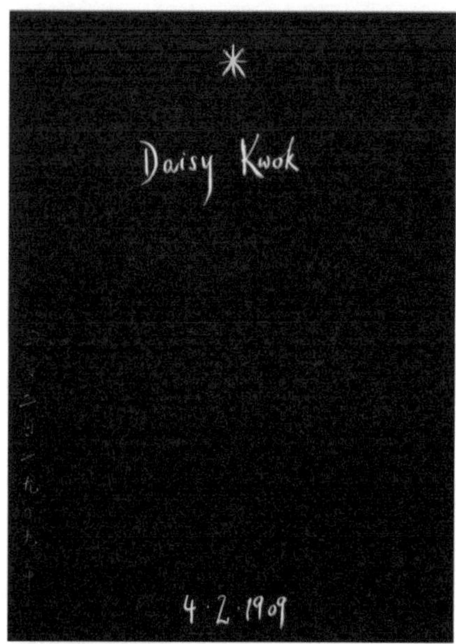

Daisy Kwok
4·2·1909

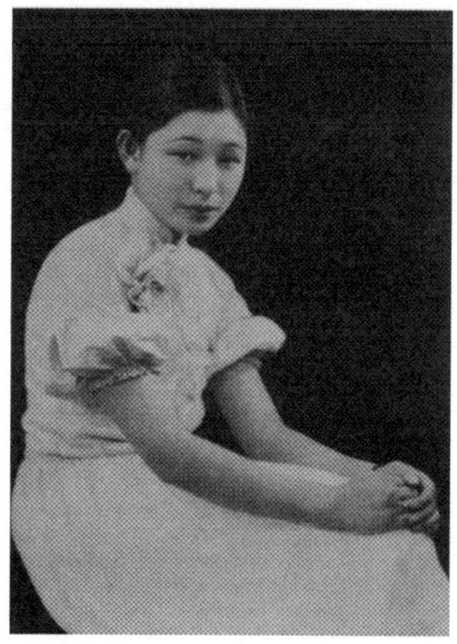

McTyeire School for
Girls, Shanghai 1928
with the Soong Sisters
Yenching University, Beijing
Heiress to the Wing On
fortune. Purity and
tenacity of character
MARX'S   CAPITAL
POLLYANNA

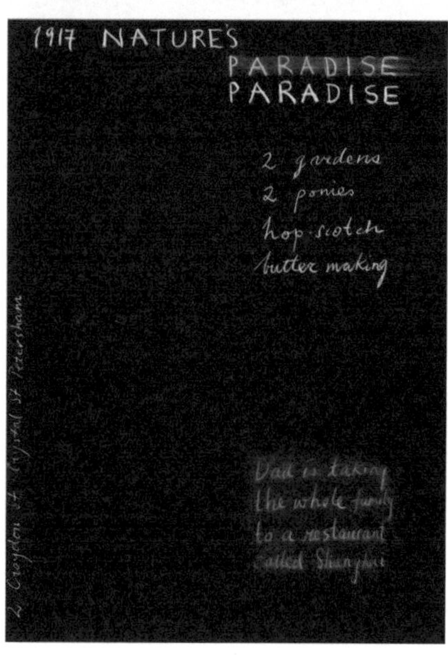

1917 NATURE'S
PARADISE
PARADISE
2 gardens
2 ponies
hop-scotch
butter making
Dad is taking
the whole family
to a restaurant
called Shanghai

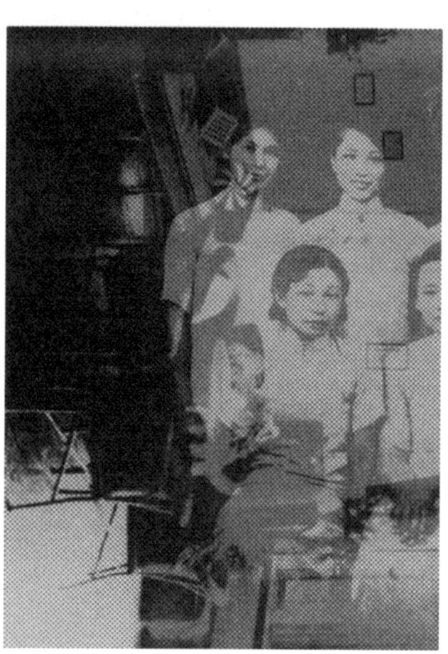

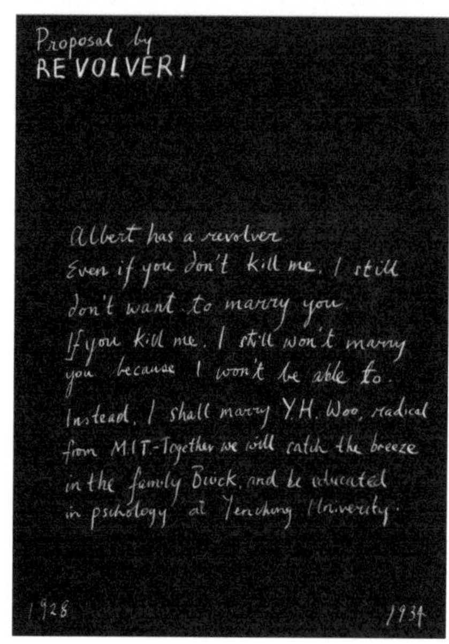

Proposal by
REVOLVER!
Albert has a revolver.
Even if you don't kill me, I still
don't want to marry you.
If you kill me, I still won't marry
you because I won't be able to.
Instead, I shall marry Y.H. Woo, radical
from MIT.-Together we will catch the breeze
in the family Buick, and be educated
in psychology at Yenching University.
1928   1934

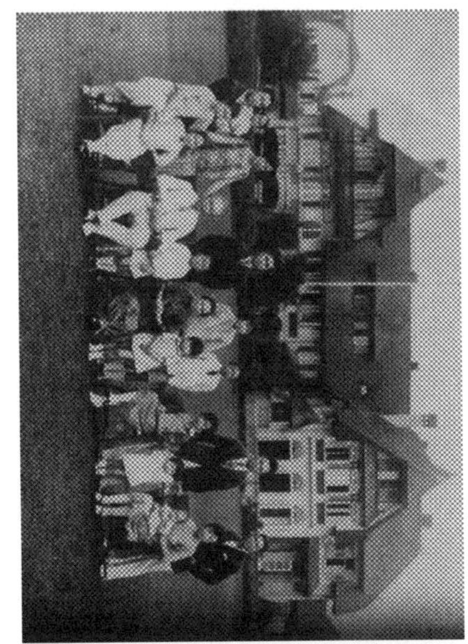
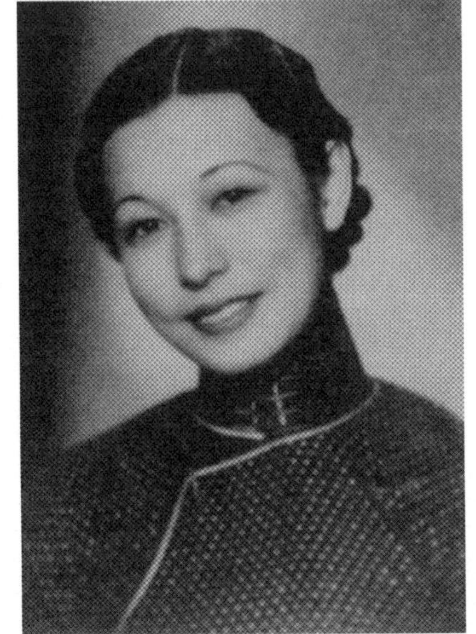
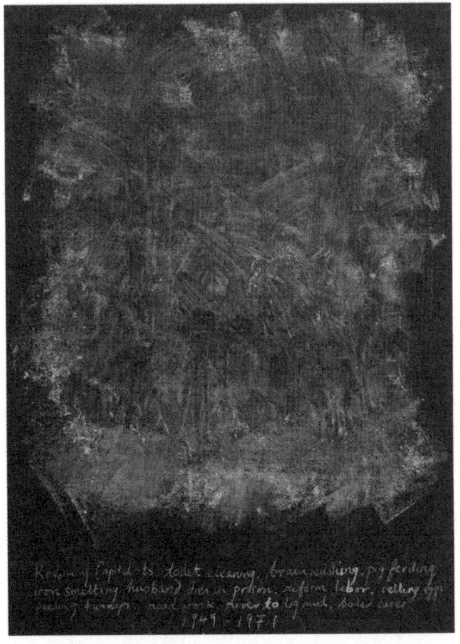
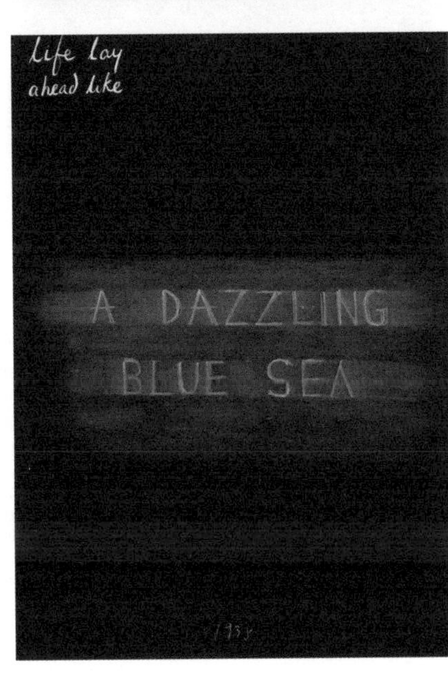
life lay
ahead like
A DAZZLING
BLUE SEA
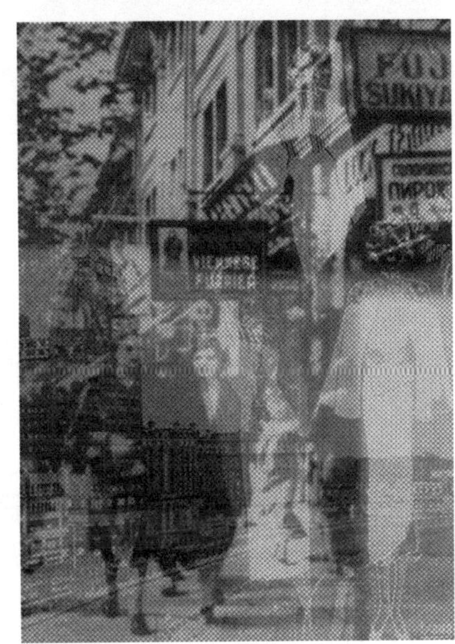
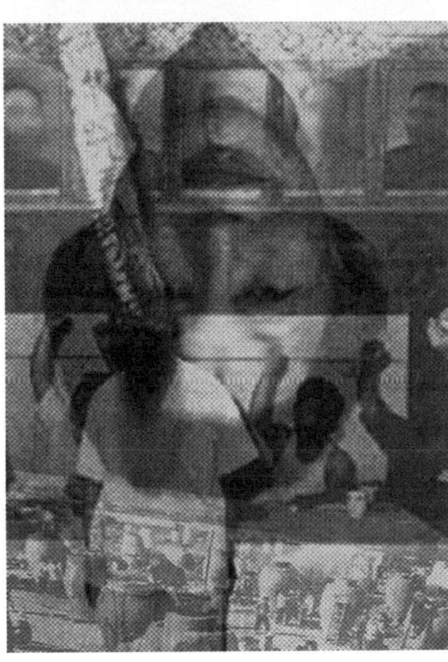

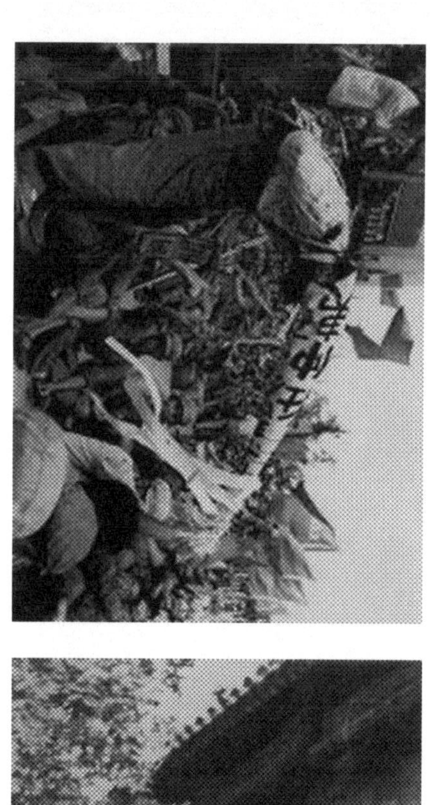

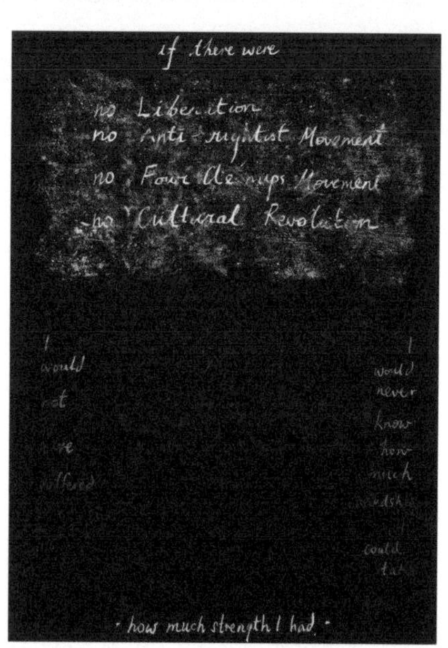
if there were
no Liberation
no Anti-rightist Movement
no Four Clean-ups Movement
no 'Cultural Revolution'
I would not have suffered
I would never know how much hardship I could take
· how much strength I had ·

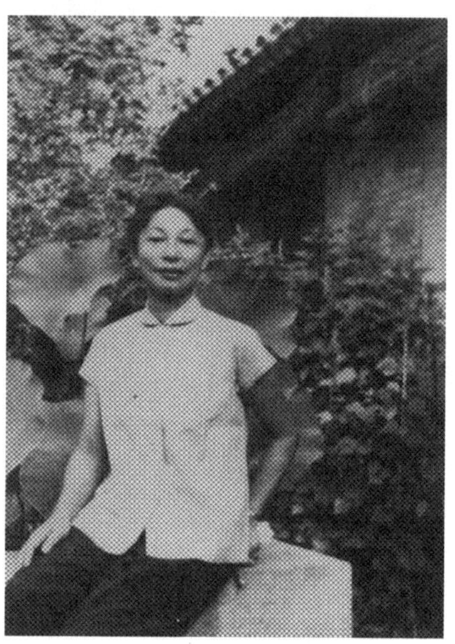

18 years old - the soul and spirit emitted a fragrance that normal life had concealed
· how much strength I had ·
社會的道德規範是力下一代而沒

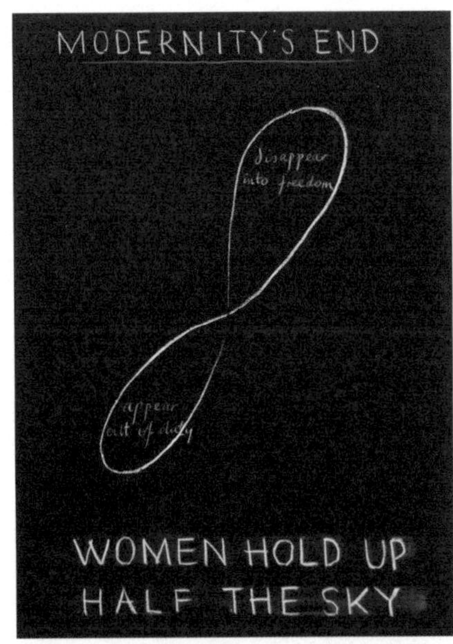

MODERNITY'S END
disappear into freedom
appear out of duty
WOMEN HOLD UP HALF THE SKY

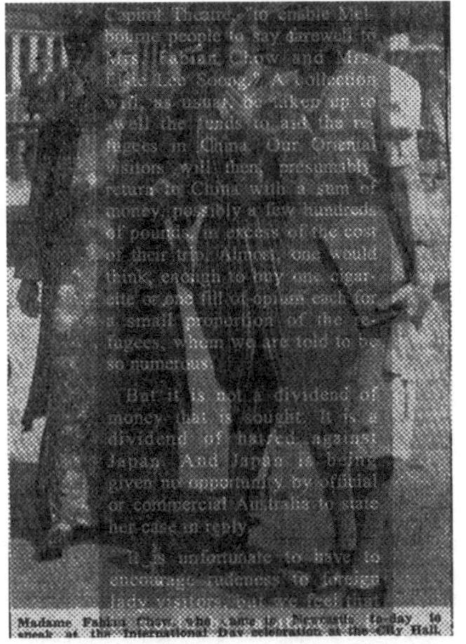

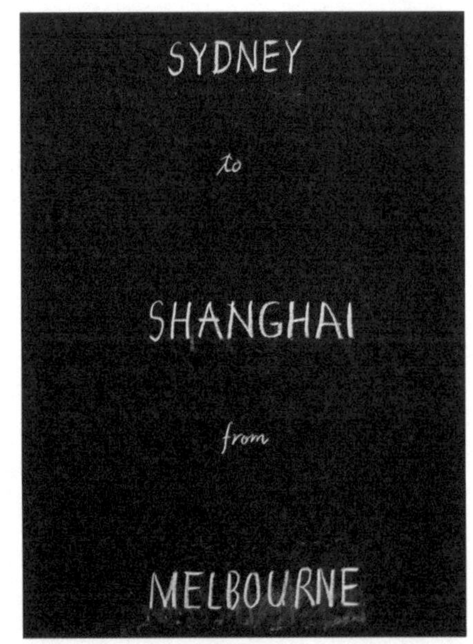

SYDNEY
to
SHANGHAI
from
MELBOURNE

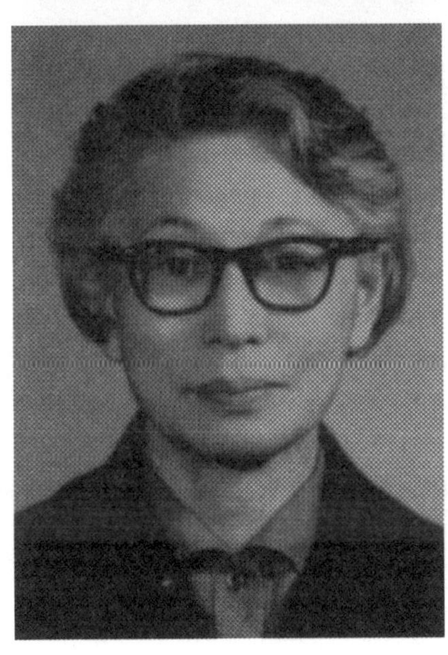

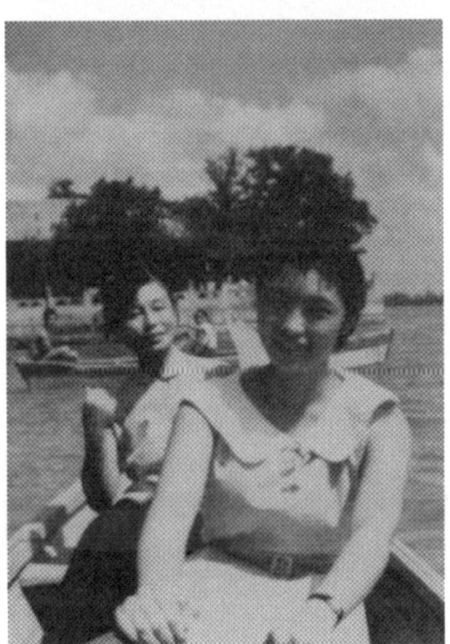

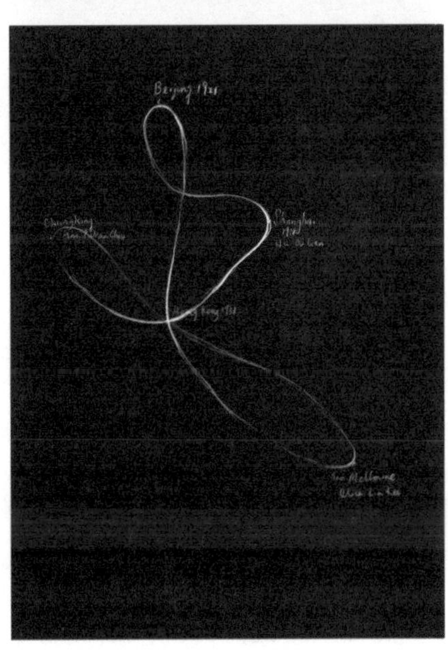

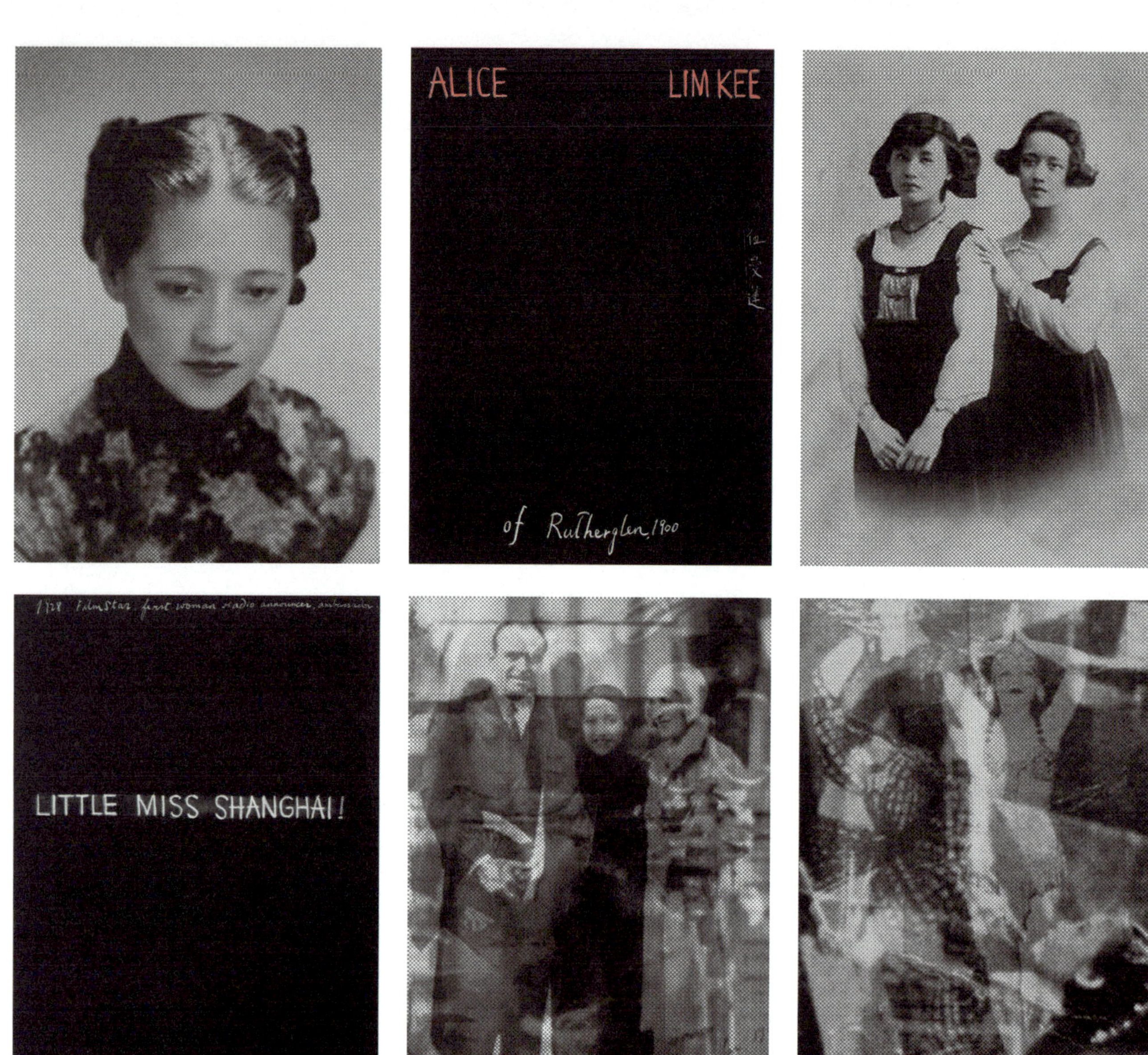

pages 291–92
Modernity's End: Half the Sky (Alice Lim Kee) 2016
Digital print on photographic paper and chalk on
blackboard-painted archival cotton paper, 16 units,
210 × 470 cm

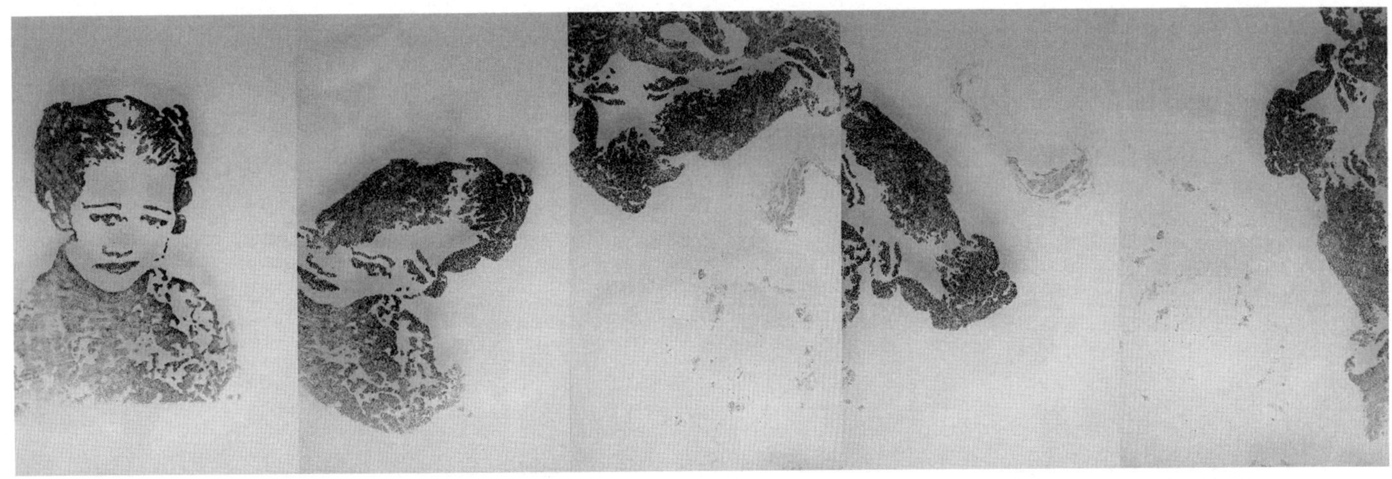

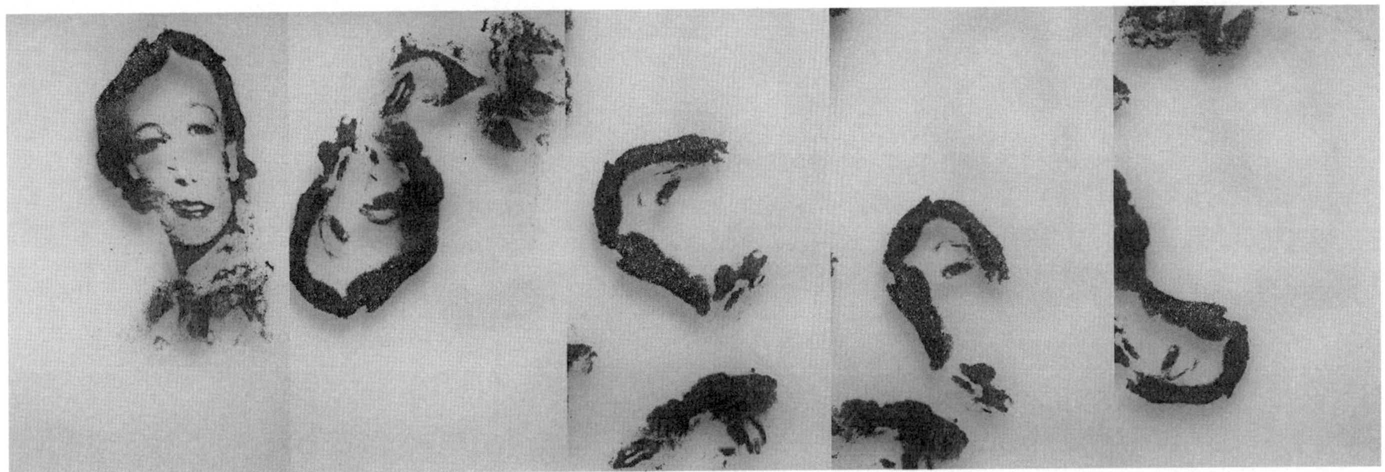

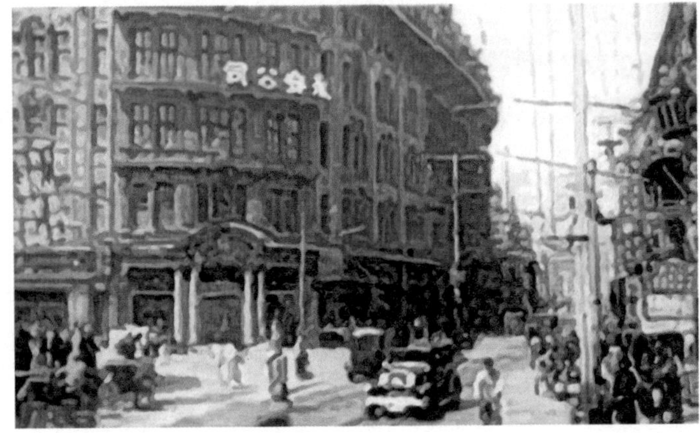

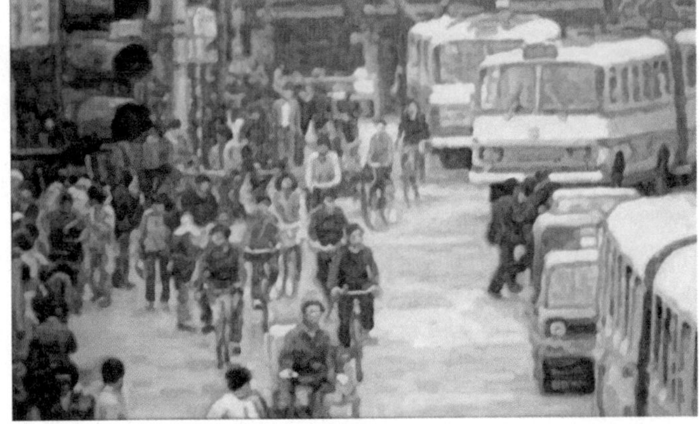

NONE LIVING KNOWS

2017

JOHN YOUNG
NONE LIVING KNOWS

During the late nineteenth century, Chinese immigrants and miners walked from Darwin through the vast northern territories. Trekking along the Overland Telegraph to Tennant Creek, then east across the Barkly Tablelands some reached as far as Cairns on Queensland's east coast - at times, in search of gold. Intermittent and often alone, the walkers trailed a perilous and unmapped two thousand kilometres. *None Living Knows* is a meditation on this walk; imagining the mental and spiritual passage of culturally displaced men in pursuit of a new life.

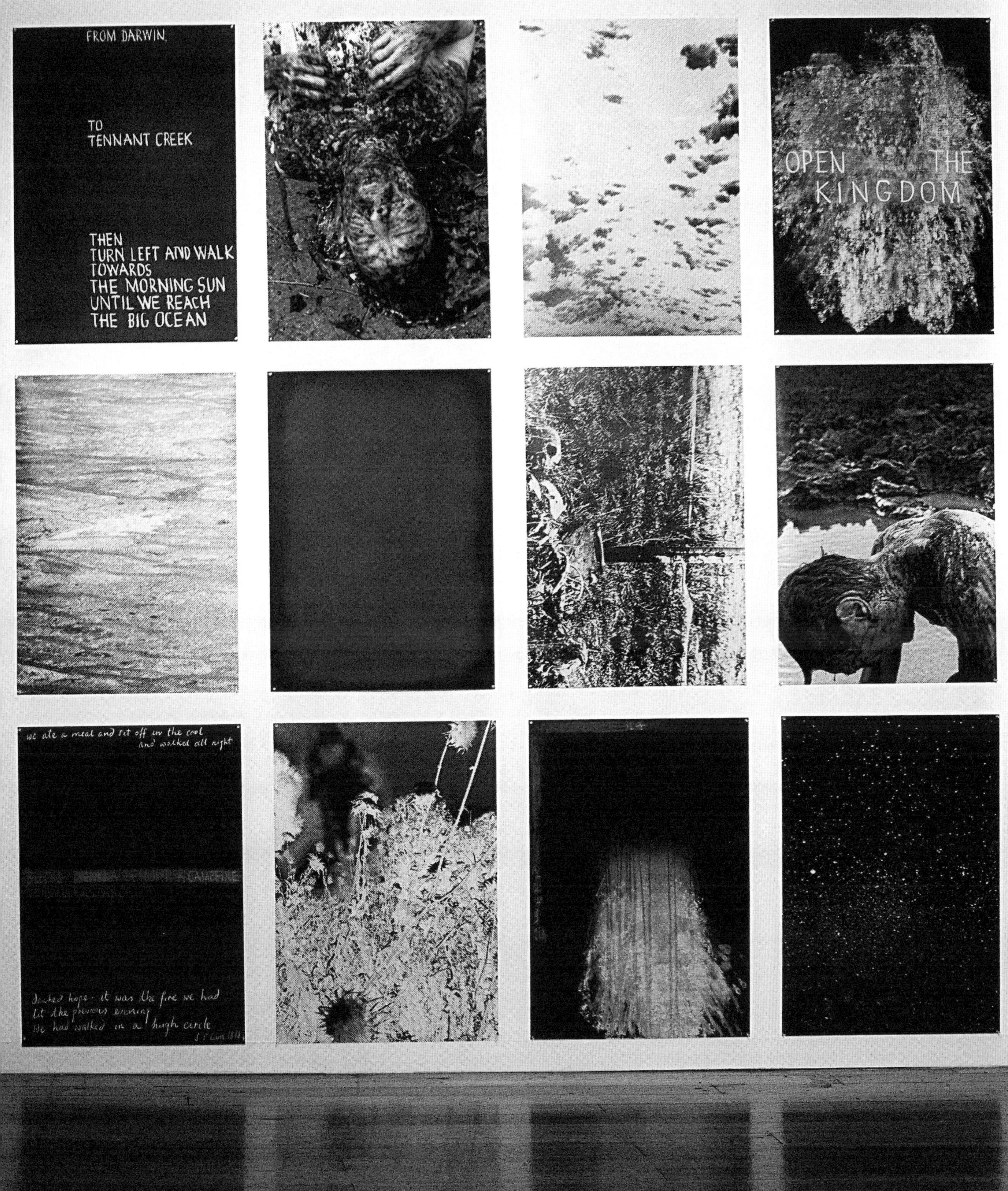
FROM DARWIN.
TO
TENNANT CREEK
THEN
TURN LEFT AND WALK
TOWARDS
THE MORNING SUN
UNTIL WE REACH
THE BIG OCEAN
OPEN   THE
KINGDOM
we ate a meal and set off in the cool
and walked all night

NONE LIVING KNOWS

OUTLINE

In the late nineteenth century, Chinese migrants walked some 2500 kilometres across Australia to avoid the Victorian ten-pound poll tax and other forms of restriction to Chinese migration introduced from 1855. As well as the more common walk from Robe, South Australia, to the Victorian goldfields of Ararat, Ballarat, Castlemaine and Bendigo (16,261 Chinese men, and one woman landed in Robe between 1857 and 1863), smaller numbers of newly arrived Chinese also travelled by foot and occasionally on horseback from Darwin, through the Northern Territory to the Queensland border towns of Burketown, Camooweal and Urandangi, with some settling in far North Queensland, where gold had initially been found at Palmer River. Without guides, and often travelling alone, the walkers trailed a perilous and uncharted route, with little water and no supplies, risking attack by Indigenous clans or arrest as illegal migrants—a tenacious endeavour that resulted in many deaths.

None Living Knows (2017) consists of a series of abstract paintings and an installation of chalkboard drawings and digital prints from archival photographs. The installation work, titled *Open the Kingdom*, comprises twelve works in a three-row grid (320 × 310 cm total) in which layered archival images of the raw Australian landscape and abject human figures are paired with the sparse instructions given to Chinese migrants by their compatriots to guide their route. Alongside these are chalkboard drawings, many of which feature areas of erased and overwritten text.

The painting series *None Living Knows #1–7* (86.5 × 102.5 cm) and the pair *None Living Knows I* and *II* (238 × 156 cm each) are luminescent abstractions of the Barkly Tableland, an area of grasslands running from eastern Northern Territory into Western Queensland, which formed part of the walk taken by Chinese migrants on the route south from Darwin.

For further information on the march from Robe and elsewhere by Chinese migrants, see Gordon Grimwade, *Australia's Long March: The exhibition*, Queensland, 2013 and Grimwade, 'Tenacity in the Tropics: Chinese Overland Migration in Northeast Australia during the Nineteenth Century', *Chinese Southern Diaspora Studies*, issue 8, 2019, pp. 168–89.

ARTIST STATEMENT

Catalogue entry (July 2017)

> Perhaps in the world's destruction
> it would be possible at last to see how it was made.
> Oceans, mountains. The ponderous counter spectacle of
> things ceasing to be. The sweeping waste, hydroptic and
> coldly secular. The silence.
> - Cormac McCarthy, *The Road*

> The stranger's out on the road … isn't just wandering
> about, with nowhere to go. All the time, he's
> coming closer to a place he can call his own.
> - Martin Heidegger

'None living knows' are words taken from section VI, 'His Memories', of the W. B. Yeats poem 'A Man Young and Old' (*The Tower*, MacMillan, 1928), and are evocative of an event in Australia that to this date has barely been documented. The works in this exhibition are a meditation on this walk, a walk by men who had departed their original Chinese world, and were denied their new world on arrival.

Reflection (2022)

This momentous event can and will only be posed as a question. When an event is drained of historical facts, whether because it is devoid of reportage or because of its remoteness in time, we can never truly know the experience of those who lived it. What inhabited the minds of those who took the walk? Their wretchedness, their demons, their loss or transcendence are inaccessible to us. I somehow had no doubt that the three words 'open the kingdom' came into the minds of these walkers— three words from a Philip Glass opera that once upon a time shot through me like a bolt. This request, this demand through trauma for a moment of transcendence, for a mystical answer that may stand so near when life comes near to its end, and all the while accompanied by art and its limits.

We can imagine and make real the arduous bodies, perhaps grasping a somatic parallel by retracing such paths or a protracted, disciplined rendering of a series of rhythmical paintings over the course of a year. The paintings in *None Living Knows* were painted with the ground of the work built up gradually through repetitive horizontal, meditative brush strokes, onto which were added multiple layers of glazing to replicate the repetitive breath when walking, and the visual effect of the Australian landscape resolving itself into an abstract haze over time. This process-based method is also reminiscent of my early series of pencil on paper works, *Drawing in Ten Parts* (1981). It was my hope that this rhythmical and repetitive way of working may, intermittently, evoke some remote resonance and sonance … a semblance of understanding, towards a hope.

THE BODY IN THE MUD:
JOHN YOUNG'S HISTORY PROJECTS
AND TRUTH-TELLING IN CHINESE
AUSTRALIAN HISTORY

Sophie Loy-Wilson

I first saw one of John Young's History Projects in 2016. Along with his *Double Ground Paintings* (1993–2005), that work —*Modernity's End: Half the Sky*, at Incinerator Art Space, Sydney—was the result of Young's long engagement with the history of the Chinese in Australia since 1840. For just as Europeans disembarked in the Australian colonies—part of an invasion so destructive that James Belich has called it 'explosive settlement'—so too did many Chinese settlers.[1] Young and I are both pre-occupied with what happened next—the legacies of Chinese migration to Australia. These legacies are many and yet little known. They run through the land, through our blood, through our language and through our history. They are troubling and exciting in equal measure. They speak to the power of historical denialism; to what Anna Clark calls 'the ease with which colonial discourse accounted for murder'.[2] And, as many Chinese Australians stayed on this land and made it their home, they demonstrate survival. But unlike historians such as myself, bent on pulling the stories together into a historical narrative, Young is a contemporary artist who is 'trying to maintain some freedom within the historical discourse'.[3] At a time when Chinese Australian historians are increasingly pressured (I feel) into fixing their historical subjects in victim and perpetrator roles, Young's work refuses such closed truths. Instead, his art looks for 'a resolution with indigeneity, with a new sense of place and nature in Australia, while inevitably drawing on one's cultural memory from elsewhere'.[4] It is not that his work refuses historical truth, but that it insists on a complex multiplicity of truths, all connected, all part of this place—an ethics of remembrance rather than a national story. Young once described his approach as akin to hearing a chorus of voices. It is not his job to interpret them, or appease them:

> There is some feeling of voices rising up from the depths of history. I think that's a real contrast, between working in an artistic domain and with these poetic dimensions as opposed to the conventionally historical domain: you can really refuse people closure over a story. You're not possessing the full story, but you're also not allowing the audience to possess the full story.[5]

Chinese Australians arrived in Australia only shortly after the Europeans. The material remains of Chinese settlement are everywhere, gathering dust in museums or sitting forgotten in the irrigation ditches of old market gardens: red and gold temple altars, glass bottles, ginger jars, stone grinders that once turned wheat into flour. Chinese Australian genetic inheritance turns up in ancestry DNA tests, or is evidenced in old photographs, waiting in family albums.

Chinese settler testimony is all through the English-language archival record. Immigration records, court records, land records, petitions, political pamphlets; these are all full of Chinese voices. But we've only recently begun to listen to them. Modern

Australian history only began to acknowledge Chinese Australian settlers in the 1970s, at the end of the White Australia Policy.[6] Prior to this, historians wrote of Chinese gold miners, but not settlers, they hinted at terrible anti-Chinese violence, but stopped short of spelling it out—'all that excitement', a journalist for *Walkabout* magazine wrote in the 1970s, referring to the Buckland anti-Chinese riots of 1857: 'You won't find too many traces of all that excitement now, but given a little imagination, you can see it all in your mind's eye'.[7]

For me, archival practice in Chinese Australian history has been a journey from the confident proclamations made as a young historian on anti-Chinese racism, motivated by my desire for atonement, to a more circumspect approach—for, what can I know about Chinese Australian lives? The gap between what we know and what we don't know can feel so big, can gape so wide, and yet the desire for knowledge about our Chinese past is only growing, partly because this past was neglected for so long. For Chinese Australians, the scars of the past sit just below the skin, on the tip of the tongue, like a grandmother shifting in her chair before speaking, for now she is ready and her family knows to fall silent.

—

When I walked into John Young's exhibition in 2017, it was a hot Sydney day and the cicadas were loud outside, but inside the air was sharp and cool. The exhibition was held at a gallery in Willoughby on Sydney's north shore, in an old incinerator next to a wide green oval. The light was low and bright at the same time, and on one of the walls I saw Young's famous grid structure, a hallmark of the History Projects, 'forc[ing] the viewer to construct the narrative by moving across the grid rather than via a linear progression through a story'.[8]

The exhibition, *Modernity's End: Half the Sky*, featured two Chinese Australian women who grew up in Australia but ended their lives in Shanghai: Alice Lee Kim and Daisy Kwok. Alice and Daisy were Australian-born; they were second generation Chinese Australians. Both had migrated to China in the 1920s and 1930s, the heady days of jazz-age Shanghai, and their portraits from this era (included in Modernity's End) evoke everything we have come to associate with interwar capitalist modernity in China—glamour, luxury, consumerism, and a new kind of female power. Daisy Kwok is said to have been the first woman in Shanghai to drive her own car.

The coda to John's exhibition, however, told the second part of Alice and Daisy's life stories. After the Japanese invasion and Communist revolution, a second imagining of this female power emerged, encapsulated by Mao's famous declaration: 'Women hold up half the sky'. And yet this promise was hollow: 'In reality, women were required to perform the same work as their male counterparts in addition to family duties.'[9] For Daisy Kwok, hailing from a famous capitalist family, Communist liberation brought great loss; her husband died in prison, her property was confiscated and she was 'sent down' to the countryside to work at a pig farm and then a vegetable factory. Young referenced this time in *Modernity's End*, writing the following words in chalk at the bottom of a black panel, underneath a large smear of smudged chalk:

> Reforming capitalists, toilet cleaning, brain washing, pig feeding, iron smelting, husband dies in prison, selling eggs, peeling turnips, river to dig mud, boiler carer 1949–1971

The quote hung in the air, scrawled as if on a dirty school board, and lay adjacent to newspaper articles overlaying black-and-white photographs. Young's printing technique

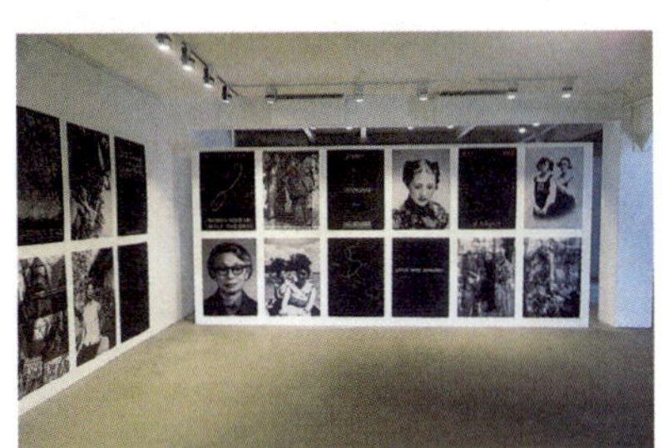

Modernity's End: Half the Sky 2016
Installation view, Incinerator Art Space,
Willoughby City Council, Sydney, 2016

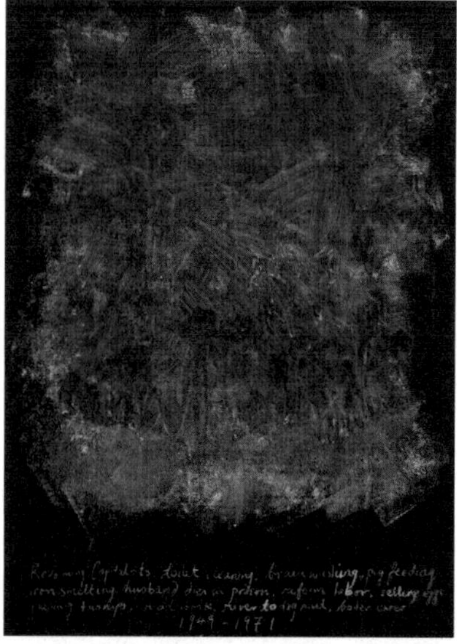

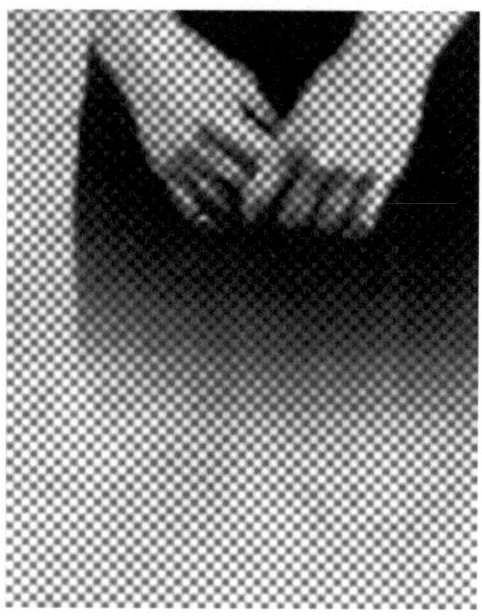

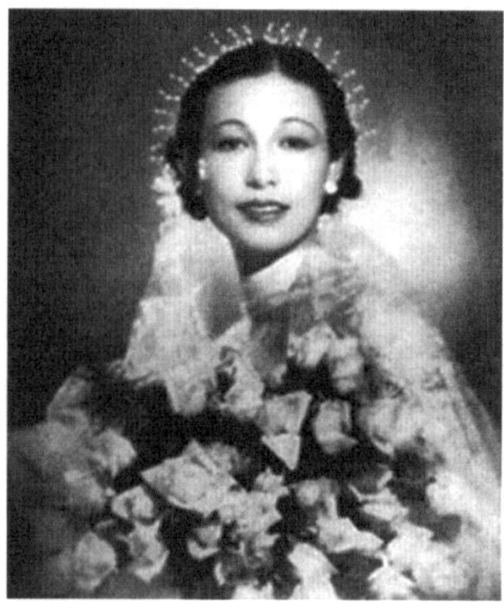

1949–1971 2016
Chalk on blackboard-painted archival
cotton paper, 100 × 70 cm

Detail from *Sisters* 2016
Digital print on photographic paper and chalk
on blackboard-painted archival cotton paper,
100 × 70 cm

Daisy Kwok, wedding photograph, c. 1930s

is intentional. His photographs and newspaper article reproductions are so granulated that they contain large half-tone dots. As he explained in 2017:

> Those dots actually withhold such a lot of information … The image pretends to be documentational and denotational but when you walk up to it, and if you think about it, it's actually not at all. It's almost acting in bad faith to truth. It's supposed to tell some truth, but it actually doesn't. If there is any truth in the work, it lies elsewhere. Not in the literal archival content.[10]

I had written a history of Daisy Kwok, and Young and I had used some of the same archival material in our work.[11] Like Young, I had immersed myself in photographs, newspapers, archives, gathering paper and quotes and firsthand accounts, photographs and maps and timelines, names, birth certificates, travel documents and obituaries. I had travelled to Shanghai and Hong Kong looking for remnants of Daisy's life. I had visited her family's old mansion in Shanghai—now dwarfed by a gleaming hospital building, and shoulder to shoulder with a freeway—and had run my hands along the still-beautiful 1930s tiles in one of the bathrooms. They were a dark green. In an apartment in the French Concession, I had interviewed her friend, Tess Johnson, one of the first United States diplomats in Shanghai after China's late-1970s 'reform and opening', who had compiled Daisy's writing to be deposited in the Hoover Institute. There, on Tess's dresser, was a 1930s photograph of Daisy in a stunning wedding dress, taken by a Russian portrait photographer famous in Shanghai at the time. Daisy had given it to Tess, and Tess had kept it.

Eventually, I had written about Daisy; a historical piece, neatly stating my case. I argued that the large Chinese Australian community in Shanghai functioned as a bridge for Australians invested in radical interwar ideas (international socialism, cosmopolitanism, anti-colonialism) and looking to a future beyond the British empire. Adam McKeown, a renowned historian of overseas Chinese peoples (who passed away young and in tragic circumstances), wrote the following about historical practice in Chinese Australian history: 'Historical writing is a constant conversation between the specific histories of individuals, locations and institutions and the more general narratives of peoples, nations, regions and the world'.[12] Daisy's life mattered because it underscored the forgotten contributions Chinese Australians made to China Australia relations, while also demonstrating the price they paid for living between two nations in a time of White Australia Policy and Chinese isolationism. I made decisions about chronology. This involved papering over some of the gaps in my source material. I knew far more about Daisy's life under capitalism than I did under communism, for example, and I knew little about the effects of racism on her family at the turn of the century, though Daisy's childhood spanned the Federation decades, a high-water mark for anti-Chinese sentiment in Australia. But this is history writing, we take pieces of the archive and search for coherence, and for greater meaning; we place individual lives in patterns and contexts. For in the end, a story had to be told. I saw my quest as an ethical one, a chance to re-balance the scales, to bring Chinese Australians into Australian national history. And then I closed the page on Daisy, put away my paper, and gave birth to my first child weeks later. It was July 2016. I was later told that my work was used by a DFAT official to assist then Prime Minster Malcolm Turnbull in Shanghai. He used the story of Daisy's family in a speech, to demonstrate Australia's deep historical ties to the city.

I stood facing Modernity's End in 2017 feeling uncomfortable. The textures in the exhibition left my hands itchy; I wanted to touch the images, to cross the empty space between me and the work, to feel the texture of the paper. It was the plain black squares in the grid that unnerved me the most. Large blank squares of black. On some squares Young drew loops and figure eights, sometimes writing place names on the curves of these loops in chalk:

Melbourne, 1900, Alice Lim Kee
Beijing, 1921
Shanghai, 1928, Wu Ai Lien
Hong Kong, 1938
Chungking, Mrs. Fabian Chow[13]

I felt at sea without a point of departure or arrival, for the loops of time and movement didn't deliver such demarcations. There was no 'story' to be told here, and time did not move neatly, evenly along birth, life, departure, arrival, death and remembrance. Sadness was undeniably present in the room. Bodies were there, too, in photographs. Aged bodies, dead bodies, Chinese Australian bodies, female bodies. Voices were recorded in chalk. And yet Young refused to provide a reason for any of it; that is, he refused to perform a fundamental expectation of modern historical practice. He made no overarching argument; he didn't articulate the point of it all. Who was responsible for what Daisy endured? Would a collation of archives get us any closer to the truth of Daisy's life?

Young explained his relationship to historical practice in an interview with Genevieve Trail in 2021:

> Whereas when I started doing the History Projects, it became immediately obvious that when you are working with archives and in the historical domain, there is a sense of justice that one has to acknowledge with regard to people's suffering, because of racism, sexism, colonialism or whatever it is. But at the same time, I'm not necessarily one who, like some historians, are adamantly in pursuit of indelible truths, because I don't really believe in that, or at least not in timeless truth as socially or politically objective. On the other hand, I'm totally aware that there are different rhetorics in the way you can present truths.[14]

In eschewing a dominant narrative voice in Modernity's End, Young brought me face-to-face with the power I wield as a storyteller. For historians do more than paper over gaps in the archive. They work within the constraints of their own culture, feeling around the edges of its curiosity, sense-checking our hunger for the past. What are we craving to know? Historians offer resolutions, they build a recognition between the present and the past, and to do so they refer to a common humanity, to shared investments in human pain, dignity, strength, justice, anger, pleasure, suffering. But they also make choices, intuiting the aspects of the past that won't find recognition in the present, the unwelcome historical guests, the lives that fall on the cutting room floor. And it is this detail that leads us to the unspoken limitations of historical compassion—for every story we welcome into the present, that we make familiar in the present, there are many others we are simply not prepared to hear.

—

We are driving along a highway near Bega. The road runs along a high ridge between green valleys, and we look down onto dairy farms. The clouds are big in the sky and sit heavily on the hills. I'm directing my husband towards Brogo, a small town 20 kilometres north of Bega. There is enough phone reception for me to search digitised Australian newspapers for local histories of the area, and I've found something at Brogo.

I'm searching for Chinese Australians and I have been for a long time. I have no Chinese Australian ancestry, but I lived in China in the late 1990s and early 2000s—the early Hanson era—and I have been trying to reconcile this experience ever since, rummaging through colonial archives, listening to oral history interviews and now lost in Yuin country, directing my weary husband off the highway 'one last time'. It is January 2020 and I have just started a big research project. I type phrases into my phone: 'Chinese fishing camp—Moruya', 'Chinese market garden—Wapongo', 'Chinese shop—Bega.'

I've been doing this all week, as we snake through the Eurobodalla region, a landscape only just recovering from the Black Summer bushfires. I've walked through Moruya and Mogo cemeteries looking for Chinese miners and fishermen. I've stood on the edge of Lake Wapongo, laced with oyster farms, where newspaper articles from the 1880s tell me that Chinese fishermen lived, their catch supplying the growing township of Bega. I badly want to find the location of their camps. I spend a lot of time walking through wet grass and mud in the wrong shoes. In Moruya cemetery it was so wet my feet sank into the ground, amongst the dead.

The landscape doesn't offer me much, and why should it? It owes me nothing, and I don't know how to read the tides. The archaeologist Alister Bowen spent months excavating a Chinese fishing camp at Point Albert because he knew from old maps that dozens of these camps dotted the Gippsland coast in the nineteenth century. He dug systematically into the muddy bank to find Chinese medicine bottles and opium pipes, belt buckles, copper nails, fish bones and pig bones. It took a long time and much archaeological expertise before he could produce his now famous study, *Archaeology of the Chinese Fishing Industry in Colonial Victoria* (2008).[15] And here I am, a creature of the air-conditioned archives, with a phone, a digitised newspaper article and a hunger for Chinese Australian history that I don't quite understand, and which sometimes makes me uncomfortable.

What gives me the right to think this land will give up its secrets? I don't find Chinese graves in Moruya or in Mogo, even though my phone's 'grave finder' app assures me these Chinese graves exist; and when I stare hard at Lake Wapongo, willing it to tell me where the Chinese fishing camps might have been (is there a hut, a plaque, a market garden?) all I hear is the crunch of thousands of oyster shells underfoot as I walk along the lake's edge. At night I type ferociously onto my laptop as my family sleeps, alternating between multiple digital databases (Google maps, immigration records, newspaper records, heritage reports, local histories) hoping to pin down a location. If the many Chinese migrants who moved through this region didn't leave a trace on the land, surely they left a trace on paper. I can almost hear the search engines humming as I type: Chinese fisherman, Merimbula; Chinese fisherman, Wapongo; Chinese fisherman, Narooma; 'prohibited immigrant'; 'exempted from the dictation test'.

But one day on the road to Bega, I find something. It's an article about an assault, what was described as a 'stoning', that took place on the road between Brogo and Bega in summer 1885.[16] Six boys, aged between thirteen and sixteen, were accused of attacking Ah Poon, who was so badly injured that he had trouble speaking in court. It's not what I wanted to find and when I read about Ah Poon, I get a nauseous feeling. This is precisely the kind of story my colleagues in Chinese Australian history and I are trying to avoid, because it's the kind of story that speaks so loudly in Chinese Australian history and we worry it will drown out other voices. We don't want the stories we tell to be always about anti-Chinese violence because often, then, the focus becomes white Australians, *their* nationalism, *their* racism, *their* lives. And now, post-White Australia

Policy, *their* guilt. Indigenous historians have long argued for 'extra-colonial histories', histories that prove that Indigenous lives did not 'revolve around settler colonial domination, expropriation, exploitation or elimination.'[17]

But these stories are inescapable. Anti-Chinese violence is all through the Australian historical record. And so, I find it even when I'm not looking for it. Even when I'm explicitly avoiding it.

On 19 December 1885 the Bega Gazette and Eden District Southern Advertiser sent a journalist to Bega Police Court to cover Ah Poon's case. Ah Poon brought his attackers to court. He testified through a translator called Ching Roy. His testimony was extensive despite 'appear[ing] to be in a state of partial coma'.[18] Whoever the newspaper sent to cover the case wrote a lot of copy—thousands of words—and I read them, 136 years later, in the passenger seat of our family car, possibly the first person to read Ah Poon's testimony in a while.

Six boys, aged between thirteen and sixteen, were accused of attacking Ah Poon on Sunday 5 December 1885. The boys were sitting by the Brogo River while Ah Poon was trying to cross. They threw sand at him; he ran through the river. They threw stones at him. He remembered running:

> [F]ollowed by a shower of stones. He then went up to the creek, followed
> by the boys still stoning him; soon he was knocked down, and became
> insensible for a few minutes. He was taken to the camp at Mr. Henry
> Otton's, and lay there for two days suffering severely, when he was brought
> to Bega in a cart.[19]

There were numerous witnesses, but their testimony was conflicting. Some claimed that Ah Poon had also armed himself with stones. Others claimed the boys were assisted by an older man. One witness, James Howard, said he 'saw a road man give one of the boys a bottle and told the boys to hit the Chinaman over the face'.[20] Another of the boys claimed this man urged them to 'use a stick', not a bottle. No one disputed that Ah Poon was left injured; some of the boys thought they had killed him. Eventually, someone called Robert Sharpe helped Ah Poon off the road:

> Robert Sharpe testified to having seen three Chinese men going along
> the road towards Brogo on the day in question; some 4 or 5 boys followed
> them, throwing stones and clods; witness thought he knew one of the
> boys who was on horseback. One of the Chinese men fell or lay down,
> and some of the boys ran off through Mr Wood's corn […] Witness lifted
> the Chinese man, who was crying, from the ground, stayed with him for
> some minutes; could not say whether the man was conscious.[21]

One witness—Samuel Britton—spoke of a large crowd of men watching the assault, with a man named Foley or All Sorts 'urging the boys on'.

It's a gruesome scene, one at odds with the bucolic landscape around me. I read the article aloud to my husband as we search for Brogo. 'What do you think you'll find there?' he asks me sceptically. We arrive in the town, but it's really a cluster of houses along the road. I get out of the car and listen for running water. The grass is long and green. There is a new-ish log house flying a Eureka flag. Where was the exact spot of the stoning? I will never know, of course. We drive off towards Bega. I search Bega cemetery for Chinese gravestones, but don't find any. Ah Poon's story slides out of my mind, I don't know where to put it. I think a lot about the stones.

Historians have long worked to explain anti-Chinese violence in Australia, or anti-Chinese hostility as it was often called. The competition for resources (water, gold); the competition for wages. Labour historians tussled with the ugly side of the nineteenth-century union movement—utopian dreams of labour rights but for white men only.[22] National historians wrote of social Darwinism and its disturbing collision with racism, and race-based nationalism.[23] Feminist historians wondered if colonial Australian men, crippled by a sense of colonial inferiority, felt threatened by a potential Chinese invasion, and used anti-Chinese racism to hone their masculinity, to assert their unity against a common enemy.[24] Historians of the family wondered about homophobia—all these Chinese men living together with few Chinese women, perhaps, they thought, this triggered white male fears over repressed homosexuality.[25] Global historians saw a pattern—the same anti-Chinese violence across the white world: in the United States, England, Canada, South Africa, New Zealand, Australia. Marilyn Lake and Henry Reynolds called it *Drawing The Global Colour Line*.[26] In America, a young historian called Beth Lew Williams, whose grandfather was a Chinese miner in California, opens her book with a photograph showing the lynching of a Chinese man. She calls the book *The Chinese Must Go* and shows that American nationalism *needed* anti-Chinese violence to survive, that this nationalism thrived on such violence.[27]

In Canada, Iyko Day turned back to Marx, to capitalism, to help her understand anti-Chinese violence. The business of colonialism is dirty, Day explained, especially settler colonialism, because the invaders never go home.[28] Rather, they stay, taking the land; but to work the land they need a cheap, disposable, compliant labour force, so they bring in indentured labourers or 'coolie' labourers, or at least they try to. Over time this unseemly side of capitalism gets racialised because the indentured labourers—often Asian—come to represent all that is bad about capitalism. The new nations, with their romantic, egalitarian ideas and their Eureka Stockades, their workers' unions and dreams of labour equality, couldn't stand to be reminded that their nation was built not by them, but by the people they displaced and the workers they exploited. So, they expelled the symbols of this bad capitalism, as if by keeping these Asian workers out, they would also keep at bay all the evil aspects of capitalism; sweat shops, low wages, poor living conditions, broken families, squalor, disease: 'This alignment [between Asians and capitalism] allowed white settlers to gloss over and expunge their complicity with capitalist exploitation from their collective memory'.[29]

I've studied such explanations for years; in fact, it was anti-Chinese racism that drew me to history in the first place. In Brogo, though, as I read the report from the trial, I don't find an explanation. The boys never gave their reasons. I grasp at details. James Howard's testimony that he 'saw a road man give one of the boys a bottle and told the boys to hit the Chinaman over the face'.[30] Three Chinese men. Six boys, one an orphan (Michael Bray, fourteen). A river. Sand. Stones. Numerous witnesses. Serious injuries. A court case. Verdict unknown.

The oldest of the boys, George Edwards, is portrayed as the ringleader. He had shaved off his beard soon after the assault, an act the prosecution interpreted as an admission of guilt. I find his descendants on *Ancestry.com*—the family history they share on the website could easily be my own. One descendent has shared a wedding photo of Edwards, who married his wife Phoebe soon after the Ah Poon trial. Almost immediately after they were married, Edwards was jailed for another assault and this time sentenced to six months imprisonment in Bega jail, with hard labour. Although my curiosity has got the better of me, I feel ashamed as I leave the ancestry site, a recognition that perhaps other historians are doing the same to me, linking my ancestors to similar misdeeds.

In 2017, John Young exhibited a new series in the History Project called *None Living Knows*, quoting from W.B. Yeats for his title. *None Living Knows* also follows a grid structure, and uses chalk on black painted paper squares, with black-and-white reproductions of photographs—what Young refers to as a kind of a fake documentary style, a slight of hand, presented as 'true' but, on closer inspection, one that is revealed to be constructed and staged. He based the exhibition on the true story of Chinese miners who walked vast distances into Northern Australia looking for gold. Usually alone, they walked up to 2000 kilometres, 'resulting in many deaths'.[31] The first panel reads, in chalk: 'From Darwin, to Tennant Creek, then turn left and walk towards the morning sun, until we reach the big ocean'. On another panel, a skeleton lies forgotten in the bush; on another, a man rises from a water hole with his head down, dripping mud, as if exhausted, as if bowing to the land. When I see it, I feel mud caking on my skin, the images reaching out of the computer screen. Many of the images are presented turned on their side, as if the viewer is lying on the ground. Stars float in a black sky and dry grass parts to reveal a blurry figure. The effect is hallucinatory: *None Living Knows*.

Tam How Kee was one of many Chinese who embarked on such a journey. He had arrived in Palmerston (now Darwin) from Hong Kong only to be told the gold fields were depleted and that he should move on to Cooktown, but he had no more money.[32] Tam died long ago, but his daughter Felicia How Kee kept his stories for him, repeating them to historians, and also to reporter Jason Tin on her 100th birthday in 2009, in Cairns:

> Mrs Lee Long's story begins with her father Tam How Kee. Mr How Kee migrated from China to Darwin in 1875 only to find he couldn't pay for the passage of eight pennies and the NSW landing tax of ten pounds. Instead of staying in Darwin, or returning to China, Mr How Kee decided to walk the 2000 kilometres to the Palmer River Goldfields west of Cooktown. The journey took him a year to complete. Mr Lee Long said the directions given by the local fishing villagers were simple. 'They told him to walk towards the morning sun and when you hit the big ocean, you turn left', Mrs Lee Long said.[33]

For over a hundred years, ships pulled up on Australian shores, on the lands of hundreds of different Indigenous nations, and strangers arrived—from Europe, from Asia. Tam How Kee arrived from Hong Kong on Larrakia country. My Dutch ancestors jumped ship near Geelong, swimming to Colo Bay to join the Victorian goldrush. They didn't know, and I doubt they asked, but they were on Wadawurrung country, near a place called Djiland, the Wadawurrung name for Geelong, 'the tongue of the land'.

In *None Living Knows* the land is storyteller and narrator; it is the horizon meeting the sun, the water mixing the dirt into mud. Bodies move across the land because they must, the ships have left them there, the decision they made to board that ship long past, and perhaps they survive—as Tam did—or perhaps they don't. It is not their land, they fight it to survive, and sweat drips from their faces onto the earth.

Historian Anna Clarke lives near the town of Brogo, on land adjoining Lake Wapongo. Her grandparents, Manning and Dymphna Clark, bought the land in the 1970s, partly to preserve its history, which they knew held sites of significance for Indigenous Australians. Before I leave the Eurobodalla, I message Anna about Chinese Australian history. She tells me that locals have often spoken to her of the Chinese fishermen on Lake Wapongo. And she sends me two photographs—a kurrajong tree

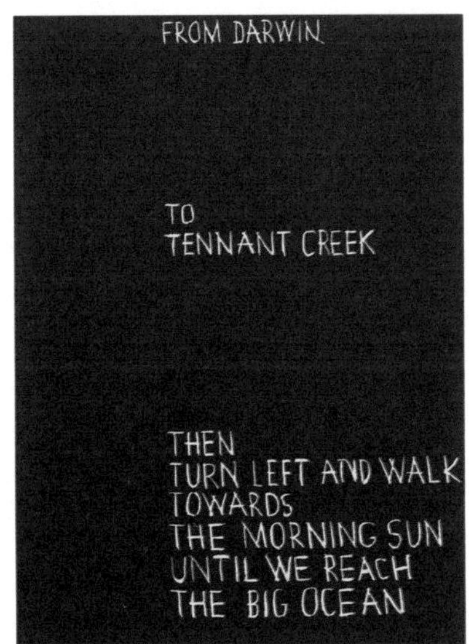

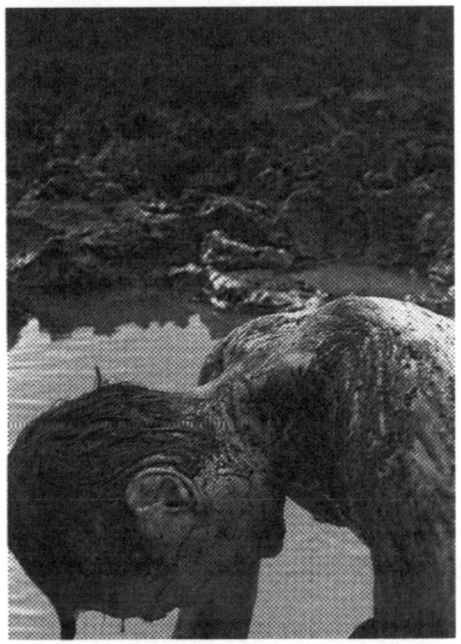

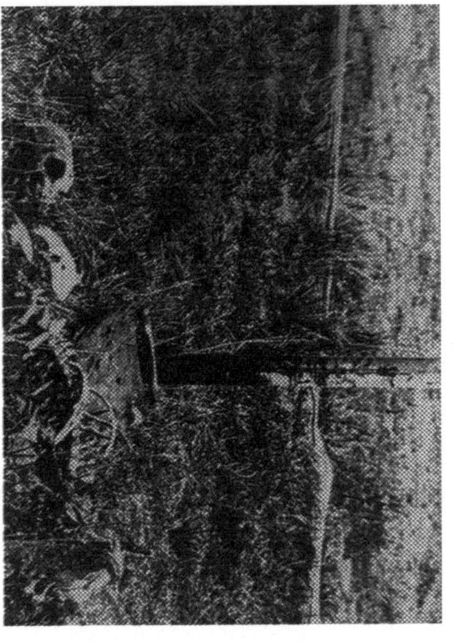

From Darwin 2017
Chalk on blackboard-painted archival
cotton paper, 100 × 70 cm

Waterhole 2 2017
Digital print on photographic paper,
100 × 70 cm

NLK 2017
Digital print on photographic paper,
100 × 70 cm

in the middle of a field, and a bright yellow flower in the middle of a field. The field, she says, is an old Chinese market garden. The kurrajong trees were important for Indigenous fisherman, as they were used to make fishing wire, and Anna believes the Chinese market gardeners left the trees—conspicuous in the middle of their otherwise cleared land—out of respect for Indigenous locals. As for the yellow flower: it is an Indigenous yam that Anna thinks was also preserved out of cross-cultural respect. So, the land is not as silent as I thought. Anna reads it for me; she has lived on it her whole life.

After Bega, my family and I keep driving, we are heading for the abandoned town of Buckland, site of the Buckland race riots. A recent newspaper article on the riots describes them this way:

> Chinese miners all along the Buckland were beaten as they fled, at least 750 of their tents were torn down and incinerated, 30 Chinese stores were robbed and burned and a newly constructed joss house, the first place of worship in the district—a scandalous presumption so far as the white miners were concerned—was put to the torch. No one knows how many Chinese men died on that winter day.[34]

To get to Buckland, we pass through Omeo, where I wander along the river looking for the old Chinese camp that was demolished in the 1970s. Ron, whose land I am trespassing on, tells me that old mines still dot the riverbank. 'You can tell the Chinese mines because they were square', he says, 'whereas the Europeans dug round holes'. We cross the Victorian alps and arrive at Harrietville where archaeologists are conducting annual digs at an old Chinese township. Soon we arrive in Bright. My children and I swim in the Ovens River. I want to go to Buckland, even though not much remains there; in Bright they call it 'one of Victoria's most notable ghost towns'. We arrive in Buckland late the following afternoon, pulling into the cemetery. All the shadows are long, and everything is golden: golden light, golden grass, golden sheep, golden bark on the trees. The cemetery has two Chinese graves. I can't read them, but I've seen a photograph of these graves in a newspaper article, a Chinese Australian descendent standing beside them. The Tony Wright article, quoted above, included a photograph of Eva Park. Eva is descended from Ah Sue, who died during the riots. She was shown standing behind one of the last three remaining graves of the Buckland victims.

There is a book available for purchase in Bright and I buy it. In the 2000s, the Bright and District Historical Society began compiling all the information they could on the Buckland riots, based on firsthand accounts. On the 150th anniversary of the riots in 2007 they release their findings, introducing their work in the following way:

This event was spoken of guardedly for generations and the whispers of what occurred on July 4th 1857 have carried down through the years. One of the most repeated stories tells of how hundreds of Chinese miners were murdered and that their bodies were hastily thrown into disused mine shafts. Other tales tell of the decomposed remains of Chinese found years later in remote gullies, supposed to have frozen to death on that fateful day. When time or old age began to loosen tongues (or embroider the truth) the names of perpetrators started to surface, and the location of hidden graves were spoken of [...] The consensus that a conspiracy of silence among those involved and the residents of the Buckland has been further fuelled over the years by the fact that *most of the official material relating to the trials of the rioters has vanished* [my emphasis].[35]

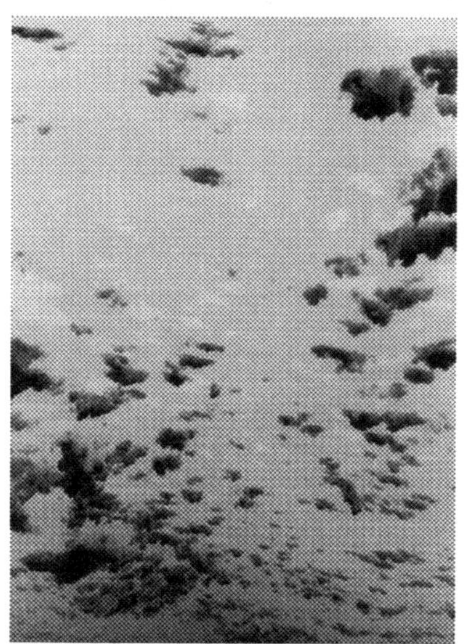

Clouds 2017
Digital print on photographic paper,
100 × 70 cm

Around the same time, a La Trobe University team begins mapping the Chinese cemetery that runs down the field from the temple and two Chinese Australian societies in Melbourne erect plaques; one on the site of the old Chinese cemetery, and one in the adjacent cemetery, near the site of the three remaining Chinese graves:

> This memorial was erected on 9th November 2008 by The See Yup Society of Victoria to the memory of our early Chinese settlers who were killed in the unfortunate Buckland Riot of July 4th 1857. It is to commemorate their energy, travails, courage and their sacrifices in paving the way for future generations of Australian Chinese. It is to be hoped that these future generations remember them fondly with pride and respect.

Brian Castro is a Chinese Australian writer, and friend and colleague of Young's. He wrote his award-winning novel *Birds of Passage* in 1983, the year I was born, and just as the emergence of a multicultural Australia was stimulating historians to imagine a new Australian past.[36] In *Birds of Passage*, Seamus O'Young, an Australian-born Chinese, reconstructs his past through the eyes of his ancestor Shan, who came to Australia in the 1880s. 'We will celebrate our lives together', Seamus tells Shan, 'I will not let you, Shan, drown in a wild river. I will bring your words, hermeneutically sealed to the light'.[37] Shan is assaulted on the Victorian goldfields by a German miner:

> He was kicked from behind and he sprawled in the mud. Tears of frustration formed in his eyes. A bottle was thrown. It hit him on the side of his face. The two Chinamen ran for their lives … A rock split his mouth. They stopped. He lay panting on the ground. The blood tasted like water from the inside of a fish. He was hauled to his feet. Blood dripped into his eyes.[38]

In 2021, John Young lay in the mud. He had walked, covered in mud, retracing the route Chinese miners had taken during the Lambing Flat race riots on 30 June 1861, running to save their lives. Three photographs document Young's performance *(Action: Covering 1, 2* and *3)* as part of *The Burrangong Affray* exhibition project:

> When he lies down, exhausted, an anonymous figure comes to cover him with a blanket, offering benevolent care in a manner proximate to that given by the farmer James Roberts, who sheltered some 1200 Chinese refugees on his property in the few weeks after the riot, giving them blankets, shelter and food. Rather than focusing only on the horror of the Lambing Flat Riots, Young chooses to centre this act of benevolence in the work to show how the strength of shared humanity can cross cultural divides.[39]

I look at these images often. I reflect on my own desire to identify with moral good. In Young's vision of Australia's past, as his body lies in the mud, victims are perpetrators and perpetrators are victims and the mud mixes with the blood and bones of the dead. Young forces an identification with the perpetrator as well as the victim. The land overpowers his body, looming over his frame, no match for the bright Australian light, the long grass, the brown gum leaves framing his body. The power of the land, the place, the site of the violence communicates truth, for on this land, near to the place Young lies, violence indisputably took place and in that knowledge there is truth, in the mud, where everyone stepped and struggled and got dirty.

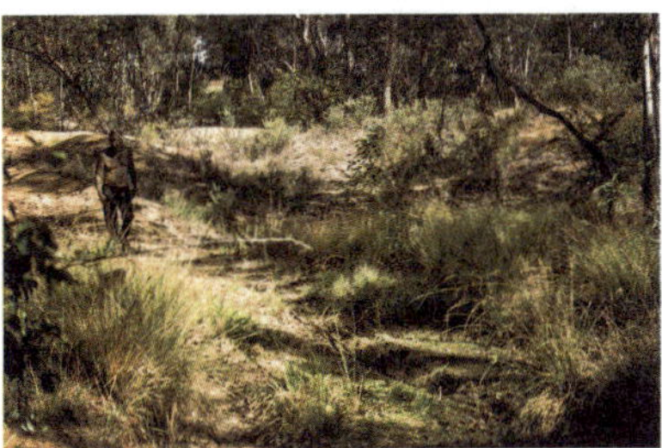

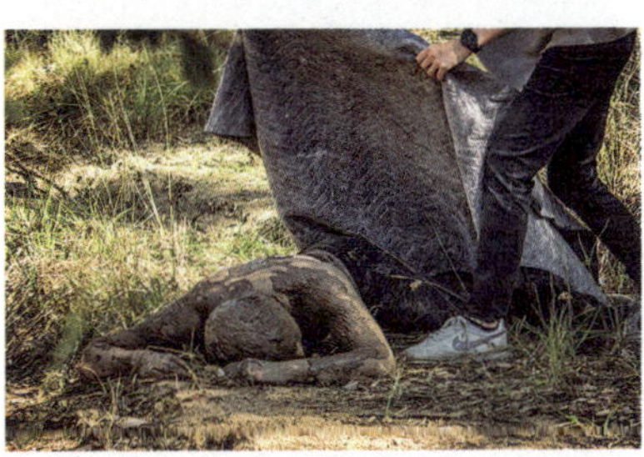

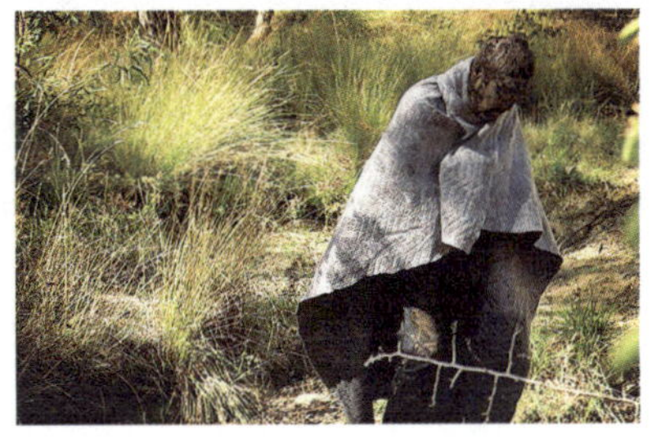

Action: Covering 1 2018
Action: Covering 2 2018
Action: Covering 3 2018
Editioned photographs, 121 × 81 cm each

1. James Belich, *Replenishing the Earth: The Settler Revolution and the Rise of the Anglo-World, 1783–1939*, Oxford University Press, Oxford, 2009.

2. Anna Clark, *Making Australian History*, Vintage, Sydney, 2022, p. 176.

3. John Young and Genevieve Trail, 'Diaspora, Psyche: Conversation—John Young and Genevieve Trail', in *John Young Diaspora, Psyche*, Bunjil Place Gallery, Melbourne, 2021, p. 45.

4. Young and Trail, p. 44.

5. Ibid., p. 46.

6. Sophie Loy-Wilson, 'Introduction' in *South Flows the Pearl: Chinese Australian Voices*, Sydney University Press, Sydney, 2021, p. 6.

7. Barbara Roger, 'Autumn is King in the Ovens Valley', *Walkabout*, March 1970, p. 57.

8. Young and Trail, p. 46.

9. Exhibition notes for John Young's *Modernity's End: Half the Sky*, Incinerator Art Gallery, 2016. See also Paul Macgregor and Sophie Loy-Wilson, 'Exploring Chinese Modernity—the lives of Alice Lim Kee & Daisy Kwok' in *Modernity's End: Holding up Half the Sky*, exhibition catalogue, Willoughby City Council, Sydney, 2017, pp. 20–23.

10. Young and Trail, p. 46.

11. Sophie Loy-Wilson, 'Daisy Kwok's Shanghai: Life in China before and after 1949', in K. Bagnall and J. T. Martínez (eds), *Locating Chinese Women: Historical Mobility between China and Australia*, Hong Kong University Press, Hong Kong, 2021, pp. 230–54.

12. Adam McKeown, 'Introduction', in Sophie Couchman, John Fitzgerald and Paul Macgregor (eds), *After the Rush: Regulation, Participation and Chinese Communities in Australia 1860–1940, Otherland*, issue 9, December 2004, pp. 10–11.

13. These refer to where and when Alice Lim Kee travelled, as well as the names she used at the time.

14. Young and Trail, p. 45.

15. Alistair Bowen, *Archaeology of the Chinese fishing industry in colonial Victoria*, Sydney University Press, in association with the Australasian Society for Historical Archaeology, Sydney, 2008.

16. 'Bega Police Court,' *Bega Gazette and Eden District or Southern Coast Advertiser*, 19 December 1885.

17. Shino Konishi, 'Feeling the Past: Indigenous History and Emotions', *Journal of Australian Studies*, vol. 44, no. 2, 2020, pp. 135–39.

18. 'Bega Police Court'.

19. Ibid.

20. Ibid.

21. Ibid.

22. Ann Curthoys and Andrew Markus (eds) *Who are our enemies? Racism and the Australian Working Class*, Hale & Iremonger, Sydney, 1978.

23. John Hirst, *Australian History in 7 Questions*, Black Inc, Melbourne, 2014.

24. Patricia Grimshaw, Marilyn Lake, Ann McGrath, Marion Quartly (eds), *Creating a Nation*, McPhee Gribble, Ringwood, 1994.

25. Alan Mayne, 'What you want John? Chinese-European interactions on the lower Turon goldfields', *Journal of Australian Colonial History*, vol. 6 (January 2004), pp. 1–13.

26. Henry Reynolds and Marilyn Lake, *Drawing The Global Colour Line: White Men's Countries and the Question of Racial Equality*, Melbourne University Press, Melbourne, 2008.

27. Beth Lew Williams, *The Chinese Must Go: Violence, Exclusion, and the Making of the Alien in America*, Harvard University Press, Cambridge, MA, 2021.

28. Iyko Day, *Alien Capital: Asian racialization and the logic of settler colonial capitalism*, Duke University Press, Durham, NC, 2016.

29. Ibid., p. 15.

30. 'Bega Police Court'.

31. John Young, *None Living Knows*, ARC ONE Gallery, Melbourne, 2017, https://www.johnyoungstudio.com/w/none-living-knows.

32. 'Tam How Kee', *Re-discovering Buk Ti: Chinese settlers in the lower Herbert district*, Cairns Museum, 19 February–13 May 2022.

33. Jason Tin, 'Felicia Lee Long turns 100', *ABC Local News*, online, 8 July 2009.

34. Tony Wright, 'A thorny trail from Buckland to our battles with Beijing', *The Age*, 5 December 2020.

35. Diann Talbot, *The Buckland Valley Riot: the Rebellion that culminated in the infamous Buckland Riot of July 4th 1857*, produced by the Bight & District Historical Society Inc. for the 150th anniversary of the Buckland Riot, 4 July 1857–4 July 2007, p. 4.

36. John Young collaborated with Brian Castro on the book *Macau Days* (2017), addressed in a conversation in this volume, see pp. 188–193.

37. Brian Castro, *Birds of Passage: A Novel*, Allen & Unwin, Sydney, 1983, p. 4.

38. Ibid., p. 109.

39. From project notes on the performance photographs, as part of *The Burrangong Affray*, 4A Centre for Contemporary Art, 2018, https://www.johnyoungstudio.com/w/the-burrangong-affray/5.

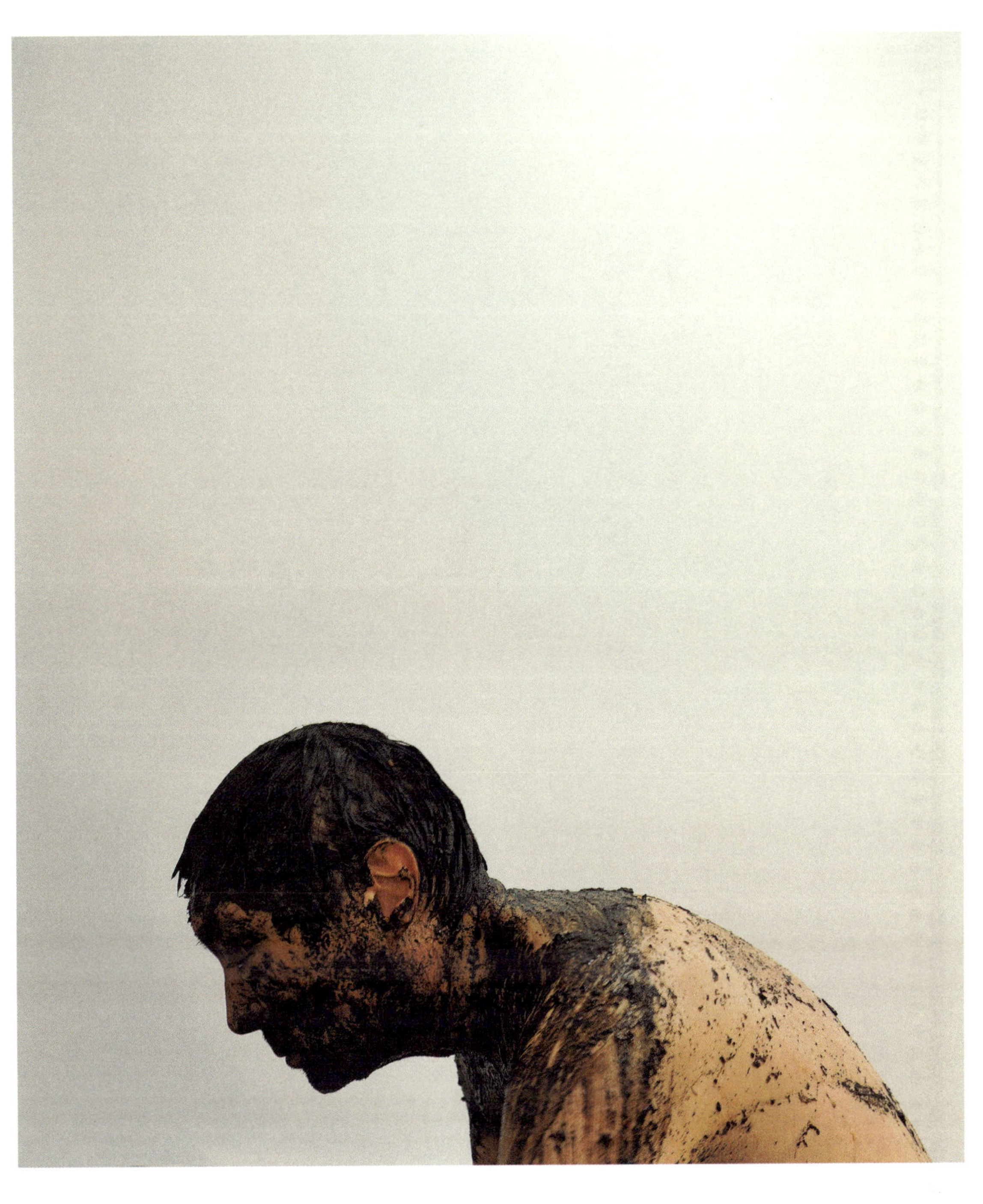

Preparatory still for
Open the Kingdom 2017

6.1.2017

1888
6122 Chinese
1144 European

Zero lines to
east coast
north to

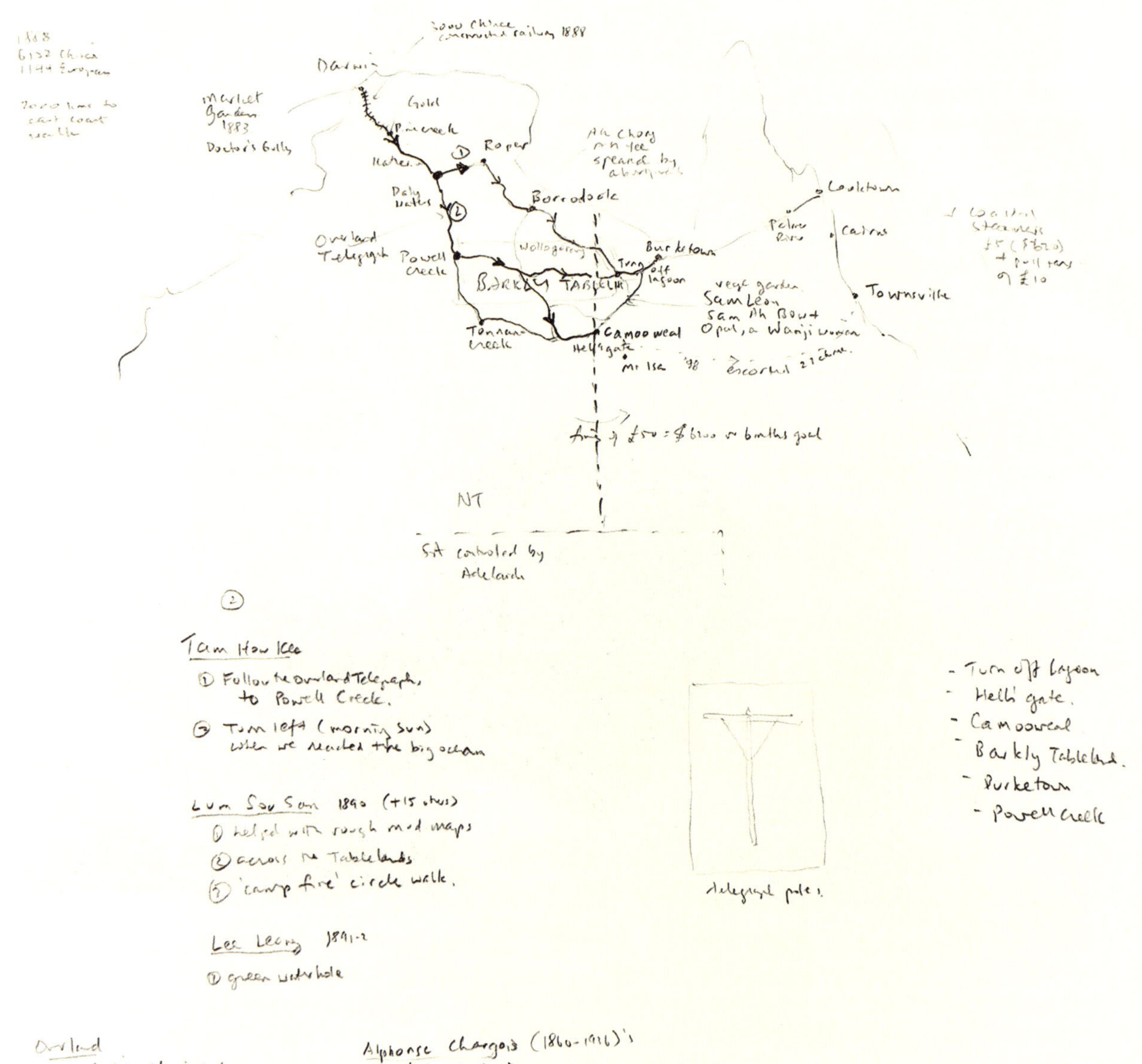

2

<u>Tam How Kee</u>
1. Follow the Overland Telegraph,
   to Powell Creek.
2. Turn left (morning sun)
   when we reached the big ocean

<u>Lum Sou Son</u> 1890 (+15 others)
1. helped with rough mud maps
2. across the Tablelands
3. 'camp fire' circle walk.

<u>Lee Leong</u> 1891-2
1. green waterhole

<u>Overland</u>
1. hostile Aborigines
2. few shops, water problematic

wet season
1. too wet to travel
2. waterholes, that turns into
   cracked clay by mid year

Alphonse Chargois (1860-1916)'s
4 photos of chinese
illegal immigrants

- Turn off lagoon
- Hells gate
- Camooweal
- Barkly Tableland.
- Burketown
- Powell Creek

Between where the concept & the vision
collides (1982)

"Open the
heaven"

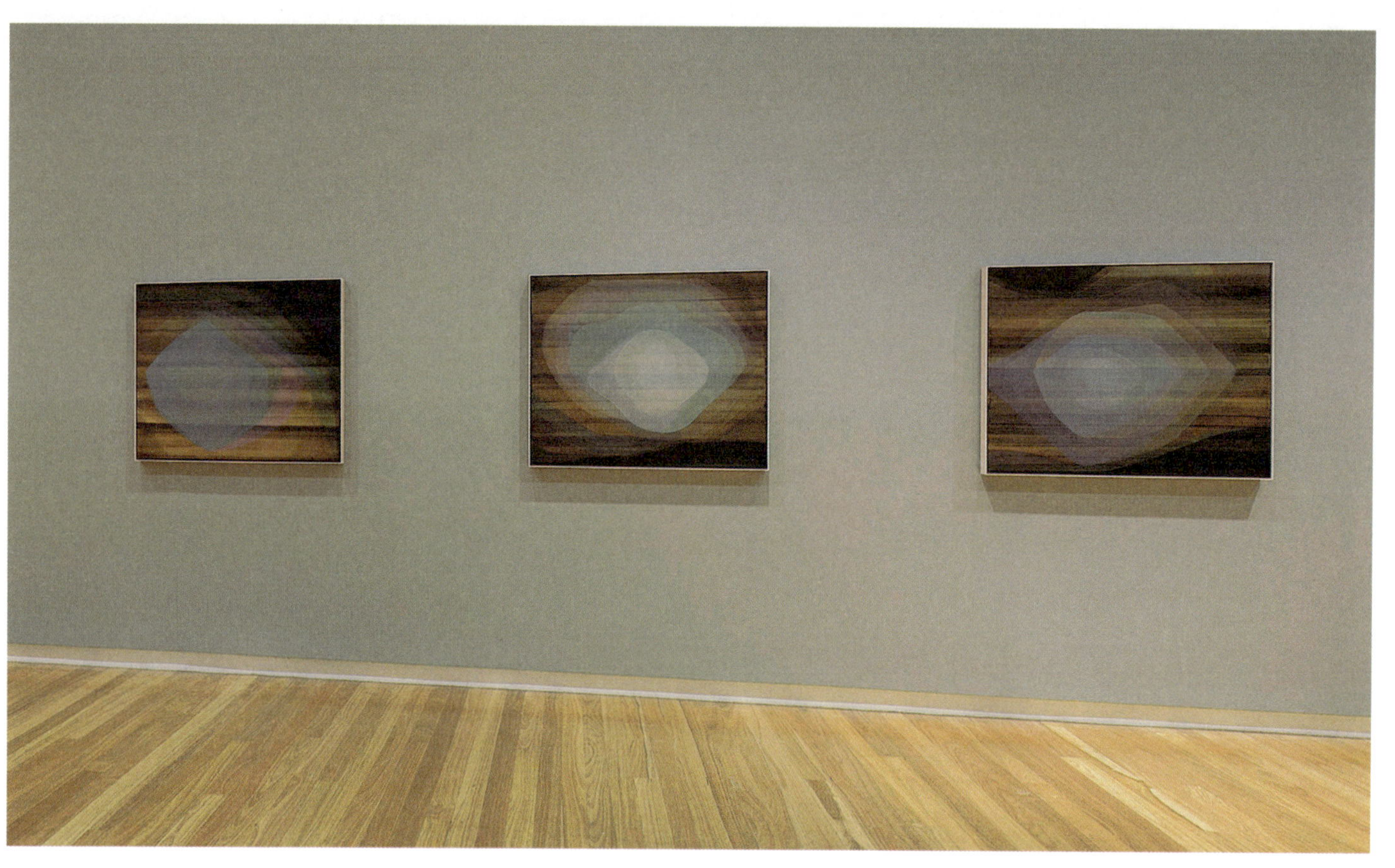

above
None Living Knows 2017
Installation view, *John Young: Diaspora, Psyche,*
Bunjil Place, Narre Warren, 2021

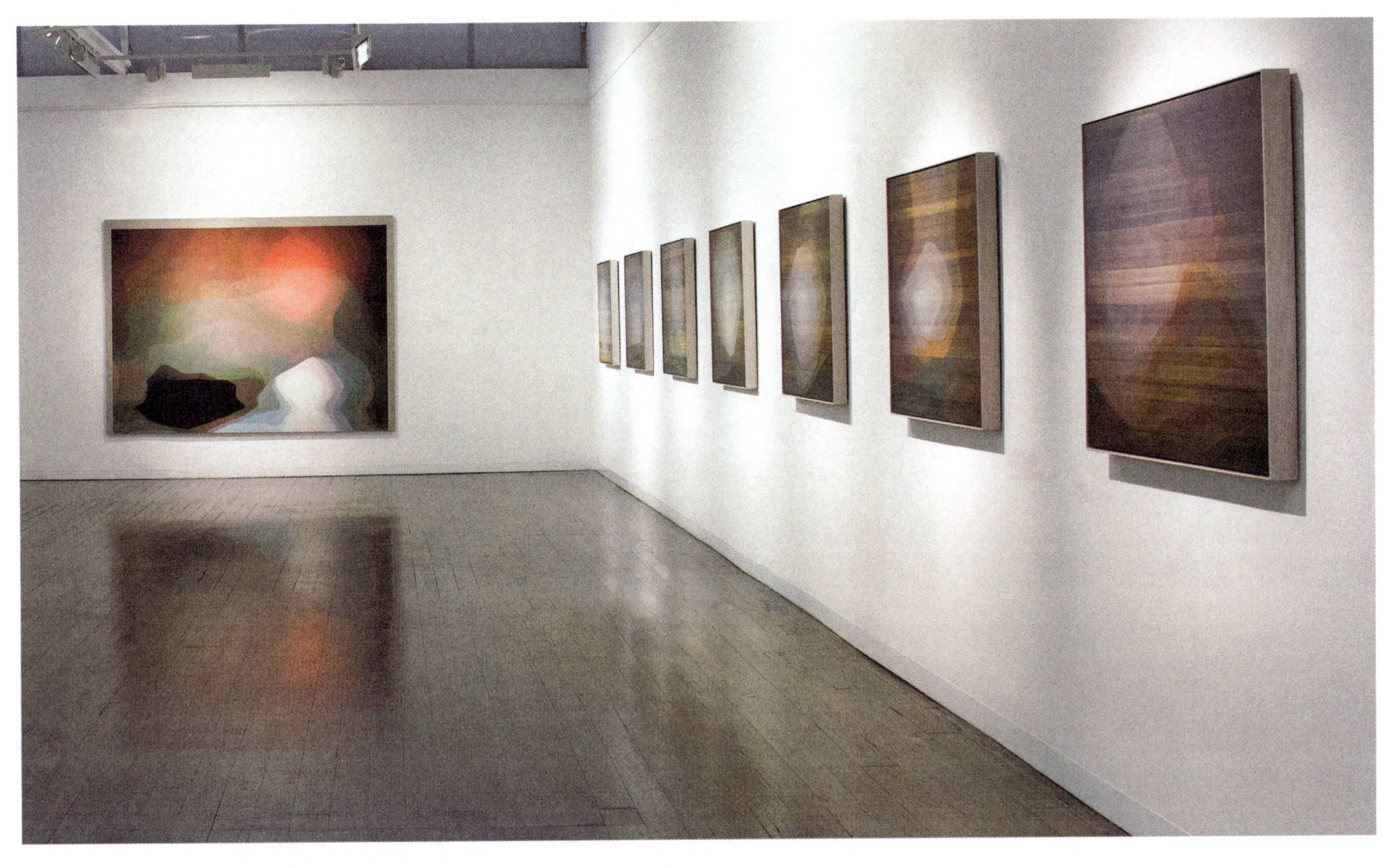

None Living Knows 2017
Installation view, ARC ONE Gallery,
Melbourne, 2017

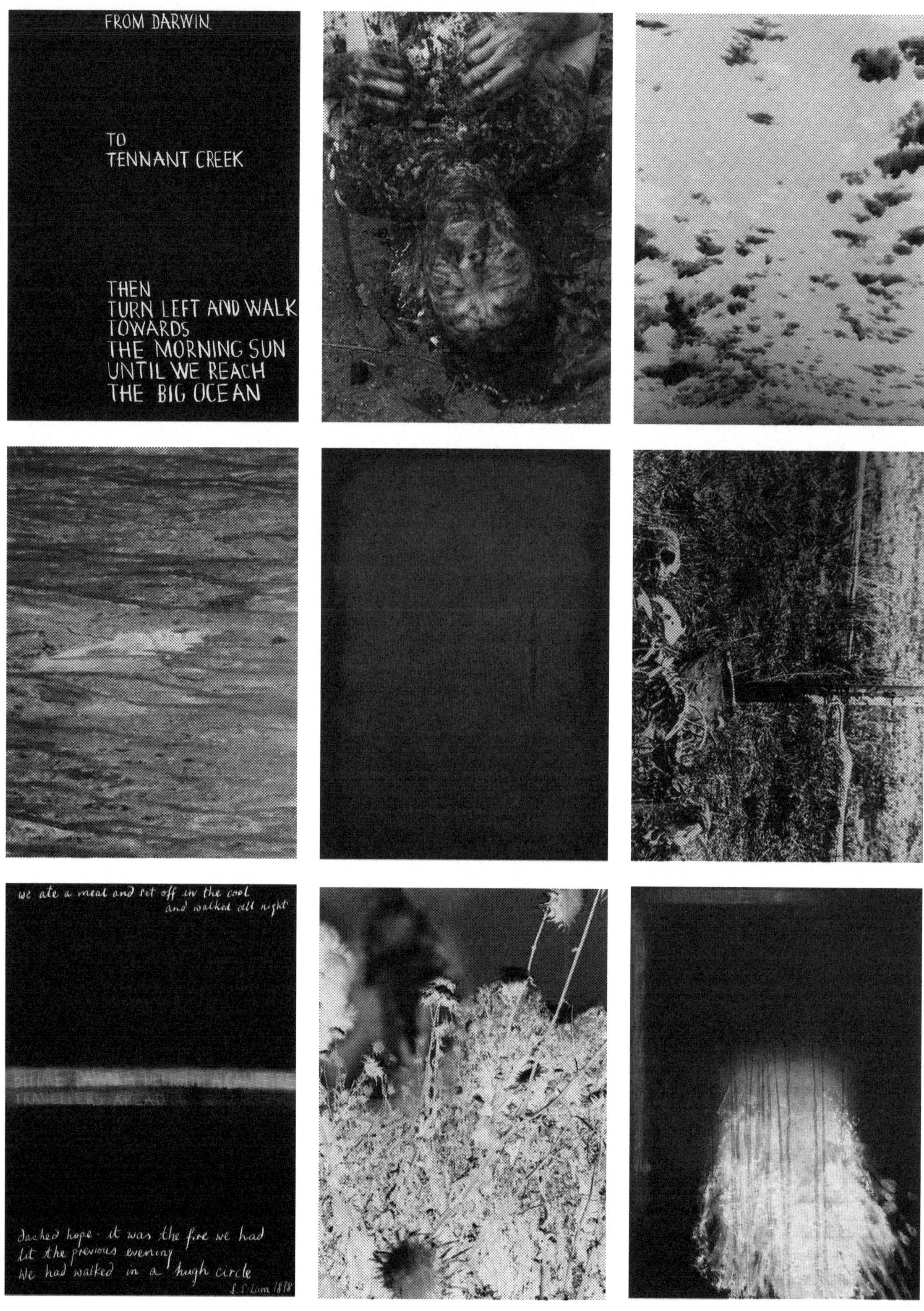
FROM DARWIN

TO
TENNANT CREEK

THEN
TURN LEFT AND WALK
TOWARDS
THE MORNING SUN
UNTIL WE REACH
THE BIG OCEAN

we ate a meal and set off in the cool
and walked all night

dashed hope - it was the fire we had
lit the previous evening
We had walked in a hugh circle
J. S. Lim 1878

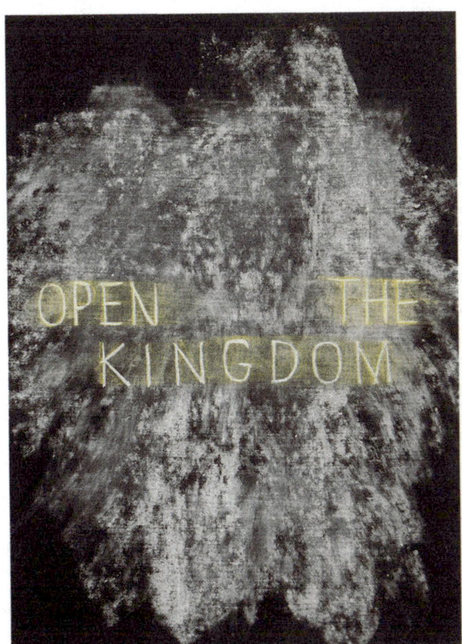

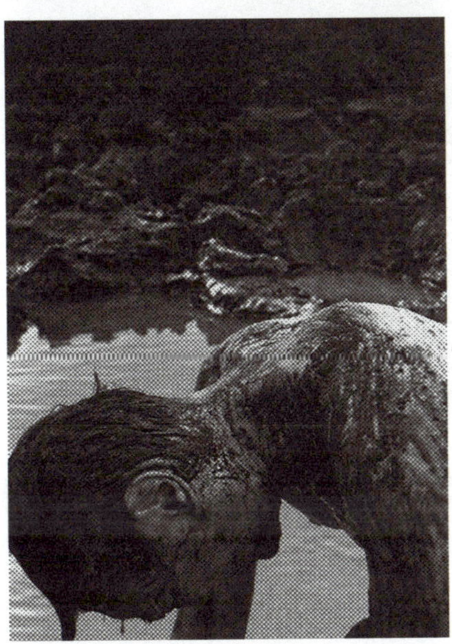

Open the Kingdom 2017
Digital print on photographic paper and
chalk on blackboard-painted cotton archival
paper, 12 units, 320 × 310 cm

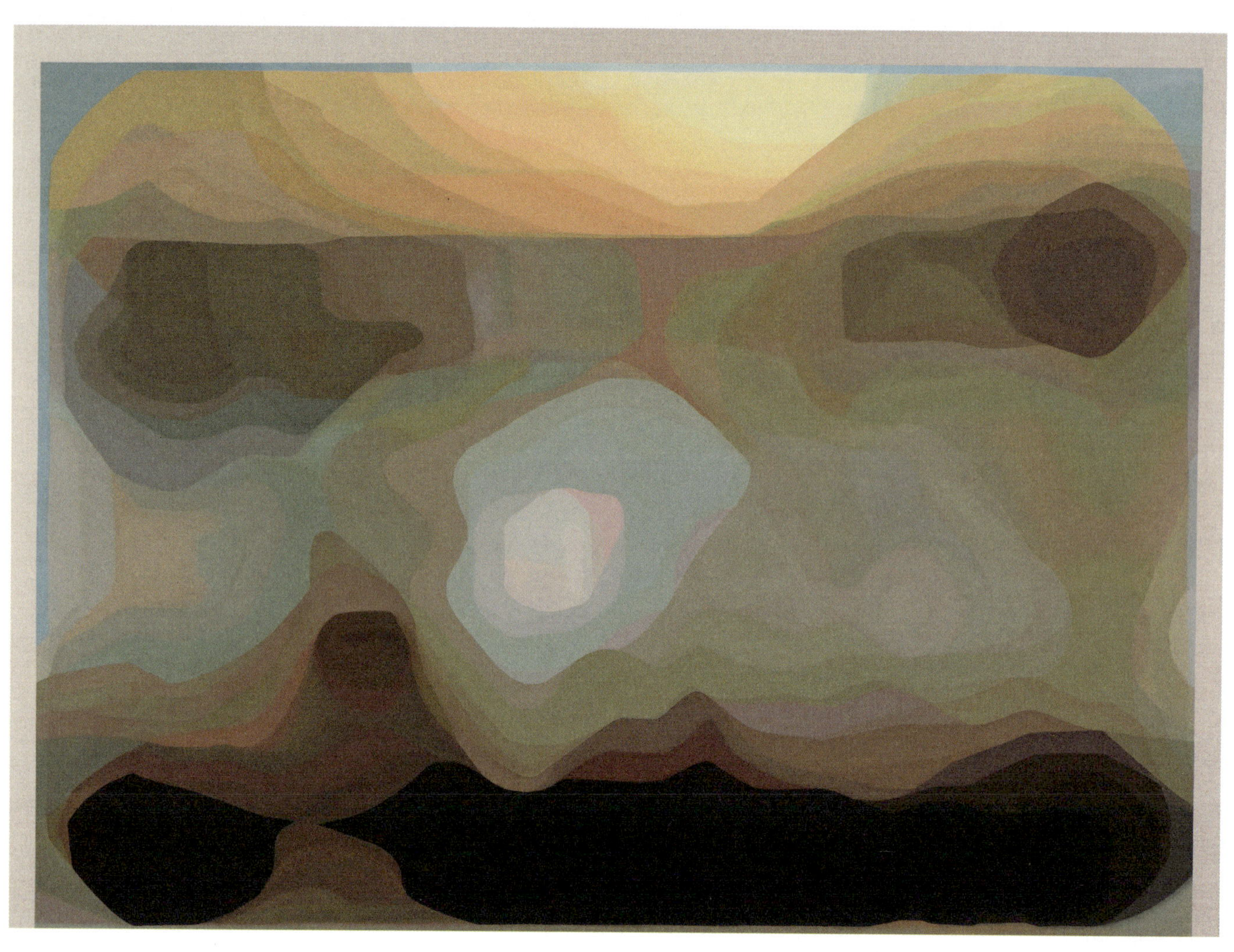

Naive and Sentimental Painting XI 2016
Oil on linen, 203 × 270 cm
Private collection, Melbourne

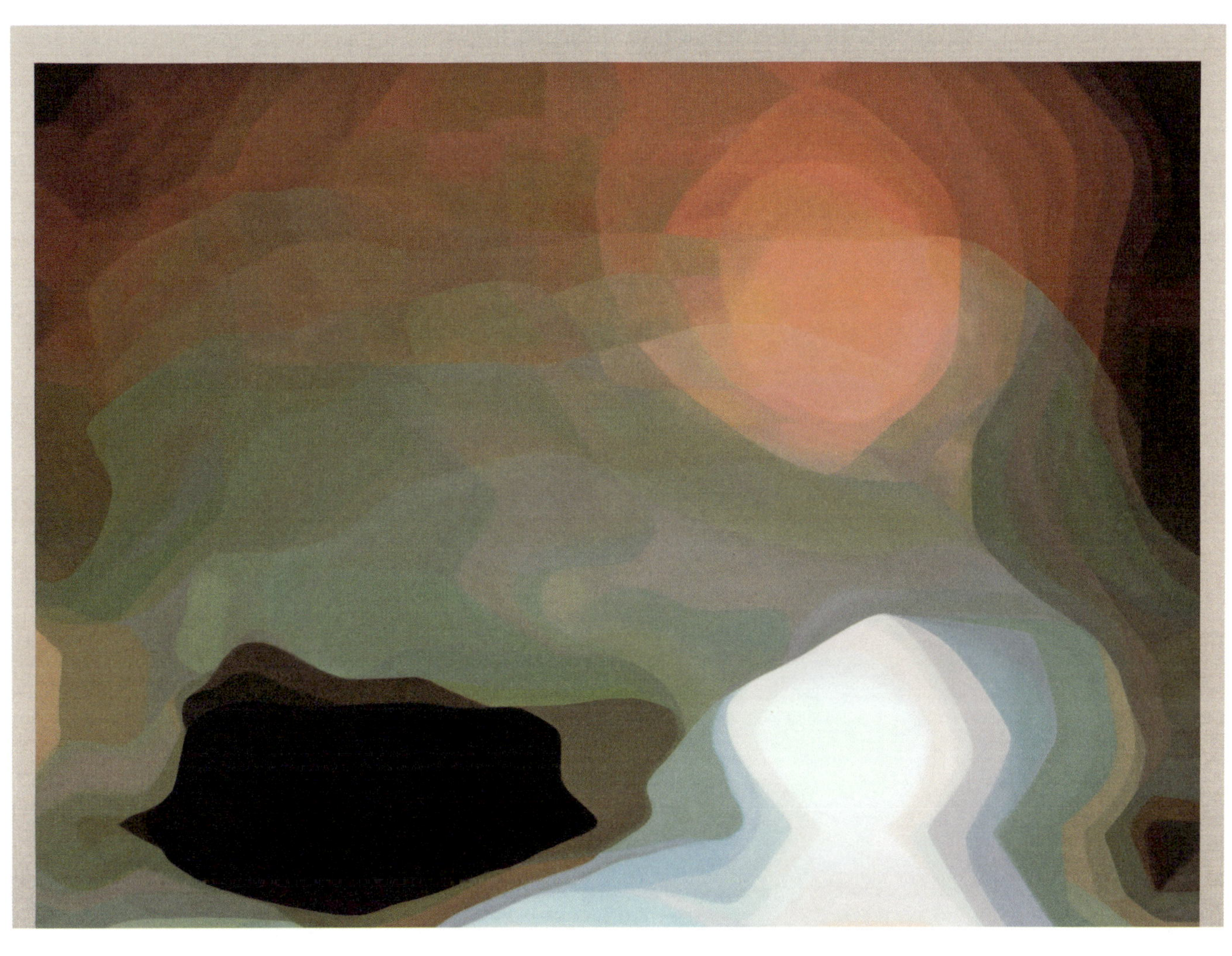

Naive and Sentimental Painting XII 2016
Oil on linen, 203 × 270 cm
Private collection, Sydney

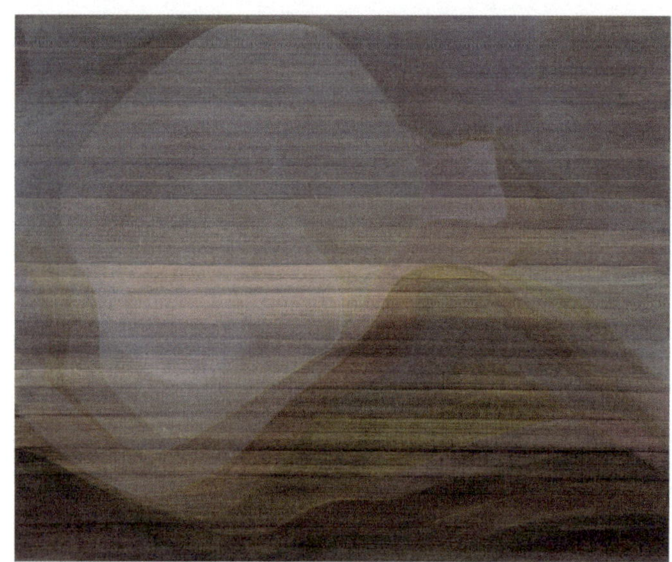 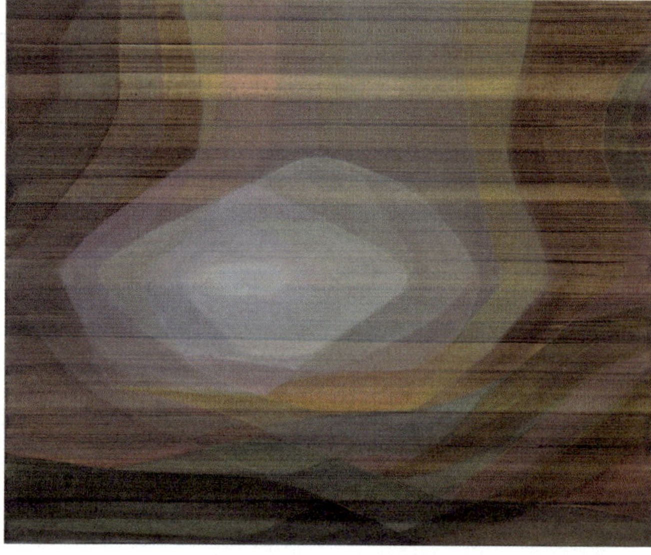

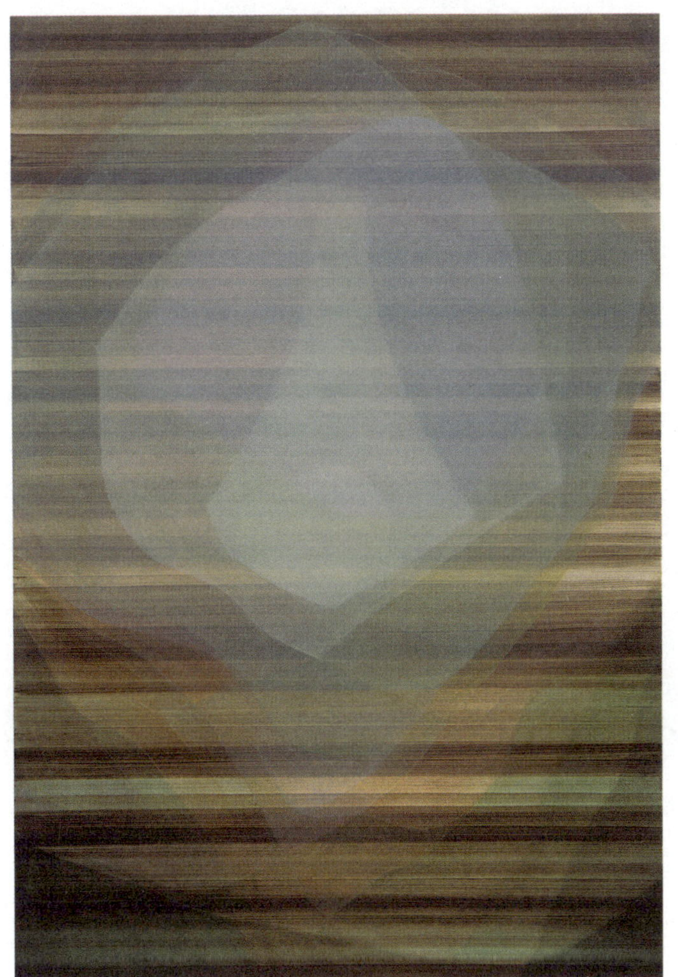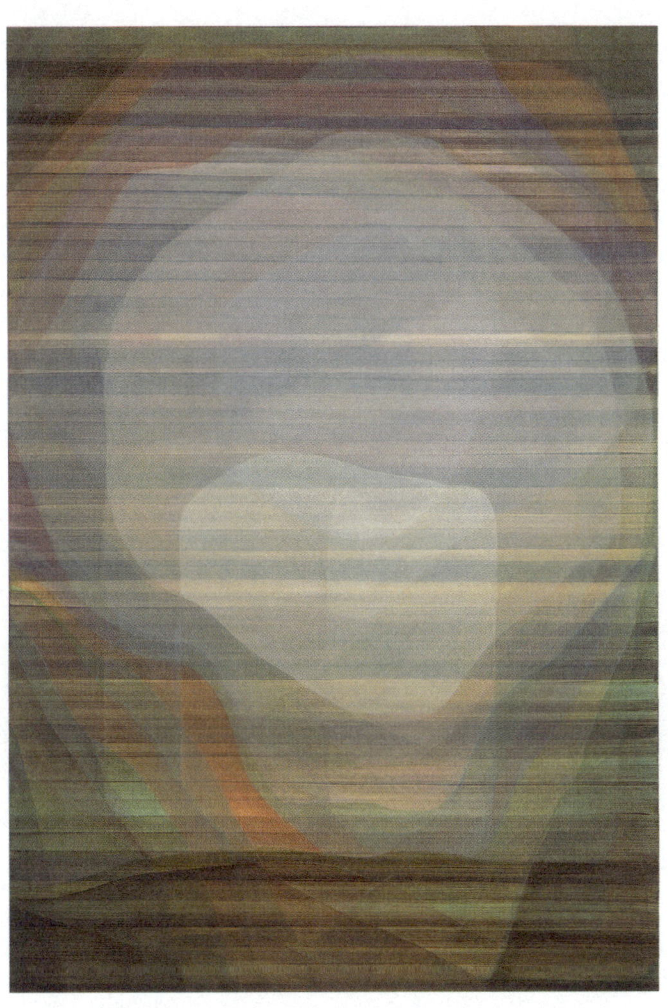

left
None Living Knows I 2017
Oil and acrylic on linen, 238 × 156 cm

right
None Living Knows II 2017
Oil and acrylic on linen, 238 × 156 cm

THE BURRANGONG AFFRAY

2018

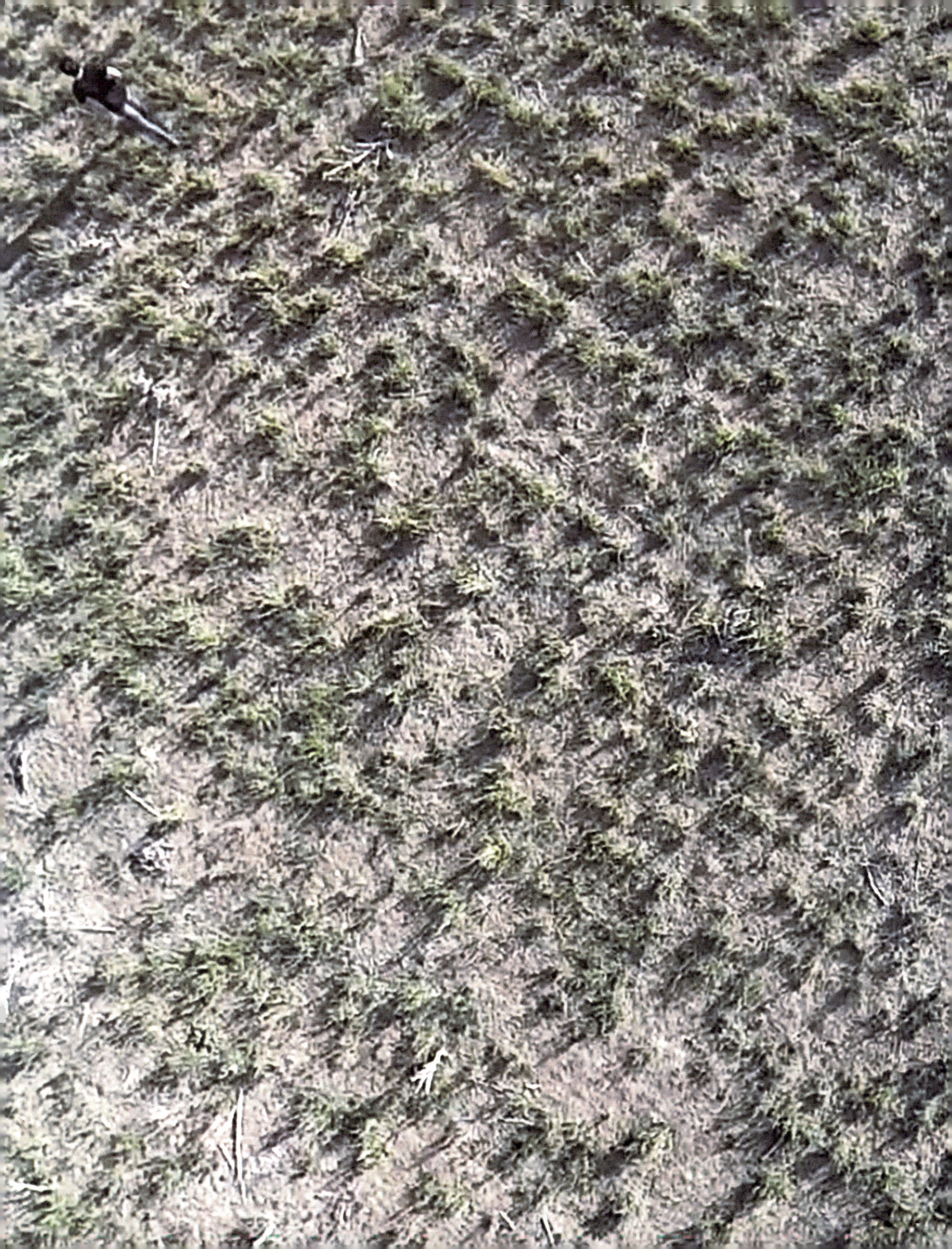

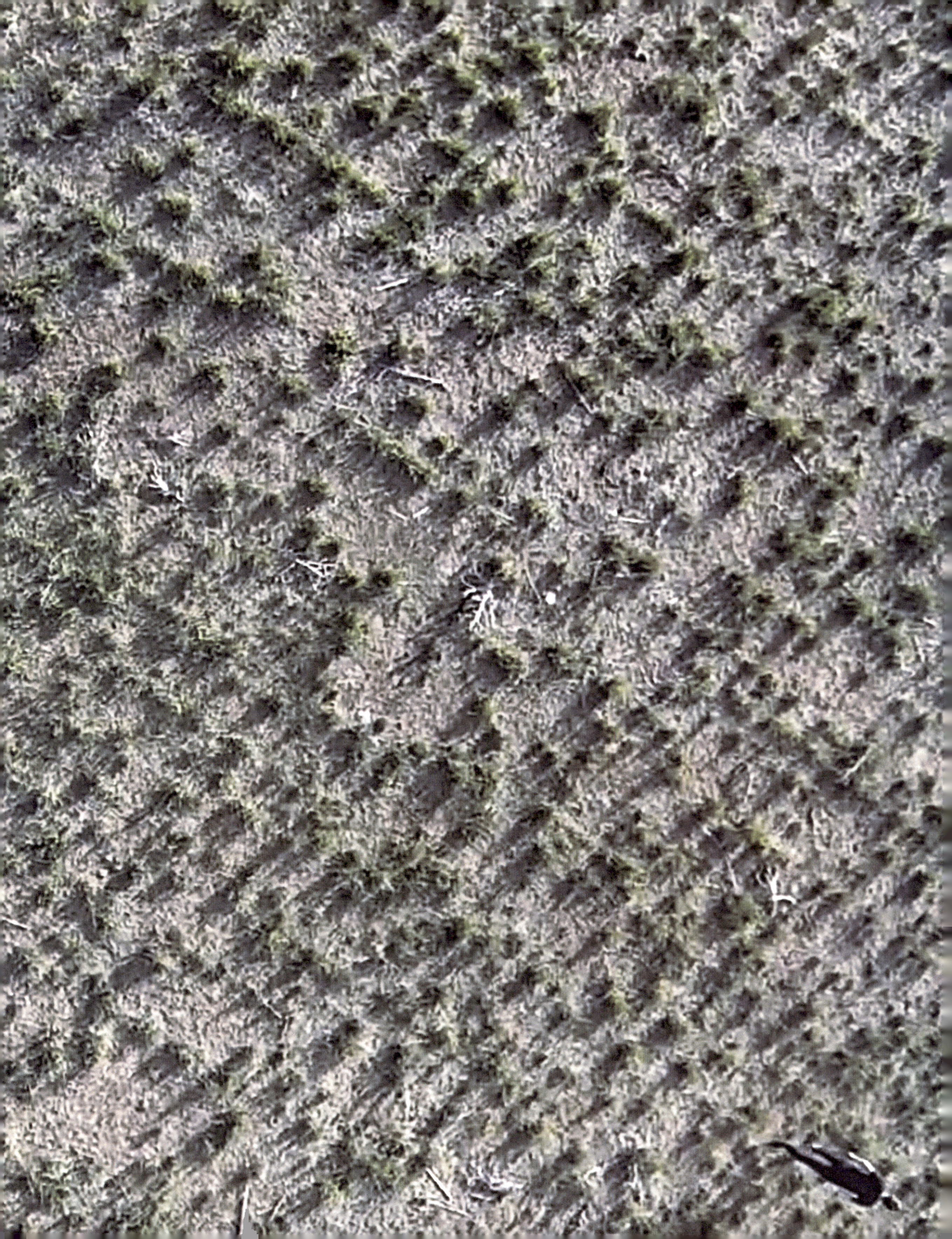

THE BURRANGONG AFFRAY

Between 1860 and 1861, a series of anti-Chinese demonstrations took place
on the goldfields at Burrangong, New South Wales. The most violent of these
was the Lambing Flat Riots of 30 June 1861, when between 2000 and 3000
European, North American and Australian-born miners attacked approximately
2000 of their Chinese counterparts and drove them from their diggings. The
Chinese were cruelly beaten, some were scalped of their traditional queues and
their campsites were looted and destroyed. The riots were the culmination of years
of anti-Chinese sentiment across Australia's colonies and played out against a
backdrop of contentious debate taking place in the New South Wales parliament
over immigration restriction. Many Chinese were sheltered by local farmer James
Roberts, who allowed some 1200 fleeing miners to camp on his station over the
course of a few months, risking his family's livelihood.

The Burrangong Affray consists of four artworks, originally developed for an
eponymous project at 4A Centre for Contemporary Asian Art in 2018. *Lambing
Flat* (2018), the central installation work, is a grid of 27 chalkboard drawings and
digital prints, in three rows of nine works each (320 × 710 cm total). The installation
interpolates archival photographs of Chinese miners, the Australian landscape, and
the interior of the Roberts family's farmhouse at Currawong (where fleeing Chinese
miners were sheltered) with references to episodes in the attacks. Also introduced
here is the intersection between Australia's Chinese and Indigenous histories, with
visual references to breastplates along with text recognising the Wiradjuri people
(traditional custodians of the area) and the names of southern Chinese towns
from which many miners typically hailed.

The Field (2018) is a looping video installation (8 minutes, 5 seconds), Young's first
significant work in this medium. In the video, a hand reaches into the frame to
tug at the long braid of a red-headed white woman, shown in profile; fake freckles
have been added to her complexion to accentuate her stereotypical 'Anglo Saxon'
appearance. As the hand tugs her hair, the girl's expression moves ambiguously
between a smile and a grimace, making the intent of the act unclear. Later, her braid
is cut off entirely and dragged in a red smear across a white ground, symbolically
referencing the scalping of Chinese miners during the riots. This violence contrasts
with the final scene in which a woman lays a felt blanket over the camera lens,
so that the viewer is gazing up from the perspective of the fallen.

Action: Covering 1, 2, and *3* (2018) is a series of three framed photographs (each
121 × 81 cm), which document the eponymous site-specific performance Young
made at Blackguard Gully, a former Chinese mining camp that was the main site
of the 1861 attack. In the original performance, Young, with bare torso and covered
in mud, walks across the site; he then lays down in a trench until a member of the
audience walks over to cover him with a grey blanket. This 'covering' was repeated
several times until all the audience had taken part. 'Artefacts' from the performance,
including a felt blanket, copper spade and a mud-encrusted steel bucket from
Blackguard Gully were also displayed in the original exhibition of this project
at the 4A Centre for Contemporary Asian Art, Sydney, in 2018.

Finally, *Circles 369: A Proposal for Three Monuments* (2018) is a framed work on
paper, presented as a poster. This is a conceptual proposal of three monuments
designed for Blackguard Gully, Currawong Farm and Murrumburrah Cemetery—
key sites of remembrance for the riots. Each monument is conceived to form
a circular 'garden', featuring two large boulders and three trees, in different
configurations at each site. The title thus refers to three gardens, six rocks, nine trees.

Reflection (2022)

An event that affected many was to be recounted, to be reflected upon by many. 'We' is the pronoun that was fundamental to the project. Prior to the 2010s, then director of 4A Centre for Contemporary Asian Art, Aaron Seeto, wrote about looking at the Lambing Flat Riots as a project, and many years later the new director, Mikala Tai, alongside co-curator Micheal Do, coined the title *The Burrangong Affray*. They initiated this as a project with two artists—the youthful Jason Phu and myself—and a wise historian, Karen Schamberger. They then provided the conditions for us to work on this event. After all, the Lambing Flat Riots were the biggest civil unrest in Australian history. This exceptional event inspired the realisation of paintings, drawings, photographs, performances, sculptures and video works, as well as a proposal for three public monuments.

The Burrangong Affray exhibition itself also became something of an event, attracting a wide public reaction from the socially progressive media, as well as socially regressive online vilification from the racist alt-right. Best of all, however, was the help we received from the descendants of James Roberts, the man who sheltered and fed over a thousand Chinese miners on the night they were displaced and for many weeks after. The Roberts family were indeed most generous. This may attest that memory and resonance are ever implicated in our present, not necessarily only through trauma but also through benevolence. Here, engaging in a relational process through artistic practice through a focus on an exceptional historical moment made sense. The gravity of the contents potentially forecloses this art event from degenerating into a socialite, spectacular, populist farce. The aesthetics here are forged from a necessity to transubstantiate the history.

pages 324–25
Still from *The Field* 2018
HD video loop, 8 min. 5 sec.

METHODOLOGIES FOR EMPATHY:
THE BURRANGONG AFFRAY AS HISTORY PAINTING

Mikala Tai

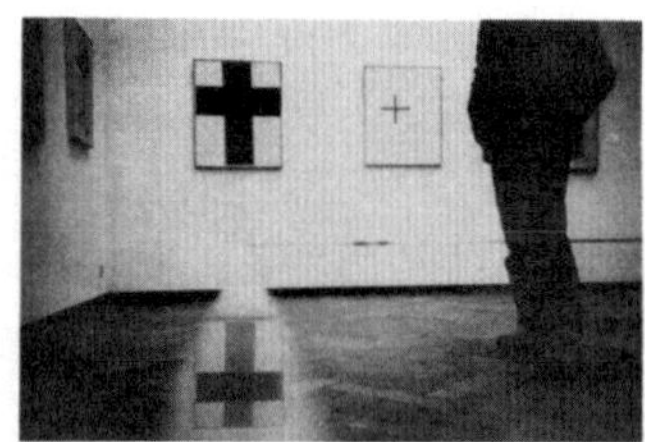

The Second Mirage 1982
Invitation to the artist's first solo exhibition
Rosroe, Connemara, Ireland, 1982

Australia's collective memory is marked by cultural amnesia and deliberate erasure. Crafted by politicised myth-making and evidenced by performative gestures, the public retelling of Australia's history is largely restricted to that of the colonial settler. Further, the political mobilisation of remembrance, which began in the 1990s, has recast historical moments into a form of commemorative nation building and diminished our complex and nuanced histories to become a taut linear narrative.[1] For contemporary Australian artist John Young, it is an uncomfortable and unsettling narrative. It is a narrative that fails to recognise that Australia has been, and continues to be, uniquely shaped by Indigenous peoples whose histories should—and must—be a focal point of national remembrance, but it also fails to recognise the centuries of non-Euramerican migration and contact that has actively contributed to contemporary Australia. For Young, this exclusion is personal. Young migrated to Australia in 1967 as a young boy, became a citizen in 1980 and has played an active role in civic cultural life, yet his story, and that of generations of Chinese Australians, remains on the fringe of Australia's history.

While now acknowledged as a leading Australian artist, Young is by training a philosopher. In 1977 he studied Philosophy of Science and Aesthetics at the University of Sydney, where he completed his honours thesis on Ludwig Wittgenstein and aesthetics. This formalist background underpins a practice in which philosophy anchors his artistic enquiry. Young's artistic methodology has long examined the persuasive power of empathy. Empathy is, according to the Greater Good Science Centre—a research institute that studies psychology, sociology, and neuroscience of wellbeing—'a building block of morality'.[2] It enables us to understand the perspective or experience of another, in both an emotional and cognitive sense. Young's practice has explored the capacity for empathy to foster understandings between those of vastly different lived experiences.

With this philosophical foundation Young entered art school at the Sydney College of the Arts (SCA), where he undertook studies in both painting and sculpture. It was a period of fervent conceptualism at SCA, during which Young, along with others such as David Ahern and Imants Tillers, embraced postmodern theory and sought to create new visual languages to articulate the contemporary Australian experience. Together they tested artistic boundaries, experimenting with formalist structures and collapsing them into new multi-layered and sometimes multi-artform bodies of work. Young's philosophical outlook remained at the heart of this experimentation, with his first solo exhibition *The Second Mirage* predicated on chance encounters that challenged the concepts of time and space. By the late 1980s and early 1990s Young had gallery representation with both United Artists Gallery (now Anna Schwartz Gallery) in Melbourne and Sherman Galleries in Sydney, had a solo exhibition at the Institute of Modern Art in Brisbane, exhibited extensively in Asia and become a lecturer in painting at SCA. However, it was in 1993 that Young began to play an active role in shaping Australia's cultural landscape.

Informed by his study of philosophy, and over a decade of artistic practice, Young became increasingly engaged with the politics of culture—a focus that continues to this day. In 1993, he was one of the chief organisers of the influential symposium, 'Australian Visual Arts in an Asian Context', held at SCA, which addressed the profound cultural contribution of Asian migration to Australia and the need to support Australia's cultural relationships with the region. Delivered in the midst of the Keating era, this conference aligned with the increasingly inclusive politics of the day that sought to foster greater economic and cultural links with Asia. The momentum of the conference also fuelled Young and his fellow organisers to expand the conversation they had begun. By meeting regularly, they quickly identified a need to establish an organisation that would recognise, document and foster Asian Australian art activities at a national level, to publicly push the boundaries and expectations for what 'Australian' art could be.

By 1996, they had established the Asian Australian Artists' Association—a group of young artists, curators and theatre-makers, and by 1997 the organisation unveiled its first gallery space, Gallery 4A, in Sydney's Chinatown. As president of the organisation, Young played an active role in the conceptualisation and establishment of Gallery 4A, developing—together with the likes of Melissa Chiu, Emil Goh, Vicente Butron and Felicia Kan—a clear and compelling strategy to challenge the infrastructure of Australia's cultural ecology. In this space they created a new framework for engaging with contemporary art, one that was inclusive and experimental, that both celebrated and nurtured Australia's ongoing cultural relations with the wider Asian region.

Pivotal in the inception of the organisation, now known as 4A Centre for Contemporary Asian Art (4A), Young remained a key member of its board until late 2020. As a former director of 4A, I can trace much of the organisation's ethos to Young's championing of artistic experimentation and creative innovation in those early days. He imbued the organisation with a strong sense of how history and lived experience can be shared and examined to enable new prisms of understanding for contemporary culture. This transhistorical and transcultural approach centred empathy as a foundational pillar of the organisation. And, while 4A is often understood as expanding the boundaries of contemporary Australian art by foregrounding Asian Australian perspectives, it has also played a sustained role in fostering greater Asian cultural literacy in Australia over the past twenty-five years.

Young's engagement with the politics of culture has not been confined to his teaching and industry positions, it is embedded throughout his practice. From early works such as *Manchurian Snow Walk* (1979) to more recent works such as the series *None Living Knows* (2017), Young has continuously experimented with ways to articulate pockets of near-forgotten Australian histories of both personal and national importance. Through these works Young has built a sustained articulation of Australia's historic, and ongoing, connection with Asia and illustrated a collection of histories that sit parallel to mainstream, white-settler understandings of Australian culture. Young embarked on the History Projects from 2005 and, over the last fifteen years, this body of work has become one of the most compelling examples of his artistic methodology.

It is as if all of Young's works before the History Projects were a rehearsal. The History Projects, and in particular the chalkboard drawings or history paintings, as I see them, encompass Young's philosophical persuasion, his distinctive layering

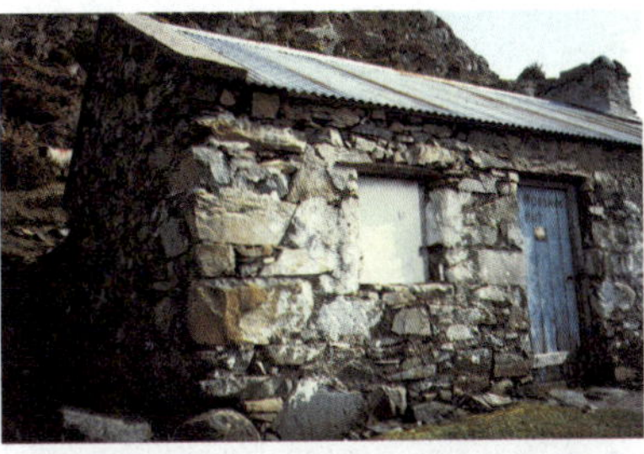

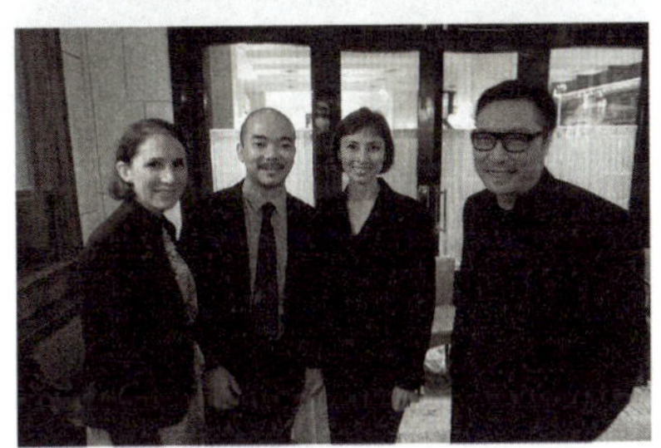

The Second Mirage 1982
Installation view, Rosroe, Connemara, Ireland 1982

Left to right: Kate Mizrahi, Aaron Seeto, Melissa Chiu, and the artist at a 4A event Cipriani, Hong Kong, 2011

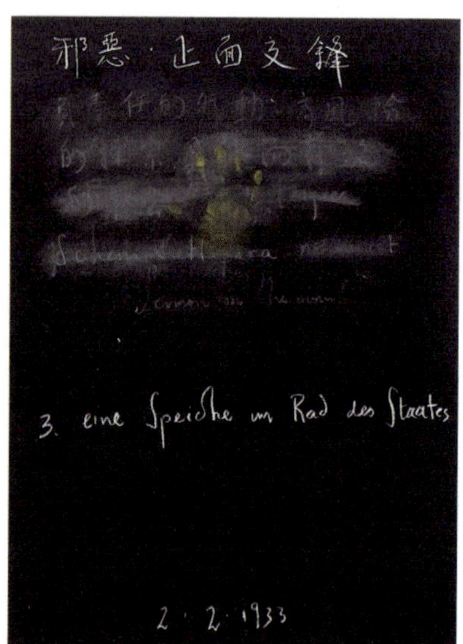

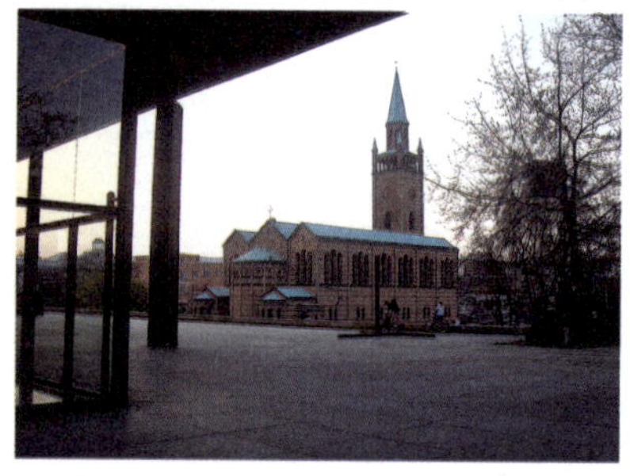

Politics 2008
Chalk on blackboard-painted archival
cotton paper, 100 × 70 cm

St Matthäus Church, Kulturforum, Berlin, 2009
Photograph by the artist

of imagery and his rigorous academic research. Throughout the development of the History Projects, Young has produced abstract oil-on-canvas paintings in tandem, which often address the same historical moments or issues. While these are exemplary in their own right, and related to his earlier practice, here I will focus on the chalkboard history paintings. This new artistic framework of enquiry allows for a sophisticated contemplation of history, yet it is underpinned by a great respect, not only for the events the projects seek to excavate but also for the audience that encounters them. They support the viewer to map their own reading of the work, offering a multiplicity of access points that each elucidate personal understandings of complex historical narratives.

Young first developed the chalkboard history paintings as an artistic methodology when he was developing work for the series *Bonhoeffer in Harlem* (2009). While the project itself was realised across multiple mediums, including tapestry and painting, it included eleven chalkboard history paintings, with each panel 100 cm by 70 cm. *Bonhoeffer in Harlem* was an ambitious project that was developed at the invitation of gallerist and curator Alexander Ochs in Berlin.[3] For Young, Dietrich Bonhoeffer (1906–1945) is a figure of benevolence who, informed by studies and work in New York's Harlem in his twenties, actively sought to consider life through the perspective of those who suffer oppression. This characterised his life's work and informed his decision to speak out against the Nazis, despite knowing it placed him in grave danger. Bonhoeffer's transcultural humanitarianism deeply impacted Young and it has become a defining characteristic of his chalkboard history paintings.

The chalkboard history paintings are a mixture of chalk on blackboard paint on paper, with digitally printed photomontages. The photomontages are linked to Young's oeuvre and exhibit his ability to select imagery that can poignantly speak to complex historical contexts. The chalk paintings were a new visual idiom for Young; this was the first time he incorporated text in his work: recording dates, writing and erasing names and key words, as well as presenting stylised, almost infographic, drawings. Each panel is symbolic of a season of Bonhoeffer's story and together they trace a complex, international life of resistance and compassion.

However, what is of particular interest in the *Bonhoeffer* panels is the appearance of traditional Chinese script, which interweaves some of Young's personal history with that of Bonhoeffer. This initial investigation of his own heritage becomes a focal point in his second series of chalkboard history paintings, *Safety Zone* (2010). *Safety Zone* expanded this methodology into a sixty-panel work that visually documents the violent and bloody Japanese invasion and occupation of the Chinese city of Nanjing in 1937, widely known as the 'Rape of Nanking'. Young's work focuses on the actions of twenty-one foreigners who saved the lives of some 200,000–250,000 Chinese citizens by sheltering them within an international concession that formed a 'safety zone'. Unlike the works that comprise the *Bonhoeffer in Harlem* series, which were first exhibited across various walls of a church, *Safety Zone* was conceived cohesively as a form of contemporary history painting, displayed in a grid of three rows of twenty columns. Together they become an artistic monument to acts of altruism and compassion.

The sheer scale of *Safety Zone*, combined with its restricted, predominately monochrome colour palette, dwarfs and immerses the viewer. Unlike *Bonhoeffer in Harlem*, where each panel is numbered, in *Safety Zone* there is no fixed way to navigate the work. The panels, each with their own distinct exploration of a facet of the massacre, combine to become a visually open account of this complex historical event. Interwoven throughout Young's layered visual documentation of the Nanjing Massacre are memories of the victims, which appear as stories, from mapped diagrams to lists. Young focuses on two figures, John Rabe and Minnie Vautrin, who helped protect and provide for the Chinese refugees within the city's safety zone. Like *Bonhoeffer in Harlem*, the work continues Young's exploration of both the resilience and benevolence of humanity and further enables viewers to piece together an understanding of the events from a poignantly personal perspective rather than an authoritative or official historical account.

An important development occurred two years after *Safety Zone*, when Young was awarded a Visual Arts Fellowship from the Australia Council for the Arts, which supported two years of research examining the Chinese diaspora in Australia. The impact of this fellowship was immense. It enabled Young to focus on his ongoing commitment to expanding the parameters of Australian culture and agitating for more pluralistic historical and cultural narratives. Afforded the time and support to undertake extensive research, he was able to sift through archives, conduct fieldwork and immerse himself in Chinese Australian histories. While in *Bonhoeffer in Harlem* and *Safety Zone* he had examined international historical moments, the fellowship enabled him to hone his visual methodology on a history in which he himself was implicated. And, as in his previous History Projects, it was the personal narratives within the overarching tales of the Chinese diaspora that he was drawn to.

Four series of chalkboard history paintings were informed by Young's Fellowship research: *The Worlds of Lowe Kong Meng and Jong Ah Siug* (2015), *The Lives of Daisy Kwok and Alice Lim Kee* (2016), *Open Kingdom* (2017), as well as *Open Monument* (2015)—a public sculpture commissioned by the City of Ballarat, in Victoria. In each of these series, Young utilises the framework of his chalkboard history paintings to investigate forgotten and marginalised historical moments for contemporary audiences. They embody Young's sustained engagement with Australian cultural politics and work to fragment the singular collective narrative of Australianness.

All of Young's History Projects explore the concept of memory and the act of remembrance. Rather than co-opting remembrance into deliberate, orchestrated gestures for the nation, Young encourages viewers to reflect on personal experiences of memory through carefully considered open-ended provocations. These works trace the lives of generations of Chinese Australians that are little known but have had historical and cultural impact in the construction of contemporary Australia. In these works, Young imagines the interweaving lives of the influential and educated merchant Lowe Kong Meng and the illiterate and incarcerated Jong Ah Siug, the adventures and misfortunes of Australian-born Alice Lim Kee and Daisy Kwok who migrated to Shanghai in the 1920s, the trauma of the nameless Chinese immigrant miners who walked overland from Robe or Darwin in search of gold in the late nineteenth century, and the Chinese community that has contributed to and influenced the growth of Ballarat and its surrounds since the 1850s. Each of these historical explorations expands our understanding of the roles Chinese Australians have played in Australian history beyond the gold miner and market gardener.

Empathy remains a critical concept in these works. The histories they explore are often traumatic, filled with misfortune or marked by sustained and significant anti-Chinese racism. Yet Young's exploration of transcultural humanitarianism and powerful gestures of benevolence, big and small, evidence his continuing optimism and belief in humanity. It was this series of works that compelled me to invite Young to return to 4A Centre for Contemporary Asian Art in 2018 as a collaborating artist.

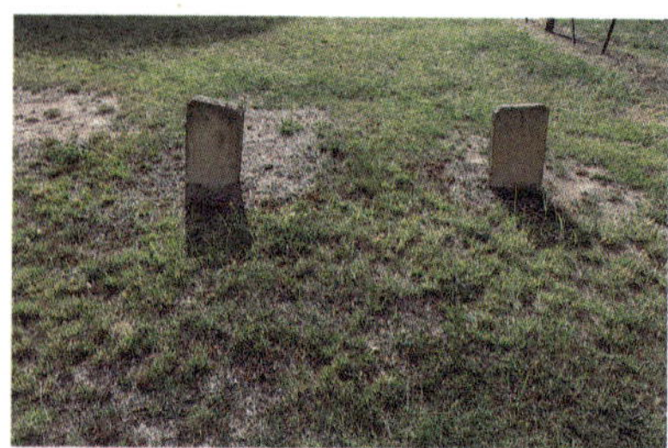

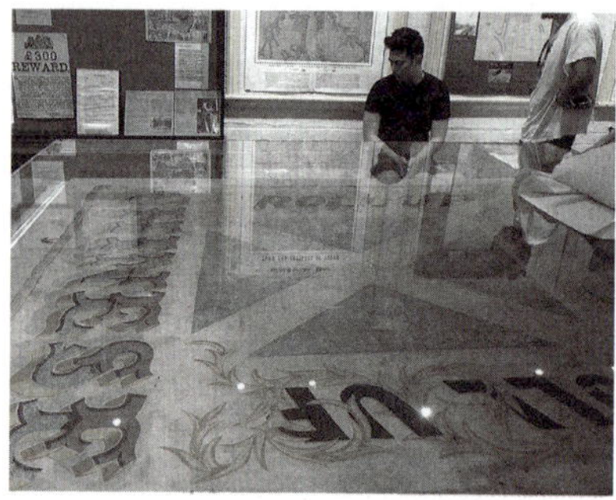

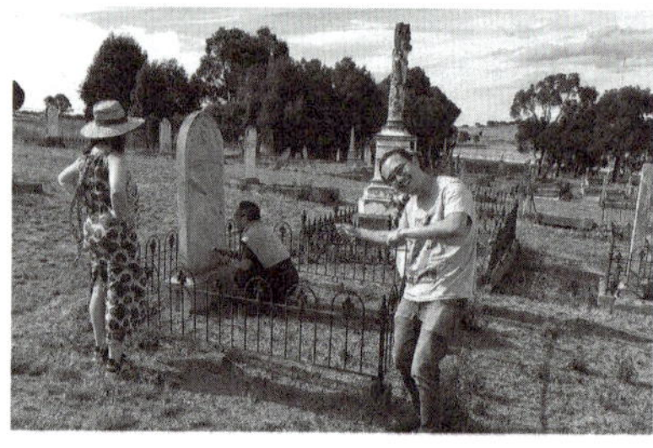

Unmarked Chinese gravestones, Young Cemetery
Hilltops Council, New South Wales, 2018
Photograph by the artist

Micheal Do with *Roll Up No Chinese* banner
Lambing Flat Folk Museum, Hilltops Council,
New South Wales, 2018
Photograph by the artist

Left to right: Mikala Tai, John Young, and Jason Phu
Young Cemetery
Hilltops Council, New South Wales, 2018

When inviting him to be involved in what would become *The Burrangong Affray* project (2018), I was aware that this would represent more than simply an exhibition for Young. The project folded both his industry advocacy and his long-term artistic enquiry into a single undertaking. This coalescence was all the more meaningful for being produced by the organisation he had helped found. While 4A is located in Sydney and Young is now based in Melbourne, he has always supported emerging Asian Australian creatives there in a manner similar to that which he instilled in 4A, fostering the Asian Australian community to work together, to share, and to lean on each other. As the team at 4A prepared to work on *The Burrangong Affray*, we felt that a historical moment such as this would benefit from the philosophical approaches of both Young and emerging artist Jason Phu. While vastly different in medium and discipline, they had mutual respect for each other, and I was hopeful that Young's considered and expansive understanding of how engaging with history can drive contemporary discourse would push Phu in new directions. Equally, I hoped Phu's unfettered and often outlandish experimentation would challenge and inspire Young.

The Burrangong Affray was an eighteen-month research-led art project supported curatorially by co-curator Micheal Do and I, as well as historian Dr Karen Schamberger. The project began as an examination of the Lambing Flat Riots, which occurred between November 1860 and September 1861 on the New South Wales goldfields at Burrangong, near the present-day township of Young. These attacks remain Australia's largest racially motivated riot. Rising antagonism over gold mining access and cultural habits saw trivial misunderstandings intensify into racial tensions that erupted into violence across the goldfields. Over ten months, Chinese miners were subjected to threats, robbery and sustained acts of violence. This anti-Chinese sentiment swept through the goldfields of Victoria in the 1850s and, by the early 1860s, reached a flashpoint in New South Wales, provoking public discussion and debate.

For both artists, it was the documentation, newspaper clippings and cultural artefacts from the main riot that captured their attention. In the depths of the winter of 1861, on the land of the Burrowmunditory people of the Wiradjuri nation—in the present-day township of Young—anti-Chinese sentiments had escalated to violence. Fractious relationships between European, North American and Australian-born miners and their Chinese counterparts on the Burrangong goldfields had grown increasingly precarious over several months, culminating in an attack led by a mob of thousands that destroyed the Chinese campsite.[4] Over ten months, in a series of organised skirmishes, thousands threatened, robbed, scalped and fought Chinese miners, culminating in an act that decimated the Chinese campsite and drove them into the night on 30 June 1861. Under the cloak of darkness, over one thousand injured Chinese clambered their way to the safety of James Roberts' farm, 20 kilometres away in Currawong. By the end of the riots, the anti-Chinese violence had again provoked public opinion and widespread debate. The NSW Parliament responded to the conflict by passing the *Chinese Immigration Regulation and Restriction Act* (1861) and then the *Chinese Restriction Act* (1881) to curb Chinese immigration.[5] These discriminatory laws mirrored those of Victoria and South Australia and have been historicised as the prelude to what would become the White Australia Policy.[6]

For Young, the story of James Roberts and his magnanimous act embodied the benevolent transcultural humanitarianism that the History Projects have sought to elucidate. Roberts sheltered hundreds of Chinese miners who sought refuge, clothing and feeding them.[7] A key part of the research process that supported *The Burrangong Affray* was a series of fieldwork trips the team undertook in the township of Young and its surrounds, which were deeply unsettling and emotional for all four of us. Young, Phu, Do and I do not have family connections to Chinese mining labour—all of our families having migrated to Australia from the 1960s onwards—so we initially approached the project from a more conceptual position. However, this all changed once we were in the township of Young.

Our research was supported by a number of locals living in and around Young who had traced this story in both a formal and informal manner; in particular our fieldwork was enabled through the generosity of the Thorsby family—descendants of James Roberts who still reside on Roberts' Currawong farm. Brad Thorsby and his family facilitated Young and Phu working on their land, documenting the site where the miners were sheltered and tracing the steps they took that winter's night. Thorsby retold the story that was so familiar to us from our research but in a manner that made it personal. Inviting us to hop into the tray of his ute, he drove to the highest point on his farm, and there we stood, among wild chocolate mint, as he pointed out the treacherous walk the miners took. As we clung to the cab on the way back down the property, he finally took us to the stretch of land where the miners took shelter—a plot of land with no defining features that felt overwhelmingly small for the number of people it had once sheltered. Throughout this visit Young was using a digital camera to take photos—in the moment it looked casual. Taking no time to set the shot up, he snapped effortlessly and unobtrusively.

On the way back to town we decided to find Blackguard Gully, the site of the Chinese campsite where the riot began. It is a moment that is seared into my memory. Blackguard Gully is on the outskirts of the township of Young and is only modestly marked. The old alluvial mining locale remains exposed, with crumbling undulations of earth providing evidence of a once active mining site. As we approached the site, we were overwhelmed by the haunting eeriness of the place. With our car parked on the bend of a country road, our short walk into the bushland placed us on the old campsite. As we each slowly walked through the abandoned site, we were able to identify mining tools, as if they had been left there only yesterday. None of us spoke. We split off and walked alone in the overgrown bush. When we all eventually got back into the car, and into the relief of the air conditioning, we studiously avoided talking about what we had just experienced.

Later that evening, after a requisite meal at the local Chinese restaurant, we shared a few bottles of red in our Airbnb. Young was the first to bring up Blackguard Gully and encouraged us all to reflect on the visceral experience. Responses tumbled out in haphazard form: from our shock at the raw emotional effect that standing on the land had on us, to the reflections and memories it had stirred up. Young, ever the mentor, encouraged us to each find ourselves in this moment and to examine our connection. It was that conversation that shifted the project from something we knew was historically important to something that felt innately personal. When we returned from that field trip, the project changed: all of us were motivated by a need to create an exhibition that would impart and evoke empathy and understanding in the audience.

Phu worked away, prolific at the last minute, producing a video that traced the car journeys of the creative team, poetry, human-sized ghost puppets that honoured those lost, wall paintings, photographs of performances held on the Thorsby's farm, and a series of four canvases entitled *ROLLING ROLLS ROLLED ROLL* (2018). Inspired by the structure of Young's chalkboard history series, each of Phu's canvases celebrated Chinese contributions to Australian society, from spring rolls to furniture making.

Hung alongside Phu's canvas works was Young's new series of chalkboard panels, *Lambing Flat*. In this series, Young explores, over twenty-seven emotive panels, the events and repercussions of this period of civil disobedience. The panels are comprised

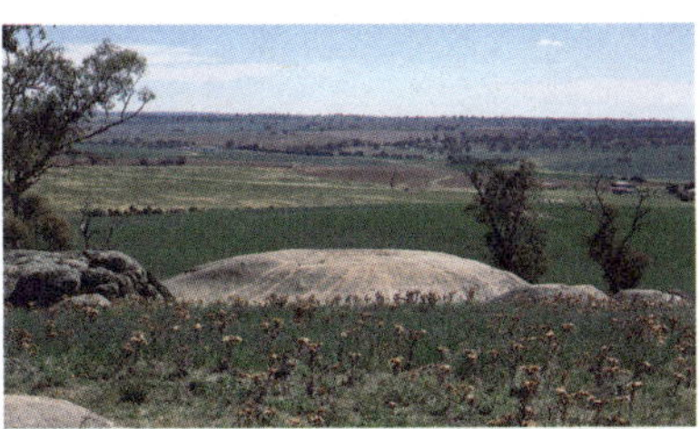

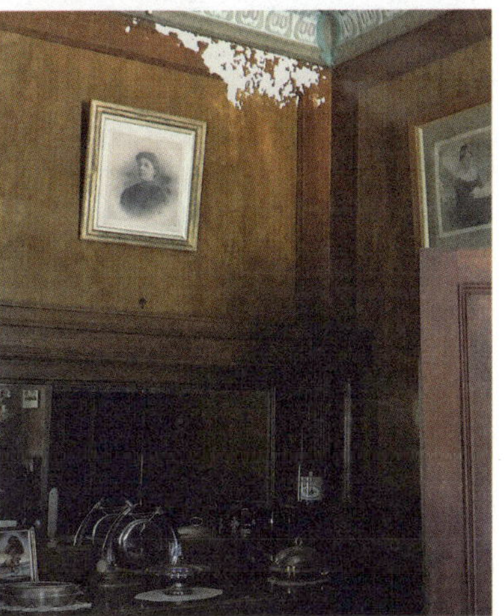

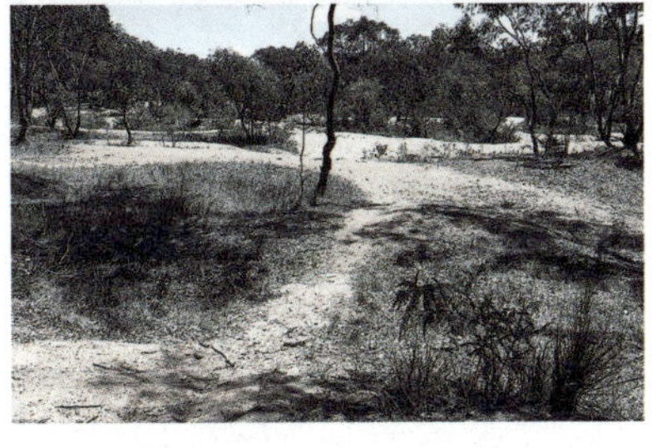

Currawong Farm
Young, New South Wales, 2018
Photograph by the artist

Thorsby/Roberts farmhouse interior,
Currawong Farm
Young, New South Wales, 2018
Photograph by the artist

Blackguard Gully with exposed diggings
still in sight
Hilltops Council, New South Wales, 2018
Photograph by the artist

of a multiplicity of source material, including archival documentation from the Australian National Archives, as well as images made by Young himself at both Currawong and the local folk museum. Stripped of colour, these images are layered and digitally graded, becoming episodic historical anecdotes amidst Young's hand-painted chalkboard panels. These panels are immediately emotive, concise but compelling as they integrate a complex historical moment into personal narratives—real and imagined—of a night of trauma and an act of compassion.

Stretching to almost seven metres, the panels should be viewed as one of the most significant history paintings in Australian art. They reveal a moment that remains, inexplicably, on the edges of our national history, passing each year without commemoration. In *Lambing Flat*, Young creates a contemporary marker for the violence and suffering of that one night in 1861, which has left an indelible mark on Australian society as a precursor to the White Australia Policy. It is an incident of national importance.

In addition to the *Lambing Flat* series, Young created a video work titled *The Field* (2018). While Young's work is often informed by and made with lens-based media, *The Field* was the first time he had presented video work in an exhibition. The idea for the piece emerged during the field trip, when Micheal Do and I suddenly became camera operators, holding a small digital point-and-shoot camera to capture Young and Phu wrestling in some long grass on the outskirts of the township of Young. It was the kind of spontaneity that Phu embraces, and it was exciting to see Young exploring this side of his practice. The final work is hypnotic. With a soundtrack devised by Ian Parkinson, its crisp white aesthetic and additional casting of a stereotypically 'white Australian' redhead woman having her neat plait pulled from behind, creates a reversal of subject positions that brings a historical moment into contemporary conversation.

On the final field trip, Phu performed to a small audience and so did Young. Performance has not been at the core of Young's practice but in discussions throughout the project he had warmed to the idea of exploring his work through the body in movement. While Phu returned to the place of shelter—the Thorsby's farm—Young chose to perform at Blackguard Gully. The place that we had all found so unsettling is depicted as a character of its own in both the performance and the resulting photographs, in which Young casts himself as a miner on that desperate night. For those that witnessed the performance it remains seared in our memories. The photographs from the performance are just as powerful. By placing a body into this landscape, the historical imaginings of this moment become visceral. This series of three photographs, *Action: Covering*, forms part of the final suite of works displayed next to the photo documentation of Phu's performance, *Do not stick your hand in the fire, sit near it and observe stars*.

Both the performances and photographs were created in collaboration, and together they trace the journey of the miners that night. They are a coalescence of two artists grappling in tandem with a complex and nuanced historical moment. While the rest of the exhibition honours their distinct art forms, this photographic series illustrates where their practices briefly converged. As one of the curators, I feel that these two series of photographs represent the core of the project, where exchange and mutual vulnerabilities were tabled for all the creative team to explore and respond to the events of 30 June 1861.

The public response to the *The Burrangong Affray* exhibition and Young and Phu's works was overwhelmingly positive. In art circles, these works were seen as exemplary contemporary mediations with the forces of identity, economics, race and otherness in Australia today, and they received widespread coverage.[8] However, surprisingly, Young's

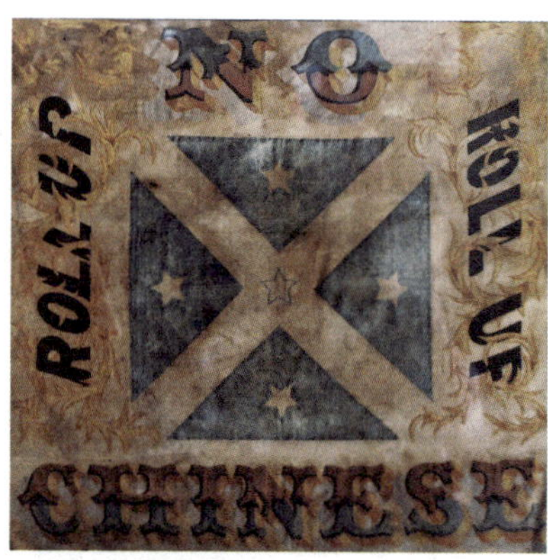

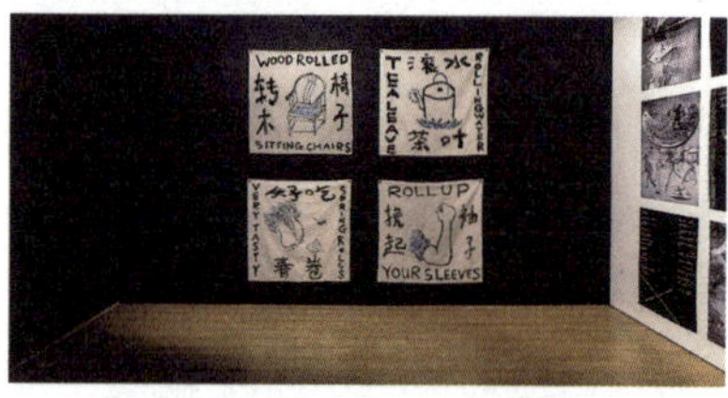

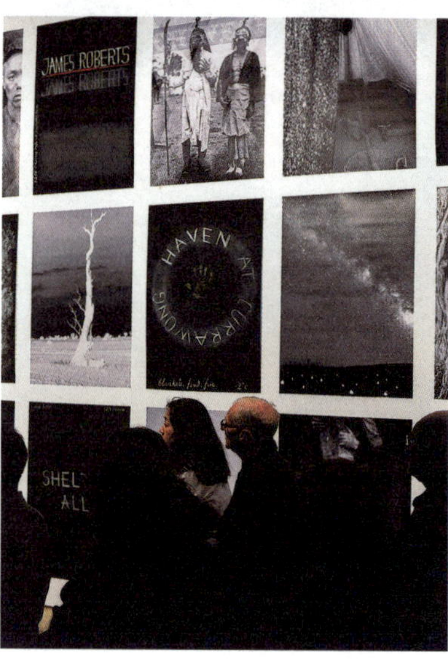

Anonymous
Roll Up No Chinese 1861
Banner, 120 × 120 cm
Collection of Lambing Flat Folk Museum,
Hilltops Council, New South Wales

Jason Phu
ROLLING ROLLS ROLLED ROLL 2018
Installation view, 4A Centre for Contemporary Asian
Art, Sydney, 2018

Opening of *The Burrangong Affray*
4A Centre for Contemporary Asian Art, Sydney, 2018
Opened by Mikala Tai and Edmund Capon

work was not collected by any major Australian institution. In fact, to date none of his chalkboard history paintings have been. These monumental historical markers contribute to an expanded and inclusive concept of Australian history but they have failed to be acknowledged by the institutions that are the custodians of our national cultural history. This omission speaks to the wider systemic challenges that many Australian artists face as they agitate for a more pluralistic and encompassing cultural landscape.

Compounding this omission was the targeted racial vitriol that Young and the project received from the far-right Australia First Party. Through a dedicated website, the far-right tried to weaponise the exhibition to incite further discrimination towards Chinese Australians, claiming that Young and Phu were 'two sad disorientated Chinese agents [who] have been staging an anti-Australian Digger propaganda art expo' and that 4A, 'in Sydney's Chinatown ghetto—is the only place that would exhibit their anti-White Australian hate'.[9] This posting was followed by a series of anonymous emails to the gallery elaborating on the website's brazen hate speech. This critical, institutional and public response was indicative of the ongoing complexity and challenges of expanding cultural conversation in Australia.

Young's artistic methodology in the later History Projects has enabled the development of significant and monumental Australian history paintings. Underpinned by extensive research and fieldwork, accessible and compelling to audiences, this body of works forms a substantial contribution to contemporary Australian art. By exploring benevolence, Young finds hope in humanitarianism. These demonstrations of compassion seek to foster cross-cultural understanding and empathy. In an age of precarity, where economic and cultural division threaten social cohesion, Young's works remind us that, amongst chaos, trauma and violence, we have the capacity to forge new connections.

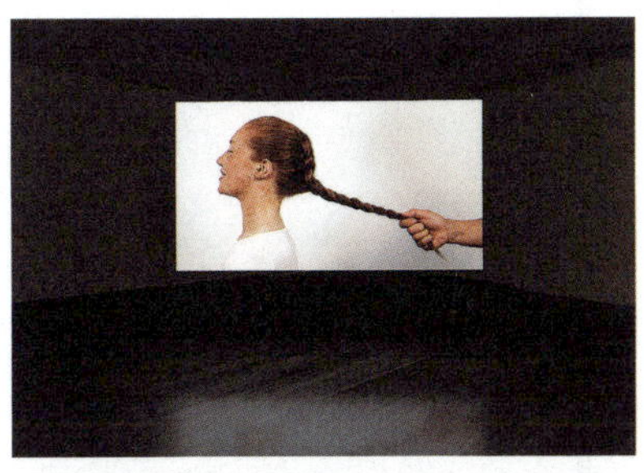

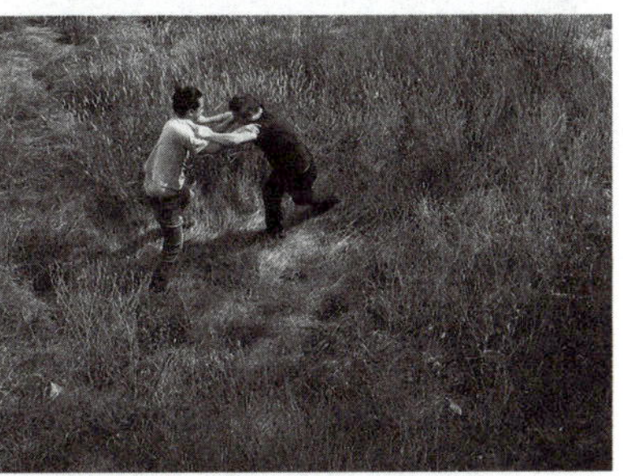

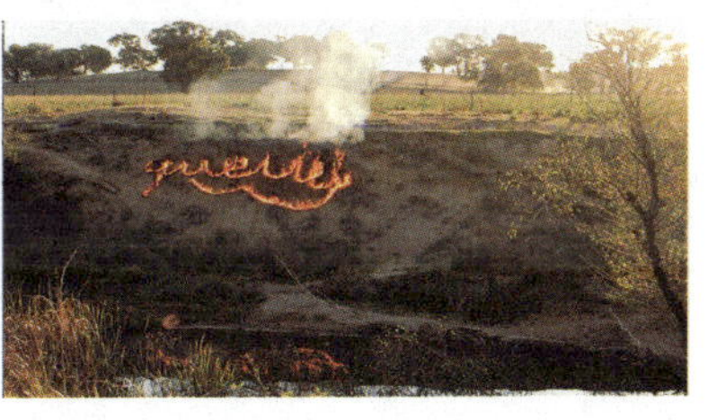

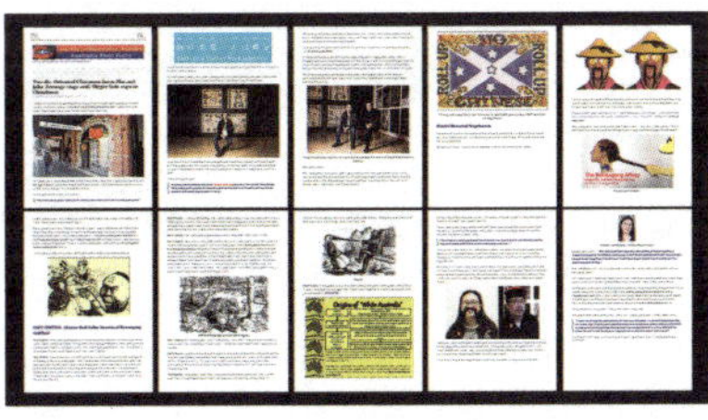

The Field 2018
Installation view, Hawthorn Arts Centre, Boroondara Arts, Melbourne, 2019

Still from *The Field* 2018
HD video loop, 8 min. 5 sec.

Jason Phu
Queue 2018
Fire installation, Currawong Farm
Young, New South Wales, 2018

John Hood
'Two dis-Oriented Chinamen Jason Phu and John Zerunge stage anti-Digger hate expo in Chinatown', Australia First Party website, 25 August 2018
Ten pages written in response to *The Burrangong Affray*, 4A Centre for Contemporary Asian Art, Sydney, 2018

1. Jenny Macleod, 'The Fall and Rise of Anzac Day: 1965 and 1990 Compared', *War & Society*, vol. 20, no. 1, 2000, pp. 149–68.

2. Greater Good Science Center, 'Empathy Defined: Why Practice It?', *Greater Good Magazine*, University of California Berkley, https://greatergood.berkeley.edu/topic/empathy/definition#why-practice-empathy. Viewed 2 March 2022.

3. In 2007 Young undertook fieldwork in Berlin ahead of his exhibition and, with Ochs, visited St Matthäus Church where he first began working towards a project centred on the life of Dietrich Bonhoeffer (1906–1945). See essays by Lo (p. 137), Volz (p. 92) and Glöde (p. 148) in this volume.

4. Karen Schamberger, 'Difficult History in a Local Museum: The Lambing Flat Riots at Young, New South Wales', *Australian Historical Studies*, vol. 48, no. 3, 2017, pp. 436–41.

5. These pieces of legislation restricted the number of Chinese migrants who could enter the colony of NSW. The laws introduced a poll tax and a limit on how many Chinese people could arrive by boat (determined by cargo-to-people ratios).

6. Australian Government, 'Australia's multicultural policy history', Department of Home Affairs, 2020, https://www.homeaffairs.gov.au/about-us/our-portfolios/multicultural-affairs/about-multicultural-affairs/our-policy-history.

7. 'Lambing Flat Riots', *The Argus*, 10 July 1861, p. 6. James Roberts clothed and fed the Chinese miners who found his property by following the path of a river. According to the special commissioner and other firsthand reports, European and British miners scalped Chinese miners, holding up their pigtails as trophies. According to *The Argus*, 'one man returned with 8 pigtails attached to a flag'.

8. See for example: Teresa Tan, 'A new exhibition explores the history and legacy of the anti-Chinese race riots at Lambing Flats' in *ABC Arts*, 21 July 2018; Lauren Carroll Harris, 'The riots history erased: reckoning with the racism of Lambing Flat', *The Guardian*, 7 August 2018; Sophia Cai, 'The Burrangong Affray', *Un Projects*, 2018; Jason Phu, 'The Lambing Flat Riots', *The Saturday Paper*, 25–31 August 2018.

9. John Hood, 'Two dis-oriented Chinamen Jason Phu and John Zerunge stage anti-Digger hate expo in Chinatown', *Australia First Party*, 25 August 2018, https://australiafirstparty.net/two-disoriented-chinamen-jason-phu-and-john-zerunge-stage-anti-digger-hate-expo-in-chinatown.

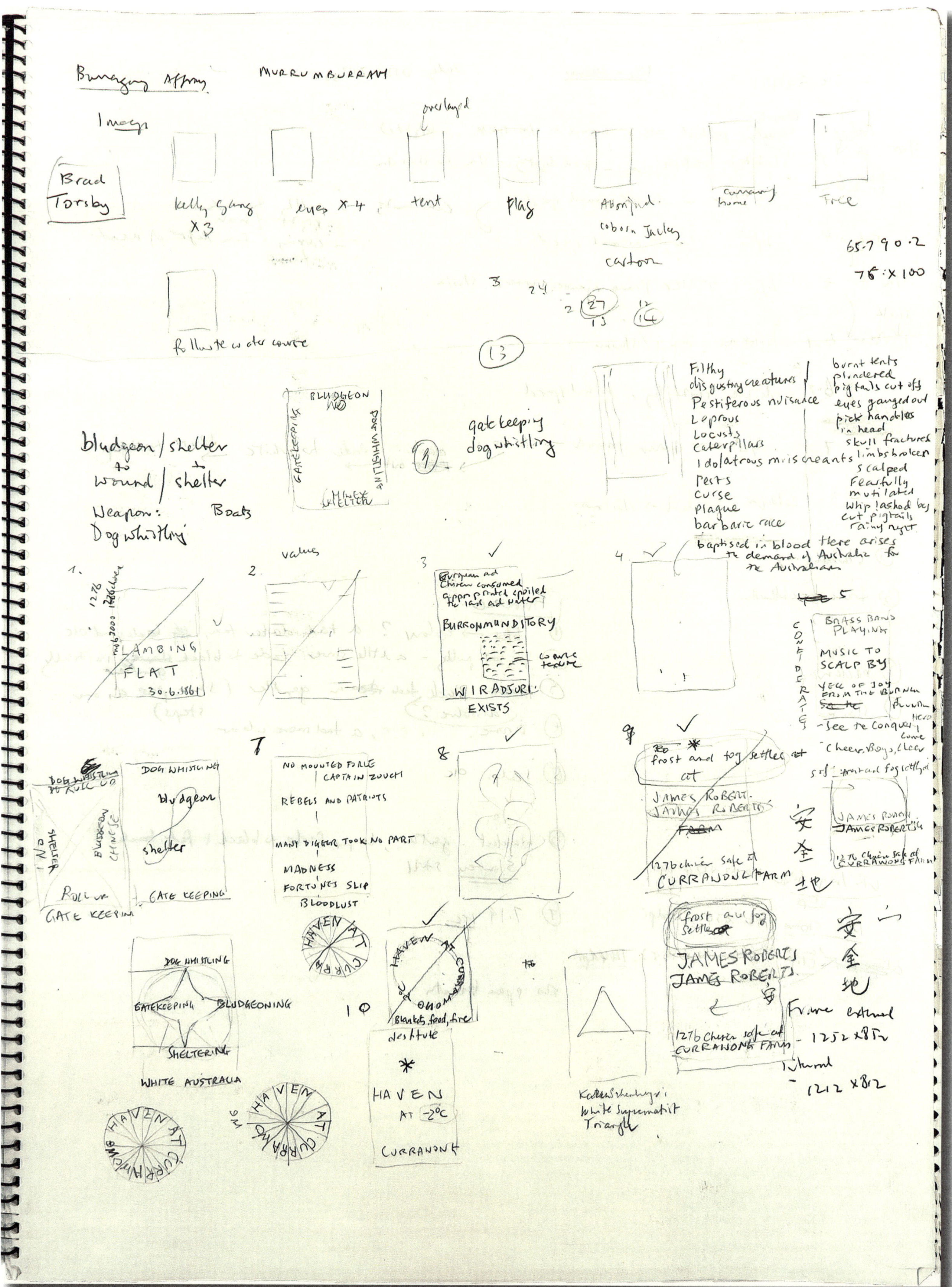

Bunagang Affray
MURRUMBURRAH
Image
Brad Torsby
Kelly gang x3
eyes x4
tent
flag
Aboriginal coborn Jacky cartoon
currawong home
Tree
65.790.2
78 x 100
follow the water course
BLUDGEON WD
GATEKEEPING
WHISTLING ARSE
MINER SHELTER
bludgeon / shelter to wound / shelter
Weapon: Boats
Dog whistling
gate keeping
dog whistling
Filthy
disgusting creatures
Pestiferous nuisance
Leprous
Locusts
Caterpillars
Idolatrous miscreants
Pests
Curse
Plague
barbaric race
burnt tents
plundered
pigtails cut off
eyes gauged out
pick handles in head
skull fractured
limbs broken
scalped
Fearfully mutilated
Whip lashed
cut pigtails
rainy night
baptised in blood there arises the demand of Australia for the Australian
1.
2. values
3. European and Chinese consumed upon printed spoiled the last and water
BURRONMUNDI STORY
WIRADJURI EXISTS
4.
LAMBING FLAT 30.6.1861
BRASS BAND PLAYING
MUSIC TO SCALP BY
YELL OF JOY FROM THE BURNING
5
CONFEDERATES
See the Conqueror
Cheer, Boys, Cheer
frost and fog settled
JAMES ROBERTS
FARM
127b chinese safe at CURRANDULL FARM
frost and fog settled
JAMES ROBERTS
JAMES ROBERTS
7
DOG WHISTLING TO ROLL UP
DOG WHISTLING
bludgeon
shelter
GATE KEEPING
NO SHELTER
BLUDGEON CHINESE
ROLL UP
GATE KEEPING
NO MOUNTED FORCE
CAPTAIN ZOUCH
REBELS AND PATRIOTS
MANY DIGGER TOOK NO PART
MADNESS
FORTUNES SLIP
BLOODLUST
8
frost and fog settled
JAMES ROBERTS
JAMES ROBERTS
127b chinese safe at CURRAWONG FARM
9
DOG WHISTLING
GATEKEEPING BLUDGEONING
SHELTERING
WHITE AUSTRALIA
HAVEN AT CURRA
HAVEN AT CURRA
10
Blankets food, fire
destitute
HAVEN AT -2°C
CURRANONG
HAVEN AT CURRAWONG
HAVEN AT CURRA
Kadinsky's White Suprematist Triangle
JAMES ROBERTS
JAMES ROBERTS
127b chinese safe at CURRANONG FARM
Frame external
- 1252 x 852
Internal
- 1212 x 812
安全地

336

14/3/2015

26   15.

26   大畜
The Taming Power of the Great

     Holding firm
     Holding still
     Holding back
     carrying far, nourishing

Perseverance furthers
Not eating at home brings good fortune
It furthers one to cross the great water

Strong creative power
Firmness & truth →
light and clarity

daily renewal.
power of the personality
Eat one's bread by entering into public office
In harmony with heaven

Heaven within the mountain
The image of the Taming Power of the great
Thus the superior man acquaints himself with
many sayings of antiquity
and many deeds of the past
In order to strengthen his character thereby

Hidden treasures from ~~birds~~ words and deeds of the past
give actuality to the past

① Danger is at hand. It furthers one to desist
     Do not force an advance
     compose himself & wait
② The axle trees are taken from the wagon
     Contents himself with waiting → energy accumulates

③ One attains the way of heaven. Success
     Time of obstruction is past
     ~~energy~~ Energy dammed up by inhibition
     forces its way out and achieves great success
     man is honored by the ruler and whose
     principles now prevail and shape the world

15   謙
     modesty

Modesty creates success
The superior man carries things through

man according to his behaviour exposes
himself to the influence of the benevolent or
destructive forces.
When a man holds a high position and is
nevertheless modest, he shines with the light
of wisdom
The superior man carries out his work to the end
without boasting of what he has achieved

Within the earth, a mountain
The image of modesty
Thus the superior man reduces that which is too much
And augments that which is too little
He weighs things and makes them equal.

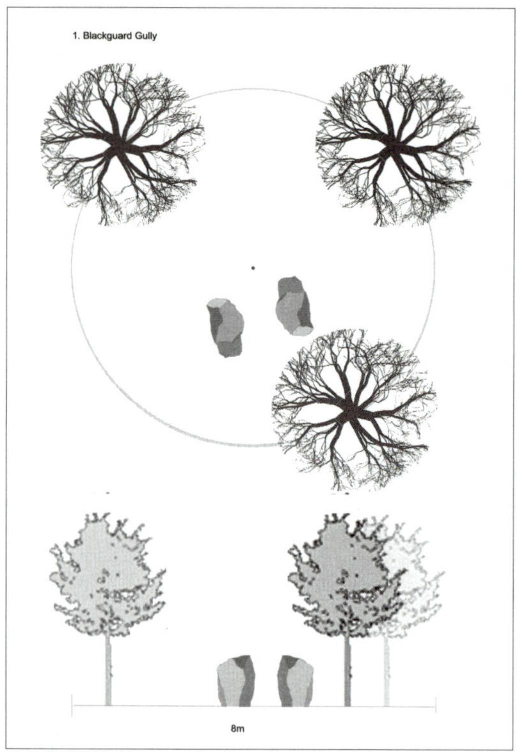

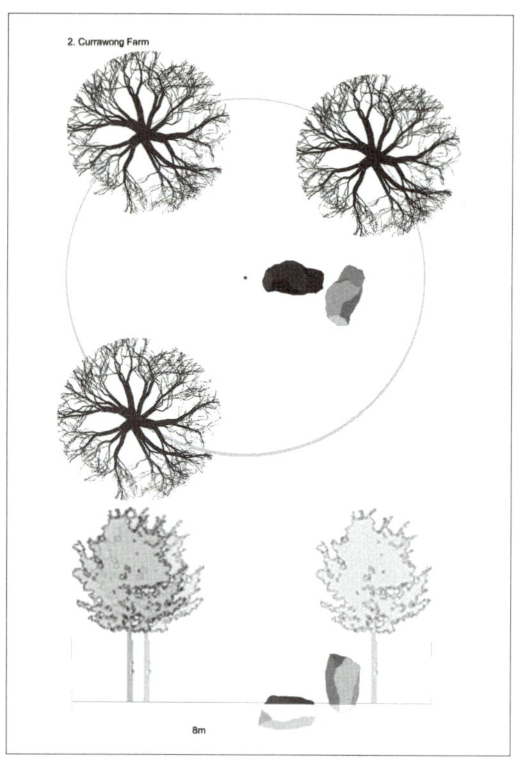

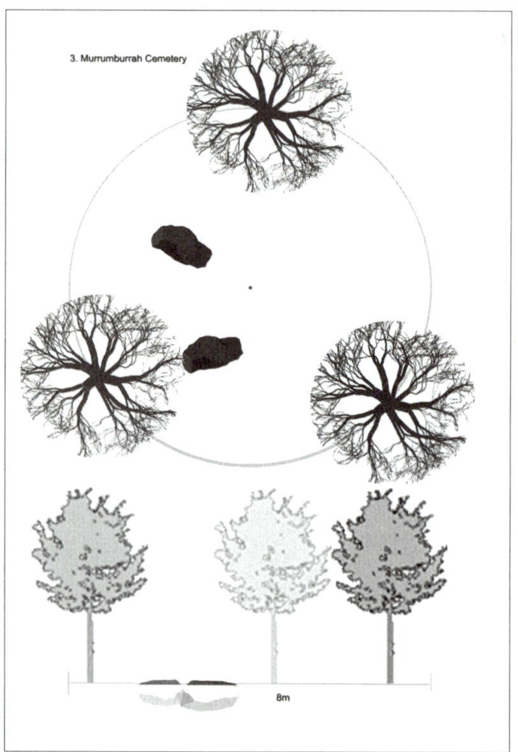

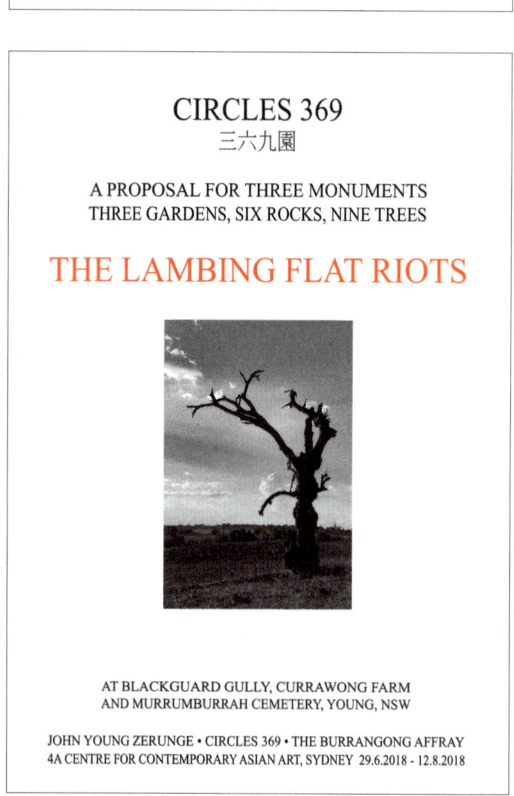

pages 336–37
Pages from the artist's notebook (JYNP2018)

above
Three drawings for *Circles 369:*
A Proposal for Three Monuments 2018
Digital composite sketch, dimensions variable

Circles 369: A Proposal for Three Monuments 2018
Digital print on photographic paper, edition of 3,
framed, 92 × 68 cm

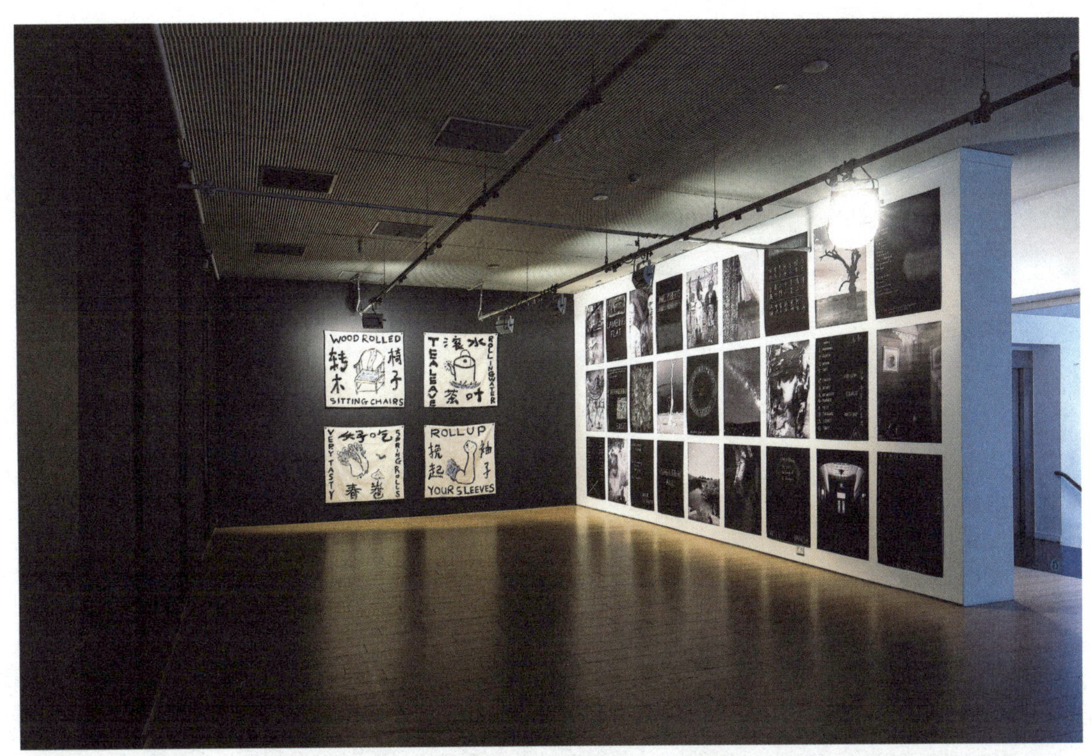

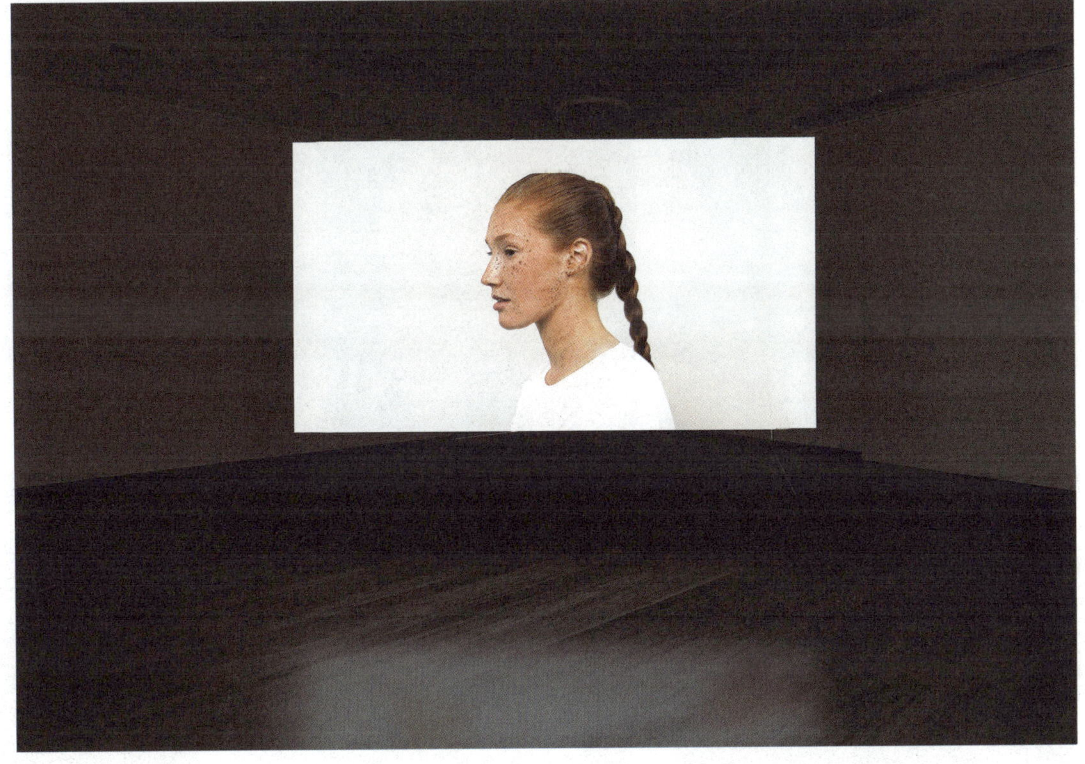

top
The Burrangong Affray 2018
Installation view, 4A Centre for Contemporary
Asian Art, Sydney, 2018
Left: Jason Phu, *Rolling Rolls Rolled Roll* 2018
Ink on sheet, four works, 120 × 120 cm each
Right: John Young, *Lambing Flat* 2018
Digital print on paper, chalk and paint on paper,
27 works, 100 × 70 cm each
Image: Document Photography

bottom
The Field 2018
Installation view, Hawthorn Arts Centre,
Boroondara Arts, Melbourne, 2019

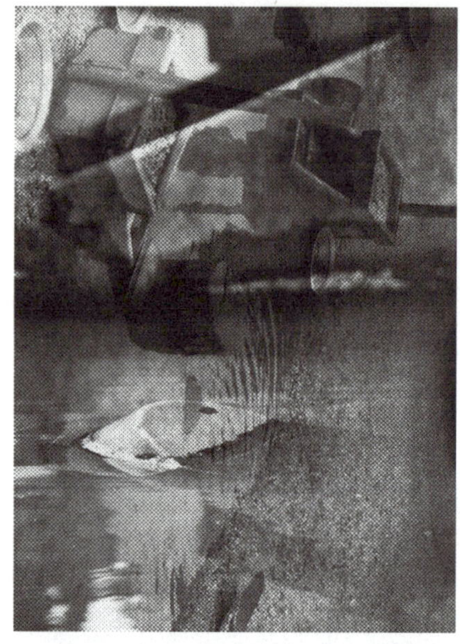

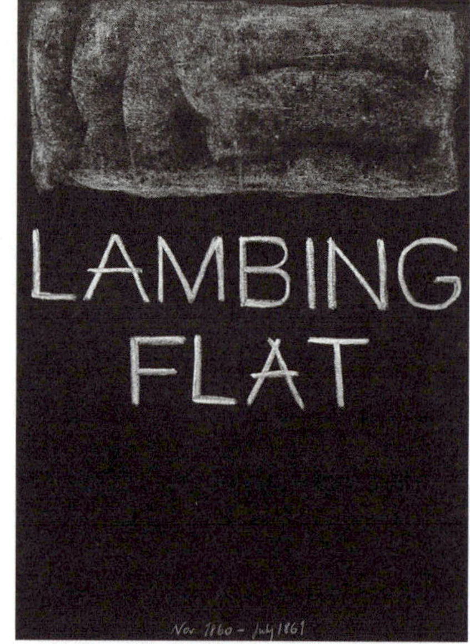

LAMBING
FLAT
Nov 1860 – July 1861

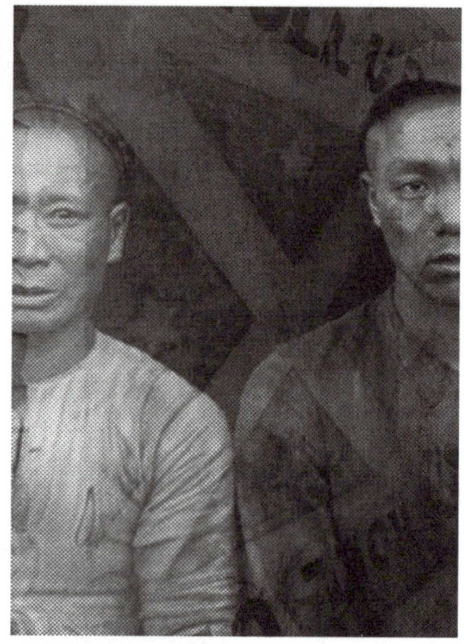

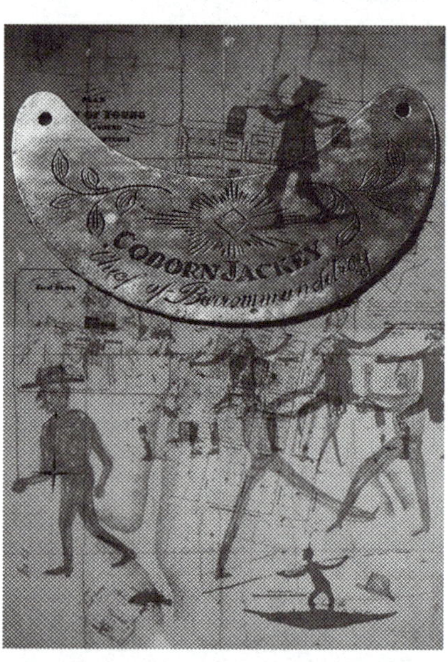

CODORN JACKEY
Chief of Burrowmundairy

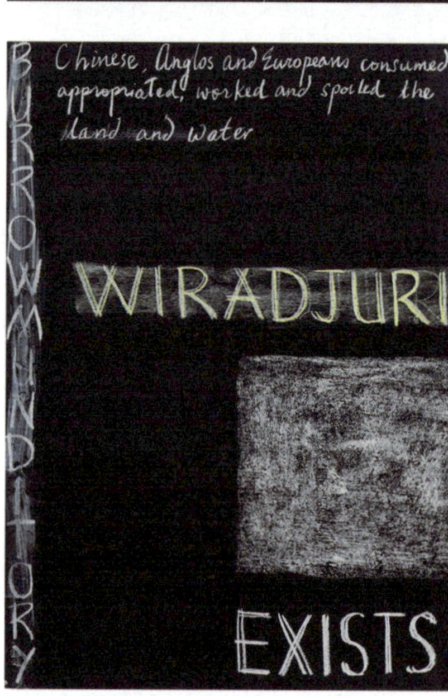

BURROWMUNDAITORY
Chinese, Anglos and Europeans consumed,
appropriated, worked and spoiled the
land and water
WIRADJURI
EXISTS

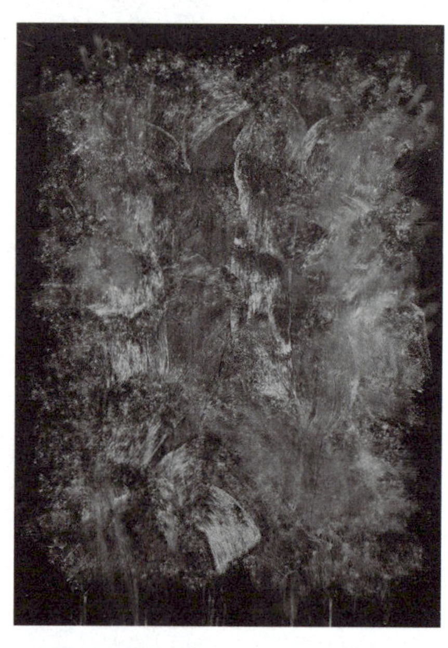

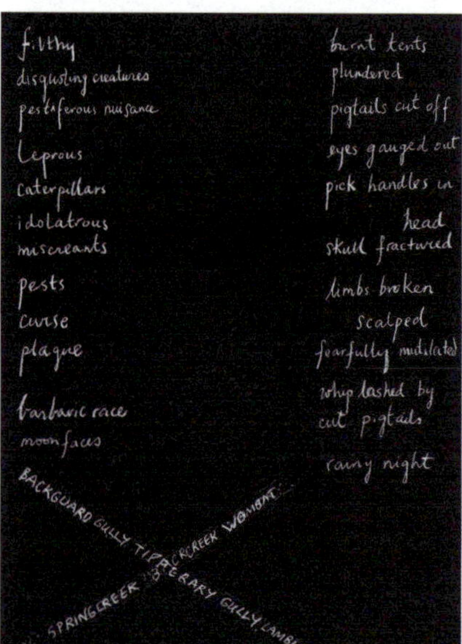

filthy
disgusting creatures
pestiferous nuisance
Leprous
Caterpillars
idolatrous
miscreants
pests
curse
plague

barbaric race
moon faces

burnt tents
plundered
pigtails cut off
eyes gauged out
pick handles in
head
skull fractured
limbs broken
scalped
fearfully mutilated
whip lashed by
cut pigtails
rainy night

BACKGUARD GULLY TIPPERARY GULLY LAMBING FLAT
SPRING CREEK BLACKGUARD GULLY

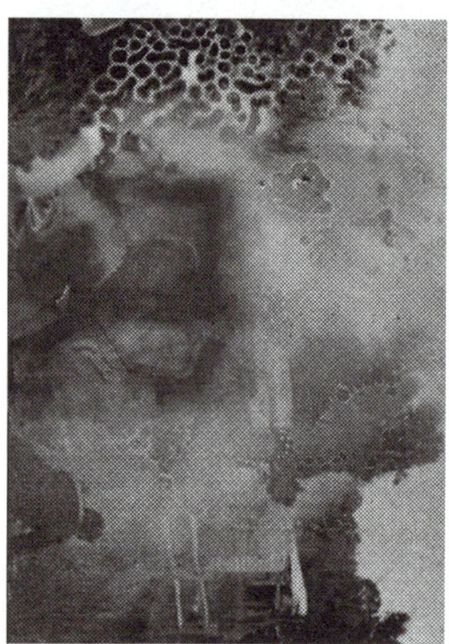

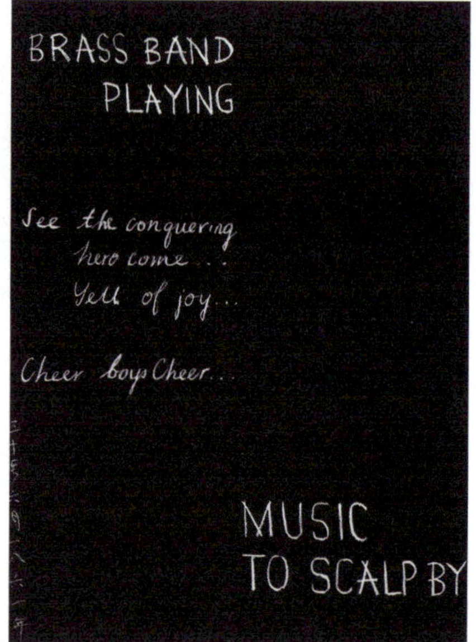

BRASS BAND
PLAYING

See the conquering
hero come...
Yell of joy...

Cheer boys Cheer...

MUSIC
TO SCALP BY

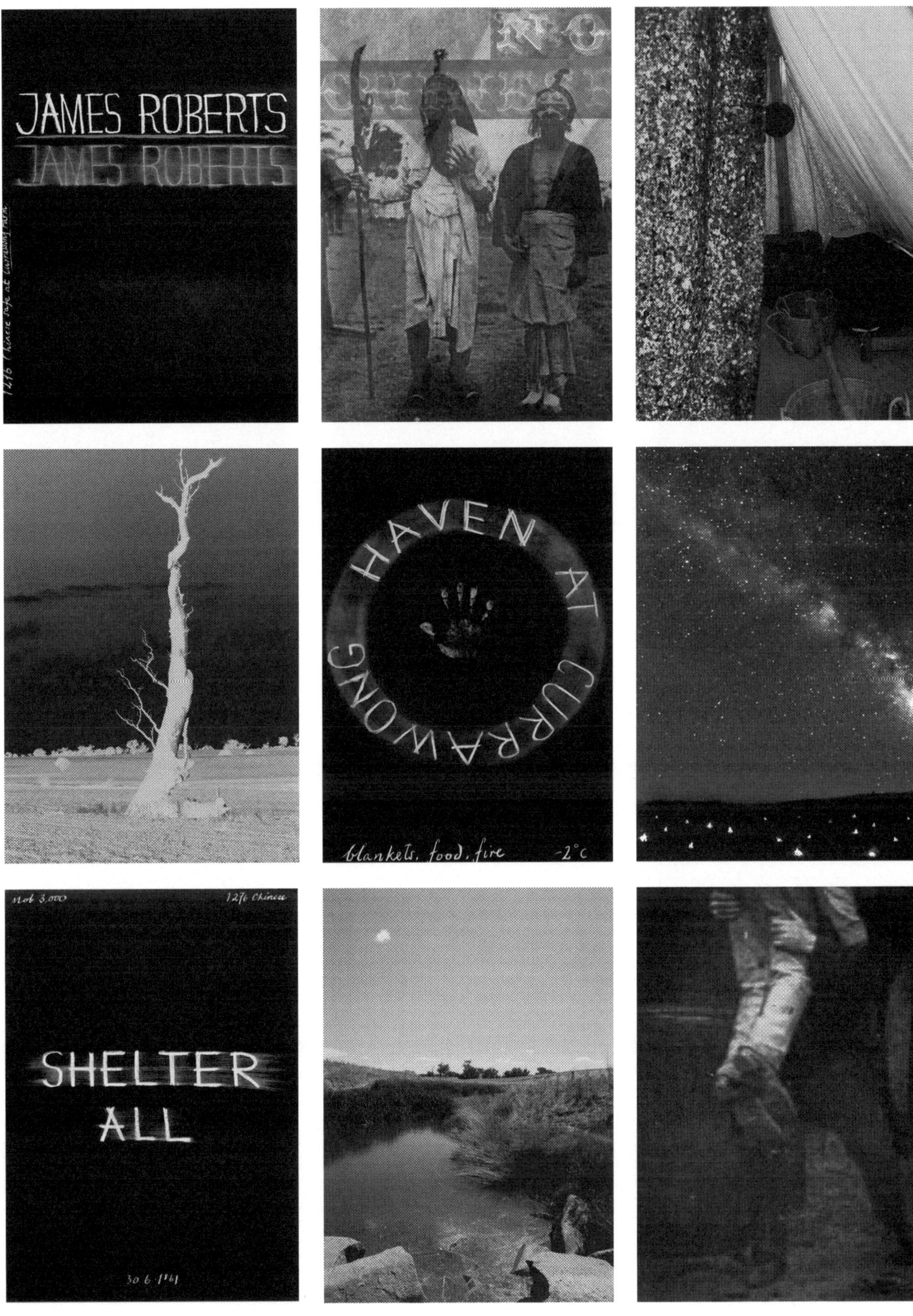
JAMES ROBERTS
JAMES ROBERTS
HAVEN AT CURRAWONG
blankets, food, fire   -2°C
SHELTER
ALL

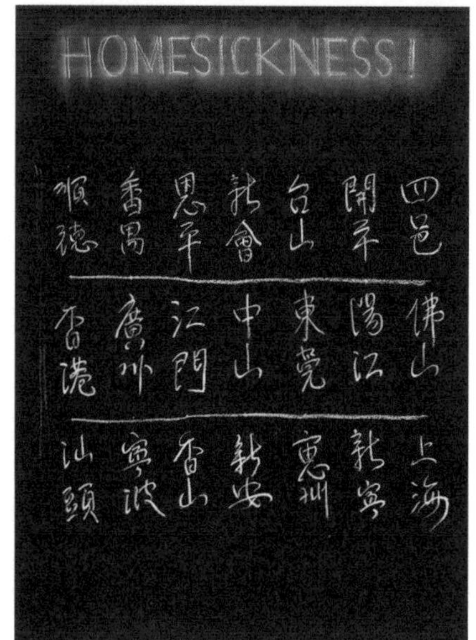
HOMESICKNESS!

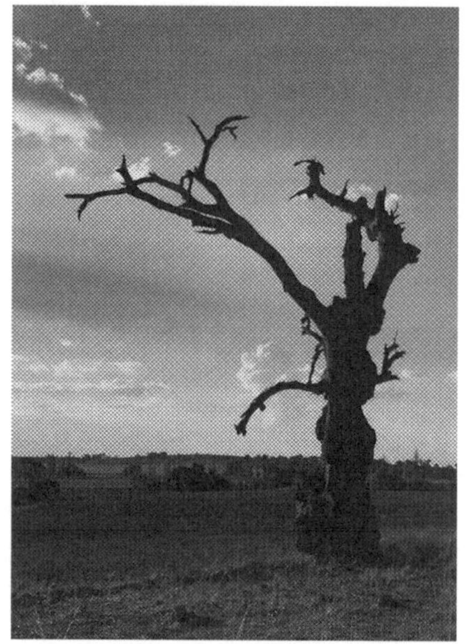

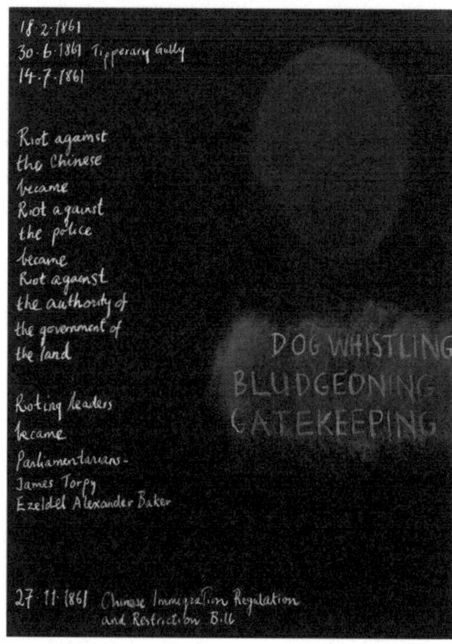
18·2·1861
30·6·1861 Tipperary Gully
14·7·1861

Riot against
the Chinese
became
Riot against
the police
became
Riot against
the authority of
the government of
the land

Rioting leaders
became
Parliamentarians –
James Torpy
Ezeldel Alexander Baker

27·11·1861 Chinese Immigration Regulation
and Restriction Bill

DOG WHISTLING
BLUDGEONING
GATEKEEPING

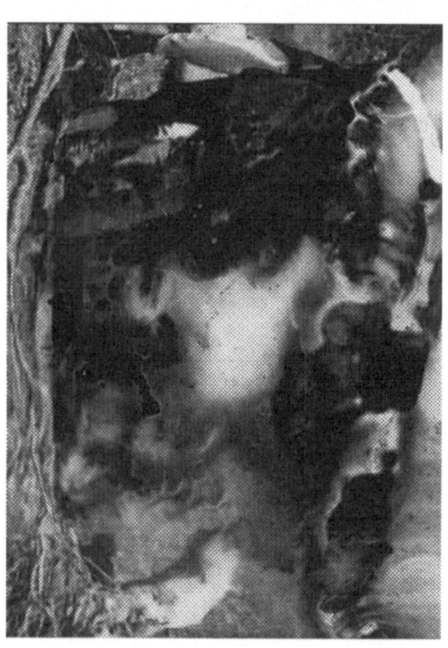

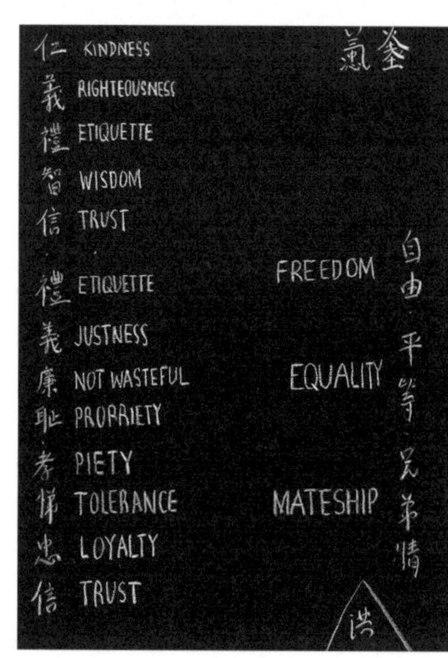
仁 KINDNESS
義 RIGHTEOUSNESS
禮 ETIQUETTE
智 WISDOM
信 TRUST

禮 ETIQUETTE   FREEDOM   自由
義 JUSTNESS
廉 NOT WASTEFUL   EQUALITY   平等
恥 PROPRIETY
孝 PIETY
悌 TOLERANCE   MATESHIP   兄弟情
忠 LOYALTY
信 TRUST

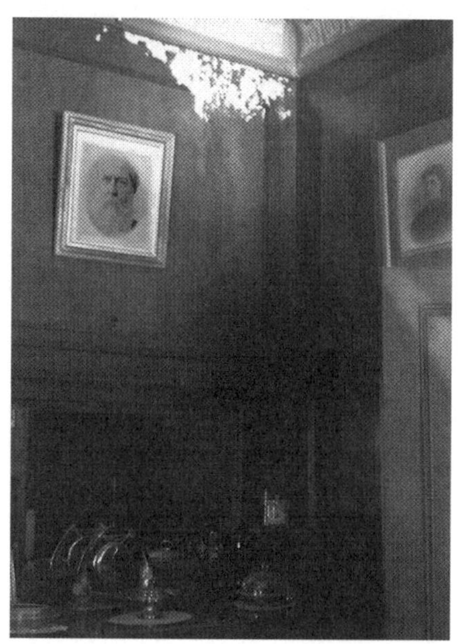

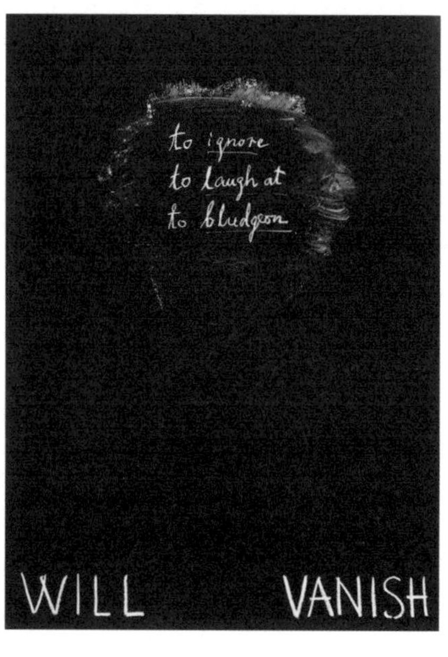
to ignore
to laugh at
to bludgeon

WILL   VANISH

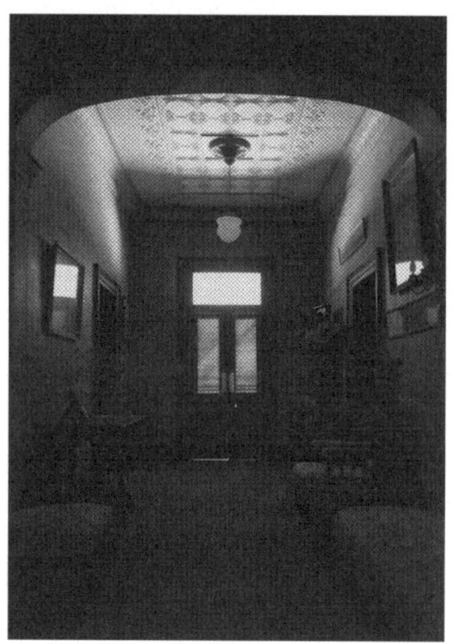

TRANSLATORS

TRIUMPH!

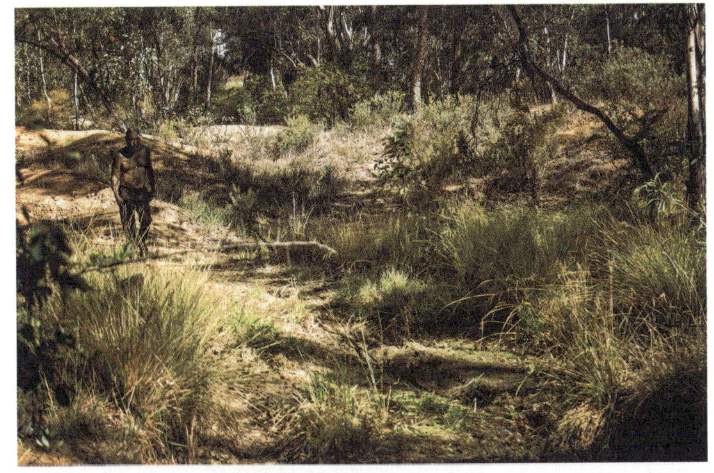

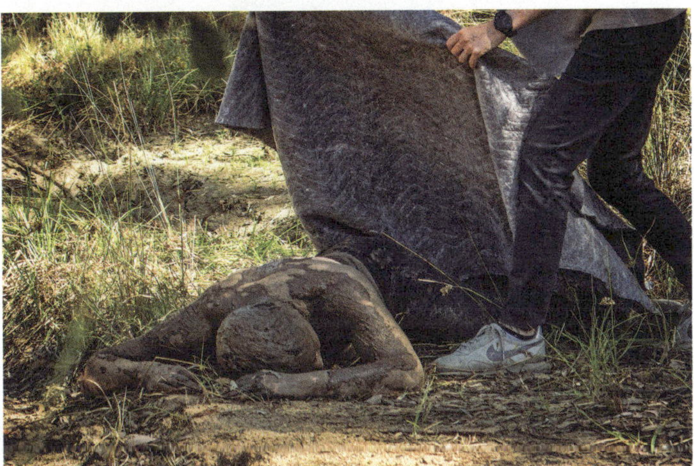

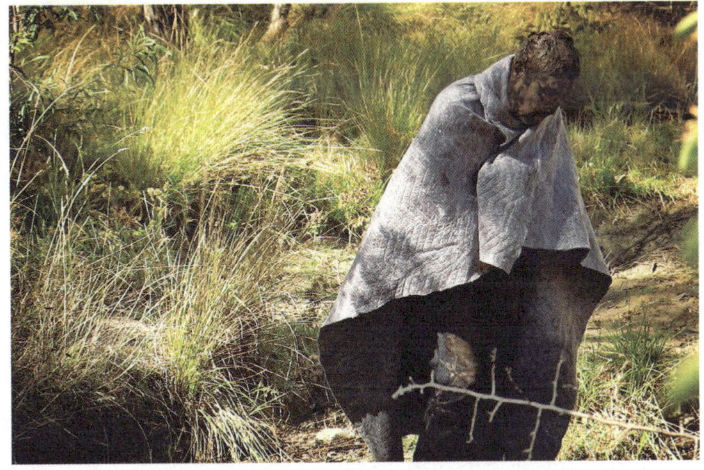

Action: Covering 1 2018
Action: Covering 2 2018
Action: Covering 3 2018
Editioned photographs, 121 x 81 cm each

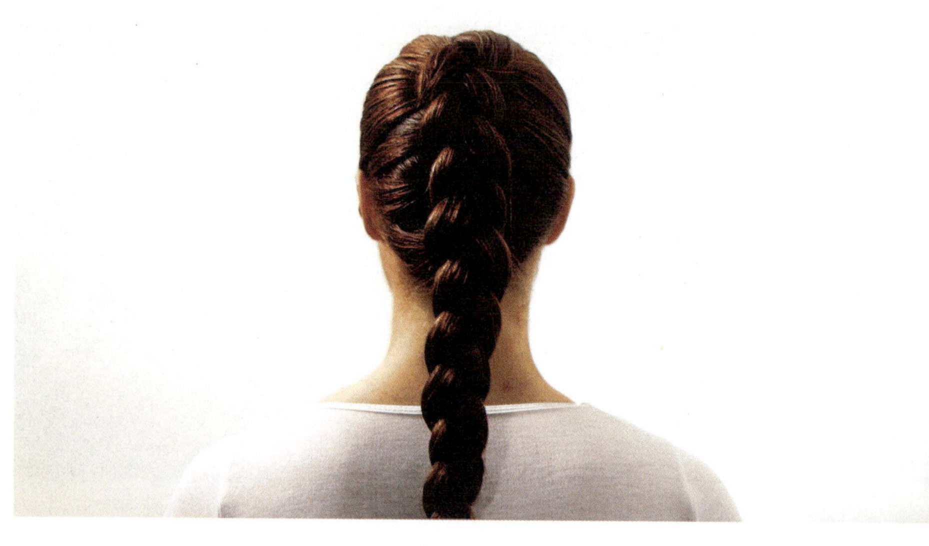

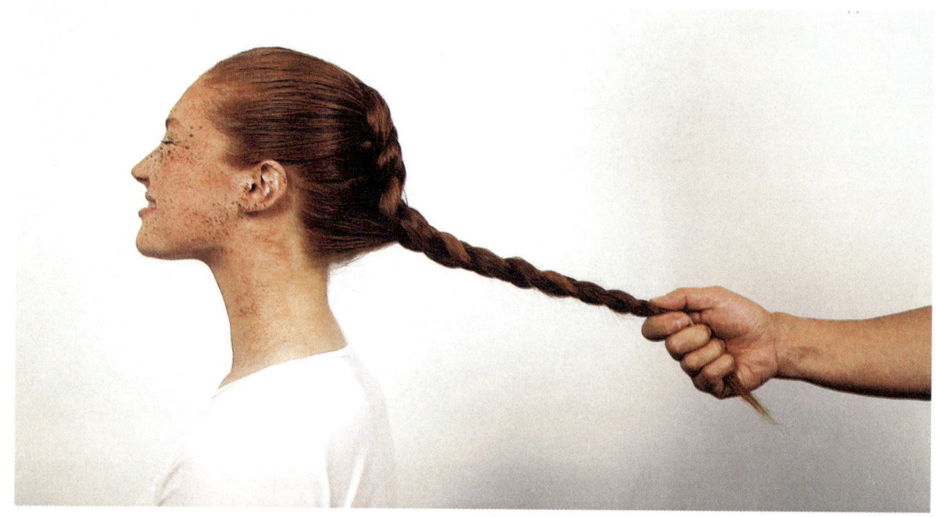

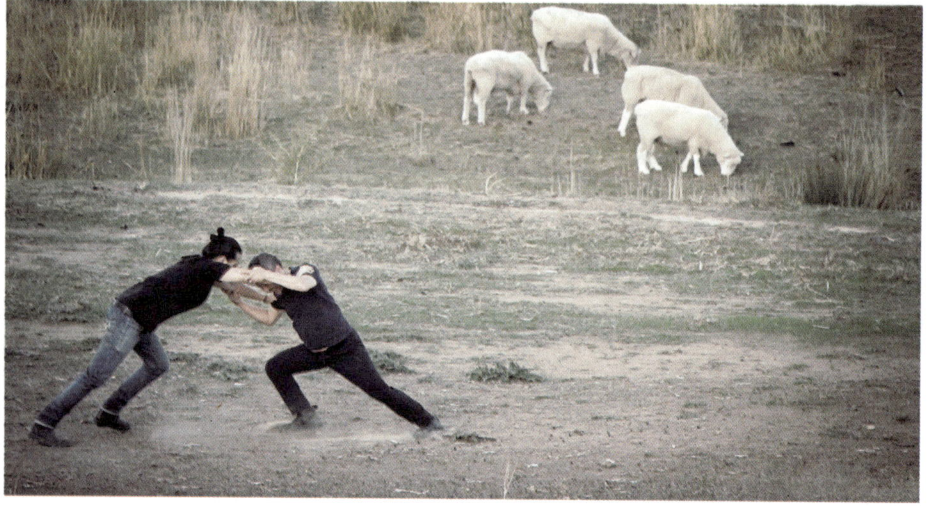

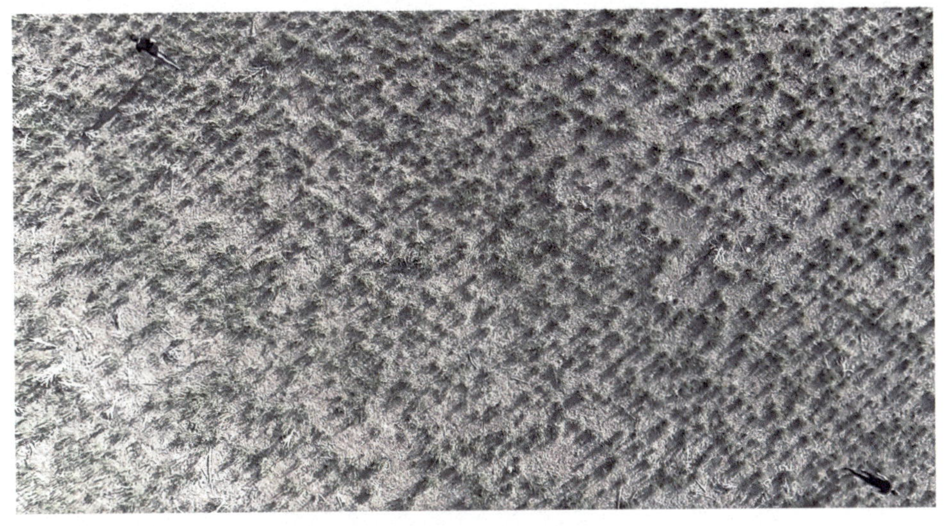

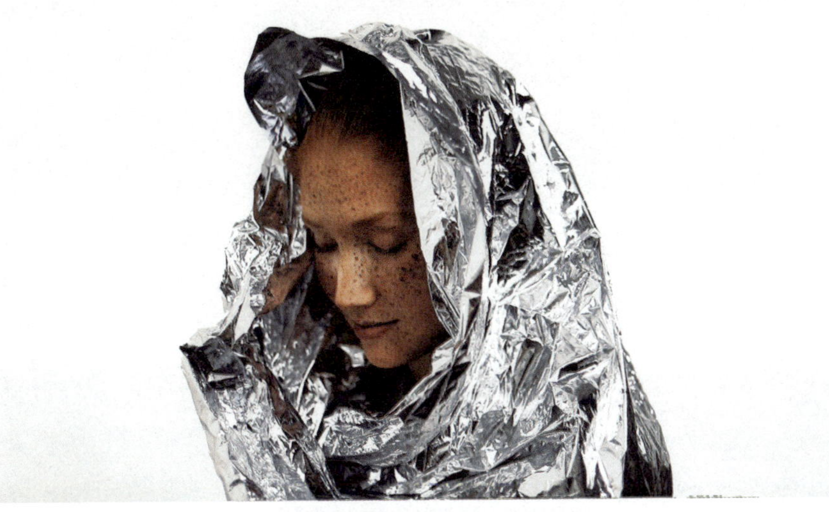

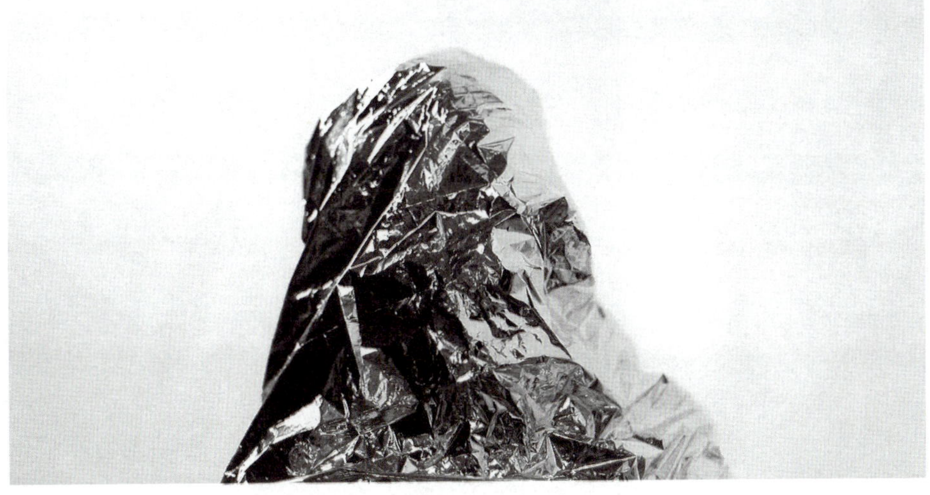

Stills from *The Field* 2018
HD video loop, 8 min. 5 sec.

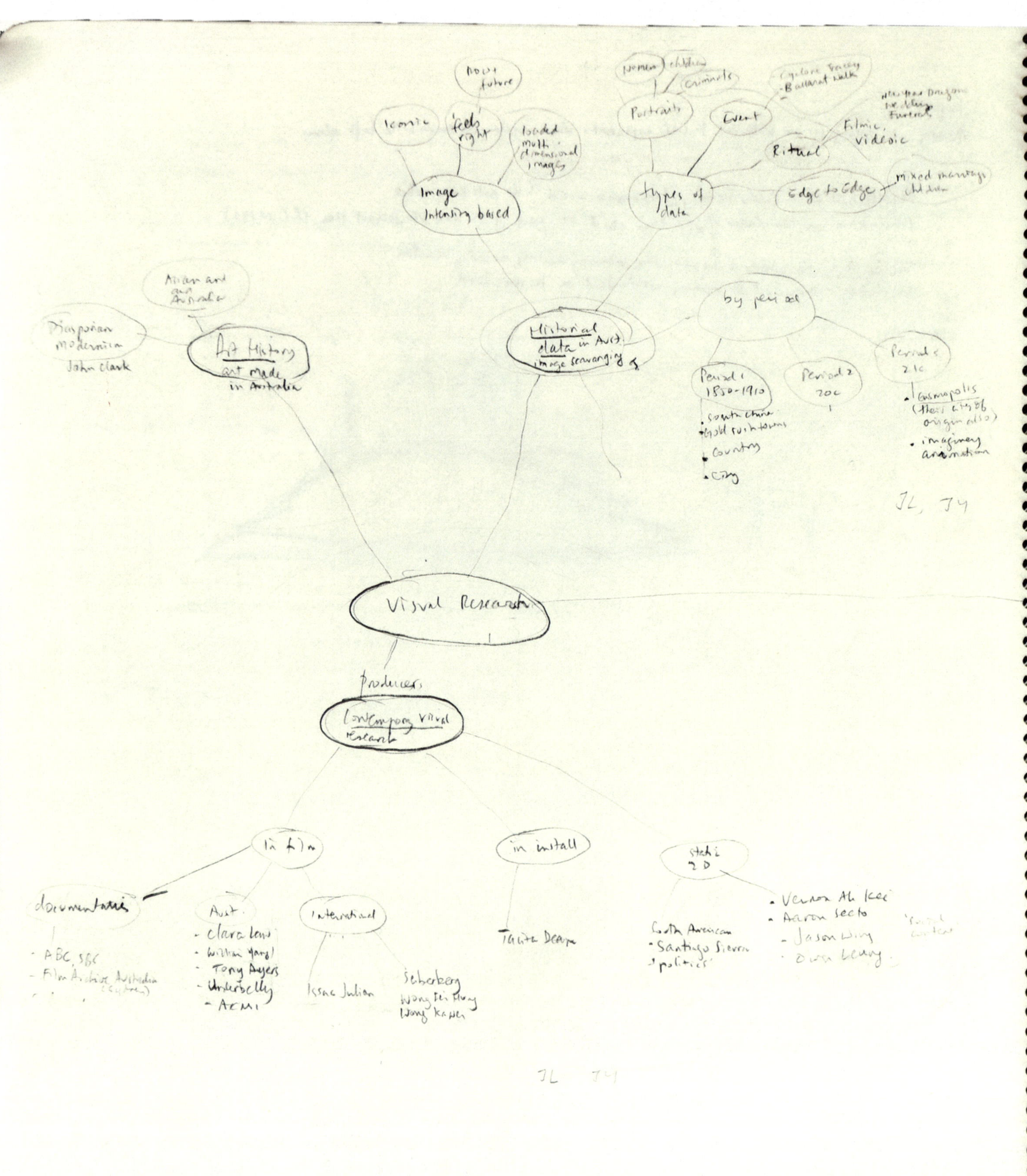

now / future
iconic
feels right
loaded multi dimensional images
Image Intensity based
women / children
criminals
Portraits
Event
Cyclone / Ballarat walk
Ritual
Filmic, videoic
types of data
edge to edge
mixed meanings children
Asian and Australian
Diasporian Modernities
John Clark
Art History
art made in Australia
Historical data in Aust
image scavenging
by period
Period 1 1850-1910
south china
gold rush towns
country
city
Period 2 20c
Period 3 21c
Cosmopolis (their city of origin also)
imaginary animation
JL, JY
Visual Research
Producers
Contemporary Visual Research
in film
documentaries
ABC, SBS
Film Archive Australian (explore)
Aust.
Clara Law
William Yang
Tony Ayres
Underbelly
ACMI
International
Issac Julian
Seberberg
Wong Sei Hong
Wong Kar Wei
in install
Tacita Deam
static 2D
South American
Santiago Sierra
politics
Vernon Ah Kee
Aaron Secto
Jason Wing
Owen Leong
JL JY

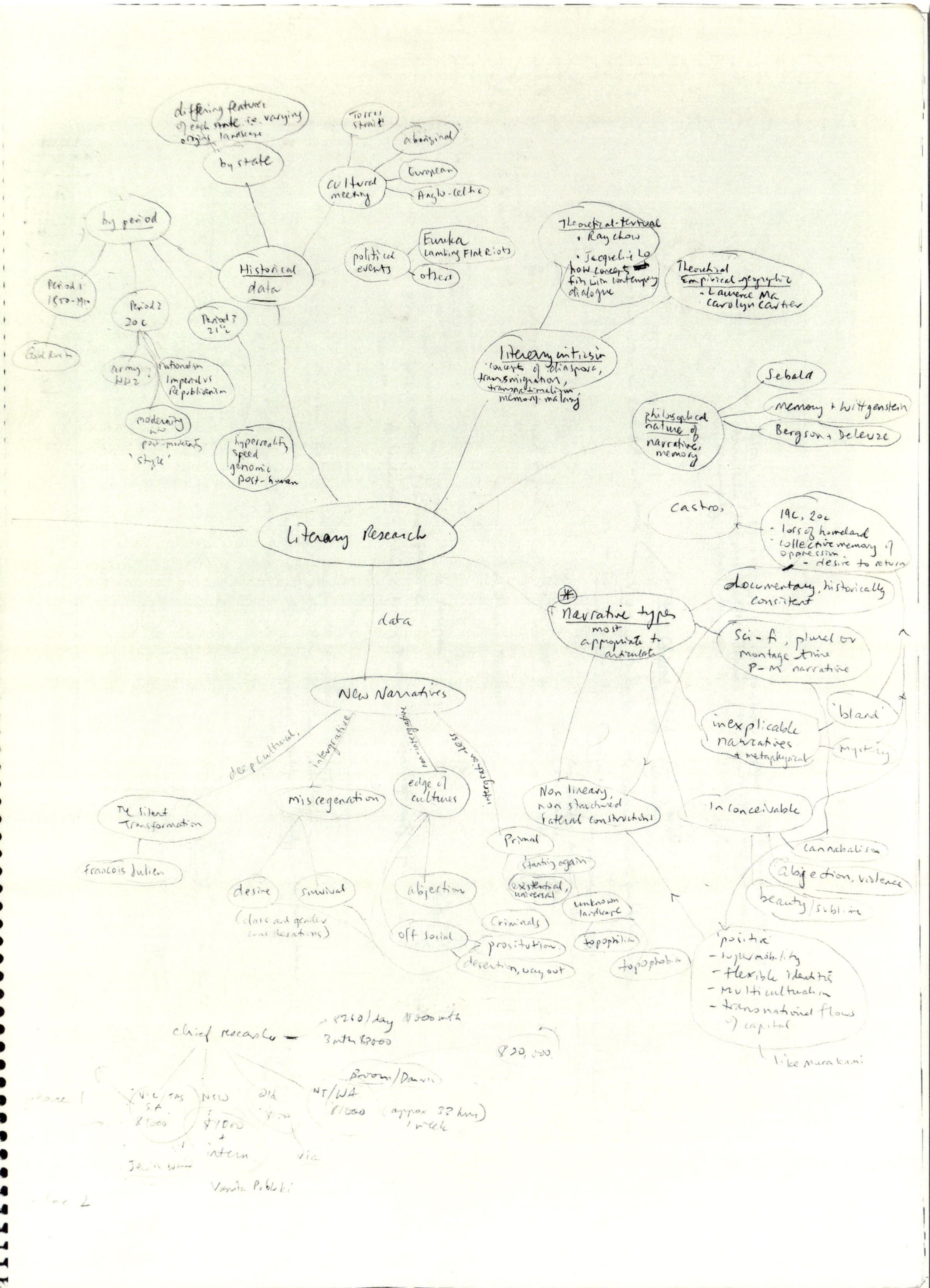

differing features of each state i.e. varying origins, landscape
by state
Torres Strait
aboriginal
European
Anglo-Celtic
Cultural meeting
by period
Historical data
political events
Eureka
Lambing Flat Riots
others
Period 1 1850-1900
Period 2 20 c
Period 3 21st c
Gold Rush
Army NP2
Nationalism Imperial vs Republicanism
modernity and post-modernity 'style'
hyperreality speed genomic post-human
Theoretical-textual + Ray Chow
+ Jacqueline Lo how concepts fits with contemporary dialogue
Theoretical Empirical geographic + Laurence Ma Carolyn Cartier
Literary criticism concepts of diaspora, transmigration, transnationalism, memory, malaxy
Sebald
Memory + Wittgenstein
Bergson + Deleuze
philosophical nature of narrative, memory
Castro
19c, 20c - loss of homeland - collective memory of oppression - desire to return
documentary, historically consistent
Literary Research
Narrative types most appropriate to articulate
Sci-fi, plural or Montage three P-M narrative
'bland'
inexplicable narratives + metaphysical
mystery
Inconceivable
cannibalism
Abjection, violence
beauty/sublime
data
New Narratives
desp cultural
integrative
non-assimilationist subjectivities
TV Silent Transformation
Francois Julien
Miscegenation
edge of cultures
Non lineary, non structured lateral constructions
Primal
starting again
existential, universal
unknown landscape
desire
survival
(class and gender considerations)
abjection
oft social
Criminals
prostitution
desertion, way out
topophilia
topophobia
positive - hypermobility - flexible identity - multiculturalism - transnational flows of capital
like Murakami
chief researcher
$260/day $5000 mth 3 mth $8000
$20,000
Broom/Darwin
Vic/Tas SA $8000
NSW
Qld
NT/WA $1000 (approx ?? hrs) 1 week
intern
via
Vesna Pobloki

THE POLITICS OF DISPLAY:
A CONVERSATION WITH
MATT COX

The following is an edited exchange between John Young and Matt Cox that took place via email correspondence and an online conversation between February and March 2022.

Matt Cox is a curator and art historian with expertise in Asian and particularly Indonesian modern and contemporary art. He has also been deeply engaged with curating contemporary Australian art, often with artists from diverse cultural experiences and backgrounds. In 2021, he was co-curator (with Erin Vink) of the Art Gallery of New South Wales' presentation of *The National 2021: New Australian Art*.

This conversation was conceived as an opportunity to critically reflect on Young's practice from the perspective of curatorial and museum practices, with the knowledge of alternative histories to the contemporary in Australian art. The exchange began with a set of reflective questions from Cox, in which he addresses the museum context through some of Young's early works in the Art Gallery of New South Wales collection.

pages 348–49
Pages from the artist's notebook (JYNP2012-14)

Matt Cox: In thinking about how museums operate as institutions of historical enquiry
and how they allow us to share time with the past, I wonder what it means for you to have
your work collected by the Art Gallery of New South Wales and how might we understand
its association and relationship with other works in the collection?

In some regard, each work reminds me of a photograph collected within an album—each
is individual and yet also selected based on certain criteria and its relationship to the other
works in the collection. Following the logic of Hans Belting, we form our understanding of
images in comparison to every other image we have ever encountered.[1] So, when we view an
artwork in a gallery setting, we bring all those other free-floating images to the conversation.
Curators sometimes seek to bypass these free-floating associations by tightening the rope
around the number of comparative objects to create particular narratives. Despite this,
objects often remain unruly and fugitive to curatorial directives. Realising the disruptive nature
of association, [Aby] Warburg relinquished curatorial control, or instead, with anachronistic
'montage-collisions', he applied a different curatorial methodology as an attempt to undermine
meta-narratives and clear chronological schemas for organising art history.

Perhaps, almost accidently, or as an indirect consequence of curatorial department structures
and cataloguing systems, museum collections find themselves grouped into more unlikely
sequences. For instance, when searching the words 'Hong Kong' on the Art Gallery's online
database, I found your works among a number of closely and sometimes distantly related
objects.[2] Interestingly the curatorial divides of 'Australian', 'International' or 'Asian' no
longer guide the contours and perimeters of the group. Instead, it is the city of Hong Kong
that becomes a multivalent site of magnetism and connection. On this page your works sit
alongside contemporaries like Paul Chan, but also an earlier generation of photographers like
Lewis Morley and even a Vietnamese dragon ewer, which speaks to global and anachronistic
relationships.

John Young: This is a perspicuous description of contemporary archiving and curatorial
directions. Whilst the rhizomatic impulse, as a foil against the logocentricism of the meta-
narrative, is indeed a positive move away from colonial historical discourses, the overdrive
towards the *Wunderkammer* assumes an audience who wants to learn with a sense of
wonder. Often, in a media-saturated environment, this condition of 'wonder' may become
interchangeable with 'spectacularity' or indeed entertainment. Once again, this institutional
black hole ultimately substitutes the wonders of difference with entertaining indifference.
What is then lost are values. Pedagogically retaining different values was one of the aims
of my discussions with Thomas Berghuis, and of coining the term 'Situational Ethics':
universal values of care and empathy within difference. This was the sort of direction [Joseph]
Beuys was intimating—Situational Ethics as an alternate position to the well-worn condition
of Relational Aesthetics.[3]

Belting's theory-laden observation of images also forms an intriguing background when
we shift frames to reading imagery, say from a historical museum context to a gallery context.
Regarding the History Projects, I tend to use the 'truth' rhetoric associated with historical
photographic images as a ruse to make convincing re-imagined narratives in the gallery.
It's an intriguing area in art making, the re-articulation of apparent indelible truths.

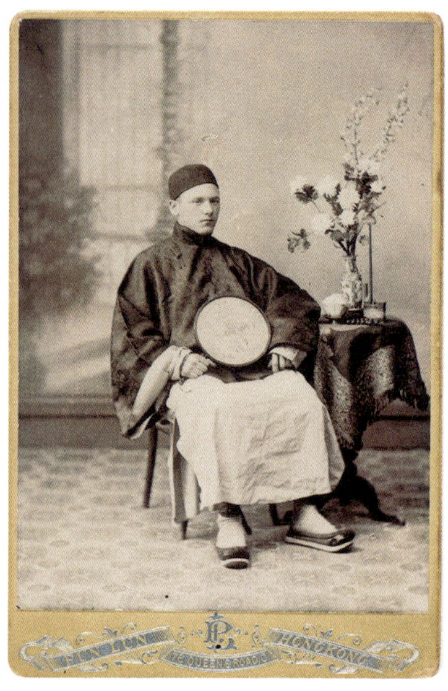

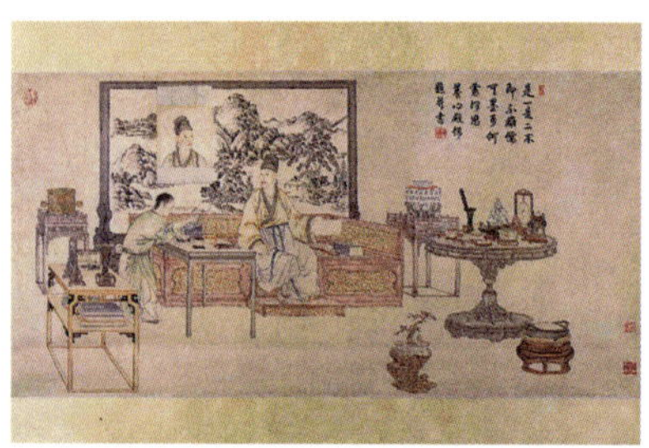

Pun Lun Studio, Hong Kong (1864–1907)
Seated man c. 1900
albumen print, 14.6 × 10 cm image
Collection of Art Gallery of New South Wales,
donated through the Australian Government's
Cultural Gifts Program by Gael Newton, 2021;
image courtesy of Art Gallery of
New South Wales, 326.2021

'One or Two' (Mental Cultivation Version)
c. 18th century
Hanging scroll, ink and colour on paper
Collection of the Palace Museum, Beijing
Image courtesy of the Palace Museum, Beijing
Artist's note: the work is a double portrait of
the Emperor Qianlong (1711–1799)

MC: These connections [across the Art Gallery's collection] also raise questions around the technologies of the specific mediums: the relationship between painting and photography, for instance, which also arises in many of your works. We know that early studio photography mimicked earlier painted portraits and many photographers were also painters.

The Art Gallery recently acquired two photographs made in Hong Kong studios around the turn of the twentieth century. I'm interested in what these images tell us about the period and what they tell us about today? Can these images transcend their own history and how can they transform the museum experience? Perhaps this is a point of departure to think about the selection of photographs and their efficacy in *Open Monument* (2015), in which the city of Ballarat is the focal point of connection.

JY: Of course, from the perspective of a contemporary reading, these photographs reveal much about the socio-ideological conditions of the time, such as patriarchy and chauvinism. However, I'm more interested in their worldview, and how that resonates through the new medium of photography. In its infancy, any new media mimics the representational order of the previous visual paradigm.

Hence the echo of the genre of Chinese ink portraiture and its worldview is certainly evident in these early photos. Ontologically, I'm reminded of the fascinating early-modern double portraits of Emperor Qianlong, in which the definition and character of a subject is diffused amongst motifs, via the surrounding objects and their signification.[4]

These photos from Hong Kong studios, in fact, resonate with a more distant pre-modern visuality, especially in contrast to the Qianlong portrait. Even though, with these two portraits, the body does not really come into play as a definition of character. The sitters here are engaged in a simpler subscription to social positioning via generic pose, appropriate clothing and seemingly prerequisite furnishings, rather than any form of modern identity as a subject capable of reflection—which the Qianlong portrait is the beginnings of (the objects are *his* objects that define *his* character). Hence, with the two Hong Kong images, it is as though the pre-modern visual paradigm is grafted onto a modern medium: photography.[5]

The early twentieth century photographs used in *Open Monument* reveal vastly different orders of signification. The Chinese within the Australian context were not able to employ the same paradigms to signify power and social positioning as those of their home country—as no one would visually understand the signification. Just like multilingualism in language, there are multiple forms of visual signification. Hence, if the early photos of Chinese Australians were taken by Anglo-Australians they were often depicted as curios, or objects of fascination or abjection. One of my tasks in the History Projects was to reframe some of these images, to turn the Chinese Australian subjects into something more than objects of curiosity or abjection—to open these images out, so to speak, away from the historical determinants of their signification, and give these images (and the depicted subjects), viewed today and in the future, a new sense of agency, for example by repositioning the reading of subjects by cropping, layering and including identifiable Ben Day dots.

MC: There are a few things I'd like to respond to: one is an agreement with you around the perils of the Wunderkammer. In thinking about curiosity in the museum I wonder how we can deal with difference without having a reductive impulse of pleasure. That seems to be the curatorial aim sometimes—to derive pleasure through a simplistic understanding of complex things. I wonder whether it's a revamped kind of fascination with the Wunderkammer as a device for thinking about difference. There is more to talk about here, including a contemporary curatorial fetish to reinvent the Wunderkammer, as well as the work of Silvia Spitta in *Misplaced Objects—Migrating Collections and Recollections in Europe and the Americas* [2009].[6] Spitta's work was introduced to me by artist Leyla Stevens, and I have found her ideas on the dislocation of objects very relevant to contemporary curating. For example, she refers to [Michel] Foucault's 'order of things' and how, from around the sixteenth century, the arrival of objects from South America in Europe really destabilised the accepted sense of order, the genealogy of ideas, and a contemporary commitment to certain structures. I find when those kinds of ideas are now reinserted into a conversation, they are at risk of being tokenistic rather than disruptive.

The second thing is the ethics of care you mentioned. In the essay I wrote for *The National*, I referred to two sessions called 'Care: Forging an Alternative Ethic through Contemporary Art', conducted by Catriona Moore and Jacqueline Millner at the 2018 AAANZ conference. They cited the American contemporary artist from the 1960s, Mierle Laderman Ukeles, who wrote a manifesto for 'Maintenance Art' and its related notions of care.[7] I found this a very interesting way to consider the curator–artist relationship and also a good model for a kind of embodied care between institutions, arts workers and collections.

Thirdly, in regard to the historical photographs, you touched on the period context of those photographs from Hong Kong, in particular you mentioned the expression of chauvinism and patriarchy. You also argued that the kind of opportunities for the expressions of power were very different from those men and women in Ballarat included in your work *Open Monument*; they weren't able to employ the same kind of devices for presenting themselves in the same way as their contemporaries elsewhere. So, one of the reasons I introduced those photographs, when we're thinking about history is to ask: How do we share time with the past? How do we live alongside those objects and allow them to live alongside us without relegating them to the past as historical artefacts, with all the issues that we now imagine them to have?

JY: In terms of care, I was talking about empathy in relation to the producer—to the artist— in the sense that the modernist artist has always constructed themselves as a subject capable of carrying some aspect of value. I was trying to shift the discussion towards a situation where the artist is not actually the expressive subject, but rather the learner, who learns traditional senses of value, or whatever it is, from the past. In that sense, the care also extends towards the process of production, as well as exhibiting the work. That was what I was really trying to do in the History Projects—get to a point where the artist is really part and parcel of the process. Sometimes it could be relational, with other artists or curators. Through a more philosophical cultural lens, I was trying to shift the discussion towards the sense of the artist as a learner, as a subject; somebody who is actually taking in new values of difference rather than just expressing their identity and their difference towards whatever it is.

MC: When working with [artist] Khaled Sabsabi in 2019, I really enjoyed hearing him talk about a form of art practice that works to negate the artistic expressive self, in favour of allowing difference to occupy the space. This approach is differentiated from relational aesthetics; it seems more attuned to a collaborative type of approach with a community. I don't know whether I've described it correctly or how one might choose a community, but I'm really open to finding a similar way of working in my curatorial practice. Curators have a position of authority to make decisions, and yet we need to find a way to relinquish some of that authority when we work collaboratively with artists. I would like to hear more about how you do that— How do you open that authority up to the 'other', such as practitioners, collaborators or historians?

JY: I think that an example would be my project *Bonhoeffer in Harlem*, where I was invited to do an exhibition in a Lutheran church. Because it was such a mono-cultural place, I wanted to shift the frame of exhibiting; also, because even for Bonhoeffer himself, it was a question of learning differences and trying to defend differences. I decided to do the tapestry, based on a stained-glass window in a church in Harlem. It was going to be woven in Nepal by Tibetan weavers, but when the actual tapestry came back to Berlin, I was shocked. I felt initially it had nothing to do with my intentions and my expectations of the image. But in the end, I felt I had to accept it because I created this process, to insert this sort of transculturality into a Lutheran church, which is already the point.

The whole discussion about the expression of the subject is very much a first world thing. So, that level of compromise was a letting go of the artist's intentions for the image (not of the process necessarily). It was something that really shifted my whole worldview, in terms of the artist as the producer. That forms a point of view of what I meant by care in a much wider sense. But of course, once again, when it moves into the exhibiting frame, within a museum or within a church or within the gallery, it shifts again. I think then intentionality gets passed on, passed on to the curator in a sense.

MC: It's interesting, the insistence we have to narrate the course of things. I think there is a desire, or at least a willingness, among many curators now to relinquish some of that control over objects. This is particularly the case in postcolonial discourses or in the attempt to decolonise the museum: on the one hand, how we understand objects that come from or belong to different communities, and have been dislocated or removed from those places, and on the other, how to display them without insisting upon a certain narrative, or a certain intention that might be perceived as reluctance on the part of the curator, an unwillingness to generate a narrative. But I think there's also the potential to allow some space for these objects to generate their own narratives.

JY: Yes. There is the question of where you conceive of the *artwork*. Is the artwork in the process of letting go of the artwork? For example, in *Bonhoeffer*, is the 'artwork' the introduction of this transculturality into the church, or is it in the objects? If this was just about the process, then in a sense, I haven't really let go that much; if it was just purely aesthetic, then of course, I've let go of everything. Since the end of the object in art making, art making has gone into completely process-oriented works. How does one actually define the artwork? This is one question that is always in my mind as well: even after you let go, the whole question of the depth of the work is also an issue. I mean, as somebody whose education background is almost completely from Euro-American ground rules, jettisoning all that, for ethical reasons, and losing a lot of the

continuous depth in the inside about artwork, is also quite complex. This is
why I chose to do the History Projects, because at least with the History Projects
there seems (I hope) to be something in the content that one could hold on to
while discussing all the things around it.

MC: It can be challenging, especially when we have spent years of our lives
developing specialisations in certain areas, and then seem to have to forego that
specialisation. At the same time, I think it has been a great learning opportunity
for me. Museums grapple with disrupting the canon, including all kinds of artworks;
it does start to dissolve the categories that define art, on which our knowledge
is based.

Anthropologists like Alfred Gell talk about the efficacy of the object, yet it is still
grounded and situated in a historical kind of knowledge.[8] But they also speak about
the object's capacity to be fugitive, and disobedient, through its own optical presence.
So, there's a kind of collision we're dealing with, that is, the need or desire to know
more thoroughly the origins and processes, with the thing that is most appealing
about art—the visual, which is where this spectacle arises. These are the two forces
pulling us. Can we have both or do we need to prioritise one over the other? It
seems that sometimes this conundrum is playing out in the display of art. Sometimes
the spectacle can be very distracting, but sometimes it also can bring people to art.

JY: I think we're not talking about spectacle in relation to entertainment, to design
and so on. We're really talking about the spectacle in relation to the body, this sort
of phenomenological side; of how it affects our body. I agree that things get pulled
on either side, and I don't really know what the answer is. The more we enter into this
level of plurality, somehow the institution enters into spectacularity, and its need for
spectacularity, in the old sort of Baudrillardian sense, really enters into the discussion.[9]
It overtakes a lot of talk about differences in value and inclusion and hospitality, in the
end, because there are no ground rules or values for the judgement of art. We more-
or-less siloed off Euramerican criteria into being the only criteria, so the sense of
judgement for artworks has become very slippery. Quite often, what then happens
is that spectacularity takes over, just like advertising.

There was a position that we arrived at, even in the 1980s or 1990s. But since then,
postcolonial discourse, and so on, has taken over, in terms of encouraging this level
of difference. But at the same time, I don't think that comprehension of this difference
is actually possible, or effective, especially from an epistemological viewpoint.

MC: There are definitely conversations about difference taking place in museums
at the moment and in the postcolonial context there is an expectation to be
representative of difference. But I feel there is also a risk of flattening that difference.
Rasheed Araeen wrote about this in his review of [the exhibition] *Magiciens de la
Terre* (1989)[10], this flattening of difference into aesthetics, when things can be aligned
aesthetically, or presented aesthetically. However, when these things are presented
without proper reference to discourse, they become (as you articulated) a sort of
advertising. How do you see that now compared to what was happening in the 1990s,
especially around the discourse of hyphenated identities?

JY: I started the History Projects, which dealt with conflict and lesser violence,
because I was fed up with the question of identity. I really felt it was going nowhere;
in terms of people's insistence on a different voice, based on difference of identity—it
didn't seem to be making sense or achieving much depth. So, instead, I tried to look

at scenarios where there are conflicts between difference—historical situations
where in fact the differences are acute and tragic situations happen—through which
people are forced to make some sort of existential value decision. For example, the
Nanjing Massacre: twenty foreigners actually defended 200,000–300,000 Chinese
citizens. They could have just left but they decided to stay and protect them. Now, call
that universal values or universal human rights, or whatever, but somebody decided
to protect those citizens.

But I think that there's more to it, more than just universal human rights. The other
thing that really shifted my thinking was that I've always thought that differences
of cultural values are incommensurable, non-translatable. Yet when I was talking with
[art historian] John Clark, he was absolutely insistent that most things are translatable,
and as soon as he saw it that way, I felt that all these issues about defence and
protection of values shifted.

What I'm trying to say is, I was really trying to shift that identity discourse away from
just being about this object or subject here having a sense of presence, and moving
towards a situation where people are forced to negotiate different identities through
empathy, or whatever it is, like in conflicts. When you're left with almost nothing,
you just make very basic human decisions. And that's a value in itself.

MC: What you're presenting there is a kind of comparison between historical
conflict, where people don't really have choice—well, they can make a choice, but
it's under very compromised circumstances—and a situation of choice. This suggests
that the current insistence upon identity is, in some regards, a position of privilege.

JY: Absolutely. Whereas the historical encounter is actually an opportunity for
empathy and ambivalence, or a dual position.

AUSTRALIAN ART SINCE THE 1990s

MC: What do you think has happened in the Australian art landscape since the
nineties, since the formation of ARX, APT and Gallery 4A for example?[11] When
I talked to students a couple of years ago there seemed to be an amnesia or a lack
of knowledge around what happened in the nineties, yet it is a precondition to
what's going on now. We imagined that those ideas would be carried forward, but
it appears there's been some kind of lag or forgetting.

JY: I guess I can describe my understanding of that situation from two viewpoints.
One is that from the nineties, from a political standpoint, the problem with Australia,
in terms of its push for different cultural positions, is that it runs by election cycles.
Unfortunately, institutions follow this very short cycle, and public policies are actually
pushed in this way, which isn't very good for development for artists—every four
years, you have to change your entire context to make sense of where you're standing
culturally, or at least reconfigure your project to have a livelihood. An artist needs
to be doing things that are of the present, but also relevant way past the present,
so their work retains a significance that is past their lifetime, if possible.

But the other difficulty is the collapse of criticism in Australia. If you look at the
development from the establishment of *Art & Text*, all the way to the end of Paul

Taylor's editorship, or Bernice Murphy and Leon Paroissien's short-lived *Visual Arts and Culture* which ushered in the postcolonial context in the early 1990s—Australia was still pretty tight in terms of art criticism in relation to artistic practice.[12] But now there's a dislocation between art criticism—or the shrinking area of art criticism, barring perhaps Helen Hughes, Nick Croggon and David Homewood's journal *Discipline*—and artistic practice. So, in that sense, the depth to which one can negotiate ideas in making art has been eroded. Art criticism is based on pretty superficial, immediate criteria, like identity or different social issues. Our condition doesn't reach a certain depth or resonance, because if you're looking at different contemporary cultural practices, you also have to look at art criticism in the language of that culture. I think that because we're not in general multilingual, we can't actually access art criticism to really look at the depths of difference.

MC: For me, what you're saying about a dearth of criticism speaks to a lack or unwillingness to accept difference of opinion, which I think is also based in a kind of general antipathy towards expertise that has its correlations in universities as well. I wonder whether that's also something that's manifesting within cultural critique and art criticism more generally—a kind of distrust or a lack of interest in in-depth analysis?

JY: Yes, and it's not necessarily white society's fault. As things get globalised, affected, most of us only speak one or two languages, really restricting the possibility of getting deep into another language's cultural or art criticism. That is one issue, and there are a lot of other issues that affect the First World which are still playing out. But one of the most prevalent issues for me in Australia is that although the whole discourse on diasporas is starting to be advanced (in literature, for example), in the visual arts it's just beginning.

I feel the other crucial discussion in Australia must be about the relationship between Indigeneity and diaspora, because people are from an Irish diaspora, a German diaspora, a Chinese diaspora, and so on—or they are Indigenous. I don't want to necessarily put things into a binary situation, but I do think that there's a lot of discussion to be had there. I have not read a lot on this, although I do understand the context. I've not followed closely writings on indigeneity such as Imants Tillers' work and the critical relationships between diaspora and the Indigenous context. Tillers, of course, enunciated the whole idea of diaspora in the visual arts. It was David Malouf who entertained the idea of diaspora many years ago; but Tillers at least announced it in the art context, and his relationship with Gordon Bennett, for example, is very interesting. I don't know how far that sort of understanding has taken us but at least that context is visualised. And to a certain degree, that's where the context is at present. Where does Asia fit in this relationship? Does it fit only within the diaspora conversation, or is it something else?

MC: The discussion of Asian–Indigenous relationships disrupts the binary of the white settler–Indigenous narrative, and also disrupts the idea of settlement as well, which can be interesting. I was talking about sharing time—what you described as the maturation of ideas, which also speaks to the idea that multiple temporal understandings exist at the same time; it isn't necessarily a linear trajectory. I wonder whether we could think about that in relation to geographies and cultures, especially with the relocation of historical material and objects from one country to another.

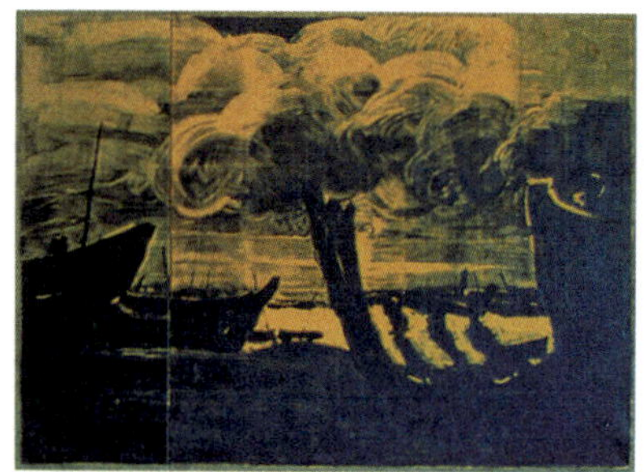

Compulsory Power Morality 1986
Oil on linen, 152 × 203 cm
Collection of Art Gallery of New South Wales,
Sydney

When I was in conversation with [artist] James Nguyen, he spoke about the repatriation of objects, in particular a drum in the Art Gallery's collection, a [bronze] Đông Sơn drum.[13] James talked about a theory of 'rematriation', which he says has been borrowed from Indigenous intellectual thought, that emphasises the reinvigoration of living culture tied to material culture.[14] So, in the case of the drum—which has an origin story contested by more than one modern nation state—having it in Australia may open up engagement with that drum, irrespective of national identity or state boundaries. Floating is not the right word, but it may become open to more universal humanist values rather than those dictated by specific temporal, cultural or national boundaries.

JY: I totally agree, in the sense that reality for disaporans is really memory, it's not place. I'm thinking of this old Bergsonian idea about how we understand time: we shouldn't think of time spatially, time is a thing of past, present and future, as if it were these identifiable spots that you can locate. It's a process, it overlaps, and the past is always in the present; it's durational. In that sense, the fluidity of the diaspora and the values within diaspora through memory are much more of a reality than actual movement and place.

But this is the whole issue that we're faced with: you have an Indigenous discourse that insists on complete connection to place as a foundational position, whereas you have a bunch of diasporan people, like us, for whom memory is probably more important than space or place. There is this deep philosophical discussion that can be opened up. But I also get your point in relation to art objects—that drum, for example, does have much more agency within different subsets of ownership if it's located here rather than places where they claim to have [certain] identities.

———

3–17 MARCH 2022

MEMORY AND COUNTRY

MC: I'd like to continue the discussion on diasporic communities and their relationship to Country in Australia, and the memory of Country. I'd also like to consider the ways that memory might manifest in objects that are either transported with people or removed and housed separately within galleries and museums.

But first, can we look back at some of your paintings in the Art Gallery's collection again? Your earliest work in the collection is a painting you did with oils on linen in 1986, titled *Compulsory power morality*, acquired a year later.

In the early 2000s, the Art Gallery acquired two more paintings—*Clouds and generic flower study no. 2* and *Hermit painting #3*, both painted over two seasons—summer to autumn of 1998 and winter to spring of 1999, respectively.

Both works were also made using a composite of technologies: NECO scan and oil paint, and Vutak digital scan and oil paint respectively. Both the labour of production and the technologies are revealed in this core data, which places the works in a historical period and reveals something about the processes of representation and translation that are at stake. Both works draw on generic images scanned from reproductions and invite a cross-cultural reading, but they also appear to convey a sense of the overlapping and shared history of images across geographies and times, made possible by the technologies of print and photographic reproduction.

Would it be accurate to say that the deliberate choice of generic images reflects postmodern concerns regarding authenticity, appropriation and the conflation of popular and high art, rather than any postcolonial concerns regarding the position of Asian Australian artists or issues of identity politics?

JY: All three paintings in fact deal with civilisational issues. Though they were painted ten years apart, the second two negotiated with reproductive technologies in a more direct way.

In 1981, I wrote an essay in *Art & Text* regarding hyperreality—the Baudrillardian media black hole, to be specific.[15] At the same time, I was working closely and in dialogue with Imants Tillers regarding the development of appropriation. I decided over a period of eight years (1981–89) to only appropriate the works of Andre Derain, a most untimely, regressive painter whom I admired while living in Paris at the Power Studios. At that point, Paul Taylor was developing a context in Australia with [the 1982 exhibition] *Popism*, and all of these tendencies seemed to me to still belong ultimately to a sort of modernist, avant-garde, progressive trajectory, even when they were couched as postmodern.

There was no word like 'Eurocentric' in those days, but what I felt to be lacking in most of the discourse in contemporary Australian art was any comprehension of *deep time*, except in Indigenous art, which was essentially kept at arm's length. Derain's work, such as the image used in *Compulsory Power Morality* (1986), was of course an exception in its reference to archaic time, and he rang true to the retrogressive or circular conception of time in which Chinese ink painting has historically been grounded. I initially bypassed the use of Chinese art in appropriation out of concern that it would have turned my project into a willing product of exoticisation— producing a popular Chinoiserie persona in search of professional profit while I meanwhile lost my own sense of agency. It was important that my work stay at the margins. Using Derain made this possible because of peoples' lack of immediate recognition of this artist (since appropriation was based so much on sign recognition/valorisation).

Yet, having been trained in minimalism, my preoccupation was never a question of interpretation. The painting process had to be deeply embedded in its undeniable materiality: the way you lay paint down, the way that something is dispassionately organised (the grid), the *fact* that it was an Andre Derain image used. So, you had this head-on clash between the use of late-modern minimalist processes, with the appropriated image of an anti-modern artist, Derain. The appropriated Derain image barely had any materiality—it was just faintly hovering in drab oil grisaille. This image is silhouetted by these intense minimalist materials and processes. I think there is, in retrospect, a sort of resonance with the late music pieces of Philip Glass. If there is any postmodernism in these works, it is in the thickness of their processes. Thus, they were named the *Silhouette Series*. The Derain image on the surface, silhouetted by the colour field, which is silhouetted by the raw linen, which is silhouetted by the stretcher, silhouetted by the wall and the white cube. So, there were a lot of pitfalls and necessary circumventions in order to maintain my sense of agency over this period. Which is to say, there is a difference in the comprehension of time between different cultural ontologies, and contemporary Australian art needed to recognise this.[16]

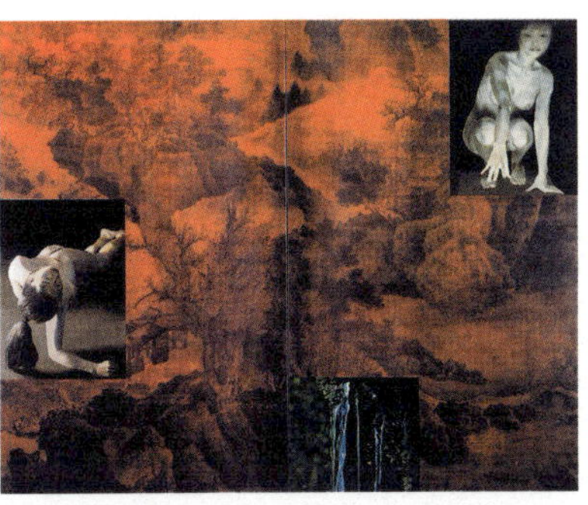

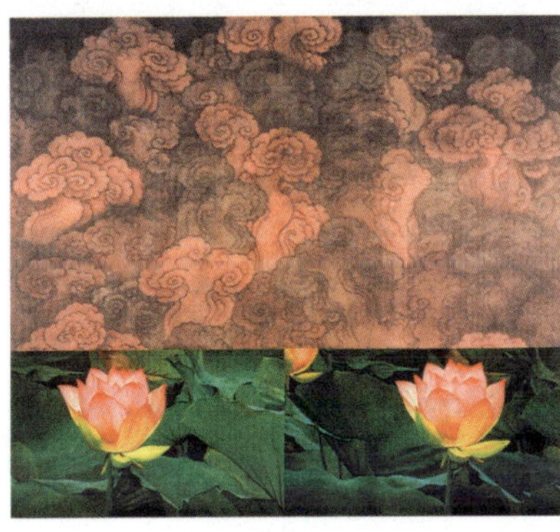

Hermit Painting #3 1999
Digital print and oil on canvas, 226 × 273 cm
Collection of Art Gallery of New South Wales, Sydney

Cloud and *generic flower study #2* 1998
Digital print and oil on canvas, 183 × 203 cm
Collection of Art Gallery of New South Wales, Sydney

From the *Silhouette Series*, I had learnt how costly it was to pose even one clearly articulated philosophical question regarding pluralism. The issues in the postmodern context—authenticity, appropriation, high-pop conflation—were the inevitable direction of the Australian art world of the 1990s, and yet also resulted in a quagmire of socialite artists who never learnt the good lessons from late Euramerican modernism—such as the notions of dissent (say Dada); art made on a consciously epistemological level (Cezanne-Cubism); xenophilia devoid of the imperial or the colonial motive ([Robert] Rauschenburg); process as the work of art, and the ethics of reduction (minimalism and conceptualism). Instead, part of the Australian 1980s and 90s regressed to naïve forms of representation, interpretation and—God forbid—style. This may have facilitated a cynicism with mature art comprehension that one may find difficult to get out of today.

I went through a period of indifference and kitsch in the *Polychrome Paintings* and, coming out of that, began to produce the *Double Ground Paintings*—the series that the latter two works that the Art Gallery acquired are from. Within these works, generic and kitsch types of still life, figure and landscape are lovingly painted in the foreground, and imagery resonating with high art is dispassionately digitally printed, producing a sort of impossible affect scenario. In *Hermit Painting #3*, for example, evocative nudes are painted in the foreground, while in the background you have the world view of the Chinese imagery where the concept of the idealised nude had never existed. Here you see the tensions of those in a diaspora, living in the liminal space of two worldviews. These works were not cynical in themselves, they merely tried to lay bare the conditions through which such melancholy exists.

TRANSHISTORICAL IMAGES

JY: Matt, I'd like to hear more on your insights as a curator, specifically regarding the articulation of complex art-making by artists when such works are shown in a museum. I have in mind our mature (though not necessarily progressive) education in late Euramerican art. Yet, at present in the museum, we are also confronted with plural or liminal cultural contexts that may undermine some valued modernist levels of complexity. Can we avoid falling into a populist comprehension based on the simple 'recognition' of representational imagery?

In order to make hospitable space for plural cultural recognition, does one have to give up a mature level of perceptual development in late Euramerican modernism? Your expertise is Southeast Asian art, for instance—is it necessary for an audience to approach a work with a Southeast Asian critical framework in mind?

MC: The short answer is no; I don't think so. There is no need to abandon Euro-American training or art historical disciplinary understanding as such. However, one might complicate this training with an approach that acknowledges autonomous histories and curatorial strategies that move beyond national and canonical frameworks. The move to regional or world art histories is at least one way that art history might decolonise itself. This doesn't mean taking a universal approach, rather an approach that acknowledges global networks and includes local scholarship, oral histories and community engagement.[17]

However, as you rightly identify, curators, museums and museum visitors do seem to have turned away from displays and engagement with art that contextualises works within specific histories, towards a more immediate apprehension of art as image and image as representation. I believe that the relationship to images has been significantly altered by their consumption through the new technologies of digital media. The screen-based circulation of images appears to have had the dual effect of rendering images devoid of materiality yet escalating their potency as signs. What I mean by this is that interest in how or why something is made is eclipsed by an interest in what the sign says. This in turn has the potential of moving art from the domains of abstraction, intrigue, criticality and ambiguity towards ideology.

Having said that, I wouldn't advocate for art devoid of politics, but rather a renewed focus on the politics of engagement. Equally, the computer-like binary default relationship that many people have to images, based on social media experiences of 'like' or 'dislike',[18] means that their durational engagement with images has dwindled in favour of quickly reached conclusions. This mode of processing images has the potential to relieve the image of evidence of its labour and conditions of production. When this happens, 'hospitable spaces' for plural cultural recognition are equally at risk of collapsing into flattened spaces that reproduce market-ready representations of difference.

In later works, including *Open Monument* (2015), you incorporate personal and perhaps even private images, made public through your artwork. Although different from a gallery, *Open Monument* does offer a comparative site of display, a site where objects belonging to a personal history are shared with a larger and transhistorical public. Can you talk about the ethics of representation in this case?

JY: The images cannot be objects of their history, they need to be the subjects of their history. From a theoretical viewpoint, the agency of the images was so critical. Hence even the values described in the texts had to be scribed, calligraphically felt. The visceral relation between the body and this public history became paramount, more so than any other time this process was undertaken in the History Projects. Yet, as you aptly point out, the work is transhistorical, and I was aware that each generation will come to this monument wanting to read a different narrative and make it their own.

MC: The title *Open Monument* alludes to your intention to create something non-definitive, a site of memory, but a memory open to new interpretation. Can you talk further about your interest in history, which would seem to be not an academic interest but an interest in how history can be reinvigorated? Moreover, in what ways do you play with the competing qualities of the photograph as an instrument to both document and to contrive reality—as both a historical archive and a fictional rendering?

JY: In the most general sense, within my practice, history is really a shorthand for the reassessment of the place for narration, memory and affect in contemporary art. Gerhard Richter and Sigmar Polke's coining of Capitalist Realism, and Nam June Paik's activities in electronic art at the end of the last century, culminated in a sort of focus on information—the sensorial functions in our consciousness. Yet, my position is one of a pursuit for individuation. Hence, in a very crude sense, my interest is also in the counter function of feeling, which, in the libidinal realm, is so critical in relation to the rise of robotics and the posthuman. Then there are also the ethical modes of creativity that have been forgotten since Marcel Duchamp, whose cynical legacy can be felt as all-encompassing, from art making to institutional developments.

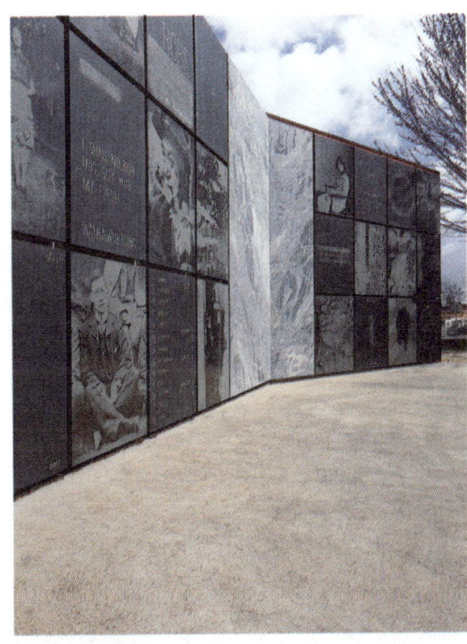

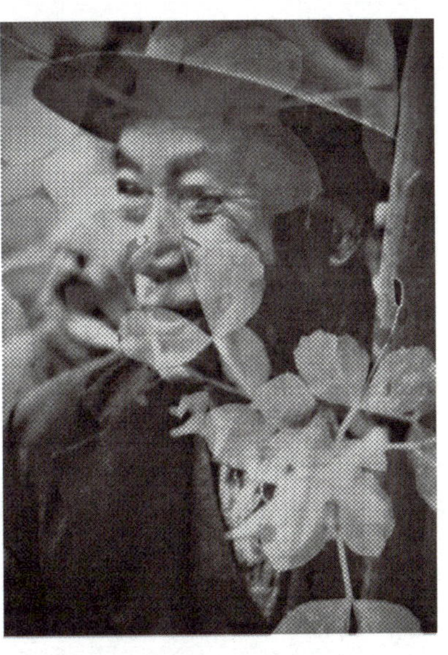

Open Monument 2015
Architectural monument, 430 sq m
Len T. Fraser Reserve, Ballarat
Collection of Ballarat City Council

Original drawing for *Transculture*,
part of *Open Monument* 2015

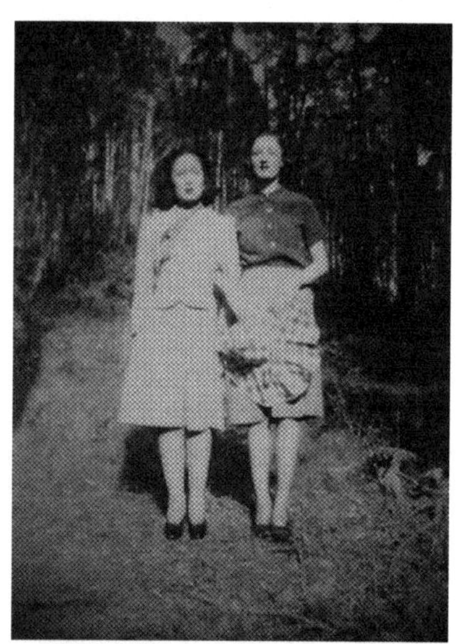

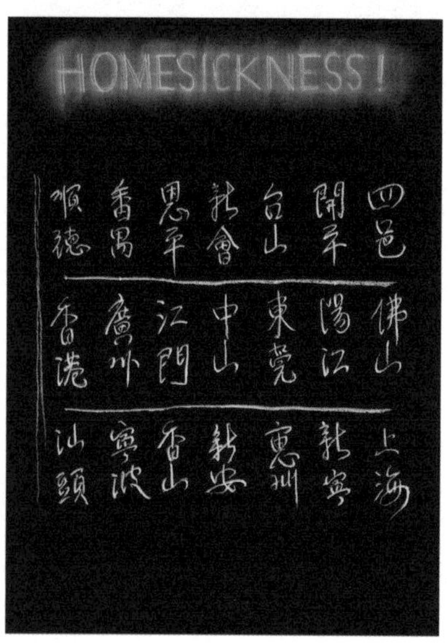

Original drawings for *Transculture,*
part of *Open Monument* 2015

MC: This use of the photographic image as performative and generative rather than fixed comes to the fore in *The Burrangong Affray* (2018), where images are purposed to recalibrate the binary of Asian/White Australian, especially in relation to Indigenous Australia. What does the reversal of the roles in these images say about the possibility of a shared future?

JY: Becoming allows us to take on the values and realities of the Asian, the White and the Indigenous. I'm not sure if the use of photographic images reverses these roles. I suspect that the aim is for the content and unfamiliar values to produce an affect that opens us up to this becoming. Indeed, I feel this was effective, as the exhibition of *The Burrangong Affray* attracted viscous vilification from the extreme right. By that, I mean that there was an adverse reaction to the way in which the work asked us to become the Other. The extreme right, typically, resisted hospitality in favour of defence.

Our shared future is the shared future of an immense flexibility in values, of a plurality in ways of feeling, in the recollection of imagined memories. A future where the margins are always pushed, and the margins inhabit the centre. From your perspective, as our population in the city has a multicultural depth, does that necessitate a different sort of cultural comprehension, curatorially?

MC: In her discussion of your early work, Jacqueline Lo has argued that the paradigm of orthodox multiculturalism operating in the 1990s tended 'to over-emphasise the biographical and ethnic identification of Asian Australian artists as the primary means for elucidating the artworks'.[19] The current situation, although motivated by a different set of circumstances, risks returning to this orthodoxy.

The challenge of accounting for difference without reverting to ethnography is something I spoke about in my essay for *The National.* I also spoke of the risk attached to a focus on certain postcodes as foci of marginalised cultural difference or as more representative of cultural authenticity.[20] If a curatorial comprehension is needed in relation to Australia's diverse population, then providing a space where difference can function critically remains a core challenge. Lo identified a failure in 1990s Australia; Rasheed Araeen identified the same failure in 1980s France.[21] This failure persists in large-scale thematic exhibitions where the arrangement of works from diverse locations is presented based on visual similarity with little attention to historical contexts or political inequity, and in cases where difference is reduced to an aesthetic sign.

In conjunction with the need to facilitate critical difference, there is the need to reconcile the exclusion of tradition, ceremony, ritual and sacredness from definitions of the contemporary art of today. In doing this, difference may manifest materially and critically by embodying different modes of production and different epistemological positions and modes of enquiry.

1. Hans Belting, 'Image, Medium, Body: A New Approach to Iconology', *Critical Inquiry*, vol. 31, no. 2, 2005, pp. 302–19.

2. See 'Hong Kong' search in the online collection of the Art Gallery of New South Wales, Sydney, https://www.artgallery.nsw.gov.au/collection/works/?q=hong+kong.

3. Nicholas Bourriaud, *Relational Aesthetics*, Les Presse Du Reel, Dijon, 1998.

4. The pictured painting is one of four extant versions of a double portrait commissioned by the Emperor Qianlong, known as 'One or Two' (是一是二圖), following the inscription upper right. For a recent discussion of this set of paintings, see Kristina Kleutghen, 'One or Two, Repictured', *Archives of Asian Art*, issue 62, pp. 25–46. We thank the anonymous reviewer for this reference.

5. On the agency and creativity of studio sitters in China in this period, see Roberta Wue, 'Group Encounters: Milton M. Miller's Hong Kong and Canton Photographs', in L. Gartlan and R. Wue (eds), *Portraiture and Early Studio Photography in China and Japan*, Routledge, New York, 2017, pp. 41–58.

6. Silvia Spitta, *Misplaced Objects—Migrating Collections and Recollections in Europe and the Americas*, University of Texas Press, Austin, 2009.

7. Written by Mierle Laderman Ukeles in 1969, her 'manifesto' was an exhibition proposal to bring the 'maintenance work' of caring—cooking, cleaning, mothering, and so on—into the museum as art. See Mierle Laderman Ukeles, 'Manifesto: Proposal for an Exhibition', written in Philadelphia, PA, 1969, https://queensmuseum.org/wp-content/uploads/2016/04/Ukeles-Manifesto-for-Maintenance-Art-1969.pdf.

8. Alfred Gell, *Art and Agency: An Anthropological Theory*, Clarendon Press, Oxford, 1998.

9. For example, see Jean Baudrillard, Kathy Acker et al., *Spectacular Optical*, TRANS> arts.cultures.media, 1998, and the writings of Guy Debord.

10. Rasheed Araeen, 'Our Bauhaus Others' Mudhouse', *Third Text*, vol. 3, no. 6, 1989, pp. 3–14.

11. Artist Regional Exchange (ARX) included five artist-led exhibitions held between 1987 and 1999, featuring artists from Australia and the Asia-Pacific. The Asia-Pacific Triennial (APT) was launched in 1993 at the Queensland Art Gallery, to feature and acquire the work of Asia-Pacific artists, and continues to be held every three years. Gallery 4A is an exhibition space established in Sydney's Chinatown (Haymarket) in 1996, by the Asian Australian Artists Association (of which Young was a leading member) to support Asian Australian artists.

12. For example, the early postmodern writings in *Art & Text* vis-à-vis the founding editor Paul Taylor, and his curatorial role in launching 'Popism' in the Australian art scene following the eponymous exhibition he curated in 1982 at the National Gallery of Victoria.

13. Unknown artist, *Drum*, (c. 500CE–1000CE), Art Gallery of New South Wales, Sydney, gift of Dr J. L. Shellshear, https://www.artgallery.nsw.gov.au/collection/works/9032/#exhibitions. Such a drum forms part of James Nguyen and Victoria Pham's collaborative project *Re:Sounding* (2020–ongoing).

14. On rematriation, see Steven Newcomb, 'PERSPECTIVES: Healing, Restoration, and Rematriation', *News & Notes*, American Indian Ritual Object Repatriation Foundation, 1995, p. 3; and Eve Tuck, 'Rematriating Curriculum Studies', *Journal of Curriculum and Pedagogy*, vol. 8, no. 1, 2001, pp. 34–37.

15. John Young and Terry Blake, 'On Some Alternatives to the Code in the Age of Hyperreality, the Hermit and the City Dweller', *Art & Text*, no. 2, 1981, pp. 4–17.

16. Emphasis by Young in the original correspondence.

17. As remarked upon by Sujath Arundathi Meegama, 'Must We Decolonise the Museum? Sacred and Ritual Art and the Raffles Collection in Singapore', *Decolonising, Curating and the Museum in Southeast Asia*, SOAS, 21 October 2021. https://www.soas.ac.uk/cseas/events/seminars/07oct2021-decolonising-curating-and-the-museum-in-southeast-asia.html.

18. See James Bridle, *New Dark Age: Technology and the end of the future*, Verso, London and New York, 2019.

19. Jacqueline Lo, 'Diaspora, art and empathy', in *John Young. The Bridge and the Fruit Tree*, Drill Hall Gallery, Australian National University, Canberra, 2013, p. 24, and in this volume p. 137.

20. Matt Cox, 'Sharing time with the past and caring for the future', *The National 4: Australian Art Now*, exhibition catalogue, Art Gallery of New South Wales, Sydney, 2021. https://www.the-national.com.au/essays/sharing-time-with-the-past-and-caring-for-the-future.

21. See Lo, p. 22; and Araeen, 'Our Bauhaus Others' Mudhouse'.

FAIRWEATHER TRANSFORMATIONS

2015–

FAIRWEATHER TRANSFORMATIONS

OUTLINE

The *Fairweather Transformations* is an ongoing series of paintings begun in 2015, for which Young applies his process of 'automated' abstraction to create digitally mediated oil paintings that respond to specific works by Ian Fairweather (1891–1974).

Fairweather was a Scottish-born artist who lived the majority of his life peripatetically. Although frequently claimed by Australia, Fairweather lived and travelled extensively across China, Indonesia and the Philippines, before eventually settling on Bribie Island, off the coast of Queensland, in 1953 at the age of sixty-three, where he built a hut-cum-studio and pursued an ascetic existence of painting and translation. Chinese culture and language—which Fairweather was first exposed to during evening classes in Chinese and Japanese languages at London University while studying at the Slade School of Fine Art in the early 1920s—exerted a significant and, until recently, underappreciated influence on Fairweather's work, as did Indigenous Australian art.

There is a total of twenty-one paintings in the series to date, all rendered with oil on linen. Young's abstract paintings are typically based on generic or vernacular photographs, such that their source imagery becomes unrecognisable. In the *Fairweather Transformations*, however, each work is based on a single painting by Fairweather. Despite the application of a digital process of abstraction, much of the composition and colour palette from the original remains in Young's transformed work, though it is softened to form a colour field. Texture, and hence materiality, is reintroduced into these flattened images through the application of light impasto highlights. Young has responded to works from across Fairweather's oeuvre, from his earlier figurative landscapes of China to his later abstractions.

'Context behind developing this process of abstracting imagery' (2008)

The everyday use of computing and the perception of images as mediated by computerisation has been with us since the turn of the century. The change in nature and perception of the image, and the role of the artist as subject, has been re-defined since the onset of digitalisation. Aspects lost from traditional paintings as a result of this transformation include the aura of the artwork (due to its now infinite reproducibility); there is a kind of flattening, and an equalisation of colour and form (due to the electronic eye's dispassionate reading of an image). In short, the expressive subject of the artist based on gestural expression, density of materiality on the surface of the painting, and the unique mark, are all lost. What remains in this process are the colour relations and some hint of resonance based on colour and form residues.

The *Abstract Paintings* work within the mood registers of mourning, melancholy and hope. They mourn for the loss of the treasured values in painting outlined above, and remain in a melancholic state that this virtual, technological and digital world has placed upon us. The paintings hope for a sort of rescue, a rescue of some human elements from the residues of the technological rout.

The Body

The act of repainting these digitally transformed images using traditional skills and material (oil painting) hopes to resuscitate some elements of the human body in the virtual world. Though devoid of the kind of obvious gestural expressive intentionality historically ascribed to the artistic subject, these works—by following the overall schema of the digital image, minute interruptions through chance, inaccuracies, and bodily tremors in the mark making—resuscitate a corporeal presence. It is a hope that some corporeality may be regained in the world of virtuality. It is what, in several press interviews, I called 'The Human-Technology Friendship' (ironically after the German electro-punk band Deutsch Amerikanische Freundschaft (German-American Friendship)).

Studio notes on Aeneid I and II (2016)

These new paintings, mediated by the computer, propose a way of making paintings by humans, re-thought and re-felt. Re-thought, as it is the original Fairweather image that passes through Hades' underworld (computer imaging), yet re-felt, by the affectionate re-painting, by our human hands. 'Aeneid', the title of these paintings, cites Seamus Heaney's account of Virgil's *Aeneid*, in which Aeneas travels into the underworld to meet the spirit of his father.

pages 366–67
The Chinese Room (Mangrove) 2022
Oil on Belgian linen, two panels,
88.6 × 128.5 cm
Collection of Art Gallery South Australia,
Adelaide

UNSETTLING ART: JOHN YOUNG, 'HISTORY PAINTING' AND THE *FAIRWEATHER TRANSFORMATIONS*

Claire Roberts

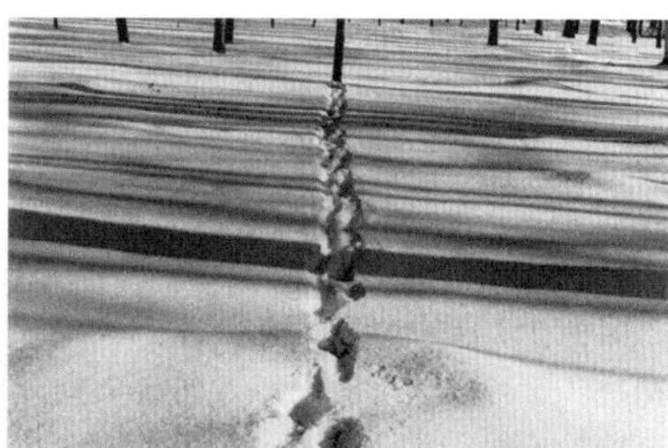

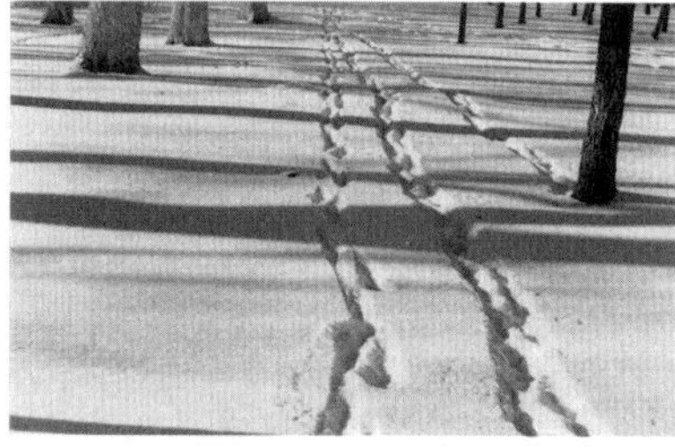

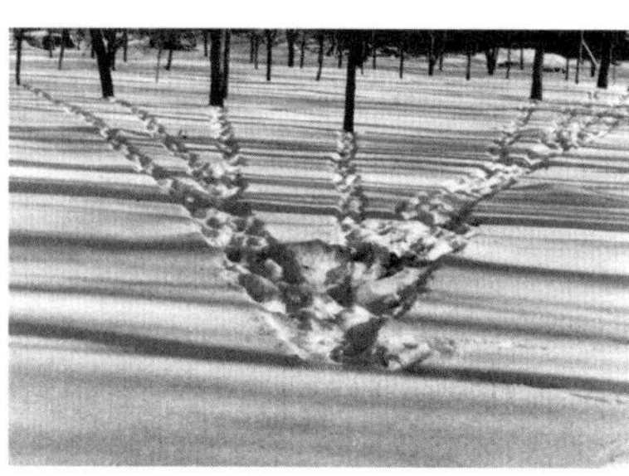

Documentation from *Manchurian Snow Walk* 1979
Silver gelatin prints, three units, 26 x 80 cm each
From top: Walking to the first tree; walking from
the seventh tree; side view of completed walk.
For the full series of 16 photographs, see p.394.

Manchurian Snow Walk (1979) is a product of John Young's trip to mainland China in 1979. A series of sixteen black-and-white photographs records the tracks he made walking through fresh snow in a sparsely wooded forest in Changchun, north-eastern China. The images are cropped so that the viewer focuses on the linear traces of Young's presence in the landscape, walking back and forth from a similar point of origin. These more or less straight lines intersect with horizontal shadows cast by trees that are otherwise illegible. The images abut one another in two horizontal strips, inspired by minimalist practice with a nod to the idea of the landscape format and perhaps even the monochrome brush-and-ink painted handscroll, though here the images are read from left to right and not right to left in the Chinese manner. With its oblique cultural reference points and multivalent visual form, which places the artist both within and outside the image, *Manchurian Snow Walk* is an early example of Young's searching, transcultural practice. The trip to Beijing, Changchun, Shenyang and Harbin was made at the suggestion of his father when travel to China became possible after the 'ten lost years' of the Cultural Revolution (1966–76).[1] It occurred during the long summer break while the artist was studying painting at the Sydney College of the Arts (SCA). The experience was unsettling. While connecting him with the country of his ancestors, at the same time it reinforced his association with the art world in Australia, however culturally limiting.

Young was born in Hong Kong and moved to Sydney for schooling at the age of eleven. That was in 1967, following the launch of the Great Proletarian Cultural Revolution in Mainland China, ripples of which threatened the stability of the British island colony. Both of Young's parents were educated in Hong Kong, which had long been a home to waves of migrants and refugees from the mainland, particularly from Guangzhou and Shanghai. He grew up in a cosmopolitan Catholic family in Repulse Bay, one of the most exclusive districts in Hong Kong. His father, Norman Sze Kuen (SK) Young, born in Zhongshan, Guangdong province, worked as a sales agent for the British company Imperial Chemical Industries (ICI, China). In the late 1940s he established Yuen Hing Hong & Co. Ltd (YHH), one of the earliest local Chinese suppliers of plastic raw materials in Hong Kong. A canny businessman and inventor, he was a leader in the new plastics industry and became Chairman of the Hong Kong Plastic Manufacturers Association. In the 1950s he led a plastics delegation to Australia, where his children would later be educated. Annie Lam-Young, Young's mother, had French, Dutch and Chinese ancestry. Together with her husband, she was a director of YHH and other family companies. She was the first female Justice of the Peace in Hong Kong and Chair of the Hong Kong Chinese Women's Club, a community organisation that played an important role advocating for southern Chinese, Shanghainese and Eurasian women in Hong Kong. She loved Cantonese opera and had a good voice. Young grew up with the sound of his mother singing

Cantonese opera accompanied by his father playing the erhu.[2] Young's elder brother Paul came to study at the University of New South Wales in the early 1960s. John followed, initially as a boarder at the Waverly Christian Brothers' School and then as a day student at the Jesuit St Aloysius College, navigating life in a new country on his own. Dealing with racism, intolerance and the ongoing legacy of the White Australia Policy, he forged a new identity as John Young, letting his other names go—Young Zerunge, Zerunge Young and 楊子榮—at least in public.

Throughout his artistic career John Young has actively worked across cultural and disciplinary boundaries. Using a wide range of practices, including painting (the production of which he later described as a 'Jurassic' technology), writing and self-publishing, while also curating exhibitions and organising conferences, he has given expression to a complex lived identity. Much of his work has involved collaboration of one kind or another in a determination to expand cultural conversations. An early example was his role in the formation of the Asian Australian Artists Association and Gallery 4A in Sydney's Chinatown in 1996, with Manila-born artist Vicente Butron and others. Today the 4A Centre for Contemporary Asian Art is Australia's leading non-profit gallery for the work of Asian Australian and Asian artists. In the early 1990s Young began to work with highly trained studio assistants in the creation of his paintings, a practice that he describes as developing out of a passion for art that is shared between artists.[3] Art is not only a sophisticated visual language with its own inner logic for him, but a way of thinking and expressing cultural and situational being. Through the process of making and directing artmaking, he seeks to unsettle and complicate our understanding of art. For many years Young's art has been concerned with issues of intercultural communication, translation, and different ways of seeing and knowing. His own life trajectory and a curiosity to understand (and be understood) lies behind the substantial research (he has always been a great reader) he undertakes for many of his painting series. The fruits of that research are incorporated into his practice, not in a rigid or didactic manner, but openly and thoughtfully, as part of a process of asking questions, creating connections, moving beyond limitations of time and place.

Young's History Projects focus on stories and events associated with the histories of Chinese communities in Australia, modern Chinese art histories, and cross-cultural histories more generally, in which he situates himself through enquiry and creative intervention. While applied by Young to indicate specific projects, the History Projects arise from a consciousness that permeates Young's artistic practice. Working as an artist and teller of what he calls 'broken stories', he has made visible forgotten historical figures and uncomfortable events from the past, inserting or reinserting them into contemporary consciousness. Young works with a sense of historical and

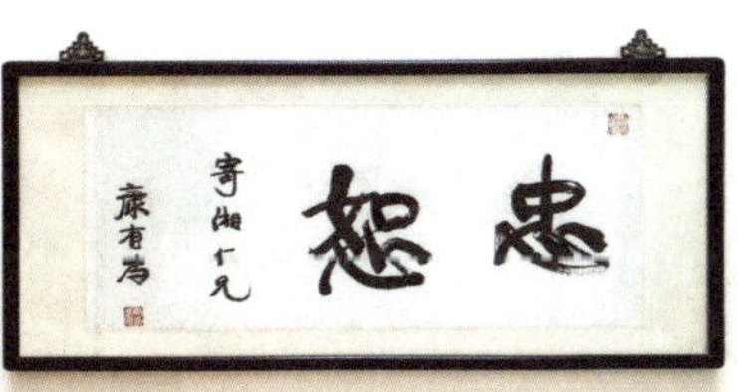

Kang Youwei (Hong Yauh-waih 康有為, 1858–1927)
Zhongshu (Loyalty)
Framed calligraphy
Installation view, John Young's childhood home, Hong Kong
Artist's note: The nineteenth century reformist and philosopher Kang Youwei fled from China to Hong Kong, Japan, and finally to Saltsjobaden, Sweden, after his failed Hundred Days Reform (11 June–22 September 1898).

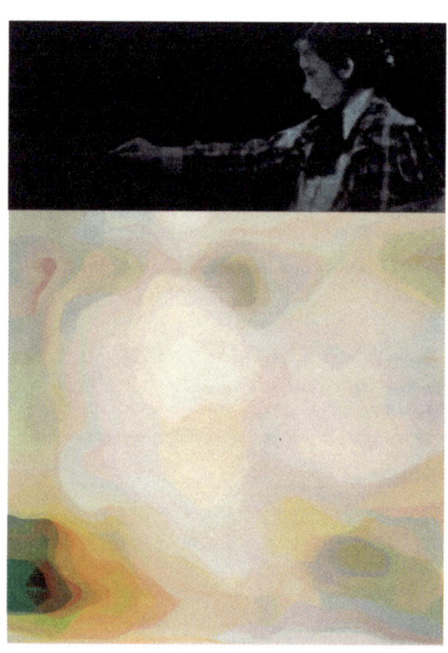

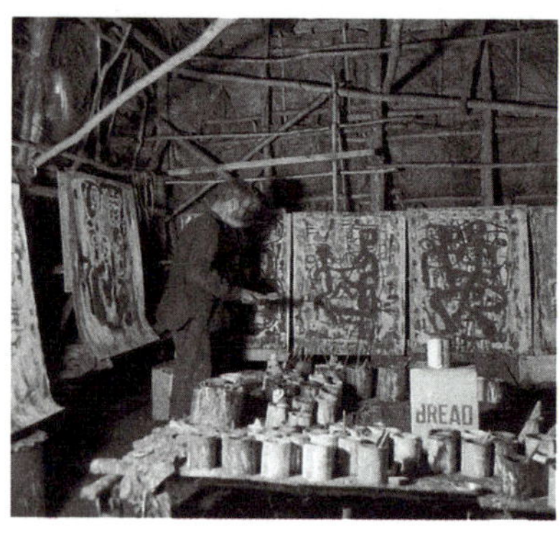

Storm *Resurrection I*, 2016
Digital print and oil on linen, in two parts,
287 × 200cm

Robert Walker (1922–2007)
Ian Fairweather on Bribie Island, Queensland
c. 1966
Collection of Art Gallery of New South Wales
Archive; image courtesy of the estate of
Robert Walker

art historical awareness and social purpose that goes beyond the usual understanding of the role and function of contemporary art.[4] This (art) historically informed, questioning approach is evident in his early series, such as *The Polychrome Paintings* (1989–92), *Double Ground Paintings* (from 1993), and the more recent *Abstract Paintings* series, begun in 2006—which includes the *Fairweather Transformations*, and continues in the *Storm Resurrection* series (2016). Maintaining a practice used in the earlier series, Young's *Abstract Paintings* are painted by hand in oil by studio assistants who actively contribute to the process of visual translation.[5] Each painting is based on an image that has been downloaded from the internet and processed using an algorithm that translates the image into an abstract form, replacing gestural or authorial detail with zones of colour. Initially, the downloaded images were completely random, with one image selected from a daily batch of 1000. Later, certain categories of image were downloaded, such as modernist paintings by particular artists or groups of artists, including the Storm Society (Juelanshe) art group in Shanghai and the paintings of Ian Fairweather, reflecting Young's fascination with a Chinese-inflected modernism.

Young's interest in Chinese-inflected modernism emerged after he attended the art history conference 'Modernism and Postmodernism in Asian Art' at the Australian National University in March 1991. Young became aware of the Storm Society, established in Shanghai in 1931, and the modernist work of its members, including Ni Yide (1901–1970), Qiu Ti (1906–1958), Wang Jiyuan (1893–1975) and Guan Liang (1900–1986).[6] Prior to then, Young had begun to look more closely at the paintings of Scottish-born painter Ian Fairweather (1891–1974), following his contact with Imants Tillers at SCA. Tillers had appropriated elements from Fairweather's paintings and incorporated them into his early canvas board works, including *The Great Metaphysical Interior*, *Solar Light Radiations* and *Spirit of Place*, paintings that grapple with ideas of place and belonging, all created in 1983.[7] Fairweather is a significant figure for Tillers, and for many Australian artists, owing to his total commitment to painting and the philosophically inclined semi-abstract nature of the works that he created during the last decades of his life, in a hut self-made from bush materials on Bribie Island, off the coast of Queensland. In 1962, *Sydney Morning Herald* art critic Wallace Thornton provocatively named Fairweather Australia's 'greatest painter'.[8] Fairweather would become a touchstone artist for Young too, who describes him as 'absolutely crucial to the diaspora and the understanding of the cross-cultural condition': 'I really consider Fairweather one of the origins of my work', Young explains, 'because of his capacity to hold two world views together'.[9]

Slade School of Fine Art-trained Fairweather is exceptional among modern artists for his experience of Chinese life and culture. Fairweather lived and worked in China for extended periods, from 1929 to 1933 and 1935 to 1936. He learnt the Chinese language, and later, from his base on Bribie Island, published *The Drunken Budda* (1965), a book-length translation of the popular Qing dynasty Chinese novel *The Complete Biography of* [Monk] *Jigong (Jigong Quanzhuan)* by eighteenth-century writer Guo Xiaoting. Fairweather's engagement with the principles of Chinese art and thought was longstanding and profound.[10] As a young art student in London, he spent all his time looking at 'wallpapers, tapestries and furniture' in the Victoria and Albert

Museum and Byzantine reliefs at the British Museum, having got 'nothing from any of the galleries with paintings'.[11] 'Imitative painting', Fairweather wrote, 'makes me feel quite ill'.[12] From an early age he sought alternatives to art based on verisimilitude and single point perspective, which included Chinese and Japanese art.

Young has admitted that he initially had difficulty looking at Fairweather's paintings. The honesty with which Fairweather painted was direct and painful. For Young, the paintings were 'too existentially real'.[13] Fairweather's works have an intense, layered, even visceral physicality; created out of deeply felt experience, they were made using whatever materials were at hand. There is an urgency about them, as if the built-up surfaces of the paintings are part of a conscious practice of visual thinking, to express and conceal, work and rework, a process of conjuring form from an acknowledged complexity of being.

In the mid 1990s Young acquired Fairweather's *Composition 1* (c. 1961), which dates from the period in which Fairweather actively pursued abstraction and then had difficulty returning from it.[14] He never regarded himself as an abstract artist. More than any other work in the artists' oeuvre, *Composition 1* has the appearance of being based on a Chinese word or character. The bold gestural lines have an affinity with ancient Chinese calligraphy, specifically Seal Script, which Fairweather was known to admire. It was perhaps this cultural resonance that attracted Young's attention. In any case, the painting appears to signify Fairweather's achievement in bringing together two very different artistic paradigms to create a transcultural practice that is not forced or clichéd. Following his own artistic training at SCA, artist residencies in Europe, and his lived experience with Chinese language and culture, Young sought to draw the artistic traditions of Chinese and European art into a productive creative dialogue. Like Fairweather, he consciously pursued a transcultural artistic practice— but Young's starting point was Hong Kong, the opposite end of the cultural spectrum to Fairweather's.

For many years Fairweather's *Composition 1* hung in Young's dining room in Melbourne, bringing its creative energy into the artist's private realm. Was it Young's familiarity with *Composition 1* that led him to apply his method of abstraction (in the *Abstract Paintings*) to paintings by Fairweather? Young's earliest Fairweather renditions are six paintings in the *Moment* (2015) series. They are based on digital images of works by Fairweather in public and private collections that were downloaded from the internet. The title, 'Moment', implies the fleeting passage of time; that there is a before and an after, and that there is change and also loss. The series includes artistic transformations of some of Fairweather's most ambitious paintings, including the magisterial *Monastery* (1960), in the National Gallery of Australia collection, and *Gethsemane* (1958), formerly owned by the writer Patrick White and now in the collection of the Queensland Art Gallery. Young's *Moment V* (2015), which is based on *Monastery*, is virtually illegible as a Fairweather painting. The cubist lapidary structure has been transmuted into rounded-off interlinking forms, as if the whole painting is being viewed through a kaleidoscope. *Moment VI* (2015), on the other hand, retains recognisable elements of the remembered landscape paintings

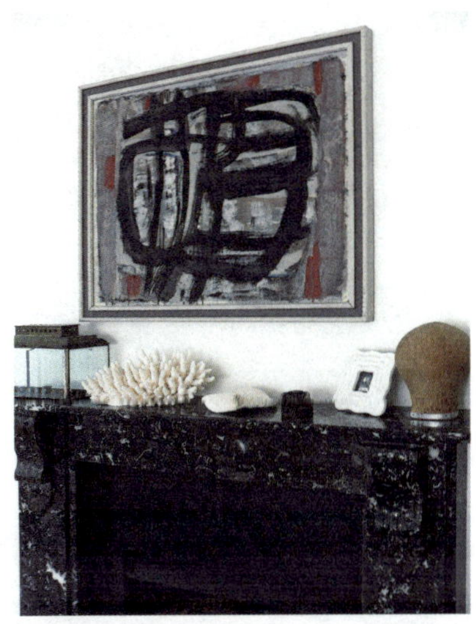

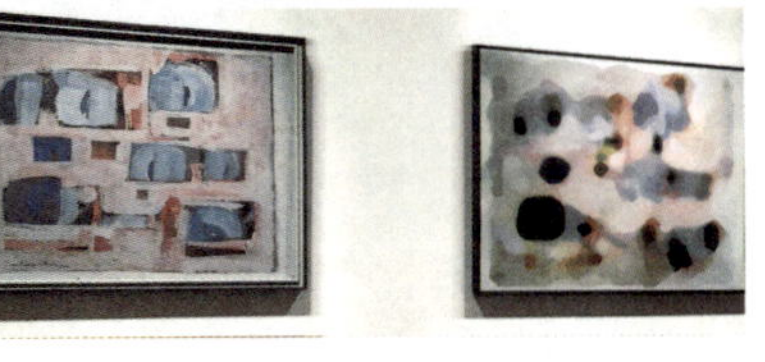

Ian Fairweather (1891–1974)
Composition 1 1961
Synthetic polymer paint and gouache on cardboard on hardboard, 67.5 × 83.5 cm
Installation view, John Young's home, Melbourne, 2005

Installation view of Ian Fairweather's *Painting 1*, 1960 (left), and John Young's *Moment 1 (Fairweather Transformation 1)*, 2015 (right)
Philip Bacon Galleries, Brisbane

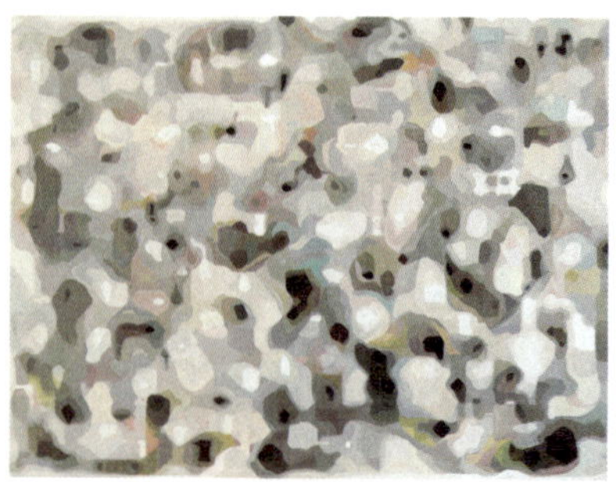

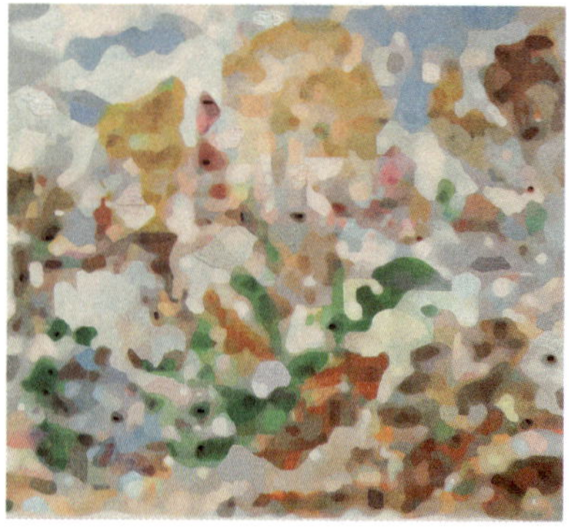

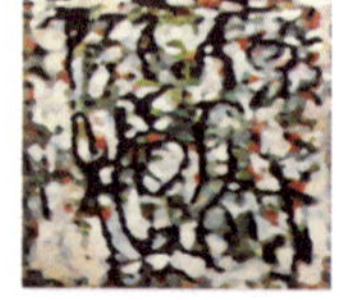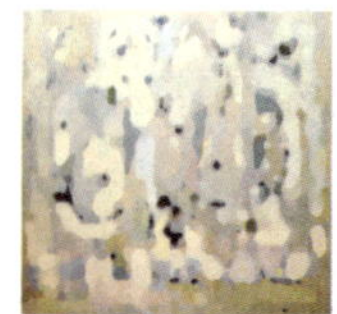

Moment V
(Fairweather Transformation V) 2015
oil on Belgian linen, 76 × 98 cm

Fairweather Transformation XII
(Tombs in Peking) 2015
Oil on Belgian linen, 76 × 80.4 cm
Private collection, Brisbane

Aenid I and II 2016
Installation view
Private collection, Brisbane

of China, which Fairweather created in Calcutta in 1941. Having been filtered through an algorithm, the emotion of the experience of place originally expressed by Fairweather through his application of paint has been removed but there remains an identifiable Fairweather palette of warm earth colours and brilliant Reckitt's blue. What was a spirited composite landscape has become, through Young's practice, a silent vestigial image in which the possibility of focus is occluded by atmospheric passages of white.

Young's later works *Aeneid I* (2016) and *Aeneid II* (2016), also based on images of Fairweather's paintings, were inspired by the translation of Book VI of Virgil's epic poem *The Aeneid* by the poet Seamus Heaney, published in 2016. Aeneas' journey to the underworld to meet the spirit of his father becomes a metaphor for the encounter between the original work of art and the digital simulacrum in which it is easy to lose direction. The privileging of the electronic eye and mathematical algorithms produces a flattened image in which the details of brush strokes and gestural marks are removed. The personality of the artist is expunged. 'What remains', says Young, 'are the colour relations, some hint of resonance based on colour and form residues'.[15]

Aeneid I, based on Fairweather's painting *Pelléas et Melisande* (1959), is like a mirage. Rounded zones of flat colour further abstract Fairweather's imagery, creating a camouflage-like pattern that, in spite of its fixed form, appears to move and shimmer as though animated by an inner force. The palette of soft creams, violets, greens, browns and greys—warm and cool colours held in balance—reveal Fairweather's mastery and sensitivity as a colourist. *Aeneid II*, based on *Triple Portrait*, also known as *(Elephant)* (c. 1970–71) in the collection of the Art Gallery of New South Wales, creates a very different effect. The clear black outlines of the original painting remain but have been released from any representational role. Instead, they hover on the surface of the image as if moving into and out of a dappled phosphorescent ground.

Following the inclusion of *Aeneid I* and *Aeneid II* in the 2016 Rockhampton Art Gallery Gold Award exhibition, Young was commissioned to create *Standing Figures Revisited* (2018). Arranged by Philip Bacon Galleries in Brisbane, a gallery with a longstanding interest in the work of Ian Fairweather, the commission resulted in Young's painting joining Fairweather's *Standing Figures* (c. 1971–74) in a private collection in Brisbane, creating a direct encounter between the 'father' and 'son' works. The painterly specificity of the Fairweather work with its confidently brushed overlay of black outlined figures and dripping paint is nowhere present in *Revisited*, which instead appears like an out-of-focus detail of reptilian skin or a section of dark camouflage material, a digitally generated pattern created to deceive or deter. The two works are the same but different. *Standing Figures Revisited* boldly asserts its legitimacy as the 'son' image.

In Young's *Fairweather Transformation XII* (2019), based on the 1936 painting *Tombs in Peking*, the vibrant palette of springtime colours, including pink and green, is retained. The bright pale blue of the sky and earthbound ground colours help orient the viewer and signal the landscape referent. In a surprisingly discordant move, a few areas of textured paint have been added to the abstracted zones of flat colour, reintroducing the idea of the handmade. Brush strokes are visible in small raised areas of impasto paint, albeit restrained and contained within the boundaries of their respective fields of colour. *Fairweather Transformation XIV* (2019), based on Fairweather's *Temple Yard, Peking* (1936), is treated in a similar manner. The textured areas of brushwork are at once affecting and disturbing, a poignant reminder of the hands that have carefully re-thought and re-felt Fairweather's paintings at one remove. The patches of impasto colour bring the viewer back to the real world with a jolt, reminding us of the importance of touch. When viewed in relation to the original paintings, the *Fairweather Transformations* read as glorious afterimages created in response to the flattened virtual world of print and screen culture. It is as if we have viewed the originals in extreme light and for too long; we can no longer see clearly and must instead rely on memory to translate them into being.

Fairweather's works are so materially rich that Young's *Fairweather Transformations* could be construed as artistic acts of provocation. What is it that motivates Young to create artworks that are apparently at such a remove from Fairweather's expressive practice? Is Young's method partly a response to the difficulty he first experienced viewing Fairweather's paintings, finding their honesty too direct, painful and existentially real, and a need, therefore, to find a way to process that energy using a detached, analytical mode—a chameleon-like approach that in its own way reveals and conceals? According to Young, it is precisely the loss of gesture and individuality in the renditions that is the point; the impossibility of reducing and reproducing Fairweather's art, which is so defined by gesture and emotion.[16] In that case, the *Fairweather Transformations* offer a critique of the flattening of the physical world and the widespread acceptance and dependence on digital media. The paradoxical, even absurd, process of painstakingly hand-painting the *Fairweather Transformations* in oil on Belgian linen may be understood as an extreme act of re-evaluation on the one hand and of introducing the handmade into digitally generated images on the other—a mode of production that questions the ontology of art.

The use of emerging or alternative visual technologies by artists is nothing new. When living in Shanghai, Fairweather used a Leica camera to record scenes that he wanted to commit to memory and a projector to scale up his images.[17] Later, on Bribie Island, he used a Box Brownie to document his paintings, as 'something to remember them by' or as 'an asset to study', but also as an aid to see more clearly what he was painting.[18] Following the visit of Craig MacGregor and the photographer David Beal to Bribie Island in 1968, for the book *In the Making* (1969), Fairweather wrote to thank Beal for sending him copies of photographs that he had taken. 'One ought to have photographs all the time, to help one see what one is doing. I am most delighted with the ones you sent. Though much regret there were not a few more – a bit nearer to realisation – But such as they are – they are a great help – I can see and hope to correct many mistakes.'[19] Beal's photographs of Fairweather's paintings presented the artist's works back to him in a different form; objectified in black and white they allowed him to 'see' his paintings in a way that was not possible in the studio. Fairweather appreciated the technology for its capacity to take him outside the process of painting. He wrote to his nephew in New Zealand, an artist and graphic designer, advising him not to follow the 'terrible lonely way of life' of an artist, but to use the camera and 'belong to the world of today'. 'I belong to the world of yesterday', he wrote, 'which has ceased to exist'.[20] In a much earlier letter, written to William Frater in 1938, Fairweather lamented the solitary world of the artist with its precarity and impecunity and instead pointed to prospects in the film and animation industry: 'I think it's in the direction of Walt Disney', he wrote, 'it is something many can work at and many can appreciate'.[21]

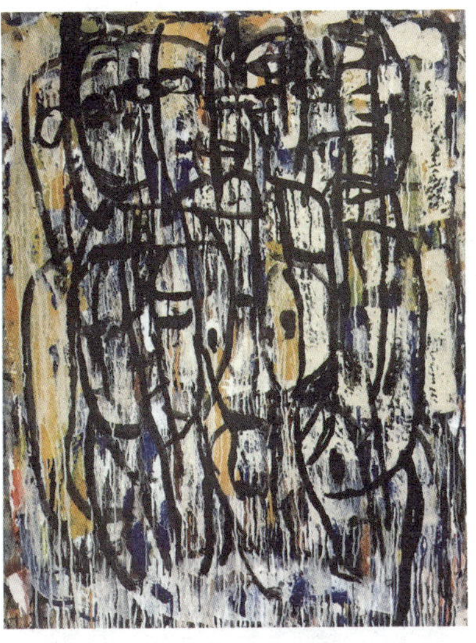

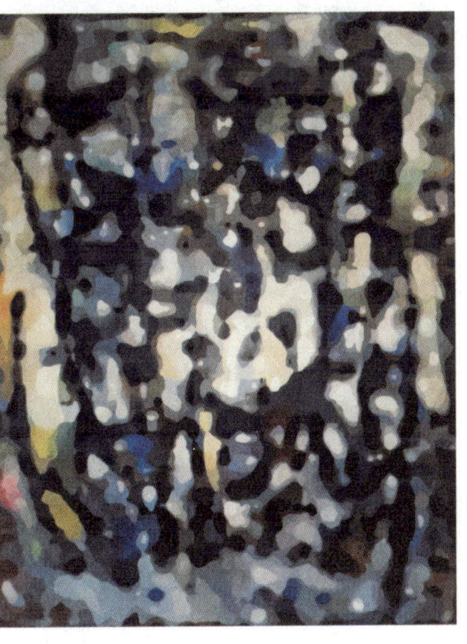

Ian Fairweather
Standing Figures 1971–74
Oil on carboard on composition board,
106.5 × 76.5 cm
Private collection, Brisbane; image courtesy
of the Design and Artists Copyright Society/
Copyright Agency, 2023

*Standing Figures Revisited (Fairweather
Transformation X)* 2018
Oil on Belgian linen, 107 × 77 cm
Private collection, Brisbane

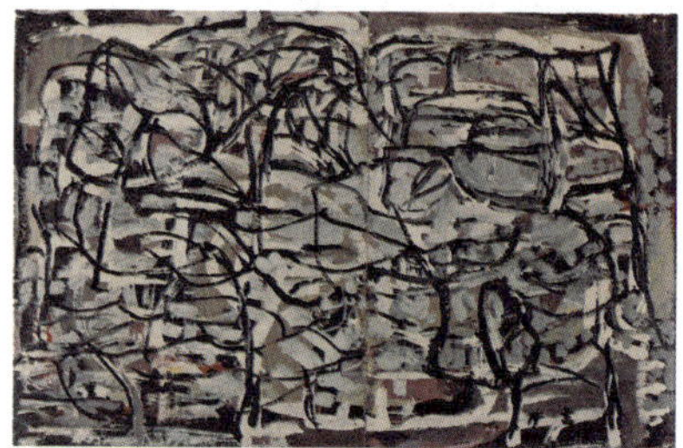

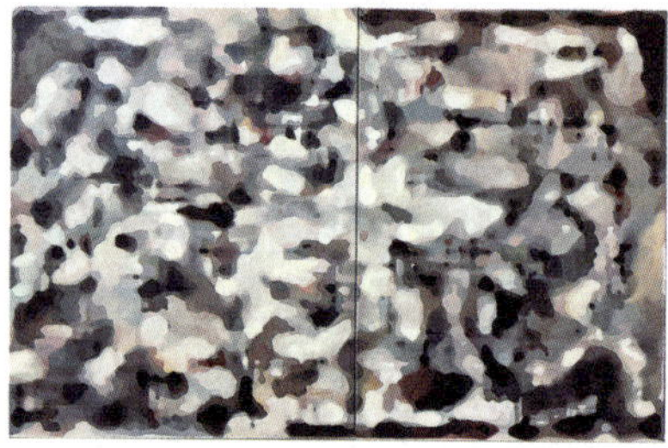

Ian Fairweather (1891–1974)
Mangrove 1961–62
Synthetic polymer paint, gouache on hardboard,
2 panels, 82 × 122 cm
Collection of Art Gallery of South Australia,
Adelaide; image courtesy of Design and Artists
Copyright Society/Copyright Agency, 2023

The Chinese Room (Mangrove) 2022
Oil on Belgian linen, two panels,
88.6 × 128.5 cm
Collection of Art Gallery of South Australia,
Adelaide

Fairweather distrusted reproductions, famously disowning numerous of his own works when he saw them in print, further highlighting the process of conceptual distancing that occurs in the photographic translation of artworks into digital files. Young's application of mathematical algorithms to images of Fairweather's paintings in effect translates Fairweather's works into fields of non-objective colour, allowing us to appreciate that aspect of Fairweather's art more clearly. 'I am more of a colourist than a draughtsman', Fairweather confided to Craig McGregor. 'I see things as colour first of all. It's hard for me to put form into it'.[22] In notebooks Fairweather would record the colours of paints, lists of colours that he needed to purchase, or notes about a painting. As early as 1913 he listed some twenty oil colours in a diary, including Yellow Ochre, Chinese Vermillion, Light Rose Madder, French Ultramarine and Van Dyke Brown. And in notes made when he was a student at the Slade School of Fine Art, there is a poetic dimension to his shorthand description of paintings: 'soft yellow, tinge purple here & there, ground of pink grey | olive green, indigo, tourquoise [sic] & light blue | v. pale blue stained with rust | Bt. Sienna pure-black – dull lilac grey'.[23]

In the *Fairweather Transformations*, Young transmutes Ian Fairweather's paintings into the essentials of colour, but this uncomplicated reading overlooks the significance of Young's practice on its own terms and in the context of art history. It appears that the challenge Young has set himself is to create an artistic practice that expresses the complexity of contemporary being while holding together two world views—a project that he and Fairweather share.

The History Projects in general, and the *Fairweather Transformations* in particular, are part of John Young's ongoing activity to challenge the idea that art arises out of untroubled monocultures, disconnected from their (art) historical pasts. The process of translating digital images of Fairweather's paintings into visual information, or code, draws attention to the importance of touch and the haptic dimension of art through which individuality, complexity and humanity are asserted. Young's *Fairweather Transformations* are intriguing paintings that are visually seductive and have a beauty and presence of their own while at the same time being contingent and dependent, making it impossible for the art historian to divorce them from the originals from which they were generated. They are self-consciously connected to multiple people and processes, and to art and history.

Moreover, the *Fairweather Transformations* contribute to Young's ongoing trans-medial project to complicate and unsettle the idea of Australian art. Created to hover in our minds, they shimmer like mirages. Products of the new algorithmic sublime, they are no longer site specific but generalised, out of time and out of place.[24] We might think of the *Fairweather Transformations* and related series as a new form of 'history painting', an attempt to bridge the gulf between the digital and the real, untethered from any particular location or moment. And perhaps we can understand their creation—by studio assistants working under Young's direction, hand-painting digitally processed images of the Fairweather originals—as a form of artistic learning in the Chinese tradition of copying 'old master' works, acknowledging artistic connections and lineages and recognising that making is an always complex and often fraught process of realisation and becoming.

1. Carolyn Barnes, 'Towards a layered imaginary', in Carolyn Barnes, *John Young*, Craftsman House, Fishermans Bend, Victoria, 2005, p. 30.

2. John Young, conversation with the author, 20 August 2019, and John Young email communication, 30 November 2020.

3. Barnes, p. 39, and note 42.

4. John Young Studio, 'The Lives of Celestials: John Young Zerunge', unpublished exhibition essay, Town Hall Gallery, Hawthorn Arts Centre, Boroondara, 31 August–20 October 2019.

5. The backs of the paintings are signed by Young and the studio assistants.

6. Barnes, pp. 41–42.

7. See Claire Roberts, 'Displacement Thinking: Yirrkala and Ian Fairweather', in Charles Green and Ian McLean (eds), *What is Postnational Art History*, Perimeter Editions, Melbourne, 2023, pp. 224–25.

8. Wallace Thornton, 'Fairweather Now Seen as Our Greatest Painter', *Sydney Morning Herald*, 15 August 1962.

9. John Young, conversation with the author, Melbourne, 20 August 2019.

10. See Claire Roberts, *Fairweather and China*, Melbourne University Press, Melbourne, 2021.

11. Ian Fairweather, letter to Clark Massie, Bribie Island, 18 July [1964], in Claire Roberts and John Thompson (eds), *Ian Fairweather: A Life in Letters*, Text Publishing, Melbourne, 2019, p. 363.

12. Ibid.

13. John Young, conversation with the author, Melbourne, 20 April 2017.

14. Many works by Fairweather are owned or have been owned by artists, indicating a deeply felt interest in his paintings.

15. John Young, notes on *The Fairweather Transformations*, 2017, unpublished.

16. John Young email communication, 30 November 2020.

17. Ian Fairweather letter to Annette Waters, Bribie Island, March [1963] and Ian Fairweather letter to Ian Alister Fairweather, Bribie Island, [early June 1971], in Roberts and Thompson (eds), *Ian Fairweather: A Life in Letters*, pp. 324; 492–93.

18. Ian Fairweather letter to Treania Smith, Bribie Island, 22 April [1960], in *Ian Fairweather: A Life in Letters*, p. 247.

19. Ian Fairweather letter to David Beal, Bribie Island, 14 April [1968], unpublished. With thanks to David Beal for providing me with a copy of the letter.

20. Ian Fairweather letter to Ian Alister Fairweather, Bribie Island, [early June 1971], in *Ian Fairweather: A Life in Letters*, p. 492.

21. Ian Fairweather letter to William Frater, Manila, 8 May [1938], in *Ian Fairweather: A Life in Letters*, p. 79.

22. Craig McGregor, David Beal et al., *In the Making*, Thomas Nelson Limited, Sydney, 1969, p. 150.

23. Ian Fairweather, diary, Fairweather family archive, and notes inscribed in Laurence Binyon, *The Flight of the Dragon: An Essay on the Theory and Practice of Art in China and Japan Based on Original Sources*, Wisdom of the East series, John Murray, London, 1914, gifted by Fairweather to Norman Sterling.

24. Edwin Heathcote, 'How do machines see the world?', *FT Weekend*, 26–27 September 2020, p. 12.

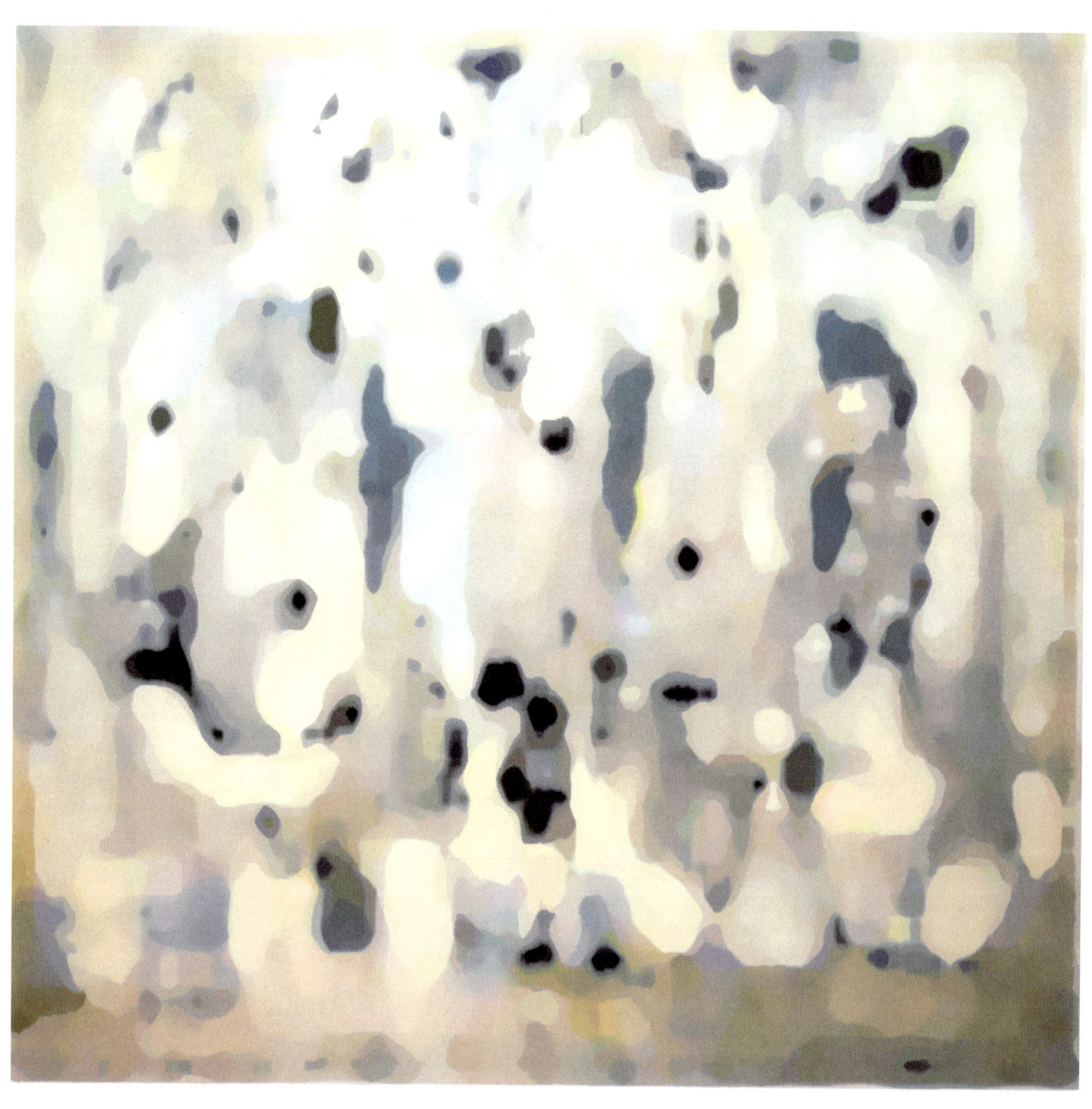

Aeneid I (Fairweather Transformation VII) 2016
Oil on Belgian linen, 200 × 200 cm

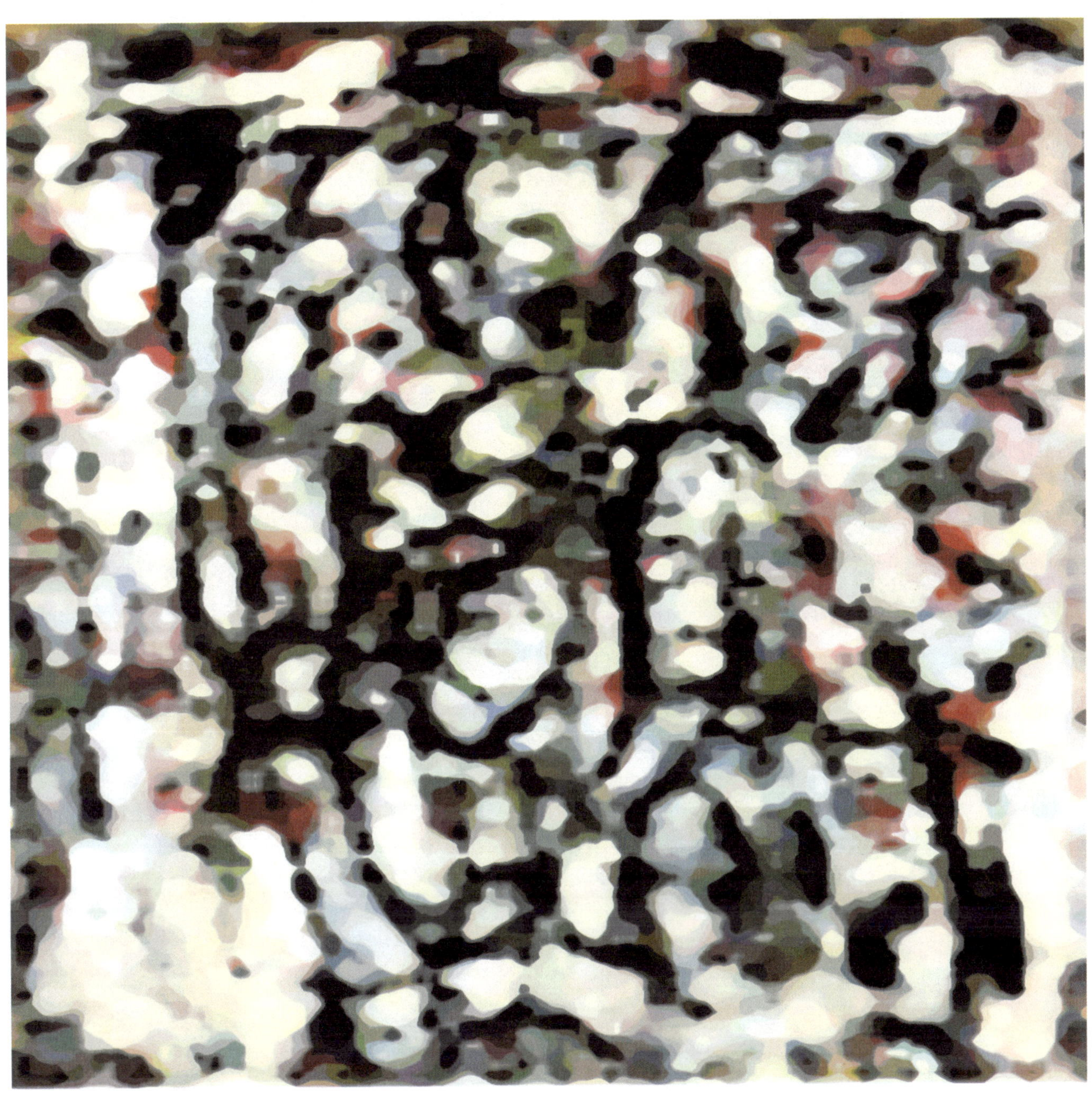

Aeneid II (Fairweather Transformation VIII) 2016
Oil on Belgian linen, 200 × 200 cm
Private collection, Brisbane

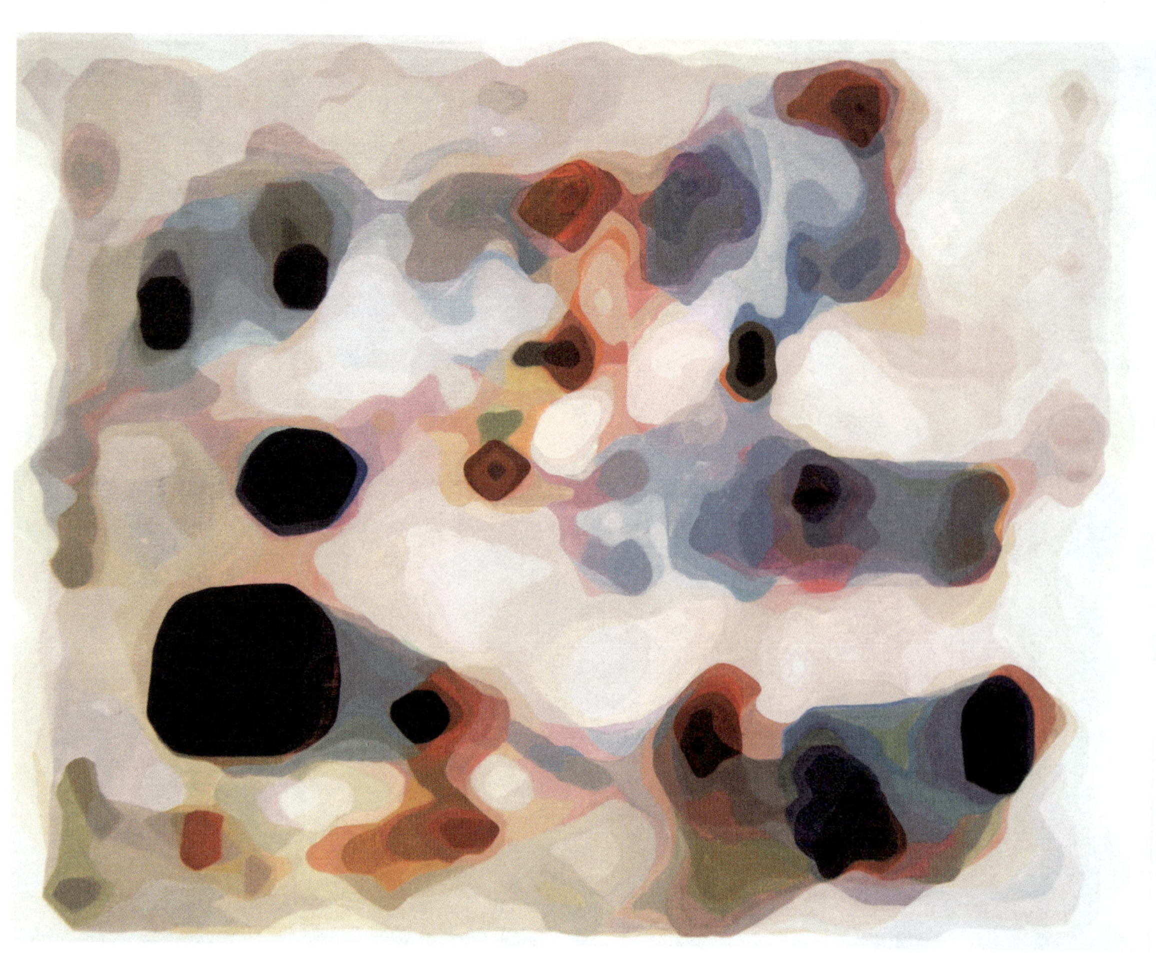

Moment I (Fairweather Transformation I) 2015
Oil on Belgian linen, 76 x 96 cm
Private collection, Brisbane

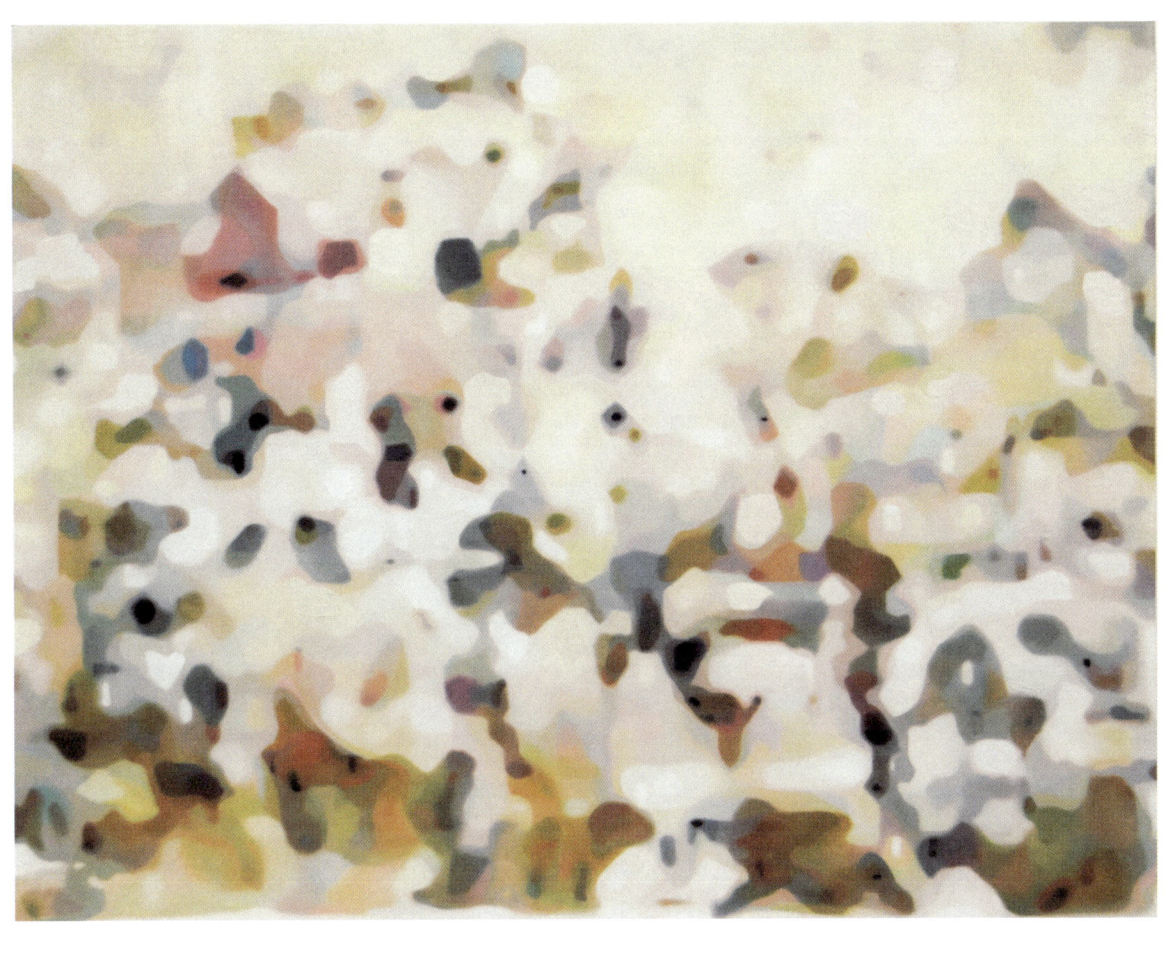

381

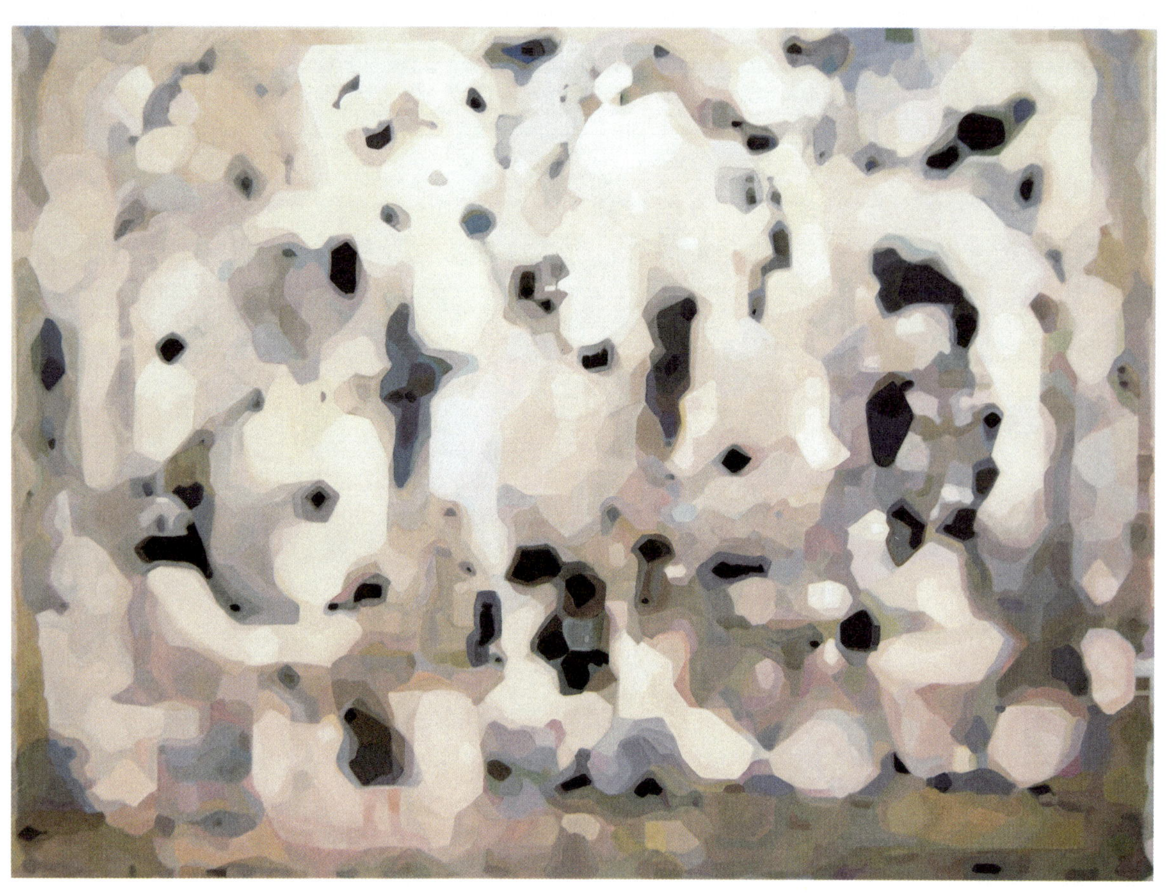

Moment III (Fairweather Transformation III) 2015
Oil on Belgian linen, 76 × 103 cm
Collection of University of Queensland Art
Museum, Brisbane

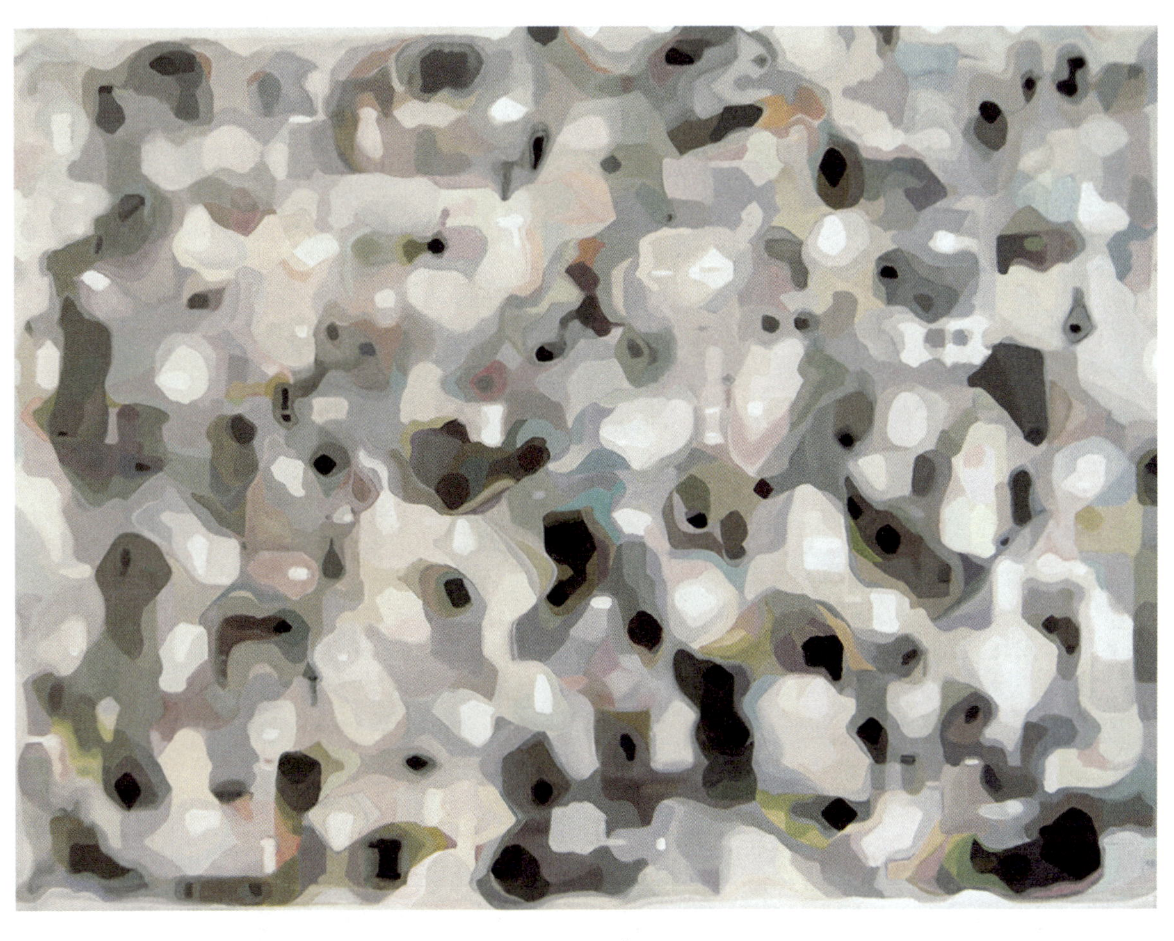

Moment V (Fairweather Transformation V) 2015
Oil on Belgian linen, 76 × 98 cm

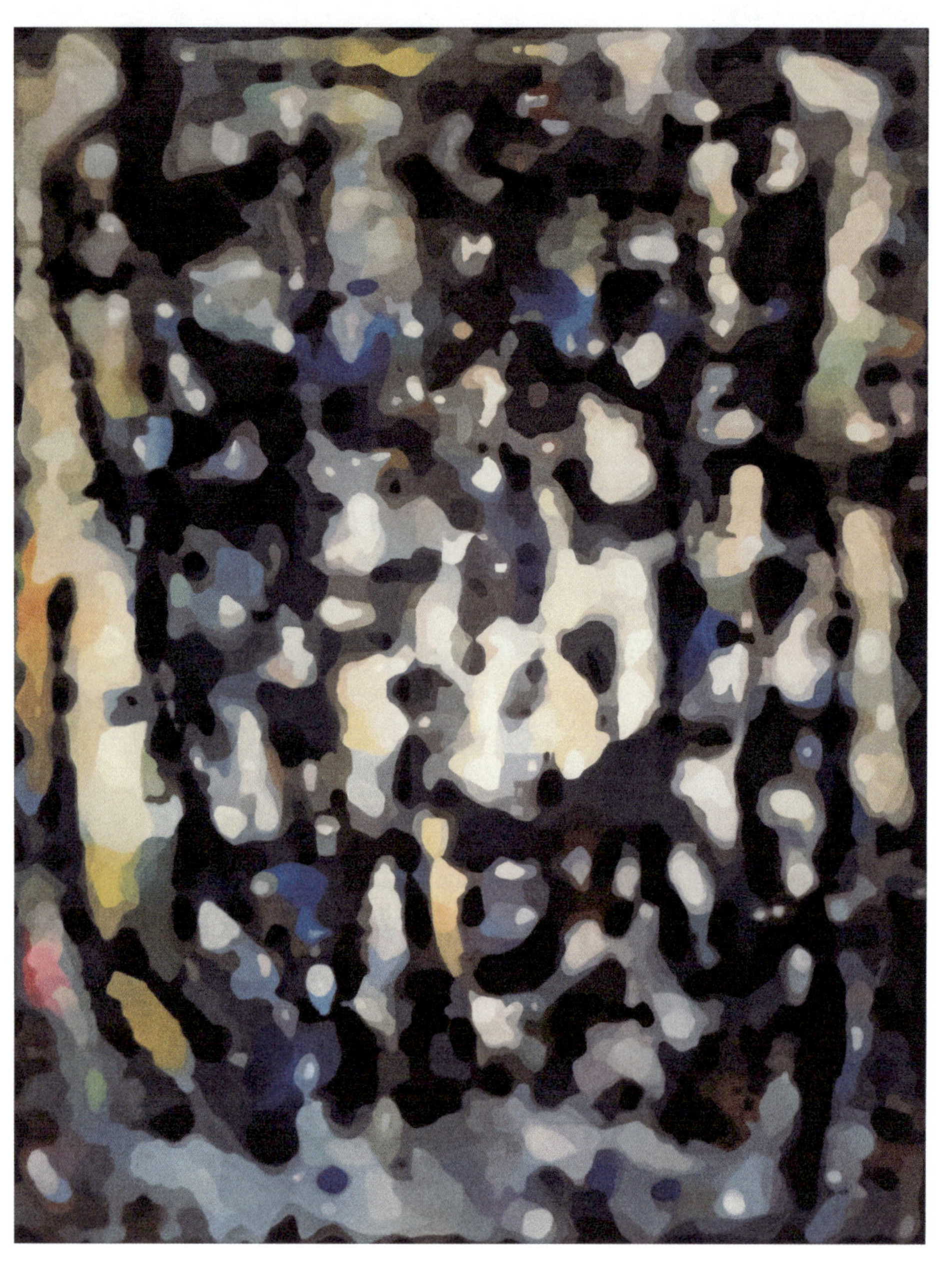

Standing Figures Revisited (Fairweather Transformation X) 2018
Oil on Belgian linen, 107 × 77 cm
Private collection, Brisbane

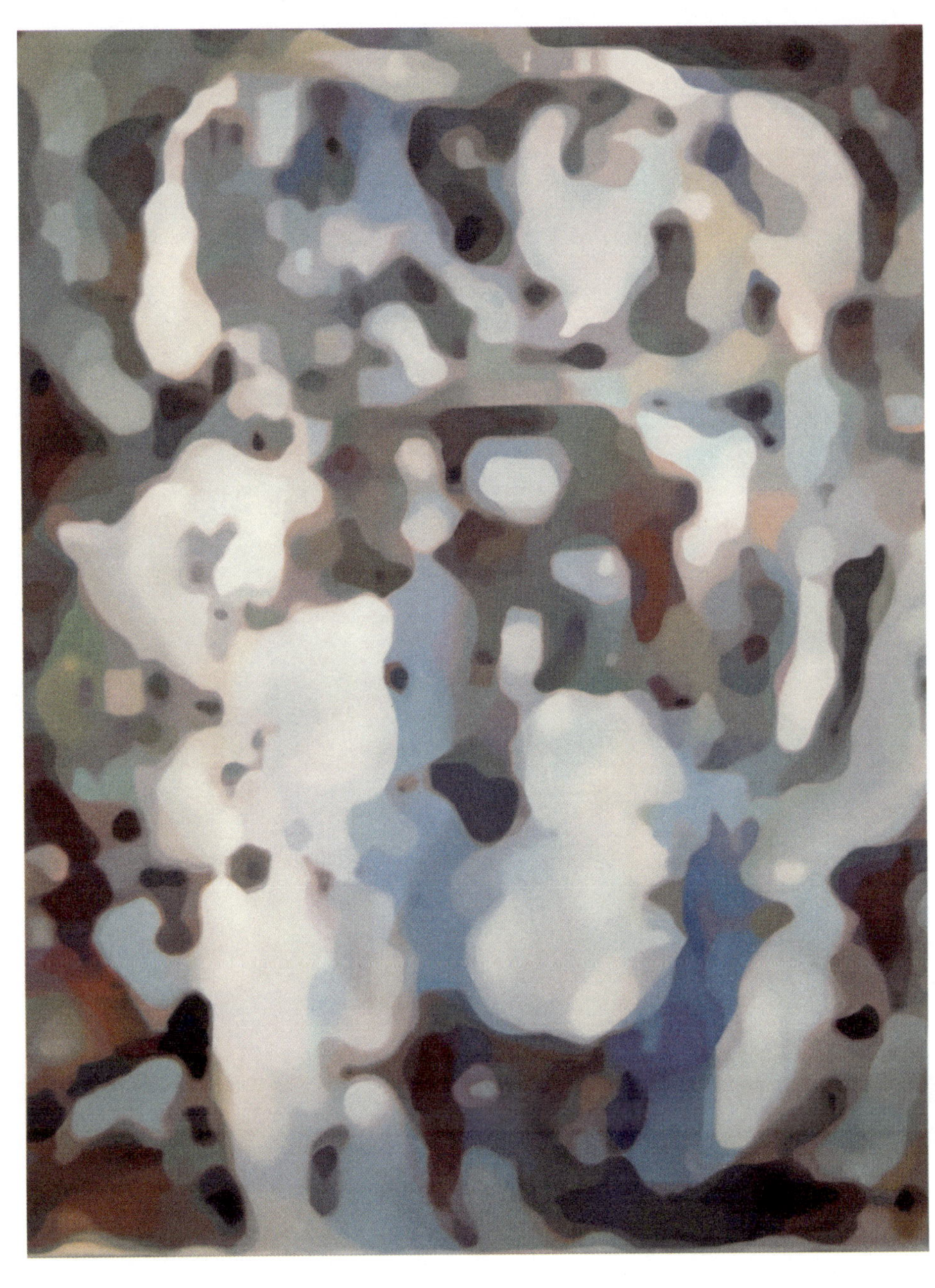

Fairweather Transformation XIII 2019
Oil on Belgian linen, 106 x 76 cm
Private collection, Melbourne

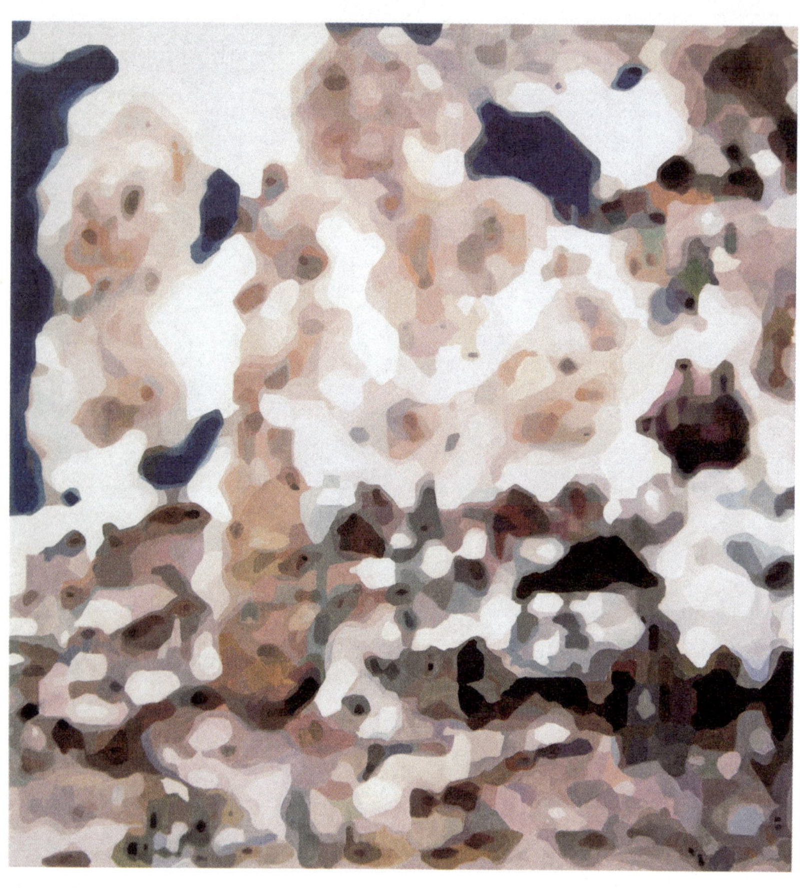

Fairweather Transformation XI 2019
Oil on Belgian linen, 76 × 72 cm

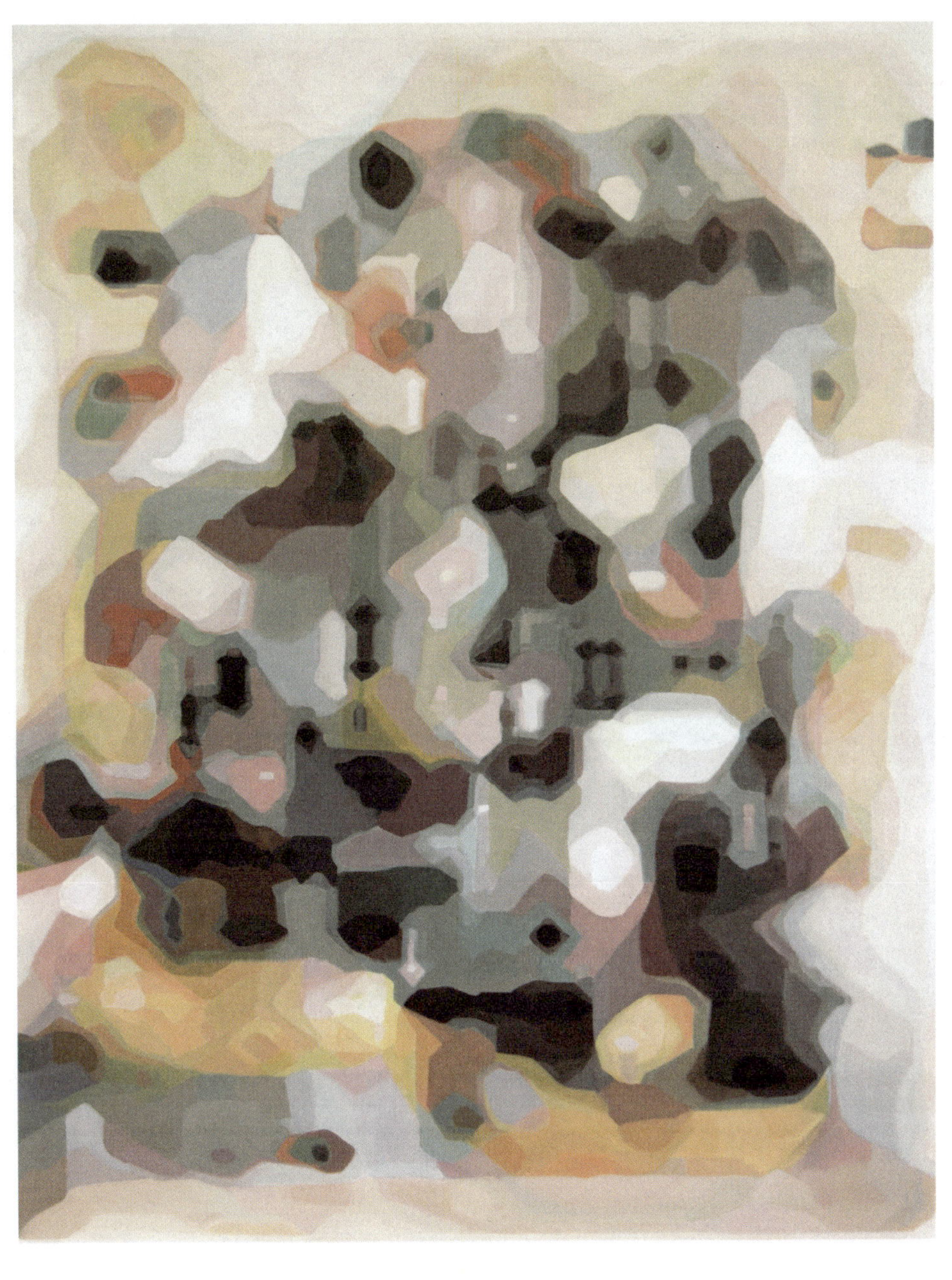

Moment II (Fairweather Transformation II) 2015
Oil on Belgian linen, 97 × 71 cm
Private collection, Brisbane

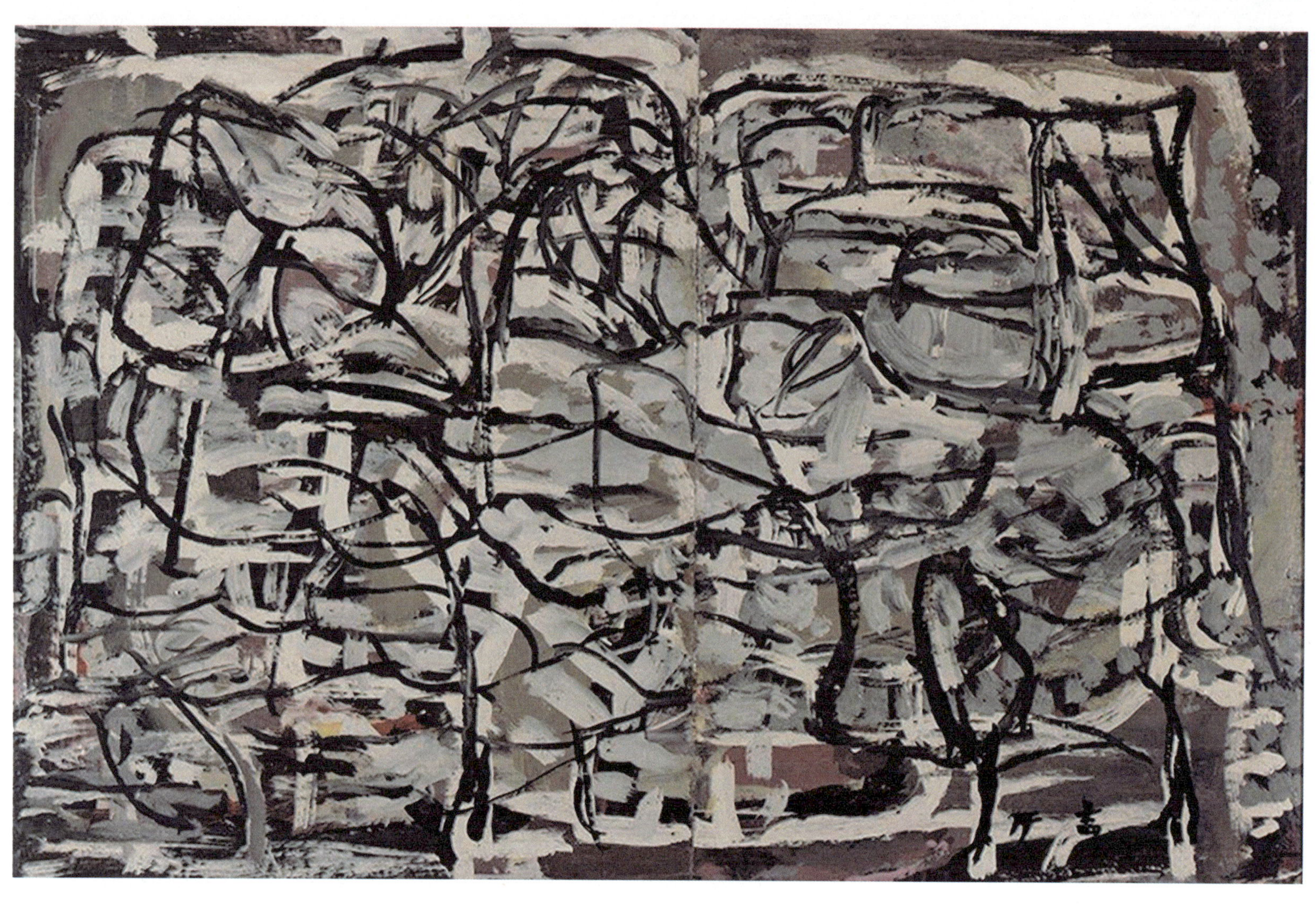

Ian Fairweather (1891–1974)
Mangrove 1961–62
Synthetic polymer paint, gouache on hardboard,
2 panels, 82 × 122 cm
Collection of Art Gallery of South Australia,
Adelaide; image courtesy of Design and Artists
Copyright Society/Copyright Agency, 2023

The Chinese Room (Mangrove) 2022
Oil on Belgian linen, two panels,
128.5 × 88.6 cm
Collection of Art Gallery of South Australia,
Adelaide

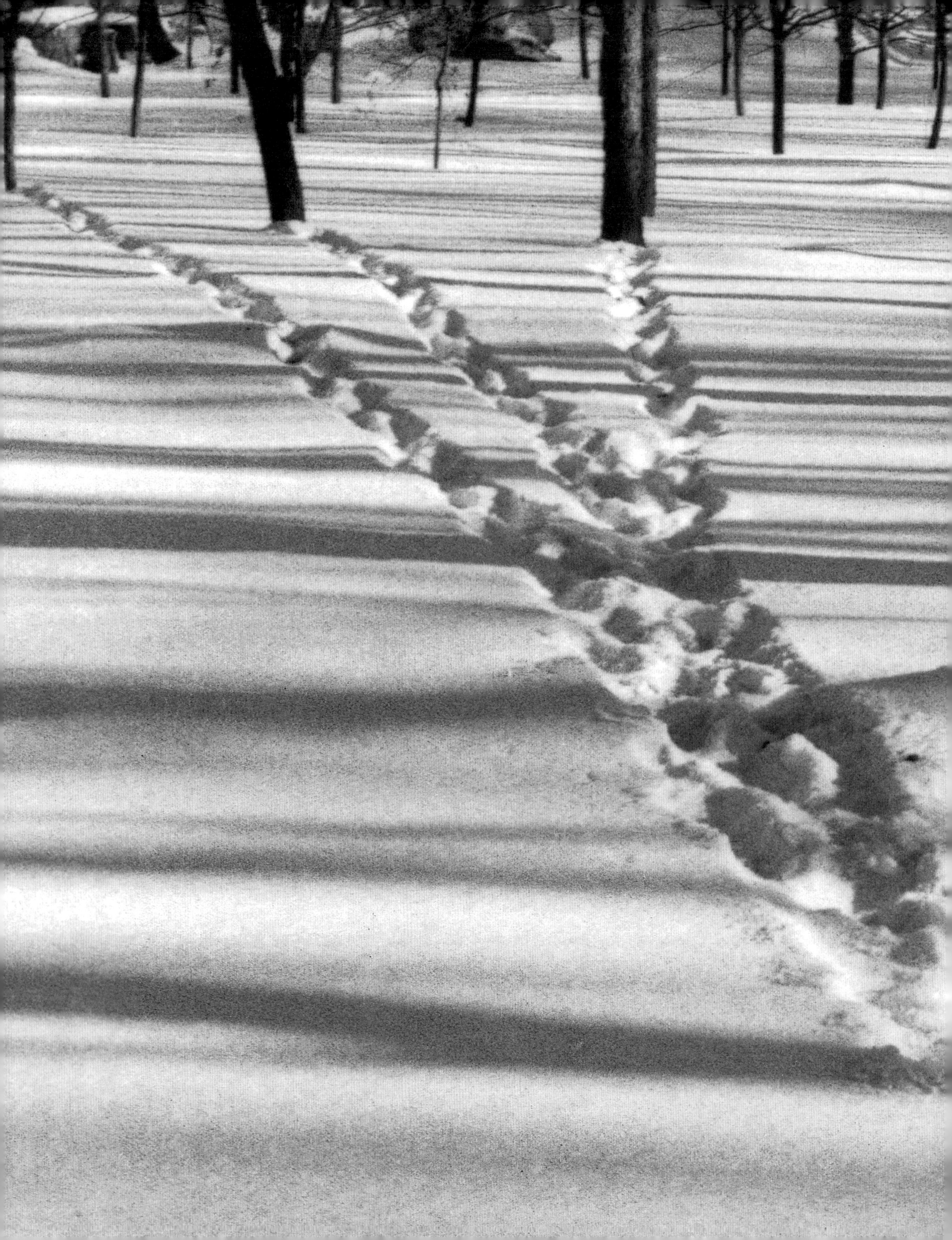

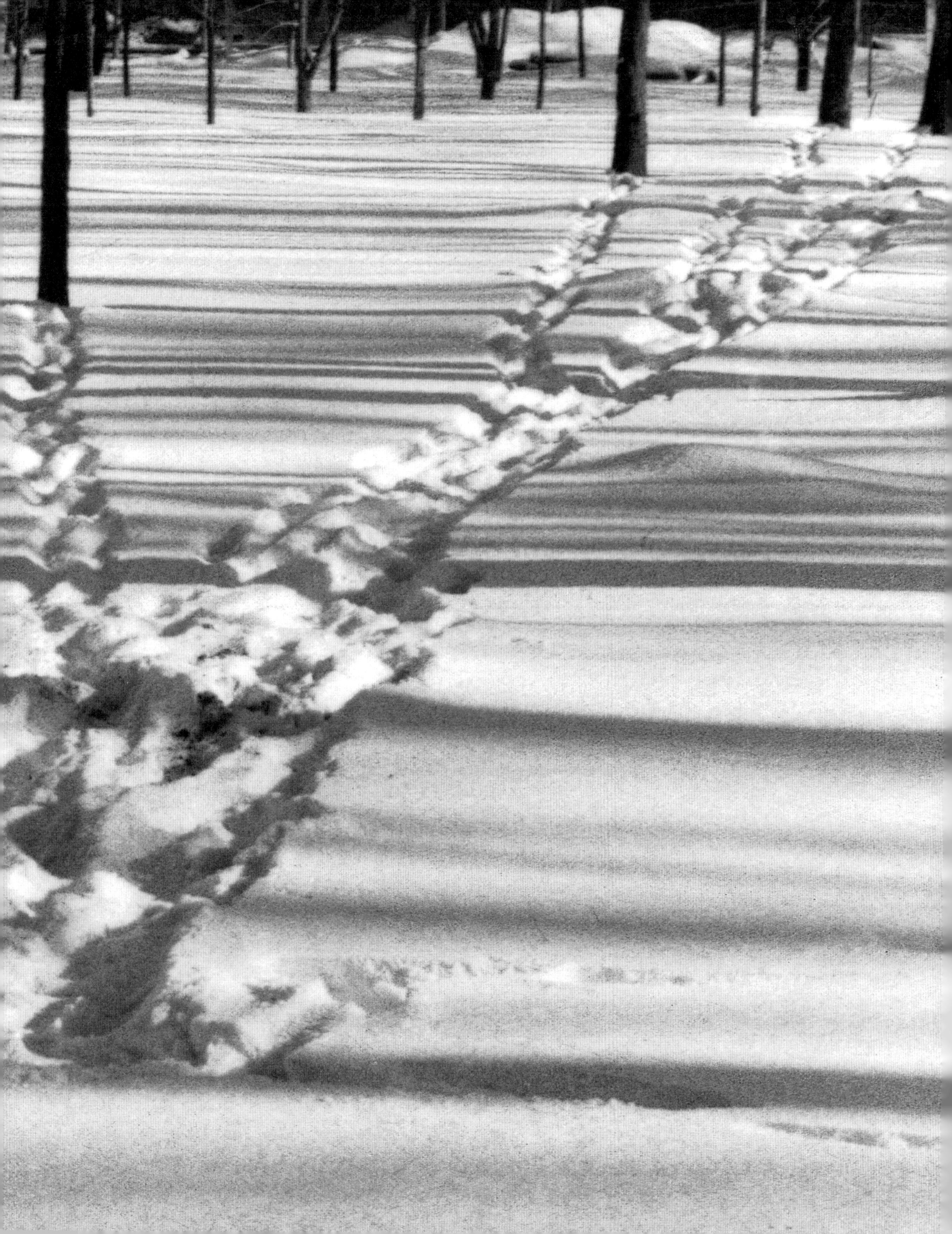

CODA: A CONVERSATION WITH AARON SEETO

This text is the culmination of three conversations between Aaron Seeto and John Young held from July to September 2022, between Yogyakarta, Jakarta and Melbourne, conducted via email and online. As an artist, and later as curator and director of 4A Centre for Contemporary Asian Art in Sydney, Seeto has a specific familiarity with different dimensions of Young's practice, foregrounded in the informality of the final text. Invited to approach this conversation as a 'coda', Seeto used the opportunity to revisit some of Young's earliest works, based on his curatorial experience with Young's practice, drawing suggestive connections between methodologies and interests in Young's works of the 1970s, later developments in The History Projects and key intervening series.

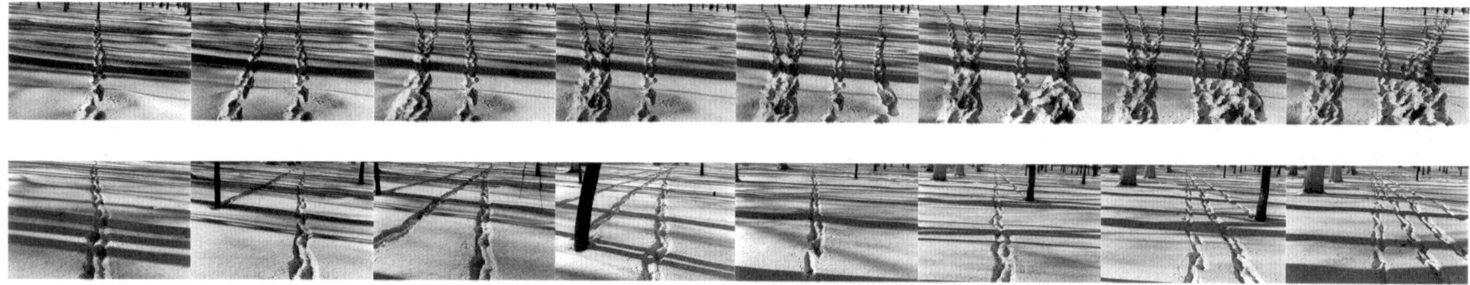

pages 392–93

Manchurian Snow Walk (completed) 1979
Silver gelatin print, 60.5 × 80 cm

Manchurian Snow Walk 1979
16 photographs; silver gelatin prints,
two units, 26 × 263 cm each

Aaron Seeto: One of the strange things about this pandemic, because of its
forced social disconnection and isolation, is that it has made me realise things that
probably should have been more evident earlier. Your work touches on the historical,
art historical, political, curatorial and artistic. Since I first came across it, it has had
a deep impact on my conceptual development as both a curator and a young artist.
It provided me with a framework to understand the power relations within art
worlds and knowledge systems, especially the politics and operations of diaspora
in the Australian system. And as I reflect on your work, now, I've had some time
to pause and reflect on our relationship.

We met properly, probably around 2008 or 2009, when I took on the directorship
of 4A, an organisation that you had an early connection with. The political work that
was being accomplished through this organisation has had a profound impact upon
my experience of the Australian art world—probably more so than the theoretical
training one has from art school. The 4A days have framed all of my work, and
I think that guidance, those conversations we've had, have in essence revolved
around the possibility of Australian art opening up to a broader set of interests.
For me, it actually comes back to the primary problem of epistemes. It's an
epistemological issue.

The role of a coda is to restate and come back to the very beginning; to recapitulate
key themes and ideas. In this conversation, I'd like to review some of the concerns
of your work, in the present, and to look back at a few key moments in your practice:
Manchurian Snow Walk, the *1967Dispersion* and *Double Ground* series of images
of oceans (from the early 2000s), and the History Projects generally. I think these
works are all tied together.

I want to start with *Manchurian Snow Walk*, to better understand how your
understanding of epistemes and knowledge systems may have developed since
the 1970s. You studied philosophy and have talked about [Ludwig] Wittgenstein in
the context of this early seminal work. What was it about Wittgenstein that was
influential to you in the late 1970s?

John Young: Well, this is the first time I've talked about Wittgenstein in
relationship to my art making. I mean, implicitly I've talked to other writers such
as Carolyn Barnes about this, but I've always been a bit reticent in talking about
his philosophy. When we talk about the interest in epistemological levels of things,
it is important to understand that my first level of research was really to demonstrate
that artistic practice was a very legitimate form of knowledge acquisition, as opposed
to the high church of science for example, and Wittgenstein provided a way into
that level of pluralism of knowledge and knowledge acquisition.

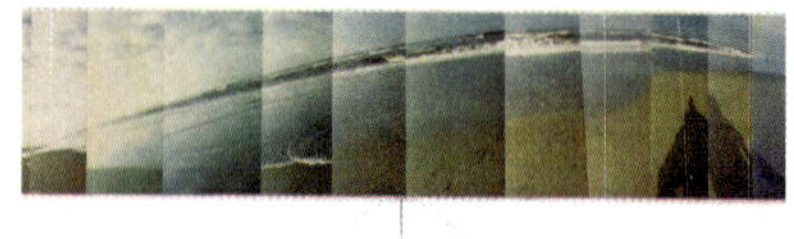

Jan Dibbets (1941–)
*Panorama Dutch Mountain 12 x 15°
Sea II A* 1971
12 photographs, colour, on paper,
75.1 × 99.8 cm support
Collection of Tate, London; image courtesy of
Jan Dibbets. Artists Rights Society/Copyright
Agency, 2023, T01745

That dovetailed with my interest in another writer, Paul Feyerabend, who wrote the book *Against Method* [1975], which attacked the notion that science is the only way in which we could actually acquire knowledge through different scientific revolutions and paradigms—that other forms from other cultures which bore techniques, such as acupuncture or witchcraft and so on, are just as legitimate in terms of acquiring a plural sense of knowledge, which may potentially be very useful for us in the future.

That was how I started when I first went to art school. I had already developed a framework to work in, that I was first and foremost interested in—not so much social issues or the representational function of art, but rather the capacity of art to be one form of knowledge acquisition. And I found that the only person who understood my position then was Imants Tillers. We actually shared a common interest at that point in Paul Feyerabend's work, because Imants had also discovered Feyerabend's work through another academic in the same year. This book, *Against Method* was very important for us.[1]

AS: As a young artist, how do you actually go about applying these ideas?

JY: Of course the issue is—when you're interested in art and are also interested in knowledge acquisition—the context of perception always comes into it; and the limits of perception and the limits in the way our whole worldview is defined by what we know in the Western episteme. The earliest work I did, the minimal works, dealt with paradoxes since the limits of one's perception is the visual paradox. In a most populist way, you think of someone like [MC] Escher's illustrations, but more sophisticatedly, the minimalist Robert Mangold. They are the logical limits in which Western perception is defined; I was very interested in that.

Of course, the other issue that determines the whole notion of perception in the Western episteme in the late twentieth century was still photography. But the problem was that everybody's understanding of photography at this point was representational, and they were really only interested in photography from a formal aesthetic point of view or a social point of view. They weren't interested in it from an epistemological point of view. The only people that I found interested in pushing that were artists like Jan Dibbets, whose serial photographic work turned photography from a representational medium into a generative, presentational medium—through *Dutch Mountain* [1971] and all these sort of works, he was actually creating something out of photography rather than trying to represent something from the so called external world. In philosophy it's what may be termed the theory-ladenness[2] of observation, rather than an empirical position that the world exists primarily outside of us. Thus, the claim is that our perception is dependent on our world views.

AS: What you're saying is that you were interested in the generative potential of photography to allow us to see, rather than to just represent, and that there is some validity in non-rational esoteric forms to help us see differently?

How does an immigrant to Australia—and I've never actually heard you call yourself this—but how does a person who was born outside of Australia and only recently arrived, become interested in these high-level philosophical conversations about epistemes and knowledge systems? Was there a social and political context for your interests? Were you also beginning to understand and interrogate the knowledge and power systems of Australian culture and society?

JY: I guess in those days, in the late 1970s, when I was starting to be active in the art world after leaving art school, in high Euramerican modernism, there was still room for this sort of discussion. There was still room for investigation through minimalism and conceptualism, which was legitimate enough for artists like Mel Bochner, and to

a certain degree Sol Lewitt, On Kawara and Sherrie Levine, to exist, and of course
Jan Dibbets. And there was historical room as well, because I discovered Tillers was
interested in Surrealism and pataphysics, all these other moments in our history
when epistemes were questioned. I concentrated on looking at those limits in the
Western episteme so that I could find room to investigate other forms of knowledge
acquisition, say from the East.

Of course, over time, what I discovered were some weaknesses of Euramerican
modernism, which was that it was progressive; it was actually almost, in a sense,
ahistorical—it wanted to overturn everything, through one movement after another.
Whereas from the East, there's a lot more resonance in the way knowledge systems
actually continue or are backward-looking in time. I guess at that point, I felt the
social came *after* the epistemological, and was working out what kind of room I had
in Australian artistic practice to look at the epistemological aspect of the work of art.

AS: These early works are quite formal; they are investigations into the limits and
relationships between the object and knowledge production. But the location for
Manchurian Snow Walk is very specific. I've always read into it a different overlay,
a different set of cultural parameters. What takes you to Manchuria?[3] Why that
location or, indeed, any other location?

JY: My father bought me a ticket to go to Manchuria for completely mysterious
reasons! He's now gone, I can't ask him. However, I think that the interesting thing is
that I have gone to a lot of extreme places like Antarctica or Alice Springs, the desert
and other remote places, to do work that I feel was significant for me. I think that also
has a lot to do with looking at the parameters of being in a diaspora. How far do you
have to bloody go before you can actually make sense of yourself? Standing in that
snow forest, where your mortality was at stake—it was so cold! The transience of the
work, and thus my mark on the world, was at stake; the snow would melt when the
work was done, it sort of disappears.

In fact, it was in Manchuria where nobody had any concept of what I was doing.
It was during a time in China when it was still Socialist Realism; during the making
of that work, the Stars Group hadn't even started I don't think, or maybe just, in 1979.
So, in that sense, nobody knew what I was doing. But it was culturally, perhaps, a way
for me to clarify for myself, my background, my education, my philosophical interests;
and it was a very spontaneous thing. I never actually planned it. I was walking through
this forest, which is just near the hotel, and lo and behold—I was standing in front
of this forest and the idea came to me to do this work.

For some mysterious reason I was really thinking about the difference between the
Copernican system of the universe and the Ptolemaic! The law about Ptolemaic is
that you're the centre of the world, everything revolves around you. Whereas the
Copernican one is where the Earth revolves around the Sun, so you are actually on
the periphery all the time, revolving around the centre. So, this work, finding an
arbitrary spot and looking, walking towards different trees and coming back, made
this arbitrary spot more and more significant every time when I went to a new tree.

This was a very spontaneous idea—to wade through this deep snow in a forest
and make a mark, a temporary mark, which would disappear the next day because
the snow would have melted, but it was a sort of documentation of an event. And
it became of interest because it probably said something to myself, it said that being
from a diaspora you feel as if you're a nobody or nothing, anywhere you go, nobody
knows you. But the more you go elsewhere, the more significantly you feel where you
came from …

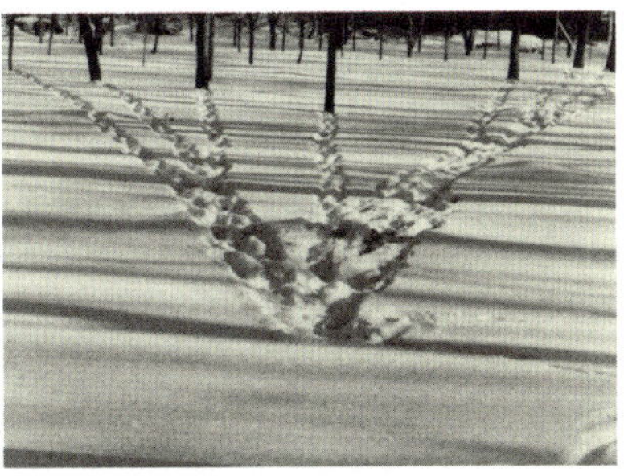

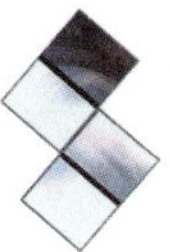

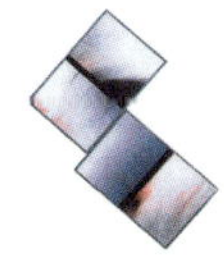

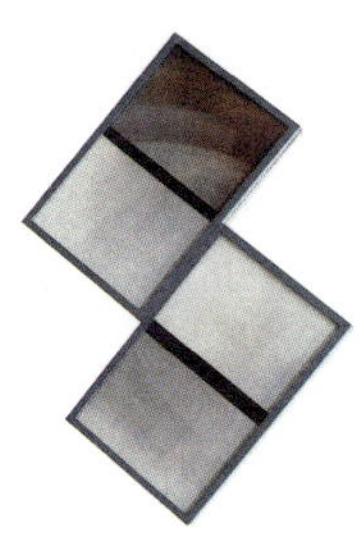

Manchurian Snow Walk (completed) 1979
Silver gelatin print, 60.5 × 80 cm

That Which is in Favour of No Centre 1981
Cibachrome print, two units, 70 × 50 cm each

Detail from *That Which is in Favour
of No Centre* 1981
Cibachrome print, 70 × 50 cm

AS: Were you already aware of these terms, I mean, diaspora probably wasn't yet a word that was widely used for people like yourself?

JY: I was aware of the context but not the term, because I'd shared a lot of conversations with Tillers and he, as you know, is from the Latvian diaspora. He had not known that word at that stage, it was still a few more years before [the writer] David Malouf used this particular word—*diaspora*—and Tillers then did a very significant related work later on.[4] But, we were certainly talking about it, we were talking about immigrants. I said to him, you know, you're a White Russian, so you're ahead of me in the queue, as far as being accepted; I'm an Asian, and I was later on in the queue, and he said, 'I suppose that's true'. So, I was acutely aware of my positioning in the art world; that it was my ambition to somehow make sense of being in the Australian art world. Yet, I knew that because of the political and social prejudices, I was pretty much at the back of the queue, as far as having agency in making art, or even being allowed to make sense of being in any diaspora. It took a few very enlightened curators, especially William Wright, but also Bernice Murphy and Leon Paroissien, who assured me that I could have that sense of agency.

AS: So these are photographic and serial works. They are process driven. But they're also quite sensual, because they point to something human or even existential, in the sense that you're trying to locate the position of the camera, and by default the position of the artist in relationship to a real, distant, and maybe also a psychological, landscape. I understand the logical and serial nature of these early works, but there's also something else that has been niggling me. I've always imagined that they talk about other issues that appear much later in your practice, which have more to do with the political and social experiences of people who are diasporic. Do you think this is the wrong way to look at these works, retrospectively?

JY: When I was making the work, it was like doing visual logic, because it didn't consciously have that social imperative. Yet, I think that social aspect—the diasporan existential world feeling—was inherently there, because somehow my psyche made me do this work, felt it was necessary to do so, and that it felt right. It wasn't just visual logic, the interest in visual logic was the appropriate cognitive means to do this work. It was something else that made me do this, and that is the interesting part. That one is willing to do it. There's a certain trust in making art with some level of intuitive certainty. Now, in retrospect, more than forty years since I did this work—you start to understand that there were psychological and social motivations and ramifications in doing it.

AS: When I came across your work, I was a young artist. There was something quite seductive and powerful about the idea of being able to imagine an Asian body in a landscape. In this set of works, the fact we only see it as a document, and that the physical trace had melted away, resonated with me. Your logical and serial experiments provoked lots of latent political ideas. These ideas are partly what drove a lot of my own photographic and artistic experiments. It was a time when I was trying to come to terms with what Australian art meant, and yours didn't quite fit the stereotype of what 'migrant art' looked like; it wasn't strictly representational.

JY: I get the drift of where you're heading and deeply agree. In a sense, that is what's happening at this point, when you have so many different diasporas in Australia trying to gain a cultural position, it's really a game. It's about people occupying certain spaces in the Australian culture. But the problem is that there's a lack of depth in terms of its art making, let alone an understanding of the different epistemes that we are coming from to actually negotiate within this place called Australia. I think it is too much of a spatial occupation, the way in which the diaspora dialogue has been articulated at this point. Like, 'I just want to be in the art world, and I will do anything to get into the art world, to get a sense of agency'—but the depth of the dialogue is lacking.

AS: Your work is dealing with something much more complicated. This is why it continues to resonate—because it's not just about the occupation of space, it has more to do with the systems of art and knowledge production that govern the entry to those spaces. The work's logical construction, and serial nature, provoked in me a realisation that these issues of knowledge and power are also systems, and drove questions about what kinds of actions are required in order to challenge the system.

JY: I was brought up with a conceptually oriented work process, and the system or paradigm I was challenging was the one based on representation and interpretation. I've never done any work where I felt it was important that the work needed to be interpreted. We live in such a communication obsessed time. For me, then, the process of making a meaningful work is objective, factual. With *Manchurian Snow Walk*, the process of this work is: you do a walk in the forest, with a certain procedure—from spot to tree, back again and so forth. Nobody can say that you were walking somewhere else, you know, or that you were dancing or something, you're actually walking in the forest. So the factuality of the process, which is not open to interpretation, was very important. Any interpretation comes later. But I have come to the understanding that perhaps some interpretations, like the 'diasporan's existential world-feeling' we talked about earlier, may resonate more with the process here. And that's why you were saying that I was very concerned about the clarity of the methodology and the process by which I made a work. All the way from the *Silhouette Paintings* to the *Polychrome Paintings* through to the *Double Ground Paintings*—they were all well thought through; the process is the first order of the work, and that's where I got to trying to develop a sort of method.

1967DISPERSION:
PHOTOGRAPHY, HISTORY AND TECHNO-ABSTRACTION

AS: I'd like to switch gears a little and talk about a body of work which I think illustrates a bit of a shift in your methodology. These are the paintings that refer to oceans and the blue and white check patterns, that refer to refugees, made around a similar time to the *1967Dispersion* paintings.

JY: So the Ocean paintings, the refugee ones that I did, are called the *Refugee Patterns* series (2003), the dispersal ones are *1967Dispersion* (2008). The 'dispersion' is the idea of people dispersing from different parts of the world or to different possible worlds; 1967 was when the riots happened in Hong Kong, so I put those two things together: *1967Dispersion*, people leaving Hong Kong.

It's not exactly made with the same process as *The Double Ground Paintings*. I think that the *Abstract Paintings* were the beginning of me trying to make art out of a concern with technology in a post posthuman context, by placing algorithms in the creative process—which I'm doing in full force now.

In *1967Dispersion* I was giving these abstract paintings a head-on clash with documentary photography. You know, there are these documentary photographs, photographs that people believed were factual and representational truths about the Hong Kong riots. So I was giving them the head-on clash between one panel, which was documentary, and the other panel, which was totally contingent, abstract and presentational. That's one level. The other level about these abstracts was that they

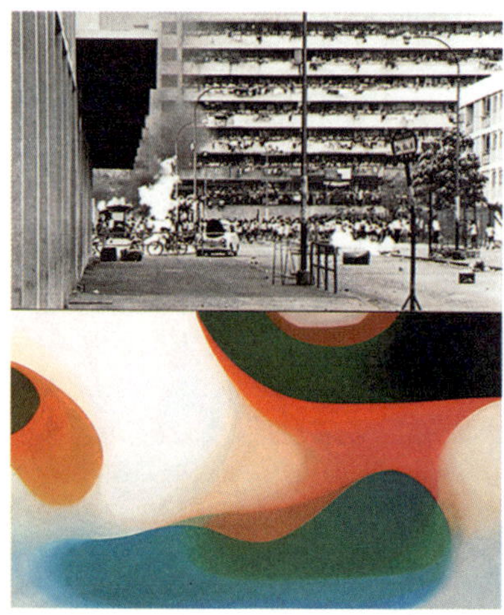

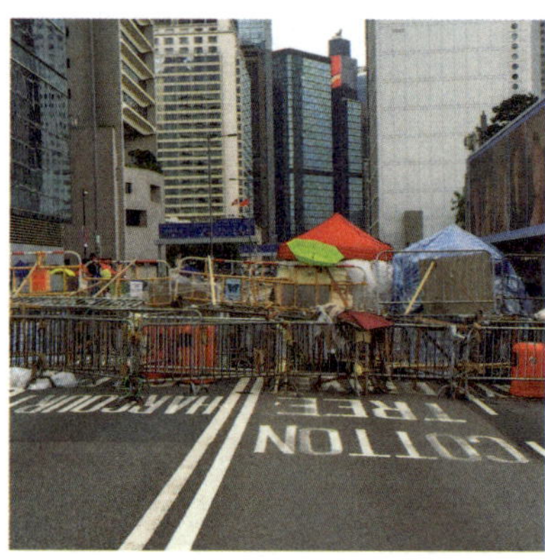

Riot 2008
Digital print and oil on linen, two panels,
170 × 125 cm
Collection of M+, Hong Kong

Umbrella Revolution city blockade
Hong Kong, 2014
Photograph by the artist

looked like American sixties abstraction, bourgeois Greenbergian abstraction, and that had social implications (class distinctions) in relationship to the Hong Kong riots. Workers producing plastic products in a factory started rioting and it was a whole issue of the working class rioting against the bourgeoisie, the factory owners. So, it was just a butting up of the two contexts in the crudest way, because there was no other way to think through how to clash these two ways of working and these two distinct economic classes, to make a work that works. What underpins a lot of this series, and thus the logic of dispersion or diaspora is civil unrest or violence.

AS: That's a methodology but tell me about the source material.

JY: The documentary photographs were all from *South China Morning Post* in 1966 and 1967, when the riots happened. I got permission to reproduce those which were taken by photographers then. The bottom abstract works were from a process that I developed: I was getting 1000 random photos from the internet, scanning them through the computer and transforming them via algorithms into 1000 abstract images. When I started doing this the images were very sweet and looked like American abstraction. So that's why I used those ones.

You're right, in a sense they're very unusual because I started using the documentary photographic part for the History Projects, and then the abstract stuff I started using for the *Abstract Paintings*. They really were a very aggressive abutting of two different processes that I had in my hands. Though, you know, the twentieth century was about the clash between painting and photography—look at [Gerhard] Richter, look at everybody, it's really between photography and painting. But painting was metamorphosising because we were entering into photography, and now we're entering into the digital world, and we're entering into the posthuman through AI and augmentation. I see these works as pretty classically 'twentieth century' in a way, done belatedly in the twenty-first century [laughs]!

AS: I think there's a big shift though, John—why Hong Kong? You could have been sourcing almost any image from anywhere, at this point, that related to globalised violence, for instance the Abu Ghraib images that were beginning to circulate.

What was it about these images? Because they're more than just random, you have classified these works as 'History' paintings.

JY: Yeah, I think you're right, because a lot of the earlier *Double Ground Paintings* implicitly address social issues like Abu Ghraib and the vilification of Persian culture during the time of the Iraq invasion, refugees and so on. So, there were nods to all these situations by being positive. However, by the time of *1967 Dispersion* there was a sense of urgency, it was already almost ten years since Hong Kong returned to China.

I worked with some artists in Hong Kong, and they had a totally different understanding of Hong Kong returning to China at that point. Of course, now they have a different understanding again, as they were in the Umbrella Revolution as well as the Revolution of Our Time. But at that point, in 2007, it was almost like a feeling that something else was going to change, and I really wanted to use this demonstration from '67 as a sort of model towards something that I've felt: that Hong Kong was definitely changing even ten years after the Handover.

AS: You said that you really wanted to use these 1967 images as a model. Where does that model lead you to?

JY: Lead to? That's a really interesting question, because it was like a premonition for me about Hong Kong. But what that model actually led me to was a greater sense of didacticism in my work and a sense of directness. I was using documentary photographs, of course, but I was aware that they're not documentary—you know, rhetorically the documentary points to truth, but we all know about photography, and this presupposes objectivity, which is really just a rhetoric. It's not *really* the real world. So, it led me to become a lot more interested in this urgency, a didactic sense of wanting to show something rather than alluding to it, or doing work just based on the resonance from the past. I used a lot of old Chinese historical allusions that were all really resonances from a non-Western episteme. But here is something in the present, something that needs to be shown. Yet I didn't know how to clearly do this; you can't just say it literally, it's art, you know. I didn't feel that you could just say it. I needed to develop some sort of model to articulate the urgency, the social urgency of things.

AS: I think that the other shift is that this is also part of your history. I mean, this is your hometown, it's not a random selection of images. When I look at your work, there's always a very clear process of selection. And if you're not talking about the historical resonance anymore maybe you're talking about something that's much more sensual, or maybe embodied. That's where I think that the sense of urgency and the sensual go hand in hand with this work. I wonder if there's a shift from the rules and the logic—from the 'scientific' approach to locating the artist in the landscape, to now being more emotionally attached, perhaps?

JY: Yes, ironically. The History Projects, even though they look so rigid and grid-bound, they're almost more poetic than the methodologically structured works like the *Double Ground Paintings*.

BEGINNING THE HISTORY PROJECTS

AS: Let's just pick up from the beginning of the History Projects.

The History Projects are one of your key bodies of work, which have touched on geographies that cross China, Germany, Australia, and cultural contexts impacted by genocide, political violence, and diaspora. Can you tell me about the first set of History Projects—how did you begin them and why?

JY: I think it was with *1967Dispersion*, which is a group of paintings rather than chalk drawings.[5] And that series was done quite a number of years before I started, technically, on the History Projects, which really came to the fore with *Bonhoeffer in Harlem*. But I think that *1967Dispersion* is critical in the sense that it was the first time that I specified a particular event in time in any of my work; also retrospectively, looking at the riots in Hong Kong.

So, even though the form of the work was not the same, there's a sort of intention going back to a very specific event; to look at the event and try to clarify some aspects about that. That violent event also created the diaspora from Hong Kong to Australia. 1967 was probably like a second wave of Hong Kong people coming to Australia— the first wave was the Gold Rush, while the second wave from southern China was probably from Hong Kong in 1967.

AS: Let's talk about *Bonhoeffer* first: at other times you've spoken about Alexander Ochs, your gallerist, as having given you an opportunity, but tell me more about how you were invited to do the work, and what motivated you to take on such a big idea?

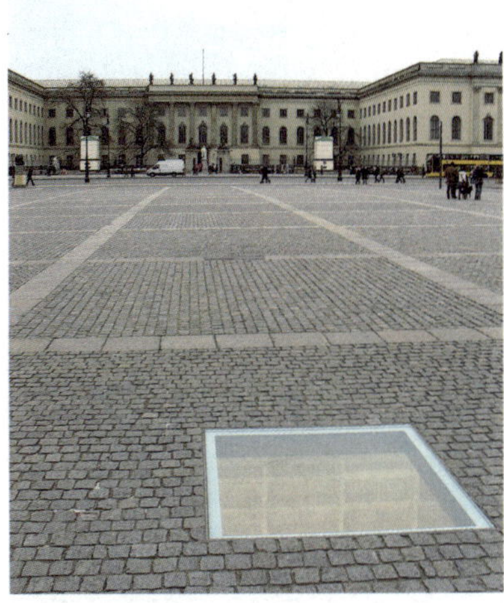

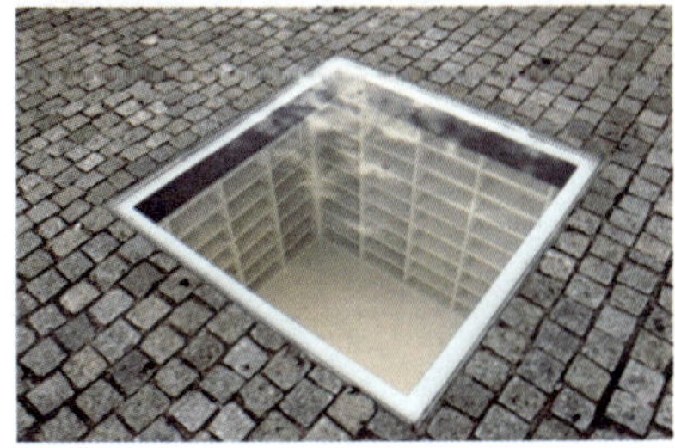

Micha Ullman (1939–)
The Empty Library 1995
Bebelplatz, Berlin
Photograph by the artist
Artist's note: The work acts as a site of remembrance for the Nazi book burnings of May 1933.

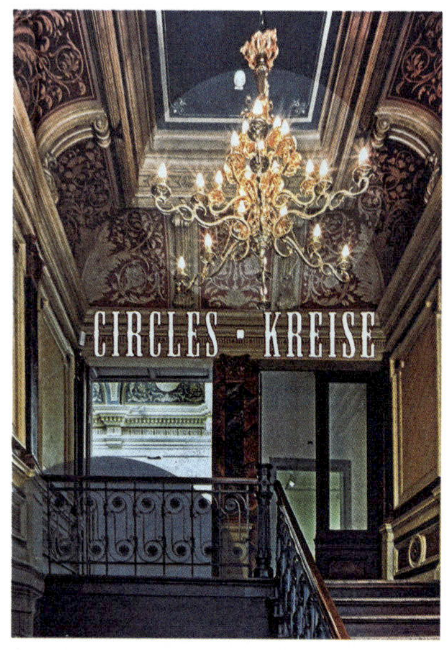

Circles exhibition catalogue
Bamberg, 2013

JY: I think you know Alexander Ochs invited me to Berlin. Years prior, I already had an interest in contemporary German art, meeting up with Erhard Klein (the gallerist who showed [Sigmar] Polke) and having several meetings (and getting drunk!) with Martin Kippenberger—but that was Koln, very different from the politics of Berlin. At that time, Ochs was the biggest gallerist promoting contemporary Chinese art in Europe. But I didn't feel particularly comfortable doing the sort of 'Chinese art' that he was interested in, whether political art or cynical art or more conceptual approaches—you know, like Fang Lijun, Yang Shaobin or even Xu Bing and Yin Xiuzhen, all artists he was dealing with. I felt I was already living a more transcultural life than those people, and I really wanted to do something very specifically located in Germany. So, he invited me to actually go spend some weeks in Berlin first, then go back to Australia and think about a project.

I thought of lots of different projects for Berlin, based on my impressions of it, looking at Walter Benjamin, Robert Musil, the Fassbinder Foundation too, and of course events of World War II. In retrospect, another great inspiration was seeing Micha Ullman's *The Empty Library* [1995] at Bebelplatz—truly a masterpiece. But ultimately, I stumbled on the *Bonhoeffer* project by chance, just going with Ochs into this church in the Tiergarten; and he told me Bonhoeffer was actually ordained there. I found that historically interesting, the more I got into it. I looked at the church and I thought it was such a monocultural Lutheran church. It was bare, with nothing on the walls, and I really wanted to shift the frame of looking at that church, so I invited all these people and wanted to do a tapestry woven by Dolma Lob Sang in Nepal.

I gave you a very descriptive answer, but I think I was trying to look at Berlin as a monocultural place and shifting the frame of that church into a more multicultural way of looking, I guess.

AS: It's a very specific subject, isn't it? It's not just about multiculturalism. It's also dealing with German history. Was there something else that you were attracted to in the figure of Bonhoeffer—or was it simply the church, and you wanting to turn it into a different kind of space?

JY: I must admit that it was also friendship with Alexander. We had discussed the commercialisation of the art world, particularly through [the art fair] Art Basel and all that, and he was very dissatisfied. He was heading towards a more ethical position, which resulted in not wanting to show at any art galleries or fairs. Instead he wanted to show art in churches, as he did in Bamberg some years later, then in a significant way in Berlin. I really took that on board to a degree and I felt that there probably was an ethical dimension that I needed to look at, when making.

AS: What exactly was this ethical dimension for you?

JY: I felt someone like Bonhoeffer had made a decision to defend a group of people (the Jewish people) in the Third Reich, and was subsequently hanged for it. This story pointed to a different modality in working in art at that point, you know.

AS: Do you have a particular affinity to the Jewish context?

JY: Not really. I mean, you know my wife is partly Jewish. It was just a question of somebody like Bonhoeffer leaving his own episteme, making a very courageous ethical decision—contrary to his own deeply held Christian values—to assassinate someone. I think that interested me, but then it also bore a lot of fruit in making art in that

context. It led me to throw away my sense of self as an artist who always insists on creating
something that is precise and perfect. Through Tibetans weaving this tapestry in Nepal,
which was a very poor place, it allowed me to accept the fact that things that can be created
don't necessarily have to be formally perfect. In fact, I'm not necessarily just the creator of
all these works. I might have come up with the concept, but things changed so much in the
process of the weaving that it actually became something else altogether. That was a very
big change.

AS: What kind of research went into this project? How did you go about it? What
decisions went into the image selection and the construction of the works?

JY: I sort of approached it like a filmmaker. Of course, there are a set of narratives about
a person's life or what they did. But I really listened to the things that resonated in the
whole narrative, not just in Bonhoeffer's own writings, but the sentences and the voices
that made sense to me at that point. That's why in many of my drawings there's a lot of
repetition. It's like an act of teaching myself something new in terms of value, and I think
that's how I actually chose words or sentences, ideas or concepts to work with.

AS: These works are also very connected to ideas about transculturalism that you
explore at other times. If you look at some of the blackboard drawings, there are
inscriptions or quotations in German and also Chinese. What's going on there?

JY: Well, that was definitely for the context of Euramerican art in Australia, since up to
that point I hadn't seen many works which are done bilingually or trilingually in Australia.
So, I think that was important for me, to use a multilingual context for making art. I think
that's an important thing. But once you do that, you realise that there's incompleteness in
comprehension; not many people can actually completely understand those works because
some languages they don't know and, you know, a Chinese may not know German and
vice versa. So there's very interesting lapses or gaps in the work, which one could never
really grasp as a whole.

AS: With the Chinese inscriptions, what is being written?

JY: Some of them are from translations from his works, and at other times they are sort
of echoes from earlier works. There are cross-project echoes that go on in different
languages, when they make sense in the particular narrative that I'm working on.

AS: These black drawings use a very particular material, especially in the German art
historical context. What is your relationship with the work of Joseph Beuys? Is he an artist
that you were channeling at this time?

JY: I think Joseph Beuys is incredibly important. But also, the didacticism used in
Rudolf Steiner's work as well. That sort of spiritualism. Both of them were critical in the
development of Euramerican modernism—Steiner in relationship to Theosophy, and Beuys'
ethical dimension, the value of care, which I found very instructive, and I still feel that he's
probably very underrated. You know, I think he's the new [Johann Wolfgang von] Goethe
of Germany, but as a philosopher artist, he's also one of the founders of the Green Party,
which has such ramifications nowadays. So, I think that he probably represented somebody
who's sort of universally interested in the world, rather than being compartmentalised into
any sort of specific modernist context. Not that that's necessarily possible anymore, but
I think that Beuys was really quite special in that way.

AS: Was Beuys also connected to your ethical awakening? Correct me if I'm wrong, but
I think this was the first time that you were using this material?

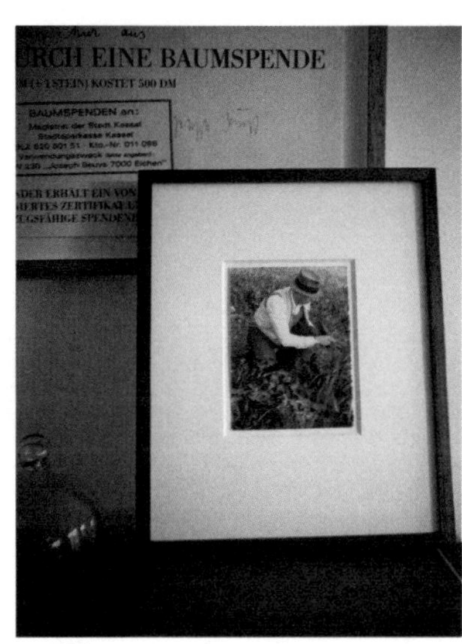

Buby Durini (1924–)
The Shaman of Art – Joseph Beuys 1972
(background)
Joseph Beuys (1921–1986)
7000 Eichen in Kassel 1982 (foreground)
Installation view, the artist's home,
Melbourne, 2021

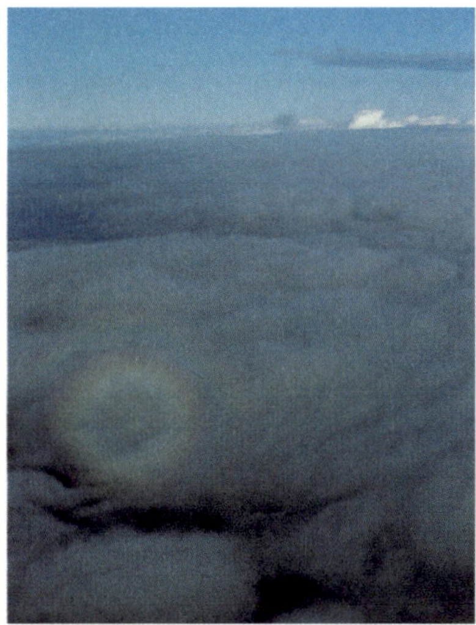

'Buddha's Ray' captured by the artist in transit from Cologne to Berlin, 2008

JY: It was the first time. It was also the first time that I didn't have any professional motivations in doing so.

AS: I find these works interesting because there is a question of legibility emerging in these drawings. I imagine people are approaching these works with multilingual modalities, perhaps with a grasp of German or Chinese but not necessarily both; or with a grasp of neither but an understanding of the relationship of the material (the blackboard and chalk) to their own education experience; or with an understanding of Beuys, and his ideas about the generative opportunity of education and the world. It raises interesting questions about legibility, and your processes of abstraction.

The whole project consists of different aesthetic approaches—these black board drawings, photographic reproductions, painterly abstractions and, for the centerpiece, a commissioned tapestry. Let's discuss your ideas of abstraction, and how you choose the various source materials that go into a work.

JY: Definitely. I mean, that's the reason I did this project, because he took an understanding from a transcultural situation, like when he was in Harlem, went back to Germany, and understood that the Jews were being persecuted like Black Americans were in the United States. The fact that something ethical was learnt from a transcultural situation was critical in making this work, and that's where I think it fits like a jigsaw puzzle for me, personally.

AS: What is it that brought you to think about Nanjing after Nazi Germany?

JY: Before I went to Germany, on Och's invitation to do [the citywide exhibition project] 'Berlin Reflections', as I mentioned earlier, I did some thorough research about Berlin. I also stumbled onto the story of a person called John Rabe, who was the man who saved 300,000 Chinese at the Nanjing Massacre in 1937. I did a little bit of research about that. I was in Nanjing previously because I had made another tapestry called *Open World* (2005). But when I was in Nanjing the Massacre Museum was closed, so I never got to see it.

So, previously being in Nanjing wasn't the inspiration for me to do this work *Safety Zone*. It was actually being in Berlin. I saw this crazy rainbow in the sky, a perfectly round rainbow as I was flying from Cologne to Berlin. This rainbow was a complete circle, which I recalled Chinese people call 'Buddha's Ray', and the interesting thing is that it reminded me that after John Rabe saved all these citizens in Nanjing, the Chinese used to call him the 'living Buddha of China'. So I just put the two ideas together, and I felt the synchronic moment must be telling me to do something.

These are things in our makeup which I really love—the fact that things are initiated by chance, and synchronic moments make you draw lateral relationships. And it takes a facilitator like Ochs and a researcher like Sylvia Volz, who believed that there was a point to this sort of synchronicity to act on it, buying me a train ticket to go and meet up with John Rabe's grandson, Dr Thomas Rabe. I learnt a lot of stories about the Nanjing Massacre, and that's where all the unpublished information I used in the work came from.

AS: When did you start applying the term 'History Projects' to these projects? Was this a conscious decision as you were doing them or was it something that happened after you had a number of works?

JY: I think probably around the time when I did *1866: The Worlds of Lowe Kong Meng and Jong Ah Siug*. I knew that I really wanted to do a visualisation of the history of the Chinese in Australia. I think that was when I thought of doing a series of projects related to Chinese Australian history, and that's when the notion of history actually became far more prevalent for me.

AS: What makes you turn to Chinese Australian history? This is a very decisive move; I think in 2015? Your earlier works were referring to classical and intellectual traditions that obliquely relate to the aesthetic influence of China, then, all of a sudden there is a shift toward the social history of Chinese Australians?

JY: Well, like I was saying, I felt we needed the Chinese Australian history and that this history needed to be written or visualised by Chinese Australians. I really felt there was a rift between narratives by historians, where there was a need for a certain factual accuracy or truth, and making art or literature in relation to that. I looked at people who turned historical narratives into artistic form, for example the writings of Brian Castro—such as his *Birds of Passage*, or Peter Carey in relation to Ned Kelly. I also got the Australia Council Fellowship to do research about the history of the Chinese in Australia. I had two or three researchers working with me for a whole year and a half; we found 105 very interesting narratives of the Chinese in Australia, going from 1840 onwards. So, I think there was a methodological change when that happened, when the momentum of research came along, I really had to develop a systematic method of creating works in relation to the vast amount of information that was being researched. This was not predicated so much on how to properly use iconic historic Chinese cultural imagery, like in the *Double Ground Paintings*, but somehow learning or re-imagining those significant narratives we have discovered.

AS: I remember we spoke a few years back about the fact that you were engaging with a number of younger historians in this project. You've used researchers before, but this, I think is a more conscious political decision to work with young people. What was your underlying research methodology, and what was your relationship to these historians?

JY: We were very ambitious, we actually had a small team first, about three people inside the studio. Then we got some crazy idea of farming out the research. We got a team of people in India to start looking at the history of the Chinese in Australia online! Which they did to a certain degree, but it failed because they just couldn't do that level of deep research from so far away. There was a lot of empirical research that needed to be done, field work. So then we allocated one person per state, who we contracted to research and find narratives about the history of the Chinese in those states. And of course, I also met up with a lot of historians at the Dragon Tails conferences at that stage.[6] I met so many passionate historians, particularly Kate Bagnall, John Fitzgerald and many others, without whom there wouldn't be a chapter on Chinese in Australia in Australian history. But when I talked to some of these historians, they also felt that different ways of writing and visualising this history was very important for the future.

AS: Do you think that by this time your method had changed? Have your ideas about diaspora also changed through these projects?

JY: Well, I learnt a lot more from outside my own experience of coming to Australia. I also learnt that diasporas change because people from different classes in China came to Australia, for example there were educated political dissidents and those who came as indentured labor, who were illiterate. I learned that, certainly, the notion of the Chinese diaspora in Australia wasn't the one that had been painted by White Australia—that we were all abject miners, looking to profit from finding gold. The reason why some men came to Australia was not only to profit; some of the young

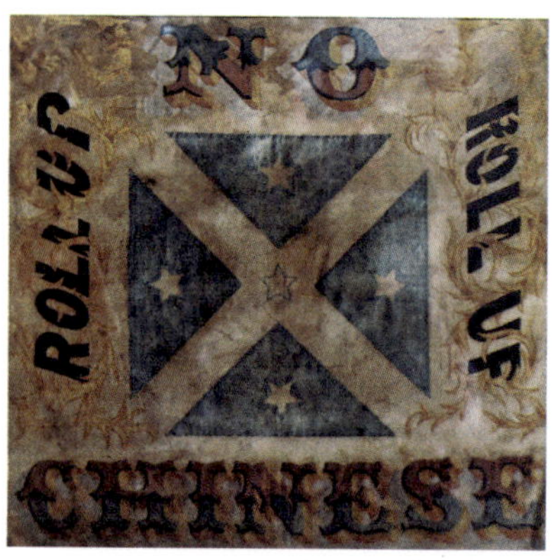

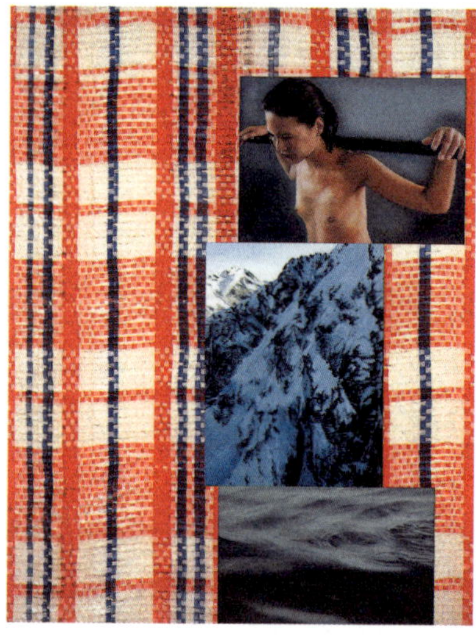

Anonymous
Roll Up No Chinese 1861
Banner, 120 × 120 cm
Collection of Lambing Flat Folk Museum,
Hilltops Council, New South Wales

Red Grid 2003
Digital print and oil on linen, 200 × 150 cm

people came to Australia, or to San Francisco, as a rite of passage. They would leave southern China, go to San Francisco or Ballarat, and then come to hopefully find enough money to go back to southern China, marry and settle down. Some never did of course. So there were a lot of characterisations in the history, within popular understanding, that needed to be recast. And of course, for example, this particular work—*1866*—was a way of bookending the two different classes of Chinese present at that time: a very successful merchant and a very abject situation, where a near illiterate young man was cast as insane and locked up for the rest of his days.

AS: Does your intellectual understanding of diaspora change?

JY: Definitely, and even my education—like the latitude of people and their reasons for coming to Australia, there were just so many different contexts.

AS: You describe the History Projects as being almost more poetic than rigid—what you just called ambiguous, poetic ways of dealing with images. But there's also something, perhaps, that is reacting to the world that's going on around you. There's a shift from the poetic towards archival kinds of approaches to histories. You're working with historians, and, with the Chinese Australian projects, you're dealing with the political framings by identifying the absence of Chinese people in the narrative of Australia, or dealing with real life situations of dispersion. I suggest that these works are somewhat autobiographical and connected to real social histories.

JY: Well, I felt that it was a learning process by that stage. I didn't forget what I learnt about letting go of my ego and the autonomy of the artist, and in *Bonhoeffer* and the idea of *Safety Zone*—of atonement and such ethical aspects. But I think that with this group there were two ideas that I was learning from the Chinese diaspora: the idea of benevolence and the objective creation of artworks.

I must say that I know the narrative of the Lambing Flat Riots was originally your idea, at 4A; that you had actually wanted to do this show for a long time. We picked up on that and ran with it, and that was the perfect time for me to learn from doing that show because it was about the benevolence of the Roberts family who housed all these Chinese miners. I think that was brilliant insight on your part, to look at that, but I suspect that you were probably waiting to find the right artists to do the project, and it had to take time.

AS: I remember that. One of the things I was very interested in exploring with respect to *Lambing Flat* was historical reenactment and what that means in the twenty-first century, and how historical reenactments of such terrible race-based violence function, as remembrance, as a warning. And, ultimately, who is it for? Which I suppose is somewhat similar to the processes of abstraction and fragmentation, and the issues of legibility and opacity and all those things that we see in your work.

I wonder whether your interest in the political and historical reality of Chinese Australia begins to seep into the highly classical, aesthetic, intellectual position that you were developing two decades prior. I sense that in the *Refugee Patterns* series, which you began around 2001 and 2002. These works, with their interwoven grids, of red, blue and white—reminiscent of the heavy-duty bags that lots of migrants of a particular class are familiar with—become very specific abstractions, which resonate with the politics of that moment. It's the time of the Tampa Incident. If we recall, the captain of the Tampa was also faced with a perverse ethical dilemma.

JY: Oh, totally. I absolutely felt there was a relationship but I've always shied away from a literal tackling of any political circumstance—that's the job of the media, which is based on a short temporal cycle. That's why, for example, the *Persian Paintings* were done during the Iraq War, Abu Ghraib, but I only mentioned the situation in the catalogue, not in the works.[7]

Funnily enough, the 'Refugee' patterns are very sweet. But there's nothing sweet about being a refugee. Do I think now that this sort of irony is enough? No. But, I think that what was lacking at that point, in terms of my insight, was that there was a rift between what I considered as being aesthetic and what I considered as being ethical, and now I just see those as one. If there is an ethical position I need to take, I think the aesthetic just follows. I don't believe there is this realm of the aesthetics of beauty, because as far as I'm concerned, the beauty is the good, now it's got nothing to do with this artificial idea of an idealised sense of perceptual configuration which encapsulates 'the beautiful'. I guess I've grown older in understanding this. In that sense, there is definitely a political relationship, but I think the way I tackled it was a lot more head-on with the History Projects.

TO LIVE IN THE PRESENT

AS: One of the things that I learnt by looking at your practice was that it didn't give me the exact answer that I was looking for. Yet, I think that we've arrived at very similar expectations of the role of art and history with respect to experiences of diaspora. You have arrived at this position from a more classical education, expressed through art history, aesthetics and philosophy, compared to say the cultural studies that people of my generation experienced.

I wonder, however, whether the concepts of diaspora have changed. Right from the beginning until now, the thing that I think is underlying all your work is actually the issue of diaspora. But even now, when we think about the social history side of the diaspora, there's something quite beautiful about the intellectual position of melancholia and how we can approach reading and writing these types of histories of place and position.

JY: We were talking about different epistemes and the interest in knowledge paradigms. If you look at the early works like the *Silhouette Paintings*, the images were appropriated only from one person, André Derain, as opposed to any other appropriation people were doing. Derain is this totally unpopular artist who was not a modernist anymore, because he went back into a sort of regressive historicism. His paintings were the antithesis of works appropriated by Australian 'appropriation' artists in the 1980s; paintings or images which were often curatorially expedient, valorised—bellwether works. Derain was certainly not very popular by the 1980s. Yet the reason I was interested was because it felt Chinese or sort of othered. It felt as if he was backward looking, in some sort of cyclical time rather than a uni-directional modernist, progressive time. And, I must say, it took bit of courage to use his work, because nobody in Australia knew why I was using this artist's images, as they were so unpopular.

So, if you want to talk about having different epistemes or presenting different epistemes in our cultural context, I think that right from the start I was interested in presenting something that had a different conception of time, with Derain's regressive, arcadian or 'classicist' paintings. Derain's conception of time changed radically after

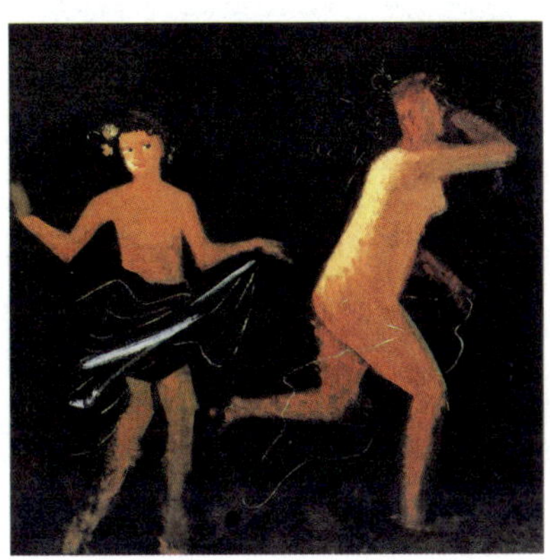

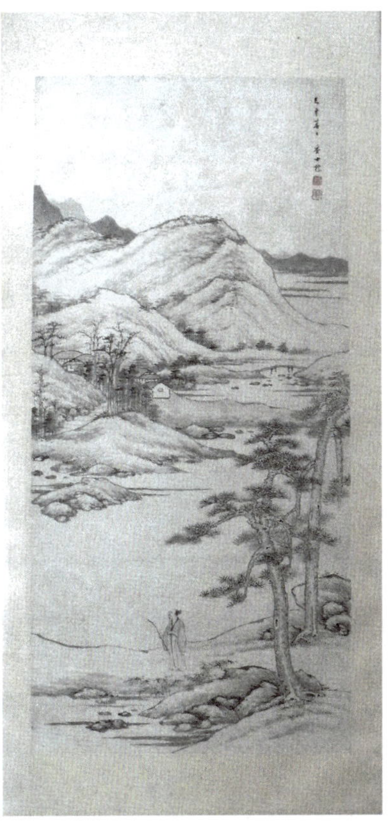

André Derain (1880–1954)
Black Binge 1943
Oil on canvas

Zha Shibiao 查士標 (1615–1698)
Landscape c. 1650
Ink on rice paper, 124 × 61cm
Collection of the artist

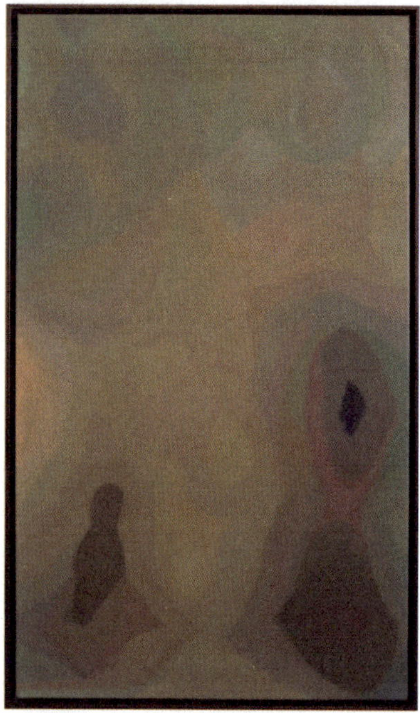

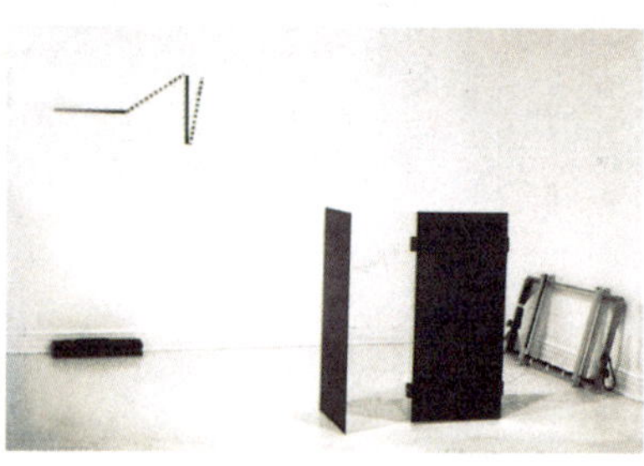

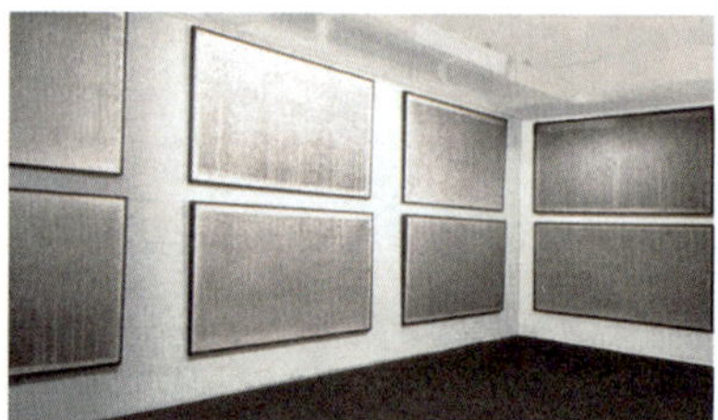

Northern Song V 2007
Oil on linen, 90 × 50 cm

Synchronic Screen 1980
Glass and steel hinged screen, positive and
negative film on aluminum, hardbound
instruction manual, dimensions variable

Drawing in Ten Parts 1981
Pencil on paper, ten units, 127 × 228 cm each

his Fauvist period. His later 'classicist' works were more akin to the Greek-Arcadian conception of time, with some qualification, as his work also incorporated a French sense of subjectivity contrary to fascist imagery. Derain's works had a sort of resonance with Chinese ink painting, which looks 'back' to an archaic time rather than being progressive. In that sense, making the *Silhouette Paintings* was a very epistemological statement.

AS: Tell me about your pre-university education—for instance, where does this understanding of the ancient Chinese conception of time come from?

JY: I think it came from just having Chinese paintings in my home as I was growing up. This sort of archaism and backward-looking sensibility I found incredibly resonant, even when they were hanging in my home.

You know, I think that that's where the power of Chinese art really is—the ability to draw you into this notion of time that was not Western. You could look at it and you could somehow imagine a different sense of time about it. So, I guess it was just from where I grew up, from the environment.

AS: There's something also particular and researched about your interest in Chinese painting though. You have referenced Song painting in other works, so do you think that this is just by exposure? Not every Chinese person has Chinese paintings on the walls and an understanding of, say, Song Dynasty painting!

JY: I think I know where you're heading, and it's a sort of diasporic intersectionality!

Yes, I did have the privilege of growing up with these evocative Qing Dynasty ink paintings—by Zha Shibiao, for example, or calligraphy by Kang Youwei.[8] Good ink paintings hanging on the walls. When I was growing up, there were so many fascinating works, the Song Dynasty ones were actually copies, as I discovered, but the Qing paintings and other calligraphy were authentic works. I think that growing up with them is where I naturally absorbed this different sense of time.

AS: The images in *1967Dispersion* are quite dramatic, they're not generalised abstract images; as you've said, they rely on the news and the rhetoric of documentary photography. Was it a traumatic transition from Hong Kong to Australia?

JY: Totally. The paradigmatic shift, in my worldviews, was quite distinct. It was traumatic if only for the fact that nobody actually understood what my worldview was, where it came from. If people in Australia understood what existential position and worldview I had, I don't think it would have been as traumatic. It was the shock of being in Australia, and people's unwillingness to learn and understand other worldviews, that really disturbed me. I think that people were quite convinced that being in Australia was the best place to be, 'the lucky country'. And that 'you come to us', you know.

AS: Were you thinking of this as a young person though?

JY: Of course I was thinking of that. I was very resentful of the fact that everywhere you went you had to go to them, or they felt that the other diasporan had to come to them. Somehow, by having to do that, you lose your sense of certainty; you feel nobody is quite willing to understand your world. So, you lose your sense of certainty, except for memory of course.

I thank you very much for this question. Because, actually, I think it gives me some hint as to how to think about trauma in relationship with diasporans in the future. You know, it's not just historical circumstances of violence or war that causes trauma in the diaspora. It's the disjunction and the unwillingness of a certain population to imagine themselves in your position.

AS: This is one of the ways I've read *Manchurian Snow Walk* (1979) and also the early serial photography: there is an existential questioning, trying to position yourself in view. And even if you have done this by a rules-based method, a methodical model in a sense, it's trying to locate the relationship between the landscape and the camera. Even the I Ching-based processes in *Synchronic Screen* (1980) and the tai chi drawing practice in *Drawing in Ten Parts* (1981) I read as trying to locate a sense of self within nature, within your surroundings. This is very different to other forms of practice by diasporan artists who may be more about representing their cultural difference.

JY: Probably, I mean, the process was sort of advocating for Chinese practices or values. It was probably a way for me to work out my existential position living in Australia. But I was aware that there were modernists using the I Ching, like John Cage; or Nam June Paik—who I spoke with several times in Koln, and who was also a good calligrapher. There was this knowledge of the I Ching amongst some white artists, even in Australia, in the 1960s and 1970s. So it was like a door that was slightly ajar, within the context of art, that I could put my toe in, you know, the door to see whether I can participate with my own worldview.

It's all very personal. I can't imagine how to make work that is purely abstracted. Yet there is objectivity in the work of course. But the personal, I often feel it's my own quest for individuation, so I rarely feel it has relevance to others, or its relevance, if there is any, is coincidental. Like the *1967Dispersion* works—I identify more with those American abstraction panels in the paintings because my upbringing in Hong Kong was very privileged, and I hated that privilege in a way. In that sense, creating a head-on clash between that abstraction and the documentary photographs—which I saw was really the working class—was actually a very personal sort of ambivalence on my part. Yet, I don't really want to say that; it's not my place as an artist to flaunt my personal problems. I'm here to clarify the use of visuality.

AS: I also see Barnett Newman in some of the early works. That's what led me to the thinking around the existential positioning.

JY: Your observations are very precise because the early works, like the *Silhouette Paintings*, are definitely Newman; because Newman's got this thing called the 'zip', which is the present, and it's actually very Jewish. It's like you have to come to a recognition of the past in order to be able to live in the present.

And that is one thing that I learnt from doing *Safety Zone*, for example, that in World War II, unlike the Germans who came to terms with their past, through atoning for the atrocities in the Holocaust, the Japanese population never did. They didn't admit to, say, the Nanjing Massacre; this event was never in schoolbooks in Japan. And because they couldn't admit to or atone for the past they could never live in the present.

So, the Japanese Zeitgeist actually produced a future to dwell in—all the time in fantasy, you know, whereas the Germans are actually living very much in the present now, because they've atoned for the past. So, I mean, that's definitely a Barnett Newman 'zip', in a way, the ability to live in the present.

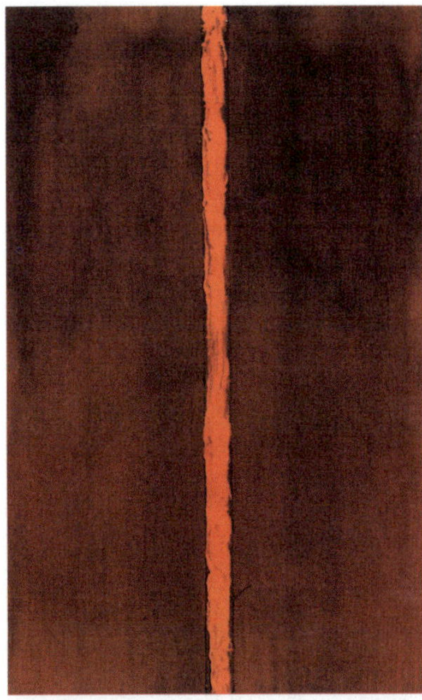

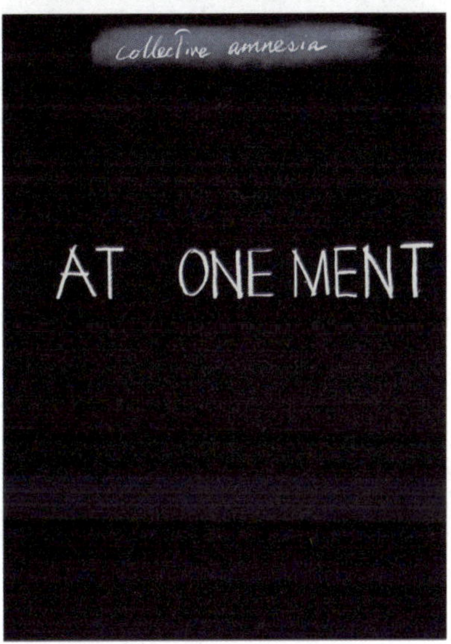

Barnett Newman (1905–1970)
Onement I 1948
Oil and masking tape on canvas, 69.2 × 41.2 cm
Collection of Museum of Modern Art,
New York

Atonement 2010
Chalk on blackboard-painted archival
cotton paper, 100 × 70 cm

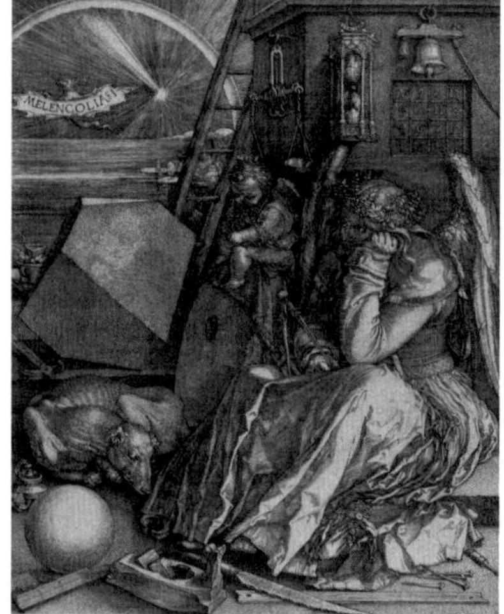

Albrecht Dürer (1471–1528)
Melencolia I 1514
Engraving, Edition ii of two states,
23.9 × 18.9 cm platemark;
34.0 × 27.0 cm sheet
Collection of Art Gallery of New South Wales,
Sydney, purchased with funds provided by the
Tony Gilbert Bequest, 2013

DIASPORA AND MELANCHOLY

AS: Would you say, that all your History Projects have to do with histories of diaspora?

JY: Absolutely, but of course in different modalities. I think that all the History Projects have to do with memory. The most important thing about the diaspora is not space, it's not going from one place to another—the most important thing is memory. Because, for us, memory is in the present. It exists at the same time as the present; it determines everything that we do. And in that sense, I think that this is something very unique, because we can't say that we have any specific claim to land, like Indigenous people do. Diasporans only have claim to their memories. And I think that this is a potential strength, but it's also a potential problem in the future.

AS: Can we talk about the relationship between diaspora and melancholy? It's a reference to Benjamin that curator Terence Maloon brought up in a dialogue between you and Jacqueline Lo at an exhibition that included some of your history paintings in 2013.[9]

JY: I think one of the crucial things about melancholy is that there's always a sense of loss. I've discussed this with Brian Castro, as well; he was quite deeply interested in Benjamin and particularly in the notion of melancholy.[10] Melancholy can also be a sort of positive sense too, in which you have this whole sea of plurality that is very different from a literal association. You know, there's a distance between you and the plural sea of possibilities out there, whether it's in the past or whether it's a potential in the future. I think melancholy is an acceptance of the ocean of plurality. It doesn't necessarily have to be abject loss or emotively melancholic in the traditional sense of the word. I think I see sublimity in the immense plurality which diasporans may actually experience.

AS: After that talk, I went back to look at some of your earlier paintings, like the *Double Ground Paintings*, and wondered whether or not melancholia was part of these strategies from the earliest paintings—were you dealing with diaspora all the way along?

JY: The *Double Ground Paintings* were always describing where all these images lie. Whether they want to have historical resonance or whether they're kitsch, it's a process of describing where things lie, in a clearer way. But when you do that, you sort of leave things alone. You know, they're out here, and they're laid out as they are. And in that sense, it's melancholic. But maybe now it's shifted, I've wound it up one more notch in the History Projects, where you're starting to look at the emotive side, you're starting to look at trauma, you're starting to look at benevolence—and that's where the poetic comes in as well. You're starting to look at these human qualities in a melancholy way, not just intellectually, like the *Double Ground Paintings*, but in an engaged and embodied way. If you look at cultural values or cultural images in a plural way, that's just looking at something from a distance, you know—you push yourself away, as if to say, I'm just trying to clarify all these situations. Whereas now, with the History Projects, they're actually highly emotive, highly charged situations of trauma, violence and benevolence. I think the melancholy is somehow different; you're submerged within that sea of emotions and affect.

I've also changed a bit too. I was really forced to understand, since *Bonhoeffer in Harlem*, that when you cross cultures, you need to have some universal human values. I don't necessarily believe that different epistemologies are incommensurate and need different ethics, for example. Now, I really feel that the resolution to transculturalism is that we need to have a sense of empathy with the other person, to understand that violence is done to them, or agency is taken away or denied to them. We need to help them.

AS: Let me ask you about your interest in other artists: you are also a collector, and there has always seemed to be an intellectual relationship between what you collect and your own work. We've discussed Ian Fairweather extensively over the years[11], but we've never really discussed Robert Rauschenberg.

For both these artists, there's an aesthetic play within their work, but there's also a political and social context from which they emerge. I have a sense that you're interested in Fairweather because he's such an anomaly; he doesn't fit into the establishment, he wasn't really part of the scene. He isn't even technically an Australian artist, even though the establishment appears to have adopted him, and maybe slightly sanitised him. He's been inserted into the Australian history, but when you read his biographies, I wonder if he ever really belongs.

JY: Yes, I think you're absolutely right. The interesting thing about Fairweather is that he didn't fit. Because of his travels in China and learning Chinese, and feeling 'Chinese', I'm sure—through his interest in calligraphy and other activities, like translating the *Drunken Buddha*, he feels there is a part of him which is Chinese— and that just didn't fit in the Australia of that time. There was a part of him that nobody understood. It just didn't matter what he did. His only resolution was to become a hermit and do this self-imposed exile. Which brings me to this interesting proposition—that I'm interested in him because he's a model for me, because I feel that whatever is important might not be realised for twenty years, or for fifty or 200 years. But somehow, somewhere along the way, it gets realised—not with the word 'appreciation', but I mean, realised in the sense of being understood. And I think we're starting to have this sort of multicultural society in Australia, which finally understands Fairweather for who he was, because he held two cultures deeply in his consciousness.

AS: I don't think we've ever spoken of Rauschenberg in the past. I can see the interest in the image construction, and the systems of image proliferation in his work that would be interesting to you. We are talking about an artist who really attempted to straddle different worlds and open a way of communicating beyond Cold War dichotomies, especially through his ideas of cultural exchange and his *Rauschenburg Overseas Cultural Interchange* projects.[12] I wonder if your interest is also in his politics?

JY: Yes, I'm sure he had the same depth of ambitions in the 1960s decade of male dominated art as Andy Warhol or Jasper Johns had. You know, whereas Warhol just stuck completely to capitalism, I think Rauschenberg somehow tried to find a way out, through his plural understanding of things in concurrent ways, as John Cage probably did. The most interesting part of his practice, I find, was his travels to all the 'Stans', making the fabric works—and that's why I bought one, with the little money that I had at that point. It's not worth much now, that work, I don't know why!

People talk about xenophobia—I think that for me, or for Rauschenberg, and maybe for you, there is actually a *xenophilia*. There's a love for difference rather than the other way round, this is the interesting thing I find about him. Whereas, Warhol, because he kissed capitalism so closely, he couldn't look at the love of the other at all, even though he was gay himself, but the interesting thing was that Rauschenberg quite obviously was xenophilic.

AS: So this is an attitude towards the transcultural as well?

JY: Yes, like John Cage, and Fluxus as well. I think this is the same attitude.

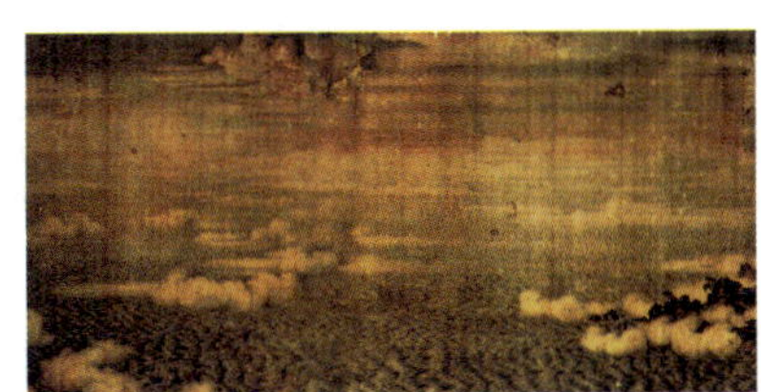

Giuseppe Castiglione
(Lang Shining 郎世寧, 1688–1766)
Rising Sun Against Oceanic Sky 海天旭日圖
c. 1765
Ink and colour on silk, 93.7 × 182.2 cm
Collection of The Palace Museum, Beijing

AS: Australia's alignment with Euramerica is part of its political history, and it has obscured a more complicated understanding of the other historical, political and cultural forces that are fundamental to a broader participation in Asia. We lack the ability to see the nuance, maybe because Australia is monolingual. I wonder if this also plays into the kinds of questions that you and I have had about White Australia's challenge in engaging with its own Indigenous, First Nations as well as migrant histories?

JY: Do you think this is only a question of time? I find now in Australia, you have the beginnings of serious research on, for example, something as regionally specific as the history of Hong Kong art—the specificity of 'Hong Kong', not just as a place but as a *concept*. That would have been totally unheard of a couple of decades back. Back then were people doing this? They might have been researching Chinese contemporary art, but certainly nothing as specific as Hong Kong. So do you think with that level of scholarship, as Australia becomes more multiculturally conscious, that the dominant population will have a better sense in time?

Thinking of artists' engagement, you've got two types: the artists that are just culturally interested, so they will engage anyway, regardless of politics; then you've got a majority who are Euramerican-centric, and still consider a cultural engagement or professional pathway in that direction, due potentially to a subscription to historical national politics.

AS: Yes, I think it's not just a question of time, as you say, there's also curiosity. But I am a little troubled by the phrase: 'as Australia becomes a lot more multiculturally conscious', because Australia has been aware of its multicultural context since 1901—it federated to deal with the so-called 'problem'! Race politics and fear drove so much of the discussion in the lead up to Federation, we should see it as one of the founding cornerstones of Australian modernity. So, I don't quite understand when people say that they're just becoming aware of the existence of other people from other cultures! But now I believe that it requires representation not acceptance. And this is probably what drew both of us to the work of 4A all those years ago.

We need a renewed imagination when it comes to these issues. I'm always drawn to Arjun Appadurai's use of the word 'imagination' when it comes to issues of structure and power. He suggests that 'social exclusion is ever more tied to epistemological exclusion'[13] and that how we address the biases found within the structure of discourse—which 'experts' we rely on and which voices we deem of value; which forms of art reach outside of their immediate locales of production and thinking; which narratives are privileged, and why—requires different kinds of imagination to break and to become more equitable, closer to reality perhaps? Perhaps this resonates with what you described earlier about the ethical questions you faced in relation to the History Projects. He describes how, within the drive for an expanded imagination of the global, and as we become more curious about local conditions, we should also pay attention to small narratives that help us to perceive how power is distributed. In doing so we need to be aware of 'our own first-order, necessarily parochial, world pictures', and that local places have their own imagination—their own autonomy, whereby 'regions also imagine their own worlds'.[14]

We've skirted around lots of issues and ideas in this conversation, John, a conversation that is underpinned by your interest in seriality, diaspora and history.

We've crisscrossed parts of your own biography and White Australia. But let's
end with a very direct question: What is your interest in these structural issues
of White Australia?

JY: Why am I interested in these kinds of structural issues in White Australia and the
wider Australian art world? At the end of the day, for me, it's about a sort of advocacy
for plural epistemes to be culturally meaningful in Australia. And being interested in
the structural issues of art institutions and their discourse, thus looking at what can be
done within one's lifetime. The obstacles to cultural pluralism are not just colonialism
from two centuries ago and racial policies from 1901, but issues related to the imperial
aspects of Euramerican modernity, parts of which are congruent with capitalism, as
well as issues of the posthuman condition of this century, and maybe something worse
than neoliberalism.

The Indigenous position in relationship to Country is established in harmony through
a very long mythological history. Yet, the issue with different diasporas coming to
Australia is that we've been faced with only one governing powerful episteme that
champions the abstract and the theoretical, which in a way had already finished with
Niels Bohr. This is the Western modernist worldview dovetailed with the discourses
of industrial revolution and now the information revolution. Hence, meaningful
existence is bracketed by these paradigms and their associated means of expression.

This land, Australia, for better or for worse, has had no plural paradigms or epistemes
tested, amongst which we may then live meaningfully and in harmony. So this sort
of efficacy to me is part of a long term hope of cultural place-building, and ushers us
into a world that is post-empirical, a mythological science that quantum mechanics
has already hinted at.

I feel that my hope of learning from both phases of Wittgenstein (*Tractatus* and
Philosophical Investigations) very early on, perhaps over forty years ago, was to put some
philosophical, aesthetic and artistic questions in order—an untying, a dissolution and
perspicuous clarification of philosophical issues. To tackle such issues is not a question
of expertise, nor could one wear it with a sense of pride in questioning. Really, to
tackle philosophical questions is an ethical obligation, especially as a basis for art
making. The dominance of chauvinistic high-modern aesthetic, artistic and cultural
canons, was in a sense, already messily dissolved by deconstruction in the 1990s.
This is not so much to my liking, in terms of the hope of an enlightened dissolution,
but nonetheless the art world became more anarchic, unpredictable and thus
generative. Deconstruction challenged the domination of one particular cultural
trajectory—that is, modernism.

I think that Wittgenstein was laying bare those sorts of questions that I have also
hoped to help clarify, or discard, in cultural practice, specifically visual culture—with
an ambition towards *description*, a therapeutic description of the limits of visual
discourse in contemporary Australian art making, in terms of presumptions we have
of time, resonance and the visual modalities we practice with. This was my ambition
in the earlier series, and I feel resolved with those years of work. In the last fifteen
years, the History Projects asks more, I feel, through the reckoning of plural world-
pictures, or epistemes, for a future Australia. It demands us to ask, as you said, with
imagination, but also with our hearts.

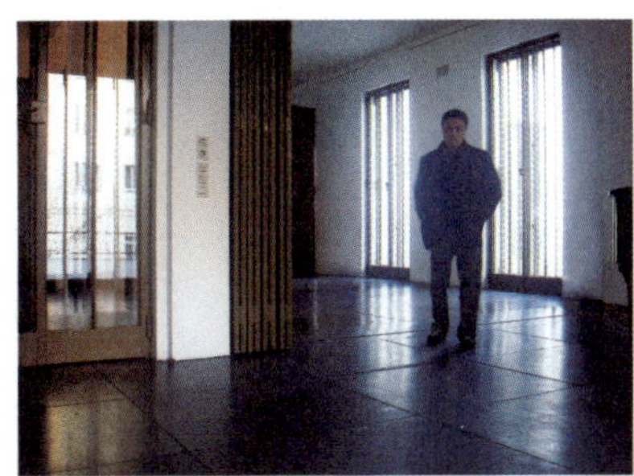

The artist in Stonborough House, built by
Ludwig Wittgenstein and Paul Engelmann in 1928
Kundmanngasse, Vienna, 2008

1. Paul Feyerabend, *Against Method: Outline of an Anarchistic Theory of Knowledge*, New Left Books, London, 1975.

2. In the philosophy of science, the notion that observations are 'theory-laden' understands that the observer's perception is generated by preconceived ideas; it is associated with the work of Paul Feyerabend among others.

3. Manchuria is a historical name referring to the traditional homeland of the Manchu people, who conquered and ruled China as the Qing dynasty from the mid-seventeenth century to 1911; it is the area that comprises most of northeast China today.

4. Imants Tillers, *Diaspora* (1992), oilstick, gouache and synthetic polymer paint on 228 canvas boards, nos. 34,000–38,183, 305 × 915 cm, collection of the Museum of New Zealand Te Papa Tongarewa.

5. On *1967Dispersion*, see the essay in this volume by Olivier Krischer, p. 60.

6. *Dragon Tails*, a bi-annual conference held in Australia/New Zealand on the history of the Chinese in Australia and New Zealand. Please refer to research acknowledgments in Projects (pp. 419–26) for more historians who have contributed.

7. See *Persian Paintings*, exhibition catalogue, Sherman Galleries, Sydney, 2004.

8. Zha Shibiao (查士标, 1615–1698), from Anhui, was a painter associated with the Xinan, also known as Anhui School, known for 'dry' brushstrokes and sparse compositions. Zha was from an aristocratic Ming dynasty family with a significant collection of paintings and antiquities. He had passed the Ming administration's civil service exams in his twenties but chose not to pursue office under the Manchu regime, instead settling in Yangzhou as a painter and calligrapher. Kang Youwei (康有為, 1858–1927), from Guangdong, was one of the most prominent early reformist political thinkers in twentieth century China, though he remained committed to a form of constitutional monarchy. While he had passed the civil service exams in the 1880s, he studied foreign affairs and development and travelled widely overseas, notably in Chinese diaspora communities including in the United States, Australia and Southeast Asia. He was also a prominent calligraphy researcher and practitioner, even relying on the sale of his works in later life, when his political fortunes had very much changed.

9. *The Bridge and the Fruit Tree*, exhibition catalogue, Drill Hall Gallery, Australian National University, Canberra, 2013.

10. See the conversation between Young and Castro in this volume, p. 188.

11. In 2013, Young's work was featured in the exhibition *ORIENTing: With Or Without You*, curated by Aaron Seeto and Toby Chapman for 4A Centre for Contemporary Asian Art, to consider Ian Fairweather's work and 'the significance of place, identity and landscape'. It was held in parallel with the exhibition *ORIENTing: Ian Fairweather in Western Australian Collections*, curated by Ted Snell and Sally Quin at Lawrence Wilson Art Gallery, University of Western Australia. See https://archive.4a.com.au/orienting/ and the exhibition publication by Ted Snell, Aaron Seeto et al, *Orienting: An exhibition in two parts. Ian Fairweather in Western Australian Collections. With or Without You*, Lawrence Wilson Art Gallery, Perth, 2013.

12. See a brief overview of ROCI projects at https://www.rauschenbergfoundation.org/art/art-context/roci.

13. Arjun Appadurai, 'Grassroots Globalization and the Research Imagination,' *Public Culture*, vol. 12, no. 1, 2000, p. 2.

14. Ibid., p. 8.

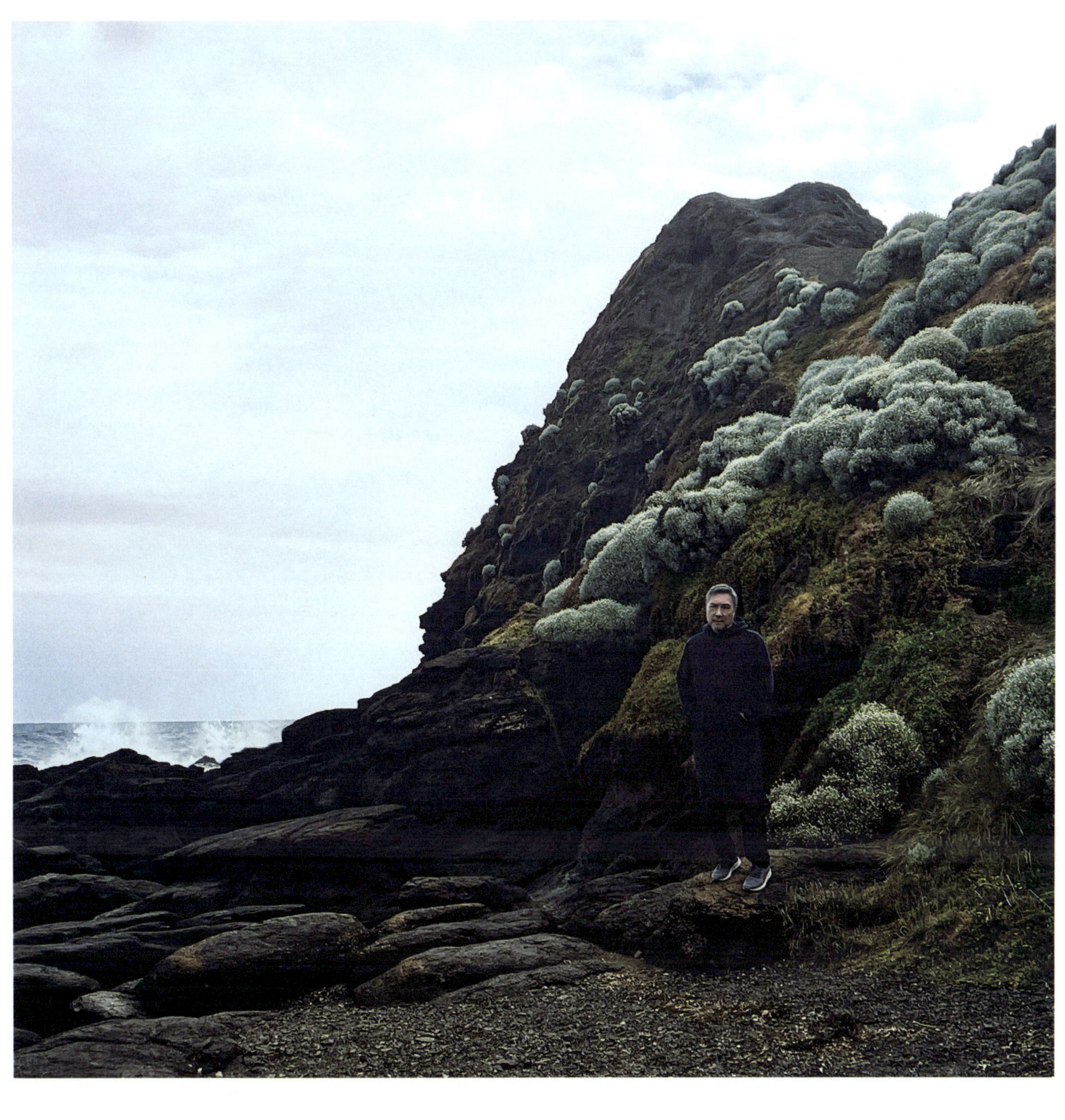

The artist at Flinders, Victoria, 2023
Photograph by Charlotte-Persia Young

pages 416–17
Pages from the artist's notebook (JYNB2017)

Australian National Portrait Gallery. <u>A self portrait</u>

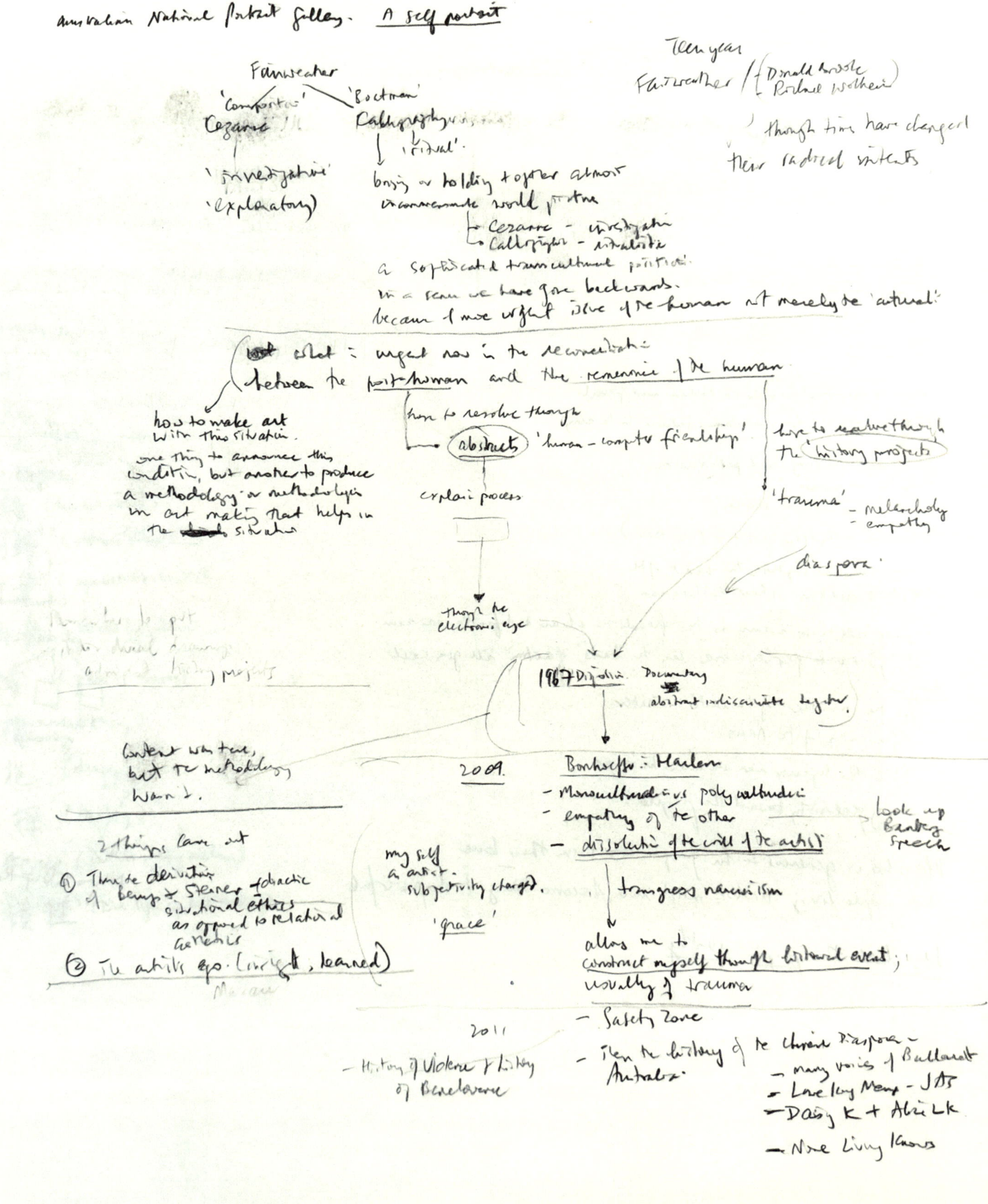

Fairweather

'Composition'   'Boatman'
Cezanne !   Calligraphy ...
                           { 'ritual'.

'investigative'   basis ... holding together almost
'exploratory'   incommensurate world pictures
                                   └─ Cezanne – investigative
                                   └─ Calligraphy – ritualistic
                           a sophisticated transcultural position.
                           in a sense we have gone backwards.
                           because I ... urgent idea of the human not merely the 'actual'.

Ten year
Fairweather / { Donald Brook
                Richard Wollheim)

' though times have changed
  their radical intents

what is urgent now in the reconciliation
between the post-human and the remnants / the human

how to make art   how to resolve through   have to resolve through
with this situation.   ── (abstracts) 'human–computer friendship'   the 'history projects'
one thing to announce this
condition, but another to produce   explain process   'trauma' – melancholy
a methodology or methodologies   – empathy
in art making that helps in
the ─── situation   diaspora

                             through the
                             electronic age

                                         1967 Diptych. Documentary
                                                        abstract indiscernible together.

Context was there,   2009.   Bonhoeffer: Harlem
but the methodology   - Monocultural vs polycultural   look up
wasn't.   my self   - empathy of the other   Barth's
                             as artist.   - dissolution of the will of the artist speech
2 things I am about   subjectivity changed.   transgress narcissism
① Then the derivation   'grace'   allow me to
  of beuys + Steiner +   construct myself through historical event;
  ... didactic   usually of trauma
  oppositional ethics
  as opposed to relational
  aesthetics   2011   - Safety Zone
② The artist's ego (invented, learned)   - then the history of the Chinese Diaspora –
                             - History of Violence + History   - many voices of Ballarat
                               of Benevolence   - Love ley Meng – SAS
                                                                 - Daisy K + Alice Lk
                                                                 - Nine Living Knons

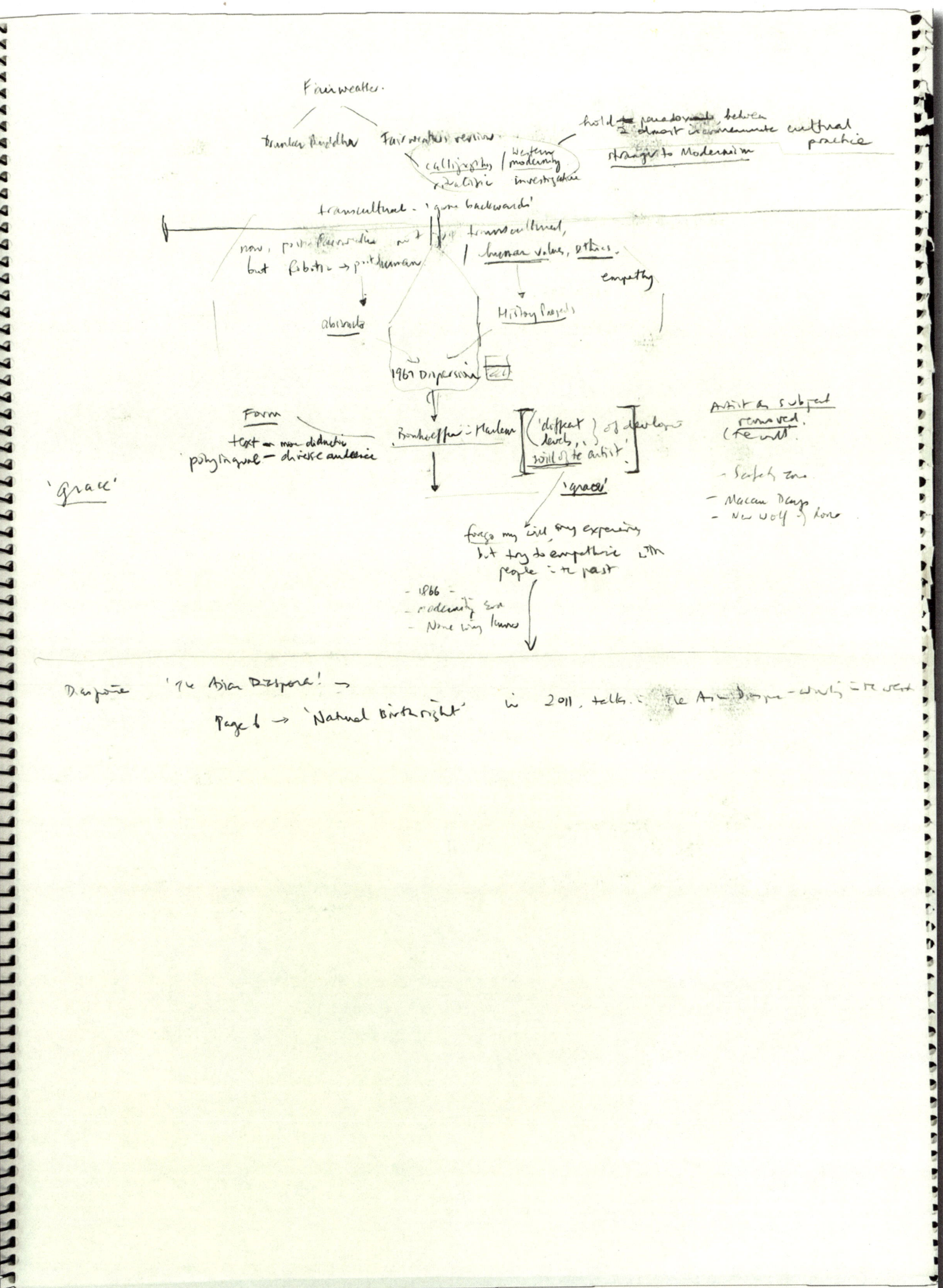

PROJECTS

Note: Images of works by John Young and references to these works are listed below. Locators given in **_bold italics_** indicate the images. Art works by John Young which are not listed here may be found in the Index at **Young, John: works of art**.

OPEN WORLD

Outline, 40; artist's statement, 41; interview with ATW director and weavers, 42–9; weavers' reflections, 50–1.

Exhibition

Cowen Gallery, State Library of Victoria, Melbourne, 2006

Mitchell Library, State Library of New South Wales, Sydney, 2006

Queensland Art Gallery, Brisbane, 2006

Melbourne Art Fair, Melbourne, 2006

Nanjing Library Gallery, Nanjing, 2007

Collection

Nanjing Library, Nanjing

Works

Open World 2005
Cotton and wool tapestry, 330 × 365 cm
Collection of Nanjing Library, Nanjing
31, *38–9*, 40, *42*, *43*, *44*, 45, *49*, *53*

ACKNOWLEDGEMENTS
Research
Jennifer Brown

With thanks to
Hon. Steve Bracks
Amanda Browne
Hon. Mary Delahunty
Carrillo Gantner AC
Penny Hutchinson
Director General Mr Zhang Jianhua (Department of Culture of Jiangsu Province)
Jonah Jones
Guan Jun
Michael Nation
Director General Mr Na Ning (Nanjing Library)
Alexander Ochs-Barwinek
Alan Rubenstein
Anna Schwartz AM
Susie Shears
Antonia Syme AM
Sue Walker
Joanna Zhu

Tapestry (woven by)
Amy Cornall
Kate Durham
Rachel Hine
Milena Paplinska
Caroline Tully

Institutions
Australian Tapestry Workshop, Melbourne
Creative Victoria, Melbourne
Department of Culture of Jiangsu Province, Nanjing
Department of Premier and Cabinet, Victoria
Nanjing Library, Nanjing
Queensland Art Gallery, Brisbane
State Library of New South Wales, Sydney
State Library of Victoria, Melbourne

1967DISPERSION

Outline, 58; artist's statement, 59; discourse, 60–9.

Exhibition
10 Chancery Lane Gallery, Hong Kong, 2008

Collection
M+ Museum Collection, Hong Kong
Collection of the artist

Works
Wishforce 2008
Digital print and oil on linen, two panels
151 × 180 cm
Collection of M+ Museum, Hong Kong
58, 66, *66*, *71*

Riot 2008
Digital print and oil on linen, two panels
170 × 125 cm
Collection of M+ Museum, Hong Kong
65, *73*, 138, *138*, 400, *400*

Flood 2008
Digital print and oil on linen, two panels
170 × 125 cm
Collection of M+ Museum, Hong Kong
64, *64*, *72*

Riot – Flowers 2008
Digital print and oil on linen, four panels
147 × 146 cm
Collection of M+ Museum, Hong Kong
65, *73*, 138, 400, *400*

Folks 2008
Digital print and oil on linen, two panels
169 × 118 cm
Collection of the artist
65, *75*, *141*

Riot – Fire 2008
Digital print and oil on linen, two panels
170 × 98 cm
Collection of the artist
74

Dispersion 2008
Digital print and oil on linen, three panels
85 × 395 cm
Collection of M+ Museum, Hong Kong
56–7, *59*

ACKNOWLEDGEMENTS
With thanks to
Katie de Tilly
Georges de Tilly
Claire Hsu
His Excellency Mr. Les Luck, Australian Consul-General, Hong Kong
Tina Pang
Suhanya Raffel

Institutions
10 Chancery Lane Gallery, Hong Kong
Australian Consulate-General, Hong Kong; Macau,
M+ Museum of Art, Hong Kong

BONHOEFFER IN HARLEM

Outline, 90; artist's statement, 91; concept, 31–2; concept development notes, *96*; discourses, 10, 16, 21, 27–8, 32, 44, 64, 87–106, 134–6, 143–4, 150–2, 328–35, 354; tapestry rug, 44; use of proverbs, 106.

Exhibition
St Matthäus Church, Kulturforum, Berlin, in conjunction with Alexander Ochs Galleries Berlin/ Beijing, 2009
10, 16, 27–8, *28*, 32, 44, 64, 82, *88–9*, 90, *108–9*, *142*, *143*, *156*, *157*, 330–1, 354, 401, 410

The Bonhoeffer Concept, Alexander Ochs Galleries, Berlin, 2011

Erlöserkirche, Bamberg, as part of the Circles festival curated by Alexander Ochs-Barwinek, 2013
107, *112–13*

The repetition of the good. The repetition of the bad Centrum Judaicum, New Synagogue, Berlin, curated by Alexander Ochs-Barwinek, 2016
152, 156–8, *157*

Collection
Erlöserkirche, Bamberg
Private collections
Collection of the artist

Works
Bonhoeffer in Harlem 2009
Chinese silk tapestry, 303 × 119 cm
Collection of Erlöserkirche, Bamberg
44, 82, 96, *142*, 151, *151*

Bonhoeffer in Harlem I 2009
Oil on linen, 190 × 150 cm
Collection of the artist
98

Bonhoeffer in Harlem II 2009
Oil on linen, 190 × 150 cm
Collection of the artist
98

Birth 2008
Digital prints on photographic paper and chalk on blackboard-painted archival cotton paper, framed, 100 × 70 cm each
Collection of Erlöserkirche, Bamberg
114

Children 2008
Digital prints on photographic paper and chalk on blackboard-painted archival cotton paper, framed, 100 × 70 cm each
Collection of Erlöserkirche, Bamberg
114

Harlem 2008
Digital prints on photographic paper and chalk on blackboard-painted archival cotton paper, framed, 100 × 70 cm each
Collection of Erlöserkirche, Bamberg
96, *114*

Politics 2008
Digital prints on photographic paper and chalk on blackboard-painted archival cotton paper, framed, 100 × 70 cm each
Collection of Erlöserkirche, Bamberg
95, *96*, *105*, 105, *114*, *330*

ACKNOWLEDGEMENTS
With thanks to
Katherine Barwinek
Jürgen Dahlmanns, Rug Star, Berlin
Bishop Dr H. C. Wolfgang Huber
His Excellency Mr. Ian Kemish AM
Pfarrerin Dorothea Münch
Dr Christhard-Georg Neubert
Alexander Ochs-Barwinek
Hon. Kevin Rudd
Dolma Lob Sang and the team of weavers
Dr Sylvia D. Volz

Institutions
Alexander Ochs Galleries, Berlin, Beijing
St Staatsbibliothek zu Berlin, Berlin
Erlöserkirche, Bamberg
Centrum Judaicum, New Synagogue, Berlin
St Matthäus Church, Kulturforum, Berlin

SAFETY ZONE

Exhibition

Collection

All works collection of the artist

Works

ACKNOWLEDGEMENTS
Research
Dr Jennifer Brown
Dr Thomas Rabe
Dr Sylvia D. Volz

With thanks to
Dr Thomas Berghuis
Julian Burnside AO KC
Georgia Cribb
Kate Durham
Michele Helmrich
Dr Linda Jaivin
Robert Loh
Terence Maloon
Anthony Oates
Alexander Ochs-Barwinek
Anna Schwartz AM
Jane Smith
Penny Teale

Institutions
Anna Schwartz Gallery, Melbourne
Bunjil Place Gallery, Narre Warren
Centrum Judaicum, New Synagogue, Berlin
Drill Hall Gallery, Australian National University,
Canberra
Museum of Australian Democracy at Eureka,
Ballarat
University of Queensland Art Museum,
Brisbane

THE MACAU DAYS

Outline, 182; artist's statement and reflection, 22, 183; discourses, 11, 13, 21–2, 188–93, 215–7.

Selected poems (Brian Castro) 184–7.

Exhibitions
10 Chancery Lane Gallery, Hong Kong, 2012
22, 194, 195

The Script Road, Macau Literary Festival, Macau, 2017
183

Migration Museum, Adelaide, 2017

John Young: Diaspora, Psyche, Bunjil Place Gallery, Narre Warren, curated by Penny Teale, 2021
180–1

Entire group reproduced in Brian Castro and John Young, *Macau Days*, Art + Australia, Victorian College of the Arts, University of Melbourne, with assistance from the J. M. Coetzee Centre for Creative Practice, University of Adelaide, 2017

Book Launches
Migration Museum, Adelaide
OzAsia Festival, Adelaide, with Brian Castro
Macau Literary Festival, Macau, with Brian Castro
Readings Bookshop, Melbourne
M Pavilion, Melbourne, with Brian Castro, moderated by Natalie King

Collections
Private collections
Collection of the artist

Works
The Macau Days 2012
Digital print on photographic paper and chalk on blackboard painted cotton archival paper, 15 units
320 × 390 cm
Collection of the artist
196–7

Mazu, Goddess of the Sea I (Mazu Saves) 2012
Oil on linen, 190 × 145 cm
Private collection, Melbourne

Mazu, Goddess of the Sea II (The Drowning of Mazu) 2012
Oil on linen, 190 × 145 cm
Collection of the artist
195

Mazu, Goddess of the Sea III (Mazu Swimming Amongst the Pantheon of Idiots) 2012
Oil on linen, 190 × 145 cm
Collection of the artist
198

Marienbad 2012
Digital print and oil on canvas, 185 × 270 cm
Collection of the artist
200–1

I Sailed with Women Pirates 2017
Digital print on photographic paper, 14 units
74 × 90 cm each
Private collection, Melbourne
Collection of the artist
182, *203*

Brian Castro and John Young
Macau Days
Art + Australia, Victorian College of the Arts, University of Melbourne, with assistance from the J. M. Coetzee Centre for Creative Practice, University of Adelaide, 2017

ACKNOWLEDGEMENTS

Research
Claire Hielscher
Eliette Rosich

With thanks to
Prof. Su Baker AM
Dr Paul Carter
Prof. Brian Castro
Dorothy Coetzee
John Coetzee OMG
Dr Isabel Maria de Costa Morais
Katie de Tilly
Dr Edward Colless
Geraldine Cosnuau
Prof. Natalie King OAM
Dr Luke Harrald
Celine Ho
Graca Pacheco Jorge
Prof. Nicholas Jose
Joseph Mitchell
Mandy Paul
Eliette Rosich
Prof. Jennifer Rutherford
Geoffrey Silagy

Institutions
10 Chancery Lane Gallery, Hong Kong
Bunjil Place Gallery, Narre Warren
J. M. Coetzee Centre for Creative Practice, Adelaide
Macau Literary Festival, Macau
Migration Museum, Adelaide
Oz Asia Festival, Adelaide
Art + Australia, Melbourne

THE NEW WOLF OF ROME

Outline, 208; artist's statement, 208; discourses, 11, 13, 21, 209–17.

Exhibitions
Philip Bacon Galleries, Brisbane, 2012
208

The Bridge and the Fruit Tree; John Young – a survey, Drill Hall Gallery, Australian National University, Canberra, curated by Anthony Oates and Terence Maloon, 2013

ARC ONE Gallery, Melbourne, 2023

Collections
Private collections
Collection of the artist

Works
Through the Eyes of the Wolf: Ancient Waters 2012
Digital print on photographic paper and chalk on blackboard painted archival cotton paper
145.2 × 102.4 cm
Collection of the artist
206–7, 211, *212, 218*

Through the Eyes of the Wolf: Awakening 2012
Digital print on photographic paper and chalk on blackboard painted archival cotton paper
145.2 × 102.4 cm
Private collection, Melbourne
219

Through the Eyes of the Wolf: Deep Solitude 2012
Digital print on photographic paper and chalk on blackboard painted archival cotton paper
145.2 × 102.4 cm
Private collection, Brisbane
211, *212, 219*

Through the Eyes of the Wolf: Dark Waters 2012
Digital print on photographic paper and chalk on blackboard painted archival cotton paper
145.2 × 102.4 cm
Collection of the artist
218

Through the Eyes of the Wolf: A Traveller's Mind Rinsed 2012
Digital print on photographic paper and chalk on blackboard painted archival cotton paper
145.2 × 102.4 cm
Collection of the artist
220

Through the Eyes of the Wolf: Floating Clouds 2012
Digital print on photographic paper and chalk on blackboard painted archival cotton paper
145.2 × 102.4 cm
Collection of the artist
220

Born from Ice 2012
Oil on linen, 190 × 144 cm
Collection of the artist
208, *214, 223*

Repose 2012
Oil on linen, 190 × 144 cm
Collection of the artist
211

ACKNOWLEDGEMENTS

With thanks to
Philip Bacon AO
Fran Clark
Elizabeth Errol
Lachlan Henderson
Terrance Maloon
Anthony Oates

Institutions
ARC ONE Gallery, Melbourne
Drill Hall Gallery, Australian National University, Canberra
Philip Bacon Galleries, Brisbane

1866: THE WORLDS OF LOWE KONG MENG AND JONG AH SIUG

ACKNOWLEDGEMENTS

Research
Jessica Lucas,
Dr Ember Parkin

With thanks to
Charlotte Christie
Fran Clark
Elle Groch Hale
Sue Hampel
Martin King
Rachel Kier-Smith
Dr Nadia Rhook
Stephanie Sacco
Anne Virgo OAM
Theodore Whong

Institutions
ARC ONE Gallery, Melbourne
City Library, Melbourne
Hawthorn Arts Centre, Melbourne
Australian Print Workshop, Melbourne

OPEN MONUMENT

Exhibition
Len T Fraser Reserve, Ballarat, 2015

Collection
Len T Fraser Reserve, Ballarat;
permanent architectural monument

Works
John Young and Times Two Architects

Open Monument 2015
430m² permanent architectural monument
Len T Fraser Reserve, Ballarat
Commissioned by Sovereign Hill in association
with the City of Ballarat
Outline, 262; artist's statement, 263; concept
drawings, *268*; construction, *271*; discourses, 28, 41,
81, 264–9; original drawings, *361–2*; page from JY's
notebook, *270*; photographs, *260–1, 264,
272, 352, 361*; *'The Shovel'* prototype sketch, *267*;
'The Shovel', view, 267; Uncle Byron Powell, smoking
ceremony, *269*

Transculture from *Open Monument* 2015
Laser-etched granite, thirty-three panels
100 × 70 cm each
Collection of Ballarat City Council
32, 82, 272, 274–7; detail, *32*; granite panels and
documentation, *267*

Timeline (1850-2010-2170) from *Open Monument*
2015
Bluestone and 34 laser-etched granite panels
embedded in ground
4000 × 42 cm
Collection of Ballarat City Council
269

ACKNOWLEDGEMENTS
Research
Georgina Cue
Shirley Doon
Jess Lucas
Dr Ember Parkin
Jim Quinn
Prof. Kier Reeves

Construction
Butler Excavations, Victoria
DJ Projects
Derek John
Pyrenees Quarries, Victoria
Vivid Civil & Structural Engineering, Melbourne

With thanks to
Michelle Black
A/Prof. Richard Black
Julie Collins
Daniel Henderson
Jeremy Johnson
Emeritus Prof. Terry Lloyd
Venita Poblocki
Henry Thai
Times Two Architects, Melbourne
Charles Zhang

Institutions
The Ballarat China Community Committee
Ballarat Chinese Community Association Inc.
Chinese Australian Cultural Society Ballarat Inc.
City of Ballarat
Public Art Advisory Committee, Ballarat
Sovereign Hill Museums Trust Board, Sovereign Hill

**The following generous donors to this project
are acknowledged with gratitude:**
Association of Chinese from Vietnam, Cambodia
and Laos
Association of Vic. Inc.
Australian Lian Jiang Association
Ballarat Chinese Community Association Inc.
Bright Moon Buddhist Society
Charity & Multi Art Association of Victoria Inc.
Chinese Australian Cultural Society Ballarat Inc.
Chinese Masonic Association Inc.
City of Ballarat
Elderly Chinese Home Inc.
The Federation of Chinese Associations (Vic.) Inc.
Nam Pon Soon Club House
See-Yup Society
The Sovereign Hill Museum Association

A full list of donors is acknowledged at the site

The artist would also like to acknowledge that
Open Monument stands on the unceded lands of
the Wadawurrung and Dja Dja Wurrung people.

MODERNITY'S END:
HALF THE SKY

Outline, 282–3; artists' statements: Cyrus Tang,
284; John Young, 284; Pei Pei He, 285; discourses,
13, 28, 282–3, 285, 300–3.

Exhibitions
Modernity's End: Half the Sky, Incinerator Art Space,
Willoughby City Council, Sydney, curated by Venita
Poblocki, 2016
installation view, Incinerator Art Space, Sydney, *286,
287, 301*

The Lives of Celestials: John Young Zerunge, Town Hall
Gallery, Hawthorn Arts Centre, Boroondara Arts,
Melbourne, curated by Charlotte Christie, Rachel
Kier-Smith, Stephanie Sacco and Elle Groch Hale,
2019

Collections
Willoughby City Council Collection, Sydney
Private collection
Collection of the artist

Works
Modernity's End: Half the Sky (Daisy Kwok) 2016
Digital print on photographic paper and chalk on
blackboard painted archival cotton paper, 16 units
210 × 630 cm
Collection of the artist

Modernity's End: Half the Sky (Alice Lim Kee) 2016
Digital print on photographic paper and chalk on
blackboard painted archival cotton paper, 12 units
210 × 470 cm
Collection of the artist
291–2

Modernity's End 2016
Single thread hand-sewn embroidery and digital
print on silk, 41 × 42 cm
Collection of Willoughby City Council

Pei Pei He
Era in Daisy Kwok's Life (1920s–1940s) 2016
Oil on canvas, 42 × 66 cm
Private collection, Sydney
286

Pei Pei He
Era in Daisy Kwok's Life (1960s–1980s) 2016
Oil on canvas, 42 × 66 cm
Private collection, Sydney
286

Cyrus Tang
The Final Cast Off 2016
HD video loop, 16 min. 11 sec.
286

Theodore Wohng
Half the sky 2016
Organum for female choir, glass harmonica,
synthesiser & the Earth atmosphere (NASA)
3 min. 17 sec.

ACKNOWLEDGEMENTS
Research
Claire Hielscher
Jessica Lucas

With thanks to
Dr Kate Bagnall
Charlotte Christie
Elle Groch Hale
Rachel Kier-Smith
Paul McGregor
Kathie Najar
Venita Poblocki
Stephanie Sacco

Invited artists
Pei Pei He
Cyrus Tang
Theodore Wohng

Institutions
Hawthorn Arts Centre, Boroondara Arts,
Melbourne
Incinerator Art Space, Willoughby City Council,
Sydney

NONE LIVING KNOWS

Outline, 298; artist's statement and reflection,
299; discourses, 12, 298–9, 307, 329.

Exhibitions
ARC ONE Gallery, Melbourne, 2017
296–7, 315

Lucky?, Bundoora Homestead Art Centre,
Bundoora, curated by Sophie Cai and Claire
Watson, 2018–2019

John Young: Diaspora, Psyche, Bunjil Place Gallery,
Narre Warren, curated by Penny Teale, 2021
314

Moore Contemporary, Perth, 2022

Collections
Victoria University Art Collection, Melbourne,
gifted by Dr Fiona Myer
Private collections, Melbourne
Collection of the artist

Works
Open the Kingdom 2017
Digital print on photographic paper and chalk on
blackboard painted cotton archival paper, 12 units
320 × 310 cm
Collection of the artist
298, *311, 317*

None Living Knows #1 2017
Oil on canvas, 86.5 × 102.5 cm
Private collection, Melbourne
320

None Living Knows #2 2017
Oil on canvas, 86.5 × 102.5 cm
Collection of the artist

None Living Knows #3 2017
Oil on canvas, 86.5 × 102.5 cm
Collection of Victoria University, Melbourne
320

None Living Knows #4 2017
Oil on canvas, 86.5 × 102.5 cm
Collection of the artist

None Living Knows #5 2017
Oil on canvas, 86.5 × 102.5 cm
Collection of the artist

None Living Knows #6 2017
Oil on canvas, 86.5 × 102.5 cm
Collection of the artist

None Living Knows #7 2017
Oil on canvas, 86.5 × 102.5 cm
Collection of Victoria University, Melbourne

None Living Knows I 2017
Oil and acrylic on linen, 238 × 156 cm
Collection of the artist
321

Collection of the artist
None Living Knows II 2017
Oil and acrylic on linen, 238 × 156 cm
Collection of the artist
321

ACKNOWLEDGEMENTS
Historian
Gordon Grimwade

With thanks to
Sophie Cai
Fran Clark
Sue Hampel
Margaret Moore
Dr Fiona Myer
Penny Teale
Claire Watson

Institutions
ARC ONE Gallery, Melbourne
Bundoora Homestead Art Centre, Bundoora
Bunjil Place Gallery, Narre Warren
Hawthorn Arts Centre, Melbourne
Moore Contemporary, Perth
Victoria University, Melbourne

Fairweather Transformation XII 2019
Oil on Belgian linen, 76 × 80.5 cm
Private collection, Brisbane

Fairweather Transformation XIII 2019
Oil on Belgian linen, 106 × 76 cm
Private collection, Melbourne
385

Fairweather Transformation XIV 2019
Oil on Belgian linen, 76 × 96 cm
Private collection, Brisbane
381

Fairweather Transformation XV 2019
Oil on Belgian linen, 76 × 109.7 cm
Collection of the artist

Fairweather Transformation XVI 2019
Oil on Belgian linen, 76 × 117.5 cm
Collection of the artist

Fairweather Transformation XVII 2019
Oil on Belgian linen, 107.5 × 76 cm
Collection of the artist

Fairweather Transformation XVIII 2019
Oil on Belgian linen, 70 × 50 cm
Collection of the artist

Fairweather Transformation XIX 2019
Oil on Belgian linen, 70 × 50 cm
Collection of the artist

Fairweather Transformation XX 2019
Oil on Belgian linen, 70 × 50 cm
Collection of the artist

The Chinese Room (Mangrove) 2022
Oil on Belgian linen, two panels, 128.5 × 88.6 cm
Collection of Art Gallery of South Australia,
Adelaide
366–7, 376, 389

ACKNOWLEDGEMENTS

With thanks to
Philip Bacon AO
A/Prof. Carolyn Barnes
Prof. John Clark
Rhana Devenport ONZM
Prof. Mark Ledbury
Prof. Jacqueline Lo
Dr Fiona Myer
Sidney Myer AM
Lara Nicholls
Tim Olsen
Dr Maudie Palmer AO
A/Prof. Claire Roberts
Hon. Bin Tschen
A/Prof. Caroline Turner

Institutions

ARC ONE Gallery, Melbourne
Art Gallery of South Australia, Adelaide
Olsen Gallery, Sydney
Philip Bacon Galleries, Brisbane
Rockhampton Museum of Art, Rockhampton

ARTIST'S ACKNOWLEDGEMENTS

STUDIO

Research
Ashlee Baldwin, Jennifer Brown, Georgina Cue,
Antoinette Dillon, Claire Hielscher, Jessica Lucas,
Ember Parkin, Stephanie Sacco, Genevieve Trail

Assistants (2007 onwards)
Senior Assistants – Colleen Ahern, Amanda Marburg,
Mateja Simenko, Noël Skrzypczak
Assistants – Yvette Coppersmith, Georgina Cue,
Kirsty Budge, Edie Duffy, Anthea Kemp, Madeline
Kidd, Jessica Lucas, Tully Moore, Bryan Spier, Michelle
Ussher, Alice Wormald

Management (2007 onwards)
Ashlee Baldwin, Jacqueline Fraser, Elle Groch Hale,
Sarah Lammardo, Stephanie Sacco, Genevieve Trail,
Emily Winslade

GENERAL

Historians and advisors
Dr Kate Bagnall, Prof. John Fitzgerald AM, Dr Grace
Gassin, Gordon Grimwade, Dr Sophie Loy-Wilson,
Paul McGregor, Prof. Kier Reeves, Dr Nadia Rhook,
Dr Karen Schamberger, Senator Bin Tschen

With thanks to
Katrina Arent, Philip Bacon AO, Prof. Su Baker AM,
A/Prof. Caroline Barnes, Julian Burnside AO KC,
Vicente Butron, Prof. Brian Castro, Fran Clark,
Prof. John Clark, Dr Edward Colless, Georgia
Cribb, Kate Durham, Elizabeth Errol, Marianne
Fenton, Carrillo Gantner AC, Sue Hampel, Michele
Helmrich, Lachlan Henderson, Prof. Maria Jaschok,
Dr Olivier Krischer, Prof. Mark Ledbury, Prof.
Jacqueline Lo, Terence Maloon, Thomas Melick,
Kate Mizrahi, Susan Mizrahi, Margaret Moore,
Dr Fiona Myer, Anthony Oates, Alexander
Ochs-Barwinek, Tim Olsen, Dr Maudie Palmer AO,
Venita Poblocki, Eliette Rosich, Hon. Kevin Rudd,
Prof. Jennifer Rutherford, Anna Schwartz AM,
Aaron Seeto, Gene Sherman AM, Antonia
Syme AM, Senator Bin Tschen, Dr Mikala Tai, Penny
Teale, Katie de Tilly, Georges de Tilly, A/Prof. Caroline
Turner AM, Marni Williams, Cecilia Young,
Charlotte-Persia Young, Jasper Young

Galleries
10 Chancery Lane Gallery, Hong Kong; Alexander
Ochs Gallery, Berlin, Beijing; Anna Schwartz Gallery,
Melbourne; ARC ONE Gallery, Melbourne; Bunjil
Place Gallery, Narre Warren; Drill Hall Gallery,
ANU, Canberra; Hawthorn Arts Centre, Melbourne;
Moore Contemporary, Perth; Olsen Gallery, Sydney;
Pearl Lam Gallery, Shanghai, Singapore; Philip Bacon
Galleries, Brisbane; Sherman Galleries, Sydney

Organisations
Asia Art Archive, Hong Kong; Art + Australia,
Melbourne; ANU Centre for European Studies,
Canberra; Asialink, Melbourne; Creative Australia;
Creative Victoria; J. M. Coetzee Centre for Creative
Practice, Adelaide; Di'van Journal, Sydney; Power
Institute Foundation for Art and Visual Culture,
Sydney; Victorian College of the Arts, Melbourne

Photography
Christian Capurro, Robert Colvin, Dan Mahon,
Ian Wilson

EDITOR'S ACKNOWLEDGEMENTS

A book of this kind takes on a life of its own as it
touches and is touched by the many contributors
that bring it into being. It is (and should be) the
work of many hands, before and after my own.
John Young has always been earnest and open, and
it would not have been possible to arrive here
without his warm energy at every stage. I must then
acknowledge Venita Poblocki, whose earlier work as
'founding editor' made the current volume possible.
Genevieve Trail has been an invaluable assistant
to the project, not only for her attention to detail
but her own keen knowledge of John's work and
archive. Similarly, Vicente Butron is both an old and
new friend, whose design further elucidates aspects
of John's practice to which he has been a witness
for many decades. Power Publications' support and
advice reflected a genuine belief in the work and
what this book could do, for which special thanks
are due to Tom Melick, Naomi Riddle and Marni
Williams. Finally, a heartfelt thanks to the many
authors, some of whom meet for the first time in
these pages. Thanks for their insight and patience,
and their tacit belief in the spirit in which this book
has been made.

AUTHORS

CAROLYN BARNES

is Deputy Chair of the Department of
Communication Design and Digital Media Design
and Academic Director of Research Training in
the School of Design at Swinburne University of
Technology, where she teaches research methods
for academic and practice applications at Honours
and Masters level. Her art writing focuses on
artist-initiated activity, artist's networks and the
legacy of modernism in Australian non-objective
and concrete art post 1980. Carolyn is an associate
editor of the *International Journal of Design* and
a member of the editorial board of *The Journal
of Visual Arts Practice*.

THOMAS BERGHUIS

is a curator and art historian specialising in
contemporary art and performance art, based
in Leiden, the Netherlands. He was formerly
the Robert H. Ho Curator of Chinese Art at
the Guggenheim Museum in New York, and first
director of Museum MACAN in Jakarta, Indonesia.
He is the author of *Performance Art in China*
(Timezone 8, 2006); *Suspended Histories* (Museum
Van Loon, 2013); *Wang Jianwei: Time Temple*
(Guggenheim Museum, 2014); and *Home and the
World* (Museum Van Loon, 2024).

BRIAN CASTRO

is the author of eleven novels, a volume of essays
and a visual/poetic collaboration with John Young.
His novels include the multi-award-winning *Double-
Wolf* (Wakefield Press, 1991) and *Shanghai Dancing*
(Giramondo, 2003). He was the 2014 winner of the
Patrick White Award for Literature and the 2018
Prime Minister's Prize for Poetry. He is Emeritus
Professor of Creative Writing at Adelaide University.

JOHN CLARK

is Professor Emeritus in Art History at the
University of Sydney where he taught for twenty-
one years. He published *Modern Asian Art* in 1988
with Craftsman House, Sydney, and University of
Hawai'i Press. His book *Asian Modernities: Chinese
and Thai Art of the 1980s and1990s* was published
by Power Publications, Sydney, in 2010. His book
The Asian Modern, which examines twenty-five
Asian artists in five generations from the 1850s
to 1990s, was published by the National Gallery
of Singapore in 2021.

MATT COX

is Curator of Asian Art at the Art Gallery of New
South Wales, where he is broadly engaged with
historical and contemporary art from Asia and the
world. He recently curated *The National 2021:
New Australian Art; A Promise: Khaled Sabsabi* (2020);
Walking with Gods (2019); *Playback: Dobell Australian
Drawing Biennale* 2018; and *Passion and Procession*
(2017). He has published widely on Asian art,
photography and architecture including publications
with the National Gallery of Australia, Amsterdam
University Press, and the National University of
Singapore.

MARC GLÖDE

is a curator, critic and film scholar. His work focuses
on the relationship between images, technology,
space, and the body. It also examines the dynamics
between art, architecture and film. He has curated
exhibitions and programs with institutions globally
and has published widely. Previously the senior
curator of Art Basel's film program (2008–14),
Glöde is currently Assistant Professor and Co-
Director of the MA in Museum Studies
and Curatorial Practices at the School of Art,
Design and Media, Nanyang Technological
University, Singapore.

CLAIRE HIELSCHER

spends her time working on projects and initiatives
that help people to live more interconnected,
enriching and sustainable lives. This commitment
has led her to work as a writer and strategist across
the academic and civic spectrum with governments,
cultural institutions, not-for-profits and commercial
businesses. Her background in history, commerce
and public policy has shaped her belief that words
can lead to positive action, especially if they are
thoughtful and purpose-driven.

WOLFGANG HUBER

is a German theologian and ethicist. Huber served
as Bishop of the Evangelical Church of Berlin-
Brandenburg-Silesian Upper Lusatia from 1993
until November 2009. From 1998 to 2001 Huber
served as a member of the Central and Executive
Committees of the World Council of Churches.
He continues to be engaged in public ethical
debates and was chosen by the German Cabinet
to serve on Germany's Ethics Council in 2010.

OLIVIER KRISCHER

is a historian and curator of modern and
contemporary art from East Asia and its diasporas,
with a particular interest in photomedia. He is
a lecturer at the University of New South Wales
School of Art & Design. His curatorial projects
include *Assembly* (2024), featuring eight Hong
Kong-born artists; *Abridge* (2022), an exhibition
of the work of photomedia artist Wei Leng Tay;
and *Wayfaring: Photography in 1970s–80s Taiwan*
(co-curated with Shuxia Chen, 2021), curated
from the National Taiwan Museum of Fine Arts
collection. He is currently working on a co-edited,
co-authored volume titled *Wayfaring: Photography
in Taiwan, 1950s–1980s* (forthcoming, 2025).

"

JACQUELINE LO

is Director of the Indo-Pacific Research Centre at Murdoch University. She is also Honorary Professor at the Australian National University (ANU) and Chair of the Asian Australian Studies series with ANU Press. An internationally recognised Humanities scholar and pioneer of Asian Australian Studies, her work on multiculturalism, diaspora and public policy has influenced academic and policy sectors in Australia and overseas.

SOPHIE LOY-WILSON

is a Senior Lecturer in Australian History at the University of Sydney where she specialises in the history of Chinese Australian communities. She is the author of *Australians in Shanghai: Race, Rights and Nation in a Treaty Port China* (Routledge, 2017), and is currently working on her new book project, *Chinese Business: Economic and Social Survival in White Australia, 1870–1940*.

JENNIFER MACKENZIE

is a poet and reviewer, focusing on writing from and about the Asian region. Her most recent book is *Navigable Ink* (Transit Lounge, 2020), a homage to the Indonesian writer, Pramoedya Ananta Toer.

VENITA POBLOCKI

graduated with a Master of Art Administration from the College of Fine Arts (University of New South Wales). Venita has worked as a curator and writer to further pursue her interests in notions of national identity, expressions of cultural identity, and Australia's history of migration. Venita has worked with John Young in many creative capacities since 2012, notably as curator for the exhibition, *Modernity's End: Half the Sky* at Incinerator Artspace (2016).

NADIA RHOOK

is a non-Indigenous historian, poet and educator born in Naarm / Melbourne. She has a PhD in History from La Trobe University, and has lectured at La Trobe and the University of Western Australia. Her research has focused on intersections between language, law, race, and medicine in colonial Victoria. She has designed and delivered public walking tours and heritage exhibitions, including *'Moving Tongues: Language and Migration in 1890s Melbourne'*. Nadia is also the author of two history-themed poetry collections: *boots* (UWA Publishing, 2020), and *Second Fleet Baby* (Fremantle Press, 2022).

CLAIRE ROBERTS

is an art historian and a curator with an interest in modern and contemporary Chinese art, and cultural flows between Australia and Asia. She is Professor of Art History in the School of Culture and Communication at the University of Melbourne and a Fellow of the Australian Academy of the Humanities.

ANETTE SIMOJOKI

is a Pastor at the Erlöserkirche (Evangelical Lutheran Church of the Redeemer) in Bamberg.

AARON SEETO

is the Deputy Director of the Smithsonian's Hirshhorn Museum and Sculpture Garden, Washington DC. He was previously the Director of the Museum of Modern and Contemporary Art in Nusantara (Museum MACAN) in Jakarta. He is a curator and museum professional with a background in contemporary Asian art. In Indonesia, he presented major exhibition projects by artists including Agus Suwage, Melati Suryodarmo, Arahmaiani, Lee Mingwei, Xu Bing, Yayoi Kusama and Chiharu Shiota. He was formerly Curatorial Manager of Asian and Pacific Art at the Queensland Art Gallery, Australia, and Director of 4A Centre for Contemporary Asian Art, Sydney.

MIKALA TAI

Mikala Tai is a curator, researcher and academic specialising in contemporary Asian and Australian art. She is currently the Head of Visual Arts at Creative Australia and is a previous director of 4A Centre for Contemporary Asian Art.

CAROLINE TURNER

is a curator and academic. She was previously Deputy Director of the Queensland Art Gallery and of the Humanities Research Centre at the Australian National University. She has published extensively on contemporary Asian art. Her latest publication with Elly Kent and Virginia Hooker is *Living Art: Indonesian Artists Engage Politics, Society and History* (ANU Press, 2023).

SYLVIA DOMINIQUE VOLZ

is an Austrian-based art historian (formerly of Berlin, Germany). She has worked as an art consultant for many years, advising international collectors and artists, and has also served as editor-in-chief of several editions of the *BMW Art Guide by Independent Collectors*, the global online guide to private collections of contemporary art. Since 2021, Sylvia has also worked as a coach and mentor for creatives in the field of personal development. She completed her PhD on the genesis of the portrait medal genre at the end of the Trecento in Padua. Her most recent publication is *Ruprecht von Kaufmann: Leben zwischen den Stühlen (Life between the Chairs)* (Distanz Verlag, 2020).

JEN WEBB

is Professor of Creative Practice at the University of Canberra, and co-author with Caroline Turner of *Art and Human Rights: Contemporary Asian Contexts* (Manchester University Press, 2016). Her most recent publication is *Gender and the Creative Labour Market* (with S. Brook et al., Palgrave, 2022).

INDEX

435

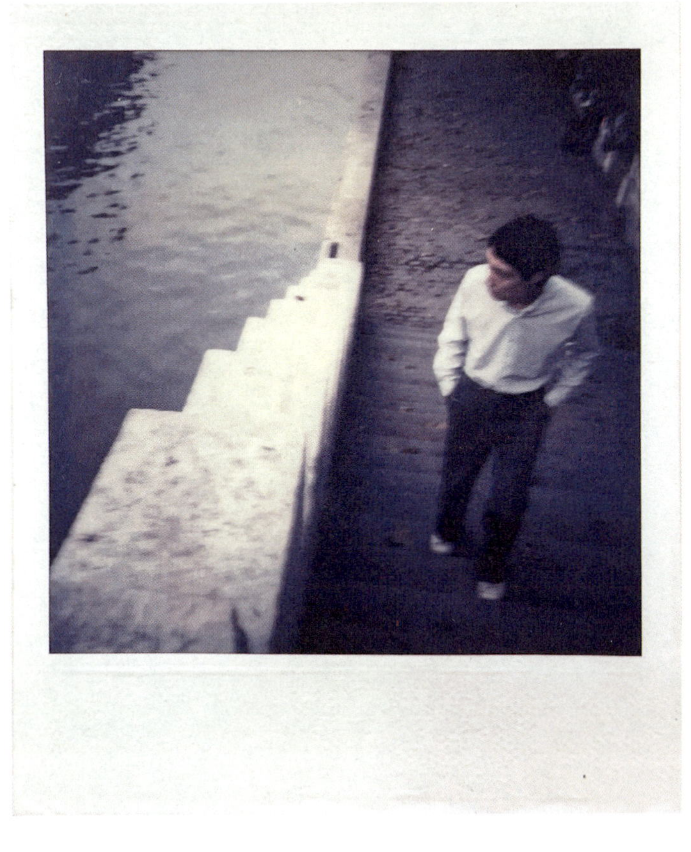

John Young walking along the Seine River, Paris, in 1982, at the site of Yves Klein's *Zone of Immaterial Pictorial Sensibility* (1962). Polaroid photograph by Steven Beyer and Laura Blau

Editor: Olivier Krischer
Foundation Editor: Venita Poblocki
Assistant Editor: Genevieve Trail
Project Management: Marni Williams, Thomas Melick
Book Design: Vicente Butron (BA&D)
Imaging Support: Edie Duffy, Sarah Lammardo, Emily Winslade
Copy Editing: Naomi Riddle
Proofreading: Kay Campbell, The Comma Institute
Indexing: Miranda Fyfield

Published by Power Institute Foundation for Art and Visual Culture,
The University of Sydney
Printed by Pristone, Singapore, on Munken White 90gsm
Typeset in Adobe Caslon Pro and Gill Sans

ISBN 978-0-909952-41-9

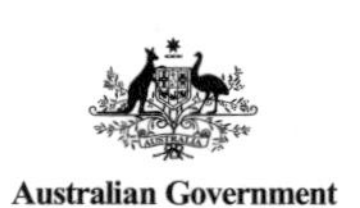

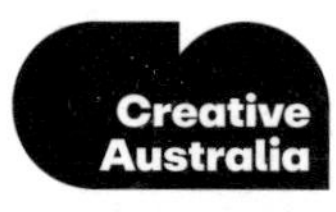

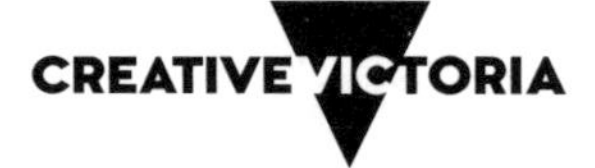

POWER PUBLICATIONS